NARRATIVE AND CRITICAL

HISTORY OF AMERICA

Justin Winsor

Aboriginal

America

NARRATIVE AND CRITICAL

HISTORY OF AMERICA

EDITED

By JUSTIN WINSOR

LIBRARIAN OF HARVARD UNIVERSITY

CORRESPONDING SECRETARY MASSACHUSETTS HISTORICAL SOCIETY

VOL. I. — PART I.

BOSTON AND NEW YORK

HOUGHTON, MIFFLIN AND COMPANY

The Riverside Press, Cambridge

The Riverside Press, Cambridge, Mass., U. S. A.
Electrotyped and Printed by H. O. Houghton & Company.

To

CHARLES WILLIAM ELIOT, LL. D.

PRESIDENT OF HARVARD UNIVERSITY.

DEAR ELIOT:

Forty years ago, you and I, having made preparation together, entered college on the same day. We later found different spheres in the world; and you came back to Cambridge in due time to assume your high office. Twelve years ago, sought by you, I likewise came, to discharge a duty under you.

You took me away from many cares, and transferred me to the more congenial service of the University. The change has conduced to the progress of those studies in which I hardly remember to have had a lack of interest.

So I owe much to you; and it is not, I trust, surprising that I desire to connect, in this work, your name with that of your

Obliged friend,

Justin Winsor

CAMBRIDGE, 1889.

CONTENTS AND ILLUSTRATIONS.

[*The cut on the title represents a mask, which forms the centre of the Mexican Calendar Stone, as engraved in D. Wilson's Prehistoric Man, i. 333, from a cast now in the Collection of the Society of Antiquaries of Scotland.*]

INTRODUCTION.

CHAPTER I.

CHAPTER II.

CHAPTER III.

CHAPTER IV.

CHAPTER V.

CHAPTER VI.

APPENDIX.

Justin Winsor.

INTRODUCTION.

By the Editor.

Part I. AMERICANA IN LIBRARIES AND BIBLIOGRAPHIES.

HARRISSE, in the Introduction of his *Bibliotheca Americana Vetustissima*, enumerates and characterizes many of the bibliographies of Americana, beginning with the chapter, "De Scriptoribus rerum Americanarum," in the *Bibliotheca Classica* of Draudius, in 1622.[1] De Laet, in his *Nieuwe Wereldt* (1625), gives a list of about thirty-seven authorities, which he increased somewhat in later editions.[2] The earliest American catalogue of any moment, however, came from a native Peruvian, Léon y Pinelo, who is usually cited by the latter name only. He had prepared an extensive list; but he published at Madrid, in 1629, a selection of titles only, under the designation of *Epitome de la biblioteca oriental i occidental*,[3] which included manuscripts as well as books. He had exceptional advantages as chronicler of the Indies.

In 1671, in Montanus's *Nieuwe weereld*, and in Ogilby's *America*, about 167 authorities are enumerated.

Sabin[4] refers to Cornelius van Beughem's *Bibliographia Historica*, 1685, published at Amsterdam, as having the titles of books on America.

The earliest exclusively American catalogue is the *Bibliothecæ Americanæ Primordia* of White Kennett,[5] Bishop of Peterborough, published in London in 1713. The arrangement of its sixteen hundred entries is chronological; and it enters under their respective dates the sections of such collections as Hakluyt and Ramusio.[6] It particularly pertains to the English colonies, and more especially to New England, where, in the eighteenth century, three distinctively valuable American libraries are known to have existed, — that of the Mather family, which was in large part destroyed during the battle of Bunker Hill, in 1775; that of Thomas Prince, still in large part existing in the Boston Public Library; and that of Governor Hutchinson, scattered by the mob which attacked his house in Boston in 1765.[7]

In 1716 Lenglet du Fresnoy inserted a brief list (sixty titles) in his *Méthode pour étudier la géographie*. Garcia's *Origen de los Indias de el nuevo mundo*, Madrid, 1729, shows a list of about seventeen hundred authors.[8]

In 1737–1738 Barcia enlarged Pinelo's work, translating all his titles into Spanish, and added

[1] Herrera failed to add a list of authors to the original edition of his *Historia* (1601–1615), but one of about thirty-three entries is found in later editions.

[2] See Vol. IV. p. 417.

[3] Sabin, vol. x. no. 40,053; Carter-Brown, vol. ii. no. 347; Rich (1832), no. 188; Trübner, *Bibliographical Guide to American Literature*, p. viii; Murphy, no. 1,471.

[4] *Dictionary*, vol. ii. no. 5,102.

[5] For an account of a likeness, see J. C. Smith's *British Mezzotint Portraits*, iv. no. 1,694.

[6] The book, of which 250 copies only were printed, is rare, and Quaritch prices it at £3 (Sabin, vol. ix. no. 37,447). It preserves some titles which are not otherwise known; and represents a library which Kennett had gathered for presentation to the Society for the Propagation of the Gospel in Foreign Parts. Rich (*Bibl. Amer. nova*, i. 21) says the index was made by Robert Watts. Although Stevens (*Historical Collections*, i. 142) says that the books were dispersed, the library is still in existence in London, though it lacks many titles given in the printed catalogue, and shows others not in that volume. Cf. *Mass. Hist. Soc. Proc.*, xx. 274; Allibone, ii. 1020; James Jackson's *Bibliographies géographiques* (Paris, 1881), no. 606; Trübner's *Bibliographical Guide*, p. ix; Sabin, *Bibliography of Bibliographies*, p. lxxxvii.

[7] *Memorial History of Boston*, vol. i. pp. xviii, xix; vol. ii. pp. 221, 426.

[8] The original edition was Valencia, 1607. Carter-Brown, vol. ii. no. 52.

numerous other entries which Rich[1] says were "clumsily thrown together."

Charlevoix prefixed to his *Nouvelle France*, in 1744, a list with useful comments, which the English reader can readily approach in Dr. Shea's translation. A price-list which has been preserved of the sale in Paris in 1764, *Catalogue des livres des ci-devant soi-disans Jésuites du Collége de Clermont*, indicates the lack of competition at that time for those choicer Americana, now so costly.[2] The *Regio patronatu Indiarum* of Frassus (1775) gives about 1505 authorities. There is a chronological catalogue of books issued in the American colonies previous to 1775, prepared by S. F. Haven, Jr., and appended to the edition of Thomas's *History of Printing*, published by the American Antiquarian Society. Though by no means perfect, it is a convenient key to most publications illustrative of American history during the colonial period of the English possessions, and printed in America. Dr. Robertson's *America* (1777) shows only 250 works, and it indicates how far short he was of the present advantages in the study of this subject. Clavigero surpassed all his predecessors in the lists accompanying his *Storia del Messico*, published in 1780, — but the special bibliography of Mexico is examined elsewhere. Equally special, and confined to the English colonies, is the documentary register which Jefferson inserted in his *Notes on Virginia;* but it serves to show how scanty the records were a hundred years ago compared with the calendars of such material now. Meuzel, in 1782, had published enough of his *Bibliotheca Historica* to cover the American field, though he never completed the work as planned.

In 1789 an anonymous *Bibliotheca Americana* of nearly sixteen hundred entries was published in London. It is not of much value. Harrisse and others attribute it to Reid; but by some the author's name is differently given as Homer, Dalrymple, and Long.[3]

An enumeration of the documentary sources (about 152 entries) used by Muñoz in his *Historia del nuevo mundo* (1793) is given in Fustér's *Biblioteca Valenciana* (ii. 202–234) published at Valencia in 1827–1830.[4]

There is in the Library of Congress (Force Collection) a copy of an *Indice de la Coleccion de manuscritos pertinecientes a la historia de las Indias*, by Fraggia, Abella, and others, dated at Madrid, 1799.[5]

In the Sparks collection at Cornell are two other manuscript bibliographies worthy of notice. One is a *Biblioteca Americana*, by Antonio de Alcedo, dated in 1807. Sparks says his copy was made in 1843 from an original which Obadiah Rich had found in Madrid.[6]

Harrisse says that another copy is in the Carter-Brown Library; and he asserts that, excepting some additions of modern American authors, it is not much improved over Barcia's edition of Pinelo. H. H. Bancroft[7] mentions having a third copy, which had formerly belonged to Prescott.

The other manuscript at Cornell is a *Bibliotheca Americana*, prepared in twelve volumes by Arthur Homer, who had intended, but never accomplished, the publication of it. Sparks found it in Sir Thomas Phillipps's library at Middlehill, and caused the copy of it to be made, which is now at Ithaca.[8]

In 1808 Boucher de la Richarderie published at Paris his *Bibliothèque universelle des voyages*,[9] which has in the fifth part a critical list of all voyages to American waters. Harrisse disagrees with Peignot in his favorable estimate of Richarderie, and traces to him the errors of Faribault and later bibliographers.

The *Bibliotheca Hispano-Americana* of Dr. José Mariano Beristain de Souza was published in Mexico in 1816–1821, in three volumes. Quaritch, pricing it at £96 in 1880, calls it the rarest and most valuable of all American bibliographical works. It is a notice of writers who were born, educated, or flourished in Spanish America, and naturally covers much of interest to the historical student. The author did not live to complete it, and his nephew finished it.

1 *Catalogue* (1832), no. 188. Cf. Carter-Brown, vol. iii. no. 568; Trübner, *Bibliographical Guide*, p. ix; Sabin, vol. i. no. 3,349. The portion on America is in vol. ii.

2 For example, the Champlain of 1613, 3 fr.; that of 1632, 4 fr.; 21 volumes of the *Relations* of the Jesuits, 18 fr.

3 Sabin, *Dictionary*, vol. ii. no. 5,198; and *Bibliography of Bibliographies*, p. xviii; *Hist. Mag.*, i. 57; and Allibone, ii. 1764, who calls him Reid, an American resident in London, and says he issued the bibliography as preparatory to a history of America. Jackson's *Bibliographies géographiques*, no. 611, and Trübner, *Bibliographical Guide*, p x, call it by the name of the publisher, Debrett.

4 Jackson's *Bibliographies géographiques*, no 621.

5 Jackson, *Bibliographies géographiques*, no. 612; *Serapeum* (1845), p. 223; Trübner, *Bibliographical Guide*, p. xxv

6 Sparks, *Catalogue*, no. 1,635; Jackson's *Bibliographies géographiques*, no. 613; Trübner, p. xxv.

7 *History of Mexico*, iii. 512, where is an account of Alcedo's historical labors.

8 Sparks, *Catalogue*, no. 1,635 *a*, and p. 230.

9 Sabin, *Bibliography of Bibliographies*, p. xxiv; H. H. Bancroft, *Central America*, ii. 700, 760.

In 1818 Colonel Israel Thorndike, of Boston, bought for $6,500 the American library of Professor Ebeling, of Germany, estimated to contain over thirty-two hundred volumes, besides an extraordinary collection of ten thousand maps.[1] The library was given by the purchaser to Harvard College, and its possession at once put the library of that institution at the head of all libraries in the United States for the illustration of American history. No catalogue of it was ever printed, except as a part of the General Catalogue of the College Library issued in 1830–1834, in five volumes.

Another useful collection of Americana added to the same library was that formed by David B. Warden, for forty years United States Consul at Paris, who printed a catalogue of its twelve hundred volumes at Paris, in 1820, called *Bibliotheca Americo-Septentrionalis*. The collection in 1823 found a purchaser at $5,000, in Mr. Samuel A. Eliot, who gave it to the College.[2]

The Harvard library, however, as well as several of the best collections of Americana in the United States, owes more, perhaps, to Obadiah Rich than to any other. This gentleman, a native of Boston, was born in 1783. He went as consul of the United States to Valencia in 1815, and there began his study of early Spanish-American history, and undertook the gathering of a remarkable collection of books,[3] which he threw open generously, with his own kindly assistance, to every investigator who visited Spain for purposes of study. Here he won the respect of Alexander H. Everett, then American minister to the court of Spain. He captivated Irving by his helpful nature, who says of him:

EBELING.[4]

"Rich was one of the most indefatigable, intelligent, and successful bibliographers in Europe. His house at Madrid was a literary wilderness, abounding with curious works and rare editions.

[1] Quincy's *Harvard University*, ii. 413, 596. It is noteworthy, in view of so rich an accession coming from Germany, that Grahame, the historian of our colonial period, says that in 1825 he found the University Library at Göttingen richer in books for his purpose than all the libraries of Britain joined together.

[2] This collection is also embraced in the Catalogue of the College Library already referred to. Mr. Warden began the collection of another library, which he used while writing the American part (10 vols.) of the *Art de vérifier des Dates*, Paris, 1826–1844, and which (1,118 works) was afterward sold to the State Library at Albany for $4,000. Dr. Henry A. Homes, the librarian at Albany, informs me that when arranged it made twenty-one hundred and twenty-three volumes. Warden's *Bibliotheca Americana*, Paris, 1831, reprinted at Paris in 1840, is a catalogue of this collection. Mr. Warden died in 1845, aged 67. Cf. Ludewig in the *Serapeum*, 1845, p. 209; Muller, *Books on America* (1872), no. 1734; Allibone, iii. 2,579; S. G. Goodrich, *Recollections*, ii. 243; Jackson's *Bibl. Géog.*, nos. 617, 618; Trübner, *Bibliographical Guide*, p. xiv. There was a final sale of Mr. Warden's books by Horatio Hill, in New York, in 1846.

[3] This collection was offered to Congress for purchase through Edward Everett in December, 1827. The printed list, with nearly a hundred entries for manuscripts and three hundred and eighty-nine for printed books, covering the years 1506–1825, was printed as Document 37 of the 1st session of the 20th Congress. The sale was not effected. Rich had been able to gather the books at moderate cost because of the troubled political state of the peninsula. Trübner, *Bibliographical Guide*, p. xv.

[4] This portrait of one of the earliest contributors to the bibliography of American history follows an engraving in the *Allgemeine geographische Ephemeriden*, May, 1800, p. 395. Ebeling was born Nov. 20, 1741, and died June 30, 1817, and his own contributions to American History were—

(*a*) *Amerikanische Bibliothek* (Zwei Stücke), Leipzig, 1777.

(*b*) *Erdbescreibung und Geschichte von America*, Hamburg, 1795–1816, in seven vols.; the author's interleaved copy, with manuscript notes, is in Harvard College Library.

(*c*) With Professor Hegewisch, *Americanisches Magazin*, Hamburg, 1797.

There are other likenesses,—one a large lithograph published at Hamburgh; the other a small profile by C. H. Kniep. Both are in the collection of the American Antiquarian Society.

... He was withal a man of great truthfulness and simplicity of character, of an amiable and obliging disposition and strict integrity." Similar was the estimation in which he was held by Ticknor, Prescott, George Bancroft, and many others, as Allibone has recorded.[1] In 1828 he removed to London, where he established himself as a bookseller. From this period, as Harrisse [2] fitly says, it was under his influence, acting upon the lovers of books among his compatriots, that the passion for forming collections of books exclusively American grew up.[3] In those days the cost of books now esteemed rare was trifling compared with the prices demanded at present. Rich had a prescience in his calling, and the beginnings of the great libraries of Colonel Aspinwall, Peter Force, James Lenox, and John Carter Brown were made under his fostering eye; which was just as kindly vigilant for Grenville, who was then forming out of the income of his sinecure office the great collection which he gave to the British nation in recompense for his support.[4] In London, watching the book-markets and making his catalogue, Rich continued to live for the rest of his life (he died in February, 1850), except for a period when he was the United States consul at Port Mahon in the Balearic Islands. His bibliographies are still valuable, his annotations in them are trustworthy, and their records are the starting-points of the growth of prices. His issues and reissues of them are somewhat complicated by supplements and combinations, but collectors and bibliographers place them on their shelves in the following order:

1. *A Catalogue of books relating principally to America, arranged under the years in which they were printed* (1500–1700), London, 1832. This included four hundred and eighty-six numbers, those designated by a star without price being understood to be in Colonel Aspinwall's collection. Two small supplements were added to this.

2. *Bibliotheca Americana Nova, printed since* 1700 (to 1800), London, 1835. Two hundred and fifty copies were printed. A supplement appeared in 1841, and this became again a part of his

3. *Bibliotheca Americana Nova*, vol. i. (1701–1800); vol. ii. (1801–1844), which was printed (250 copies) in London in 1846.[5]

It was in 1833 that Colonel Thomas Aspinwall, of Boston, who was for thirty-eight years the American consul at London, printed at Paris a catalogue of his collection of Americana, where seven hundred and seventy-one lots included, beside much that was ordinarily useful, a great number of the rarest of books on American history. Harrisse has called Colonel Aspinwall, not without justice, "a bibliophile of great tact and activity." All but the rarest part of his collection was subsequently burned in 1863, when it had passed into the hands of Mr. Samuel L. M. Barlow,[6] of New York.

M. Ternaux-Compans, who had collected — as Mr. Brevoort thinks [7] — the most extensive library of books on America ever brought together, printed his *Bibliothèque Américaine*[8] in 1837 at Paris. It embraced 1,154 works, arranged chronologically, and all of them of a date before 1700. The titles were abridged, and accompanied by French translations. His annotations were scant; and other students besides Rich have regretted that so learned a man had not more benefited his fellow-students by ampler notes.[9]

Also in 1837 appeared the *Catalogue d'ouvrages sur l'histoire de l'Amérique*, of G. B. Faribault, which was published at Quebec, and was more specially devoted to books on New France.[10]

With the works of Rich and Ternaux the bibliography of Americana may be considered to have acquired a distinct recognition; and the succeeding survey of this field may be

1 *Dictionary*, ii. 1788.

2 *Bibl. Amer. Vet.*, p. xxix.

3 Dibdin (*Library Companion*, edition 1825, p. 467) refers to this spirit, hoping it would lead to a new edition of White Kennett, perfected to date.

4 *Bibliotheca Grenvilliana* (London, 1842), now a part of the British Museum.

5 Sabin, *Bibliog. of Bibliog.*, p. cxxi; Allibone, *Dictionary*, p. 1787; Trübner, *Bibliographical Guide to American Literature*, Introduction, p. xiv; Jackson's *Bibl. Géog.*, no. 623, etc.; *Mass. Hist. Soc. Proc.*, i. 395; *Historical Magazine*, iii. 75; *Menzies Catalogue*, no. 1,690; Ternaux-Compans, *Bibliothèque Américaine*, Preface. Puttick and Simpson's *Catalogues*, London, June 25, 1850, and March, April, and May, 1872, note some of his books, besides manuscript bibliographies.

After Mr. Rich's death Mr. Edward G. Allen took the business, and issued various catalogues of books on America in 1857–1871. Cf. Jackson's *Bibliog. Géog.*, nos. 677–682.

6 See Vol. III. p. 159. The catalogue, being without date, is sometimes given later than 1833. Cf. Jackson, *Bibliog. Géog.*, no. 636; and no. 690. A new *Rough List* of the Barlow Collection was printed in 1885.

7 *Magazine of American History*, iii. 177. This library was sold in November, 1836, as Raetzel's; the numbers 908–2,117 concerned America. Trübner (*Bibliographical Guide*, p. xviii) says the collection was formed by Ternaux probably with an ultimate view to sale. Ternaux did not die till December, 1864.

8 Now worth 40 or 50 francs.

9 Trübner, *Bibliographical Guide*, p. xvi.

10 See Vol. IV. p. 367. Cf. also Trübner, *Bibliographical Guide*, p. xviii; and Daniel's *Nos Gloires Nationales*, where will be found a portrait of Faribault.

more conveniently made if we group the contributors by some broad discriminations of the motives influencing them, though such distinctions sometimes become confluent.

First, as regards what may be termed professional bibliography. One of the earliest workers in the new spirit was a Dresden jurist, Hermann E. Ludewig, who came to the United States in 1844, and prepared an account of the *Literature of American local history*, which was published in 1846. This was followed by a supplement, pertaining wholly to New York State, which appeared in *The Literary World*, February 19, 1848. He had previously published in the *Serapeum* at Leipsic (1845, pp. 209) accounts of American libraries and bibliography, which were the first contributions to this subject.[1] Some years later, in 1858, there was published in London a monograph on *The Literature of the American Aboriginal Linguistics*,[2] which had been undertaken by Mr. Ludewig but had not been carried through the press, when he died, Dec. 12, 1856.[3]

We owe to a Franco-American citizen the most important bibliography which we have respecting the first half century of American history; for the *Bibliotheca Americana Vetustissima* only comes down to 1551 in its chronological arrangement. Mr. Brevoort[4] very properly characterizes it as "a work which lightens the labors of such as have to investigate early American history."[5]

It was under the hospitable roof of Mr. Barlow's library in New York that, "having gloated for years over second-hand compilations," Harrisse says that he found himself "for the first time within reach of the fountain-heads of history." Here he gathered the materials for his *Notes on Columbus*, which were, as he says, like "pencil marks varnished over." These first appeared less perfectly than later, in the *New York Commercial Advertiser*, under the title of "Columbus in a Nut-shell." Mr. Harrisse had also prepared (four copies only printed) for Mr. Barlow in 1864 the *Bibliotheca Barlowiana*, which is a descriptive catalogue of the rarest books in the Barlow-Aspinwall Collection, touching especially the books on Virginian and New England history between 1602 and 1680.

Mr. Barlow now (1864) sumptuously printed the *Notes on Columbus* in a volume (ninety-nine copies) for private distribution. For some reason not apparent, there were expressions in this admirable treatise which offended some; as when, for instance (p. vii), he spoke of being debarred the privileges of a much-vaunted public library, referring to the Astor Library. Similar inadvertences again brought him hostile criticism, when two years later (1866) he printed with considerable typographical luxury his *Bibliotheca Americana Vetustissima*, which was published in New York. It embraces something over three hundred entries.[6] The work is not without errors; and Mr. Henry Stevens, who claims that he was wrongly accused in the book, gave it a bad name in the *London Athenæum* of Oct. 6, 1866, where an unfortunate slip, in making "Ander Schiffahrt"[7] a personage, is unmercifully ridiculed. A committee of the Société de Géographie in Paris, of which M. Ernest Desjardins was spokesman, came to the rescue, and printed a *Rapport sur les deux ouvrages de bibliographie Américaine de M. Henri Harrisse*, Paris, 1867. In this document the claim is unguardedly made that Harrisse's book was the earliest piece of solid erudition which America had produced, — a phrase qualified later as applying to works of American bibliography only. It was pointed out that while for the period of 1492–1551 Rich had given twenty titles, and Ternaux fifty-eight, Harrisse had enumerated three hundred and eight.[8]

Harrisse prepared, while shut up in Paris during the siege of 1870, his *Notes sur la Nouvelle France*, a valuable bibliographical essay referred to elsewhere.[9] He later put in shape the material which he had gathered for a supplemental volume to his *Bibliotheca Americana Vetustissima*, which he called *Additions*,[10] and published it in Paris in 1872. In his introduction to this latter volume he shows how thoroughly he has searched the libraries of Europe for new evidences of interest in America during the first half century after its discovery. He notes the depredations upon the older libraries which have been made in recent years, since the prices for rare Americana have ruled so high. He finds[11] that the Biblioteca Colom-

[1] Sabin, x. nos. 42,644–42,645.

[2] Sabin, x. 42,643; Trübner, *Bibliographical Guide*, p. xxi.

[3] *Historical Magazine*, xii. 145; Allibone, ii. p. 1142. The sale of Mr. Ludewig's library (1,380 entries) took place in New York in 1858.

[4] In his *Verrazano*, p. 5.

[5] Cf. also D'Avezac in his *Waltzemüller*, p. 4.

[6] Sabin, viii. p. 107; Jackson, *Bibliog. Géog.*, no. 696. The edition was four hundred copies.

[7] An error traced to the proof-reader, it is said in Sabin's *Bibliog. of Bibliog.*, p. lxxiv.

[8] Stevens noticed this defence by reiterating his charges in a note in his *Bibliotheca Historica*, 1870, no. 860.

[9] Vol. IV. p. 366.

[10] Sabin, *Bibliography of Bibliographies*, p. lxxv.

[11] *Grandeur et décadence de la Colombine*, Paris, 1885.

bina at Seville, as compared with a catalogue of it made by Ferdinand Columbus himself, has suffered immense losses. "It is curious to notice," he finally says, "how few of the original books relating to the early history of the New World can be found in the public libraries of Europe. There is not a literary institution, however rich and ancient, which in this respect could compare with three or four private libraries in America. The Marciana at Venice is probably the richest. The Trivulgiana at Milan can boast of several great rarities."

For the third contributor to the recent bibliography of Americana, we must still turn to an adopted citizen, Joseph Sabin, an Englishman by birth. Various publishing enterprises of interest to the historical student are associated with Mr. Sabin's name. He published a quarto series of reprints of early American tracts, eleven in number, and an octavo series, seven in number.[1] He published for several years, beginning in 1869, the *American Bibliopolist*, a record of new books, with literary miscellanies, largely upon Americana. In 1867 he began the publication (five hundred copies) of the most extensive American bibliography yet made, *A Dictionary of books relating to America, from its discovery to the present time*. The author's death, in 1881,[2] left the work somewhat more than half done, and it has been continued since his death by his sons.[3]

In the *Notas para una bibliografia de obras anonimas i seudonimas* of Diego Barros Arana, published at Santiago de Chile in 1882, five hundred and seven books on America (1493–1876), without authors, are traced to their writers.

As a second class of contributors to the bibliographical records of America, we must reckon the students who have gathered librari for use in pursuing their historical studie Foremost among such, and entitled to b esteemed a pioneer in the modern spirit research, is Alexander von Humboldt. H published his *Examen critique de l'histoire de géographie du nouveau continent*,[4] in five volume between 1836 and 1839.[5] "It is," says Brevoort "a guide which all must consult. With a maste hand the author combines and collates a attainable materials, and draws light fro sources which *he* first brings to bear in h exhaustive investigations." Harrisse calls "the greatest monument ever erected to th early history of this continent."

Humboldt's library was bought by Hen Stevens, who printed in 1863, in London, catalogue of it, showing 11,164 entries; but th was not published till 1870. It included a s of the *Examen critique*, with corrections, and th notes for a new sixth volume.[7] Harrisse, wh it is believed contemplated at one time a ne edition of this book, alleges that through th remissness of the purchaser of the library th world has lost sight of these precious memoria of Humboldt's unperfected labors. Stevens, the *London Athenæum*, October, 1866, rebuts th charge.[8]

Of the collection of books and manuscrip formed by Col. Peter Force we have no sep rate record, apart from their making a pc tion of the general catalogue of the Libra of Congress, the Government having boug the collection in 1867.[9]

The library which Jared Sparks forme during the progress of his historical labors w sold about 1872 to Cornell University, and now at Ithaca. Mr. Sparks left behind hi "imperfect but not unfaithful lists of his books

[1] *J. J. Cooke Catalogue*, no. 2,214; *Griswold Catalogue*, nos. 730, 731. The editions were fifty copi on large paper, two hundred on small. It may be worth record that Gowan, a publisher in New York, w the earliest (1846) to instigate a taste for large paper copies among American collectors, by printing in th style Furman's edition of Denton's *Description of New York*, after the manner of the English purveyors book-fancying.

[2] See *Proceedings of the Numismatic and Antiquarian Society*, Philadelphia, 1881, p. 28.

[3] Mr. Wilberforce Eames is the new editor. A list of the catalogues prepared by Mr. Sabin is given in h *Bibliography of Bibliographies*, p. cxxiv, etc.

[4] The German translation, *Kritische Untersuchungen*, was made by J. I. Ideler, Berlin, 1852, in 3 vo It has an index, which the French edition lacks.

[5] Sabin, viii. 539. The edition of Paris, without date, called *Histoire de la géographie du nouvea continent*, is the same, with a new title and an introduction of four pages, La Cosa's map being omitted.

[6] *Verrazano*, p. 4.

[7] In his *Cosmos* Humboldt gives results, which he says are reached in his unpublished sixth volume of th *Examen critique*.

[8] The Humboldt Library was burned in London in June, 1865. Nearly all of the catalogues were destroy at the same time; but a few large paper copies were saved, which, being perfected with a new title (Londo 1878), have since been offered by Stevens for sale. Portions of the introduction to it are also used in an artic by Stevens on Humboldt, in the *Journal of Sciences and Arts* January, 1870. Various of Humbold manuscripts on American matters are advertised in Stargardt's *Amerika und Orient*, no. 135, p. 3 (Berli 1881).

[9] Cf. *Historical Magazine*, vol. ix. no. 335; *Magazine of American History*, vol. ii. pp. 193, 221, 56 *Amer. Antiq. Soc. Proc.*, April, 1868. Colonel Force died in January, 1868.

which, after some supervision by Dr. Cogswell and others, were put in shape for the press by Mr. Charles A. Cutter of the Boston Athenæum, and were printed, in 1871, as *Catalogue of the Library of Jared Sparks.* In the appendix was a list of the historical manuscripts, originals and copies, which are now on deposit in Harvard College Library.[1]

In 1849 Mr. H. R. Schoolcraft[2] printed, at the expense of the United States Government, a *Bibliographical Catalogue of books, etc., in the Indian tongues of the United States,* — a list later reprinted with additions in his *Indian Tribes* (in 1851), vol. iv.[3]

In 1861 Mr. Ephraim George Squier published at New York a monograph on authors

[1] Mr. Sparks died March 14, 1866. Tributes were paid to his memory by distinguished associates in the Massachusetts Historical Society (*Proceedings*, ix. 157), and Dr. George E. Ellis reported to them a full and appreciative memoir (*Proceedings*, x. 211). Cf. also *Amer. Antiq. Soc. Proc.*, March, 1866; *Historical Magazine*, May, 1866; Brantz Mayer before the Maryland Historical Society, 1867, etc.

[2] Cf. *Historical Magazine*, vol. ix. p. 137.

[3] The principal interpreter of the Indian languages of the temperate parts of North America has been Dr. J. Hammond Trumbull, of Hartford, for whose labor in the bibliography of the subject see a chapter in vol i. of the *Memorial History of Boston.* There is also a collection edited by him, of books in and upon the Indian languages, in the *Brinley Catalogue*, iii. 123–145. He gave in the *Proceedings* of the American Antiquarian Society, and also separately in 1874, a list of books in the Indian languages, printed at Cambridge and Boston, 1653–1721 (Field, *Indian Bibliography*, no. 1,571). Cf. also Ludewig's *Literature of American Aboriginal Languages*, mentioned on an earlier page. It was edited and corrected by William W. Turner. (Cf. *Pinart-Brasseur Catalogue*, no. 565; Field, *Indian Bibliography*, no. 959).

Icazbalceta published in 1866, at Mexico, a list of the writers on the languages of America; and Romero made a similar enumeration of those of Mexico, in 1862, in the *Boletin de la Sociedad Mexicana de Geografia*, vol. viii. Dr. Daniel G. Brinton has made a good introduction to the literary history of the native Americans in his *Aboriginal American Authors*, published by him at Philadelphia in 1883. For his own linguistic contributions, see Field, *Indian Bibliography*, no. 187, etc. One of the earliest enumerations of linguistic titles can be picked out of the list which Boturini Benaduci, in 1746, appended to his *Idea de una nueva historia general de la America septentrional.*

The most extensive enumeration of the literature of all the North American tongues is doubtless to be the *Bibliography of North American Linguistics*, which is preparing by Mr. James C. Pilling of the Bureau of Ethnology in Washington, and which will be published in due time by that bureau. A preliminary issue (100 copies) for corrections is called *Proof-sheets of a Bibliography of the Indian Languages of North America* (pp. xl, 1135).

The *Bibliotheca Americana* of Leclerc (Paris, 1879) affords many titles to which a preliminary "Table des Divisions" affords an index, and most of them are grouped under the heading "Linguistique," p. 537, etc. The third volume of H. H. Bancroft's *Native Races*, particularly in its notes, is a necessary aid in this study; and a convenient summary of the whole subject will be found in chapter x. of John T. Short's *North Americans of Antiquity.* J. C. E. Buschmann has been an ardent laborer in this field; the bibliographies give his printed works (Field's *Indian Bibliography*, p. 208, etc.), and Stargardt's *Catalogue* (no. 135, p. 6) shows some of his manuscripts. The Comte Hyacinthe de Charencey has for some years, from time to time, printed various minor monographs on these subjects; and in 1883 he collected his views in a volume of *Mélanges de philologie et de paléographie Américaines.*

The Abbé Brasseur de Bourbourg, in his *Bibliothèque Mexico-Guatemalienne* (Leclerc, nos. 81, 1,084), has given for Central America a very excellent list of the works on the linguistics of the natives, which are all contained also in the *Catalogue* of the Pinart-Brasseur sale, which took place in Paris in January and February, 1884. Cf. the paper on Brasseur by Dr. Brinton, in *Lippincott's Magazine*, vol. i.; and the enumeration of his numerous writings in Sabin's *Dictionary*, ii. 7,420; also Leclerc, Field, and Bancroft.

Dr. Félix C. Y. Sobron's *Los Idiomas de la America Latina,* — *Estudios Biografico-bibliograficos*, published a few years since at Madrid, gives, according to Dr. Brinton, extended notices of several rare volumes; but on the whole the book is neither exhaustive nor very accurate.

Julius Platzmann's *Verzeichniss einer Auswahl Amerikanischer Grammatiken*, etc. (Leipsic, 1876), is a small but excellent list, with proper notes. These bibliographies will show the now numerous works upon the aboriginal tongues, their construction and their fruits.

There are several important series interesting to the student, which are found in the catalogues. Such are the *Bibliothèque linguistique Américaine*, published in seven volumes by Maisonneuve in Paris (Leclerc, no. 2,674); the *Coleccion de linguistica y etnografia Americanas*, or *Bibliothèque de linguistique et d'Ethnographie Américaines*, 1875, etc., edited by A. L. Pinart; the *Library of American Linguistics*, in thirteen volumes, edited by Dr. John G. Shea (Cf. *Brinley Catalogue*, vol. iii. no. 5,631; Field, no. 1,396); *Brinton's Library of Aboriginal American Literature*, published by Dr. D. G. Brinton in Philadelphia; and Brasseur de Bourbourg's *Collection de documents dans les langues indigènes*, Paris, 1861–1864, in four volumes (cf. Field, p. 175).

The earliest work printed exclusively in a native language was the *Catecismo de la Doctrina Cristiana en lengua Timuiquana*, published at Mexico in 1617 (cf. Sabin, vol. xiv. no. 58,580; Finotti, p. 14). This is the statement often made; but Mr. Pilling refers me to references in Icazbalceta's *Zumárraga* (vol. i. p. 290)

who had written in the languages of Central America, enumerating one hundred and ten, with a list of the books and manuscripts on the history, the aborigines, and the antiquities of Central America, borrowed from other sources in part. At the sale of Mr. Squier's library in 1876, the catalogue[1] of which was made by Mr. Sabin, the entire collection of his manuscripts fell, as mentioned elsewhere,[2] into the hands of Mr. Hubert Howe Bancroft of San Francisco.

Probably the largest collection of books and manuscripts[3] which any American has formed for use in writing is that which belongs to Mr. Bancroft. He is the organizer of an extensive series of books on the antiquities and history of the Pacific coast. To accomplish an examination of the aboriginal and civilized history of so large a field[4] as thoroughly as he has unquestionably made it, within a lifetime, was a bold undertaking, to be carried out in a centre of material rather than of literary enterprise. The task involved the gathering of a library of printed books, at a distance from the purely intellectual activity of the country, and where no other collection of moment existed to supplement it. It required the seeking and making of manuscripts, from the labor of which one might well shrink. It was fortunate that during the gathering of this collection some notable collections — like those of Maximilian,[5] Ramirez, and Squier, not to name others — were opportunely brought to the hammer, a chance by which Mr. Bancroft naturally profited.

Mr. Bancroft had been trained in the business habits of the book trade, in which he had established himself in San Francisco as early as 1856.[6] He was at this time twenty-four years old, having been born of New England stock in Ohio in 1832, and having had already four years residence — since 1852 — in San Francisco as the agent of an eastern bookseller. It was not till 1869 that he set seriously to work on his history, and organized a staff of assistants.[7] They indexed his library, which was now large (12,000 volumes) and was kept on an upper floor of his business quarters, and they classified the references in paper bags.[8] His first idea was to make an encyclopædia of the antiquities and history of the Pacific Coast; and it is on the whole unfortunate that he abandoned the scheme, for his methods were admirably adapted to that end, but of questionable application to a sustained plan of historical treatment. It is the encyclopedic quality of his work, as the user eliminates what he wishes, which makes and will continue to make the books that pass under his name of the first importance to historical students.

In 1875 the first five volumes of the series, denominated by themselves *The Native Races of the Pacific States*, made their appearance. It was

to an earlier edition of about 1547; and in the same author's *Bibliografia Mexicana* (p. 32), to one of 1553. Molina's *Vocabulario de la lengua Castellana y Mexicana*, placing the Nahuatl and Castilian in connection, was printed at Mexico in 1555. The book is very rare, five or six copies only being known; and Quaritch has priced an imperfect copy at £72 (Quaritch, *Bibliog. Géog. linguistica*, 1879, no. 12,616; Carter-Brown, vol. i. no. 206; *Brinley Catalogue*, vol. iii. no, 5,771). The edition of 1571 is also rare (*Pinart-Brasseur Catalogue*, no. 630; Carter-Brown, vol. i. nos. 285, 286; Quaritch, 1879, no. 12,617). The first edition of Molina's Aztec grammar, *Arte de la lengua Mexicana y Castellana*, was published the same year (1571). Quaritch (1879, no. 12,615) prices this at £52 10*s*. Cf. also Carter-Brown, vol. i. no. 284. One of the chief of the more recent studies of the linguistics of Mexico is Francisco Pimentel's *Cuadro descriptivo y comparativo de las lenguas indigenas de México*, Mexico, 1862–1865; and second edition in 1874–1875.

This subject has other treatment later in the present volume.

1 It included two thousand and thirty-four items, ninety-four of which were Mr. Squier's own works.

2 Vol. II. p. 578.

3 He says that up to 1881 he had gathered 35,000 volumes, at a cost of $300,000, exclusive of time and travelling expenses. His manuscripts embraced 1,200 volumes. The annual growth of his library is still 1,000 volumes.

4 One twelfth of the earth's surface, as he says.

5 Cf. account of Maximilian's library in the *Bookworm* (1869), p. 14.

6 These biographical data are derived from a tract given out by himself which he calls *A brief account of the literary undertakings of Hubert Howe Bancroft* (San Francisco, A. L. Bancroft & Co. [his own business house], 1882, 8vo, pp. 12). Other accounts of his library will be found in the *American Bibliopolist*, vii. 44; and in Apponyi's *Libraries of California*, 1878. Descriptions of the library and of the brick building (built in 1881) which holds it, and of his organized methods, have occasionally appeared in the *Overland Monthly* and in other serial issues of California, as well as in those of the Atlantic cities. He has been free to make public the most which is known regarding his work. He says that the grouping and separating of his material has been done mostly by others, who have also written fully one half of the text of what he does not hesitate to call *The Works of Hubert Howe Bancroft;* and he leaves the reader to derive a correct understanding of the case from his prefaces and illustrative tracts. Cf. J. C. Derby's *Fifty Years among authors, books, and publishers* (New York, 1884), p. 31.

7 Averaging twelve from that time to this; a hundred persons were tried for every one ultimately retained as a valuable assistant, — is his own statement.

8 At a cost, as he says, of $80,000 to 1882.

clear that a new force had been brought to bear upon historical research, — the force of organized labor from many hands; and this implied competent administrative direction and ungrudged expenditure of money. The work showed the faults of such a method, in a want of uniform discrimination, and in that promiscuous avidity of search, which marks rather an eagerness to amass than a judgment to select, and give literary perspective. The book, however, was accepted as extremely useful and promising to the future inquirer. Despite a certain callowness of manner, the *Native Races* was extremely creditable, with comparatively little of the patronizing and flippant air which its flattering reception has since begotten in its author or his staff. An unfamiliarity with the amenities of literary life seems unexpectedly to have been more apparent also in his later work.

In April, 1876, Mr. Lewis H. Morgan printed in the *North American Review*, under the title of "Montezuma's Dinner," a paper in which he controverted the views expressed in the *Native Races* regarding the kind of aboriginal civilization belonging to the Mexican and Central American table-lands. A writer of Mr. Morgan's reputation commanded respect in all but Mr. Bancroft, who has been unwise enough to charge him with seeking "to gain notoriety by attacking" his (Mr. B.'s) views or supposed views. He dares also to characterize so well-known an authority as "a person going about from one reviewer to another begging condemnation for my *Native Races*." It was this ungracious tone which produced a divided reception for his new venture. This, after an interval of seven years, began to make its appearance in vol. vi. of the "Works," or vol. i. of the *History of Central America*, appearing in the autumn of 1882.

The changed tone of the new series, its rhetoric, ambitious in parts, but mixed with passages which are often forceful and exact, suggestive of an ill-assorted conjoint production; the interlarding of classic allusions by some retained reviser who served this purpose for one volume at least; a certain cheap reasoning and ranting philosophy, which gives place at times to conceptions of grasp; flippancy and egotism, which induce a patronizing air under the guise of a constrained adulation of others; a want of knowledge on points where the system of indexing employed by his staff had been deficient, — these traits served to separate the criticism of students from the ordinary laudation of such as were dazed by the magnitude of the scheme.

Two reviews challenging his merits on these grounds [1] induced Mr. Bancroft to reply in a tract [2] called *The Early American Chroniclers*. The manner of this rejoinder is more offensive than that of the volumes which it defends; and with bitter language he charges the reviewers with being "men of Morgan," working in concert to prejudice his success.

But the controversy of which record is here made is unworthy of the principal party to it. His important work needs no such adventitious support; and the occasion for it might have been avoided by ordinary prudence. The extent of the library upon which the work [3] is based, and the full citation of the authorities followed in his notes, and the more general enumeration of them in his preliminary lists, make the work pre-eminent for its bibliographical extent, however insufficient, and at times careless, is the bibliographical record.[4]

The library formed by the late Henry C. Murphy of Brooklyn to assist him in his projected history of maritime discovery in America, of which only the chapter on Verrazano [5] has been printed, was the creation of diligent search for many years, part of which was spent in Holland as minister of the United States. The earliest record of it is a *Catalogue of an American library chronologically arranged*, which was

[1] They appeared in *The Nation* and in the *New York Independent* early in 1883. The first aimed to show that there were substantial grounds for dissent from Mr. Bancroft's views regarding the Aztec civilization. The second ignored that point in controversy, and merely proposed, as was stated, to test the "bibliographic value" which Mr. Bancroft had claimed for his book, and to point out the failures of the index plan and the vicarious system as employed by him.

[2] Seemingly intended to make part of one of the later volumes of his series, to be called *Essays and Miscellanies*.

[3] With a general title (as following his *Native Races*) of *The History of the Pacific States*, we are to have in twenty-eight volumes the history of Central America, Mexico, North Mexico, New Mexico, Arizona, California, Nevada, Utah, Northwest Coast, Oregon, Washington, Idaho, Montana, British Columbia, and Alaska, — to be followed by six volumes of allied subjects, not easily interwoven in the general narrative, making thirty-nine volumes for the entire work. The volumes are now appearing at the rate of three or four a year.

[4] The list which is prefixed to the first volume of the *History of California*, forming vol. xiii. of his Pacific States series, is particularly indicative of the rich stores of his library, and greatly eclipses the previous lists of Mr. A. S. Taylor, which appeared in the *Sacramento Daily Union*, June 25, 1863, and March 13, 1866. Cf. Harrisse, *Bibl. Amer. Vet.*, p. xxxix. A copy of Taylor's pioneer work, with his own corrections, is in Harvard College Library. Mr. Bancroft speaks very ungraciously of it.

[5] See Vol. IV., chap. i. p. 19.

JAMES CARSON BREVOORT.

privately printed in a few copies, about 1850, and showed five hundred and eighty-nine entries between the years 1480 and 1800.[1]

There has been no catalogue printed of the library of Mr. James Carson Brevoort, so well known as a historical student and bibliographer, to whom Mr. Sabin dedicated the first volume of his *Dictionary*. Some of the choicer portions of his collection are understood to have become a part of the Astor Library, of which Mr. Brevoort was for a few years the superintendent, as well as a trustee.[2]

The useful and choice collection of Mr. Charles Deane, of Cambridge, Mass., to which, as the reader will discover, the Editor has often had recourse, has never been catalogued. Mr. Deane has made excellent use of it, as his tracts and papers abundantly show.[3]

A distinct class of helpers in the field of American bibliography has been those gatherers of libraries who are included under the somewhat indefinite term of collectors, — owners of books, but who make no considerable dependence

[1] Jackson, *Bibl. Géog.*, no. 639; *Menzies Catalogue*, nos. 1,459, 1,460; Wynne's *Private Libraries of New York*, p. 335. Mr. Murphy died Dec. 1, 1882, aged seventy-two; and his collection, then very much enlarged, was sold in March, 1884. Its *Catalogue*, edited by Mr. John Russell Bartlett, shows one of the richest libraries of Americana which has been given to public sale in America. It is accompanied by a biographical sketch of its collector. Cf. Vol. IV. p. 22.

[2] Cf. Wynne's *Private Libraries of New York*, p. 106. Mr. Brevoort died December 7, 1887.

[3] Cf. Sabin, v. 283; Farnham's *Private Libraries of Boston*.

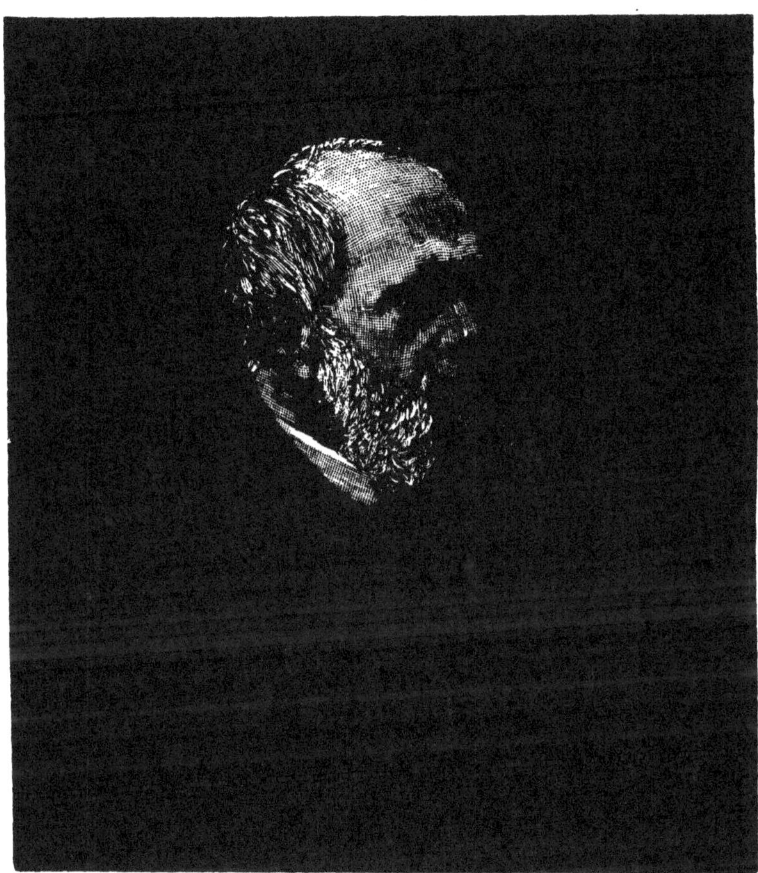

CHARLES DEANE.

upon them for studies which lead to publication. From such, however, in some instances, bibliography has notably gained, — as in the careful knowledge which Mr. James Lenox sometimes dispensed to scholars either in privately printed issues or in the pages of periodicals.

Harrisse in 1866 pointed to five Americana libraries in the United States as surpassing all of their kind in Europe, — the Carter-Brown, Barlow, Force, Murphy, and Lenox collections. Of the Barlow, Force (now in the Library of Congress), and Murphy collections mention has already been made.

The Lenox Library is no longer private, having been given to a board of trustees by Mr. Lenox previous to his death,[1] and handsomely housed, by whom it is held for a restricted public use, when fully catalogued and arranged. Its character, as containing only rare or unusual books, will necessarily withdraw it from the use of all but scholars engaged in recondite studies. It is very rich in other directions than American history; but in this department the partial access which Harrisse had to it while in Mr. Lenox's house led him to infer that it would hold the first rank. The wealth of its alcoves, with their twenty-eight thousand volumes, is becoming known gradually in a series of bibliographical monographs, printed as contributions to its catalogue, of which six have

1 February, 1880, aged eighty years. His father was Robert Lenox, a Scotchman, who began business in New York in 1783, and retired in 1812 with a large fortune, including a farm of thirty acres, worth then about $6,000, and to-day $10,000,000, — if such figures can be made accurate. Cf. also Charles Deane in *Amer. Antiq. Soc. Proc.*, April, 1880. Henry Stevens's *Recoll. of Lenox* is conspicuous for what it does not reveal.

thus far appeared, some of them clearly and mainly the work of Mr. Lenox himself.

Of these only three have illustrated American history in any degree, — those devoted to the voyages of Hulsius and Thévenot, and to the Jesuit Relations (Canada).[1]

The only rival of the Lenox is the library of the late John Carter Brown, of Providence, gathered largely under the supervision of John Russell Bartlett; and since Mr. Brown's death it has been more particularly under the same oversight.[2] It differs from the Lenox Library in that it is exclusively American, or nearly so,[3] and still more in that we have access to a thorough catalogue of its resources, made by Mr. Bartlett himself, and sumptuously printed.[4] It was originally issued as *Bibliotheca Americana: A Catalogue of books relating to North and South America in the Library of John Carter Brown of Providence, with notes by John Russell Bartlett*, in three volumes, — vol. i., 1493–1600, in 1865 (302 entries); vol. ii., 1601–1700, in 1866 (1,160 entries); vol. iii., 1701–1800, in two parts, in 1870–1871 (4,173 entries).

In 1875 vol. i. was reprinted with fuller titles, covering the years 1482[5]–1601, with 600 entries, doubling the extent of that portion.[6] Numerous fac-similes of titles and maps add much to its value. A second and similarly extended edition of vol. ii. (1600–1700) was printed in 1882, showing 1,642 entries. The *Carter-Brown Catalogue*, as it is ordinarily cited, is the most extensive printed list of all Americana previous to 1800, more especially anterior to 1700, which now exists.[7]

Of the other important American catalogues, the first place is to be assigned to that of the collection formed at Hartford by Mr. George Brinley, the sale of which since his death[8] has been undertaken under the direction of Dr. J. Hammond Trumbull,[9] who has prepared the catalogue, and who claims — not without warrant — that it embraces "a greater number of volumes remarkable for their rarity, value, and interest to special collectors and to book-lovers in general, than were ever before brought together in an American sale-room."[10]

The library of William Menzies, of New York, was sold in 1875, from a catalogue made by Joseph Sabin.[11] The library of Edward A. Crowninshield, of Boston, was catalogued in Boston in 1859, but withdrawn from public sale, and sold to Henry Stevens, who took a portion of it to London. It was not large, — the catalogue shows less than 1,200 titles, — and was not exclusively American; but it was rich in

1 The Lenox Library is now under the direction of the distinguished American historical student, Dr. George H. Moore, so long in charge of the New York Historical Society's library. Cf. an account of Dr. Moore by Howard Crosby in the *Historical Magazine*, vol. xvii. (January, 1870). The officer in immediate charge of the library is Dr. S. Austin Allibone, well known for his *Dictionary of Authors*.

2 Mr. Bartlett was early in life a dealer in books in New York; and the Americana catalogues of Bartlett and Welford, forty years ago, were among the best of dealers' lists. Jackson's *Bibl. Géog.*, no. 641.

3 The field of Americana before 1800 has been so nearly exhausted in its composition, that recent purchases have been made in other departments, particularly of costly books on the fine arts.

4 Cf. Vol. III. p. 380.

5 Because Greenland in the map of the Ptolemy of this year is laid down. The slightest reference to America in books of the sixteenth century have entitled them to admission.

6 The book purports to have been printed in one hundred copies; but not more than half that number, it is said, have been distributed. Some copies have a title reading, *Bibliographical notices of rare and curious books relating to America, printed in the fifteenth and sixteenth centuries, in the library of the late John Carter Brown, by John Russell Bartlett.*

7 Sir Arthur Helps, in referring to the assistance he had got from books sent to him from America, and from this library in particular, says: "As far as I have been able to judge, the American collectors of books are exceedingly liberal and courteous in the use of them, and seem really to understand what the object should be in forming a great library." *Spanish Conquest*, American edition, p. 122.

8 Cf. *Amer. Antiq. Soc. Proc.*, October, 1875.

9 Dr. Trumbull himself has been a keen collector of books on American history, particularly in illustration of his special study of aboriginal linguistics; while his influence has not been unfelt in the forming of the Watkinson Library, and of that of the Connecticut Historical Society, both at Hartford.

10 The first sale — there are to be four — took place in March, 1878, and illustrated a new device in testamentary bequests. Mr. Brinley devised to certain libraries the sum of several thousand dollars each, to be used to their credit for purchases made at the public sale of his books. The result was a competition that carried the aggregate of the sales, it is computed, as much beyond the sum which might otherwise have been obtained, as was the amount devised, — thus impairing in no degree the estate for the heirs, and securing credit for public bequests. The scheme has been followed in the sale of the library (the third part of which was Americana, largely from the Menzies library) of the late J. J. Cooke, of Providence, with an equivalent appreciation of the prices of the books. It is a question if the interests of the libraries benefited are advanced by such artificial stimulation of prices, which a factitious competition helps to make permanent.

11 *American Bibliopolist*, viii. 128; Wynne's *Private Libraries of New York*, p. 318. The collection was not exclusively American.

some of the rarest of such books, particularly in regard to the English Colonies.[1]

The sale of John Allan's collection in New York, in 1864, was a noteworthy one. Americana, however, were but a portion of the collection.[2] An English-American flavor of far less fineness, but represented in a catalogue showing a very large collection of books and pamphlets,[3] was sold in New York in May, 1870, as the property of Mr. E. P. Boon.

Mr. Thomas W. Field issued in 1873 *An Essay towards an Indian Bibliography, being a Catalogue of books relating to the American Indians*, in his own library, with a few others which he did not possess, distinguished by an asterisk. Mr. Field added many bibliographical and historical notes, and gave synopses, so that the catalogue is generally useful to the student of Americana, as he did not confine his survey to works dealing exclusively with the aborigines. The library upon which this bibliography was based was sold at public auction in New York, in two parts, in May, 1875 (3,324 titles), according to a catalogue which is a distinct publication from the *Essay*.[4]

The collection of Mr. Almon W. Griswold was dispersed by printed catalogues in 1876 and 1880, the former containing the American portion, rich in many of the rarer books.

Of the various private collections elsewhere than in the United States, more or less rich in Americana, mention may be made of the *Bibliotheca Mejicana*[5] of Augustin Fischer, London, 1869; of the Spanish-American libraries of Gregorio Beéche, whose catalogue was printed at Valparaiso in 1879; and that of Benjamin Vicuña Mackenna, printed at the same place in 1861.[6]

In Leipsic, the catalogue of Serge Sobolewski (1873)[7] was particularly helpful in the bibliography of Ptolemy, and in the voyages of De Bry and others. Some of the rarest of Americana were sold in the Sunderland sale[8] in London in 1881–1883; and remarkably rich collections were those of Pinart and Bourbourg,[9] sold in Paris in 1883, and that of Dr. J. Court,[10] the first part of which was sold in Paris in May, 1884. The second part had little of interest.

Still another distinctive kind of bibliographies is found in the catalogues of the better class of dealers; and among the best of such is to be placed the various lists printed by Henry Stevens, a native of Vermont, who has spent most of his manhood in London. In the dedication to John Carter Brown of his *Schedule of Nuggets* (1870), he gives some account of his early bibliographical quests.[11] Two years after graduating at Yale, he says, he had passed "at Cambridge, reading passively with legal Story, and actively with historical Sparks, all the while sifting and digesting the treasures of the Harvard Library. For five years previously he had scouted through several States during his vacations, prospecting in out-of-the-way places for historical nuggets, mousing through town libraries and country garrets in search of anything old that was historically new for Peter Force and his American Archives. . . . From Vermont to Delaware many an antiquated churn, sequestered hen-coop, and dilapidated flour-barrel had yielded to him rich harvests of old papers, musty books, and golden pamphlets. Finally, in 1845, an irrefragable desire impelled him to visit the Old World, its libraries and book-stalls. Mr. Brown's enlightened liberality in those primitive years of his bibliographical pupilage contributed largely towards the boiling of his kettle. . . . In acquiring *con amore* these American Historiadores Primitivos, he . . . travelled far and near. In this labor of love, this journey of life, his tracks often become your tracks, his labors your works, his

1 Memoir of Mr. Crowninshield, by Charles Deane, in *Mass. Hist. Soc. Proc.*, xvii. 356. Mr. Stevens is said to have given about $9,500 for the library. It was sold in various parts, the more extensive portion in July, 1860. Allibone, vol. ii. p. 2,248.

2 This collection — which Mr. Allan is said to have held at $15,000 — brought $39,000 at auction after his death.

3 Another catalogue rich in pamphlets relating to America is that of Albert G. Greene, New York, 1869.

4 The *Catalogue* is more correctly printed than the *Essay*. Sabin, *Bibliog. of Bibliog.*, p. cxxv.

5 *Bibliotheca Mejicana, a collection of books relating to Mexico, and North and South America;* sold by Puttick & Simpson in London, June, 1869. (About 3,000 titles.)

6 Jackson, *Bibl. Géog.*, nos. 844, 845.

7 *Catalogue de la collection précieuse de livres anciens et modernes formant la Bibliothèque de feu M. Serge Sobolewski* (*de Moscou*) Leipsic, 1873.

8 *Bibliotheca Sunderlandiana. Sale Catalogue of the Sunderland or Blenheim Library. Five Parts.* London, 1881–1883. (13,858 nos.)

9 *Catalogue de livres rares et précieux, manuscrits et imprimés, principalement sur l'Amérique et sur les langues du monde entier, composant la bibliothèque de Alphonse L. Pinart, et comprenant en totalité la bibliothèque Mexico-Guatémalienne de M. l'abbé Brasseur de Bourbourg.* Paris, 1883. viii. 248 pp. 8°.

10 *Catalogue de la précieuse bibliothèque de feu M. le Docteur J. Court, comprenant une collection unique de voyageurs et d'historiens relatifs à l'Amérique. Première partie.* Paris, 1884. (458 nos.)

11 There is an account of his family antecedents, well spiced as his wont is, in the introduction to his *Bibliotheca Historica*, 1870.

libri your *liberi*," he adds, in addressing Mr. Brown.

In 1848 Mr. Stevens proposed the publication, through the Smithsonian Institution, of a general *Bibliographia Americana*, illustrating the sources of early American history;[1] but the project failed, and one or more attempts later made to begin the work also stopped short of a beginning. While working as a literary agent of the Smithsonian Institution and other libraries, in these years, and beginning that systematic selection of American books, for the British Museum and Bodleian, which has made these libraries so nearly, if not quite, the equal of any collection of Americana in the United States, he also made the transcriptions and indexes of the documents in the State Paper Office which respectively concern the States of New Jersey, Rhode Island, Maryland, and Virginia. These labors are now preserved in the archives of those States.[2] Perhaps the earliest of his sale catalogues was that of a pseudo "Count Mondidier," embracing Americana, which were sold in London in December, 1851.[3] His *English Library* in 1853 was without any distinctive American flavor; but in 1854 he began, but suspended after two numbers, the *American Bibliographer* (100 copies).[4] In 1856 he prepared a *Catalogue of American Books and Maps in the British Museum* (20,000 titles), which, however, was never regularly published, but copies bear date 1859, 1862, and 1866.[5] In 1858 — though most copies are dated 1862[6] — appeared his *Historical Nuggets; Bibliotheca Americana, or a descriptive Account of my Collection of rare books relating to America.* The two little volumes show about three thousand titles, and Harrisse says they are printed "with remarkable accuracy." There was begun in 1885, in connection with his son Mr. Henry Newton Stevens, a continuation of these *Nuggets.* In 1861 a sale catalogue of his *Bibliotheca Americana* (2,415 lots), issued by Puttick and Simpson, and in part an abridgment of the *Nuggets* with similarly careful collations, was accepted by Maisonneuve as the model of his *Bibliothèque Américaine* later to be mentioned.[7]

In 1869–1870 Mr. Stevens visited America, and printed at New Haven his *Historical and Geographical Notes on the earliest discoveries in America*, 1453–1530, with photo-lithographic fac-similes of some of the earliest maps. It is a valuable essay, much referred to, in which the author endeavored to indicate the entanglement of the Asiatic and American coast lines in the early cartography.[8]

In 1870 he sold at Boston a collection of five thousand volumes, catalogued as *Bibliotheca Historica*[9] (2,545 entries), being mostly Americana, from the library of the elder Henry Stevens of Vermont. It has a characteristic introduction, with an array of readable notes.[10] His catalogues have often such annotations, inserted on a principle which he explains in the introduction to this one: "In the course of many years of bibliographical study and research, having picked up various isolated grains of knowledge respecting the early history, geography, and bibliography of this western hemisphere, the writer has thought it well to pigeon-hole the facts in notes long and short."

In October, 1870, he printed at London a *Schedule of Two Thousand American Historical Nuggets taken from the Stevens Diggings in September*, 1870, *and set down in Chronological Order of Printing from* 1490 *to* 1800 [1776], *described and recommended as a Supplement to my printed Bibliotheca Americana.* It included 1,350 titles.

In 1872 he sold another collection, largely Americana, according to a catalogue entitled *Bibliotheca Geographica & Historica; or, a Catalogue of* [3,109 *lots*], *illustrative of historical geography and geographical history. Collected, used, and described, with an Introductory Essay on Catalogues, and how to make them upon the Stevens system of photo-bibliography.* The title calls it a first part; but no second part ever appeared. Ten copies were issued, with about four hundred

1 Trübner, *Bibliographical Guide to American Literature* (1859), p. iv.; *North American Review*, July, 1850, p. 205, by George Livermore.

2 Allibone, ii. 2247–2248.

3 Sabin, vol. xii. no. 49,961.

4 Stevens, *Historical Collections*, i. 874. It was ostensibly made in preparation for his projected *Bibliographia Americana.*

5 *Historical Collections*, vol. i. no. 90; Allibone, vol. ii. p. 2248.

6 Allibone, ii. 2248; *Historical Collections*, vol. i. no. 875; *Bibliotheca Historica* (1870), no. 1,974.

7 Allibone, ii. 2248; *Historical Collections*, vol. i. no. 878.

8 It was first published, less perfectly, in the *American Journal of Science*, vol. xcviii. p. 299; and of the separate issue seventy-five copies only were printed. *Bibliotheca Historica* (1870), no. 1,976. It was also issued as a part of a volume on the proposed *Tehuantepec Railway*, prepared by his brother, Simon Stevens, and published by the Appletons of New York the same year. *Ibid.* no. 1,977; *Historical Collections*, vol. i. nos. 894 895; Allibone, vol. ii. p. 2348, nos. 17, 18, 19.

9 *Historical Collections*, vol. i. no. 897.

10 It is a droll fancy of his to call his book-shop the "Nuggetory;" to append to his name "G. M. B.," for Green Mountain Boy; and even to parade in a similar titular fashion his rejection at a London Club, — "Bk-bld — Ath.-Cl."

photographic copies of titles inserted. Some copies are found without the essay.[1]

The next year (1873) he issued a privately printed list of two thousand titles of American "Continuations," as they are called by librarians, or serial publications in progress as taken at the British Museum, quaintly terming the list *American books with tails to 'em*.[2]

Finally, in 1881, he printed Part I. of *Stevens's Historical Collections*, a sale catalogue showing 1,625 titles of books, chiefly Americana, and including his Franklin Collection of manuscripts, which he later privately sold to the United States Government, an agent of the Boston Public Library yielding to the nation.[3]

One of the earliest to establish an antiquarian bookshop in the United States was the late Samuel G. Drake, who opened one in Boston in 1830.[4] His special field was that of the North American Indians; and the history and antiquities of the aborigines, together with the history of the English Colonies, give a character to his numerous catalogues.[5] Mr. Drake died in 1875, from a cold taken at a sale of the library of Daniel Webster; and his final collections of books were scattered in two sales in the following year.[6]

William Gowans, of New York, was another of the early dealers in Americana.[7] The catalogues of Bartlett and Welford have already been mentioned. In 1854, while Garrigue and Christern were acting as agents of Mr. Lenox, they printed *Livres Curieux*, a list of desiderata sought for by Mr. Lenox, pertaining to such rarities as the letters of Columbus, Cartier, parts of De Bry and Hulsius, and the Jesuit Relations. This list was circulated widely through Europe, but not twenty out of the 216 titles were ever offered.[8]

About 1856, Charles B. Norton, of New York, began to issue American catalogues; and in 1857 he established *Norton's Literary Letter*, intended to foster interest in the collection of Americana.[9] A little later, Joel Munsell, of Albany, began to issue catalogues;[10] and J. W. Randolph, of Richmond, Virginia, more particularly illustrated the history of the southern parts of the United States.[11] The most important Americana lists at present issued by American dealers are those of Robert Clarke & Co., of Cincinnati, which are admirable specimens of such lists.[12]

In England, the catalogues of Henry Stevens and E. G. Allen have been already mentioned.

[1] *Historical Collections*, vol. i. no. 898.

[2] *Historical Collections*, vol. i. no. 899.

[3] The public is largely indebted to the efforts of Mr. Theodore F. Dwight, the librarian and keeper of the Archives of the Department of State at Washington, for the ultimate success of the endeavor to secure these manuscripts to the nation. Mr. Stevens had lately (1885) formed a copartnership with his son, Mr. Henry N. Stevens, and had begun a new series of Catalogues, of which No. 1 gives his own publications, and No. 2 is a bibliography of New Hampshire History. He died in London, February 28, 1886.

[4] *N. E. Hist. and Geneal. Reg.*, 1863, p. 203. Dr. Homes, of Albany, is confident Joseph Bumstead was earlier in Boston than Mr. Drake. The *Boston Directory* represents him as a printer in 1800, and as a bookseller after 1816.

[5] His earliest catalogue appeared in 1842, as of his private library. Sabin's *Bibl. of Bibl.*, p. xlix. A collection announced for sale in Boston in 1845 was withdrawn after the catalogue was printed, having been sold to the Connecticut Historical Society for $4,000. At one time he amassed a large collection of American school-books to illustrate our educational history. They were bought (about four hundred in all) by the British Museum.

[6] Cf. Jackson's *Bibl. Géog.*, no. 684, and pp. 185, 199. Also see Vol. III. 361.

[7] His catalogues are spiced with annotations signed "Western Memorabilia." Sabin (*Dictionary*, vii. 369) quotes the saying of a rival regarding Gowans's catalogues, that their notes "were distinguished by much originality, some personality, and not a little bad grammar." His shop and its master are drawn in F. B. Perkins's *Scrope, or the Lost Library. A Novel.* Mr. Gowans died in November, 1870, at sixty-seven, leaving a stock, it is said, of 250,000 bound volumes, besides a pamphlet collection of enormous extent. Mr. W. C. Prime told the story of his life, genially, in *Harper's Magazine* (1872), in an article on "Old Books in New York." Speaking of his stock, Mr. Prime says: "There were many more valuable collections in the hands of booksellers, but none so large, and probably none so wholly without arrangement." Mr. Gowans was a Scotchman by birth, and came to America in 1821. After a varied experience on a Mississippi flat-boat, he came to New York, and in 1827 began life afresh as a bookseller's clerk. Cf. *American Bibliopolist*, January, 1871, p. 5.

[8] Harrisse, *Bibl. Amer. Vet.*, p. xxx.

[9] Jackson, *Bibl. Géog.*, nos. 670–676.

[10] Jackson, no. 687. See Vol. IV. p. 435. Munsell issued privately, in 1872, a catalogue of the works printed by him. Sabin, *Bibl. of Bibl.*, p. cv. Cf. a *Biographical Sketch of Joel Munsell, by George R. Howell, with a Genealogy of the Munsell Family, by Frank Munsell.* Boston, 1880. This was printed (16 pp.) for the New England Historic Genealogical Society.

[11] Jackson, no. 669.

[12] They have been issued in 1869, 1871, 1873, 1876, 1877, 1878, 1879, 1883. Jackson, nos. 705–711. Lesser lists have been issued in Cincinnati by William Dodge. The chief dealer in Americana in Boston, who issues catalogues, is, at the present time, Mr. George E. Littlefield.

The leading English dealer at present in the choicer books of Americana, as of all other subjects — and it is not too much to say, the leading one of the world — is Mr. Bernard Quaritch, a Prussian by birth, who was born in 1819, and after some service in the book-trade in his native country came to London in 1842, and entered the service of Henry G. Bohn, under whose instruction, and as a fellow-employé of Lowndes the bibliographer, he laid the foundations of a remarkable bibliographical acquaintance. A short service in Paris brought him the friendship of Brunet. Again (1845) he returned to Mr. Bohn's shop; but in April, 1847, he began business in London for himself. He issued his catalogues at once on a small scale; but they took their well-known distinctive form in 1848, which they have retained, except during the interval December, 1854,-May, 1864, when, to secure favorable consideration in the post-office rates, the serial was called *The Museum*. It has been his habit, at intervals, to collect his occasional catalogues into volumes, and provide them with an index. The first of these (7,000 entries) was issued in 1860. Others have been issued in 1864, 1868, 1870, 1874, 1877 (this with the preceding constituting one work, showing nearly 45,000 entries or 200,000 volumes), and 1880 (describing 28,009 books).[1] In the preface to this last catalogue he says: "The prices of useful and learned books are in all cases moderate; the prices of palæographical and bibliographical curiosities are no doubt in most cases high, that indeed being a natural result of the great rivalry between English, French, and American collectors. . . . A fine copy of any edition of a book is, and ought to be, more than twice as costly as any other."[2] While the Quaritch catalogues have been general, they have included a large share of the rarest Americana, whose titles have been illustrated with bibliographical notes characterized by intimate acquaintance with the secrets of the more curious lore.

The catalogues of John Russell Smith (1849, 1853, 1865, 1867), and of his successor Alfred Russell Smith (1871, 1874), are useful aids in this department.[3] The *Bibliotheca Hispano-Americana* of Trübner, printed in 1870, offered about thirteen hundred items.[4] Occasional reference can be usefully made to the lists of George Bumstead, Ellis and White, John Camden Hotten, all of London, and to those of William George of Bristol. The latest extensive Americana catalogue is *A catalogue of rare and curious books, all of which relate more or less to America*, on sale by F. S. Ellis, London, 1884. It shows three hundred and forty-two titles, including many of the rarer books, which are held at prices startling even to one accustomed to the rapid rise in the cost of books of this description. Many of them were sold by auction in 1885.

In France, since Ternaux, the most important contribution has come from the house of Maisonneuve et Cie., by whom the *Bibliotheca Americana* of Charles Leclerc has been successively issued to represent their extraordinary stock. The first edition was printed in 1867 (1,647 entries), the second in 1878[5] (2,638 entries, with an admirable index), besides a first supplement in 1881 (nos. 2,639–3,029). Mr. Quaritch characterizes it as edited "with admirable skill and knowledge."

Less important but useful lists, issued in France, have been those of Hector Bossange, Edwin Tross,[6] and the current *Americana* series of Dufossé, which was begun in 1876.[7]

In Holland, most admirable work has been done by Frederik Muller, of Amsterdam, and by Mr. Asher, Mr. Tiele, and Mr. Otto Harrassowitz under his patronage, of which ample ac-

1 Another is now in progress.

2 With these canons Mr. Quaritch's prices can be understood. The extent and character of his stock can be inferred from the fact that his purchases at the Perkins sale (1873) amounted to £11,000; at the Tite sale (1874), £9,500; at the Didot sales (1878–1879), £11,600; and at the Sunderland sales (1883), £32,650, out of a total of £56,851. At the recent sales of the Beckford and Hamilton collections, which produced £86,444, over one half, or £44,105, went to Mr. Quaritch. These figures enable one to understand how, in a sense, Mr. Quaritch commands the world's market of choice books. A sketch, *B. Q., a biographical and bibliographical Fragment* (1880, 25 copies), in the privately printed series of monographs issued to a club in London, of which Mr. Quaritch is president, called "The Sette of Odd Volumes," has supplied the above data. The sketch is by C. W. H. Wyman, and is also reprinted in his *Bibliography of Printing*, and in the *Antiquarian Magazine and Bibliographer*, November, 1882. One of the club's "opuscula" (no. iii.) has an excellent likeness of Mr. Quaritch prefixed. Cf. also the memoir and portrait in Bigmore and Wyman's *Bibliography of Printing*, ii. 230.

3 Jackson, nos. 643–649; Trübner, *Bibliographical Guide*, p. xix.

4 Mr. Trübner died in London March 30, 1884. Cf. memorial in *The Library Chronicle*, April, 1884, p. 43, by W. E. A. Axon; also a "Nekrolog" by Karl J. Trübner in the *Centralblatt für Bibliothekswesen*, June, 1884, p. 240.

5 Cf. notice by Mr. Brevoort in *Magazine of American History*, iv. 230.

6 There is a paper on "Edwin Tross et ses publications relatives à l'Amérique" in *Miscellanées bibliographiques*, Paris, 1878, p. 53, giving a list of his imprints which concern America.

7 Jackson, nos. 689, 703, 717.

counts are given in another place.[1] Muller's catalogues were begun in 1850, but did not reach distinctive merit till 1872.[2] Martin Nijhoff, at the Hague, has also issued some American catalogues.

In 1858 Muller sold one of his collections of Americana to Brockhaus, of Leipsic, and the *Bibliothèque Américaine* issued by that publisher in 1861, as representing this collection, was compiled by one of the editors of the *Serapeum*, Paul Trömel, whom Harrisse characterizes as an "expert bibliographer and trustworthy scholar." The list shows 435 entries by a chronological arrangement (1507–1700).[3] Brockhaus again, in 1866, issued another American list, showing books since 1508, arranged topically (nos. 7,261–8,611). Mr. Otto Harrassowitz, of Leipsic, a pupil of Muller, of Amsterdam, has also entered the field as a purveyor of choice Americana. T. O. Weigel, of Leipsic, issued a catalogue, largely American, in 1877.

So well known are the general bibliographies of Watt, Lowndes, Brunet, Graesse, and others, that it is not necessary to point out their distinctive merits.[4] Students in this field are familiar with the catalogues of the chief American libraries. The library of Harvard College has not issued a catalogue since 1834, though it now prints bulletins of its current accessions. An admirable catalogue of the Boston Athenæum brings the record of that collection down to 1871. The numerous catalogues of the Boston Public Library are of much use, especially the distinct volume given to the Prince Collection. The Massachusetts Historical Society's library has a catalogue printed in 1859–60. There has been no catalogue of the American Antiquarian Society since 1837, and the New England Historic Genealogical Society has never printed any; nor has the Congregational Library. The State Library at Boston issued a catalogue in 1880. These libraries, with the Carter-Brown Library at Providence, which is courteously opened to students properly introduced, probably make Boston within easy distance of a larger proportion of the books illustrating American history, than can be reached with equal convenience from any other literary centre. A book on the private libraries of Boston was compiled by Luther Farnham in 1855; but many of the private collections then existing have since been scattered.[5] General Horatio Rogers has made a similar record of those in Providence. After the Carter-Brown Collection, the most valuable of these private libraries in New England is probably that of Mr. Charles Deane in Cambridge, of which mention has already been made. The collection of the Rev. Henry M. Dexter, D.D., of New Bedford, is probably unexampled in this country for the history of the Congregational movement, which so largely affected the early history of the English Colonies.[6]

Two other centres in the United States are of the first importance in this respect. In Washington, with the Library of Congress (of which a general consolidated catalogue is now printing), embracing as it does the collection formed by Col. Peter Force, and supplementing the archives of the Government, an investigator of American history is situated extremely favorably.[7] In New York the Astor and Lenox libraries, with those of the New York Historical Society and American Geographical Society, give the student great opportunities. The catalogue of the Astor Library was printed in 1857–66,

1 Vol. IV. chap. viii. editorial note. There is an account of Muller and his bibliographical work in the *Centralblatt für Bibliothekswesen*, November, 1884.

2 Jackson, nos. 650–654; Trübner, *Bibliographical Guide*, p. xix; Sabin, *Bibliog. of Bibliog.*, p. cv; Petzholdt, *Bibliotheca Bibliographica*.

3 This collection was subsequently, with the exception of three lots, bought of Mr. Brockhaus by Henry Stevens. *Bibliotheca Geographica*, no. 343.

4 More or less help will be derived from the American portion of the *Liste provisoire de bibliographies géographiques spéciales, par James Jackson*, published in 1881 by the Société de Géographie de Paris,—a book of which use has been made in the preceding pages.

5 See the chapter on the libraries of Boston in the *Memorial History of Boston*, vol. iv.

6 The extent of Dr. Dexter's library is evident from the signs of possession which are so numerously scattered through the 7,250 titles that constitute the exhaustive and very careful bibliography of Congregationalism and the allied phases of religious history, which forms an appendix to his *Congregationalism as seen in its Literature*, New York, 1880. He explains in the Introduction to his volume the wide scope which he intended to give to this list; and to show how poorly off our largest public libraries in America are in the earliest books illustrating this movement, he says that of the 1,000 earliest titles which he gives, and which bear date between 1546 and 1644, he found only 208 in American libraries. His arrangement of titles is chronological, but he has a full name-index.

The students of the early English colonies cannot fail to find for certain phases of their history much help from Joseph Smith's *Descriptive Catalogue of Friends' Books*, London, 1867; his *Bibliotheca Anti-Quakeriana*, 1873; and his *Bibliotheca Quakeristica*, a bibliography of miscellaneous literature relating to the Friends, of which Part I. was issued in London in 1883.

7 The private library of George Bancroft is in Washington. It is described as it existed some years ago in Wynne's *Private Libraries of New York*.

and that of the Historical Society in 1859. No general catalogue of the Lenox Library has yet been printed. An account of the private libraries of New York was published by Dr. Wynne in 1860. The libraries of the chief importance at the present time, in respect to American history, are those of Mr. S. L. M. Barlow in New York, and of Mr. James Carson Brevoort in Brooklyn. Mr. Charles H. Kalbfleisch of New York has a small collection, but it embraces some of the rarest books. The New York State Library at Albany is the chief of the libraries of its class, and its principal characteristic pertains to American history.

The other chief American cities are of much less importance as centres for historical research. The Philadelphia Library and the collection of the Historical Society of Pennsylvania are hardly of distinctive value, except in regard to the history of that State. In Baltimore the library of the Peabody Institute, of which the first volume of an excellent catalogue has been printed, and that of the Maryland Historical Society are scarcely sufficient for exhaustive research. The private library of Mr. H. H. Bancroft constitutes the only important resource of the Pacific States;[1] and the most important collection in Canada is that represented by the catalogue of the Library of Parliament, which was printed in 1858.

This enumeration is intended only to indicate the chief places for ease of general investigation in American history. Other localities are rich in local helps, and accounts of such will be found elsewhere in the present History.[2]

1 A book on the private libraries of San Francisco by Apponyi was issued in 1878.

2 An account of the libraries of the various historical societies in the United States is given in the *Public Libraries of the United States*, issued by the Bureau of Education at Washington in 1876.

INTRODUCTION.

By the Editor.

Part II. THE EARLY DESCRIPTIONS OF AMERICA AND COLLECTIVE ACCOUNTS OF THE EARLY VOYAGES THERETO.

OF the earliest collection of voyages of which we have any mention we possess only a defective copy, which is in the Biblioteca Marciana, and is called *Libretto de tutta la navigazione del Rè di Spagna delle isole e terreni nuovamente scoperti stampato per Vercellese.* It was published at Venice in 1504,[1] and is said to contain the first three voyages of Columbus. This account, together with the narrative of Cabral's voyage printed at Rome and Milan, and an original — at present unknown — of Vespucius' third voyage, were embodied, with other matter, in the *Paesi novamente retrovati et novo mondo da Alberico Vesputio Florentino intitulato,* published at Vicentia in 1507,[2] and again possibly at Vicentia in 1508, — though the evidence is wanting to support the statement, — but certainly at Milan in that year

[1] The title is quoted differently by different authorities. Harrisse, *Bibl. Amer. Vet.*, no. 32, and *Additions*, no. 16; his *Christophe Colomb*, i. 89; Humboldt, *Examen critique*, iv. 67; Sabin, *Dictionary of Books relating to America*, x. 327; D'Avezac, *Waltzemüller*, p. 79; Varnhagen, *Nouvelles Recherches*, p. 17; Irving's *Columbus*, app. ix.

[2] See Vol. IV. p. 12. The editorship is in dispute, — whether Zorzi or Montalboddo. The better opinion seems to be that Humboldt erred in assigning it to Zorzi rather than to Montalboddo. Cf. Humboldt, *Examen critique;* Brunet, v. 1155, 1158; Sabin, *Dictionary*, vol. xii. no. 50,050; D'Avezac, *Waltzemüller*, p. 80; Graesse, *Trésor;* Harrisse, *Bibl. Amer. Vet.*, nos. 48, 109, app. p. 469, and *Additions*, no. 26; *Bulletin de la Société de Géographie*, October, 1857, p. 312; Santarem's *Vespucius*, Eng. tr., p. 73; Irving's *Columbus*, app. xxx.; Navarrete, *Opúsculos*, i. 101; Harrisse, *Christophe Colomb*, i. 89. There are copies of this 1507 edition in the Lenox and Carter-Brown libraries, and in the Grenville Library; and one in the Beckford sale, 1882 (no. 186), brought £270. Cf. also *Murphy Catalogue*, no. 2,612*, and *Catalogue de la précieuse bibliothèque de feu M. le Docteur J. Court* (Paris, 1884), no. 262. The *Paesi novamente retrovati* is shown in the chapter on the Cortereals in Vol. IV. to be of importance in elucidating the somewhat obscure story of that portion of the early Portuguese discoveries in North America. Since Vol. IV. was printed, two important contributions to this study have been made. One is the monograph of Henry Harrisse, *Les Cortereal et leur voyages au Nouveau-monde. D'après des documents nouveaux ou peu connus tirés des archives de Lisbonne et de Modène. Suivi du texte inédit d'un recit de la troisième expédition de Gasper Cortereal et d'une carte nautique portugaise de* 1502 *reproduite ici pour la première fois. Mémoire lu à l'Académie des inscriptions et belles-lettres dans sa séance du* 1er *juin*, 1883, and published in Paris in 1883, as Vol. III. of the *Recueil de voyages et de documents pour servir à l'histoire de la géographie depuis le XIIIe jusqu'à la fin du XVIe siècle.* The other is the excerpt from the *Archivo des Açores*, which was drawn from that work by the editor, Ernesto do Canto, and printed separately at Ponta Delgarda (S. Miguel) in an edition of one hundred copies, under the title of *Os Corte-Reaes, memoria historica accompanhada de muitos documentos ineditos.* Do Canto refers (p. 34) to other monographs on the Portuguese discoveries in America as follows: Sebastião Francisco Mendo Trigoso, — *Ensaio sobre os Descobrimentos e Commercio dos Portuguezes em as Terras Septentrionaes da America*, presented to the Lisbon Academy (1813), and published in their *Memorias da Litteratura*, viii. 305. Joaquim José Gonçalves de Mattos Corrêa, — *Acerca da prioridade das Descobertas feitas pelos portuguezes nas costas orientaes da America do norte*, which was printed in *Annaes maritimos e Coloniaes*, Lisbon, 1841, pp. 269–423. Luciano Cordeiro, — *De la part prise par les Portugais dans le découverte de l'Amerique*, Lisbon, 1876. This was a communication made to the Congrès des Américanistes in 1875. Cf. Vol. IV. p. 15.

(1508).[1] There were later editions in 1512,[2] 1517,[3] 1519[4] (published at Milan), and 1521.[5] There are also German,[6] Low German,[7] Latin,[8] and French[9] translations.

While this Zorzi-Montalboddo compilation was flourishing, an Italian scholar, domiciled in Spain, was recording, largely at first hand, the varied reports of the voyages which were then opening a new existence to the world. This was Peter Martyr, of whom Harrisse[10] cites an early and quaint sketch from Hernando Alonso de Herrera's *Disputatio adversus Aristotelez* (1517).[11] The general historians have always made due acknowledgment of his service to them.[12]

Harrisse could find no evidence of Martyr's First Decade having been printed at Seville as early as 1500, as is sometimes stated; but it has been held that a translation of it, — though no copy is now known, — made by Angelo Trigviano into Italian was the *Libretto de tutta la navigazione del Rè di Spagna*, already mentioned.[13] The earliest unquestioned edition was that of 1511, which was printed at Seville with the title *Legatio Babylonica;* it contained nine books and a part of the tenth book of the First Decade.[14] In 1516 a new edition, without map, was printed at Alcalá in Roman letter. The part of the tenth book of the First Decade in the 1511 edition is here annexed to the ninth, and a new tenth book is added, besides two other decades, making three in all.[15]

1 Harrisse, *Bibl. Amer. Vet.*, no. 55; D'Avezac, *Waltzemüller*, p. 80; Wieser, *Magalhães-Strasse*, pp. 15, 17. There are copies in the Lenox, Carter-Brown, Harvard College, and Cincinnati Public libraries. The Beckford copy brought, in 1882, £78. Quaritch offered a copy in 1883 for £45. At the Potier sale, in 1870 (no. 1,791), a copy brought 2,015 francs; the same had brought 389 francs in 1844 at the Nodier sale. *Livres payés en vente publique* 1,000 *francs et au dessus*, 1877, p. 77. Cf. also Court, no. 263.

2 Only one copy in the United States, says Sabin.

3 In Carter-Brown and Lenox libraries; also in the Marciana and Brera libraries. Leclerc in 1878 priced a copy at 1,000 francs. Cf. Harrisse, no. 90, also p. 463, and *Additions*, no. 52; Sobolewski, no. 4,130; Brunet, v. 1158; Court, no. 264.

4 Sabin, vol. xii. no. 50,054; Leclerc, no. 2,583 (500 francs). A copy was sold in London in March, 1883. There is a copy in the Cincinnati Public Library.

5 Harrisse, no. 109; Sobolewski, no. 4,131; Carter-Brown, vol. i. no. 68; Murphy, no. 2,617.

6 *Newe unbekanthe landte* (Nuremberg, 1508), by Ruchamer; copies are in the Lenox, Carter-Brown, Congress, and Cincinnati Public libraries. Cf. Sabin, vol. xii. no. 50,056; Carter-Brown, vol. i. no. 36; Harrisse, no. 57; Murphy, no. 2,613; Sobolewski, no. 4,069; D'Avezac, *Waltzemüller*, p. 83; Rosenthal, *Catalogue* (1884), no. 67, at 1,000 marks.

7 *Nye unbekande Lande* (1508), in Platt-Deutsch, by Henning Ghetel, of Lubeck, following the German. Sabin, vol. xii. no. 50,057; Harrisse, *Additions*, no. 29. The Carter-Brown copy (*Catalogue*, vol. i. no. 37) cost about 1,000 marks at the Sobolewski (no. 4,070) sale, when it was described as an "édition absolument inconnu jusqu'au présent." Mr. C. H. Kalbfleisch has since secured a copy at 3,000 marks, — probably the copy advertised "as the second copy known," by Albert Cohn, of Berlin, in 1881, in his *Katalog*, vol. cxxxix. no. 27. Cf. *Studi biografici e bibliografici della Società Italiana*, i. 219.

8 *Itinerariū Portugallēsiū e Lusitania in Indiā* (Milan, 1508), a Latin version by Archangelus Madrinanus, of Milan. Cf. D'Avezac, *Waltzemüller*, p. 82; Sabin, vol. xii. no. 50,058; Harrisse, no. 58; Sobolewski, no. 4,128; Muller (1870), no. 1,844. There are copies in the Lenox, Barlow, Harvard College, Carter-Brown (*Catalogue*, vol. i. no. 35), and Congressional libraries. The Beckford copy (no. 1,081) brought £78. Sabin quotes Bolton Corney's copy at £137. Copies have been recently priced at £30, £36, and £45. A copy noted in the *Court Catalogue* (no. 177) differs from Harrisse's collation.

9 *Sensuyt le nouveau mõde*, supposed to be 1515; some copies vary in text. The Lenox Library has two varieties. Cf. Sabin, vol. xii. nos. 50,059, 50,061; Harrisse, no. 83, and *Additions*, no. 46; D'Avezac, *Waltzemüller*, p. 84. An edition of 1516 (*Le nouveau monde*) is in the Carter-Brown and Lenox libraries (Sabin, vol. xii. no. 50,062; Court, no. 248; Harrisse, no. 86; Sobolewski, no. 4,129). One placed in 1521 (*Sensuyt le nouveau mõde*) is in Harvard College Library (Harrisse, no. 111; Sabin, vol. xii. no. 50,063). Another (*Sensuyt le nouveau monde*) is placed under 1528 (Sabin, vol. xii. no. 50,064; Harrisse, no. 146, and *Additions*, no. 87).

10 *Bibl. Amer. Vet.*, no. 50. Harrisse also gives a chapter to Peter Martyr in his *Christophe Colomb*, i. 85.

11 See also the reference in Joannes Tritemius' *De scriptoribus ecclesiasticis* (Cologne, 1546), pp. 481-482. There have been within a few years two monographs upon Martyr: (1) Hermann A. Schumacher's *Petrus Martyr, der Geschichtsschreiber des Weltmeeres* (New York, 1879); (2) Dr. Heinrich Heidenheimer's *Petrus Martyr Anglerius und sein Opus epistolarum* (Berlin, 1881). This last writer gives a section to his geographical studies.

12 Humboldt, *Examen critique*, ii. 279; Irving, *Columbus*, app.; Prescott, *Ferdinand and Isabella* (1873), ii. 74, and *Mexico*, ii. 96; H. H. Bancroft, *Central America*, i. 312; Helps, *Spanish Conquest*. Cf. Harrisse, *Bibl. Amer. Vet.*, nos. 66 and 160.

13 Morelli's edition of *Letter of Columbus*, 1810.

14 There is an examination of this edition on page 109 of Vol. II.

15 Harrisse, *Bibl. Amer. Vet.*, no. 88; *Carter-Brown Catalogue*, vol. i. no. 50; Huth, p. 920; Brunet, i. 293; Murphy, no. 1,606; Leclerc, no. 2,647 (600 francs); Stevens, *Nuggets*, £10 10*s.*; *Bibliotheca Grenvilliana*. There is a copy in Charles Deane's collection. Tross priced a copy in 1873 at 900 francs.

There exists what has been called a German version (*Die Schiffung mitt dem landt der Gulden Insel*) of the First Decade, in which the supposed author is called Johan von Angliara; and its date is 1520, or thereabout; but Mr. Deane, who has the book, says that it is not Martyr's.[1] Some *Poemata*, which had originally been included in the publication of the First Decade, were separately printed in 1520.[2]

At Basle in 1521 appeared his *De nuper sub D. Carolo repertis insulis*, the title of which is annexed in facsimile. Harrisse [3] has called it an extract from the Fourth Decade; and a similar statement is made in the *Carter-Brown Catalogue* (vol. i. no. 67). But Stevens and other authorities define it as a substitute for the lost First Letter of Cortes, touching the expedition of Grijalva and the invasion of Mexico; and it supplements, rather than overlaps, Martyr's other narratives.[4] Mr. Deane contends that if the Fourth Decade had then been written, this might well be considered an abridgment of it.

The first complete edition (*De orbe novo*) of all the eight decades was published in 1530 at Complutum; and with it is usually found the map ("Tipus orbis universalis") of Apianus, which originally appeared in Camer's *Solinus* in 1520. In this new issue the map has its date changed to 1530.[5]

In 1532, at Paris, appeared an abridgment in French of the first three decades, together with an abstract of Martyr's *De insulis* (Basle, 1521), followed by abridgments of the printed second and third letters of Cortes, — the whole bearing the title, *Extraict ou Recueil des Isles nouuellemẽt trouuees en la grand mer Oceane*

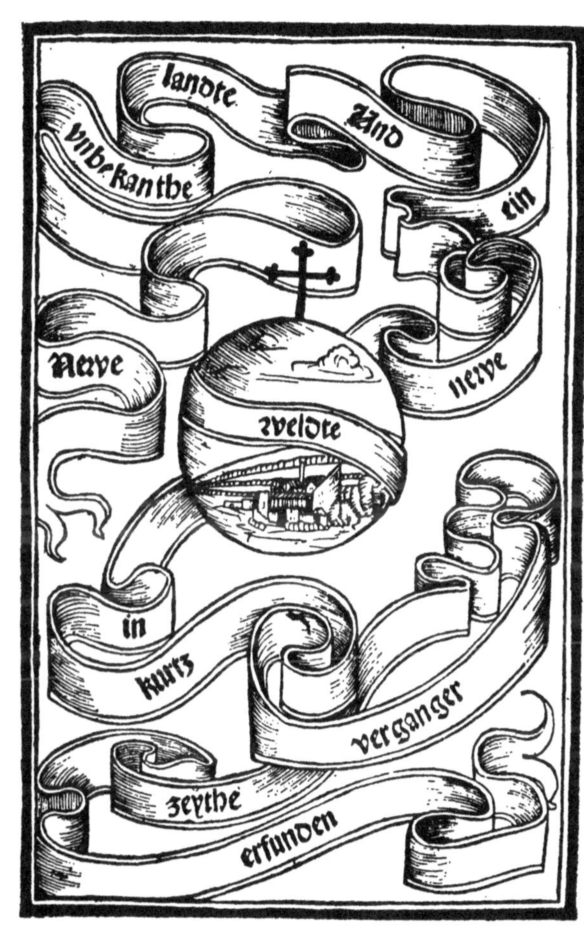

TITLE OF THE NEWE UNBEKANTHE LANDTE (REDUCED).

1 *Carter-Brown Catalogue*, vol. i. no. 61; Graesse, *Trésor*, i. 130; Sabin, i. 201, who says Rich put it under 1560.

2 *Bibl. Amer. Vet.*, no. 62; *Additions*, p. 78.

3 *Bibl. Amer. Vet.*, no. 110.

4 There are copies in Harvard College and Carter-Brown libraries. Cf. Sabin, i. 199; Leclerc, no. 24 (150 francs); Court, no. 13; Murphy, no. 1,606*; Stevens, *Historical Collection*, i. 48; his *Nuggets*, £2 2s. But recent prices have been £20 and £25; Brunet, i. 294; Ternaux, no. 24; Sunderland, vol. iv. no. 8,173. This tract was reprinted in the *Novus orbis* (Basle, 1532), and was appended to the Antwerp edition (1536) of Brocard's *Descriptio terræ sanctæ* (Harrisse, *Bibl. Amer. Vet.*, no. 218; Carter-Brown, vol. i. no. 117). It is also in the *Novus orbis* of Rotterdam, 1596 (Carter-Brown, vol. i. no. 505).

5 There are copies in the Harvard College, Lenox, and Carter-Brown libraries. It is very rare; a fair copy was priced in London, in 1881, at £62. Cf. Brunet, i. 293; *Carter-Brown Catalogue*, vol. i. no. 94; Sabin, i. 198; Harrisse, *Bibl. Amer. Vet.*, no. 154; Murphy, no. 1,607; Court, no. 14.

DE NVPER SVB D. CAROLO REPERTIS Insulis, simulq; incolarum moribus, R. Petri Martyris, Enchiridion, Dominæ Margaritæ, Diui Max. Cæs. filiæ dicatum.

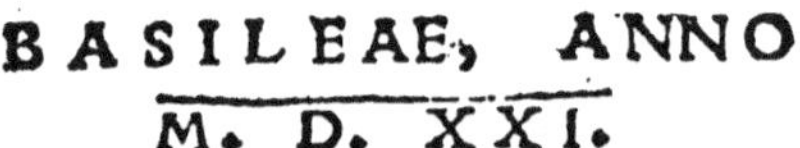

BASILEAE, ANNO M. D. XXI.

en temps du roy Despaigne Fernād & Elizabeth sa femme, faict premierement en latin par Pierre Martyr de Millan, & depuis translate en languaige francoys.[1]

In 1533, at Basle, in folio, we find the first three decades and the tract of 1521 (*De insulis*) united in *De rebus oceanicis et orbe novo.*[2]

At Venice, in 1534, the *Summario de la generale historia de l' Indie occidentali* was a joint issue of Martyr and Oviedo, under the editing of Ramusio.[3] An edition of Martyr, published at Paris in 1536, sometimes mentioned,[4] does not apparently exist;[5] but an edition of 1537 is noted by Sabin.[6] In 1555 Richard Eden's *Decades of the Newe Worlde, or West India*, appeared in black-letter at London. It is made up in large part from Martyr,[7] and was the basis of Richard Willes' edition of Eden in 1577, which included the first four decades, and an abridgment of the last four, with additions from Oviedo and others, — all under the new name, *The History of Trauayle.*[8]

There was an edition again at Cologne in 1574, — the one which Robertson used.[9] Three decades and the *De insulis* are also included in a composite folio published at Basle in 1582, containing also Benzoni and Levinus, all in German.[10] The entire eight decades, in Latin, which had not been printed together since the Basle edition of 1530, were published in Paris in 1587 under the editing of Richard Hakluyt, with the title: *De orbe novo Petri Martyris Anglerii Mediolanensis, protonotarij, et Caroli quinti senatoris Decades octo, diligenti temporum obseruatione, et vtilissimis annotationibus illustratæ, suðque nitori restitutæ, labore et industria Richardi Haklvyti Oxoniensis Angli. Additus est in vsum lectoris accuratus totius operis index.* Parisiis, apud Gvillelmvm Avvray, 1587. With its "F. G." map, it is exceedingly rare.[11]

1 The book is very rare. There is a copy in Harvard College Library. A copy was priced in London at £36; but Quaritch holds the Beckford copy (no. 2,275), in fine binding, at £148. Harrisse (*Bibl. Amer. Vet.*, no. 167) errs in his description. Cf. Brunet, i. 294; Sobolewski, no. 3,667; Sabin, i. 199; Huth, p. 920; Stevens, *Historical Collections*, i. 48; Carter-Brown, vol. i. no. 99; Murphy, no. 3,002; Court, no. 124.

2 Richard Eden's copy of this book, with his annotations, apparently used in making his translation of 1555, was sold in the Brinley sale, no. 40, having been earlier in the Judge Davis sale in 1847 (no. 1,352). The first of the Stevens copies, in his sale of 1870 (nos. 75, 1,234), is now in Mr. Deane's library. There are also copies in the Force (Library of Congress), Carter-Brown (*Catalogue*, vol. i. no. 104), and Ticknor (*Catalogue*, p. 14) collections, and in Harvard College Library. Cf. Sabin, i.; Stevens's *Nuggets*, £1 11*s.* 6*d.*; Ternaux, no. 47; Harrisse, *Bibl. Amer. Vet.*, no. 176; Muller (1877), no. 2,031; Court, no. 15; Murphy, no. 1,608; Leclerc (1878), no. 25 (80 francs); Quaritch, no. 11,628 (£3 10*s.*; again, £5 5*s.*); Sunderland, vol. iv. no. 8,176 (£50). Priced in Germany at 60 and 100 marks.

3 Ramusio's name does not appear, but D'Avezac thinks his editorship is probable; cf. *Bulletin de la Société de Géographie* (1872), p. 11. There are copies in Harvard College, Carter-Brown, J. C. Brevoort, H. C. Murphy, and Lenox libraries. For an account of a map said to belong to it, see Winsor's *Bibliography of Ptolemy*, sub anno 1540. Cf. *Bibl. Amer. Vet.*, no. 190; Stevens, *Historical Collections*, vol. i. no. 344, and *Nuggets*, vol. ii. no. 1,808; Murphy, no. 1,609; Sunderland, vol. iv. no. 8,177; Carter-Brown, vol. i. no. 107; Ternaux, no. 43; Court, no. 213. Ramusio also included Martyr in the third volume of his *Navigationi*. Cf. the opinions of Mr. Deane and Mr. Brevoort on the *Summario* as given in Vol. III. p. 20.

4 Brunet, Graesse, Ternaux.

5 Harrisse, *Bibl. Amer. Vet.*, no. 214.

6 Vol. i. p. 199.

7 See Vol. III. p. 200; Murphy, no. 1,610.

8 The book is rare; the copy in the Menzies sale (no. 1,332) brought $42.50. Cf. further in Vol. III. p. 204; also Cooke, no. 1,642.

9 It has three decades and three books of the "De Babylonica legatione." There are copies in Harvard College and the Carter-Brown libraries. Cf. Rich (1832), no. 52; *Nuggets*, £1 10*s.* 6*d.*; Sabin, i. 201; Muller, (1877), no. 2,031; Carter-Brown, vol. i. no. 295; Leclerc, no. 26 (80 francs); Harrassowitz, 35 marks; Quaritch, £1 5*s.* and £1 16*s.*; Sunderland, vol. iv. no. 8,178; O'Callaghan, no. 1,479; Cooke, no. 1,641; Court, no. 16; Murphy, no. 1,611.

10 Graesse, i. 130; Carter-Brown, vol. i. no. 344; Stevens (1870), no. 1,235.

11 The Sunderland copy (vol. iv. no. 8,179), with the map, brought £24; a French catalogue advertised one with the map for 250 francs. Without the map it is worth about $25. See further in Vol. III. p. 42; also Murphy, no. 1,612; Cooke, no. 1,643; Court, no. 17. Hakluyt's text was used by Lok in making an English version (he adopted, however, Eden's text of the first three decades), which was printed as *De Novo Orbe; or, the Historie of the West Indies.* Bibliographers differ about the editions. One without date is held by some to have been printed in 1597 (White-Kennett; Field, *Indian Bibliography*, no. 1,013; Menzies, no. 1,333, $35; Huth, p. 923); but others consider it the sheets of the 1612 edition with a new title (see Vol. III. p. 47, Field, no. 1,014; Stevens, 1870, no. 1,236; Harrisse, *Notes on Columbus*, p. 10; O'Callaghan, no. 1,481; Murphy, no. 1,612*; Carter-Brown, vol. i. nos. 129, 130). There are copies of this 1612 edition in the Boston Athenæum, Harvard College, Carter-Brown, and Massachusetts Historical Society libraries; it is worth from $30 to $40. Mr. Deane's edition of 1612 has a dedication to Julius Cæsar, the English jurist of that day, which is not in the edition without date. See Vol. III. p. 47. The same was reissued as a "second edition," with a title dated 1628, of which there is a copy in Harvard College Library (Field, no. 1,015; Stevens, *Nuggets*, £4 14*s.* 6*d.*; Menzies, no. 1,334; Griswold, no. 475; Quaritch, £9 and £12).

GRYNÆUS.[1]

As illustrating in some sort his more labored work, the *Opus epistolarum Petri Martyris* was first printed at Complutum in 1530.[2] The letters were again published at Amsterdam, in 1670,[3] in an edition which had the care of Ch. Patin, to which was appended other letters by Fernando del Pulgar.[4]

The most extensive of the early collections was the *Novus orbis*, which was issued in separate editions at Basle and Paris in 1532. Simon Grynæus, a learned professor at Basle, signed the preface; and it usually passes under his name. Grynæus was born in Swabia, was a friend of Luther, visited England in 1531, and died in Basle, in 1541. The compilation, however, is the work of a canon of Strasburg, John Huttich (born about 1480; died, 1544), but the labor of revision fell on Grynæus.[5] It has the first three voyages of Columbus, and those of Pinzon and Vespucius; the rest of the book is taken up with the travels of Marco Polo and his successors to the East.[6] It

1 Fac-simile of cut in Reusner's *Icones* (Strasburg, 1590), p. 107.

2 Brunet, i. 294; Harrisse, *Notes on Columbus*, p. 10; *Bibl. Amer. Vet.*, no. 160; Carter-Brown, vol. i. no. 93; Sunderland, vol. iv. no. 8,174, (£61). There is also a copy in Harvard College Library.

3 Sabin, i. 200. Copy in Harvard College Library; it was printed at the Elzevir Press (Harrisse, *Notes on Columbus*, p. 11; Carter-Brown, vol. ii. no. 1,036; Sunderland, vol. iv. no. 8,175).

4 Prescott's copy is in Harvard College Library (*Ferdinand and Isabella*, 1873, ii. 76).

5 Cf. Arana, *Bibliog. de obras anon.* (1882), no. 373.

6 There are copies of this Basle edition in the Boston Public, Harvard College, Carter-Brown, Lenox, Astor, and Barlow libraries. Münster's map, of which an account is given elsewhere, is often wanting; the price for a copy with the map has risen from a guinea in Rich's day (1832), to £5. Cf. Harrisse, no. 171; Leclerc, no. 411; Muller (1877), no. 1,301; Ternaux, no. 38; Sabin, vol. ix. no. 34,100; Court, no. 249. The Paris edition has the Orontius Finæus map properly, though others are sometimes found in it. Cf. Harrisse,

next appeared in a German translation at Strasburg in 1534, which was made by Michal Herr, *Die New Welt*. It has no map, gives more from Martyr than the other edition, and substitutes a preface by Herr for that of Grynæus.[1] The original Latin was reproduced at Basle again in 1537, with 1536 in the colophon.[2] In 1555 another edition was printed at Basle, enlarged upon the 1537 edition by the insertion of the second and third of the Cortes letters and some accounts of efforts in converting the Indians.[3] Those portions relating to America exclusively were reprinted in the Latin at Rotterdam in 1616.[4]

Sebastian Münster, who was born in 1489, was forty-three years old when his map of the world — which is preserved in the Paris (1532) edition of the *Novus orbis* — appeared. This is the first time that Münster significantly comes before us as a describer of the geography of the New World. Again in 1540 and 1542 he was associated with the editions of Ptolemy issued at Basle in those years.[5] It is, however, upon his *Cosmographia*, among his forty books, that Münster's fame chiefly rests. The earliest editions are extremely rare, and seem not to be clearly defined by the bibliographers. It appears to have been originally issued in German, probably in 1544 at Basle,[6] under the mixed title: *Cosmographia. Beschreibūg aller lender Durch Sebastianum Munsterum. Getruckt zü Basel durch Henrichum Petri, Anno MDxliiij.*[7] He says that he had been engaged upon it for eighteen years, keeping Strabo before him as a model. To the section devoted to Asia he adds a few pages "Von den neüwen inseln" (folios

nos. 172, 173; Carter-Brown, vol. i. no. 102; Sabin, vol. ix. nos. 34,101, 34,102; Leclerc, nos. 412 (150 francs), 2,769; Stevens, *Bibliotheca geographica*, p. 124; Cooke, no. 2,879; Court, no. 250; Sunderland, no. 263; Muller (1872), no. 1,847; Quaritch (1883) £12 16*s*. The Lenox Library has copies of different imprints, — "apud Galeotum" and "apud Parvum." There are other copies in the Barlow and Carter-Brown libraries. Good copies are worth about £10.

1 Sabin (vol. ix. p. 30) says it is rarer than the original Latin. There are copies in Harvard College, Congressional, and Carter-Brown libraries. Cf. Rich (1832), £1 1*s*.; Ternaux, no. 45; Sabin, vol. ix. no. 34,106; Grenville, p. 498; Harrisse, no. 188, with references; Stevens (1870), no. 1,419; Muller (1872), no. 1,853, and (1877) no. 1,309 (40 florins), with corrections of Harrisse; Sobolewski, no. 3,857; Carter-Brown, vol. i. no. 110; Huth, vol. iii. nos. 1,050–1,051. Quaritch and others of late price it at £3. It was from this German edition of the *Novus orbis* that the collection, often quoted as that of Cornelis Ablyn, and called *Nieuwe Weerelt*, was made up in 1563, with some additional matter. It is in the dialect of Brabant, and Muller (*Books on America*, 1872, no. 1,854) says it is "exceedingly rare, even in Holland;" he prices it at 50 florins. Cf. Leclerc, no. 2,579 (250 francs); Sabin, vol. ix. no. 34,107; Carter-Brown, vol. i. no. 240; Huth, vol. iii. no. 1,051; A. R. Smith's Catalogue (1874), no. 8 (£2 2*s*.); Pinart, no. 668.

2 It has pp. 585–600 in addition to the edition of 1532. There are copies in the Cornell University (*Sparks Catalogue*, no. 1,107), Lenox, Carter-Brown, Barlow, J. C. Brevoort, and American Antiquarian Society libraries. One of the two copies in Harvard College Library belonged at different times to Charles Sumner, E. A. Crowninshield (no. 796), and the poet Thomas Gray, and has Gray's annotations, and a record that it cost him one shilling and ninepence. The map of the 1532 Basle edition belongs to this 1537 edition; but it is often wanting. The *Huth Catalogue* (vol. iii. p. 1050) calls the map of "extreme rarity;" and Quaritch has pointed out that the larger names in the map being set in type in the block, there is some variation in the style of these inscriptions belonging to the different issues. Cf. Sabin, vol. ix. no. 34,103; Harrisse, no. 223; Carter-Brown, vol. i. no. 123; Leclerc, no. 413, with map (100 francs); Stevens (*Nuggets*) does not mention the map, but his *Bibliotheca historica* (1870), no. 1,455, and *Historical Collections*, p. 66, give it; Muller (1872), no. 1,850 and (1877) no. 1,306. Recent prices of good copies with the map are quoted at £4 4*s*., 57 marks, and 70 francs; without the map it brings about $4.00. Grolier's copy was in the Beckford sale (1882), no. 187.

3 There are copies in the Boston Public (two copies), Boston Athenæum, Harvard College, Carter-Brown (no. 202), and American Antiquarian Society libraries. The map is repeated from the earlier Basle editions. Cf. *Brinley Catalogue*, no. 50; *Huth Catalogue* (without map), iii. 1,050; Harrisse, no. 171; Stevens, *Historical Collection*, vol. i. no. 501; Cooke, no. 1,064; Sabin, vol. ix. no. 34,104. Rich, in 1832, priced it with map at £2 2*s*.; recent prices are £4 4*s*. and £5 5*s*.

4 Edited by Balthazar Lydius. Cf. Carter-Brown, vol. ii. no. 182; Graesse, iv. 699; Brunet, iv. 132; Sabin, vol. ix. no. 34,105; Huth, iii. 1051; Leclerc, no. 414 (40 francs); Stevens, *Nuggets*, £2 2*s*.; Court, no. 251; Muller (1872), no. 1,870. There are copies in Harvard College Library and Boston Athenæum.

5 The editions of Ptolemy recording or affecting the progress of geography in respect to the New World are noted severally elsewhere in the present work; but the whole series is viewed together in the *Bibliography of Ptolemy's Geography*, by Justin Winsor, which, after appearing serially in the *Harvard University Bulletin*, was issued separately by the University Library in 1884 as no. 18 of its *Bibliographical Contributions*.

6 H. H. Bancroft, *Mexico*, i. 258. Harrisse (*Bibl. Amer. Vet.*, no. 237) gives the date 1541 as apparently the first edition. His authority is the *Labanoff Catalogue;* but the date therein is probably an error (Sabin, vol. xii. no. 51,384). The *Athenæ Rauricæ* cites a Latin edition of 1543, — it is supposed without warrant, though it is also mentioned in Poggendorff's *Biog.-liter. Handwörterbuch*, ii. 234.

7 Harrisse (*Bibl. Amer. Vet.*, no. 258), describing a copy in the Lenox Library. The map of America in this edition is given by Santarem, and much reduced in Lelewel. There are twenty-four maps in it in all (Sabin, vol. xii. no. 51,385).

MÜNSTER.[1]

dcxxxv–dcxlij). This account was scant; and though it was a little enlarged in the second edition in 1545,[2] it remained of small extent through subsequent editions, and was confined to ten pages in that of 1614. The last of the German editions appeared in 1628.[3] The earliest

1 Fac-simile of the cut in the *Ptolemy* of 1552.

2 Also published at Basle (Harrisse, *Bibl. Amer. Vet.*, *Additions*, no. 152; Weigel, 1877, *Catalogue;* Sabin, vol. xii. no. 51,386). It has twenty-eight maps. There is a copy in the Royal Library at Munich.

3 The third and later German editions were as follows: 1546. According to the *Athenæ Rauricæ.* — 1550. Basle, 1,233 pages, woodcuts, with views of towns added for the first time, and fourteen folios of maps. Harrisse (no. 294) quotes the description in Ebert's *Dictionary*, no. 14,500. Cf. Sabin, vol. xii. no. 51,387; Leclerc, no. 396; Rosenthal (Munich, 1884), no. 52, at 80 marks. Harrisse (*Additions*, no. 179) says the Royal Library at Munich has three different German editions of 1550. — 1553. Basle. Muller (*Books on*

SEBASTIANVS MVNSTERVS
Cosmographus.

Sat linguæ fuerat fontes mihi tradere sanctæ:
Scribere sed mundi me iuuat historiam.

M. D. LII.

MÜNSTER.[1]

undoubted Latin text[2] appeared at Basle in 1550, with the same series of new views, etc., by Manuel Deutsch, which were given in the German edition of that date.[3] With nothing

America, 1872, no. 1,020; 1877, no. 2,203) cites a copy, with twenty-six maps; also Sabin (vol. xii. no. 51,388). — 1556. Cited by Sabin, vol. xii. no. 53,389. — 1561. Basle. Cf. Rosenthal, *Catalogue* (1884), no. 53. — 1564. Basle. Cf. Sabin, vol. xii. no. 51,390; *Carter-Brown Catalogue*, i. 598. It has fourteen maps, the last being of the New World. — 1569, 1574, 1578. Basle. All are cited by Ebert and Harrisse, who give them twenty-six maps, and say that the cuts are poor impressions. — 1574, 1578, 1588. Undated; but cited by Sabin, vol. xii. no. 51,391–51,393. — 1592, 1598. In these editions the twenty-six maps and the woodcuts are

1 Fac-simile of a cut in Reusner's *Icones* (Strasburg, 1590), p. 171.

2 The *Athenæ Rauricæ* gives a Latin edition of 1545.

3 This 1550 Latin edition has fourteen maps, and copies are worth from $12 to $15. Cf. *Bibl. Amer. Vet.*, no. 300; *Huth Catalogue*, iii. 1,009; Sabin, vol. xii. no. 51,379; Strutt, *Dictionary of Engravers.*

but a change of title apparently, there were reissues of this edition in 1551, 1552, and 1554,[1] and again in 1559.[2] The edition of 1572 has the same map, "Novæ insulæ," used in the 1554 editions; but new names are added, and new plates of Cusco and Cuba are also furnished.[3]

The earliest French edition, according to Brunet,[4] appeared in 1552; and other editions followed in that language.[5] Eden gave the fifth book an English dress in 1553, which was again issued in 1572 and 1574.[6] A Bohemian edition, made by Jan z Puchowa, *Kozmograffia Czieská*, was issued in 1554.[7] The first Italian edition was printed at Basle in 1558, using the engraved plates of the other Basle issues; and finally, in 1575, an Italian edition, according to Brunet,[8] appeared at Colonia.

The best-known collection of voyages of the sixteenth century is that of Ramusio, whose third volume — compiled probably in 1553, and printed in 1556 — is given exclusively to American voyages.[9] It contains, however, little regarding Columbus not given by Peter Martyr and Oviedo, except the letter to Fracastoro.[10] In Ramusio the narratives of these early voyages first got a careful and considerate editor,

engraved after new drawings. That of 1592 is in the Boston Athenæum; that of 1598 is in Harvard College Library. The likeness of Münster on the title is inscribed: "Seins alters lx jar." America is shown in the general mappemonde, and in map no. xxvi., "Die Newe Welt." Sabin, vol. xii. no. 51,394–51,395. — 1614, 1628. These Basle editions reproduced the engravings of the 1592 and 1598 editions, and are considered the completest issues of the German text. They are worth from 30 to 40 marks each. Sabin, vol. xii. no. 51,396.

1 The title of the 1554 edition as shown in the copy in the Boston Public Library reads as follows: *Cosmo | graphiae | uniuersalis Lib. VI. in | quibus iuxta certioris fidei scriptorum | traditionem describuntur, | Omnium habitabilis orbis partium situs, pro- | priæq' dotes. | Regionum Topographicæ effigies. | Terræ ingenia, quibus sit ut tam differentes & ua | rias specie res, & animatas, & inanimatas, ferat. | Animalium peregrinorum naturæ & picturæ. | Nobiliorum ciuitatum icones & descriptiones. | Regnorum initia, incrementa & translationes. | Regum & principum genealogiæ. | Item omnium gentium mores, leges, religio, mu- | tationes: atq' memorabilium in hunc usque an- | num* 1554. *gestarum rerum Historia. | Autore Sebast. Munstero.* The same edition is in the Harvard College Library; but the title varies, and reads thus: *Cosmo | graphiæ | uniuersalis Lib. VI. in | quibus, iuxta certioris fidei scriptorum | traditionem describuntur, | Omniū habitabilis orbis partiū situs, propriæq' dotes. | Regionum Topographicæ effigies. | Terræ ingenia, quibus sit ut tam differentes & uarias | specie res, & animatas & inanimatas, ferat. | Animalium peregrinorum naturæ & picturæ. | Nobiliorum ciuitatum icones & descriptiones. | Regnorum initia, incrementa & translationes. | Omnium gentium mores, leges, religio, res gestæ, mu- | tationes: Item regum & principum genealogiæ. | Autore Sebast. Munstero.* | The colophon in both reads: | *Basileæ Apvd Henrichvm Petri, | Mense Septemb. Anno Sa | lvtis M.D.LIIII.* | This copy belonged to Dr. Mather Byles, and has his autograph; the title is mounted, and may have belonged to some other one of the several "title-editions" which appeared about this time. Cf. *Harvard University Bulletin*, ii. 285; *Carter-Brown*, vol. i. no. 194; Sabin, vol. xii. no. 51,380-51,381. The account of America is on pages 1,099–1,113. These editions have been bought of late years for about $4; but Rosenthal (Munich, 1884) prices a copy of 1552 at 130 marks, and one of 1554 at 150 marks.

2 Sabin, vol. xii. no. 51,382; Muller, *Books on America* (1872), p. 11.

3 Some copies have nineteen maps, others twenty-two in all. Cf. Carter-Brown, vol. i. no. 291; Sabin, vol. xii. no. 51,383. Some passages displeasing to the Catholics are said to have been omitted in this edition. It is worth about $12 or $15.

4 *Supplément*, col. 1,129; Sabin, vol. xii. no. 51,397.

5 That of Basle, 1556, has on pp. 1,353–1,374, "Des nouvelles ilsles: comment, quand et par qui elles ont esté trouvées," with a map and fourteen woodcuts. It is usually priced at about $20; the copies are commonly worn (Sabin, vol. xii. no. 51,398). The same publisher, Henry Pierre, reissued it (without date) in 1568, with twelve folding woodcut maps, the first of which pertains to America (Carter-Brown, vol. i. no. 271; Sabin, vol. xii. no. 51,399). In 1575 a new French edition, with the cuts reduced, was issued in three volumes, folio, edited by Belleforest and others; it gives 101 pages to America. Cf. Brunet, col. 1,945; *Supplément*, col. 1,129; Stevens (1870), p. 121; Sunderland, no. 8,722 (£18 10*s*.); Porquet (1884), no. 1,673, (150 francs); Sabin, vol. xii. no. 51,400.

6 Cf. Vol. III. of the present *History*, pp. 200, 201.

7 Weigel (1877), p. 96; Sabin, vol. xii. no. 51,401.

8 *Supplément*, col. 1,129. Cf. also Weigel (1877), p. 96; Carter-Brown, vol. ii. no. 1,132; Sabin, vol. xii. nos. 51,402–51,403.

9 *Terzo volume delle navigationi et viaggi*, etc., Venice, 1556. His name is, Latinized, Ramusius.

10 Harrisse, *Notes on Columbus*, p. 46. A list of the Contents is given in the *Carter-Brown Catalogue* (vol. i. p. 181), and in Leclerc (no. 484), where a set (1554, 1583, 1565) is priced at 250 francs. Of interest in connection with the present History, there are in the first volume of Ramusio the voyages of Da Gama, Vespucius, and Magellan, as well as matter of interest in connection with Cabot (see Vol. III. p. 24); in the second volume (1559), the travels of Marco Polo, the voyage of the Zeni and of Cabot. The first edition of the first volume was published in 1550; Ramusio's name does not appear. A second edition came out in 1554. Cf. *Murphy Catalogue*, nos. 2,096–2,098; Cooke, no. 2,117.

who at this time was ripe in knowledge and experience, for he was well beyond sixty,[1] and he had given his maturer years to historical and geographical study. He had at one time maintained a school for topographical studies in his own house. Oviedo tells us of the assistance Ramusio was to him in his work. Locke has praised his labors without stint.[2]

Monardes, one of the distinguished Spanish physicians of this time, was busy seeking for the simples and curatives of the New World plants, as the adventurers to New Spain brought them back. The original issue of his work was the *Dos Libros*, published at Seville in 1565, treating "of all things brought from our West Indies which are used in medicine, and of the Bezaar Stone, and the herb Escuerçonera." This book is become rare, and is priced as high as 200 francs and £9.[3] The "segunda parte" is sometimes found separately with the date 1571; but in 1574 a third part was printed with the other two, — making the complete work, *Historia medicinal de nuestras Indias*, — and these were again issued in 1580.[4] An Italian version, by Annibale Briganti, appeared at Venice in 1575 and 1589,[5] and a French, with Du Jardin, in 1602.[6] There were three English editions printed under the title of *Joyfull Newes out of the newe founde world, wherein is declared the rare and singular virtues of diverse and sundry Herbes, Trees, Oyles, Plantes, and Stones, by Doctor Monardus of Sevill, Englished by John Frampton*, which first appeared in 1577, and was reprinted in 1580, with additions from Monardes' other tracts, and again in 1596.[7]

The Spanish historians of affairs in Mexico, Peru, and Florida are grouped in the *Hispanicarum rerum scriptores*, published at Frankfort in 1579–1581, in three volumes.[8] Of Richard Hakluyt and his several collections, — the *Divers Voyages* of 1582, the *Principall Navigations* of

MONARDES.

1 Born in 1485–1486; died in 1557. There is an alleged portrait of Ramusio in the new edition of *Il viaggio di Giovan Leone*, etc. (Venice, 1857), the only volume of it published. The portrait of him by Paul Veronese in the hall of the Great Council was burned in 1557; and Cicogna (*Biblioteca Veneziana*, ii. 310) says that the likeness now in the Sala dello Scudo is imaginary.

2 Cf. also Camus, *Mémoire sur De Bry*, p. 8; Humboldt, *Examen critique;* Hallam, *Literature of Europe;* Harrisse, *Bibl. Amer. Vet.*, no. 304; Brunet, vol. iv. col. 1100; Carter-Brown, vol. i. no. 195; Clarke's *Maritime Discovery*, p. x, where Tiraboschi's account of Ramusio is translated; and H. H. Bancroft, *Mexico*, i. 282. Ternaux mentions a second edition in 1564; but Harrisse could find no evidence of it (*Bibl. Amer. Vet.*, p. xxxiii). There was a well-known second edition of the third volume in 1565 (differing in title only from the 1556 edition), which, with a first volume of 1588 and a second volume of 1583, is thought to make up the most desirable copy; though there are some qualifications in the case, since the 1606 edition of the third volume is really more complete.

3 Carter-Brown, vol. i. no. 275.

4 Cf. Carter-Brown, vol. i. nos. 287, 288, 299, 337; Sunderland, nos. 8,569, 8,570; Brinley, no. 44; Murphy, no. 1,709; Court, no. 241.

5 Court, no. 242.

6 Carter-Brown, i. 386; ii. 12; Brinley, no. 45.

7 The different editions in the various languages are given in Sabin, xii. 282.

8 Sabin, vol. viii. no. 32,004.

PORTRAIT OF DE BRY.[1]

1589, and his enlarged edition, of which the third volume (1600) relates to America, — there is an account in Vol. III. of the present work.[2]

The great undertaking of De Bry was also begun towards the close of the same century. De Bry was an engraver at Frankfort, and his professional labors had made him acquainted with works of travel. The influence of Hakluyt and a visit to the English editor stimulated him to undertake a task similar to that of

1 This follows a print given in fac-simile in the *Carter-Brown Catalogue*, i. 316.

2 A complete reprint of all of Hakluyt's publications, in fourteen or fifteen volumes, is announced (1884) by E. and G. Goldsmid, of Edinburgh.

FEYERABEND.[1]

the English compiler. He resolved to include both the Old and New World; and he finally produced his volumes simultaneously in Latin and German. As he gave a larger size to the American parts than to the others, the commonly used title, referring to this difference, was soon established as *Grands et petits voyages*.[2] Theodore De Bry himself died in March, 1598; but the work was carried forward by his widow, by his sons John Theodore and John Israel, and by his sons-in-law Matthew Merian and William Fitzer. The task was not finished till 1634, when twenty-five parts had been printed in the Latin, of which thirteen pertain to America; but the German has one more part in the American series. His first part — which was Hariot's *Virginia* — was printed not only in Latin and German, but also in the original English[3] and in French; but there seeming to be no adequate demand in these languages, the subsequent issues were confined to Latin and German. There was a gap in the

[1] Sigmund Feyerabend was a prominent bookseller of his day in Frankfort, and was born about 1527 or 1528. He was an engraver himself, and was associated with De Bry in the publications of his *Voyages*.

[2] The title, however, as given in catalogues generally, runs: *Collectiones peregrinationum in Indiam orientalem et Indiam occidentalem, XXV partibus comprehensæ a Theodoro, Joan-Theodoro De Bry, et a Matheo Merian publicatæ. Francofurti ad Mænum*, 1590–1634.

[3] This part is of extreme rarity, and Dibdin says that Lord Oxford bought the copy in the Grenville Library in 1740 for £140. Cf. Vol. III. p. 123.

dates of publication between 1600 (when the ninth part is called "postrema pars") and 1619–1620, when the tenth and eleventh parts appeared at Oppenheim, and a twelfth at Frankfort in 1624. A thirteenth and fourteenth part appeared in German in 1628 and 1630; and these, translated together into Latin, completed the Latin series in 1634.

Without attempting any bibliographical description,[1] the succession and editions of the American parts will be briefly enumerated: —

I. *Hariot's Virginia.* In Latin, English, German, and French, in 1590; four or more impressions of the Latin the same year. Other editions of the German in 1600 and 1620.

II. *Le Moyne's Florida.* In Latin, 1591 and 1609; in German, 1591, 1603.

III. *Von Staden's Brazil.* In Latin, 1592, 1605, 1630; in German, 1593 (twice).

IV. *Benzoni's New World.* In Latin, 1594 (twice), 1644; in German, 1594, 1613.

V. *Continuation of Benzoni.* In Latin, 1595 (twice); in German, two editions without date, probably 1595 and 1613.

VI. *Continuation of Benzoni (Peru).* In Latin, 1596, 1597, 1617; in German, 1597, 1619.

VII. *Schmidel's Brazil.* In Latin, 1599, 1625; in German, 1597, 1600, 1617.

VIII. *Drake, Candish, and Ralegh.* In Latin, 1599 (twice), 1625; in German, 1599, 1624.

IX. *Acosta,* etc. In Latin, 1602, 1633; in German, probably 1601; "additamentum," 1602; and again entire after 1620.

X. *Vespucius, Hamor, and John Smith.* In Latin, 1619 (twice); in German, 1618.

XI. *Schouten and Spilbergen.* In Latin, 1619, — appendix, 1620; in German, 1619, — appendix, 1620.

XII. *Herrera.* In Latin, 1624; in German, 1623.

XIII. *Miscellaneous, — Cabot,* etc. In Latin, 1634; in German, the first seven sections in 1627 (sometimes 1628); and sections 8–15 in 1630.

Elenchus: Historia Americæ sive Novus orbis, 1634 (three issues). This is a table of the Contents to the edition which Merian was selling in 1634 under a collective title.

The foregoing enumeration makes no recognition of the almost innumerable varieties caused by combination, which sometimes pass for new editions. Some of the editions of the same date are usually called "counterfeits;" and there are doubts, even, if some of those here named really deserve recognition as distinct editions.[2]

1 The earliest description of a set of De Bry of any bibliographical moment is that of the Abbé de Rothelin, *Observations et détails sur la collection des voyages,* etc. (Paris, 1742), pp. 44 (Carter-Brown, vol. i. no. 473), which is reprinted in Lenglet du Fresnoy's *Méthode pour étudier la géographie* (1768), i. 324. Gabriel Martin, in his catalogue of the library of M. Cisternay du Fay, had somewhat earlier announced that collector's triumph in calling a set in his catalogue (no. 2,825) "exemplum omni genere perfectum," when his copy brought 450 francs. The Abbé de Rothelin aimed to exceed Cisternay du Fay, and did in the varieties which he brought together. The next description was that of De Bure in his *Bibliographie instructive* (vol. i. p. 67), printed 1763–1768; but the German editions were overlooked by De Bure, as they had been by his predecessors. The *Carter-Brown Catalogue* (vol. i. no. 473) shows Sobolewski's copy of De Bure with manuscript notes. A lifetime later, in 1802, A. G. Camus printed at Paris his *Mémoire sur les grands et petits voyages* [de De Bry] *et les voyages de Thevenot.* As a careful and critical piece of work, this collation of Camus was superior to De Bure's. A description of a copy belonging to the Duke of Bedford was printed in Paris in 1836 (6 pp.). Weigel, in the *Serapeum* (1845), pp. 65–89, printed his "Bibliographische Mittheilungen über die deutschen Ausgaben von De Bry," which was also printed separately. It described a copy now owned in New York. Muller, in his *Catalogue* (1872), p. 217, indicates some differences from Weigel's collations. The copy formed by De Bure fell into Mr. Grenville's hands, and was largely improved by him before he left it, with his library, to the British Museum. The *Bibliotheca Grenvilliana* describes it, and Bartlett (*Carter-Brown Catalogue,* i. 321) thinks it the finest in Europe. Cf. Dibdin's description, which is copied in the *American Bibliopolist* (1872), p. 13. The standard collation at present is probably that of Brunet, in his *Manuel du libraire,* vol. i. (1860), which was also printed separately; in this he follows Weigel for the German texts. This account is followed by Sabin in his *Dictionary* (vol. iii. p. 20), whose article, prepared by Charles A. Cutter, of the Boston Athenæum, has also been printed separately. The Brunet account is accompanied by a valuable note (also in Sabin, iii. 59), by Sobolewski, whose best set (reaching one hundred and seventy parts) was a wonderful one, though he lacked the English Hariot. This set came to this country through Muller (cf. his *Catalogue,* 1875, p. 387), and is now in the Lenox Library. Sobolewski's second set went into the Field Collection, and was sold in 1875; and again in the J. J. Cooke sale (*Catalogue,* iii. 297) in 1883. Cf. *Catalogue de la collection de feu M. Serge Sobolewski de Moscou,* prepared by Albert Cohn. The sale took place in Leipsic in July, 1873. Brunet and Sobolewski both point out the great difficulties of a satisfactory collation, arising from the publisher's habit of mixing the sheets of the various editions, forming varieties almost beyond the acquisition of the most enthusiastic collector, "so that," says Brunet, "perhaps no two copies of this work are exactly alike." "No man ever yet," says Henry Stevens (*Historical Collections,* vol. i. no. 179), "made up his De Bry perfect, if one may count on the three great De Bry witnesses, — the Right Honorable Thomas Grenville, the Russian prince Sobolewski, and the American Mr. Lenox, — who all went far beyond De Bure, yet fell far short of attaining all the variations they had heard of." The collector will value various other collations now accessible, like that in the *Carter-Brown Catalogue,* vol. i. no. 396 (also printed separately, twenty-five copies, in 1875); that printed by Quaritch, confined to the German texts; that in the *Huth Catalogue,* ii. 404; and that in the *Sunderland Catalogue,* nos. 2,052, 2,053.

2 There are lists of the sets which have been sold since 1709 given in Sabin (vol. iii. p. 47), from Brunet, and in the *Carter-Brown Catalogue* (vol. i. p. 408). The Rothelin copy, then esteemed the best known, brought, in 1746, 750 francs. At a later day, with additions secured under better knowledge, it again changed hands at 2,551

While there is distinctive merit in De Bry's collection, which caused it to have a due effect in its day on the progress of geographical knowledge,[1] it must be confessed that a certain meretricious reputation has become attached to the work as the test of a collector's assiduity, and of his supply of money, quite disproportioned to the relative use of the collection in these days to a student. This artificial appreciation has no doubt been largely due to the engravings, which form so attractive a feature in the series, and which, while they in many cases are the honest rendering of genuine sketches, are certainly in not a few the merest fancy of some designer.[2]

There are several publications of the De Brys sometimes found grouped with the *Voyages* as a part, though not properly so, of the series. Such are Las Casas' *Narratio regionum Indicarum;* the voyages of the "Silberne Welt," by Arthus von Dantzig, and of Olivier van Noort;[3] the *Rerum et urbis Amstelodamensium historia* of Pontanus, with its Dutch voyages to the north; and the *Navigations aux Indes par les Hollandois*.[4]

Another of De Bry's editors, Gasper Ens, published in 1680 his *West-unnd-Ost Indischer Lustgart*, which is a summary of the sources of American history.[5]

There are various abridgments of De Bry. The earliest is Ziegler's *America*, Frankfort, 1614,[6] which is made up from the first nine parts of the German *Grands Voyages*. The *Historia antipodum, oder Newe Welt* (1631), is the first twelve parts condensed by Johann Ludwig Gottfried, otherwise known as Johann Phillippe Abelin, who was, in Merian's day, a co-laborer on the *Voyages*. He uses a large number of the plates from the larger work.[7] The chief rival collection of De Bry is that of Hulsius, which is described elsewhere.[8]

Collections now became numerous. Conrad Löw's *Meer oder Seehanen Buch* was published at Cologne in 1598.[9] The Dutch Collection of Voyages, issued by Cornelius Claesz, appeared in uniform style between 1598 and 1603, but it never had a collective title. It gives the voyages of Cavendish and Drake.[10]

It was well into the next century (1613) when Purchas began his publications, of which there

francs, and once more, in 1855 (described in the *Bulletin du bibliophile*, 1855, pp. 38–41), Mr. Lenox bought it for 12,000 francs; and in 1873 Mr. Lenox also bought the best Sobolewski copy (fifty-five volumes) for 5,050 thalers. With these and other parts, procured elsewhere, this library is supposed to lead all others in the facilities for a De Bry bibliography. Fair copies of the *Grands voyages* in Latin, in first or second editions, are usually sold for about £100, and for both voyages for £150, and sometimes £200. Muller, in 1872, held the fourteen parts, in German, of the *Grands voyages*, at 1,000 florins. Fragmentary sets are frequently in the Catalogues, but bring proportionately much less prices. In unusually full sets the appreciation of value is rapid with every additional part. Most large American libraries have sets of more or less completeness. Besides those in the Carter-Brown (which took thirty years to make, besides a duplicate set from the Sobolewski sale) and Lenox libraries, there are others in the Boston Public, Harvard College, Astor, and Long Island Historical Society libraries, — all of fair proportions, and not unfrequently in duplicate and complemental sets. The copy of the Great Voyages, in Latin (all first editions), in the Murphy Library (*Catalogue*, no. 379), was gathered for Mr. Murphy by Obadiah Rich. The Murphy Library also contained the German text in first editions. In 1884 Quaritch offered the fine set from the Hamilton Library (twenty-five parts), "presumed to be quite perfect," for £670. The Earl of Crawford and Balcarres is about publishing his bibliography of De Bry.

1 There are somewhat diverse views on this point expressed by Brunet and in the Grenville Catalogue.

2 Reference has been made elsewhere (Vol. III. pp. 123, 164) to sketches, now preserved as a part of the Grenville copy of De Bry in the British Museum, which seem to have been the originals from which De Bry engraved the pictures in Hariot's *Virginia*, etc. These were drawn by Wyth, or White. A collection of twenty-four plates of such, from De Bry, were published in New York in 1841 (*Field's Indian Bibliography*, no. 1,701). Cf. *Amer. Antiq. Soc. Proc.*, Oct. 20, 1866, for other of De Bry's drawings in the British Museum. De Bry's engravings have been since copied by Picard in his *Cérémonies et coutumes religieuses des peuples idolatres* (Amsterdam, 1723), and by others. Exception is taken to the fidelity of De Bry's engravings in the parts on Columbus; cf. Navarrete, French translation, i. 320.

3 Carter-Brown, vol. i. nos. 453, 454, 455.

4 Rich (1832), £5 5*s*. Cf. P. A. Tiele's *Mémoire bibliographique sur les journaux des navigateurs Néerlandais réimprimés dans les collections de De Bry et de Hulsius*, Amsterdam, 1867.

5 Stevens (1870), no. 668; Sabin, vi. 211.

6 Carter-Brown, vol. i. no. 456; vol. ii. no. 198; Muller (1875), p. 389.

7 Carter-Brown, vol. i. nos. 457, 458; vol. ii. nos. 373, 791. There was a second edition in 1655. Cf. Muller (1872), no. 636; Sabin, vol. i. no. 50; iii. 59; Huth, ii. 612. Abelin also edited the first four volumes (covering 1617–1643) of the *Theatrum Europeum* (Frankfort, 1635), etc., which pertains incidentally to American affairs (Muller, 1872, no. 1,514). Fitzer's *Orientalische Indien* (1628) and Arthus's *Historia Indiæ orientalis* (1608) are abridgments of the *Small Voyages*.

8 Vol. IV. p. 442.

9 Sabin, vol. x. no. 42,392; Carter-Brown, vol. i. no. 530.

10 Muller (1872), no. 1,867.

is an account elsewhere.[1] Hieronymus Megiser's *Septentrio novantiquus* was published at Leipsic in 1613. In a single volume it gave the Zeni and later accounts of the North, besides narratives pertaining to New France and Virginia.[2] The *Journalen van de Reysen op Oostindie* of Michael Colijn, published at Amsterdam in 1619, is called by Muller[3] the first series of voyages published in Dutch with a collective title. It includes, notwithstanding the title, Cavendish, Drake, and Raleigh. Another Dutch folio, Herckmans' *Der Zeevaert lof*, etc. (Amsterdam, 1634), does not include any American voyages.[4] The celebrated Dutch collection, edited by Isaac Commelin, at Amsterdam, and known as the *Begin en Voortgangh van de Oost-Indische Compagnie*, would seem originally to have included, among its voyages to the East and North,[5] those of Raleigh and Cavendish; but they were later omitted.[6]

The collection of Thevenot was issued in 1663; but this has been described elsewhere.[7] The collection usually cited as Dapper's was printed at Amsterdam, 1669–1729, in folio (thirteen volumes). It has no collective title, but among the volumes are two touching America, — the *Beschrijvinge* of Montanus,[8] and Nienhof's *Brasiliaansche Zee-en Lantreize*.[9] A small collection, *Recueil de divers voyages faits en Africa et en l'Amérique*,[10] was published in Paris by Billaine in 1674. It includes Blome's Jamaica, Laborde on the Caribs, etc. Some of the later American voyages were also printed in the second edition of a Swedish *Reesa-book*, printed at Wysingzborg in 1674, 1675.[11] The Italian collection, *Il genio vagante*, was printed at Parma in 1691-1693, in four volumes.

An Account of Several Voyages (London, 1694) gives Narborough's to Magellan's Straits, and Marten's to Greenland.

The important English *Collection of Voyages and Travels* which passes under the name of its publisher, Churchill, took its earliest form in 1704, appearing in four volumes; but was afterwards increased by two additional volumes in 1733, and by two more in 1744, — these last, sometimes called the *Oxford Voyages*, being made up from material in the library of the Earl of Oxford. It was reissued complete in 1752. It has an introductory discourse by Caleb Locke; and this, and some other of its contents, constitutes the *Histoire de la navigation*, Paris, 1722.[12]

John Harris, an English divine, had compiled a *Collection of Voyages* in 1702 which was a rival of Churchill's, differing from it in being an historical summary of all voyages, instead of a collection of some. Harris wrote the Introduction; but it is questionable how much else he had to do with it.[13] It was revised and reissued in 1744–1748 by Dr. John Campbell, and in this form it is often regarded as a supplement to Churchill.[14] It was reprinted in two

1 Vol. III. p. 47. Cf. Carter-Brown, vol. ii. nos. 159, 169, 189, 223, 308, 330, 397. Sobolewski's copy was in the Menzies sale (no. 1,649). Quaritch's price is from £75 to £100, according to condition, which is the price of good copies in recent sales.

2 Muller (1872), no. 2,067.

3 *Catalogue* (1875), no. 3,284; (1877), no. 1,627; Tiele, no. 1.

4 Muller (1872), no. 1,837.

5 This collection also includes the voyages of Barentz, and of Hudson, as well as several through Magellan's Straits, with Madriga's voyage to Peru and Chili.

6 The collection, as it is known, is sometimes dated 1644 and 1645, but usually 1646 (Muller, 1872, no. 1,871; Tiele, *Mémoire bibliographique*, p. 9; Carter-Brown, vol. ii. nos. 567, 586; Sabin, iv. 315, 316). A partial English translation appeared in London in 1703 (Muller, 1872, no. 1,886). The *Oost-Indische Voyagien*, issued at Amsterdam in 1648 by Joost Hartgers, is a reprint of part of Commelin, with some additions. Only one volume was printed; but Muller thinks (1872 *Catalogue*, no. 1877) that some separate issues (1649–1651), including Vries's voyage to Virginia and New Netherland, were intended to make part of a second volume. Cf. Sabin, viii. 118; Stevens, *Nuggets*, no. 1,339.

7 Vol. IV. p. 219.

8 The original of Ogilby's *America*: cf. Vol. III. p. 416.

9 Muller (1872), no. 1,884. Another Dutch publication, deserving of a passing notice, which, though not a collection of voyages, enlarges upon the heroes of such voyages, is the *Leeven en Daden der doorluchtigste Zee-helden* (Amsterdam, 1676), by Lambert van den Bos, which gives accounts of Columbus, Vespucius, Magellan, Drake, Cavendish, the Zeni, Cabot, Cortereal, Frobisher, and Davis. There was a German translation at Nuremberg in 1681 (Carter-Brown, vol. ii. no. 1,149; Stevens, 1870, no. 231).

10 Carter-Brown, vol. ii. no. 1,111. A second edition was printed by the widow Cellier in Paris in 1683 (Muller, 1875, p. 395), containing the same matter differently arranged.

11 An earlier edition (1667) did not have them (Muller, 1875, p. 394). Capel's *Vorstellungen des Norden* (Hamburg, 1676) summarizes the voyages of the Zeni, Hudson, and others to the Arctic regions.

12 Sabin, iv. 68; Carter-Brown, vol. iii. no. 50. It includes in the later editions Castell's description of America, with other of the Harleian manuscripts, and gives Ferdinand Columbus' life of his father.

13 *Historical Magazine*, i. 125.

14 Allibone; Bohn's *Lowndes*, etc.

volumes, folio, with continuations to date, in 1764.[1]

The well-known Dutch collection (*Voyagien*) of Vander Aa was printed at Leyden in 1706, 1707. It gives voyages to all parts of the world made between 1246 and 1693. He borrows from Herrera, Acosta, Purchas, De Bry, and all available sources, and illuminates the whole with about five hundred maps and plates. In its original form it made twenty-eight, sometimes thirty, volumes of small size, in black-letter, and eight volumes in folio, both editions being issued at the same time and from the same type. In this larger form the voyages are arranged by nations; and it was the unsold copies of this edition which, with a new general title, constitutes the edition of 1727. In the smaller form the arrangement is chronological. In the folio edition the voyages to Spanish America previous to 1540 constitute volumes three and four; while the English voyages, to 1696, are in volumes five and six.[2]

In 1707 Du Perier's *Histoire universelle des voyages* had not so wide a scope as its title indicated, being confined to the early Spanish voyages to America;[3] the proposed subsequent volumes not having been printed. An English translation, under Du Perier's name, was issued in London in 1708;[4] but when reissued in 1711, with a different title, it credited the authorship to the Abbé Bellegarde.[5] In 1711, also, Captain John Stevens published in London his *New Collection of Voyages;* but Lawson's Carolina and Cieza's Peru were the only American sections.[6] In 1715 the French collection known as Bernard's *Recueil de voiages au Nord*, was begun at Amsterdam. A pretty wide interpretation is given to the restricted designation of the title, and voyages to California, Louisiana, the Upper Mississippi (Hennepin), Virginia, and Georgia are included.[7] Daniel Coxe, in 1741, united in one volume *A Collection of Voyages*, three of which he had already printed separately, including Captain James's to the Northwest. A single volume of a collection called *The American Traveller* appeared in London in 1743.[8]

The collection known as *Astley's Voyages* was published in London in four volumes in 1745–1747; the editor was John Green, whose name is sometimes attached to the work. It gives the travels of Marco Polo, but has nothing of the early voyages to America,[9] — these being intended for later volumes, were never printed. These four volumes were translated, with some errors and omissions, into French, and constitute the first nine volumes of the Abbé Prevost's *Histoire générale des voyages*, begun in Paris in 1746, and completed, in twenty quarto volumes, in 1789.[10] An octavo edition was printed (1749–1770) in seventy-five volumes.[11] It was again reprinted at the Hague in twenty-five volumes quarto (1747–1780), with considerable revision, following the original English, and with Green's assistance; besides showing some additions. The Dutch editor was P. de Hondt, who also issued an edition in Dutch in twenty-one volumes quarto, — including, however, only the first seventeen volumes of his French edition, thus omitting those chiefly concerning America.[12] A small collection of little moment, *A New Universal Collection of Voyages*, appeared in London in 1755.[13] De Brosses' *Histoire des navigations aux terres australes depuis 1501* (Paris, 1756), two volumes quarto, covers Vespucius, Magellan, Drake, and Cavendish.[14]

1 Carter-Brown, vol. iii. no. 1,400; Sabin, viii. 92; Muller (1872), no. 1,901.

2 H. H. Bancroft, *Central America*, ii. 745, who errs somewhat in his statements; *Murphy Catalogue*, no. 1,074; Carter-Brown, vol. iii. no. 88, with full table of contents. The best description is in Muller (1872), no. 1,887. Although Vander Aa says, in the title of the folio edition, that it is based on the Gottfriedt-Abelin *Newe Welt*, this new collection is at least four times as extensive.

3 Carter-Brown, vol. iii. no. 96.

4 Carter-Brown, iii. 110.

5 Carter-Brown, iii. 150.

6 The publication began in numbers in 1708, and some copies are dated 1710 (Carter-Brown, vol. iii. no. 158).

7 Carter-Brown, vol. iii. no. 208, in ten vols., 1715–1718. H. H. Bancroft (*Central America*, ii. 749), cites an edition (1715–1727) in nine vols. Muller (1870, no. 2,021) cites an edition, ten vols., 1731–1738.

8 Sabin, vol. i. no. 1,250.

9 Carter-Brown, vol. iii. no. 792; H. H. Bancroft, *Central America*, ii. 747.

10 Volumes xii. to xv. are given to America; the later volumes were compiled by Querlon and De Leyre.

11 Different sets vary in the number of volumes.

12 Muller (1872), nos. 1,895–1,900; Carter-Brown, vol. iii. no. 831; H. H. Bancroft, *Central America*, ii. 746. A German translation appeared at Leipsic in 1747 in twenty-one volumes.

13 H. H. Bancroft, *Central America*, ii. 750.

14 Muller (1872), nos. 1,980, 1,981. There was a German translation, with enlargements, by J. C. Adelung, Halle, 1767; an English translation is also cited. A similar range was taken in Alexander Dalrymple's *Historical Collection of Voyages in the South Pacific Ocean* (London, 1770), of which there was a French translation in 1774 (Carter-Brown, vol. iii. no. 1,730). The most important contribution in English on this

Several English collections appeared in the next few years; among which are *The World Displayed* (London, 1759–1761), twenty vols. 16mo, — of which seven volumes are on American voyages, compiled from the larger collections,[1] — and *A Curious Collection of Travels* (London, 1761) is in eight volumes, three of which are devoted to America.[2]

The Abbé de la Porte's *Voyageur François*, in forty-two volumes, 1765–1795 (there are other dates), may be mentioned to warn the student of its historical warp with a fictitious woof.[3] John Barrows' *Collection of Voyages* (London, 1765), in three small volumes, was translated into French by Targe under the title of *Abrégé chronologique.* John Callender's *Voyages to the Terra australis* (London, 1766–1788), three volumes, translated for the first time a number of the narratives in De Bry, Hulsius, and Thevenot. It gives the voyages of Vespucius, Magellan, Drake, Galle, Cavendish, Hawkins, and others.[4] Dodsley's *Compendium of Voyages* was published in the same year (1766) in seven volumes.[5] The *New Collection of Voyages*, generally referred to as Knox's, from the publisher's name, appeared in seven volumes in 1767, the first three volumes covering American explorations.[6] In 1770 Edward Cavendish Drake's *New Universal Collection of Voyages* was published at London. The narratives are concise, and of a very popular character.[7] David Henry, a magazinist of the day, published in 1773–1774 *An Historical Account of all the Voyages Round the World by English Navigators*, beginning with Drake and Cavendish.[8]

La Harpe issued in Paris, 1780–1801, in thirty-two volumes, — Comeyras editing the last eleven, — his *Abrégé de l'histoire générale des voyages*, which proved a more readable and popular book than Prévost's collection. There have been later editions and continuations.[9]

Johann Reinhold Forster made a positive contribution to this field of compilation when he printed his *Geschichte der Entdeckungen und Schifffahrten im Norden* at Frankfort in 1785.[10] He goes back to the earliest explorations, and considers the credibility of the Zeno narrative. He starts with Gomez for the Spanish section. A French collection by Berenger, *Voyages faits autour du monde* (Paris, 1788–1789), is very scant on Magellan, Drake, and Cavendish. A collection was published in London (1789) by Richardson on the voyages of the Portuguese and Spaniards during the fifteenth and sixteenth centuries. Mavor's *Voyages, Travels, and Discoveries* (London, 1796–1802), twenty-five volumes, is a condensed treatment, which passed to other editions in 1810 and 1813–1815.

A standard compilation appeared in John Pinkerton's *General Collection of Voyages* (London, 1808–1814), in seventeen volumes,[11] with over two hundred maps and plates, repeating the essential English narratives of earlier collections, and translating those from foreign languages afresh, preserving largely the language of the explorers. Pinkerton, as an editor, was learned, but somewhat pedantic and over-confident; and a certain agglutinizing habit indicates a process of amassment rather than of selection and assimilation. Volumes xii., xiii., and xiv. are given to America; but the operations of the Spaniards on the main, and particularly on the Pacific coast of North America, are rather scantily chronicled.[12]

In 1808 was begun, under the supervision of Malte-Brun and others, the well-known *Annales des voyages*, which was continued to 1815, making twenty-five volumes. A new series, *Nouvelles annales des voyages*, was begun in 1819. The whole work is an important gathering of original sources and learned comment, and is in considerable part devoted to America. A French *Collection abrégée des voyages*, by Bancarel, appeared in Paris in 1808–1809, in twelve volumes.

The Collection of the best Voyages and Travels, compiled by Robert Kerr, and published in Edinburgh in 1811–1824, in eighteen octavo volumes, is a useful one, though the scheme was not wholly carried out. It includes an historical essay on the progress of navigation and discovery by W. Stevenson. It also includes among others the Northmen and Zeni voyages, the travels of Marco Polo and Galvano, the African discoveries of the Portuguese. The voyages of Columbus and his successors begin in vol. iii.;

subject, however, is in Dr. James Burney's *Chronological History of Discovery in the South Sea* (1803–1817), five volumes quarto.

1 Dr. Johnson wrote the Introduction; there was a third edition in 1767 (Bohn's *Lowndes*, p. 2994).

2 H. H. Bancroft, *Central America*, ii. 750.

3 H. H. Bancroft, *Central America*, ii. 754.

4 Carter-Brown, vol. iii. no. 1,494.

5 Sabin, v. 473; H. H. Bancroft, *Central America*, ii. 750.

6 Sabin, ix. 529; Carter-Brown, vol. iii. no. 1,602; H. H. Bancroft, *Central America*, ii. 750.

7 Carter-Brown, vol. iii. no. 1,733; H. H. Bancroft, *Central America*, ii. 751.

8 H. H. Bancroft, *Central America*, ii. 751; Allibone.

9 H. H. Bancroft, *Central America*, ii. 749.

10 H. H. Bancroft, *Central America*, ii. 752.

11 There was a quarto reprint in Philadelphia of a part of it in 1810–1812.

12 There is a catalogue of voyages and an index in vol. xvii. Cf Allibone's *Dictionary.*

and the narratives of these voyages are continued through vol. vi., though those of Drake, Cavendish, Hawkins, Davis, Magellan, and others come later in the series.

The *Histoire générale des voyages*, undertaken by C. A. Walkenaer in 1826, was stopped in 1831, after twenty-one octavos had been printed, without exhausting the African portion.

The early Dutch voyages are commemorated in Bennet and Wijk's *Nederlandsche Ontdekkingen in America*, etc., which was issued at Utrecht in 1827,[1] and in their *Nederlandsche Zeereizen*, printed at Dordrecht in 1828–1830, in five volumes octavo. It contains Linschoten, Hudson, etc.

Albert Montémont's *Bibliothèque universelle des voyages* was published in Paris, 1833–1836, in forty-six volumes.

G. A. Wimmer's *Die Enthüllung des Erdkreises* (Vienna, 1834), five volumes octavo, is a general summary, which gives in the last two volumes the voyages to America and to the South Seas.[2]

In 1837 Henri Ternaux-Compans began the publication of his *Voyages, relations, et mémoires originaux pour servir à l'histoire de la découverte de l'Amérique*, of which an account is given on another page (see p. vi).

The collection of F. C. Marmocchi, *Raccolta di viaggi dalla scoperta del Nuevo Continente*, was published at Prato in 1840–1843, in five volumes; it includes the Navarrete collection on Columbus, Xeres on Pizarro, and other of the Spanish narratives.[3] The last volume of a collection in twelve volumes published in Paris, *Nouvelle bibliothèque des voyages*, is also given to America.

The Hakluyt Society in London began its valuable series of publications in 1847, and has admirably kept up its work to the present time, having issued its volumes generally under satisfactory editing. Its publications are not sold outside of its membership, except at second hand.[4]

Under the editing of José Ferrer de Couto and José March y Labores, and with the royal patronage, a *Historia de la marina real Española* was published in Madrid, in two volumes, 1849 and 1854. It relates the early voyages.[5] Édouard Charton's *Voyageurs anciens et modernes* was published in four volumes in Paris, 1855–1857; and it passed subsequently to a new edition.[6]

A summarized account of the Portuguese and Spanish discoveries, from Prince Henry to Pizarro, was published in German by Theodor Vogel, and also in English in 1877.

A *Nouvelle histoire des voyages*, by Richard Cortambert, is the latest and most popular presentation of the subject, opening with the explorations of Columbus and his successors; and Édouard Cat's *Les grandes découvertes maritimes du treizième au seizième siècle* (Paris, 1882) is another popular book.

[1] Stevens, *Bibliotheca geographica*, no. 317.

[2] Muller (1872), no. 1,842.

[3] Muller (1875), no. 3,303.

[4] Complete sets are sometimes offered by dealers at £30 to £35.

[5] H. H. Bancroft, *Central America*, ii. 757.

[6] A Spanish translation of the modern voyages by Urrabieta was published in Paris in 1860–1861. The Spanish *Enciclopedia de viajes modernos* (Madrid, 1859), five volumes, edited by Fernandez Cuesta, refers to the later periods (H. H. Bancroft, *Central America*, ii. 758).

NARRATIVE AND CRITICAL

HISTORY OF AMERICA

CHAPTER I.

THE GEOGRAPHICAL KNOWLEDGE OF THE ANCIENTS CONSIDERED IN RELATION TO THE DISCOVERY OF AMERICA.

BY WILLIAM H. TILLINGHAST,

Assistant Librarian of Harvard University.

AS Columbus, in August, 1498, ran into the mouth of the Orinoco, he little thought that before him lay, silent but irrefutable, the proof of the futility of his long-cherished hopes. His gratification at the completeness of his success, in that God had permitted the accomplishment of all his predictions, to the confusion of those who had opposed and derided him, never left him; even in the fever which overtook him on the last voyage his strong faith cried to him, "Why dost thou falter in thy trust in God? He gave thee India!" In this belief he died. The conviction that Hayti was Cipangu, that Cuba was Cathay, did not long outlive its author; the discovery of the Pacific soon made it clear that a new world and another sea lay between the landfall of Columbus and the goal of his endeavors.

The truth, when revealed and accepted, was a surprise more profound to the learned than even the error it displaced. The possibility of a short passage westward to Cathay was important to merchants and adventurers, startling to courtiers and ecclesiastics, but to men of classical learning it was only a corroboration of the teaching of the ancients. That a barrier to such passage should be detected in the very spot where the outskirts of Asia had been imagined, was unexpected and unwelcome. The treasures of Mexico and Peru could not satisfy the demand for the products of the East; Cortes gave himself, in his later years, to the search for a strait which might yet make good the anticipations of the earlier discoverers. The new interpretation, if economically disappointing, had yet an interest of its own. Whence came the human population of the unveiled continent? How had its existence escaped the wisdom of Greece and Rome? Had it done so? Clearly, since the whole human race had been renewed through Noah, the red men of America must have descended from the patriarch; in some way, at some time, the New World had been discovered and populated from the Old. Had knowledge of this event lapsed from the minds of men before their memories were committed to writing, or did reminiscences exist in ancient literatures, overlooked, or misunderstood by modern ignorance? Scholars were not wanting, nor has their line since wholly failed, who freely devoted their ingenuity to the solution of these questions, but with a success so diverse in its results, that the inquiry is still pertinent, especially since the pursuit, even though on the main point it end in reservation of judgment, enables us to understand from what source and by what channels the inspiration came which held Columbus so steadily to his westward course.

Although the elder civilizations of Assyria and Egypt boasted a cultivation of astronomy long anterior to the heroic age of Greece, their cosmographical ideas appear to have been rude and undeveloped, so that whatever the Greeks borrowed thence was of small importance compared with what they themselves ascertained. While it may be doubted if decisive testimony can be extorted from the earliest Grecian literature, represented chiefly by the Homeric and Hesiodic poems, it is probable that the people among whom that literature grew up had not gone, in their conception of the universe, beyond simple acceptance of the direct evidence of their senses. The earth they looked upon as a plane, stretching away from the Ægean Sea, the focus of their knowledge, and ever less distinctly known, until it ended in an horizon of pure ignorance, girdled by the deep-flowing current of the river Oceanus. Beyond Oceanus even fancy began to fail: there was the realm of dust and darkness, the home of the powerless spirits of the dead; there, too, the hemisphere of heaven joined its brother hemisphere of Tartarus.[1] This conception of the earth was not confined to Homeric times, but remained the common belief throughout the course of Grecian history, underlying and outlasting many of the speculations of the philosophers.

That growing intellectual activity which was signalized by a notable development of trade and colonization in the eighth century, in the seventh awoke to consciousness in a series of attempts to formulate the conditions of existence. The philosophy of nature thus originated, wherein the testimony of nature in her own behalf was little sought or understood, began with the assumption of a flat earth, variously shaped, and as variously supported. To whom belongs the honor of first propounding the theory of the spherical form of the earth cannot be known. It was taught by the Italian Pythagoreans of the sixth century, and was probably one of the doctrines

[1] The plane earth cut the cosmic sphere like a diaphragm, shutting the light from Tartarus.

> αὐτὰρ ὕπερθεν
> γῆς ῥίζαι πεφύασι καὶ ἀτρυγέτοιο θαλάσσης.
> (Hesiod, *Theog.* 727.)

> "and above
> Impend the roots of earth and barren sea."
> (*The remains of Hesiod the Ascræan*, etc., translated by C. A. Elton, 2d ed. London, 1815.)

Critics differ as to the age of the vivid description of Tartarus in the Theogony.

of Pythagoras himself, as it was, a little later, of Parmenides, the founder of the Eleatics.[1]

In neither case can there be a claim for scientific discovery. The earth was a sphere because the sphere was the most perfect form; it was at the centre of the universe because that was the place of honor; it was motionless because motion was less dignified than rest.

Plato, who was familiar with the doctrines of the Pythagoreans, adopted their view of the form of the earth, and did much to popularize it among his countrymen.[2] To the generation that succeeded him, the sphericity of the earth was a fact as capable of logical demonstration as a geometrical theorem. Aristotle, in his treatise "On the Heaven," after detailing the views of those philosophers who regarded the earth as flat, drum-shaped, or cylindrical, gives a formal summary of the grounds which necessitate the assumption of its sphericity, specifying the tendency of all things to seek the centre, the unvarying circularity of the earth's shadow at eclipses of the moon, and the proportionate change in the altitude of stars resulting from changes in the observer's latitude. Aristotle made the doctrine orthodox; his successors, Eratosthenes, Hipparchus, and Ptolemy, constituted it an inalienable possession of the race. Greece transmitted it to Rome, Rome impressed it upon barbaric Europe; taught by Pliny, Hyginus, Manilius, expressed in the works of Cicero, Virgil, Ovid, it passed into the schoolbooks of the Middle Ages, whence, reinforced by Arabian lore, it has come down to us.[3]

That the belief ever became in antiquity or in the Middle Ages widely spread among the people is improbable; it did not indeed escape opposition among the educated; writers even of the Augustan age sometimes appear in doubt.[4]

[1] Pythagoras has left no writings; Aristotle speaks only of his school; Diogenes Laertius in one passage (*Vitae*, viii. 1 (Pythag.), 25) quotes an authority to the effect that Pythagoras asserted the earth to be spherical and inhabited all over, so that there were antipodes, to whom that is *over* which to us is *under*. As all his disciples agreed on the spherical form of the earth while differing as to its position and motion, it is probable that they took the idea of its form from him. Diogenes Laertius states that Parmenides called the earth round (*στρογγύλη*, viii. 48), and also that he spoke of it as spherical (*σφαιροειδῆ*, ix. 3); the passages are not, as has been sometimes assumed, contradictory. The enunciation of the doctrine is often attributed to Thales and to Anaximander, on the authority of Plutarch, *De placitis philosophorum*, iii. 10, and Diogenes Laertius, ii. 1, respectively; but the evidence is conflicting (Simplicius, *Ad Aristot.*, p. 506 b. ed. Brandis; Aristot., *De caelo*, ii. 13; Plutarch, *De plac. phil.* iii., xv. 9).

[2] Plato, *Phaedo*, 109. Schaefer is in error when he asserts (*Entwicklung der Ansichten der Alten ueber Gestalt und Grösse der Erde*, 16) that Plato in the *Timaeus* (55, 56) assigns a cubical form to the earth. The question there is not of the shape of the earth, the planet, but of the form of the constituent atoms of the element earth.

[3] Terra pilae similis, nullo fulcimine nixa,
  Aëre subjecto tam grave pendet onus.
[Ipsa volubilitas libratum sustinet orbem:
  Quique premit partes, angulus omnis abest.
Cumque sit in media rerum regione locata,
  Et tangat nullum plusve minusve latus;
Ni convexa foret, parti vicinior esset,
  Nec medium terram mundus haberet onus.]
Arte Syracosia suspensus in aëre clauso
  Stat globus, immensi parva figura poli;
Et quantum a summis, tantum secessit ab imis
  Terra. Quod ut fiat, forma rotunda facit.
(Ovid, *Fasti*, vi. 269–280.)

The bracketed lines are found in but a few MSS. The last lines refer to a globe said to have been constructed by Archimedes.

[4] Plato makes Socrates say that he took up the works of Anaxagoras, hoping to learn

The sphericity of the earth once comprehended, there follow certain corollaries which the Greeks were not slow to perceive. Plato, indeed, who likened the earth to a ball covered with party-colored strips of leather, gives no estimate of its size, although the description of the world in the *Phaedo* seems to imply immense magnitude;[1] but Aristotle states that mathematicians of his day estimated the circumference at 400,000 stadia,[2] and Archímedes puts the common reckoning at somewhat less than 300,000 stadia.[3] How these figures were obtained we are not informed. The first measurement of the earth which rests on a known method was that made about the middle of the third century B. C., by Eratosthenes, the librarian at Alexandria, who, by comparing the estimated linear distance between Syene, under the tropic, and Alexandria with their angular distance, as deduced from observations on the shadow of the gnomon at Alexandria, concluded that the circumference of the earth was 250,000 or 252,000 stadia.[4] This result, owing to an uncertainty as to the exact length of the stade used in the computation, cannot be interpreted with confidence, but if we assume that it was in truth about twelve per cent. too large, we shall probably not be far out of the way.[5] Hipparchus, in many matters

whether the earth was round or flat (*Phaedo*, 46, Stallb. i. 176). In Plutarch's dialogue "*On the face appearing in the orb of the moon*," one of the characters is lavish in his ridicule of the sphericity of the earth and of the theory of antipodes. See also Lucretius, *De rerum nat.*, i. 1052, etc., v. 650; Virgil, *Georgics*, i. 247; Tacitus, *Germania*, 45.

1 That extraordinary picture could, however, hardly have been intended for an exposition of the actual physical geography of the globe.

2 Aristotle, *De caelo*, ii. 15.

3 Archimedes, *Arenarius*, i. 1, ed. Helbig. Leipsic, 1881, vol. ii. p. 243.

4 The logical basis of Eratosthenes's work was sound, but the result was vitiated by errors of fact in his assumptions, which, however, to some extent counterbalanced one another. The majority of ancient writers who treat of the matter give 252,000 stadia as the result, but Cleomedes (*Circ. doctr. de subl.*, i. 10) gives 250,000. It is surmised that the former number originated in a desire to assign in round numbers 700 stadia to a degree. Forbiger, *Handbuch der alten Geographie*, i. 180, n. 27.

5 The stadium comprised six hundred feet, but the length of the Greek foot is uncertain; indeed, there were at least two varieties, the Olympic and the Attic, as in Egypt there was a royal and a common ell, and a much larger number of supposititious feet (and, consequently, stadia) have been discovered or invented by metrologists. Early French scholars, like Ramé de l'Isle, D'Anville, Gosselin, supposed the true length of the earth's circumference to be known to the Greeks, and held that all the estimates which have come down to us were expressions of the same value in different stadia. It is now generally agreed that these estimates really denote different conceptions of the size of the earth, but opinions still differ widely as to the length of the stadium used by the geographers. The value selected by Peschel (*Geschichte der Erdkunde*, 2d ed., p. 46) is that likewise adopted by Hultsch (*Griechische und Römische Metrologie*, 2d ed., 1882) and Muellenhof (*Deutsche Alterthumskunde*, 2d ed., vol. i.). According to these writers, Eratosthenes is supposed to have devised as a standard geographical measure a stadium composed of feet equal to one half the royal Egyptian ell. According to Pliny (*Hist. Nat.*, xii. 14, § 5), Eratosthenes allowed forty stadia to the Egyptian schonus; if we reckon the schonus at 12,000 royal ells, we have stadium $= \frac{12{,}000}{40} \times .525^{m} = 157.5^{m}$. This would give a degree equal to $110{,}250^{m}$, the true value being, according to Peschel, $110{,}808^{m}$. To this conclusion Lepsius (*Das Stadium und die Gradmessung des Eratosthenes auf Grundlage der Aegyptischen Masse*, in *Zeitschrift für Aegypt. Sprache u. Alterthumskunde*, xv. [1877]. See also *Die Längenmasse der Alten*. Berlin, 1884) objects that the royal ell was never used in composition, and that the schonus was valued in different parts of Egypt at 12,000, 16,000, 24,000, *small* ells. He believes that the schonus referred to by Pliny contained 16,000 small ells, so that Eratosthenes's stadium $= \frac{16{,}000}{40} \times .450^{m} = 180^{m}$

It is possible, however, that Eratosthenes did not devise a new stadium, but adopted that in current use among the Greeks, the Athenian stadium. (I have seen no evidence that the long

the opponent of Eratosthenes, adopted his conclusion on this point, and was followed by Strabo,[1] by Pliny, who regarded the attempt as somewhat over-bold, but so cleverly argued that it could not be disregarded,[2] and by many others.

Fortunately, as it resulted, this over-estimate was not allowed to stand uncontested. Posidonius of Rhodes (B. C. 135–51), by an independent calculation based upon the difference in altitude of Canopus at Rhodes and at Alexandria, reached a result which is reported by Cleomedes as 240,000, and by Strabo as 180,000 stadia.[3] The final judgment of Posidonius apparently approved the smaller number; it hit, at all events, the fancy of the time, and was adopted by Marinus of Tyre and by Ptolemy,[4] whose authority imposed it upon the Middle Ages. Accepting it as an independent estimate, it follows that Posidonius allowed but 500 stadia to a degree, instead of 700, thus representing the earth as about 28 per cent. smaller than did Eratosthenes.[5]

To the earliest writers the known lands constituted the earth; they were girdled, indeed, by the river Oceanus, but that was a narrow stream whose

Olympic stadium was in common use.) This stadium is based on the Athenian foot, which, according to the investigations of Stuart, has been reckoned at .3081^{m}, being to the Roman foot as 25 to 24. This would give a stadium of 184.8^{m}, and a degree of 129,500^{m}. Now Strabo, in the passage where he says that people commonly estimated eight stadia to the mile, adds that Polybius allowed 8⅓ stadia to the mile (*Geogr.*, vii. 7, § 4), and in the fragment known as the Table of Julian of Ascalon (Hultsch, *Metrolog. script. reliq.*, Lips., 1864, i. 201) it is distinctly stated that Eratosthenes and Strabo reckoned 8⅓ stadia to the mile. In the opinion of Hultsch, this table probably belonged to an official compilation made under the emperor Julian. Very recently W. Dörpfeld has revised the work of Stuart, and by a series of measurements of the smaller architectural features in Athenian remains has made it appear that the Athenian foot equalled .2957^{m} (instead of .3081^{m}), which is almost precisely the Roman foot, and gives a stadium of 177.4^{m}, which runs 8⅓ to the Roman mile. If this revision is trustworthy, — and it has been accepted by Lepsius and by Nissel (who contributes the article on metrology to Mueller's *Handbuch der klassischen Alterthumswissenschaft*, Nordlingen, 1886, etc.), — it seems to me probable that we have here the stadium used by Eratosthenes, and that his degree has a value of 124,180^{m} (Dörpfeld, *Beiträge zur antiken Metrologie*, in *Mittheilungen des deutschen Archaeolog. Instituts zu Athen*, vii. (1882), 277).

1 Strabo, *Geogr.*, ii. 5, § 7; the estimate of Posidonius is only quoted hypothetically by Strabo (ii. 2, § 2).

2 Pliny, *Hist. Nat.* ii. 112, 113. There is apparently some misunderstanding, either on the part of Pliny or his copyists, in the subsequent proposition to increase this estimate by 12,000 stadia. Schaefer's (*Philologus*, xxviii. 187) readjustment of the text is rather audacious. Pliny's statement that Hipparchus estimated the circumference at 275,000 stadia does not agree with Strabo (i. 4, § 1).

3 The discrepancy is variously explained. Riccioli, in his *Geographia et hydrographia reformata*, 1661, first suggested the more commonly received solution. Posidonius, he thought, having calculated the arc between Rhodes and Alexandria at 1-48 of the circumference, at first assumed 5,000 stadia as the distance between these places: $5{,}000 \times 48 = 240{,}000$. Later he adopted a revised estimate of the distance (Strabo, ii. ch. v. § 24), 3,750 stadia: $3{,}750 \times 48 = 180{,}000$. Letronne (*Mém. de l'Acad. des Inscr. et Belles-Lettres*, vi., 1822) prefers to regard both numbers as merely hypothetical illustrations of the processes. Hultsch (*Griechische u. Römische Metrologie*, 1882, p. 63) follows Fréret and Gosselin in regarding both numbers as expressing the same value in stadia of different length (Forbiger, *Handbuch der alten Geographie*, i. 360, n. 29). The last explanation is barred by the positive statement of Strabo, who can hardly be thought not to have known what he was talking about: κἂν τῶν νεωτέρων δὲ ἀναμετρήσεων εἰσάγηται ἡ ἐλαχίστην ποιοῦσα τὴν γῆν, οἵαν ὁ Ποσειδώνιος ἐγκρίνει περὶ ὀκτωκαίδεκα μυριάδας οὖσαν, (*Geogr.*, ii. 2, § 2.)

4 *Geographia*, vii. 5.

5 $1° = 500$ stadia $= 88{,}700^{m}$, which is about one fifth smaller than the truth.

further bank lay in fable-land.[1] The promulgation of the theory of the sphericity of the earth and the approximate determination of its size drew attention afresh to the problem of the distribution of land and water upon its surface, and materially modified the earlier conception. The increase of geographical knowledge along lines of trade, conquest, and colonization had greatly extended the bounds of the known world since Homer's day, but it was still evident that by far the larger portion of the earth, taking the smallest estimate of its size, was still undiscovered, — a fair field for speculation and fantasy.[2]

We can trace two schools of thought in respect to the configuration of this unknown region, both represented in the primitive conception of the earth, and both conditioned by a more fundamental postulate. It was a near thought, if the earth was a sphere, to transfer to it the systems of circles which had already been applied to the heavens. The suggestion is attributed to Thales, to Pythagoras, and to Parmenides; and it is certain that the earth was very early conceived as divided by the polar and solstitial circles into five zones, whereof two only, the temperate in either sphere, so the Greeks believed, were capable of supporting life; of the others, the polar were uninhabitable from intense cold, as was the torrid from its parching heat. This theory, which excluded from knowledge the whole southern hemisphere and a large portion of the northern, was approved by Aristotle and the Homeric school of geographers, and by the minor physicists. As knowledge grew, its truth was doubted. Polybius wrote a monograph, maintaining that the middle portion of the torrid zone had a temperate climate, and his view was adopted by Posidonius and Geminus, if not by Eratosthenes. Marinus and Ptolemy, who knew that commerce was carried on along the east coast of Africa far below the equator, cannot have fallen into the ancient error, but the error long persisted; it was always in favor with the compilers, and thus perhaps obtained that currency in Rome which enabled it to exert a restrictive and pernicious check upon maritime endeavor deep into the Middle Ages.[3]

[1] Xenophanes is to be excepted, if, as M. Martin supposes, his doctrine of the infinite extent of the earth applied to its extent horizontally as well as downward.

[2] The domain of early Greek geography has not escaped the incursions of unbalanced investigators. The Greeks themselves allowed the Argonauts an ocean voyage: Crates and Strabo did valiant battle for the universal wisdom of Homer; nor are scholars lacking to-day who will demonstrate that Odysseus had circumnavigated Africa, floated in the shadow of Teneriffe — Horace to the contrary notwithstanding, — or sought and found the north pole. The evidence is against such vain imaginings. The world of Homer is a narrow world; to him the earth and the Ægean Sea are alike boundless, and in his thought fairy-land could begin west of the Lotos-eaters, and one could there forget the things of this life. There is little doubt that the author of the Odyssey considered Greece an island, and Asia and Africa another, and thought the great ocean eddied around the north of Hellas to a union with the Euxine.

[3] Quinque tenent caelum zonae: quarum una corusco
Semper sole rubens, et torrida semper ab igni;
Quam circum extremae dextra laevaque trahuntur
Caeruleae glacie concretae atque imbribus atris;
Has inter mediam duae mortalibus aegris
Munere concessae divom.
(Virgil, *Georg.* i. 233.)

The passage appears to be paraphrased from similar lines which are preserved in Achilles Tatius (*Isag. in Phænom. Arat.*; Petavius, *Uranolog.*

Upon the question of the distribution of land and water, unanimity no longer prevailed. By some it was maintained that there was one ocean, confluent over the whole globe, so that the body of known lands, that so-called continent, was in truth an island, and whatever other inhabitable regions might exist were in like manner surrounded and so separated by vast expanses of untraversed waves. Such was the view, scarcely more than a survival of the ocean-river of the poets deprived of its further bank by the assumption of the sphericity of the earth, held by Aristotle,[1] Crates of Mallus, Strabo, Pliny, and many others. If this be called the oceanic theory, we may speak of its opposite as the continental: according to this view, the existing land so far exceeded the water in extent that it formed in truth the continent, holding the seas quite separate within its hollows. The origin of the theory is obscure, even though we recall that Homer's ocean was itself contained. It was strikingly presented by Plato in the *Phaedo,* and is implied in the Atlantis myth; it may be recalled, too, that Herodotus, often depicted as a monster of credulity, had broken the bondage of the ocean-river, because he could not satisfy himself of the existence of the ocean in the east or north; and while reluctantly admitting that Africa was surrounded by water, considered Gaul to extend indefinitely westward.[2] Hipparchus revived the doctrine, teaching that Africa divided the Indian Ocean from the Atlantic in the south, so that these seas lay in separate basins. The existence of an equatorial branch of the ocean, a favorite dogma of the other school, was also denied by Polybius, Posidonius, and Geminus.[3]

The reports of traders and explorers led Marinus to a like conclusion; both he and Ptolemy, misinterpreting their information, believed that the eastern coast of Asia ran south instead of north, and they united it with the eastern trend of Africa, supposing at the same time that the two continents met also in the west.[4] The continental theory, despite its famous disciples, made no headway at Rome, and was consequently hardly known to the Middle Ages before its falsity was proved by the circumnavigation of Africa.[5]

p. 153), and by him attributed to the *Hermes* of Eratosthenes. See also Tibullus, *Eleg.* iv., Ovid, and among the men of science, Aristotle, *Meteorol.*, ii. 5, §§ 11, 13, 15; Strabo, *Geogr.*, i. 2, § 24; ii. 5, § 3; Pliny, *Hist. Nat.*, ii. ch. 68; Mela, *De chorographia*, i. 1; Cicero, *Republ.*, vi. 16; *Tusc. Disp.*, i. 28.

[1] Aristotle, *Meteorol.*, ii. 1, § 10; ii. 5, § 15; *De caelo*, ii. 14 *ad fin.* Letronne, finding the latter passage inconvenient, reversed the meaning by the arbitrary insertion of a negative (*Discussion de l'opinion d'Hipparque sur le prolongement de l'Afrique au sud de l'Equator* in *Journal des Savans,* 1831, pp. 476, 545). The theory which he built upon this reconstructed foundation so impressed Humboldt that he changed his opinion as to the views of Aristotle on this point (*Examen critique*, ii. 373). Such an emendation is only justifiable by the sternest necessity, and it has been shown by Ruge (*Der Chaldäer Seleukos,* Dresden, 1865), and Prantl (*Werke des Aristoteles uebersetzt und erläutert*, Bd. ii.; *Die Himmelsgebäude*, note 61), that neither sense nor consistency requires the change.

[2] Herodotus, ii. 23; iii. 115; iv. 36, 40, 45.

[3] Geminus, *Isagoge.* Polybius's work on this question is lost, and his own expressions as we have them in his history are more conservative. It is, he says, unknown, whether Africa is a continent extending toward the south, or is surrounded by the sea. Po[illegible] *Hist.* iii. 38; Hampton's translation (London, 17[illegible]), i. 334.

[4] Ptolemy, *Geogr.*, vii. 3, 5.

[5] The circumnavigation of Africa by Phœni-

That portion of Europe, Asia, and Africa known to the ancients, whether regarded as an island, or as separated from the rest of the world by climatic conditions merely, or by ignorance, formed a distinct concept and was known by a particular name, ἡ οἰκουμένη. Originally supposed to be circular, it was later thought to be oblong and as having a length more than double its width. Those who believed in its insularity likened its shape to a sling, or to an outspread chlamys or military cloak, and assumed that it lay wholly within the northern hemisphere. In absolute figures, the length of the known world was placed by Eratosthenes at 77,800 stadia, and by Strabo at 70,000. The latter figure remained the common estimate until Marinus of Tyre, in the second century A. D., receiving direct information from the silk-traders of a caravan route to China, substituted the portentous exaggeration of 90,000 stadia on the parallel of Rhodes, or 225°. Ptolemy, who followed Marinus in many things, shrank from the naïveté whereby the Tyrian had interpreted a seven months' caravan journey to represent seven months' travelling in a direct line at the rate of twenty miles a day, and cut down his figures to 180°, or 72,000 stadia.[1] It appears, therefore, that Strabo considered the known world as occupying not much over one third of the circuit of the temperate zone, while Marinus, who adopted 180,000 stadia as the measure of the earth, claimed a knowledge of two thirds of that zone, and supposed that land extended indefinitely eastward beyond the limit of knowledge.

What did the ancients picture to themselves of this unknown portion of the globe? The more imaginative found there a home for ancient myth and modern fable; the geographers, severely practical, excluded it from the scope of their survey; philosophers and physicists could easily supply from theory what they did not know as fact. Pythagoras, it is said, had taught that the whole surface of the earth was inhabited. Aristotle demonstrated that the southern hemisphere must have its temperate zone, where winds similar to our own prevailed; his successors elaborated the hint into a systematized nomenclature, whereby the inhabitants of the earth were divided into four classes, according to their location upon the surface of the earth with relation to one another.[2]

cians at the command of Necho, though described and accepted by Herodotus, can hardly be called an established fact, in spite of all that has been written in its favor. The story, whether true or false, had, like others of its kind, little influence upon the belief in the impassable tropic zone, because most of those who accepted it supposed that the continent terminated north of the equator.

[1] Ptolemy, *Geogr.*, i. 11–14. Eratosthenes and Strabo located their first meridian at Cape St. Vincent; Marinus and Ptolemy placed it in the Canary group. See Vol. II. p. 95.

[2] Geminus, *Isagoge*, ch. 13; Achilles Tatius, *Isagoge in Phænom. Arati;* Cleomedes, *De circulis sublimis*, i. 2. The first two are given in the *Uranologion* of Petavius, Lond., Paris, 1630, pp. 56, 155.

The classes were always divided on the same principle, and each contained two groups so related that they could apply to one another reciprocally the name by which the whole class was designed. These names, however, are not always applied to the same classes by different writers. 1. The first class embraced the people who lived in the same half of the same temperate zone; to them all it was day or night, summer or winter, at the same time. They were called *σύνοικοι* by Cleomedes, but *περίοικοι* by Achilles Tatius. 2. The second class included such peoples as lived in the same temperate zone, but were

This system was furthest developed by the oceanic school. The rival of Eratosthenes, Crates of Mallus (who achieved fame by the construction of a large globe), assumed the existence of a southern continent, separated from the known world by the equatorial ocean; it is possible that he introduced the idea of providing a distinct residence for each class of earth-dwellers, by postulating four island continents, one in each quarter of the globe. Eratosthenes probably thought that there were inhabitable regions in the southern hemisphere, and Strabo added that there might be two, or even more, habitable earths in the northern temperate zone, especially near the parallel of Rhodes.[1] Crates introduced his views at Rome, and the oceanic theory remained a favorite with the Roman physicists. It was avowed by Pliny, who championed the existence of antipodes against the vulgar disbelief. In the fine episode in the last book of Cicero's *Republic*, the younger Scipio relates a dream, wherein the elder hero of his name, Scipio Africanus, conveying him to the lofty heights of the Milky Way, emphasized the futility of fame by showing him upon the earth the regions to which his name could never penetrate: "Thou seest in what few places the earth is inhabited, and those how scant; great deserts lie between them, and they who dwell upon the earth are not only so scattered that naught can spread from one community to another, but so that some live off in an oblique direction from you, some off toward the side, and some even dwell directly opposite to you."[2] Mela confines himself to a mention of the *Antichthones*, who live in the temperate zone in the south, and are cut off from us by the intervening torrid zone.[3]

divided by half the circumference of that zone; so that while they all had summer or winter at the same time, the one group had day when the other had night, and *vice versa*. These groups could call one another περίοικοι according to Cleomedes, but ἀντίχθονες according to Tatius. 3. The third class included those who were divided by the torrid zone, so that part lived in the northern temperate zone and part in the southern, but yet so that all were in the same half of their respective zones; *i. e.*, all were in either the eastern or western, upper or lower, hemisphere. Day and night were shared by the whole class at once, but not the seasons, the northern group having summer when the southern had winter, and *vice versa*. These groups could call one another ἄντοικοι. 4. The fourth class comprised the groups which we know as antipodes, dwelling with regard to one another in different halves of the two temperate zones, so that they had neither seasons nor day or night in common, but stood upon the globe diametrically opposed to one another. All writers agree in calling these groups ἀντίποδες. The introduction of the word *antichthones* in place of *perioeci* was due, apparently, to a misunderstanding of the Pythagorean *antichthon*. This name was properly applied to the imaginary planet invented by the early Pythagoreans to bring the number of the spheres up to ten; it was located between the earth and the central fire, and had the same period of revolution as the earth, from the outer, Grecian, side of which it was never visible. This "opposite earth," *Gegenerde*, was later confused with the other, western, or lower hemisphere of the earth itself. It was also sometimes applied to the inhabitants of the southern hemisphere, as by Cicero in the *Tusculan Disputations* (i. 28), "duabus oris distantibus habitabilem et cultum; quarum altera quam nos incolimus,

> Sub axe posita ad stellas septem unde horrifer
> Aquiloni stridor gelidas molitur nives,

altera australis, ignota nobis, *quam vocant Græci* ἀντίχθονα." Mela has the same usage (i. 4, 5), as quoted below. Macrobius, *Comm. in Somn. Scip.* lib. ii. 5, uses the nomenclature of Cleomedes. Reinhardt, quoted in Engelmann's *Bibliotheca classica Græca*, under Geminus, I have not been able to see.

[1] Strabo, i. 4, § 6, 7; i. 2, § 24. Geminus, *Isagoge*, 13. Muellenhof, *Deutsche Alterthumskunde*, i. 247–254. Berger, *Geogr. Fragmente d. Eratosthenes*, 8, 84.

[2] Cicero, *Respubl.*, vi. 15 . . . sed partim obliquos, partim transversos, partim etiam adversos stare vobis. Some MSS. read aversos. See also *Tusc. Disp.*, i. 28; *Acad.*, ii. 39.

[3] Antichthones alteram [zonam], nos alteram

Indeed, the southern continent, the other world, as it was called,[1] made a more distinct impression than the possible other continents in the northern hemisphere. Hipparchus thought that Trapobene might be a part of this southern world, and the idea that the Nile had its source there was wide-spread: some supposing that it flowed beneath the equatorial ocean; others believing, with Ptolemy, that Africa was connected with the southern con-

MACROBIUS.*

tinent. The latter doctrine was shattered by the discovery of the Cape of Good Hope; but the continent was revived when Tierra del Fuego, Australia, and New Zealand were discovered, and attained gigantic size on the

incolimus. Illius situs ob ardorem intercedentis plagae incognitus, huius dicendus est. Haec ergo ab ortu porrecta ad occasum, et quia sic iacet aliquanto quam ubi latissima est longior, ambitur omnis oceano. Mela, *Chor.*, i. 4, 5. Because Mela says that the known world is *but little* longer than its width, it has been supposed that he was better informed than his contemporaries, and attributed something like its real extent to Africa. Thomassy (*Les papes géographiques*, Paris, 1852, p. 17) finds in his work a rival system to that of Ptolemy. The discovery of America, he thinks, was due to Ptolemy; that of the Cape of Good Hope to Mela. It was the good fortune of Mela that his work was widely read in the Middle Ages, and had great influence; but we owe him no new system of geography, since he simply adopted the oceanic theory as represented by Strabo and Crates. That he slightly changed the traditional proportion between the length and breadth of the known world is of small importance. The known world, he states, was surrounded by the ocean, and there is nothing to show that he supposed Africa to extend below the equator. In his description of Africa he applies the terms length and breadth not as we should, but with contrary usage: "Africa ab orientis parte Nilo terminata, pelago a ceteris, brevior est quidem quam Europa, quia nec usquam Asiae et non totis huius litoribus obtenditur, longior tamen ipsa quam latior, et qua ad fluvium adtingit latissima," etc., i. 20. (Ed. Parthey, 1867.)

[1] Mela, i. 54, "Alter orbis." Cicero, *Tusc. Disp.*, i. 28, "Ora Australis."

* From *Macrobii Ambrosii Aurelii Theodosii in Somnium Scipionis, Lib. II.* (Lugduni, 1560).

maps of the sixteenth and seventeenth centuries; only within the last two centuries has it shrunk to the present limits of the antarctic ice.

The oceanic theory, and the doctrine of the Four Worlds, as it has been termed,[1] *terra quadrifiga*, was set forth in the greatest detail in a commentary on the Dream of Scipio, written by Macrobius, probably in the fifth century A. D. In the concussion and repulsion of the ocean streams he found a sufficient cause for the phenomena of the tides.[2]

Such were the theories of the men of science, purely speculative, originating in logic, not discovery, and they give no hint of actual knowledge regarding those distant

MACROBIUS.*

[1] Hyde Clarke, *Atlantis*, in the *Transactions of the Royal Historical Society*, London, New Series, vol. iii.; Reinaud, *Relations politiques*, etc., *de l'empire Romaine avec l'Asie orientale*, etc., in the *Journal Asiatique*, 1863, p. 140.

[2] The exposition of Macrobius is so interesting as illustrating the mathematical and physical geography of the ancients, and as showing how thoroughly the practical consequences of the sphericity of the earth were appreciated; it is so important in the present connection as demonstrating that the whole idea of inhabited lands in other parts of the earth was based on logic only, not on knowledge, that I have ventured to quote from it somewhat freely.

Macrobius, *Comm. in Somn. Scipionis*, ii. 5.—"Cernis autem eamdem terram quasi quibusdam redimitam et circumdatam cingulis, e quibus duos maxime inter se diversos, et caeli verticibus ipsis ex utraque parte subnixos, obriguisse pruina vides; medium autem illum, et maximum, solis ardore torreri. Duo sunt habitabiles: quorum australis ille, in quo qui insistunt, adversa vobis urgent vestigia, nihil ad vestrum genus; hic autem alter subjectus aquiloni, quem incolitis, cerne quam tenui vos parte contingat. Omnis enim terra, quae colitur a vobis, angusta verticibus, lateribus latior, parva quaedam insula est. . . ." (Cicero.) . . . Nam et septentrionalis et australis extremitas perpetua obriguerunt pruina. . . . Horum uterque habitationis impatiens est. . . . Medius cingulus et ideo maximus, aeterno afflatu continui caloris ustus, spatium quod et lato ambitu et prolixius occupavit, nimietate fervoris facit inhabitabile victuris. Inter extremos vero et medium duo majores ultimis, medio minores ex utriusque vicinitatis intemperie temperantur. . . . Licet igitur sint hae duae . . . quas diximus temperatas, non tamen ambae zonae hominibus nostri generis indultae sunt: sed sola superior, ... incolitur ab omni, quale scire possumus, hominum genere, Romani Graecive sint, vel barbari cujusque nationis. Illa vero . . . sola ratione intelligitur, quod propter similem temperiem similiter incolatur, sed a quibus, neque licuit unquam nobis nec licebit cognoscere: interjecta enim torrida utrique hominum generi commercium ad se denegat commeandi . . . Nec dubium est, nostrum quoque septentrionem [ventum] ad illos qui australi adjacent, propter eamdem rationem calidum pervenire, et austrum corporibus eorum gemino aurae suae rigore blandiri. Eadem ratio nos non permittit ambigere quin per illam quoque superficiem terrae quae ad nos habetur inferior, integer zonarum ambitus quae hic temperatae sunt, eodem ductu temperatus habeatur; atque ideo illic quoque eaedem duae zonae a se distantes similiter incolantur. . . . Nam si nobis vivendi facultas est in hac terrarum parte quam colimus, quia, calcantes humum, caelum suspicimus super verticem, quia sol nobis et oritur et occidit, quia circumfuso fruimur aere cujus spiramus haustu, cur non et illic aliquos vivere credamus ubi eadem semper in

* From *Avr. Theodosii Macrobii Opera* (Lipsiæ, 1774).

regions with which they deal. From them we turn to examine the literature of the imagination, for geography, by right the handmaid of history, is easily perverted to the service of myth.

MACROBIUS.*

The expanding horizon of the Greeks was always hedged with fable: in the north was the realm of the happy Hyperboreans, beyond the blasts of Boreas; in the east, the wonderland of India; in the south, Panchæa and the blameless Ethiopians; nor did the west lack lingering places for romance. Here was the floating isle of Æolus, brazen-walled; here the mysterious Ogygia, navel of the sea;[1] and on the earth's extremest verge were the Elysian Fields, the home of heroes exempt from

promptu sunt? Nam, qui ibi dicuntur morari, eamdem credendi sunt spirare auram, quia eadem est in ejusdem zonalis ambitus continuatione temperies. Idem sol illis et obire dicitur nostro ortu, et orietur quum nobis occidet: calcabunt aeque ut nos humum, et supra verticem semper caelum videbunt. Nec metus erit ne de terra in caelum decidant, quum nihil unquam possit ruere sursum. Si enim nobis, quod asserere genus joci est, deorsum habitur ubi est terra, et sursum ubi est caelum, illis quoque sursum erit quod de inferiore suspicient, nec aliquando in superna casuri sunt.

Hi quos separat a nobis perusta, quos Graeci ἀντοικοὺς vocant, similiter ab illis qui inferiorem zonae suae incolunt partem interjecta australi gelida separantur. Rursus illos ab ἀντοικοῖς suis, id est per nostri cinguli inferiora viventibus, interjectio ardentis sequestrat: et illi a nobis septentrionalis extremitatis rigore removentur. Et quia non est una omnium affinis continuatio, sed interjectae sunt solitudines ex calore vel frigore mutuum negantibus commeatum, has terrae partes quae a quattuor hominum generibus incoluntur, maculas habitationum vocavit. . . .

9. Is enim quem solum oceanum plures opinantur, de finibus ab illo originali refusis, secundum ex necessitate ambitum fecit. Ceterum prior ejus corona per zonam terrae calidam meat, superiora terrarum et inferiora cingens, flexum circi equinoctialis imitata. Ab oriente vero duos sinus refundit, unum ad extremitatem septentrionis, ad australis alterum: rursusque ab occidente duo pariter enascuntur sinus, qui usque ad ambas, quas supra diximus, extremitates refusi occurrunt ab oriente demissis; et, dum vi summa et impetu immaniore miscentur, invicemque se feriunt, ex ipsa aquarum collisione nascitur illa famosa oceani accessio pariter et recessio. . . . Ceterum verior, ut ita dicam, ejus alveus tenet zonam perustam; et tam ipse qui equinoctialem, quam sinus ex eo nati qui horizontem circulum ambitu suae flexionis imitantur, omnem terram quadrifidam dividunt, et singulas, ut supra diximus, habitationes insulas faciunt . . . binas in superiore atque inferiore terrae superficie insulas. . . .

[1] Mr. Gladstone (*Homer and the Homeric age*, vol. iii.) transposes these Homeric localities to the east, and a few German writers agree with him. President Warren (*True key to ancient cosmologies*, etc., Boston, 1882) will have it that Ogygia is neither more nor less than the north pole. Neither of these views is likely to displace the one now orthodox. Mr. Gladstone is so much troubled by Odysseus's course on leaving Ogygia that he cannot hide a suspicion of corruption in the text. President Warren should remember that Ogygia apparently enjoyed the common succession of day and night. In Homeric thought the western sea extended northward and eastward until it joined the Euxine.

* After Santarem's *Atlas*, as a "mappemonde tirée d'un manuscrit de Macrobe du Xème siècle."

death, "where life is easiest to man. No snow is there, nor yet great storm nor any rain, but always ocean sendeth forth the breeze of the shrill west to blow cool on men."[1] Across the ocean river, where was the setting of the sun, all was changed. There was the home of the Cimmerians, who dwelt in darkness; there the grove of Persephone and the dreary house of the dead.[2]

In the Hesiodic poems the Elysian Fields are transformed into islands, the home of the fourth race, the heroes, after death: —

> "Them on earth's utmost verge the god assign'd
> A life, a seat, distinct from human kind:
> Beside the deepening whirlpools of the main,
> In those blest isles where Saturn holds his reign,
> Apart from heaven's immortals calm they share
> A rest unsullied by the clouds of care:
> And yearly thrice with sweet luxuriance crown'd
> Springs the ripe harvest from the teeming ground."[3]

"Those who have had the courage to remain stedfast thrice in each life, and to keep their souls altogether from wrong," sang Pindar, "pursue the road of Zeus to the castle of Cronos, where o'er the isles of the blest ocean breezes blow, and flowers gleam with gold, some from the land on glistering trees, while others the water feeds; and with bracelets of these they entwine their hands and make crowns for their heads."[4]

The Islands of the Blest, μακάρων νῆσοι, do not vanish henceforward from the world's literature, but continue to haunt the Atlantic through the Roman period and deep into the Middle Ages. In the west, too, were localized other and wilder myths; here were the scenes of the Perseus fable, the island of the weird and communistic sisters, the Graeae, and the Gorgonides, the homes of Medusa and her sister Gorgons, the birthplace of the dread Chimaera.[5] The importance of the far west in the myths connected

Ogygia, located northwest of Greece, would be the centre, *omphalos*, of the sea, as Delphi was later called the centre of the land-masses of the world.

[1] *Odyssey*, iv. 561, etc.

[2] It is well known that whereas Odysseus meets the spirits of the dead across Oceanus, upon the surface of the earth, there is in the *Iliad* mention of a subterranean Hades. The Assyrio-Babylonians had also the idea of an earth-encircling ocean stream, — the word 'Ωκεανὸς the Greeks said was of foreign origin, — and on the south of it they placed the sea of the dead, which held the island homes of the departed. As in the *Odyssey*, it was a place given over to dust and darkness, and the doors of it were strongly barred; no living being save a god or a chosen hero might come there. Schrader, *Namen d. Meere in d. Assyrischen Inschriften* (*Abhandl. d. k. Akad. d. Wiss. zu Berlin*, 1877, p. 169). Jeremias, *Die Babylonisch-Assyrischen Vorstellungen vom Leben nach dem Tode* (Leipzig, 1887). The Israelites, on the other hand, imagined the home of the dead as underground. *Numbers*, xvi. 30, 32, 33.

Buchholtz, *Die Homerische Realien*, i. 55, places Hades on the European shores of Ocean, but the text of the Odyssey seems plainly in favor of the site across the stream, as Völcker and others have understood.

[3] Hesiod, *Works and Days*, 166–173; Elton's translation, London, 1815, p. 22. Paley marks the line Τηλοῦ ἀπ' ἀθανάτων τοῖσιν Κρόνος ἐμβασιλεύει as probably spurious. Cronos appears to have been originally a Phœnician deity, and his westward wandering played an important part in their mythology. We shall find further traces of this divinity in the west.

[4] Pindar, *Olymp.*, ii. 66–85, Paley's translation, London, 1868, p. 12. See also Euripides, *Helena*, 1677.

[5] Æschylus, in the *Prometheus bound*, introduced the Gorgon islands in his epitome of the wanderings of Io, and certainly seems to speak

with Hercules is well known. In the traditionary twelve labors the Greek hero is confused with his prototype the Tyrian Melkarth, and those labors which deal with the west were doubtless borrowed from the cult which the Greeks had found established at Gades when trade first led them thither. In the tenth labor it is the western isle Erytheia, which Hercules visits in the golden cup wherein Helios was wont to make his nocturnal ocean voyage, and from which he returns with the oxen of the giant Geryon. Even more famous was the search for the apples of the Hesperides, which constituted the eleventh labor. This golden fruit, the wedding gift produced by Gaa for Hera, the prudent goddess, doubtful of the security of Olympus, gave in charge to the Hesperian maids, whose island garden lay at earth's furthest bounds, near where the mysterious Atlas, their father or their uncle, wise in the secrets of the sea, watched over the pillars which propped the sky, or himself bore the burden of the heavenly vault. The poets delighted to depict these isles with their shrill-singing nymphs, in the same glowing words which they applied to the Isles of the Blessed. "Oh that I, like a bird, might fly from care over the Adriatic waves!" cries the chorus in the Crowned Hippolytus,

"Or to the famed Hesperian plains,
Whose rich trees bloom with gold,
To join the grief-attuned strains
My winged progress hold:
Beyond whose shores no passage gave
The ruler of the purple wave;

"But Atlas stands, his stately height
The awfull boundary of the skies:
There fountains of Ambrosia rise,
Wat'ring the seat of Jove: her stores
Luxuriant there the rich soil pours
All, which the sense of gods delights."[1]

When these names first became attached to some of the Atlantic islands is uncertain. Diodorus Siculus does not apply either term to the island discovered by the Carthaginians, and described by him in phrases applicable to both. The two islands described by sailors to Sertorius about 80 B. C. were depicted in colors which reminded Plutarch of the Isles of the Blessed, and it is certain that toward the close of the republic the name *Insulae Fortunatae* was given to certain of the Atlantic islands, including the Canaries. In the time of Juba, king of Numidia, we seem to distinguish at least three groups, the *Insulae Fortünatae*, the *Purpurariae*, and the *Hesperides*, but beyond the fact that the first name still designated some of the Canaries identification is uncertain; some have thought that different groups among the Canaries were known by separate names, while others

of them as in the east; the passage is, however, imperfect, and its interpretation has overtasked the ablest commentators.

[1] Euripides, *Hippolytus*, 742–751; Potter's translation, i. p. 356. See also Hesiod, *Theog.*, 215, 517–519.

hold that one or both of the Madeira and Cape de Verde groups were known.[1] The Canaries were soon lost out of knowledge again, but the Happy or Fortunate Islands continued to be an enticing mirage throughout the Middle Ages, and play a part in many legends, as in that of St. Brandan, and in many poems.[2]

Beside these ancient, widespread, popular myths, embodying the universal longing for a happier life, we find a group of stories of more recent date, of known authorship and well-marked literary origin, which treat of western islands and a western continent. The group comprises, it is hardly necessary to say, the tale of Atlantis, related by Plato; the fable of the land of the Meropes, by Theopompus; and the description of the Saturnian continent attributed to Plutarch.

The story of Atlantis, by its own interest and the skill of its author, has made by far the deepest impression. Plato, having given in the *Republic* a picture of the ideal political organization, the state, sketched in the *Timaeus* the history of creation, and the origin and development of mankind; in the *Critias* he apparently intended to exhibit the action of two types of political bodies involved in a life-and-death contest. The latter dialogue was unfinished, but its purport had been sketched in the opening of the *Timaeus*. Critias there relates "a strange tale, but certainly true, as Solon declared," which had come down in his family from his ancestor Dropidas, a near relative of Solon. When Solon was in Egypt he fell into talk with an aged priest of Saïs, who said to him: "Solon, Solon, you Greeks are all children, — there is not an old man in Greece. You have no old traditions, and know of but one deluge, whereas there have been many destructions of mankind, both by flood and fire; Egypt alone has escaped them, and in Egypt alone is ancient history recorded; you are ignorant of your own past." For long before Deucalion, nine thousand years ago, there was an Athens founded, like Saïs, by Athena; a city rich in power and wisdom, famed for mighty deeds, the greatest of which was this. At that time there lay opposite the columns of Hercules, in the Atlantic, which was then navigable, an island larger than Libya and Asia together, from which sailors could pass to other islands, and so to the continent. The sea in front of the straits is indeed but a small harbor; that which lay beyond the island, however, is worthy of the name, and the land which surrounds that greater sea may be truly called the continent. In this island of Atlantis had grown up a mighty power, whose kings were descended from Poseidon, and had

[1] Mela, iii. 100, 102, etc. The chief passage is Pliny, *Hist. Nat.*, vi. 36, 37, who took his information from King Juba and a writer named Statius Sebosus. Pliny, who, beside the groups named in the text, mentions the Gorgades, which he identifies with the place where Hanno met the gorillas, has probably misunderstood and garbled his authorities; his account is contradictory and illusive.

[2] Tzetzes (*Scholia in Lycophron*, 1204, ed. Mueller, ii. 954), a grammarian of the twelfth century, says that the Isles of the Blessed were located in the ocean by Homer, Hesiod, Euripides, Plutarch, Dion, Procopius, Philostratus and others, but that to many it seems that Britain must be the true Isle of the Blessed; and in support of this view he relates a most curious tale of the ferriage of the dead to Britain by Breton fishermen.

extended their sway over many islands and over a portion of the great continent; even Libya up to the gates of Egypt, and Europe as far as Tyrrhenia, submitted to their sway. Ever harder they pressed upon the other nations of the known world, seeking the subjugation of the whole. "Then, O Solon, did the strength of your republic become clear to all men, by reason of her courage and force. Foremost in the arts of war, she met the invader at the head of Greece; abandoned by her allies, she triumphed alone over the western foe, delivering from the yoke all the nations within the columns. But afterwards came a day and night of great floods and earthquakes; the earth engulfed all the Athenians who were capable of bearing arms, and Atlantis disappeared, swallowed by the waves: hence it is that this sea is no longer navigable, from the vast mud-shoals formed by the vanished island." This tale so impressed Solon that he meditated an epic on the subject, but on his return, stress of public business prevented his design. In the *Critias* the empire and chief city of Atlantis is described with wealth of detail, and the descent of the royal family from Atlas, son of Poseidon, and a nymph of the island, is set forth. In the midst of a council upon Olympus, where Zeus, in true epic style, was revealing to the gods his designs concerning the approaching war, the dialogue breaks off.

Such is the tale of Atlantis. Read in Plato, the nature and meaning of the narrative seem clear, but the commentators, ancient and modern, have made wild work. The voyage of Odysseus has grown marvellously in extent since he abandoned the sea; Io has found the pens of the learned more potent goads than Hera's gadfly; but the travels of Atlantis have been even more extraordinary. No region has been so remote, no land so opposed by location, extent, or history to the words of Plato, but that some acute investigator has found in it the origin of the lost island. It has been identified with Africa, with Spitzbergen, with Palestine. The learned Latreille convinced himself that Persia best fulfilled the conditions of the problem; the more than learned Rudbeck ardently supported the claims of Sweden through three folios. In such a search America could not be overlooked. Gomara, Guillaume de Postel, Wytfliet, are among those who have believed that this continent was Atlantis; Sanson in 1669, and Vaugondy in 1762, ventured to issue a map, upon which the division of that island among the sons of Neptune was applied to America, and the outskirts of the lost continent were extended even to New Zealand. Such work, of course, needs no serious consideration. Plato is our authority, and Plato declares that Atlantis lay not far west from Spain, and that it disappeared some 8,000 years before his day. An inquiry into the truth or meaning of the record as it stands is quite justifiable, and has been several times undertaken, with divergent results. Some, notably Paul Gaffarel[1] and Ignatius Donnelly,[2] are convinced that Plato merely adapted to his purposes a story

[1] *L'Atlantide*, by Paul Gaffarel, in the *Revue de Géographie*, April, May, June, July, 1880 (vi. 241, 331, 421; vii. 21). See also, in his *Étude sur les rapports de l'Amérique et de l'ancien continent avant Christophe Colomb* (Paris, 1869).

[2] *Atlantis: the antediluvian world*, New York, 1882.

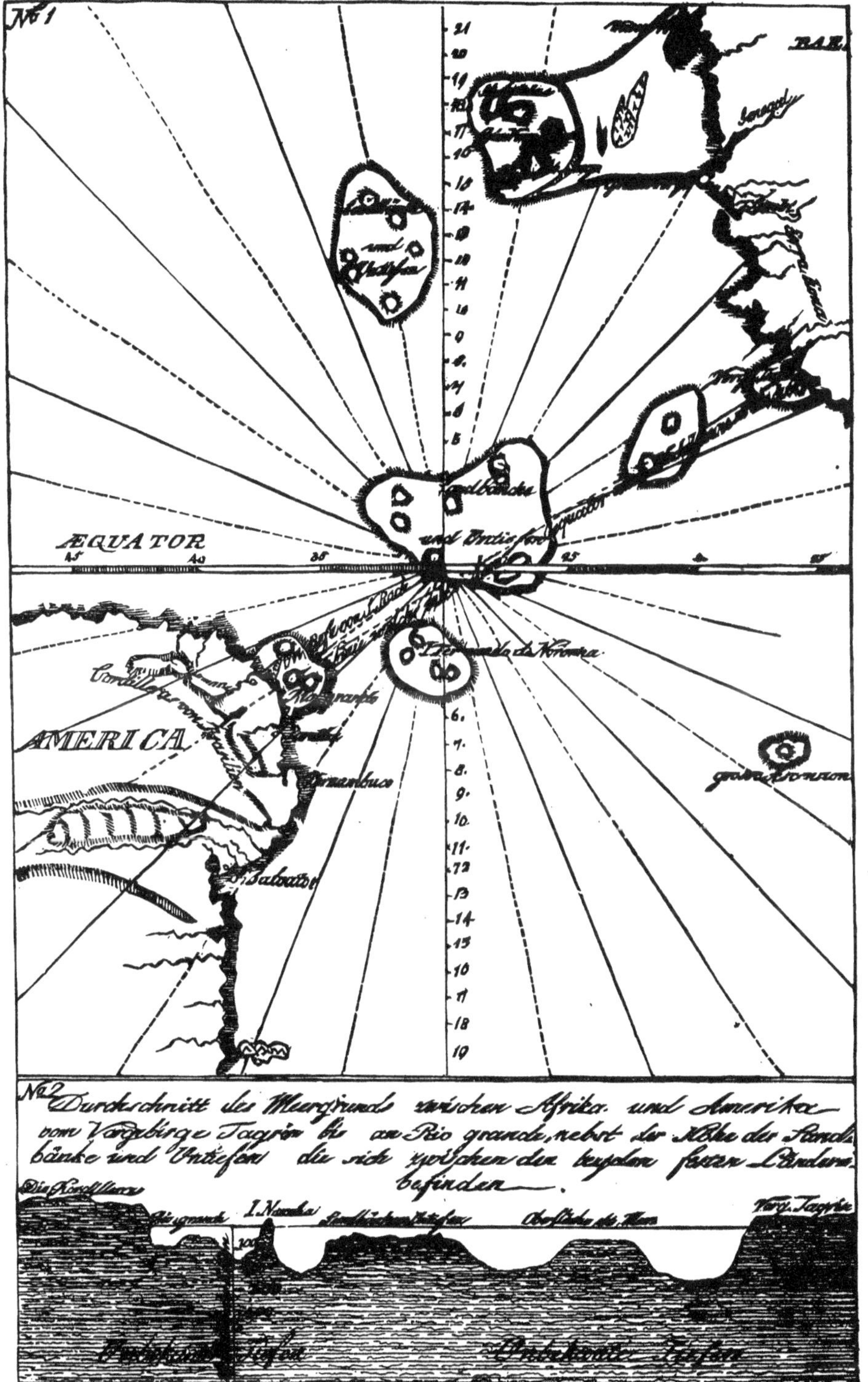

TRACES OF ATLANTIS.

Section of a map given in *Briefe über Amerika aus dem Italienischen des Hn. Grafen Carlo Carli übersetzt, Dritter Theil* (Gera, 1785), where it is called an "Auszug aus denen Karten welche der Pariser Akademie der Wissenschaften (1737, 1752) von dem Herrn von Buache übergeben worden sind."

ATLANTIS INSULA

The annexed cut is an extract from Sanson's map of America, showing views respecting the new world as constituting the Island of Atlantis. It is called: *Atlantis insula à Nicolao Sanson, antiquitati restituta; nunc demum majori forma delineata, et in decem regna juxta decem Neptuni filios distributa. Præterea insulæ, nostræq. continentis regiones quibus imperavere Atlantici reges; aut quas armis tentavere, ex conatibus geographicis Gulielmi Sanson, Nicolai filii* (Amstelodami apud Petrum Mortier). Uricoechea in the *Mapoteca Colombiana* puts this map under 1600, and speaks of a second edition in 1688, which must be an error. Nicholas Sanson was born in 1600, his son William died in 1703. Beside the undated Amsterdam print quoted above, Harvard College Library possesses a copy in which the words *Novus orbis potius Altera continent sive* are prefixed to the title, while the date MDCLXVIIII is inserted after *filii*. This copy was published by Le S. Robert at Paris in 1741.

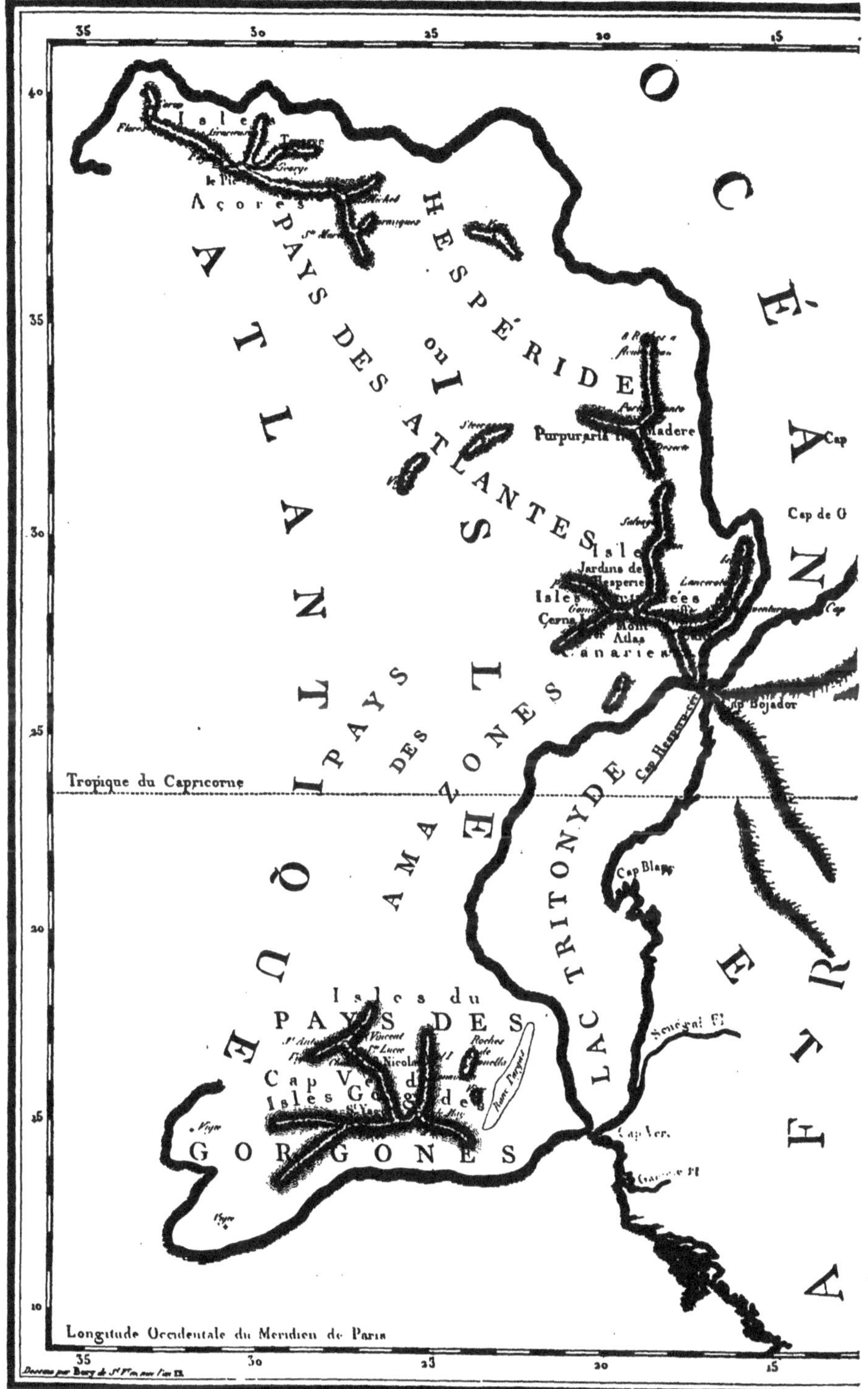

CARTE CONJECTURALE DE L'ATLANTIDE.

From a map in Bory de St. Vincent's *Essais sur les isles Fortunées*, Paris [1803]. A map in Anastasius Kircher's *Mundus Subterraneus* (Amsterdam, 1678), i. 82, shows Atlantis as a large island midway between the pillars of Hercules and America.

CONTOUR CHART OF THE BOTTOM OF THE ATLANTIC.

Sketched from the colored map of the United States Hydrographic office, as given in Alexander Agassiz's *Three Cruises of the Blake* (Cambridge, 1888), vol. i. The outline of the continents is shown by an unbroken line. The 500 fathom shore line is a broken one (—— —— —— ——). The 2,000 fathom shore line is made by a dash and dot (——. ——. ——. ——). The large areas in mid-ocean enclosed by this line, have this or lesser depths. Of the small areas marked by this line, the depth of 2,000 fathoms or less is within these areas in all cases except as respects the small areas on the latitude of Newfoundland, where the larger areas of 2,000 fathoms' depth border on the small areas of greater depth. Depths varying from 1,500 to 1,000 fathoms are shown by horizontal lines; from 1,000 to 500 by perpendicular lines; and the crossed lines show the shallowest spots in mid-ocean of 500 fathoms or less. The areas of greatest depth (over 3,500 fathoms) are marked with crosses.

which Solon had actually brought from Egypt, and which was in all essentials true. Corroboration of the existence of such an island in the Atlantic is found, according to these writers, in the physical conformation of the Atlantic basin, and in marked resemblances between the flora, fauna, civilization, and language of the old and new worlds, which demand for their explanation the prehistoric existence of just such a bridge as Atlantis would have supplied. The Atlantic islands are the loftiest peaks and plateaus of the submerged island. In the widely spread deluge myths Mr. Donnelly finds strong confirmation of the final cataclysm; he places in Atlantis that primitive culture which M. Bailly sought in the highlands of Asia, and President Warren refers to the north pole. Space fails for a proper examination of the matter, but these ingenious arguments remain somewhat top-heavy when all is said. The argument from ethnological resemblances is of all arguments the weakest in the hands of advocates. It is of value only when wielded by men of judicial temperament, who can weigh difference against likeness, and allow for the narrow range of nature's moulds. The existence of the ocean plateaus revealed by the soundings of the "Dolphin" and the "Challenger" proves nothing as to their having been once raised above the waves; the most of the Atlantic islands are sharply cut off from them. Even granting the prehistoric migration of plants and animals between America and Europe, as we grant it between America and Asia, it does not follow that it took place across the mid-ocean, and it would still be a long step from the botanic "bridge" and elevated "ridge" to the island empire of Plato. In short, the conservative view advocated by Longinus, that the story was designed by Plato as a literary ornament and a philosophic illustration, is no less probable to-day than when it was suggested in the schools of Alexandria. Atlantis is a literary myth, belonging with *Utopia*, the *New Atlantis*, and the *Orbis alter et idem* of Bishop Hall.

Of the same type is a narrative which has come down indirectly, among the flotsam and jetsam of classic literature: it is a fragment from a lost work by Theopompus of Chios, a historian of the fourth century B. C., found in the *Varia Historia* of Aelian, a compiler of the third century A. D.[1] The story is told by the satyr Silenus to Midas, king of Phrygia, and is, as few commentators have refrained from remarking, worthy the ears of its auditor.[2] "Selenus tolde Midas of certaine Islands, named Europa, Asia, and Libia, which the Ocean Sea circumscribeth and compasseth round about. And that without this worlde there is a continent or percell of dry lande, which in greatnesse (as hee reported) was infinite and unmeasurable, that it nourished and maintained, by the benifite of the greene medowes and pas-

[1] Theopomp., *Fragmenta*, ed. Wieters, 1829, no. 76, p. 72. *Geographi Graec. minores*, ed. Mueller, i. 289. Aeliani, *Var. Hist.*, iii. 18. The extracts in the text are taken from "*A Registre of Hystories, etc., written in Greeke by Aelianus, a Roman, and delivered in English by* A.[braham] F.[leming]." London, 1576, fol. 36.

[2] We owe this quip to Tertullian (he at least is the earliest writer to whom I can trace it): "Ut Silenus penes aures Midae blattit, *aptas sane grandioribus fabulis* (*De pallio*, cap. 2).

ture plots, sundrye bigge and mighty beastes; that the men which inhabite the same climats, exceede the stature of us twise, and yet the length of there life is not equale to ours." Many other wonders he related of the two cities, Machimus, the warlike, and Euseues, the city of peace, and how the inhabitants of the former once made an attack upon Europe, and came first upon the Hyperboreans; but learning that they were esteemed the most holy of the dwellers in that island, they "had them in contempte, detesting and abhorring them as naughty people, of preposterous properties, and damnable behauiour, and for that cause interrupted their progresse, supposing it an enterprise of little worthinesse or rather none at al, to trauaile into such a countrey." The concluding passage relating to the strange country inhabited by the Meropes, from whose name later writers have called the continent Meropian, bears only indirectly upon the subject, as characterizing the whole narrative.[1]

Without admitting the harsh judgment of Aelian, who brands Theopompus as a "coyner of lyes and a forger of fond fables," it is clear that we are dealing here with literature, not with history, and that the identification of the land of the Meropes, or, as Strabo calls it, Meropis, with Atlantis or with America is arbitrary and valueless.[2]

1 "Furthermore he tolde one thing among all others, meriting admiration, that certain men called Meropes dwelt in many cittyes there about, and that in the borders adiacent to their countrey, was a perilous place named Anostus, that is to say, wythout retourne, being a gaping gulfe or bottomles pit, for the ground is as it were cleft and rent in sonder, in so much that it openeth like to the mouth of insatiable hell, y[t] it is neither perfectly lightsome, nor absolutely darksome, but that the ayer hangeth ouer it, being tempered with a certaine kinde of clowdy rednes, that a couple of floodes set their recourse that way, the one of pleasure the other of sorow, and that about each of them growe plantes answearable in quantity and bignes to a great plaine tree. The trees which spring by y[e] flood of sorow yeldeth fruite of one nature, qualitie, and operation. For if any man taste thereof, a streame of teares floweth from his eyes, as out of a conduite pipe, or sluse in a running riuer, yea, such effect followeth immediately after the eating of the same, that the whole race of their life is turned into a tragical lamentation, in so much that weeping and wayling knitteth their carkeses depriued of vitall mouing, in a winding sheete, and maketh them gobbettes for the greedy graue to swallow and deuoure. The other trees which prosper vpon the bankes of the floode of pleasure, beare fruite cleane contrary to the former, for whosoeuer tasteth thereof, he is presently weined from the pappes of his auncient appetites and inueterate desires, & if he were linked in loue to any in time past, he is fettered in the forgetfulnes of them, so that al remembrance is quite abolished, by litle and litle he recouereth the yeres of his youth, reasuming vnto him by degrees, the times & seasons, long since, spent and gone. For, the frowardnes and crookednes of old age being first shaken of, the amiablenes and louelynesse of youth beginneth to budde, in so much as they put on y[e] estate of stripplings, then become boyes, then change to children, then reenter into infancie, & at length death maketh a finall end of all."

Compare the story told by Mela (iii. 10) about the Fortunate Isles: "Una singulari duorum fontium ingenio maxime insignis: alterum qui gustavere risu solvuntur, ita adfectis remedium est ex altero bibere."

It should be noted that the country described by Theopompus is called by him simply "The Great Continent."

2 Strabo, vii. 3, § 6. Perizonius makes this passage in Aelian the peg for a long note on ancient knowledge of America, in which he brings together the most important passages bearing on the subject. He remarks: "Nullus tamen dubito, quin Veteres aliquid crediderint vel scriverent, sed quasi per nebulam et caliginem, de America, partim ex antiqua traditione ab Aegyptiis vel Carthaginiensibus accepta, partim ex ratiocinatione de forma et situ orbis terrarum, unde colligebant, superesse in hoc orbe etiam alias terras praeter Asiam, Africam, & Europam." In my opinion their assumed knowledge was based entirely on ratiocination, and was not real knowledge at all; but Perizonius well expresses the other view.

The same remark applies to the account of the great Saturnian continent that closes the curious and interesting dialogue "On the Face appearing in the Orb of the Moon," attributed to Plutarch, and printed with his *Morals:*

"'An isle, Ogygia, lies in Ocean's arms,'" says the narrator, "about five days' sail west from Britain; and before it are three others, of equal distance from one another, and also from that, bearing northwest, where the sun sets in summer. In one of these the barbarians feign that Saturn is detained in prison by Zeus." The adjacent sea is termed the Saturnian, and the continent by which the great sea is circularly environed is distant from Ogygia about five thousand stadia, but from the other islands not so far. A bay of this continent, in the latitude of the Caspian Sea, is inhabited by Greeks. These, who had been visited by Heracles, and revived by his followers, esteemed themselves inhabitants of the firm land, calling all others islanders, as dwelling in land encompassed by the sea. Every thirty years these people send forth certain of their number, who minister to the imprisoned Saturn for thirty years. One of the men thus sent forth, at the end of his service, paid a visit to the great island, as they called Europe. From him the narrator learned many things about the state of men after death, which he unfolds at length, the conclusion being that the souls of men ultimately arrive at the moon, wherein lie the Elysian Fields of Homer. "And you, O Lamprias," he adds, "may take my relation in such part as you please." After which hint there is, I think, but little doubt as to the way in which it should be taken by us.[1]

That Plato, Theopompus, and Plutarch, covering a range of nearly five centuries, should each have made use of the conception of a continent beyond the Atlantic, is noteworthy; but it is more naturally accounted for by supposing that all three had in mind the continental hypothesis of land distribution, than by assuming for them an acquaintance with the great western island, America. From this point of view, the result of our search into the geographical knowledge and mythical tales of the ancients is purely negative. We find, indeed, well-developed theories of physical geography, one of which accords remarkably well with the truth; but we also find that these theories rest solely on logical deductions from the mathematical doctrine of the sphere, and on an æsthetic satisfaction with symmetry and analogy. This conclusion could be invalidated were it shown that exploration had already revealed the secrets of the west, and we must now consider this branch of the subject.

The history of maritime discovery begins among the Phœnicians. The civilization of Egypt, as self-centred as that of China, accepted only the commerce that was brought to its gates; but the men of Sidon and Tyre, with their keen devotion to material interests, their almost modern ingenuity, had early appropriated the carrying trade of the east and the west. As they looked adventurously seaward from their narrow domain,

[1] *Mare Cronium* was the name given to a portion of the northern ocean. Forbiger, *Handbuch*, ii. 3, note 9.

the dim outline of Cyprus beckoned them down a long lane of island stations to the rich shores of Spain. Even their religion betrayed their bent: El and Cronos, their oldest deities, were wanderers, and vanished in the west; on their traces Melkarth led a motley swarm of colonists to the Atlantic. These legends, filtering through Cyprus, Crete, or Rhodes, or borne by rash adventurers from distant Gades, appeared anew in Grecian mythology, the deeds of Melkarth mingling with the labors of Hercules. We do not know when the Phœnicians first reached the Atlantic, nor what were the limits of their ocean voyages. Gades, the present Cadiz, just outside the Straits of Gibraltar, was founded a few years before 1100 B. C., but not, it is probable, without previous knowledge of the commercial importance of the location. There were numerous other settlements along the adjacent coast, and the gold, silver, and tin of these distant regions grew familiar in the markets of Egypt, Mesopotamia, and India. The trade with Tartessus, the El Dorado of antiquity, gave the Phœnician merchant vessels a name among the Jews, as well in the tenth century, when Solomon shared the adventures of Hiram, as in the sixth, when Ezekiel depicted the glories of Tyrian commerce. The Phœnician seamanship was wide-famed; their vessels were unmatched in speed,[1] and their furniture and discipline excited the outspoken admiration of Xenophon. Beside the large Tarshish ships, they possessed light merchant vessels and ships of war, provided with both sails and oars, and these, somewhat akin to steamships in their independence of wind, were well adapted for exploration. Thus urged and thus provided, it is improbable that the Phœnicians shunned the great ocean. The evidence is still strong in favor of their direct trade with Britain for tin, despite what has been urged as to tin mines in Spain and the prehistoric existence of the trade by land across Gaul.[2]

Whether the Tyrians discovered any of the Atlantic islands is unknown; the adventures and discoveries attributed to Hercules, who in this aspect is but Melkarth in Grecian raiment, points toward an early knowledge of western islands, but these myths alone are not conclusive proof. Diodorus Siculus attributes to the Phœnicians the discovery, by accident, of a large island, with navigable rivers and a delightful climate, many days' sail westward from Africa. In the compilation *De Mirabilibus Auscultationibus*, printed with the works of Aristotle, the discovery is attributed to Cartha-

[1] The average of all known rates of speed with ancient ships is about five knots an hour; some of the fastest runs were at the rate of seven knots, or a little more. Breusing, *Nautik der Alten*, Bremen, 1886, pp. 11, 12. Movers, *Die Phœnizier*, ii. 3, 190. Movers estimates the rate of a Phœnician vessel with 180 oarsmen at double that of a Greek merchantman. He compares the sailing qualities of Phœnician vessels with those of Venice in the Middle Ages to the disadvantage of the latter. As the ancients had nothing answering to our log, and their contrivances for time-keeping were neither trustworthy nor adapted for use on shipboard, these estimates are necessarily based on a few reports of the number of days spent on voyages of known length, — a rather uncertain method.

[2] Tin exists in some of the islands of the Indian Ocean, and they were worked at a later period, but there is no direct evidence, as far as I am aware, that they were known at the date when Tyre was most flourishing.

ginians. Both versions descend from one original, now lost, and it is impossible to give a date to the event, or to identify the locality.[1] Those who find America in the island of Diodorus make improbabilities supply the lack of evidence. Stories seldom lose in the telling, and while it is not impossible that a Phœnician ship might have reached America, and even made her way back, it is not likely that the voyage would have been tamely described as of many *days*' duration.

When Carthage succeeded Tyre as mistress of the Mediterranean commerce, interest in the West revived. In the middle of the fifth century B. C., two expeditions of importance were dispatched into these waters. A large fleet under Hanno sailed to colonize, or re-colonize, the western coast of Africa, and succeeded in reaching the latitude of Sierra Leone. Himilko, voyaging in the opposite direction, spent several months in exploring the ocean and tracing the western shores of Europe. He appears to have run into the Sargasso Sea, but beyond this little is known of his adventures.[2]

Ultimately the Carthaginians discovered and colonized the Canary Islands, and perhaps the Madeira and Cape Verde groups; the evidence of ethnology, the presence of Semitic inscriptions, and the occurrence in the descriptions of Pliny, Mela, and Ptolemy of some of the modern names of the separate islands, establishes this beyond a doubt for the Canaries.[3] There is no evidence that the Phœnicians or Carthaginians penetrated much beyond the coast islands, or that they reached any part of America, or even the Azores.

The achievements of the Greeks and Romans were still more limited. A certain Colaeus visited Gades towards the middle of the seventh century B. C., and was, according to Herodotus, the first Greek who passed outside of the columns of Hercules. His example could not have been widely

[1] Diodorus Siculus, v. 18, 19; *De Mirab. Auscult.*, 84. Müllenhof, *Deutsche Alterthumskunde*, i., Berlin, 1870, p. 467, traces the report through the historian Timaeus to Punic sources.

[2] The narration of Hanno's voyage has been preserved, apparently in the words of the commander's report. *Geographi Graeci minores*, ed. Mueller (Paris, 1855), i. pp. 1–14. Cf. also *Prolegom.*, pp. xviii, xxiii. Our only notion of the date of the expedition is derived from Pliny, *Hist. Nat.*, v. i. § 7, who says: "Fuere et Hannonis Carthaginiensium ducis commentarii, *Punicis rebus florentissimis* explorare ambitum Africae jussi." All that is known of Himilko is derived from the statement of Pliny, *Hist. Nat.*, ii. 67, that he was sent at about the same time as Hanno to explore the distant regions of Europe; and from the poems of Avienus, who wrote in the fourth century, and professed to give, in the *Ora Maritima*, many extracts from the writings of Himilko. The description of the difficulties of navigation in the Atlantic is best known. In his *Deutsche Alterthumskunde* (Berlin, 1870), i. pp. 73–210, Muellenhof has devoted especial attention to an analysis of this record.

[3] Pliny, *Hist. Nat.*, vi. 36, 37; Mela, iii. 100, etc.; Solinus, 23, 56 [ed. Mommsen, p. 117, 230]; Ptolemy, *Geogr.*, iv. 6; *Rapport sur une mission scientifique dans l'archipel Canarienne*, par M. le docteur Verneau; 1877. In *Archives des Missions Scientifique et Litteraires*, 3e série, tom. xiii. pp. 569, etc. The presence of Semites is indicated in Gran Canaria, Ferro, Palma, and the inscriptions agree in character with those found in Numidia by Gen. Faidherbe. In Gomera and Teneriffe, where the Guanche stock is purest, there have been no inscriptions found. Dr. Verneau believes that the Guanches are not descended from Atlantes or Americans, but from the Quaternary men of Cro-magnon on the Vézère; he found, however, traces of an unknown brachycephalic race in Gomera.

followed, for we find Pindar and his successors referring to the Pillars as the limit of navigation. In 600 B. C., Massilia was founded, and soon became a rival of Carthage in the western Mediterranean. In the fourth century we have evidence of an attempt to search out the secrets of the ocean after the manner of Hanno and Himilko. In that century, Pytheas made his famous voyage to the lands of tin and amber, discovering the still mysterious Thule; while at the same time his countryman Euthymenes sailed southward to the Senegal. With these exceptions we hear of no Grecian or Roman explorations in the Atlantic, and meet with no indication that they were aware of any other lands beyond the sea than the Fortunate Isles or the Hesperides of the early poets.[1]

About 80 B. C., Sertorius, being for a time driven from Spain by the forces of Sulla, fell in, when on an expedition to Baetica, with certain sailors who had just returned from the "Atlantic islands," which they

[1] In the second century, A. D., Pausanias (*Desc. Graec.*, i. 23) was told by Euphemus, a Carian, that once, on a voyage to Italy, he had been driven to the sea outside [*ἐς τὴν ἔξω θάλασσαν*], where people no longer sailed, and where he fell in with many desert islands, some inhabited by wild men, red-haired, and with tails, whom the sailors called Satyrs. Nothing more is known of these islands. **Ἔξω** has here been rendered simply "distant"; but even in this sense it could hardly apply in the time of Pausanias to any region but the Atlantic. It is more probable that the phrase means "outside the columns."

In the first century B. C., some men of an unknown race were cast by the sea on the German coast. There is nothing to show that these men were American Indians; but since that has been sometimes assumed, the matter should not be passed over here. The event is mentioned by Mela (*De Chorogr.*, iii. 5, § 8), and by Pliny (*Hist. Nat.*, ii. 67); the castaways were forwarded to the proconsul, Q. Caecilius Metellus Celer (B. C. 62), by the king of the tribe within whose territory they were found. Pliny calls the tribe the *Suevi;* the reading in Mela is very uncertain. Parthey has *Botorum*, the older editors *Baetorum*, or *Boiorum*. The Romans took them for inhabitants of India, who had been carried around the north of Europe; modern writers have seen in them Africans, Celts, Lapps, or Caribs. A careful study of the whole subject, with references to the literature, will be found in an article by F. Schiern: *Un énigme ethnographique de l'antiquité*, contributed to the Memoirs of the Royal Society of Northern Antiquaries, New Series, 1878–83, pp. 245–288.

In the Louvre is an antique bronze which has been thought to represent one of the Indians of Mela, and also to be a good reproduction of the features of the North American Indian (Longpérier, *Notice des bronzes antiques*, etc., *du Musée du Louvre*, Paris, 1868, p. 143), but the supposition is purely arbitrary.

Such an event as an involuntary voyage from the West Indies to the shores of Europe is not an impossibility, nor is the case cited by Mela and Pliny the only one of the kind which we find recorded. Gomara (*Hist. gen. de las Indias*, 7) says some savages were thrown upon the German coast in the reign of Frederic Barbarossa (1152–1190), and Aeneas Silvius (Pius II.) probably refers to the same event when he quotes a certain Otho as relating the capture on the coast of Germany, in the time of the German emperors, of an Indian ship and Indian traders (mercatores). The identity of Otho is uncertain. Otto of Freisingen († 1158) is probably meant, but the passage does not appear in his works that have been preserved (Aeneas Silvius, *Historia rerum*, ii. 8, first edition, Venice, 1477). The most curious story, however, is that related by Cardinal Bembo in his history of Venice (first published 1551), and quoted by Horn (*De orig. Amer.*, 14), Garcia (iv. 29), and others. It deserves, however, record here. "A French ship while cruising in the ocean not far from Britain picked up a little boat made of split oziers and covered with bark taken whole from the tree; in it were seven men of moderate height, rather dark complexion, broad and open faces, marked with a violet scar. They had a garment of fish-skin with spots of divers shades, and wore a headgear of painted straw, interwoven with seven things like ears, as it were (coronam e culmo pictam septem quasi auriculis intextam). They ate raw flesh, and drank blood as we wine. Their speech could not be understood. Six of them died; one, a youth, was brought alive to Roano (so the Italian; the Latin has Aulercos), where the king was" (Louis XII.). Bembo, *Rerum Venetarum Hist.* vii. year, 1508. [*Opere*, Venice, 1729, i. 188.]

described as two in number, distant 10,000 stadia from Africa, and enjoying a wonderful climate. The account in Plutarch is quite consistent with a previous knowledge of the islands, even on the part of Sertorius. Be this as it may, the glowing praises of the eye-witnesses so impressed him that only the unwillingness of his followers prevented his taking refuge there. Within the next few years, the Canaries, at least, became well known as the *Fortunatae Insulae;* but when Horace, in the dark days of civil war, urged his countrymen to seek a new home across the waves, it was apparently the islands of Sertorius that he had in mind, regarding them as unknown to other peoples.[1]

As we trace the increasing volume and extent of commerce from the days of Tyre and Carthage and Alexandria to its fullest development under the empire, and remember that as the drafts of luxury-loving Rome upon the products of the east, even of China and farther India, increased, the true knowledge of the form of the earth, and the underestimate of the breadth of the western ocean, became more widely known, the question inevitably suggests itself, Why did not the enterprise which had long since utilized the monsoons of the Indian Ocean for direct passage to and from India essay the passage of the Atlantic? The inquiry gains force as we recall that the possibility of such a route to India had been long ago asserted. Aristotle suggested, if he did not express it; Eratosthenes stated plainly that were it not for the extent of the Atlantic it would be possible to sail from Spain to India along the same parallel;[2] and Strabo could object nothing but the chance of there being another island-continent or two in the way, — an objection unknown to Columbus. Seneca, the philosopher, iterating insistence upon the smallness of the earth and the pettiness of its affairs compared with the higher interests of the soul, exclaims: "The earth, which you so anxiously divide by fire and sword into kingdoms, is a point, a mere point, in the universe. . . . How far is it from the utmost shores of Spain to those of India? But very few days' sail with a favoring wind." [3]

[1] Nos manet Oceanus circumvagus; arva, beata
Petamus arva, divites et insulas,
Reddit ubi Cererem tellus inarata quotannis
Et inputata floret usque vinea.
. . . .
Non huc Argoo contendit remige pinus,
Neque inpudica Colchis intulit pedem;
Non huc Sidonii torserunt cornua nautae,
Laboriosa nec cohors Ulixei.
Juppiter illa piae secrevit litora genti,
Ut inquinavit aere tempus aureum;
Aere, dehinc ferro duravit saecula, quorum
Piis secunda, vate me, datur fuga.
(Horace, *Epode*, xvi.)

Virgil, in the well-known lines in the prophecy of Anchises —

Super et Garamantes et Indos
Proferet inperium; iacet extra sidera tellus,
Extra anni solisque vias, ubi caelifer Atlas
Axem humero torquet stellis ardentibus aptum —
(*Æneid*, vi. 795.)

had Africa rather than the west in mind, according to the commentators.

It is possible that the islands described to Sertorius were Madeira and Porto Santo, but the distance was much overestimated in this case.

[2] "He [Eratosthenes] says that if the extent of the Atlantic Ocean were not an obstacle, we might easily pass by sea from Iberia to India, still keeping in the same parallel, the remaining portion of which parallel . . . occupies more than a third of the whole circle. . . . But it is quite possible that in the temperate zone there may be two or even more habitable earths [οἰκουμένας], especially near the circle of latitude which is drawn through Athens and the Atlantic ocean." (Strabo, *Geogr.*, i. 4, § 6.)

[3] Seneca, *Naturalium Quaest. Praefatio.* The

Holding these views of the possibility of the voyage, it is improbable that the size of their ships and the lack of the compass could have long prevented the ancients from putting them in practice had their interest so demanded.[1] Their interest in the matter was, however, purely speculative, since, under the unity and power of the Roman empire, which succeeded to and absorbed the commercial supremacy of the Phœnicians, international competition in trade did not exist, nor were the routes of trade subject to effective hostile interruption. The two causes, therefore, which worked powerfully to induce the voyages of Da Gama and Columbus, after the rise of individual states had given scope to national jealousy and pride, and after the fall of Constantinople had placed the last natural gateway of the eastern trade in the hands of Arab infidels, were non-existent under the older civilization. It is certain, too, that the ancients had a vivid horror of the western ocean. In the Odyssey, the western Mediterranean even is full of peril. With knowledge of the ocean, the Greeks received tales of "Gorgons and Chimeras dire," and the very poets who sing the beauties of the Elysian or Hesperian isles dwell on the danger of the surrounding sea. Beyond Gades, declared Pindar, no man, however brave, could pass; only a god might voyage those waters. The same idea recurs in the reports of travellers and the writings of men of science, but here it is the storms, or more often the lack of wind, the viscid water or vast shoals, that check and appall the mariner. Aristotle thought that beyond the columns the sea was shallow and becalmed. Plato utilized the common idea of the mud-banks and shoal water of the Atlantic in accounting for the disappearance of Atlantis. Scylax reported the ocean not navigable beyond Cerne in the south, and Pytheas heard that beyond Thule sea and air became confounded. Even Tacitus believed that there was a peculiar resistance in the waters of the northern ocean.[2]

Whether the Greeks owed this dread to the Phœnicians, and whether the latter shared the feeling, or simulated and encouraged it for the purpose of concealing their profitable adventures beyond the Straits, is doubtful. In two cases, at least, it is possible to trace statements of this nature to Punic

passage is certainly striking, but those who, like Baron Zach, base upon it the conclusion that American voyagers were common in the days of Seneca overestimate its force. It is certainly evident that Seneca, relying on his knowledge of theoretical geography, underestimated the distance to India. Had the length of the voyage to America been known, he would not have used the illustration.

[1] Smaller vessels even than were then afloat have crossed the Atlantic, and the passage from the Canaries is hardly more difficult than the Indian navigation. The Pacific islanders make voyages of days' duration by the stars alone to goals infinitely smaller than the broadside of Asia, to which the ancients would have supposed themselves addressed.

[2] Aristotle, *Meteorolog.*, ii. 1, § 14; Plato, *Timaeus*; Scylax Caryandensis, *Periplus*, 112. τῆς Κέρνης δὲ νήσου τὰ ἐπέκεινα οὐκέτι ἐστὶ πλωτὰ διὰ βραχύτητα θαλάττης καὶ πηλὸν καὶ φῦκος (*Geogr. Graec. min.*, ed. Mueller, i. 93; other references in the notes). Pytheas in Strabo, ii. 4, § 1; Tacitus, *Germania*, 45, 1; *Agricola*, x. A gloss to Suidas applies the name Atlantic to all innavigable seas. Pausanias, i. ch. 3, § 6, says it contained strange sea-beasts, and was not navigable in its more distant parts. A long list of references to similar passages is given by Ukert, *Geogr. der Griechen u. Römer*, ii. 1, p. 59. See also Berger, *Wissenschaftliche Geographie*, i. p. 27, note 3, and Grote, *Hist. of Greece*, iii. ch. 18, notes.

sources, and antiquity agreed in giving the Phœnicians credit for discouraging rivalry by every art.[1]

To an age averse to investigation for its own sake, ignorant of scientific curiosity, and unimpelled by economic pressure, tales like these might seem decisive against an attempt to sail westward to India. Rome could thoroughly appreciate the imaginative mingling of science and legend which vivified the famous prophecy of the poet Seneca:

> Venient annis saecula seris
> Quibus Oceanus vincula rerum
> Laxet, et ingens patebit tellus
> Tethysque novos deteget orbes
> Nec sit terris ultima Thule.[2]

But even were it overlooked that the prophecy suited better the revelation of an unknown continent, such as the theory of Crates and Cicero placed between Europe and Asia, than the discovery of the eastern coast of India, mariners and merchants might be pardoned if they set the deterrent opinions collected by the elder Seneca above the livelier fancies of his son.[3]

The scanty records of navigation and discovery in the western waters confirm the conclusions drawn from the visions of the poets and the theories of the philosophers. No evidence from the classic writers justifies the assumption that the ancients communicated with America. If they guessed at the possibility of such a continent, it was only as we to-day imagine an antarctic continent or an open polar sea. Evidence from ethnological com-

[1] *De Mirab. Auscult.*, 136. The Phœnicians are said to have discovered beyond Gades extensive shoals abounding in fish.

> Quae Himilco Poenus mensibus vix quatuor,
> Ut ipse semet re probasse retulit
> Enavigantem, posse transmitti adserit:
> Sic nulla late flabra propellunt ratem,
> Sic segnis humor aequoris pigri stupet.
> Adjecit et illud, plurimum inter gurgites
> Extare fucum, et saepe virgulti vice
> Retinere puppim: dicit hic nihilominus,
> Non in profundum terga dimitti maris,
> Parvoque aquarum vix supertexi solum:
> Obire semper huc et huc ponti feras,
> Navigia lenta et languide repentia
> Internatare belluas.
> (Avienus, *Ora Maritima*, 115–130.)

> Hunc usus olim dixit Oceanum vetus,
> Alterque dixit mos Atlanticum mare.
> Longo explicatur gurges hujus ambitu,
> Producitur que latere prolixe vago.
> Plerumque porro tenue tenditur salum,
> Ut vix arenas subjacentes occulat.
> Exsuperat autem gurgitem fucus frequens,
> Atque impeditur aestus hic uligine:
> Vis belluarum pelagus omne internatat,
> Multusque terror ex feris habitat freta.
> Haec olim Himilcos Poenus Oceano super
> Spectasse semet et probasse retulit:
> Haec nos, ab imis Punicorum annalibus
> Prolata longo tempore, edidimus tibi. (*Ibid.* 402–415.)

Whether Avienus had immediate knowledge of these Punic sources is quite unknown.

[2] Seneca, *Medea*, 376–380.

[3] In the first book of his *Suasoriæ*, M. Annaeus Seneca collected a number of examples illustrative of the manner in which several of the famous orators and rhetoricians of his time had handled the subject, *Deliberat Alexander, an Oceanum naviget*, which appears to have been one of a number of stock subjects for use in rhetorical training. This collection thus gives a good view of the prevalent views about the ocean, and certainly tells strongly against the idea that the western passage was then known or practised. "Fertiles in Oceano jacere terras, ultraque Oceanum rursus alia littora, alium nasci orbem, . . . *facile ista finguntur; quia Oceanus navigari non potest* . . . confusa lux alta caligine, et interceptus tenebris dies, ipsum veros grave et devium mare, et aut nulla, aut ignota sidera. Ita est, Alexander, rerum natura; *post omnia Oceanus, post Oceanum nihil*. . . . Immensum, et humanae intentatum experientiae pelagus, totius orbis vinculum, terrarumque custodia, inagitata remigio vastitas. . . . Fabianus . . . divisit enim illam [quaestionem] sic, ut primum negaret ullas in Oceano, aut trans Oceanum, esse terras habitabiles: deinde si essent, perveniri tamen ad illas non posse. Hic difficultatem ignoti maris, naturam non patientem navigationis."

parisons is of course admissible, but those who are best fitted to handle such evidence best know its dangers; hitherto its use has brought little but discredit to the cause in which it was invoked.

The geographical doctrines which antiquity bequeathed to the Middle Ages were briefly these: that the earth was a sphere with a circumference of 252,000 or 180,000 stadia; that only the temperate zones were inhabitable, and the northern alone known to be inhabited; that of the southern, owing to the impassable heats of the torrid zone, it could not be discovered whether it were inhabited, or whether, indeed, land existed there; and that

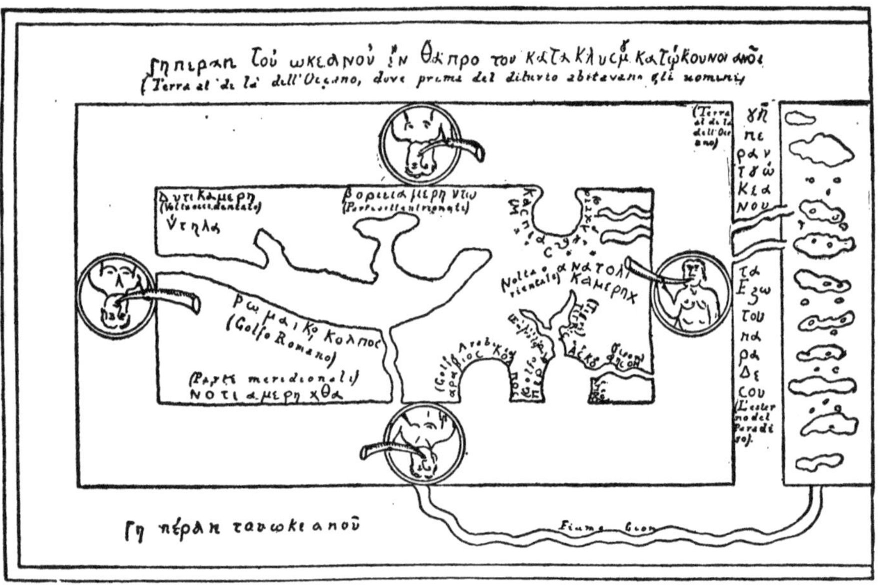

THE RECTANGULAR EARTH.*

of the northern, it was unknown whether the intervention of another continent, or only the shoals and unknown horrors of the ocean, prevented a westward passage from Europe to Asia. The legatee preserved, but did not improve his inheritance. It has been supposed that the early Middle Ages, under the influence of barbarism and Christianity, ignored the sphericity of the earth, deliberately returning to the assumption of a plane surface, either wheel-shaped or rectangular. That knowledge dwindled after the fall of the empire, that the early church included the learning as well as the religion of the pagans in its ban, is undeniable; but on this point truth prevailed. It was preserved by many school-books, in many popular

* Sketched in the *Bollettino della Società geografica italiana* (Roma, 1882), p. 540, from the original in the Biblioteca Medicea Laurenziana in Florence. The representation of this sketch of the earth by Cosmas Indicopleustes more commonly met with is from the engraving in the edition of Cosmas in Montfaucon's *Collectio nova patrum*, Paris, 1706. The article by Marinelli which contains the sketch given here has also appeared separately in a German translation (*Die Erdkunde bei den Kirchenvätern*, Leipzig, 1884). The continental land beyond the ocean should be noticed.

compilations from classic authors, and was accepted by many ecclesiastics. St. Augustine did not deny the sphericity of the earth. It was assumed by Isidor of Seville, and taught by Bede.[1] The schoolmen buttressed the doctrine by the authority of Aristotle and the living science which the Arabs built upon the Almagest. Gerbert, Albert the Great, Roger Bacon, Dante, were as familiar with the idea of the earth-globe as were Hipparchus and Ptolemy. The knowledge of it came to Columbus not as an inspiration or an invention, but by long, unbroken descent from its unknown Grecian, or pre-Grecian, discoverer.

As to the distribution of land and water, the oceanic theory of Crates, as expounded by Macrobius, prevailed in the west, although the existence of antipodes fell a victim to the union, in the ecclesiastic mind, of the heathen theory of an impassable torrid zone with the Christian teaching of the descent of all men from Adam.[2] The discoveries made by the ancients in the ocean, of the Canaries and other islands known to them, were speedily forgotten, while their geographic myths were superseded by a ranker growth. The Saturnian continent, Meropis, Atlantis, the Fortunate Isles, the Hesperides, were relegated to the dusty realm of classical learning; but the Atlantic was not barren of their like. Mediæval maps swarmed with fabulous islands, and wild stories of adventurous voyages divided the attention with tales of love and war. Antillia was the largest, and perhaps the most famous, of these islands; it was situated in longitude 330° east, and near the latitude of Lisbon, so that Toscanelli regarded it as much facilitating the plan of Columbus. Well known, too, was Braçir, or Brazil, having its proper position west and north of Ireland, but often met with elsewhere; both this island and Antillia afterward gave names to portions of the new continent.[3]

Antillia, otherwise called the Island of Seven Cities, was discovered and settled by an archbishop and six bishops of Spain, who fled into the ocean after the victory of the Moors, in 714, over Roderick; it is even reported to have been rediscovered in 1447.[4] Mayda, Danmar, Man Satanaxio, Isla Verde, and others of these islands, of which but little is known beside the names, appear for the first time upon the maps of the fourteenth and fifteenth centuries, but their origin is quite unknown. It might be thought that they were derived from confused traditions of their classical prede-

[1] Virgil, bishop of Salzburg, was accused before Pope Zacharias by St. Boniface of teaching the doctrine of antipodes; for this, and not for his belief in the sphericity of the earth (as I read), he was threatened by the Pope with expulsion from the church. The authority for this story is a letter from the Pope to Boniface. See Marinelli, *Die Erdkunde bei den Kirchenvätern*, p. 42.

[2] Cosmas, as will be seen in the cut, adhered to the continental theory, placing Paradise on the continent in the east. Paradise was more commonly placed in an island east of Asia.

[3] It has been suggested by M. Beauvois that Labrador may in the same way derive its name from *Inis Labrada*, or the Island of Labraid, which figures in an ancient Celtic romance. The conjecture has only the phonetic resemblance to recommend it. Beauvois, *L'Elysée transatlantique* (*Revue de l'Histoire des Religions*, vii. (1883), p. 291, n. 3).

[4] Gaffarel, P., *Les isles fantastiques de l'Atlantique au moyen âge*, 3.

cessors, with which they have been identified, but modern folk-lore has shown that such fancies spring up spontaneously in every community. To dream of a distant spot where joy is untroubled and rest unbroken by grief or toil is a natural and inalienable bent of the human mind. Those happy islands which abound in the romances of the heathen Celts, Mag Mell, Field of Delight, Flath Inis, Isle of the Heroes, the Avallon of the Arthur cycle, were but a more exuberant forth-putting of the same soil that produced the Elysian Fields of Homer or the terrestrial paradise of the Hebrews. The later growth is not born of the seed of the earlier, though somewhat affected by alien grafts, as in the case of the famous island of St. Brandan, where there is a curious commingling of Celtic, Greek, and Christian traditions. It is dangerous, indeed, to speak of earlier or later in reference to such myths; one group was written before the others, but it is quite possible that the earthly paradise of the Celt is as old as those of the Mediterranean peoples. The idea of a phantom or vanishing island, too, is very old, — as old, doubtless, as the fact of fog-banks and mirage, — and it is well exemplified in those mysterious visions which enticed the sailors of Bristol to many a fruitless quest before the discovery of America, and for centuries tantalized the inhabitants of the Canaries with hope of discovery. The Atlantic islands were not all isles of the blessed; there were many Isles of Demons, such as Ramusio places north of Newfoundland, a name of evil report which afterward attached itself with more reason to Sable Island and even to the Bermudas:

> "Kept, as suppos'd by Hel's infernal dogs;
> Our fleet found there most honest courteous hogs."[1]

Not until the revival of classical learning did the continental system of Ptolemy reach the west; the way, however, had been prepared for it. The measurement of a degree, executed under the Calif Mamun, seemed to the Europeans to confirm the smallest estimate of the size of the earth, which Ptolemy also had adopted,[2] while the travels of Marco Polo, revealing the great island of Japan, exaggerated the popular idea of the extent of the known world, until the 225° of Marinus seemed more probable than the 180° of Ptolemy. If, however, time brought this shrinkage in the breadth of the Atlantic, the temptation to navigators was opposed by the belief in the dangers of the ocean, which shared the persistent life of the dogma of the impassable torrid zone, and was strongly reinforced by Arab lore. Their geographers never tire of dilating on the calms and storms, mud-banks and fogs, and unknown dangers of the "Sea of Darkness." Nevertheless, as the turmoil of mediæval life made gentler spirits sigh for peace in distant homes, while the wild energy of others found the very dangers

1 Coryat's *Crudities*, London, 1611. Sig. h (4), verso.

2 The result of the Arabian measurements gave 56⅔ miles to a degree. Arabian miles were meant, and as these contain, according to Peschel (*Geschichte der Geographie*, p. 134), 4,000 ells of 540.7^{mm}., the degree equalled 122,558.6^{m}. The Europeans, however, thought that Roman miles were meant, and so got but 83,866.6^{m}. to a degree.

of the sea delightful, there was opened a double source of adventures, both real and imaginary. Those pillars cut with inscriptions forbidding further advance westward, which we owe to Moorish fancy, confounding Hercules and Atlas and Alexander, were transformed into a knightly hero pointing oceanwards, or became guide-posts to the earthly paradise.

If there be a legendary flavor in the flight of the seven bishops, we must set down the wanderings of the Magrurin[1] among the African islands, the futile but bold attempts of the Visconti to circumnavigate Africa, as real, though without the least footing in a list of claimants for the discovery of America. The voyages of St. Brandan and St. Malo, again, are distinctly fabulous, and but other forms of the ancient myth of the soul-voyages; and the same may be said of the strange tale of Maelduin.[2] But what of those other Irish voyages to Irland-it-mikla and Huitramanna-land, of the voyage of Madoc, of the explorations of the Zeni? While these tales merit close investigation, it is certain that whatever liftings of the veil there may have been — that there were any is extremely doubtful — were unheralded at the time and soon forgotten.[3]

It was reserved for the demands of commerce to reveal the secrets of the west. But when the veil was finally removed it was easy for men to see that it had never been quite opaque. The learned turned naturally to their new-found classics, and were not slow to find the passages which seemed prophetic of America. Seneca, Virgil, Horace, Aristotle, and Theopompus, were soon pressed into the service, and the story of Atlantis obtained at once a new importance. I have tried to show in this chapter that these patrons of a revived learning put upon these statements an interpretation which they will not bear.

The summing up of the whole matter cannot be better given than in the words applied by a careful Grecian historian to another question in ancient geography: "In some future time perhaps our pains may lead us to a knowledge of those countries. But all that has hitherto been written or reported of them must be considered as mere fable and invention, and not the fruit of any real search, or genuine information."[4]

CRITICAL ESSAY ON THE SOURCES OF INFORMATION.

THE views of the ancient Mediterranean peoples upon geography are preserved almost solely in the ancient classics. The poems attributed to Homer and Hesiod, the so-called Orphic hymns, the odes of Pindar, even the dramatic works of Æschylus and his successors, are sources for the earlier time. The writings of the earlier philosophers

[1] Edrisi, *Geography*, Climate, iv., § 1, Jaubert's translation, Paris, 1836, ii. 26.

[2] Found in various Celtic MSS. See Beauvois, *L'Eden occidentale* (*Rev. de l'Hist. des Relig.*), viii. (1884), 706, etc.; Joyce, *Old Celtic Romances*, 112–176.

[3] These alleged voyages are considered in the next chapter.

[4] Polybius, *Hist.*, iii. 38.

are lost, and their ideas are to be found in later writers, and in compilations like the Biographies of Diogenes Laertius (3d cent. A. D.), the *De placitis philosophorum* attributed to Plutarch, and the like. Among the works of Plato the *Phaedo* and *Timaeus* and the last book of the *Republic* bear on the form and arrangement of the earth; the *Timaeus* and *Critias* contain the fable of Atlantis. The first scientific treatises preserved are the *De Caelo* and *Meteorologica* of Aristotle.[1] It is needless to speak in detail of the geographical writers, accounts of whom will be found in any history of Greek and Roman literature. The minor pieces, such as the *Periplus* of Hanno, of Scylax of Caryanda, of Dionysius Periegetes, the Geography of Agatharcides, and others, have been several times collected;[2] and so have the minor historians, which may be consulted for Theopompus, Hecataeus, and the mythologists.[3] The geographical works of Pytheas (B. C. 350 ?), of Eratosthenes (B. C. 276–126), of Polybius (B. C. 204–122), of Hipparchus (flor. circ. B. C. 125), of Posidonius (1st cent. B. C.), are preserved only in quotations made by later writers; they have, however, been collected and edited in convenient form.[4] The most important source of our knowledge of Greek geography and Greek geographers is of course the great *Geography* of Strabo, which a happy fortune preserved to us. The long introduction upon the nature of geography and the size of the earth and the dimensions of the known world is of especial interest, both for his own views and for those he criticises.[5] Strabo lived about B. C. 60 to A. D. 24.

The works of Marinus of Tyre having perished, the next important geographical work in Greek is the world-renowned *Geography* of Ptolemaeus, who wrote in the second half of the second century A. D. Despite the peculiar merits and history of this work, it is not so important for our purpose as the work of Strabo, though it exercised infinitely more influence on the Middle Ages and on early modern geography.[6]

1 The tract *On the World* (*περὶ κόσμου, de mundo*), and the *Strange Stories* (*περὶ θαυμασίων ἀκουσμάτων, de mirabilibus auscultationibus*), printed with the works of Aristotle, are held to be spurious by critics: the former, which gives a good summary of the oceanic theory of the distribution of land and water (ch. 3), is considerably later in date; the latter is a compilation made from Aristotle and other writers. Muellenhof has sought partially to analyze it in his *Deutsche Alterthumskunde*, i. 426, etc.

2 First in *Geographica Marciani, Scylacis, Artemidoris, Dicæarchi, Isidori. Ed. a Hoeschelio* (Aug. Vind., 1600). The great collection made by Hudson, *Geographiae veteris scriptores Graeci minores* (4 vols., Oxon., 1698–1712; re-edited by Gail, Paris, 1826, 6 vols.), is still useful, notwithstanding the handy edition by C. Mueller in the Didot classics, *Geographiae Graeci minores* (Paris, 1855–61. 2 vols. and atlas).

3 *Fragmenta historicorum Graecorum. Ed. C. et T. Mueller* (Paris, Didot, 1841–68. 5 vols.).

4 *Die geographischen Fragmente des Hipparchus: H. Berger* (Leipzig, 1869); *Posidonii Rhodii reliquiae doctrinae: coll. J. Bake* (Lugd. Bat., 1810); *Eratosthenica composuit G. Bernhardy* (Berlin, 1822); *Die geographischen Fragmente des Eratosthenes: H. Berger* (Leipzig, 1880).

5 *Strabonis Geographia* (Romae, Suweynheym et Pannartz, s. a.), in 1469 or 1470, folio. First edition of the Latin translation which was made by Guarini of Verona, and Lilius Gregorius of Tiferno; only 275 copies were printed. It was reprinted in 1472 (Venice), 1473 (Rome), 1480 (Tarvisii), 1494 (Venice), 1502 (Venice), 1510 (Venice), and 1512 (Paris). *Strabo de situ orbis* (Venice. Aldus et Andr. Soc., 1516), fol., was the first Greek edition; a better edition appeared in 1549 (Basil., fol.), with Guarini's and Gregorius's translation revised by Glareanus and others. Critical ed. by J. Kramer (Berlin, 1844), 3 vols. Ed. with Latin trans. by C. Müller and F. Dübner (Paris, Didot, 1853, 1857). It has since been edited by August Meineke (Leipsic, Teubner, 1866. 3 vols. 8vo).

There was an Italian translation by Buonacciuoli, in Venice and Ferrara, 1562, 1585. 2 vols. The Γεωγραφικὰ has been several times translated into German, by Penzel (Lemgo, 1775–1777, 4 Bde. 8vo), Groskund (Berlin, Stettin, 1831–1834. 4 Thle.), and Forbiger (Stuttgart, 1856–1862. 2 Bde.), and very recently into English by H. C. Hamilton and W. Falconer (London, Bell [Bohn], 1887). 3 vols. This has a useful index.

The great French translation of Strabo, made by order of Napoleon, with very full notes by Gosselin and others, is still the most useful translation: *Géographie du Strabon trad. du grec en française* (Paris, 1805–1819). 5 vols. 4to.

6 The Geography was first printed, in a Latin translation, at Vincentia, in 1475; the date 1462 in the Bononia edition being recognized as a misprint, probably for 1482. The history of the book has been described by Lelewel in the appendix to his *Histoire de la Géographie*, and more

The astronomical writers are also of importance. Eudoxus of Cnidus, said to have first adduced the change in the altitude of stars accompanying a change of latitude as proof of the sphericity of the earth, wrote works now known only in the poems of Aratus, who flourished in the latter half of the third century B. C.[1] Geminus (circ. B. C. 50),[2] and Cleomedes,[3] whose work is famous for having preserved the method by which Eratosthenes measured the circumference of the earth, were authors of brief popular compilations of astronomical science. Of vast importance in the history of learning was the astronomical work of Ptolemy, ἡ μεγάλη σύνταξις τῆς ἀστρονομίας, which was so honored by the Arabs that it is best known to us as the *Almagest*, from *Tabric al Magisthri*, the title of the Arabic translation which was made in 827. It has been edited and translated by Halma (Paris, 1813, 1816).

Much is to be learned from the *Scholia* attached in early times to the works of Hesiod, Homer, Pindar, the *Argonautica* of Apollonius Rhodius (B. C. 276–193 ?), and to the works of Aristotle, Plato, etc. In some cases these are printed with the works commented upon; in other cases, the *Scholia* have been printed separately. The commentary of Proclus (A. D. 412–485) upon the *Timaeus* of Plato is of great importance in the Atlantis myth.[4]

Much interest attaches to the dialogue entitled *On the face appearing in the orb of the moon*, which appears among the *Moralia* of Plutarch. Really a contribution to the question of life after death, this work also throws light upon geographical and astronomical knowledge of its time.

Among the Romans we find much the same succession of sources. The poets, Virgil, Horace, Ovid, Tibullus, Lucretius, Lucan, Seneca, touch on geographical or astronomical points and reflect the opinion of their day.[5]

The first six books of the great encyclopaedia compiled by Pliny the elder (A. D. 23–79)[6] contain an account of the universe and the earth, which is of the greatest value, and was long exploited by compilers of later times, among the earliest and best of whom was Solinus.[7] Equally famous with Solinus was the author of a work of more independent character, Pomponius Mela, who lived in the first century A. D. His geography, commonly

fully in Winsor's *Bibliography of Ptolemy's Geography* (Cambridge, Mass., 1884), and in the section on Ptolemy by Wilberforce Eames in Sabin's *Dictionary*, also printed separately.

1 The *Phaenomena* of Aratus was a poem which had great vogue both in Greece and Rome. It was commented upon by Hipparchus and Achilles Tatius (both of which commentaries are preserved, and are found in the *Uranologion* of Petavius), and translated by Cicero.

2 *Gemini elementa astronomiae*, also quoted by the first word of the Greek title, *Isagoge*. First edition, Altorph, 1590. The best edition is still that in the *Uranologion* of Dionysius Petavius (Paris, 1630). It is also found in the rare translation of Ptolemy by Halma (Paris, 1828).

3 Κύκλικη θεώρια quoted as *Cleom. de sublimibus circulis*. The first edition was at Paris, 1539. 4to. It has been edited by Bake (Lugd. Bat., 1826), and Schmidt (Leips. 1832). Nothing is known of the life of Cleomedes. He wrote after the 1st cent. A. D., probably.

4 It was first printed in the Plato of Basle, 1534. There is an English translation by Thomas Taylor, *The Commentaries of Proclus on the Timaeus of Plato*, in 2 vols. (London, 1820). Proclus was also the author of astronomical works which helped to keep Grecian learning alive in the early Middle Ages.

5 The works of L. Annaeus Seneca were first printed in Naples, 1475, fol., but the *Questionum naturalium lib. vii.* were not included until the Venice ed. of 1490, which also contained the first edition of the *Suasoriae* and *Controversariae* of M. Ann. Seneca. The *Tragoediae* of L. Ann. Seneca were first printed about 1484 by A. Gallicus, probably at Ferrara.

6 *Historiae naturalis libri xxxvii.* The first edition was the famous and rare folio of Joannes de Spira, Venice, 1469. I find record of ten other editions and three issues of Landino's Italian translation before 1492.

7 *C. Julii Solini Collectanea rerum memorabilium sive polyhistor.* Solinus lived probably in the third century A. D. His book was a great favorite in the Middle Ages, both in manuscript and in print, and was known by various titles, as *Polyhistor*, *De situ orbis*, etc. The first edition appeared without place or date, at Rome, about 1473, and in the same year at Venice, and it was often reprinted with the annotations of the most famous geographers. The best edition is that by Mommsen (Berlin, 1864). See Vol. II. p. 180.

known as *De situ orbis* from the mediæval title, though the proper name is *De chorographia*, is a work of importance and merit. In the Middle Ages it had wonderful popularity.[1] Cicero, who contemplated writing a history of geography, touches upon the arrangement of the earth's surface several times in his works, as in the *Tusculan Disputations*, and notably in the sixth book of the *Republic*, in the episode known as the "Dream of Scipio." The importance of this piece is enhanced by the commentary upon it written by Macrobius in the fifth century A. D.[2] A peculiar interest attaches to the poems of Avienus, of the fourth century A. D., in that they give much information about the character attributed to the Atlantic Ocean.[3] The astronomical poems of Manilius[4] and Hyginus were favorites in early Middle Ages. The astrological character of the work of Manilius made it popular, but it conveyed also the true doctrine of the form of the earth. The curious work of Marcianus Capella gave a résumé of science in the first half of the fifth century A. D., and had a like popularity as a school-book and house-book which also helped maintain the truth.[5]

Such in the main are the ancient writers upon which we must chiefly rely in considering the present question. In the interpretation of these sources much has been done by the leading modern writers on the condition of science in ancient times; like Bunbury, Ukert, Forbiger, St. Martin, and Peschel on geography;[6] like Zeller on philosophy, not to name many others;[7] and like Lewis and Martin on astronomy;[8] but there is no occasion to go to much length in the enumeration of this class of books. The reader is referred to the examination of the literature of special points of the geographical studies of the ancients to the notes following this Essay.

Mediæval cosmology and geography await a thorough student; they are imbedded in the wastes of theological discussions of the Fathers, or hidden in manuscript cosmographies in libraries of Europe. It should be noted that confusion has arisen from the use of the word *rotundus* to express both the sphericity of the earth and the circularity of the

1 First edition, Milan, 1471. 4to. The best is that by Parthey, Berlin, 1867. A history and bibliography of this work is given in Vol. II. p. 180.

2 *Commentariorum in somnium Scipionis libri duo.* The first edition was at Venice, 1472. There has been an edition by Jahn (2 vols. Quedlinburg, 1848, 1852), and by Eyssenhardt (Leipzig, 1868), and a French translation by various hands, printed in 3 vols. at Paris, 1845–47.

3 *Descriptio orbis terrae; ora maritima.* The first edition appeared at Venice in 1488, with the *Phaenomena* of Aratus. It is included in the *Geogr. Graec. min.* of Mueller. Muellenhof has treated of the latter poem at length in his *Deutsche Alterthumskunde*, i. 73–210.

4 *Astronomicon libri v.* Manilius is an unknown personality, but wrote in the first half of the first century A. D. (First ed., Nuremberg, 1472 or 1473); Hyginus, *Poeticon Astronomicon*, 1st or 2d cent. A. D. (Ferrara, 1475).

5 *De nuptiis philologiae et Mercurii*, first ed. Vicent., 1499.

6 E. H. Bunbury, *Hist. of Anc. Geog. among the Greeks and Romans* (London, 1879), in two volumes,—a valuable, well-digested work, but scant in citations. Ukert, *Geog. der Griechen und Römer* (Weimar, 1816), very rich in citations, giving authorities for every statement, and useful as a summary.

Forbiger, *Handbuch der alten Geographie* (Hamburg, 1877), compiled on a peculiar method, which is often very sensible. He first analyzes and condenses the works of each writer, and then sums up the opinions on each country and phase of the subject.

Vivien de St. Martin, *Histoire de la Géographie* (Paris, 1873).

Peschel, *Geschichte der Erdkunde* (2d ed., by S. Ruge, München, 1877). Perhaps reference is not out of place also to P. F. J. Gosselin's *Géographie des Grecs analysée, ou les Systèmes d'Eratosthenes, de Strabon et de Ptolémée, comparés entre eux et avec nos connaissances modernes* (Paris, 1790); and his later *Recherches sur la Geographie systématique et positive des anciens* (1797–1813).

Cf. Hugo Berger, *Geschichte der wiss. Erdkunde der Griechen* (Leipzig, 1887).

7 *Geschichte der Griechischen Philosophie* (Tübingen, 1856–62).

8 Sir George Cornwall Lewis, *Historical Survey of the Astronomy of the Ancients* (London, 1862).

Theodore Henri Martin, whose numerous papers are condensed in the article on "Astronomie" in Daremberg and Saglio's *Dictionnaire de l'Antiquité.* Some of the more important distinct papers of Martin appeared in the *Mém. Acad. Inscrip. et Belles Lettres.*

known lands, and from the use of *terra*, or *orbis terrae*, to denote the inhabited lands, as well as the globe. It has been pointed out by Ruge (*Gesch. d. Zeitalters der Entdeckungen*, p. 97) that the later Middle Age adopted the circular form of the *oekoumene* in consequence of a peculiar theory as to the relation of the land and water masses of the earth, which were conceived as two intercepting spheres. The *oekoumene* might easily be spoken of as a round disk without implying that the whole earth was plane.[1] That the struggle of the Christian faith, at first for existence and then for the proper harvesting of the fruits of victory, induced its earlier defenders to wage war against the learning as well as the religion of the pagans; that Christians were inclined to think time taken from the contemplation of the true faith worse than wasted when given to investigations into natural phenomena, which might better be accepted for what they professed to be; and that they often found in Scripture a welcome support for the evidence of the senses, — cannot be denied. It was inevitable that St. Chrysostom, Lactantius, Orosius and Origines rejected or declined to teach the sphericity of the earth. The curious systems of Cosmas and Aethicus, marked by a return to the crudest conceptions of the universe, found some favor in Europe. But the truth was not forgotten. The astronomical poems of Aratus, Hyginus, and Manilius were still read. Solinus and other plunderers of Pliny were popular, and kept alive the ancient knowledge. The sphericity of the earth was not denied by St. Augustine; it was maintained by Martianus Capella, and assumed by Isidor of Seville. Bede[2] taught the whole system of ancient geography; and but little later, Virgilius, bishop of Saltzburg, was threatened with papal displeasure, not for teaching the sphericity of the earth, but for upholding the existence of antipodes.[3] The canons of Ptolemy were cited in the eleventh century by Hermann Contractus in his *De utilitatibus astrolabii*, and in the twelfth by Hugues de Saint Victor in his *Eruditio didascalica*. Strabo was not known before Pope Nicholas V., who ordered the first translation. Not many to-day can illustrate the truth more clearly than the author of *L'Image du Monde*, an anonymous poem of the thirteenth century. If two men, he says, were to start at the same time from a given point and go, the one east, the other west, —

Si que andui egaumont alassent
Il convendroit qu'il s'encontrassent
Dessus le leu dont il se mûrent.[4]

In general, the mathematical and astronomical treatises were earlier known to the West than the purely metaphysical works: this was the case in the eleventh and twelfth centuries; in the thirteenth the schoolmen were familiar with the whole body of Aristotle's works. Thus the influence of Aristotle on natural science was early important, either through Arabian commentators or paraphrasers, or through translations made from the Arabic, or directly from the Greek.[5]

Jourdain affirms that it was the influence of Aristotle and his interpreters that kept alive in the Middle Ages the doctrine that India and Spain were not far apart. He also main-

[1] See Cellarius, *Notit. orb. antiq.* i. ch. 2, *de rotunditate terrae*. See also Günther, *Aeltere und neuere Hypothese ueber die chronische Versetzung des Erdschwerpunktes durch Wassermassen* (Halle, 1878).

[2] *De Natura Rerum.*

[3] See *ante*, p. 31. In the second century St. Clement spoke of the "Ocean impassible to man, and the worlds beyond it." *1st Epist. to Corinth.* ch. 20. (*Apostolic Fathers*, Edinb. 1870, p. 22.)

[4] Legrand d'Aussy, *Image du Monde. Notices et extraits de la Bibliothèque du Roi*, etc., v. (1798), p. 260. It is also said that the earth is round, so that a man could go all round it as an insect can walk all round the circumference of a pear. This notable poem has been lately studied by Fant, but is still unprinted. It was known to Abulfeda, that if two persons made the journey described, they would on meeting differ by two days in their calendar (Peschel, *Gesch. d. Erdkunde*, p. 132).

[5] A. Jourdain, *Recherches critique sur l'âge et l'origin des traductions latines d'Aristote, et sur des commentaires Grecs et Arabes employés par les docteurs scolastiques* (Paris, 1843). See also *De l'influence d'Aristote et de ses interprètes sur la découverte du nouveau-monde, par Ch. Jourdain* (Paris, 1861).

tains that the doctrine of the sphericity of the earth was familiar throughout the Middle Age, and, if anything, more of a favorite than the other view.

The field of the later ecclesiastical and scholastic writers, who kept up the contentions over the form of the earth and kindred subjects, is too large to be here minutely surveyed. Such of them as were well known to the geographical students of the centuries next preceding Columbus have been briefly indicated in another place;[1] and if not completely, yet with helpful outlining, the whole subject of the mediæval cosmology has been studied by not a few of the geographical and cartographical students of later days.[2] So far as these studies pertain to the theory of a Lost Atlantis and the fabulous islands of the Atlantic Ocean, they will be particularly illustrated in the notes which follow this Essay.

Wm. H. Tillinghast

NOTES.

A. THE FORM OF THE EARTH.—It is not easy to demonstrate that the earliest Greeks believed the earth to be a flat disk, although that is the accepted and probably correct view of their belief. It is possible to examine but a small part of the earliest literature, and what we have is of uncertain date and dubious origin; its intent is religious or romantic, not scientific; its form is poetic. It is difficult to interpret it accurately, since the prevalent ideas of nature must be deduced from imagery, qualifying words and phrases, and seldom from direct description. The interpreter, doubtful as to the proportion in which he finds mingled fancy and honest faith, is in constant danger of overreaching himself by excess of ingenuity. In dealing with such a literature one is peculiarly liable to abuse the always dangerous argument by which want of knowledge is inferred from lack of mention. Other difficulties beset the use of later philosophic material, much of which is preserved only in extracts made by antagonists or by compilers, so that we are forced to confront a lack of

[1] See Vol. II., ch. i., Critical Essay.

[2] Cf. a bibliographical note in St. Martin's *Histoire de la Géographie* (1873), p. 296. The well-known *Examen Critique* of Humboldt, the *Recherches sur la géographie* of Walckenaer, the *Géographie du moyen-âge* of Lelewel, with a few lesser monographic papers like Fréville's "Mémoire sur la Cosmographie du moyen-âge," in the *Revue des Soc. Savantes*, 1859, vol. ii., and Gaffarel's "Les relations entre l'ancient monde et l'Amérique, étaient-elles possible au moyen-âge," in the *Bull. de la Soc. Normande de Géog.*, 1881, vol. iii. 209, will answer most purposes of the general reader; but certain special phases will best be followed in Letronne's *Des opinions cosmographiques des Pères de l'Eglise, rapprocher des doctrines philosophiques de la Grece*, in the *Revue des Deux Mondes*, Mars, 1834, p. 601, etc. The Vicomte Santarem's *Essai sur l'histoire de la cosmographie et de la cartographie pendant le moyen-âge, et sur les progrès de la géographie après les grandes découvertes du xve siècle* (Paris, 1849–52), in 3 vols., was an introduction to the great *Atlas* of mediæval maps issued by Santarem, and had for its object the vindication of the Portuguese to be considered the first explorers of the African coast. He is more interested in the burning zone doctrine than in the shape of the earth. H. Wuttke's *Ueber Erdkunde und Kultur des Mittelalters* (Leipzig, 1853) is an extract from the *Serapeum*. G. Marinelli's *Die Erdkunde bei den Kirchenvätern* (Leipzig, 1884, pp. 87) is very full on Cosmas, with drawings from the MS. not elsewhere found; Siegmund Günther's *Die Lehre von der Erdrundung u. Erdbewegung im Mittelalter bei den Occidentalen* (Halle, 1877), pp. 53, and his *Die Lehre von der Erdrundung u. Erdbewegung bei den Arabern und Hebräern* (Halle, 1877), pp. 127, give numerous bibliographical references with exactness. Specially interesting is Charles Jourdain's *De l'influence d'Aristote et de ses interprètes aux la découverte du nouveau monde* (Paris, 1861), where we read (p. 30): "La pensée dominante de Colomb était l'hypothèse de la proximité de l'Espagne et de l'Asie, et . . . cette hypothèse lui venait d'Aristote et des scolastiques;" and again (p. 24): "Ce n'est pas à Ptolémée . . . que le moyen âge a emprunté l'hypothèse d'une communication entre l'Europe et l'Asie par l'océan Atlantique. . . . Cette conséquence, qui n'avait par éschappé à Eratosthène, n'est pas énoncée par Ptolémée tandis qu'elle retrouve de la manière la plus expresse chez Aristote."

context and possible misunderstanding or misquotation. The frequent use of the word στρογγύλος, which has the same ambiguity as our word "round" in common parlance, often leads to uncertainty. A more fruitful cause of trouble is inherent in the Greek manner of thinking of the world. It is often difficult to know whether a writer means the planet, or whether he means the agglomeration of known lands which later writers called ἡ οἰκουμένη. It is not impossible that when writers refer to the earth as encircled by the river Oceanus, they mean, not the globe, but the known lands, the eastern continent, as we say, what the Romans sometimes called *orbis terrae* or *orbis terrarum*, a term which may mean the "circle of the lands," not the "orb of the earth." At a later time it was a well-known belief that the earth-globe and water-globe were excentrics, so that a segment of the former projected beyond the surface of the latter in one part, and constituted the known world.[1]

I cannot attach much importance to the line of argument with which modern writers since Voss have tried to prove that the Homeric poems represent the earth flat. That Poseidon, from the mountains of the Solymi, sees Odesseus on the sea to the west of Greece (*Od.* v. 282); that Helios could see his cattle in Thrinakia both as he went toward the heavens and as he turned toward the earth again (*Od.* xii. 380); that at sunset "all the ways are darkened;" that the sun and the stars set in and rose from the ocean, — these and similar proofs seem to me to have as little weight as attaches to the expressions "ends of the earth," or to the flowing of Oceanus around the earth. There are, however, other and better reasons for assuming that the earth in earliest thought was flat. Such is the most natural assumption from the evidence of sight, and there is certainly nothing in the older writings inconsistent with such an idea. We know, moreover, that in the time of Socrates it was yet a matter of debate as to whether the earth was flat or spherical, as it was in the time of Plutarch.[2] We are distinctly told by Aristotle that various forms were attributed to earth by early philosophers, and the implication is that the spherical theory, whose truth he proceeds to demonstrate, was a new thought.[3] It is very unlikely, except to those who sincerely accept the theory of a primitive race of unequalled wisdom, that the sphericity of the earth, having been known to Homer, should have been cast aside by the Ionic philosophers and the Epicureans, and forgotten by educated people five or six centuries later, as it must have been before the midnight voyage of Helios in his golden cup, and before similar attempts to account for the return of the sun could have become current. Ignorance of the true shape of the earth is also indicated by the common view that the sun appeared much larger at rising to the people of India than to the Grecians, and at setting presented the same phenomenon in Spain.[4] As we have seen, the description of Tartarus in the *Theogony* of Hesiod, which Fick thinks an interpolation of much later date, likens the earth to a lid.

The question has always been an open one. Crates of Mallos, Strabo, and other Homer-worshippers of antiquity, could not deny to the poet any knowledge current in their day, but their reasons for assuming that he knew the earth to be a globe are not strong. In recent years President Warren has maintained that Homer's earth was a sphere with Oceanus flowing around the equator, that the pillars of Atlas meant the axis of the earth, and that Ogygia was at the north pole.[5] Homer, however, thought that Oceanus flowed around the known lands, not that it merely grazed their southern border: it is met with in the east where the sun rises, in the west (*Od.* iv. 567), and in the north (*Od.* v. 275).

That "Homer and all the ancient poets conceived the earth to be a plane" was distinctly asserted by Geminus in the first century B. C.,[6] and has been in general steadfastly maintained by moderns like Voss,[7] Völcker,[8] Buchholtz,[9] Gladstone,[10] Martin,[11] Schaefer,[12] and Gruppe.[13] It is therefore intrinsically probable. commonly accepted, and not contradicted by what is known of the literature of the time itself.[14]

B. Homer's Geography. — There is an extensive literature on the geographic attainments of Homer, but it is for the most part rather sad reading. The later Greeks had a local identification for every place men-

1 See also *ante*, p. 37.

2 Plato, *Phaedo*, 108; Plutarch, *De facie*.

3 Aristotle, *De caelo*, ii. 13.

4 Ctesias, *On India*, ch. v. (ed. Didot, p. 80), says the rising sun appears ten times larger in India than in Greece. Strabo, *Geogr.* iii. 1, § 5, quotes Posidonius as denying a similar story of the setting sun as seen from Gades.

Whether Herodotus had a similar idea when he wrote that in India the mornings were torrid, the noons temperate and the evenings cold (Herod. iii. 104), is uncertain. Also see Dionysius Periegetes, *Periplus*, 1109–1111, in *Geographi Graeci minores. Ed. C. Mueller* (Paris, Didot, 1861), ii. 172). Rawlinson sees in it only a statement of climatic fact.

5 *The True Key to Ancient Cosmogonies*, in the *Year Book of Boston University*, 1882, and separately, Boston, 1882; and in his *Paradise Found*, 4th ed. (Boston, 1885).

6 Geminus, *Isagoge*, c. 13.

7 "Ueber die Gestalt der Erde nach den Begriffen der Alten," in *Kritische Blätter*, ii. (1790) 130.

8 *Ueber Homerische Geographie und Weltkunde* (Hanover, 1830).

9 *Homerische Realien, I. 1. Homerische Cosmographie und Geographie* (Leipzig, 1871).

10 *Homer and the Homeric Age* (London, 1858), ii. 334. The question of Aeaea, "where are the dancing places of the dawn" (*Od.* xii. 5), almost induces Gladstone to believe that Homer thought the earth cylindrical, but it may be doubted if the expression means more than an outburst of joy at returning from the darkness beyond ocean to the realm of light.

11 "Mémoire sur la cosmographie Grecque à l'époque d'Homere et d'Hesiode," in *Mém. de l'Acad. des Inscr. et des Belles Lettres*, xxviii. (1874) 1, 211–235.

12 *Entwicklung der Ansichten des Alterthums ueber Gestalt und Grösse der Erde.* Leipzig, 1868. (Gymn. z. Insterburg.)

13 *Die Kosmischen Systeme der Griechen* (Berlin, 1851).

14 See also Keppel, *Die Ansichten der alten Griechen und Römer von der Gestalt, Grösse, und Weltstellung der Erde.* (Schweinfurt, 1884.)

tioned in the *Odyssey;* but conservative scholars at present are chary of such, while agreed in confining the scene of the wanderings to the western Mediterranean. Gladstone, in *Homer and the Homeric Age*, has argued with ingenuity for the transfer of the scene from the West to the East, and has constructed on this basis one of the most extraordinary maps of "the ancient world" known. K. E. von Baer (*Wo ist der Schauplatz d. Fahrten d. Odysseus zu finden? 1875*), agreeing with Gladstone, "identifies" the Lastrygonian harbor with Balaklava, and discovers the very poplar grove of Persephone. It is a favorite scheme with others to place the wanderings outside the columns of Hercules, among the Atlantic isles,[1] and to include a circumnavigation of Africa. The better opinion seems to me that which leaves the wanderings in the western Mediterranean, which was considered to extend much farther north than it actually does. The maps which represent the voyage within the actual coast lines of the sea, and indicate the vessel passing through the Straits to the ocean, are misleading. There is not enough given in the poem to resolve the problem. The courses are vague, the distances uncertain or conventional, — often neither are given; and the matter is complicated by the introduction of a *floating* island, and the mysterious voyages from the land of the Phaeacians. It is a pleasant device adopted by Buchholtz and others to assume that where the course is not given, the wind last mentioned must be considered to still hold, and surely no one will grudge the commentators this amelioration of their lot.

C. Supposed References to America. — It is well known that Columbus's hopes were in part based on passages in classical authors.[2] Glareanus, quoting Virgil in 1527, after Columbus's discovery had made the question of the ancient knowledge prominent, has been considered the earliest to open the discussion;[3] and after this we find it a common topic in the early general writers on America, like Las Casas (*Historia General*), Ramusio (introd. vol. iii.), and Acosta (book i. ch. 11, etc.)

In the seventeenth and eighteenth centuries it was not an uncommon subject of academic and learned discussion.[4] It was a part of the survey made by many of the writers who discussed the origin of the American tribes, like Garcia,[5] Lafitau,[6] Samuel Mather,[7] Robertson,[8] not to name others.

It was not till Humboldt compassed the subject in his *Examen Critique de l'histoire de la géographie du nouveau continent* (Paris, 1836), that the field was fully scanned with a critical spirit, acceptable to the modern mind. He gives two of the five volumes which comprise the work to this part of his subject, and very little has been added by later research, while his conclusions still remain, on the whole, those of the most careful of succeeding writers. The French original is not equipped with guides to its contents, such as a student needs; but this is partly supplied by the index in the German translation.[9] The impediments which the student encounters in the *Examen Critique* are a good deal removed in a book which is on the whole the easiest guide to the sources of the subject, — Paul Gaffarel's *Etude sur les rapports de l'Amérique et de l'ancien continent avant Christophe Colomb* (Paris, 1869).[10]

The literature of the supposed old-world communication with America shows other phases of this question of ancient knowledge, and may be divided, apart from the Greek embraced in the previous survey, into those of the Egyptians, Phœnicians, Tyrians, Carthaginians, and Romans.

[1] For example, K. Jarz, "Wo sind die Homerischen Inseln Trinakie, Scherie, etc. zu suchen?" in *Zeitschr. für wissensch. Geogr.* ii. 10–18, 21.

[2] See Vol. II. p. 26. His son Ferdinand enlarges upon this. The passage in Seneca's *Medea* was a favorite. This is often considered rather as a lucky prophecy. Leibnitz, *Opera Philologica* (Geneva, 1708), vi. 317. Charles Sumner's "Prophetic Voices concerning America," in *Atlantic Monthly*, Sept. 1867 (also separately, Boston, 1874). *Hist. Mag.* xiii. 176; xv. 140.

[3] Vol. II. 25. Harrisse, *Bib. Amer. Vet.* i. 262.

[4] Perizonius, in his note to the story of Silenus and Midas, quoted from Theopompus by Ælian in his *Varia Historiæ* (Rome, 1545; in Latin, Basle, 1548; in English, 1576), quotes the chief references in ancient writers. Cf. Ælian, ed. by Perizonius, Lugd. Bat. 1701, p. 217. Among the writers of the previous century quoted by this editor are Rupertus, *Dissertationes mixtæ ad Val. Max.* (Nuremberg, 1663). Math. Berniggerus, *Ex Taciti Germaniâ et Agricolâ questiones* (Argent. 1640). Eras. Schmidt, *Dissert. de America*, which is annexed to Schmidt's ed. of Pindar (Witelsbergæ, 1616), where it is spoken of as "Discursus de insula Atlantica ultra columnas Herculis quæ America hodie dicitur." Cluverius, *Introduction in univers. geogr.*, vi. 21, § 2, supports this view, 1st ed., 1624. In the ed. 1729 is a note by Reiskius on the same side, with references (p. 667).

Of the same century is J. D. Victor's *Disputatio de America* (Jenæ, 1670).

In Brunn's *Bibliotheca Danica* are a number of titles of dissertations bearing on the subject; they are mostly old.

[5] Even the voyage of Kolaos, mentioned in Herodotus (iv. 152), is supposed by Garcia a voyage to America.

[6] *Mœurs des Sauvages* (Paris, 1724).

[7] *Attempt to show that America must have been known to the Ancients* (Boston, 1773).

[8] *History of America*, 1775.

[9] See Vol. II. p. 68. Humboldt (i. 191) adopts the view of Ortelius that the grand continent mentioned by Plutarch is America and not Atlantis. Cf. Brasseur's *Lettres à M. le Duc de Valmy*, p. 57.

[10] Gaffarel has since elaborated this part of the book in some papers, "Les Grecs et les Romains ont-ils connu l'Amérique?" in the *Revue de Géographie* (Oct. 1881, *et seq.*), ix. 241, 420; x. 21, under the heads of traditions, theories, and voyages.

There are references in Bancroft's *Native Races*, v. ch. 1; and in his *Cent. America*, vi. 70, etc.; in Short, *No. Amer. of Antiq.*, 146, 466, 474; in DeCosta's *Precolumbian Discovery*. Brasseur touches the subject in his introduction to his *Landa's Relation;* Charles Jourdain, in his *De l'influence d'Aristote et de ses interprètes sur la découverte du nouveau monde* (Paris, 1861), taken from the *Journal de l'Instruction Publique.* A recent book, W. S. Blackett's *Researches*, etc. (Lond. 1883), may be avoided.

The Egyptian theory has been mainly worked out in the present century. Paul Felix Cabrera's *Teatro critico Americano*, printed with Rio's *Palenqué* (Lond., 1822), formulates the proofs. An essay by A. Lenoir, comparing the Central American monuments with those of Egypt, is appended to Dupaix's *Antiquités Méxicaines* (1805). Delafield's *Inquiry into the Origin of the Antiquities of America* (Cincinnati, 1839), traces it to the Cushites of Egypt, and cites Garcia y Cubas, *Ensayo de an Estudio Comparativo entre las Pirámides Egipcias y Méxicanas.* Brasseur de Bourbourg discussed the question, *S'il existe des sources de l'histoire primitive du Méxique dans les monuments égyptiens de l'histoire primitive de l'ancien monde dans les monuments américains?* in his ed. of Landa's *Relations des Choses de Yucatan* (Paris, 1864). Buckle (*Hist. of Civilization*, i. ch. 2) believes the Mexican civilization to have been strictly analogous to that of India and Egypt. Tylor (*Early Hist. of Mankind*, 98) compares the Egyptian hieroglyphics with those of the Aztecs. John T. C. Heaviside, *Amer. Antiquities, or the New World the Old, and the Old World the New* (London, 1868), maintains the reverse theory of the Egyptians being migrated Americans. F. de Varnhagen works out his belief in *L'origine touranienne des américains tupis-caribes et des anciens égyptiens montrée principalement par la philologie comparée; et notice d'une émigration en Amérique effectuée à travers l'Atlantique plusieurs siècles avant notre ère* (Vienne 1876).[1]

Aristotle's mention of an island discovered by the Phœnicians was thought by Gomara and Oviedo to refer to America. The elder leading writers on the origin of the Indians, like Garcia, Horn, De Laet, and at a later day Lafitau, discuss the Phœnician theory; as does Voss in his annotations on Pomponius Mela (1658), and Count de Gebelin in his *Monde primitif* (Paris, 1781). In the present century the question has been touched by Cabrera in Rio's *Palenqué* (1822). R. A. Wilson, in his *New Conquest of Mexico*, assigns (ch. v.) the ruins of Middle America to the Phœnicians. Morlot, in the *Actes de la Société Jurassienne d'Emulation* (1863), printed his "La découverte de l'Amérique par les Phéniciens." Gaffarel sums up the evidences in a paper in the *Compte Rendu, Cong. des Amér.* (Nancy), i. 93.[2]

The Tyrian theory has been mainly sustained by a foolish book, by a foolish man, *An Original History of Anc. America* (London, 1843), by Geo. Jones, later known as the Count Johannes (cf. Bancroft's *Native Races*, v. 73).

The Carthaginian discovery rests mainly on the statements of Diodorus Siculus.[3]

Baron Zach in his *Correspondenz* undertakes to say that Roman voyages to America were common in the days of Seneca, and a good deal of wild speculation has been indulged in.[4]

D. ATLANTIS. — The story of Atlantis rests solely upon the authority of Plato, who sketched it in the *Timaeus*, and began an elaborated version in the *Critias* (if that fragment be by him), which old writers often cite as the *Atlanticus*. This is frequently forgotten by those who try to establish the truth of the story, who often write as if all statements in print were equally available as "authorities," and quote as corroborations of the tale all mentions of it made by classical writers, regardless of the fact that all are later than Plato, and can no more than Ignatius Donnelly corroborate him. In fact, the ancients knew no better than we what to make of the story, and diverse opinions prevailed then as now. Many of these opinions are collected by Proclus in the first book of his commentary on the *Timaeus*,[5] and all shades of opinion are represented from those who, like Crantor, accepted the story as simply historical, to those who regarded it as a mere fable. Still others, with Proclus himself, accepted it as a record of actual events, while accounting for its introduction in Plato by a variety of subtile metaphysical interpretations. Proclus reports that Crantor, the first commentator upon Plato (*circa* B. C. 300), asserted that the Egyptian priests said that the story was written on pillars which were still preserved,[6] and he likewise quotes from the *Ethiopic History* of Marcellus, a writer of whom

[1] Of lesser importance are these: Bancroft's *Native Races*, iv. 364, v. 55; Short, 418; Stephens's *Cent. Amer.*, ii. 438–442; M'Culloh's *Researches*, 171; Weise, *Discoveries of America*, p. 2; Campbell in *Compte Rendu, Congrès des Amér.* 1875, i. W. L. Stone asks if the mound-builders were Egyptians (*Mag. Amer. History*, ii. 533).

[2] Of less importance are: Bancroft, *Nat. Races*, v. 63–77, with references; Short, 145; Baldwin's *Anc. America*, 162, 171; Warden's *Recherches*, etc. The more general discussion of Humboldt, Brasseur (*Nat. Civ.*), Gaffarel (*Rapport*), De Costa, etc., of course helps the investigator to clues.

The subject is mixed up with some absurdity and deceit. The Dighton Rock has passed for Phœnician (Stiles' *Sermon*, 1783; Yates and Moulton's *New York*). At one time a Phœnician inscription in Brazil was invented (*Am. Geog. Soc. Bull.* 1886, p. 364; St. John V. Day's *Prehistoric Use of Iron*, Lond. 1877, p. 62). The notorious Cardiff giant, conveniently found in New York state, was presented to a credulous public as Phœnician (*Am. Antiq. Soc. Proc.*, Ap. 1875). The history of this hoax is given by W. A. McKinney in the *New Englander*, 1875, p. 759.

[3] Cf. Johr. Langius, *Medicinalium Epistolarum Miscellanea* (Basle, 1554–60), with a chapter, "De novis Americi orbis insulis, antea ab Hannone Carthaginein repertis;" Gebelin's *Monde Primitif;* Bancroft's *Native Races*, iii. 313, v. 77; Short, 145, 209.

[4] A specimen is in M. V. Moore's paper in the *Mag. of Amer. Hist.* (1884), xii. 113, 354. There are various fugitive references to Roman coins found often many feet under ground, in different parts of America. See for such, Ortelius, *Theatrum orbis terrarum*; Haywood's *Tennessee* (1820); *Hist. Mag.*, v. 314; *Mag. Amer. Hist.*, xiii. 457; Marcel de Serre, *Cosmogonie de Moise*, p. 32; and for pretended Roman inscriptions, Brasseur de Bourbourg, *Nat. Civ. Méx.*, preface; *Journal de l'Instruction Publique*, Juin, 1853; Humboldt, *Exam. Crit.*, i. 166; Gaffarel in *Rev. de Géog.*, ix. 427.

[5] *Procli commentarius in Platonis Timaeum. Rec. C. E. C. Schneider.* (*Vratislaviae*, 1847.) *The Commentaries of Proclus on the Timaeus of Plato. Translated by Thomas Taylor*, 2 vols. 4°. (London, 1820.) Proclus lived A. D. 412–485. The passages of importance are found in the translation, vol. i. pp. 64, 70, 144, 148.

[6] Taylor, i. 64.

nothing else is known, a statement that according to certain historians there were seven islands in the external sea sacred to Proserpine; and also three others of great size, one sacred to Pluto, one to Ammon, and another, the middle one, a thousand stadia in size, sacred to Neptune. The inhabitants of it preserved the remembrance, from their ancestors, of the Atlantic island which existed there, and was truly prodigiously great, which for many periods had dominion over all the islands in the Atlantic sea, and was itself sacred to Neptune.[1] Testimony like this is of little value in such a case. What comes to us at third hand is more apt to need support than give it; yet these two passages are the strongest evidence of knowledge of Atlantis outside of Plato that is preserved. We do indeed find mention of it elsewhere and earlier. Thus Strabo[2] says that Posidonius (B. C. 135–51) suggested that, as the land was known to have changed in elevation, Atlantis might not be a fiction, but that such an island-continent might actually have existed and disappeared. Pliny[3] also mentions Atlantis in treating of changes in the earth's surface, though he qualifies his quotation with "si Platoni credimus."[4] A mention of the story in a similar connection is made by Ammianus Marcellinus.[5]

In the Scholia to Plato's *Republic* it is said that at the great Panathenaea there was carried in procession a *peplum* ornamented with representations of the contest between the giants and the gods, while on the *peplum* carried in the little Panathenaea could be seen the war of the Athenians against the Atlantides. Even Humboldt accepted this as an independent testimony in favor of the antiquity of the story; but Martin has shown that, apart from the total inconsistency of the report with the expressions of Plato, who places the narration of this forgotten deed of his countrymen at the celebration of the festival of the little Panathenaea, the scholiast has only misread Proclus, who states that the *peplum* depicted the repulse of the barbarians, *i. e.* Persians, by the Greeks.[6] To these passages it is customary to add references to the Meropian continent of Theopompus,[7] the Saturnian of Plutarch, the islands of Aristotle, Diodorus and Pausanias, — which is very much as if one should refer to the *New Atlantis* of Bacon as evidence for the existence of More's *Utopia*.[8] Plutarch in his life of Solon attributes Solon's having given up the idea of an epic upon Atlantis to his advanced age rather than to want of leisure; but there is nothing to show that he had any evidence beyond Plato that Solon ever thought of such a poem, and Plato does not say that Solon began the poem, though Plutarch appears to have so understood him.[9] Thus it seems more probable that all the references to Atlantis by ancient writers are derived from the story in Plato than that they are independent and corroborative statements.

With the decline of the Platonic school at Alexandria even the name of Atlantis readily vanished from literature. It is mentioned by Tertullian,[10] and found a place in the strange system of Cosmas Indico-pleustes,[11] but throughout the Middle Ages little or nothing was known of it. That it was not quite forgotten appears from its mention in the *Image du Monde*, a poem of the thirteenth century, still in MS., where it is assigned a location in the *Mer Betée* (= coagulée).[12] Plato was printed in Latin in 1483, 1484, 1491, and in Greek in 1513, and in 1534 with the commentary of Proclus on the Timaeus.[13] The *Timaeus* was printed separately five times in the sixteenth century, and also in a French and an Italian translation.[14]

The discovery of America doubtless added to the interest with which the story was perused, and the old controversy flamed up with new ardor. It was generally assumed that the account given by Plato was not his invention. Opinions were, however, divided as to whether he had given a correct account. Of those who believed that he had erred as to the locality or as to the destruction of the island, some thought that America was the true Atlantis, while others, with whose ideas we have no concern here, placed Atlantis in Africa, Asia, or Europe, as prejudice led them. Another class of scholars, sensible of the necessity of adhering to the text of the only extant account, accepted the whole narrative, and endeavored to find in the geography of the

1 *Procl. in Tim.* (Schneider), p. 126; Taylor, i. 148. Also in *Fragmenta Historicorum Graecorum*, ed. Mueller. (Paris, 1852), vol. iv. p. 443.

2 *Geogr.* ii. § 3, § 6 (p. 103).

3 *Hist. Nat.*, ii. 92.

4 The Atlantis mentioned by Pliny in *Hist. Nat.*, vi. 36, is apparently entirely distinct from the Atlantis of Plato.

5 Amm. Marc. xvii. 7, § 13. Fiunt autem terrarum motus modis quattuor, aut enim brasmatiae sunt, . . . aut climatiae . . . aut chasmatiae, qui grandiori motu patefactis subito voratrinis terrarum partes absorbent, ut in Atlantico mare Europaeo orbe spatiosor insula, etc. (Ed. Eyssenhardt, Berlin, 1871, p. 106).

6 Martin, *Etudes sur le Timée* (1841), i. 305, 306. The passage in question is in *Schol. ad Rempubl.*, p. 327, Plato, ed. Bekker, vol. ix. p. 67.

7 Cited in Aelian's *Varia Historia*, iii. ch. 18. For the other references see above, pp. 23, 25, 26.

8 Ammianus Marcellinus (xv. 9) quotes from Timagenes (who wrote in the first century a history of Gaul, now lost) a statement that some of the Gauls had originally immigrated from very distant islands and from lands beyond the Rhine (*ab insulis extimis* confluxisse et tractibus transrhenanis) whence they were driven by wars and the incursions of the sea (Timag. in Mueller, *Frag. hist. of Graec.*, iii. 323). It would seem incredible that this should be dragged into the Atlantis controversy, but such has been the case.

9 Plutarch, *Solon*, at end. R. Prinz, *De Solonis Plutarchi fontibus* (Bonnæ, 1857).

10 *De Pallio*, 2, *Apol.*, p. 32. Also by Arnobius, *Adversus gentes*, i. 5.

11 Ed. Montfaucon, i. 114–125, ii. 131, 136–138, iv. 186–192, xii. 340.

12 Gaffarel in *Revue de Géographie*, vi.

13 *Platonis omnia opere cum comm. Proclii in Timaeum*, etc. (Basil. Valderus, 1534).

14 *Ex Platoni Timaeo particula, Ciceronis libro de universitate respondens. . . . op. Jo. Perizonii* (Paris, Tiletanus, 1540; Basil. s. a.; Paris, Morell, 1551). *Interpret. Cicerone et Chalcidio*, etc. (Paris, 1579). *Le Timée de Platon, translaté du grec en français, par L. le Roy*, etc. (Paris, 1551, 1581). *Il dialogo di Platone, intitolato il Timaeo trad. da Sb. Erizzo, nuov. mandato en luce d. Gir. Ruscellii* (Venet. 1558).

Atlantic, or as indicated by the resemblances between the flora, fauna, and civilization of America and of the old world, additional reasons for believing that such an island had once existed, and had disappeared after serving as a bridge by which communication between the continents was for a time carried on. The discussion was prolonged over centuries, and is not yet concluded. The wilder theories have been eliminated by time, and the contest may now be said to be between those who accept Plato's tale as true and those who regard it as an invention. The latter view is at present in favor with the most conservative and careful scholars, but the other will always find advocates. That Atlantis was America was maintained by Gomara, Guillaume de Postel, Horn, and others incidentally, and by Birchrod in a special treatise,[1] which had some influence even upon the geographer Cellarius. In 1669 the Sansons published a map showing America divided among the descendants of Neptune as Atlantis was divided, and even as late as 1762 Vaugondy reproduced it.[2] In his edition of Plato, Stallbaum expressed his belief that the Egyptians might have had some knowledge of America.[3] Cluverius thought the story was due to a knowledge of America.[4]

Very lately Hyde Clark has found in the Atlantis fable evidence of a knowledge of America: he does not believe in the connecting island Atlantis, but he holds that Plato misinterpreted some account of America which had reached him.[5] Except for completeness it is scarcely worth mentioning that Blackett, whose work can really be characterized by no other word than absurd, sees America in Atlantis.[6]

Here should be mentioned a work by Berlioux, which puts Euhemerus to the blush in the manner in which history with much detail is extorted from mythology.[7] He holds that Atlantis was the northwestern coast of Africa; that under Ouranos and Atlas, astronomers and kings, it was the seat of a great empire which had conquered portions of America and kept a lively commercial intercourse with that country.

Ortelius in several places speaks of the belief that America was the old Atlantis, and also attributes that belief to Mercator.[8]

That Atlantis might really have existed[9] and disappeared, leaving the Atlantic islands as remnants, was too evident to escape notice. Ortelius suggested that the island of Gades might be a fragment of Atlantis,[10] and the doctrine was early a favorite. Kircher, in his very curious work on the subterranean world, devotes considerable space to Atlantis, rejecting its connection with America, while he maintains its former existence, and holds that the Azores, Canaries, and other Atlantic islands were formerly parts thereof, and that they showed traces of volcanic fires in his day.[11]

Las Casas in his history of the Indies devoted an entire chapter to Atlantis, quoting the arguments of Proclus, in his commentary on Plato, in favor of the story, though he is himself more doubtful. He also cites confirmative passages from Philo and St. Anselm, etc. He considers the question of the Atlantic isles, and cites authorities for great and sudden changes in the earth's surface.[12]

The same view was taken by Becman,[13] and Fortia D'Urban. Turnefort included America in the list of remnants; and De la Borde followed Sanson in extending Atlantis to the farthest Pacific islands.[14] Bory de St. Vincent,[15] again, limited Atlantis to the Atlantic, and gave on a map his ideas of its contour.

D'Avezac maintains this theory in his *Iles africaines de l'Océan Atlantique*,[16] p. 5–8. Carli devoted a large part of the second volume of his *Lettere Americane* to Atlantis, controverting Baily, who placed Atlantis

[1] *Birchrodii Schediasma de orbe novo non novo* (Altdorf, 1683).

[2] The representation of Sanson is reproduced on p. 18. The full title of these curious maps is given by Martin, *Etudes sur le Timée*, i. 270, *notes*.

[3] *Plato, ed. Stallbaum* (Gothae, 1838), vii. p. 99, note E. See also his *Prolegomena de Critia*, in the same volume, for further discussion and references.

[4] Cluverius, *Introduct.*, ed. 1729, p. 667.

[5] *Examination of the legend of Atlantis in reference to proto-historic communications with America*, in the *Trans. Royal Hist. Soc.* (Lond., 1885), iii. p. 1–46.

[6] W. S. Blackett, *Researches into the lost histories of America; or, the Zodiac shown to be an old terrestrial map in which the Atlantic isle is delineated*, etc. (London, 1883), p. 31, 32. The work is not too severely judged by W. F. Poole, in the *Dial* (Chicago), Sept. 84, *note*. The author's reasons for believing that Atlantis could not have sunk are interesting in a way. The *Fourth Rept. Bur. of Ethnology* (p. 251) calls it "a curiosity of literature."

[7] E. F. Berlioux, *Les Atlantes: histoire de l'Atlantis, et de l'Atlas primitif* (Paris, 1883). It originally made part of the first *Annuaire* of the Faculté des lettres de Lyon (Paris, 1883).

[8] *Thesaurus Geogr.*, 1587, under *Atlantis*. See also under *Gades* and *Gadirus*. On folio 2 of his *Theatrum orbis terrarum* he rejects the notion that the ancients knew America, but in the index, under *Atlantis*, he says *forte America*.

[9] Bartolomé de las Casas, *Historia de las Indias. Ed. De la Fuensanto de Valle and J. S. Rayon* (Madrid, 1875), i. cap. viii. pp. 73–79.

[10] Taylor, in the introduction to the Timaeus, in his translation of Plato, regards as almost impious the doubts as to the truth of the narrative. *The Works of Plato*, vol. i. London, 1804.

[11] *Thes. Geogr.*, s. v. *Gadirus*.

[12] *Athanasii Kircherii Mundus subterraneus in xii. libros digestus* (Amsterd., 1678), pp. 80–83. He gives a cut illustrative of his views on p. 82.

[13] *Historia orbis terrarum geographica et civilis*, cap. 5, § 2, hist. insul. I. C. Becmann, 2d ed. (Francfort on Oder, 1680). Title from British Museum, as I have been unable to see the work. The *Allg. Deutsche Biographie* says the first edition appeared in 1680. It was a book of considerable note in its day.

[14] De la Borde, *Histoire abregée de la mer du Sud* (Paris, 1791).

[15] J. B. G. M. Bory de St. Vincent, *Essais sur les isles Fortunées et l'antique Atlantide* (Paris, an xi. or 1803), ch. 7. Si les Canaries et les autres isles de l'ocean Atlantique offrent les débris d'un continent. pp. 427, etc. His map is given *ante*, p. 19.

[16] This is the second part of his *Iles de l'Afrique* (Paris, 1848), belonging to the series *L'Univers. Histoire et description de tous les peuples*, etc. Cf. also his *Les iles fantastiques* (Paris, 1845).

in Spitzbergen. Carli goes at considerable length into the topographical and geological arguments in favor of its existence.[1] The early naturalists, when the doctrine of great and sudden changes in the earth's surface was in favor, were inclined to look with acquiescence on this belief. Even Lyell confessed a temptation to accept the theory of an Atlantis island in the northern Atlantic, though he could not see in the Atlantic islands trace of a mid-Atlantic bridge.[2] About the middle of this century scholars in several departments of learning, accepting the evidences of resemblances between the product of the old and new world, were induced to turn gladly to such a connection as would have been offered by Atlantis; and the results obtained at about the same time by studies in the pre-Columbian traditions and civilization of Mexico were brought forward as supporting the same theory. That the Antilles were remnants of Atlantis; that the Toltecs were descendants from the panic-stricken fugitives of the great catastrophe, whose terrors were recorded in their traditions, as well as in those of the Egyptians, was ardently urged by Brasseur de Bourbourg.[3]

In 1859 Retzius announced that he found a close resemblance between the skulls of the Guanches of the Canaries and the Guaranas of Brazil, and recalled the Atlantis story to explain it.[4] In 1846 Forbes declared his belief in the former existence of a bridge of islands in the North Atlantic, and in 1856 Heer attempted to show the necessity of a similar connection from the testimony of palæontological botany.

In 1860, Unger deliberately advocated the Atlantis hypothesis to explain the likeness between the fossil flora of Europe and the living flora of America, enumerating over fifty similar species; and Kuntze found in the case of the tropical seedless banana, occurring at once in America before 1492 and in Africa, a strong evidence of the truth of the theory.[5]

A condensed review of the scientific side of the question is given by A. Boué in his article *Ueber die Rolle der Veränderungen des unorganischen Festen im grossen Massstabe in der Natur.*[6]

The deep-sea soundings taken in the Atlantic under the auspices of the governments of the United States, England, and Germany resulted in discoveries which gave a new impetus to the Atlantis theory. It was shown that, starting from the Arctic plateau, a ridge runs down the middle of the Atlantic, broadening toward the Azores, and contracting again as it trends toward the northeast coast of South America. The depth over the ridge is less than 1,000 fathoms, while the valleys on either side average 3,000; it is known after the U. S. vessel which took the soundings as the Dolphin ridge. A similar though more uniformly narrow ridge was found by the "Challenger" expedition (1873-76), extending from somewhat north of Ascension Island directly south between South America and Africa. It is known as the Challenger ridge. There is, beside, evidence for the existence of a ridge across the tropical Atlantic, connecting the Dolphin and Challenger ridges. Madeira, the Canaries, and the Cape Verde Islands are cut off from these ridges by a deep valley, but are connected by shoals with the continent. Upon the publication of the Challenger chart (*Special Report*, vii. 1876), those who favored the theory of communication between the continents were not slow to appropriate its disclosures in their interests (*Nature*, Dec. 21, 1876, xv. 158). In March, 1877, W. Stephen Mitchell delivered a lecture at South Kensington, wherein he placed in juxtaposition the theory of Unger and the revelations of the deep-sea soundings, when he announced, however, that he did not mean to assert that these ridges had ever formed a connecting link above water between the continents.[7] Others were less cautious,[8] but in general this interpretation did not commend itself as strongly to conservative men of science as it might have done a few years before, because such men were gradually coming to doubt the fact of changes of great moment in the earth's surface, even those of great duration.

In 1869, M. Paul Gaffarel published his first treatise on Atlantis,[9] advocating the truth of the story, and in 1880 he made it the subject of deeper research, utilizing the facts which ocean exploration had placed at command.[10] This is the best work which has appeared upon this side of the question, and can only be set against

[1] G. R. Carli, *Delle Lettere Americane*, ii. (1780). Lettere, vii. and following; especially xiii. and following.

[2] Lyell, *Elements of Geology* (Lond., 1841), p. 141; and his *Principles of Geology*, 10th ed. Buffon dated the separation of the new and old world from the catastrophe of Atlantis. *Epoques de la Nat.*, ed. Flourens, ix. 570.

[3] *Quatres lettres sur la Méxique; Popul Vuh*, p. xcix, and his *Sources de l'histoire primitive du Méxique*, section viii. pp. xxiv, xxxiii, xxxviii and ix, in his edition of Diego da Landa, *Relation des choses de Yucatan* (Paris, 1864). H. H. Bancroft, *Nat. Races*, iii. 112, 264, 480; v. 127, develops Brasseur's theory. In his *Hist. Nat. Civilisées* he compares the condition of the Colhua kingdom of Xibalba with Atlantis, and finds striking similarities. Le Plongeon in his *Sacred Mysteries* (p. 92) accepts Brasseur's theory.

[4] A. Retzius, *Present state of Ethnology in relation to the form of the human skull* (Smithsonian Report, 1859), p. 266. The resemblance is not indorsed by M. Verneau, who has lately made a detailed study of the aborigines of the Canaries.

[5] F. Unger, *Die versunkene Insel Atlantis* (Wien, 1860). Translated in the *Journal of Botany* (London), January, 1865. Asa Gray had already called attention to the remarkable resemblance between the flora of Japan and that of eastern North America, but had not found the invention of a Pacific continent preferable to the hypothesis of a progress of plants of the temperate zone round by Behring's Strait (*Memoirs of the American Academy of Arts and Sciences*, vi. 377). Unger's theory has been also more or less urged in Heer's *Flora Tertiaria Helveticae* (1854-58) and his *Urwelt der Schweitz* (1865), and by Otto Ule in his *Die Erde* (1874), i. 27.

[6] *Sitzungsberichte der Math. Phys. Classe d. k. Akad. d. Wissensch.* at Vienna, lvii. (1868) p. 12.

[7] The "Lost Atlantis" and the "Challenger" soundings, *Nature*, 26 April, 1877, xv. 553, with sketch map.

[8] J. Starkie Gardner, *How were the eocenes of England deposited?* in *Popular Science Review* (London), July, 1878, xvii. 282. Edw. H. Thompson, *Atlantis not a Myth*, in *Popular Science Monthly*, Oct., 1879, xv. 759; reprinted in *Journal of Science*, Lond., Nov. 1879.

[9] *Etude sur les rapports de l'Atlantis et de l'ancien continent avant Colomb* (Paris, 1869).

[10] *Revue de Géographie*, Mars, Avril, 1880, tom. vi. et vii.

the earlier work by Martin.[1] The same theory has been supported by D. P. de Novo y Colson, who went so far as to predict the ultimate recovery of some Atlantean manuscripts from submarine grottoes of some of the Atlantic islands, — a hope which surpasses Mr. Donnelly.[2]

Winchell found the theory too useful in his scheme of ethnology to be rejected,[3] but it was reserved for Ignatius Donnelly to undertake the arrangement of the deductions of modern science and the data of old traditions into a set argument for the truth of Plato's story. His book,[4] in many ways a rather clever statement of the argument, so evidently presented only the evidence in favor of his view, and that with so little critical estimate of authorities and weight of evidence, that it attracted only uncomplimentary notice from the scientific press.[5] It was, however, the first long presentation of the case in English, and as such made an impression on many laymen. In 1882 was also published the second volume of the *Challenger Narrative*, containing a report by M. Renard on the geologic character of the mid-Atlantic island known as St. Paul's rocks. The other Atlantic islands are confessedly of volcanic origin, and this, which laymen interpreted in favor of the Atlantis theory, militated with men of science against the view that they were remnants of a sunken continent. St. Paul's, however, was, as noted by Darwin, of doubtful character, and Renard came to the conclusion that it was composed of crystalline schists, and had therefore probably been once overlaid by masses since removed.[6] This conclusion, which tended in favor of Atlantis, was controverted by A. Geikie[7] and by M. E. Wadsworth,[8] (the latter having personally inspected specimens,) on the ground that the rocks were volcanic in origin, and that, had they been schists, the inference of denudation would not follow. Dr. Guest declared that ethnologists have fully as good cause as the botanists to regard Atlantis as a fact.[9] A. J. Weise in treating of the Discoveries of America adopted the Atlantis fable unhesitatingly, and supposes that America was known to the Egyptians through that channel.[10]

That the whole story was invented by Plato as a literary ornament or allegorical argument, or that he thus utilized a story which he had really received from Egypt, but which was none the less a myth, was maintained even among the early Platonists, and was the view of Longinus. Even after the discovery of America many writers recognized the fabulous touch in it, as Acosta,[11] who thought, "being well considered, they are rediculous things, resembling rather to *Ovid's* tales then a Historie of Philosophie worthy of accompt," and "cannot be held for true but among children and old folkes" — an opinion adopted by the judicious Cellarius.[12]

1 See p. 46.

2 *Ultima teoria sobre la Atlantida.* A paper read before the Geographical Society at Lisbon. I have seen only the epitome in *Bolletino della Società Geografica Italiana*, xvi. (1879), p. 693. Apparently the paper was published in 1881, in the proceedings of the fourth congress of Americanists at Madrid.

3 Winchell, *Preadamites, or a demonstration of the existence of man before Adam*, etc. (Chicago, 1880), pp. 378 and fol.

4 Ignatius Donnelly, *Atlantis: the Antediluvian World* (N. Y., 1882).

5 His work is much more than a defence of Plato. He attempts to show that Atlantis was the terrestrial paradise, the cradle of the world's civilization. I suppose it was his book which inspired Mrs. J. Gregory Smith to write *Atla: a Story of the Lost Island* (New York, 1886).

Donnelly's book was favorably reviewed by Prof. Winchell ("Ancient Myth and Modern Fact," *Dial*, Chicago, April, 1882, ii. 284), who declared that there was no longer serious doubt that the story was founded on fact. His theory was enthusiastically adopted by Mrs. A. A. Knight in *Education* (v. 317), and somewhat more soberly by Rev. J. P. McLean in the *Universalist Quarterly* (Oct., 1882, xxxix. 436, "The Continent of Atlantis"). I have not seen an article in *Kansas Review* by Mrs. H. M. Holden, quoted in *Poole's Index* (*Kan. Rev.*, viii. 435; also, viii. 236, 640). It was more carefully examined and its claims rejected by a writer in the *Journal of Science* (London), ("Atlantis once more," June, 1883; xx. 319-327). W. F. Poole doubts whether Mr. Donnelly himself was quite serious in his theorizing ("Discoveries of America: the lost Atlantis theory," *Dial*, Sept., 1884, v. 97). Lord Arundel of Wardour controverted Donnelly in *The Secret of Plato's Atlantis* (London, 1885), and believes that the Atlantis fable originated in vague reports of Hanno's voyage — a theory hardly less remarkable than the one it aims to displace. Lord Arundel's book was reviewed in the *Dublin Review* (Plato's "Atlantis" and the "Periplus" of Hanno), July, 1886, xcix. 91.

6 Renard, M., *Report on the Petrology of St. Paul's Rocks, Challenger Report, Narrative* (London, 1882), ii. Appendix B.

7 *A search for "Atlantis" with the microscope*, in *Nature*, 9 Nov., 1882, xxvii. 25.

8 *The microscopic evidence of a lost continent*, in *Science*, 29 June, 1883, i. 591.

9 *Origines Celticae* (London, 1883), i. 119, etc.

10 *The discoveries of America to the year 1525* (New York, 1884), ch. 1. Cf. Poole's review of this jejune work, quoted above, for some healthy criticism of this kind of writing (*Dial*, v. 97). Also a notice in the *Nation*, July 31, 1884.

The scientific theory of Atlantis is, I believe, supported by M. Jean d'Estienne in the *Revue des Questiones Scientifiques*, Oct., 1885, and by M. de Marçay, *Histoire des descouvertes et conquêtes de l'Amerique* (Limoges, 1881), but I have seen neither. H. H. Howorth, *The Mammoth and the Flood* (London, 1887), is struggling to revive the credit of water as the chief agent in the transformations of the earth's surface, and relies much upon the deluge myths, but refuses to accept Atlantis. He thinks the zoölogic evidence proves the existence in pleistocene times of an easy and natural bridge between Europe and America, but sees no need of placing it across the mid-Atlantic (p. 262).

11 *The naturall and morall historie of the East and West Indies*, etc., *written in Spanish by Joseph Acosta, and translated into English by E. G[rimeston]* (London, 1604), p. 72, 73 (lib. i. ch. 22).

12 *Notitiae orbis antiquae* (Amsterdam, 1703-6), 2 vols. The first ed. was Cantab., 1703. "Atlantica insula Platonis quae similior fabulae est quam chorographiae," lib. i. cap. xi. p. 32. In the *Additamentum de novo orbe an cognatus fuerit veteribus* (tome ii. lib. iv. pp. 164-166) Cellarius speaks more guardedly, and quotes with approval the judgment of Perizonius, which has been given above (p. 22).

Among more recent writers, D'Anville, Bartoli,[1] Gosselin,[2] Ukert,[3] approved this view.

Humboldt threw the weight of his great influence in favor of the mythical interpretation, though he found the germ of the story in the older geographic myth of the destruction of Lyctonia in the Mediterranean (Orph. *Argonaut.*, 1274, etc.); [4] while Martin, in his work on the *Timaeus*, with great learning and good sense, reduced the story to its elements, concluding that such an island had never existed, the tale was not invented by Plato, but had really descended to him from Solon, who had heard it in Egypt.

Prof. Jowett regards the entire narrative as "due to the imagination of Plato, who could easily invent 'Egyptians or anything else,' and who has used the name of Solon . . . and the tradition of the Egyptian priest to give verisimilitude to his story;" [5] and Bunbury is of the same opinion, regarding the story as "a mere fiction," and "no more intended to be taken seriously . . . than the tale of Er the Pamphylian." [6] Mr. Archer-Hind, the editor of the only separate edition of the *Timaeus* which has appeared in England, thinks it impossible to determine "whether Plato has invented the story from beginning to end, or whether it really more or less represents some Egyptian legend brought home by Solon," which seems to be a fitting conclusion to the whole matter.

The literature of the subject is widely scattered, but a good deal has been done bibliographically in some works which have been reserved for special mention here. The earliest is the *Dissertation sur l'Atlantide*, by Th. Henri Martin,[7] wherein, beside a carefully reasoned examination of the story itself and similar geographic myths, the opposing views of previous writers are set forth in the second section, *Histoire des Systèmes sur l'Atlantide*, pp. 258–280. Gaffarel has in like manner given a résumé of the literature, which comes down later than that of Martin, in the two excellent treatises which he has devoted to the subject; he is convinced of the existence of such an island, but his work is marked by such care, orderliness, and fulness of citations that it is of the greatest value.[8] The references in these treatises are made with intelligence, and are, in general, accurate and useful. That this is not the case with the work of Mr. Donnelly deprives the volume of much of the value which it might have had.[9]

B. FABULOUS ISLANDS OF THE ATLANTIC IN THE MIDDLE AGES. — Fabulous islands belong quite as much to the domain of folk-lore as to that of geography. The legends about them form a part of the great mass of superstitions connected with the sea. What has been written about these island myths is for the most part scattered in innumerable collections of folk-tales and in out-of-the-way sources, and it does not lie within the scope of the present sketch to track in these directions all that has been said. It will not be out of place, however, to refer to a few recent works where much information and many references can be found. One of the fullest collections, though not over-well sorted, is by Lieut. F. S. Bassett,[10] consisting of brief notes made in the course of wide reading, well provided with references, which are, however, often so abbreviated as

[1] *Essai sur l'explication historique donnée par Platon de sa République et de son Atlantide* (in *Reflexions impartiales sur le progrès réal ou apparent que les sciences et les arts ont faits dans le xviiie siècle en Europe*, Paris, 1780). The work is useful because it contains the Greek text (from a MS. in the Bibl. du Roi. Cf. *MSS. de la bibliothèque*, v. 261), the Latin translations of Ficinus and Serranus, several French translations, and the Italian of Frizzo and of Bembo.

[2] *Recherches sur les iles de l'océan Atlantique*, in the *Recherches sur la géographie des anciens*, i. p. 146 (Paris, 1797). Also in the French translation of Strabo (i. p. 268, note 3). Gosselin thought that Atlantis was nothing more than Fortaventure or Lancerote

[3] *Geogr. d. Griechen u. Römer*, i. 1, p. 59; ii. 1, p. 192. Cf. Letronne's *Essai sur les idées cosmographiques qui se rettachent au nom d'Atlas*, in the *Bull. Univ. des sciences* (Ferussac), March, 1831.

[4] *Examen Crit.*, i. 167–180; ii. 192.

[5] *The dialogues of Plato, translated by B. Jowett* (N. Y., 1873), ii. p. 587 (Introduction to Critias).

[6] Bunbury, *History of ancient geography*, i. 402.

[7] *Etude sur le Timée de Platon* (Paris, 1841), t. i. pp. 257–333.

[8] Paul Gaffarel, *Etude sur les rapports de l'Amérique et de l'ancien continent avant Christophe Colomb* (Paris, 1869), ch. 1er; *L'Atlantide*, pp. 3–27. The same author has more lately handled the subject more fully in a series of articles: *L'Atlantide*, in the *Revue de Géographie*, April–July, 1880; vi. 241, 331, 421; vii. 21, — which is the most detailed account of the whole matter yet brought together.

[9] One of the most recent résumés of the question is that by Salone in the *Grande Encyclopédie* (Paris, 1888, iv. p. 457). The *Encyclopædia Britannica*, by the way, regards the account, "if not entirely fictitious, as belonging to the most nebulous region of history."

A few miscellaneous references, of no great significance, may close this list: *Amer. Antiquarian*, Sept., 1886; H. H. Bancroft, *Nat. Races*, v. 123; J. S. Clarke's *Progress of Maritime Discovery*, p. ii. Geo. Catlin's *Lifted and Subsided Rocks of America* (Lond., 1870) illustrates "The Cataclysm of the Antilles." Dr. Chil, in the Nancy *Congrès des Américanistes*, i. 163. Foster's *Prehistoric Races*, app. E. Haven's *Archæol. U. S.* Irving's *Columbus*, app. xxii. Major's *Prince Henry* (1868), p. 87. Nadaillac's *Les Prem. Hommes*, ii. 114, and his *L'Amérique préhistorique*, 561. John B. Newman's *Origin of the Red Men* (N. Y., 1852). Prescott's *Mexico*, iii. 356. C. S. Rafinesque's incomplete *American Nations* (Philad.), and his earlier introduction to Marshall's *Kentucky*, and his *Amer. Museum* (1832). Two articles by L. Burke in his *Ethnological Journal* (London), 1848: *The destruction of Atlantis*, July; *The continent of America known to the ancient Egyptians and other nations of remote antiquity*, Aug. The former article is only a reprint of Taylor's trans. of Plato. Roisel's *Etudes ante-historiques* (Paris, 1874), devoted largely to the religion of the Atlanteans. Léon de Rosny's "L'Atlantide historique" in the *Mém. de la Soc. d'Ethnographie* (Paris, 1875), xiii. 33, 159, or *Revue Orientale et Américaine*. Short's *No. Americans of Antiquity*, ch. 11. Daniel Wilson's *Lost Atlantis* (Montreal, 1886), in *Proc. and Trans. Roy. Soc. of Canada*, 1886, iv. Cf. also *Poole's Index*, i. 73; ii. 27; and Larousse's *Grand Dictionnaire*.

[10] *Legends and Superstitions of the Sea and of Sailors in all Lands and at all Times* (Chicago and New York, 1885).

to inflict much trouble on those who would consult them,—an all too common fault. Of interest is a chapter on *Les îles*, in a similar work by M. Paul Sebillot.[1] An island home has often been assigned to the soul after death, and many legends, some mediæval, some of great antiquity, deal with such islands, or with voyages to them. Some account of these will be found in Bassett, and particularly in an article by E. Beauvois in the *Revue de l'histoire de Religion*,[2] where further references are to be found. Wm. F. Warren has also collected many references to the literature of this subject in the course of his endeavor to show that Paradise was at the North Pole.[3] The long articles on *Eden* and *Paradise* in McClintock and Strong's *Biblical Encyclopedia* should also be consulted.

In what way the fabulous islands of the Atlantic originated is not known, nor has the subject been exhaustively investigated. The islands of classical times, in part actual discoveries, in part born of confused reports of actual discoveries, and in part probably purely mythical, were very generally forgotten as ancient civilization declined.[4] The other islands which succeeded them were in part reminiscences of the islands known to the ancients or invented by them, and in part products of a popular mythology, as old perhaps as that of the Greeks, but until now unknown to letters. The writers who have dealt with these islands have treated them generally from the purely geographic point of view. The islands are known principally from maps, beginning with the fourteenth century, and are not often met with in descriptive works. Formaleoni, in his attempt to show that the Venetians had discovered the West Indies prior to Columbus, made studies of the older maps which naturally led him to devote considerable attention to these islands.[5]

They are also considered by Zurla.[6] The first general account of them was given by Humboldt in the *Examen Critique*,[7] and to what he did little if anything has since been added. D'Avezac[8] treated the subject, giving a brief sketch of the islands known to the Arab geographers,—a curious matter which deserves more attention.

Still more recently Paul Gaffarel has treated the matter briefly, but carefully.[9] A study of old maps by H. Wuttke, in the *Jahresbericht des Vereins für Erdkunde zu Dresden*,[10] gives considerable attention to the islands; and Theobald Fischer, in his commentary on the collection of maps reproduced by Ongania, has briefly touched on the subject,[11] as has Cornelio Desimoni in various papers in the *Atti della Società Ligure di Storia patria*, xiv., and other years, in the *Atti dell' Acad. dei Nuova Lincei*, in the *Gionale ligustico*, etc. R. H. Major's *Henry the Navigator* should also be consulted.[12]

Strictly speaking, the term mythical islands ought to include, if not Frisland and Drogeo, at least the land of Bus, the island of Bimini with its fountain of life, an echo of one of the oldest of folk-tales, the island of Saxenburg, and the other non-existent islands, shoals, and rocks, with which the imagination of sailors and cartographers have connected the Atlantic even into the present century. In fact, the name is by common consent restricted to certain islands which occur constantly on old charts: the Island of St. Brandan, Antillia or Isle of the Seven Cities, Satanaxio, Danmar, Brazil, Mayda, and Isla Verte. It is interesting to note that the Arab geographers had their fabulous islands, too, though so little is known of them that it is at present impossible to say what relation they bear to those mentioned. They say that Ptolemy assigned 25,000 islands to the Atlantic, but they name and describe seventeen only, among which we may mention the Eternal Islands (Canaries? Azores?),[13] El-Ghanam (Madeira?), Island of the Two Sorcerers (Lancerote?), etc.[14]

[1] *Légendes, croyances de la mer.* 2 vols. (Paris, 1886.) See ch. 9 in 1ere série.

[2] *L'Elysée transatlantique et l'Eden Occidental* (Mai-Juin, Nov.-Dec., 1883), vii. 273; viii. 673.

[3] *Paradise Found: the Cradle of the Human Race at the North Pole* (Boston, 1885), 4th ed.

[4] Eumenius (?), in the third century A. D., is doubtful about the existence even of the Fortunate Isles (i. e. the Canaries). *Eumenii panegyricus Constantino Aug.*, vii., in Valpy's *Panegyrici veteres* (London, 1828), iii. p. 1352. Baehrens credits this oration to an unknown author. Mamertinus appears to know them from the poets only (*Ibid.* p. 1529).

[5] *Saggio sulla nautica antica dei Veneziani*, n. p., n. d. (Venice, 1783); French translation (Venice, 1788).

[6] *Il mappamondo di Fra Mauro descritto ed illustrato* (Venice, 1806). *Di Marco Polo e degli altri viaggiatori veneziani . . . con append. sopra le antiche mappe lavorate in Venezia* (Venice, 1818).

[7] ii. 156, etc.

[8] D'Avezac: *Iles d'Afrique* (Paris, 1848) 2e *partie; Iles connues des Arabes*, pp. 15; *Les îles de Saint-Brandan*, pp. 19; *Les îles nouvellement trouvées du quinzième siècle*, pp. 24. The last two pieces had been previously published under the title *Les îles fantastiques de l'Ocean occidental au moyen âge*, in the *Nouvelles Annales des Voyages* (Mars, Avril, 1845), 2d série, i. 293; ii. 47.

[9] *Les îles fantastiques de l'Atlantique au moyen âge.* Lyon [1883], pp. 15. This is apparently extracted from the *Bulletin de la Société de Géographie de Lyon* for 1883.

[In *Poole's Index* is a reference to an article on imaginary islands in *London Society*, i. 80, 150.]

[10] "Zur Geschichte der Erdkunde in der letzten Hälfte des Mittelalters. Die Karten der seefahrenden Völker Süd-Europas bis zum ersten Druck der Erdbeschreibung des Ptolemaeus." *Jahresbericht*, vi. vii. (1870). Accompanying the article are sketches of the principal mediæval maps, which are useful if access to the more trustworthy reproductions cannot be had.

[11] *Sammlung mittelalterlicher Welt- und Seekarten italienischen Ursprungs*, etc. (Venice, 1886), especially pp. 14–22, and under the notices of particular maps in the second part.

[12] *The Life of Prince Henry of Portugal, surnamed the Navigator*, etc. London, 1868.

[13] The position of these islands and the fact that the Arabs believed that they were following Ptolemy in placing in them the first meridian seems almost conclusive in favor of the Canaries; but M. D'Avezac is inclined in favor of the Azores, because the Arabs place in the Eternal Isles certain pillars and statues warning against further advance westward, which remind him of the equestrian statues of the Azores, and because Ebn Sáyd states that the Islands of Happiness lie between the Eternal Islands and Africa.

[14] D'Avezac, *Iles d'Afrique*, ii, 15. *Géographie d'Abul-Fada trad. par M. Reinaud et M. Guiyard* (Paris,

There has been some difference of opinion as to which of the Atlantic islands answer to the ancient conception of the Fortunate Islands. It is probable that the idea is at the bottom of several of these, but it may be doubted whether the island of St. Brandan is not entirely due to the christianizing of this ancient fable.

We proceed now to examine the accounts of some of these islands.

ST. BRANDAN. — St. Brandan, or Brendan, who died May 16, 577, was Abbot of Cluainfert, in Ireland, according to the legend, where he was visited by a friend, Barontus, who told him that far in the ocean lay an island which was the land promised to the saints. St. Brandan set sail for this island in company with 75 monks, and spent seven years upon the ocean, in two voyages (according to the Irish text in the MS. *book of Lismore*, which is probably the most archaic form of the legend), discovering this island and many others equally marvellous, including one which turned out to be the back of a huge fish, upon which they celebrated Easter. This story cannot be traced beyond the eleventh century, its oldest form being a Latin prose version in a MS. of that century. It is known also in French, English, and German translations, both prose and verse, and was evidently a great favorite in the Middle Ages. Intimately connected with the St. Brandan legend is that of St. Malo, or Maclovius, Bishop of Aleth, in Armorica, a disciple of St. Brandan, who accompanied his superior, and whose eulogists, jealous of the fame of the Irish saint, provided for the younger a voyage on his own account, with marvels transcending those found by Brandan. His church-day is November 17th. The story of St. Brandan is given by Humboldt and D'Avezac,[1] and by Gaffarel.[2] Further accounts will be found in the *Acta Sanctorum* of the Bollandists,[3] and in the introductions and notes to the numerous editions of the voyages, among which reference only need be made to the original Latin edited by M. Jubinal,[4] and to the English version edited by Thomas Wright for the Percy Society.[5] A Latin text of the fourteenth century is now to be found in the *Acta Sanctorum Hiberniae ex codice Salmanticensi nunc premium integre edita opera C. de Smedt et J. de Backer* (Edinb. etc., 1888), 4to, pp. 111–154. As is well known, Philoponus gives an account of the voyages of St. Brandan with a curious map, in which he places the island N. W. of Spain and N. E. of the Canaries, or *Insulae Fortunatae.*[6] The island of St. Brandan was at first apparently imagined in the north, but it afterward took a more southerly location. Honoré d'Autun identifies it with a certain island called Perdita, once discovered and then lost in the Atlantic; we have here, perhaps, some reminiscence of the name "Aprositos," which Ptolemy bestows on one of the *Fortunatae Insulae.*[7] In some of the earlier maps there is an inlet on the west coast of Ireland called *Lacus Fortunatus*, which is packed with islands which are called *Insulae Fortunatae* or *Beatae*, and sometimes given as 300 or 368 in number.[8] But the Pizigani map of 1367 puts the *Isole dicte Fortunate S. Brandany* in the place of Madeira; and Behaim's globe, in 1492, sets it down in the latitude of Cape de Verde, — a legend against it assigning the discovery to St. Brandan in 565.

It is this island which was long supposed to be seen as a mountainous land southeast of the Canaries. After the discovery of the Azores expeditions were fitted out to search for it, and were continued until 1721, which are described by Viera, and have been since retold by all writers on the subject.[9] The island was again reported as seen in 1759.

ANTILLIA, OR ISLE OF SEVEN CITIES. — The largest of these islands, the one most persistent in its form and location, is Antillia, which is depicted as a large rectangular island, extending from north to south, lying

1848–83). 2 vols. The first volume contains a treatise on Arabian geographers and their systems. *Géographie d'Edrisi trad. par M. Jaubert* (Paris, 1836–40). 2 vols. 4to (Soc. de Géogr. de Paris, *Recueil de Voyages*, v., vi.) Cf. Cherbonneau on the Arabian geographers in the *Revue de Géographie* (1881).

[1] Humboldt, *Examen Crit.*, ii. 163; D'Avezac, *Iles d'Afrique*, ii. 19; St. Malo's voyage by Beauvois, *Rev. Hist. Relig.*, viii. 986.

[2] *Les voyages de Saint Brandan et des Papoe dans l'Atlantique au moyen-âge*, published by the Soc. de Géogr. de Rochefort (1881). See also his *Rapports de l'Amérique et de l'ancien continent* (Paris, 1869), p. 173–183. The article *Brenden* in Stephen's *Dict. of National Biography*, vol. vi. (London, 1886), should be consulted.

[3] 16 May; *Maii*, tom. ii. p. 699.

[4] *La légende latine de S. Brandaines, avec une traduction inédite*, etc. (Paris, 1836). M. Jubinal gives a full account of all manuscripts.

[5] *St. Brandan, a mediæval legend of the sea, in English prose and verse* (London, 1844). The student of the subject will find use for *Les voyages de Saint Brandan à la recherche du paradis terrestre, legend en vers du XIIe siècle, avec introduction par Francisque Michel* (Paris, 1878), and "La legende Flamande de Saint Brandan et du bibliographie" by Louis de Backer in *Miscellanées bibliographiques*, 1878, p. 191.

[6] *Nova typis transacta navigatio. Novi orbis India occidentalis*, etc. (1621), p. 11.

[7] Honoré d'Autun, *Imago Mundi*, lib. i. cap. 36. In *Maxima Bibliotheca Veterum Patrum* (Lugd., 1677), tom. xx. p. 971.

[8] Humboldt (*Examen Critique*, ii. 172) quotes these islands from Sanuto Torsello (1306). They appear on a map of about 1350, preserved in St. Mark's Library at Venice (Wuttke, in *Jahresber. d. Vereins für Erdkunde zu Dresden*, xvi. 20), as "*I fortunate I beate*, 368," in connection with *La Montagne de St. Brandan*, west of Ireland. They are also in the Medicean Atlas of 1351, and in Fra Mauro's map and many others.

[9] *Noticias de la historia general de las islas de Canaria*, by D. Jos. de Viera y Clavijo, 4 vols. 4to (Madrid, 1772–83). Humboldt, *Examen*, ii. 167. D'Avezac, *Iles d'Afrique*, ii. 22, etc. *Les îles fortunées ou archipel des Canaries* [by E. Pégot-Ogier], 2 vols. (Paris, 1862), i. ch. 13. Saint-Borondon (*Aprositus*), pp. 186–198. *Teneriffe and its six satellites*, by O. M. Stone, 2 vols. (London, 1887), i. 319. This mirage probably explains the *Perdita* of Honoré and the *Aprositos* of Ptolemy. Cf. O. Peschel's *Abhandlungen zur Erd- und Völkerkunde* (Leipzig, 1877), i. 20. A similar story is connected with Brazil.

in the mid-Atlantic about lat. 35° N. This island first appears on the map of 1424, preserved at Weimar, and is found on the principal maps of the rest of the century, notably in the Bianco of 1436.[1] On some maps of the sixteenth and seventeenth centuries appears a smaller island under the name of Sette Citade, or Sete Ciudades, which is properly another name for Antillia, as Toscanelli says in his famous letter, wherein he recommended Antillia as likely to be useful as a way-station on the India voyage. We owe to Behaim the preservation on his globe of 1492 of the legend of this island. It was discovered and settled, according to him, by refugees from Spain in 714, after the defeat of King Roderick by the Moors. The settlers were accompanied by an archbishop and six bishops, each of whom built him a town. There is a story that the island was rediscovered by a Portuguese sailor in 1447.[2]

In apparent connection with *Antillia* are the smaller islands *Danmar* or *Tanmar*, *Reillo* or *Roylo*, and *Satanaxio*. The latter alone is of special interest. Formaleoni found near Antillia, on the map of Bianco of 1436, an island with a name which he read as "Yd laman Satanaxio," — a name which much perplexed him, until he found, in an old Italian romance, a legend that in a certain part of India a great hand arose every day from the sea and carried off the inhabitants into the ocean. Adapting this tale to the west, he translated the name "Island of the hand of Satan,"[3] in which interpretation Humboldt acquiesced. D'Avezac, however, was inclined to think that there were two islands, one called Delamar, a name which elsewhere appears as Danmar or Tanmar, and Satanaxio, or, as it appears on a map by Beccario at Parma, *Satanagio*,[4] and suggests that the word is a corrupt form for S. Atanaxio or S. Atanagio, *i. e.* St. Athanasius, with which Gaffarel is inclined to agree.[5]

Formaleoni saw in *Antillia* a foreknowledge of the Antilles, and Hassel believed that North and South America were respectively represented by Satanaxio and Antillia, with a strait between, just as the American continent was indeed represented after the discovery. It is certainly curious that Beccario designates the group of Antillia, Satanagio, and Danmar, as *Isle de novo reperte*, the name afterwards applied to the discoveries of Columbus; but it is not now believed that the fifteenth-century islands were aught but geographical fancies. To transfer their names to the real discoveries was of course easy and natural.[6]

BRAZIL. — Among the islands which prefigured the Azores on fourteenth-century maps appears *I. de Brazi* on the Medicean portulano of 1351, and it is apparently Terceira or San Miguel.[7] On the Pizigani map of 1367 appear three islands with this name, *Insula de Bracir* or *Bracie*, two not far from the Azores, and one off the south or southeast end of Ireland. On the Catalan map of 1375 is an *Insula de Brazil* in the southern part of the so-called Azores group, and an *Insula de Brazil* (?) applied to a group of small islands enclosed in a heavy black ring west of Ireland. The same reduplication occurs in the Solerio of 1385, in a map of 1426

[1] M. Buache in his *Mémoire sur l'Isle Antillia* (*Mém. Inst. de France*, *Sciences math. et phys.*, vi., 1806), read on a copy of the Pizigani map of 1367, sent to him from Parma, the inscription, *Ad ripas Antilliae* or *Antullio*. Cf. Buache's article in German in *Allg. Geogr. Ephemeriden*, xxiv. 129. Humboldt (*Examen*, ii. 177) quotes Zurla (*Viaggi*, ii. 324) as denying that such an inscription can be made out on the original; but Fischer (*Sammlung von Welt-karten*, p. 19) thinks this form of the name can be made out on Jomard's fac-simile. Wuttke, however, thinks that the word Antillia is not to be made out, and gives the inscription as *Hoc sont statua q fuit ut tenprs A cules*, and reads *Hoc sunt statuae quae fuerunt antea temporibus Arcules=Herculis* (Wuttke, *Zur Geschichte der Erdkunde in der letzten Haelfte des Mittelalters*, p. 26, in *Jahresbericht des Vereins für Erdkunde zu Dresden*, vi. and vii., 1870). The matter is of interest in the story of the equestrian statue of Corvo. According to the researches of Humboldt, this story first appears in print in the history of Portugal by Faria y Sousa (*Epitome de las historias Portuguezas*, Madrid, 1628. *Historia del Reynò de Portugal*, 1730), who describes on the "Mountain of the Crow," in the Azores, a statue of a man on horseback pointing westward. A later version of the story mentions a western promontory in *Corvo* which had the form of a person pointing westward. Humboldt (ii. 231), in an interesting sketch, connects this story with the Greek traditions of the columns of Hercules at Gades, and with the old opinion that beyond no one could pass; and with the curious Arabic stories of numberless columns with inscriptions prohibiting further navigation, set up by *Dhoulcarnain*, an Arabian hero, in whose personality Hercules and Alexander the Great are curiously compounded (see *Edrisi*). Humboldt quotes from Buache a statement that on the Pizigani map of 1367 there is near Brazil (Azores) a representation of a person holding an inscription and pointing westward.

[2] Fernan Colomb, *Historia*, ch. 9; Horn, *De Originibus Amer.* p. 7, quoted by Gaffarel in his *Les îles fantastiques*, p. 3, *note* 1, 2. D'Avezac, *Iles d'Afrique*, ii. 27, quotes a similar passage from Medina (*Arte naviguar*), who found it in the Ptolemy dedicated to Pope Urban (1378–1389). According to D'Avezac (*Iles*, ii. 28), a "geographical document" of 1455 gives the name as *Antillis*, and identifies it with Plato's *Atlantis*.

[3] Formaleoni, *Essai*, 148.

[4] D'Avezac marks as wrong the reading *Sarastagio* of Humboldt.

[5] D'Avezac, *Iles d'Afrique*, ii. 29; Gaffarel, *Iles fantastiques*, 12. Fischer (*Sammlung*, 20) translates *Satanaxio*, *Satanshand*, but thinks the island of *Deman*, which appears on the Catalan chart of 1375, is meant by the first half of the title. The Catalan map, fac-similed by Buchon and Foster in the *Notices et extraits des documents*, xiv. 2, has been more exactly reproduced in the *Choix des documents géographiques conservées à la Bibl. Nat.* (Paris, 1883).

[6] Peter Martyr, in 1493, states that cosmographers had determined that Hispaniola and the adjacent isles were *Antillae insulae*, meaning doubtless the group surrounding Antillia on the old maps (*Decades*, i. p. 11, ed. 1583); but the name was not popularly applied to the new islands until after Wytfliet and Ortelius had so used it (Humboldt, *Examen*, ii. 195, etc.). But Schöner, in the dedicatory letter of his globe of 1523, says that the king of Castile through Columbus has discovered *Antiglias Hispaniam Cubam quoque* (Stevens, *Schöner*, London, 1888, fac-simile of letter). In the same way the name Seven Cities was applied to the pueblos of New Mexico by their first discoverers, and Brazil passed from an island to the continent.

[7] Humboldt identified it with *Terceira*, but Fischer questions whether St. Michael does not agree better with the easterly position constantly assigned to Brazil.

preserved at Regensburg, in Bianco's map of 1436, and in that of 1448: here *de Braxil* is the easternmost of the Azores group (i. e. *y de Colombi, de Zorzi,* etc.), while the large round island — more like a large ink-blot than anything else — west of Ireland is *y de Brazil d. binar.*[1] In a map in St. Mark's Library, Venice, dated about 1450, Brazil appears in four places. Fra Mauro puts it west of Ireland,[2] and it so appears in Ptolemy of 1519, and Ramusio in 1556; but Mercator and Ortelius inscribe it northwest of the Azores.

Humboldt has shown[3] that brazil-wood, being imported into Europe from the East Indies long before the discovery of America, gave its name to the country in the west where it was found in abundance, and he infers that the designation of the Atlantic island was derived from the same source. The duplication of the name, however, seems to point to a confusion of different traditions, and in the Brazil off Ireland we doubtless have an attempt to establish the mythical island of *Hy Brazil*, or *O'Brasile*, which plays a part as a vanishing island in Irish legends, although it cannot be traced to its origin. In the epic literature of Ireland relating to events of the sixth and subsequent centuries, and which was probably written down in the twelfth, there are various stories of ocean voyages, some involuntary, some voluntary, and several, like the voyage of the sons of Ua Corra about 540, of St. Brandan about 560, and of Mailduin in the eighth century, taking place in the Atlantic, and resulting in the discovery of numerous fabulous islands.[4] The name of Brazil does not appear in these early records, but it seems to belong to the same class of legends.[5] It is first mentioned, as far as I know, by William Betoner, called William of Worcester, who calls the island *Brasyle* and *Brasylle*, and says that July 15, 1480, his brother-in-law, John Jay, began a voyage from Bristol in search of the island, returning Sept. 18 without having found it.[6] This evidently belongs to the series of voyages made by Bristol men in search of this island, which is mentioned by Pedro d'Ayala, the Spanish ambassador to England, in his famous letter of July 25, 1498, where he says that such voyages in search of *Brazylle* and the *seven cities* had been made for seven years past, "according to the fancies of the Genoese," meaning Sebastian Cabot.[7]

It would seem that the search for Brazil was of older date than Cabot's arrival. He probably gave an additional impetus to the custom, adding to the stories of the fairy isles the legends of the *Sette Citade* or *Antillia*. Hardiman,[8] quoting from a MS. history of Ireland, in the library of the Royal Irish Academy, written about 1636, mentions an "iland, which lyeth far att sea, on the west of Connaught, and some times is perceived by the inhabitants of the *Oules* and *Iris* . . . and from Saint Helen Head. Like wise several seamen have discovered it, . . . one of whom, named Captain Rich, who lives about Dublin, of late years had a view of the land, and was so neere that he discovered a harbour . . . but could never make to land" because of "a mist which fell upon him. . . . Allsoe in many old mappes . . . you still find it by the name of *O'Brasile* under the longitude of 03°, 00', and the latitude of 50° 20'."[9] In 1675 a pretended account of a visit to this island was published in London, which is reprinted by Hardiman.[10]

An account of the island as seen from Arran given in O'Flaherty's *Sketch of the Island of Arran*,[11] is quoted by H. Halliday Sterling, *Irish Minstrelsy*, p. 307 (London, 1887). Mr. Marshall, in a note in *Notes and*

[1] The Bianco map of 1436 has, on the ocean sheets, five groups of small islands, from south to north: (1) Canaries; (2) Madeira and Porto Santo; (3) *luto* and *chapisa*; (4) *d. brasil, di colonbi, d. b. ntusta, d. sanzorzi*; (5) *coriios* and *corbo marinos*; (6) *de ventura*; (7) *de brazil.* West of the third and fourth lies *Antillia*, and N. W. of the fifth a corner of *de laman satanaxio*, while west of six and seven are numerous small islands unnamed. On the ocean sheet of the Bianco of 1448, we have (2) Madeira and Porto Santo; (3) *licongi* and *coruo marin*; (4) *de braxil, zorzi,* etc.; (5) *coriim* and *coruos marinos*; (6) *y. d. mam debentum*; (7) *y. d. brazil d. binar.* There is no Antillia and no Satanaxio, but west of (3) and (4) are two other groups: (1) *yd. diuechi marini, y de falconi*; (2) *y fortunat de s°. beati. blandan, dinferno, de ipauion, beta ixola, dexerta.* There is not much to be hoped from such geography.

[2] Over against Africa he has an *Isola dei Dragoni.* On the Pizigani map of 1367 the Brazil which lies W. of North France is accompanied by a cut of two ships, a dragon eating a man, and a legend stating that one cannot sail further on account of monsters. There was a dragon in the Hesperian isles, and some have connected it with the famous dragon-tree of the Canaries.

[3] *Examen*, ii. 216, etc.

[4] For an account of the Irish MSS. see Eugene O'Curry, *Lectures on the MS. material of ancient Irish history* (Dublin, 1861), lect. ix. p. 181; H. d'Arbois de Jubainville, *Introduction a l'étude de la littérature Celtique*, 2 vols. (Paris, 1883), i. chap. 8, p. 349, etc.; also *Essa d'un catalogue de la littérature épique d'Irlande*, by the same author (Paris, 1883). For accounts of the voyages see O'Curry, p. 252, and especially p. 289, where a sketch of that of the sons of *Ua Corra* is given. A list of the voyages is given by D'Arbois de Jubainville in his *Essai*, under *Longeas* (involuntary voyages) and *Immrain* (voluntary voyages), with details about MSS. and references to texts and translations (*Mailduin*, p. 151; *Ua Corra*, 152). See also Beauvois, *Eden occidental, Rev. de l'Hist. des Relig.*, viii. 706, 717, for voyages of *Mailduin* and the sons of *Ua Corra*, and of other voyages. Also Joyce, *Old Celtic romances* (London, 1879). Is M. Beauvois in earnest when he suggests that the talking birds discovered by Mailduin (and also by St. Brandan) were probably parrots, and their island a part of South America?

[5] The name is derived by Celtic scholars from *breas*, large, and *i*, island.

[6] *Gulielmi de Worcester Itineraria*, ed. J. Nasmyth (Cantab., 1778), p. 223, 267. I take the quotation from *Notes and Queries*, Dec. 15, 1883, 6th series, viii. 475. The latter passage is quoted in full in *Bristol, past and present*, by Nicholls and Taylor (London, 1882), iii. 292. Cf. H. Harrisse's *C. Colomb.*, i. 317.

[7] *Cal. State Papers, Spanish*, i. p. 177.

[8] *Irish Minstrelsy, or bardic remains of Ireland*, etc., 2 vols. (London, 1831), i. 368.

[9] This is very nearly its position in the *Arcano del Mare* of Dudley, 1646 (Europe 28), where it is called "disabitata e incerta."

[10] i. 369. *O-Brazile, or the enchanted island, being a perfect relation of the late discovery and wonderful disenchantment of an island on the North* [*sic*] *of Ireland*, etc. (London, 1675).

[11] John T. O'Flaherty, *Sketch of the History and antiquities of the southern islands of Aran*, etc. (Dublin, 1884, in *Roy. Irish Acad. Trans.*, vol. xiv.)

Queries, Sept. 22, 1883 (6th s., viii. 224), quotes Guest, *Origines Celticae* (London, 1883), i. 126, and R. O'Flaherty, *Ogygia, sive rerum Hibernicarum chronologiae* (London, 1685; also in English translation, Dublin, 1793), as speaking of O'Brazile. The latter work I have not seen. Mr. Marshall also quotes a familiar allusion to it by Jeremy Taylor (*Dissuasive from Popery*, 1667). This note was replied to in the same periodical, Dec. 15, 1883, by Mr. Kerslake, "N." and W. Fraser. Fraser's interest had been attracted by the entry of the island — much smaller than usual — on a map of the French Geographer Royal, Le Sieur Tassin, 1634–1652, and he read a paper before the Geological Society of Ireland, Jan. 20, 1870, suggesting that Brazil might be the present *Porcupine Bank*, once above water. On the same map *Rockall* is laid down as two islands, where but a solitary rock is now known.[1] Brasil appears on the maps of the last two centuries, with *Mayda* and *Isle Verte*, and even on the great Atlas by Jefferys, 1776, is inserted, although called "imaginary island of O'Brasil." It grows constantly smaller, but within the second half of this century has appeared on the royal Admiralty charts as *Brazil Rock*.[2]

It would be too tedious to enumerate the numerous other imaginary islands of the Atlantic to which clouds, fogs, and white caps have from time to time given rise. They are marked on all charts of the last century in profusion; mention, however, may be made of the "land of *Bus*" or *Busse*, which Frobisher's expedition coasted along in 1576, and which has been hunted for with the lead even as late as 1821, though in vain.

F. Toscanelli's Atlantic Ocean. — It has been shown elsewhere (Vol. II. pp. 30, 31, 38, 90, 101, 103) that Columbus in the main accepted the view of the width of the Atlantic, on the farther side of which Asia was supposed to be, which Toscanelli had calculated; and it has not been quite certain what actual measurement should be given to this width, but recent discoveries tend to make easier a judgment in the matter.

When Humboldt wrote the *Examen Critique*, Toscanelli's letter to Columbus, of unknown date,[3] enclosing a copy of the one he sent to Martinez in 1474, was known only in the Italian form in Ulloa's translation of the *Historie del S. D. Fernando Colombo* (Venice, 1571), and in the Spanish translation of Ulloa's version by Barcia in the *Historiades primitivos de las Indias occidentales* (Madrid, 1749), i. 5 bis, which was reprinted by Navarrete, *Coleccion de los viages y descubrimientos*, etc., ii. p. 1. In the letter to Martinez, in this form, it is said that there are in the map which accompanied it twenty-six *spaces* between Lisbon and *Quisai*, each space containing 250 miles according to the Ulloa version, but according to the re-translation of Barcia 150 miles. This, with several other changes made by Barcia, were followed by Navarrete and accepted as correct by Humboldt, who severely censures Ximenes for adopting the Italian rendering in his *Gnomone fiorent.* But the Latin copy of the letter in Columbus's handwriting, discovered by Harrisse and made public (with fac-simile) in his *D. Fernando Colon* (Seville, 1871),[4] sustained the correctness of Ulloa's version, giving 250 miliaria to the space. This authoritative rendering also showed that while the translator had in general followed the text, he had twice inserted a translation of miles into degrees, and once certainly, incorrectly, making in one place 100 miles = 35 leagues, and in another, 2,500 miles = 225 leagues. Probably this discrepancy led to the omissions made by Barcia; he was wrong, however, in changing the number 250, supposing the 150 not to be a typographical error, and in omitting the phrase, "which space (from Lisbon to Quinsai) is about the third part of the sphere." The Latin text showed, too, that this whole passage about distances was not in the Martinez letter at all, but formed the end of the letter to Columbus, since in the Latin it follows the date of the Martinez letter, into which it has been interpolated by a later hand. Finally the publication of Las Casas's *Historia de las Indias* (Madrid, 1875) gave us another Spanish version, which differs from Barcia's in closely agreeing with the Ulloa version, and which gives the length of a space at 250 miles.

There were then $26 \times 250 = 6500$ miles between Lisbon and Quinsai, and this was about one third of the circumference of the earth in this latitude, but it is not clear whether Roman or Italian miles were meant.

If the MS. in the Biblioteca Nazionale at Florence [*Cod. Magliabechiano Classe* xi. *num.* 121], described by G. Uzielli in the *Bollettino della Società Geografica Italiana*, x. 1 (1873), 13–28 ("Ricerche intorno a Paolo dal Pozzo Toscanelli, ii. Della grandezza della terra secondo Paolo Toscanelli"), actually represents the work of Toscanelli, it is of great value in settling this point. The MS. is inscribed "Discorso di M° Paolo Puteo Toscanelli sopra la cometa del 1456." In it were found two papers: 1. A plain projection in rectangular form apparently for use in sketching a map. It is divided into spaces, each subdivided into five degrees, and numbers 36 spaces in length. It is believed by Sig. Uzielli that this is the form used in the map sent to Martinez. If this be so, the 26 spaces between Lisbon and Quinsai = 130°. 2. A list of the latitude and longitude of various localities, at the end of which is inscribed this table:

Gradus continet .68 miliaria minus 3ª unius.
Miliarum tria millia bracchia.
Bracchium duos palmas.
Palmus. 12. uncias. 7. filos.

The Florentine mile of 3,000 braccia da terra contains, according to Sig. Uzielli, 1653.6m. (as against

[1] *On Hy Brasil, a traditional island off the west coast of Ireland, plotted in a MS. map written by Le Sieur Tassin*, etc., in the *Journal of the Royal Geological Society of Ireland* (1879–80), vol. xv. pt. 3, pp. 128–131, *fac-simile of map.*

[2] In an atlas issued 1866, I observe *Mayda* and *Green Rock.*

[3] Harrisse would put it in 1482. See Vol. II. p. 90.

[4] Also in his *Bib. Amer. Vet.*, p. xvi.

1481m. to the Roman mile). Hence Toscanelli estimated a degree of the meridian at 111,927m, or only 552m. more than the mean adopted by Bessel and Bayer. Since, according to the letter, one space = 250 miles, and by the map one space = 5°, we have 50 miles to a degree, which would point to an estimate for a latitude of about 42°, allowing 67 2-3 miles to an equatorial degree. Lisbon was entered in the table of Alphonso at 41° N. (true lat. 38° 41′ N.) By this reckoning Quinsai would fall 124° west of Lisbon or 10° west of San Francisco. It does not appear that the Florence MS. can be traced directly to Toscanelli, but the probability is certainly strong that we have here some of the astronomer's working papers, and that Ximenes did not deserve the rebuke administered by Humboldt for allowing 250 miles to a space, and assuming that a space contained five degrees. Certainly Humboldt's use of 150 miles is unjustifiable, and his calculation of 52° as the angular distance between Lisbon and Quinsai, according to Toscanelli, is very much too small, whatever standard we take for the mile. If we follow Uzielli, the result obtained by Ruge (*Geschichte des Zeitalters der Entdeckungen*, p. 230), 104°, is also too small.[1]

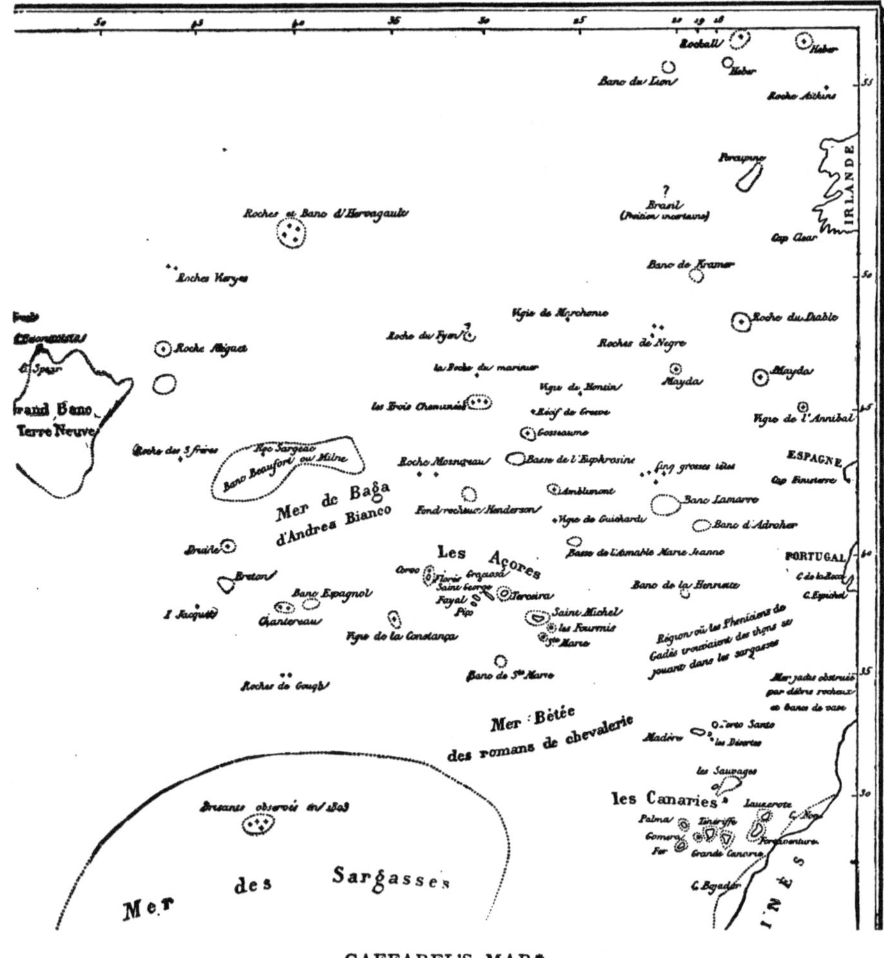

GAFFAREL'S MAP.*

[1] The various versions of the letter are as follows: *Ulloa* (*Historie*, 1571, ch. 8). Dalla città di Lisbona per dritto verso ponente sono in detta carta ventisei spazi, ciascun de' quali contien dugento, & cinquanta miglia, fino alla . . . città di Quisai, la quale gira cento miglia, che sono trentacinque leghe. . . . Questo spazio e quasi la terza parte della sfera. . . . E dalla' Isola di Antilia, che voi chiamate di sette città, . . . fino alla . . . isola di Cipango sono dieci

* From a map by Gaffarel, "L'Océan Atlantique et les restes de l'Atlantide," in the *Revue de Géographie*, vi. p. 400, accompanying a paper by Gaffarel in the numbers for April-July, 1880, and showing such rocks and islets as have from time to time been reported as seen, or thought to have been seen, and which Gaffarel views as vestiges of the lost continent.

G. Early Maps of the Atlantic Ocean. — *By the Editor.* — The cartographical history of the Atlantic Ocean is, even down to our own day, an odd mixture of uncertain fact and positive fable. The island of Bresil or Brazil was only left off the British Admiralty charts within twenty years (see Vol. II. p. 36), and editions of the most popular atlases, like Colton's, within twenty-five years have shown Jacquet Island, the Three Chimneys, Maida, and others lying in the mid-sea. It may possibly be a fair question if some of the reports of islands and rocks made within recent times may not have had a foundation in temporary uprisings from the bed of the sea.[1] We must in this country depend for the study of this subject on the great collections of fac-similes of early maps made by Santarem, Kunstmann, Jomard, and on the *Sammlung* which is now in progress at Venice, under the editing of Theobald Fischer, and published by Ongania.[2]

We may place the beginning of the Atlantic cartography[3] in the map of Marino Sanuto in 1306, who was first of the nautical map-makers of that century to lay down the Canaries;[4] but Sanuto was by no means sure of their existence, if we may judge from his omission of them in his later maps.[5]

FIFTEENTH CENTURY.*

spazi, che fanno due mila & cinquecento miglia, cioè dugento, & venticinque leghe.

Barcia. Hallareis en un mapa, que ai desde Lisboa, à la famosa ciudad de Quisay, tomando el camino derecho à Poniente, 26 espacios, cada uno de 150 millas. Quisai' tiene 35 leguas de ambitu. . . . De la isla Antilla hasta la de Cipango se quentan diez espacios, que hacen 225 leguas.

Las Casas: Y de la ciudad de Lisboa, en derecho por el Poniente, son en la dicha carta 26 espacios, y en cada uno dellos hay 250 millas hasta la . . . ciudad de Quisay, la cual etiene al cerco 100 millas, que son 25 leguas, . . . (este espacio es cuasi la tercera parte de la sfera) . . . é de la isla de Antil, . . . Hasta la . . . isla de Cipango hay 10 espacios que son 2,500 millas, es á sabre, 225 leguas.

Columbus's copy: A civitate vlixiponis per occidentem indirecto sunt .26. spacia in carta signata quorum quodlibet habet miliaria .250. usque ad nobilisim[am], et maxima ciuitatem quinsay. Circuit enim centum miliaria . . . hoc spatium est fere tercia pars tocius spere. . . . Sed ab insula antilia vobis nota ad insulam . . . Cippangu sunt decem spacia.

[1] Cf. "Les îles Atlantique," by Jacobs-Beeckmans in the *Bull. de la Soc. géog. d'Anvers*, i. 266, with map.

[2] Of these collections, those of Kunstmann and Jomard are not uncommon in the larger American libraries. A set of the Santarem series is very difficult to secure complete, but since the description of these collections in Vol. II. was written, a set has been secured for Harvard College library, and I am not aware of another set being in this country. The same library has the Ongania series. The maps in this last, some of which are useful in the present study, are the following: —

1. Arabic marine map, xiiith cent. (Milan); 2. Visconte, 1311 (Florence); 3. Carignano, xivth cent. (Florence); 4. Visconte, 1318 (Venice); 5. Anonymous, 1351 (Florence); 6. Pizigani, 1373 (Milan); 7. Anon., xivth cent. (Venice); 8. Giroldi, 1426 (Venice); 9. Bianco, 143, (Venice); 10. Anon., 1447 (Venice); 11. Bianco, 1448 (Milan); 12. Not issued; 13. Anon., Catalan, xvth cent. (Florence); 14. Leardo, 1452; 15. Fra Mauro, 1457 (Venice); 16. Cantino, 1501–3 (Modena). This has not been issued in this series, but Harrisse published a fac-simile in colors in connection with his *Les Corte-Real*, etc., Paris, 1883. 17. Agnese, 1554 (Venice). The names on these photographs are often illegible; how far the condition of the original is exactly reproduced in this respect it is of course impossible to say without comparison.

[3] The notions prevailing so far back as the first century are seen in the map of Pomponius Mela in Vol. II. p. 180.

[4] Vol. II. p. 36.

[5] Lelewel (ii. 119) gives a long account of Sanuto and his maps, and so does Kunstmann in the *Mémoires* (vii. ch. 2,

* A conventional map of the older period, which is given in Santarem's *Atlas* as a "Mappemonde qui se trouve au revers d'une Médaille du Commencement du XVe Siècle."

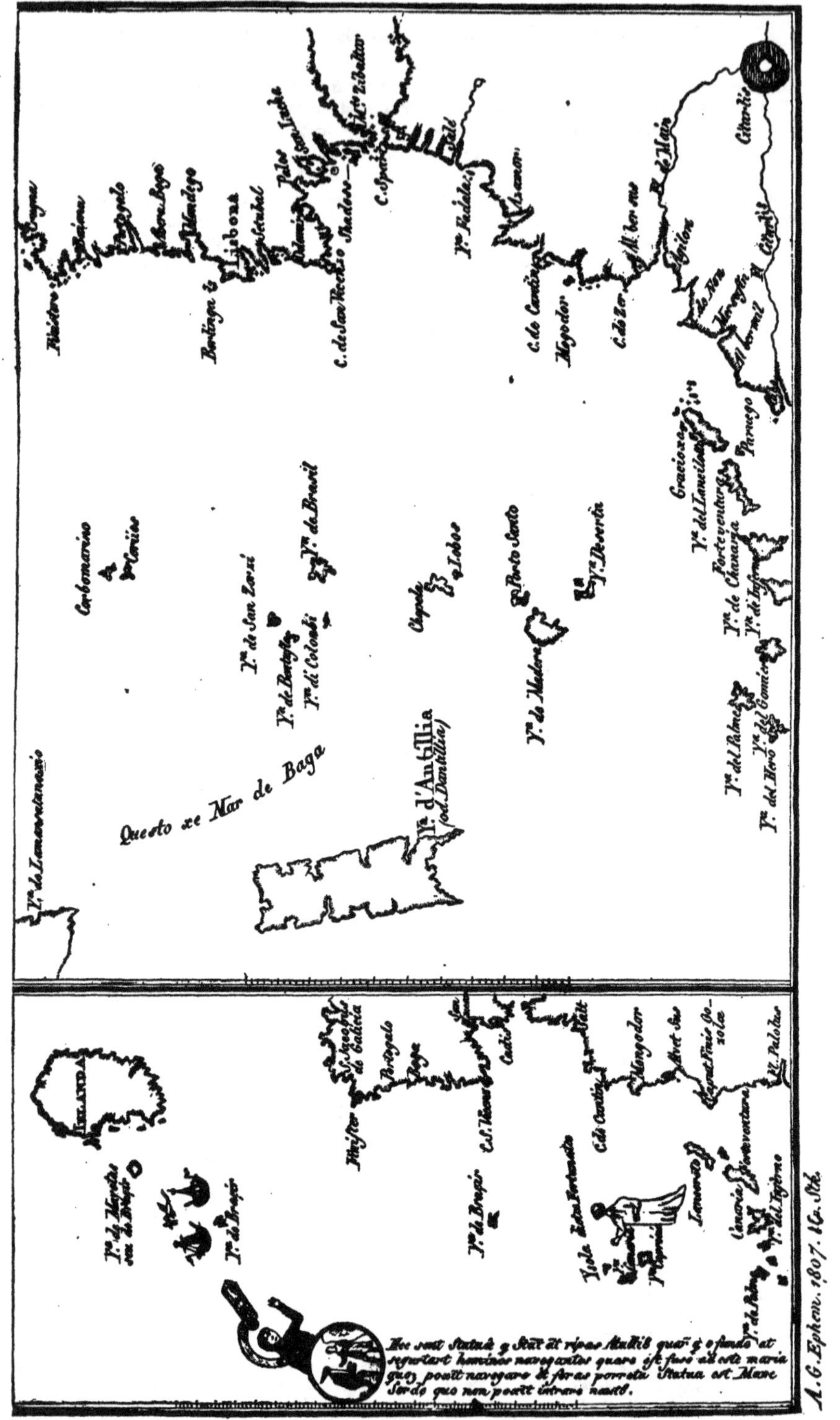

Note.—The above maps are reduced a little from the engraving in *Allgemeine Geographische Ephemeriden* (Weimar, 1807), vol. xxiv. p. 248. The smaller is an extract from that of Fr. Pizigani (1367), and the larger that of Andreas Bianco (1436). There is another fac-simile of the later in F. M. Erizzo's *Le Scoperte Artiche* (Venice, 1855).

There are two maps of Hygden (A. D. 1350), but the abundance of islands which they present can hardly be said to show more than a theory.[1] There is more likelihood of well considered work in the Portolano Laurenziano-Gaddiano (A. D. 1351), preserved in the Biblioteca Mediceo-Laurenziana at Florence, of which Ongania, of Venice, published a fac-simile in 1881.[2] There are two maps of Francisco Pizigani, which seem to give the Canaries, Madeira, and the Azores better than any earlier one. One of these maps (1367) is in the national library at Parma, and the other (1373) is in the Ambrosian library at Milan (*Studi biog. e bibliog.*, vol. ii. pp. viii, 57, 58). The 1367 map is given by Jomard and Santarem. The most famous of all these early maps is the Catalan Mappemonde of 1375, preserved in the great library at Paris. It gives the Canaries and other islands further north, but does not reach to the Azores.[3] These last islands are included, however, in another Catalan planisphere of not far from the same era, which is preserved in the national library

CATALAN MAP, 1375.*

at Florence, and has been reproduced by Ongania (1881).[4] The student will need to compare other maps of the fourteenth century, which can be found mentioned in the *Studi*, etc., with references in the *Kohl Maps*, sect. 1. The phototypic series of Ongania is the most important contribution to this study, though the yellow tints of the original too often render the details obscurely.[5] So for the next century there are the same guides; but a number of conspicuous charts may well be mentioned. Chief among them are those of Andrea Bianco contained in the Atlas (1436), in the Biblioteca Marciana at Venice, published by Ongania (1871), who also published (1881) the Carta Nautica of Bianco, in the Biblioteca Ambrosiana in Milan.[6]

1855) of the Royal Bavarian Academy; but a more perfect inventory of his maps is given in the *Studi biog. e bibliog.* of the Italian Geographical Society (1882, i. 80; ii. 50). Cf. Peschel, *Gesch. der Erdkunde*, Ruge, ed. 1877, p. 210. Sanuto's map of 1320 was first published in his *Liber Secretorum fidelium crucis* (Frankfort, 1811. Cf. reproduction in St. Martin's *Atlas*, pl. vi. no. 3). Further references are in Winsor's *Kohl Maps*, no. 12. It is in part reproduced by Santarem.

[1] Cf. *Amer. Geog. Soc. Journal*, xii. 177, and references in the *Kohl Maps*, nos. 13 and 14.

[2] Vol. II. p. 38.

[3] Cf. references in Vol. II. 38.

[4] Cf. *Studi*, etc., ii. no. 392.

[5] Cf. Desimoni's *Le carte nautiche Italiane del medio evo a proposito di un libro del Prof. Fischer* (Genoa, 1888).

[6] Cf. Vol. II. 38 for references; and Lelewel and Santarem's Atlases.

* After a sketch in St. Martin's *Atlas*, pl. vii.

The 1436 map has been reproduced in colors in Pietro Amat de San Filippo's *Planisferio disegnato del 1436* (*Bollettino Soc. Geografia*, 1879, p. 560); and a sketch of the Atlantic part is given in the *Allgem. Geog. Ephemeriden*, xxiv. no. 248.[1]

ANDREAS BENINCASA, 1476.*

During the next twenty years or more, the varying knowledge of the Atlantic is shown in a number of maps, a few of which may be named:—The Catalan map "de Gabriell de Valsequa, faite à Mallorcha en 1439," which shows the Azores, and which Vespucius is said to have owned (Santarem, pl. 54). The planisphere "in lingua latina dell' anno 1447," in the national library at Florence (Ongania, 1881). The world maps of Giovanni Leardo (Johannes Leardus), 1448 and 1452, the former of which is given in Santarem (pl. 25, — also *Hist. Cartog.* iii. 398), and the latter reproduced by Ongania, 1880. One is in the Ambrosian library, and the other in the Museo Civico at Vicenza (cf. *Studi*, etc., ii. 72, 73). In the Biblioteca Vittorio Emanuele at Rome there is the sea-chart of Bartolomaeus de Pareto of 1455, on which we find laid down the Fortunate Islands, St. Brandan's, Antillia, and Royllo.[2] The World of Fra Mauro[3] has been referred to elsewhere in the present volume.

We come now to the conditions of the Atlantic cartography immediately preceding the voyage of Columbus. The most prominent specimens of this period are the various marine charts of Grogioso and Andreas Benincasa from 1461 to 1490. Some of these are given by Santarem, Lelewel, and St. Martin; but the best enumeration of them is given in the *Studi biog. e bibliog. della Soc. Geog. Ital.* ii. 66, 77–84, 92, 99, 100. Of Toscanelli's map of 1474, which influenced Columbus, we have no sketch, though some attempts have

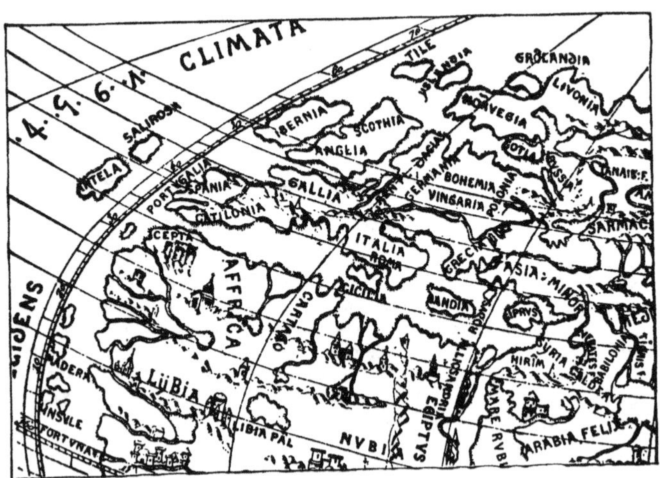

LAON GLOBE.†

[1] Cf. *Studi*, etc., vol. ii. pp. viii, 67, 72, with references.

[2] Cf. Pietro Amat in the *Mem. Soc. Geografica*, Roma, 1878; *Studi*, etc., ii. 75; Winsor's *Bibliog. Ptolemy*, sub anno 1478.

[3] Cf. account of inaugurating busts of Fra Mauro and John Cabot, in *Terzo Congresso Geografico internazionale* (held at Venice, Sept., 1881, and published at Rome, 1882), i. p. 33.

* After a sketch in St. Martin's *Atlas*, pl. vii.

† From a "projection Synoptique Cordiforme" in the *Bull. de la Soc. de Géog.*, 4e série, xx. (1860), in connection with a paper by D'Avezac (p. 398). Cf. Oscar Peschel in *Ausland*, May 12, 1861; also in his *Abhandlungen*, i. 226.

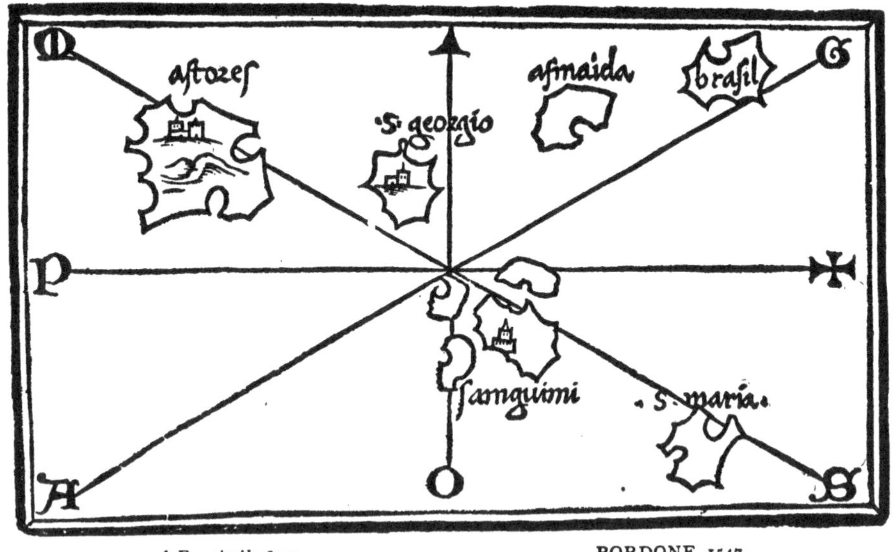

A Fac-simile from BORDONE, 1547.

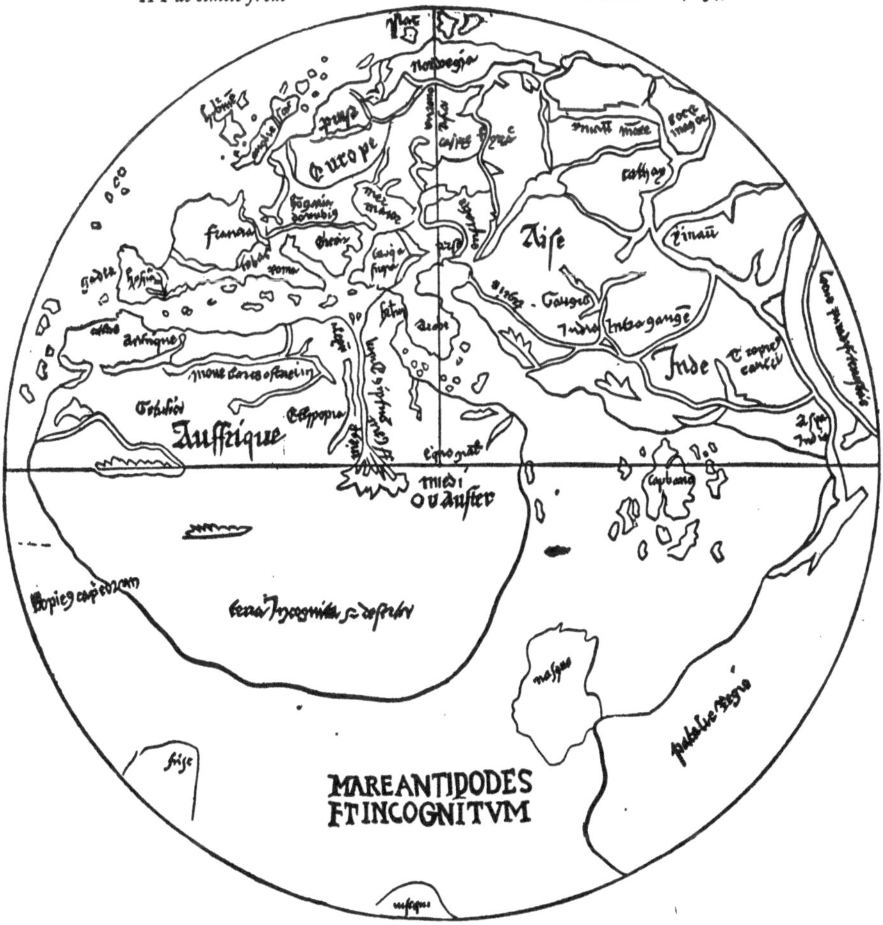

END OF FIFTEENTH CENTURY. (Santarem's *Atlas.*)

been made to reconstruct it from descriptions. (Cf. Vol. II. p. 103; Harrisse's *Christophe Colomb.*, i. 127, 129.) Brief mention may also be made of the Laon globe of 1486 (dated 1493), of which D'Avezac gives a projection in the *Bulletin de la Soc. de Géog.* xx. 417; of the Majorcan (Catalan) Carta nautica of about 1487 (cf. *Studi*, etc., ii. no. 397; *Bull. Soc. Géog.*, i. 295); of the chart in the Egerton MSS., Brit. Mus., made by Christofalo Soligo about the same time, and which has no dearth of islands (cf. *Studi*, etc., i. 89); of those of Nicola Fiorin, Canepa, and Giacomo Bertran (*Studi*, etc., ii. 82, 86, and no. 398). The globe of Behaim (1492) gives the very latest of these ante-Columbian views (see Vol. II. 105).

It took, after this, a long time for the Atlantic to be cleared, even partially, of these intrusive islands, and to bring the proper ones into accurate relations. How the old ideas survived may be traced in the maps of Ruysch, 1508 (Vol. II. 115); Coppo, 1528, with its riot of islands (II. 127); Mercator, 1541 (II. 177); Bordone, 1547; Zaltière, 1566 (II. 451); Porcacchi, 1572 (II. 453); Ortelius, 1575, 1587, — not to continue the series further.

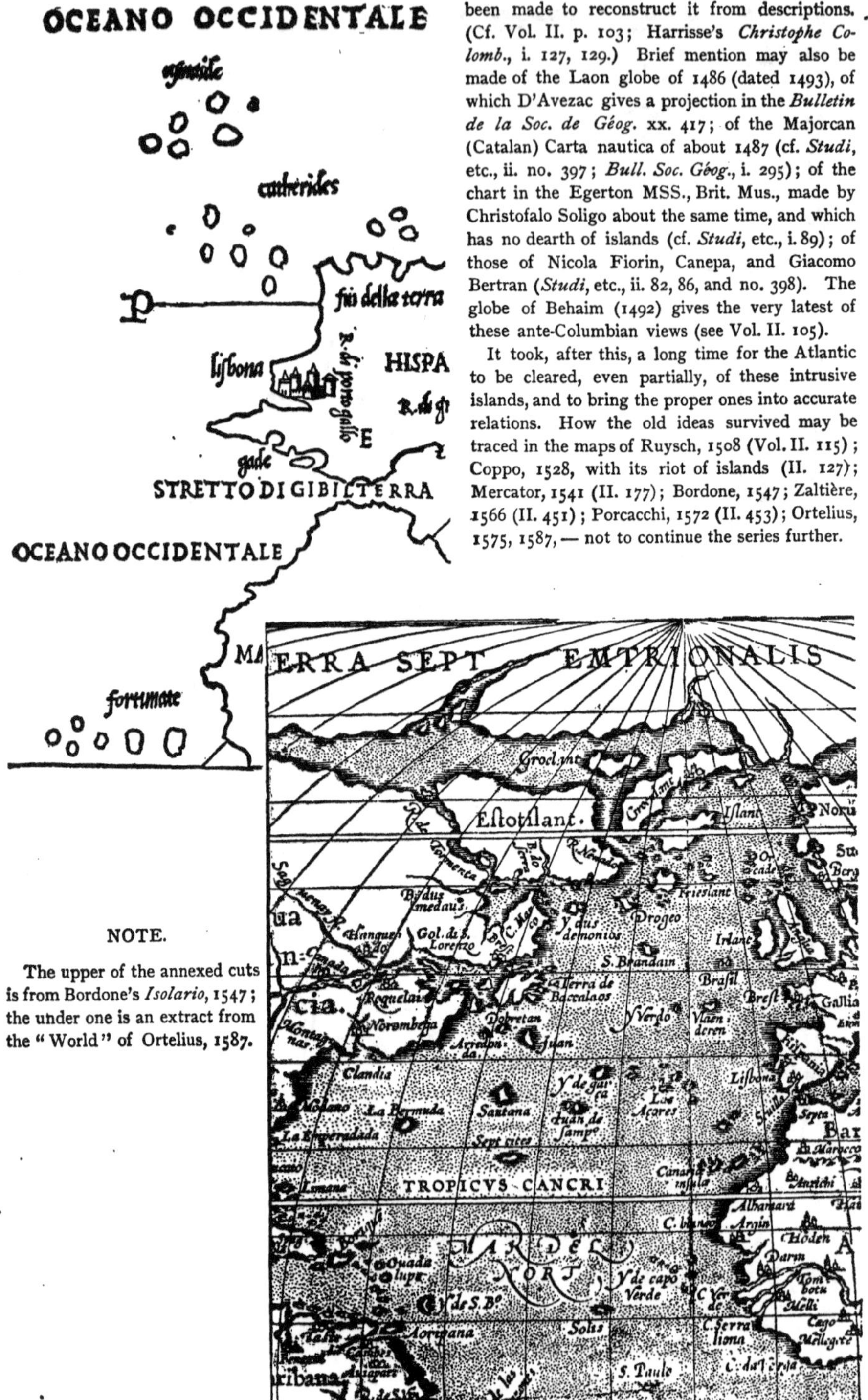

NOTE.

The upper of the annexed cuts is from Bordone's *Isolario*, 1547; the under one is an extract from the "World" of Ortelius, 1587.

CHAPTER II.

PRE-COLUMBIAN EXPLORATIONS.

BY JUSTIN WINSOR, THE EDITOR.

IN the previous chapter, in attempting to trace the possible connection of the new world with the old in the dimmest past, it was hard, if not hopeless, to find among the entangled myths a path that we could follow with any confidence into the field of demonstrable history. It is still a doubt how far we exchange myths for assured records, when we enter upon the problems of pre-Columbian explorations, which it is the object of the present chapter to discuss. We are to deal with supposable colonizations, from which the indigenous population of America, as the Spaniards found it, was sprung, wholly or in part; and we are to follow the venturesome habits of navigators, who sought experience and commerce in a strange country, and only incidentally left possible traces of their blood in the peoples they surprised. If Spain, Italy, and England gained consequence by the discoveries of Columbus and Cabot, there were other national prides to be gratified by the priority which the Basques, the Normans, the Welsh, the Irish, and the Scandinavians, to say nothing of Asiatic peoples, claimed as their share in the gift of a new world to the old. The records which these peoples present as evidences of their right to be considered the forerunners of the Spanish and English expeditions have in every case been questioned by those who are destitute of the sympathetic credence of a common kinship. The claims which Columbus and Cabot fastened upon Spain and England, to the disadvantage of Italy, who gave to those rival countries their maritime leaders, were only too readily rejected by Italy herself, when the opportunity was given to her of paling such borrowed glories before the trust which she placed in the stories of the Zeni brothers.

There is not a race of eastern Asia — Siberian, Tartar, Chinese, Japanese, Malay, with the Polynesians — which has not been claimed as discoverers, intending or accidental, of American shores, or as progenitors, more or less perfect or remote, of American peoples; and there is no good reason why any one of them may not have done all that is claimed. The historical evidence, however, is not such as is based on documentary proofs of indisputable character, and the recitals advanced are often far from precise enough to be convincing in details, if their general authenticity is allowed.

Nevertheless, it is much more than barely probable that the ice of Behring Straits or the line of the Aleutian Islands was the pathway of successive immigrations, on occasions perhaps far apart, or may be near together; and there is hardly a stronger demonstration of such a connection between the two continents than the physical resemblances of the peoples now living on opposite sides of the Pacific Ocean in these upper latitudes, with the similarity of the flora which environs them on either shore.[1] It is quite as conceivable that the great northern current, setting east athwart the Pacific, should from time to time have carried along disabled vessels, and stranded them on the shores of California and farther north, leading to the infusion of Asiatic blood among whatever there may have been antecedent or autochthonous in the coast peoples. It is certainly in this way possible that the Chinese or Japanese may have helped populate the western slopes of the American continent. There is no improbability even in the Malays of southeastern Asia extending step by step to the Polynesian islands, and among them and beyond them, till the shores of a new world finally received the impress of their footsteps and of their ethnic characteristics. We may very likely recognize not proofs, but indications, along the shores of South America, that its original people constituted such a stock, or were increased by it.

As respects the possible early connections of America on the side of Europe, there is an equally extensive array of claims, and they have been set forth, first and last, with more persistency than effect.[2]

Leaving the old world by the northern passage, Iceland lies at the threshold of America. It is nearer to Greenland than to Norway, and Greenland is but one of the large islands into which the arctic currents divide the North American continent. Thither, to Iceland, if we identify the localities in Geoffrey of Monmouth, King Arthur sailed as early as the beginning of the sixth century, and overcame whatever inhabitants he may have found there. Here too an occasional wandering pirate or adventurous Dane had glimpsed the coast.[3] Thither, among others, came the Irish, and in the ninth century we find Irish monks and a small colony of their countrymen in possession.[4] Thither the Gulf Stream carries the southern driftwood,

[1] Asa Gray, in *Darwiniana*, p. 203. Cf. his *Address* before Amer. Assoc. Adv. Science, 1827.

[2] The subject of these pre-Columbian claims is examined in almost all the general works on early discovery. Cf. Robertson's *America*; J. S. Vater's *Untersuchungen über Amerikas Bevölkerung aus dem alten Continent* (Leipzig, 1810); Dr. F. X. A. Deuber's *Geschichte der Schiffahrt im Atlantischen Ozean* (Bamberg, 1814); Ruge, *Geschichte des Zeitalters der Entdeckungen* (ch. 2); Major's *Select Letters of Columbus*, introd.; C. A. A. Zestermann's *Memoir on the Colonization of America in antehistoric times, with critical observations by E. G. Squier* (London, 1851); *Nouvelles Annales des Voyages* (ii. 404); "Les précurseurs de Colomb" in *Études par les Pères de la Compagnie de Jesus* (Leipzig, 1876); Oscar Dunn in *Revue Canadienne*, xii. 57, 194, 305, 871, 909, — not to name numerous other periodical papers. Paul Gaffarel, in his "Les relations entre l'ancien monde et l'Amérique étaient-elles possibles au moyen âge?" (*Soc. Normande de Géog. Bulletin*, 1881, p. 209), thinks that amid the confused traditions there is enough to convince us that we have no right to determine that communication was impossible.

[3] *MSS. de la bibliothèque royale* (Paris, 1787), i. 462.

[4] De Costa in *Journal Amer. Geog. Soc.* xii. (1880) p. 159, etc., with references.

suggesting sunnier lands to whatever race had been allurea or driven to its shelter.[1] Here Columbus, when, as he tells us,[2] he visited the island in 1477, found no ice. So that, if we may place reliance on the appreciable change of climate by the precession of the equinoxes, a thousand years ago and more, when the Norwegians crossed from Scandinavia and found these Christian Irish there,[3] the island was not the forbidding spot that it seems with the lapse of centuries to be becoming.

It was in A. D. 875 that Ingolf, a jarl[4] of Norway, came to Iceland with Norse settlers. They built their habitation at first where a pleasant headland seemed attractive, the present Ingolfshofdi, and later founded Reikjavik, where the signs had directed them; for certain carved posts, which they had thrown overboard as they approached the island, were found to have drifted to that spot. The Christian Irish preferred to leave their asylum rather than consort with the new-comers, and so the island was left to be occupied by successive immigrations of the Norse, which their king could not prevent. In the end, and within half a century, a hardy little republic — as for a while it was — of near seventy thousand inhabitants was established almost under the arctic circle. The very next year (A. D. 876) after Ingolf had come to Iceland, a sea-rover, Gunnbiorn, driven in his ship westerly, sighted a strange land, and the report that he made was not forgotten.[5] Fifty years later, more or less, for we must treat the dates of the Icelandic sagas with some reservation, we learn that a wind-tossed vessel was thrown upon a coast far away, which was called Ireland the Great. Then again we read of a young Norwegian, Eric the Red, not apparently averse to a brawl, who killed his man in Norway and fled to Iceland, where he kept his dubious character; and again outraging the laws, he was sent into temporary banishment, — this time in a ship which he fitted out for discovery; and so he sailed away in the direction of Gunnbiorn's land, and found it. He whiled away three years on its coast, and as soon as he was allowed ventured back with the tidings, while, to propitiate intending settlers, he said he had been to Greenland, and so the land got a sunny name. The next year, which seems to have been A. D. 985, he started on his return with thirty-five ships, but only fourteen of them

[1] Humboldt, *Views of Nature*, p. 124. He also notes the drifting of Eskimo boats to Europe.

[2] *Tratado de las cinco zonas habitables*.

[3] Respecting these Christian Irish see the supplemental chapters of Mallet's *Northern Antiquities* (London, 1847); Dasent's *Burnt Njal*, i. p. vii.; Moore's *History of Ireland;* Forster's *Northern Voyages;* Worsaae's *Danes and Norwegians in England*, 332. Cf. on the contact of the two races H. H. Howorth on "The Irish monks and the Norsemen" in the *Roy. Hist. Soc. Trans.* viii. 281.

[4] Conybeare remarks that jarl, naturalized in England as earl, has been displaced in its native north by graf.

[5] It has sometimes been contended that a bull of Gregory IV, in A. D. 770, referred to Greenland, but Spitzbergen was more likely intended, though its known discovery is much later. A bull of A. D. 835, in Pontanus's *Rerum Daniarum Historia*, is also held to indicate that there were earlier peoples in Greenland than those from Iceland. Sabin (vi. no. 22,854) gives as published at Godthaab, 1859–61, in 3 vols., the Eskimo text of Greenland Folk Lore, collected and edited by natives of Greenland, with a Danish translation, and showing, as the notice says, the traditions of the first descent of the Northmen in the *eighth* century.

reached the land. Wherever there was a habitable fiord, a settlement grew up, and the stream of immigrants was for a while constant and considerable. Just at the end of the century (A. D. 999), Leif, a son of Eric, sailed back to Norway, and found the country in the early fervor of a new religion; for King Olaf Tryggvesson had embraced Christianity, and was imposing it on his people. Leif accepted the new faith, and a priest was assigned to him to take back to Greenland; and thus Christianity was introduced into arctic

NORSE SHIP.*

* This cut is copied from one in Nordenskiöld's *Voyage of the Vega* (London, 1881), vol. i. p. 50, where it is given as representing the vessel found at Sandefjord in 1880. It is drawn from the restoration given in *The Viking ship discovered at Gokstad in Norway* (*Langskibet fra Gokstad ved Sandefjord*) *described by N. Nicholaysen* (Christiania, 1882). The original vessel owed its preservation to being used as a receptacle for the body of a Viking chief, when he was buried under a mound. When exhumed, its form, with the sepulchral chamber midships, could be made out, excepting that the prow and stern in their extremities had to be restored. In the ship and about it were found, beside some of the bones of a man, various appurtenances of the vessel, and the remains of horses buried with him. They are all described in the book above cited, from which the other cuts herewith given of the plan of the vessel and one of its rowlocks are taken. The *Popular Science Monthly*, May, 1881, borrowing from *La Nature*, gives a view of the ship as when found *in situ*. There are other accounts in *The Antiquary*, Aug., 1880; Dec., 1881; 1882, p. 87; *Scribner's Magazine*, Nov., 1887, by John S. White; *Potter's American Monthly*, Mar., 1882. Cf. the illustrated paper, "Les navires des peuples du nord," by Otto Jorell, in *Congrès Internat. des Sciences géographiques* (Paris, 1875; pub. 1878), i. 318.

Of an earlier discovery in 1872 there is an account in *The ancient vessel found in the parish of Tune, Norway* (Christiania, 1872). This is a translation by Mr. Gerhard Gadé of a Report in the Proceedings of the Society for preserving Norwegian Antiquities. (Cf. *Mass. Hist. Soc. Proc.*, xiii. p. 10.) This vessel was also buried under a mound, and she was 43½ feet long and four feet deep.

There is in the Nicholaysen volume a detailed account of the naval architecture of the Viking period, and other references may be made to Otto Jorell's *Les navires des peuples du Nord*, in the *Congrès internat. des sciences géog., compte rendu, 1875* (1878, i. 318); *Mémoires de la Soc. royal des Antiquaires du Nord* (1887, p. 280); Preble, in *United Service* (May, 1883, p. 463), and in his *Amer. Flag*, p. 159; De Costa's *Pre-Columbian Discovery of America*, p. xxxvii; Fox's *Landfall of Columbus*, p. 3; *Pop. Science Monthly*, xix. 80; *Van Nostrand's Eclectic Engineering Mag.*, xxiii. 320; *Good Words*, xxii. 759; Higginson's *Larger History U. S.* for cuts; and J. J. A. Worsaae's *Prehistory of the North* (Eng. transl., London, 1886) for the burial in ships.

There is a paper on the daring of the Norsemen as navigators by G. Brynjalfson (*Compte Rendu, Congrès des Américanistes*, Copenhagen, p. 140), entitled "Jusqu'où les anciens Scandinaves ont-ils pénétré vers le pôle arctique dans leurs expéditions à la mer glaciale?"

America. So they began to build churches[1] in Greenland, the considerable ruins of one of which stand to this day.[2] The winning of Iceland to the Church was accomplished at the same time.

There were two centres of settlement on the Greenland coast, not where they were long suspected to be, on the coast opposite Iceland, nor as supposed after the explorations of Baffin's Bay, on both the east and west side of the country; but the settlers seem to have reached and doubled Cape Farewell, and so formed what was called their eastern settlement (Eystribygd), near the cape, while farther to the north they formed their western colony (Westribygd).[3] Their relative positions are still involved in doubt.

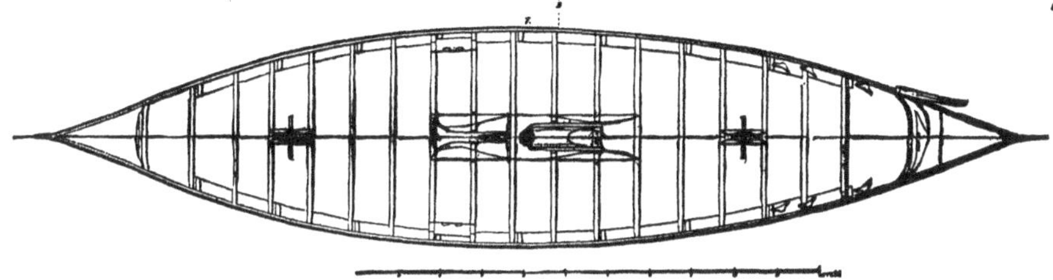

PLAN OF VIKING SHIP.

In the next year after the second voyage of Eric the Red, one of the ships which were sailing from Iceland to the new settlement, was driven far off her course, according to the sagas, and Bjarni Herjulfson, who commanded the vessel, reported that he had come upon a land, away to the southwest, where the coast country was level; and he added that when he turned north it took him nine days to reach Greenland.[4] Fourteen years later than this voyage of Bjarni, which is said to have been in A. D. 986, — that is, in the year 1000 or thereabouts, — Leif, the same who had brought the Christian priest to Greenland, taking with him thirty-five companions, sailed from Greenland in quest of the land seen by Bjarni, which Leif first found, where a barren shore stretched back to ice-covered mountains, and because of the stones there he called the region Hellu land. Proceeding farther south, he found a sandy shore, with a level forest-country back of it, and because of the woods it was named Markland. Two days later they came upon other land, and tasting the dew upon the grass they found

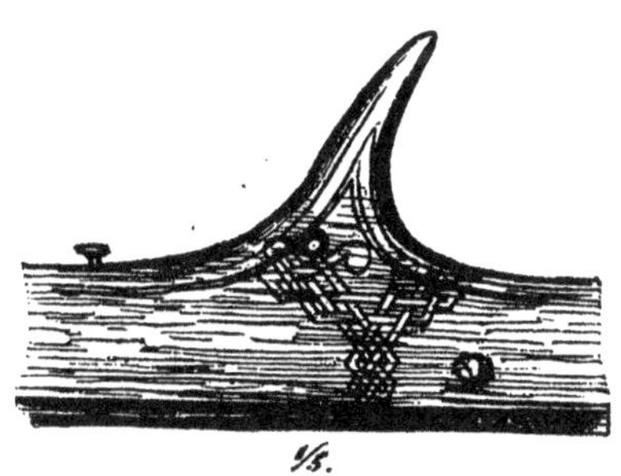

1/8.

ROWLOCK OF THE VIKING SHIP.

[1] Known as the Katortuk church.

[2] An apocryphal story goes that one of these churches was built near a boiling spring, the water from which was conducted through the building in pipes for heating it! The Zeno narrative is the authority for this. Cf. Gay's *Pop. Hist. U. S.* i. 79.

[3] The Westribygd, or western colony, had in the fourteenth century 90 settlements and 4 churches; the Eystribygd had 190 settlements, a cathedral and eleven churches, with two large towns and three or four monasteries.

[4] R. G. Haliburton, in the *Popular Science Monthly*, May, 1885, p. 40, gives a map in which Bjarni's course is marked as entering the St. Lawrence Gulf by the south, and emerging by the Straits of Belle Isle.

it sweet. Farther south and westerly they went, and going up a river came into an expanse of water, where on the shores they built huts to lodge in

NORSE BOAT USED AS A HABITATION.*

for the winter, and sent out exploring parties. In one of these, Tyrker, a native of a part of Europe where grapes grew, found vines hung with their fruit, which induced Leif to call the country Vinland.

NORMAN SHIP FROM THE BAYEUX TAPESTRY.† SCANDINAVIAN FLAGS.‡

* From Viollet-le-Duc's *Habitation humaine* (Paris, 1875).

† From Worsaae's *Danes and Norwegians in England*, etc. "With the exception of very imperfect representation carved on rocks and runic stones [see Higginson's *Larger History*, p. 27], there are no images left in the countries of Scandinavia of ships of the olden times; but the tapestry at Bayeux, in Normandy, is a contemporary evidence of the appearance of the Normanic ships."

‡ This group from Worsaae's *Danes and Norwegians in England, etc.*, p. 64, shows the transition from the raven to the cross.

Attempts have been made to identify these various regions by the inexact accounts of the direction of their sailing, by the very general descriptions of the country, by the number of days occupied in going from one point to another, with the uncertainty if the ship sailed at night, and by the length of the shortest day in Vinland, — the last a statement that might help us, if it could be interpreted with a reasonable concurrence of opinion, and if it were not confused with other inexplicable statements. The next year Leif's brother, Thorvald, went to Vinland with a single ship, and passed three winters there, making explorations meanwhile, south and north. Thorfinn Karlsefne, arriving in Greenland in A. D. 1006, married a courageous widow named Gudrid, who induced him to sail with his ships to Vinland and make there a permanent settlement, taking with him livestock and other necessaries for colonization. Their first winter in the place was a severe one; but

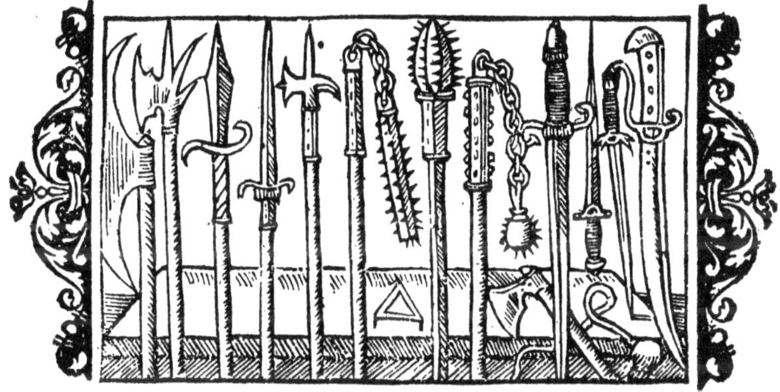

FROM OLAUS MAGNUS.*

Gudrid gave birth to a son, Snorre, from whom it is claimed Thorwaldsen, the Danish sculptor, was descended. The next season they removed to the spot where Leif had wintered, and called the bay Hóp. Having spent a third winter in the country, Karlsefne, with a part of the colony, returned to Greenland.

The saga then goes on to say that trading voyages to the settlement which had been formed by Karlsefne now became frequent, and that the chief lading of the return voyages was timber, which was much needed in Greenland. A bishop of Greenland, Eric Upsi, is also said to have gone to Vinland in A. D. 1121. In 1347 the last ship of which we have any record in these sagas went to Vinland after timber. After this all is oblivion.

There are in all these narratives many details beyond this outline, and those who have sought to identify localities have made the most they could of the mention of a rock here or a bluff there, of an island where they killed a bear, of others where they found eggs, of a headland where they buried a leader who had been killed, of a cape shaped like a keel, of broad-

* Fac-simile of Norse weapons from the *Historia* of Olaus Magnus (b. 1490; d. 1568), Rome, 1555, p. 222.

faced natives who offered furs for red cloths, of beaches where they hauled up their ships, and of tides that were strong; but the more these details are scanned in the different sagas the more they confuse the investigator, and the more successive relators try to enlighten us the more our doubts are strengthened, till we end with the conviction that all attempts at consistent unravelment leave nothing but a vague sense of something somewhere done.

Everywhere else where the Northmen went they left proofs of their occu-

FULL-SIZE FACSIMILE OF THE TABLET, *engraved by Prof. Magnus Petersen, with the Runes as he sees them.*

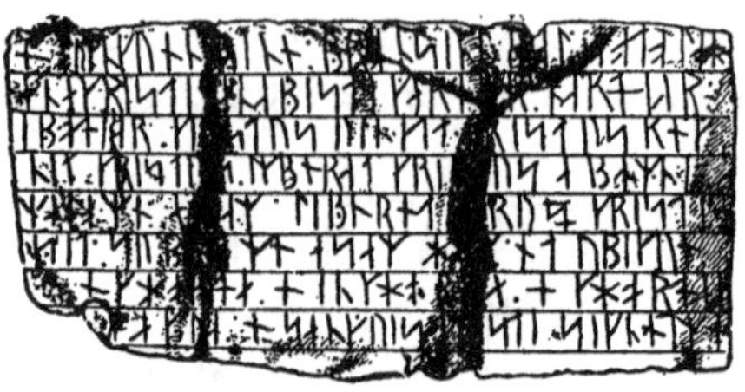

(TRANSLITERATION OF THE LEADEN TABLET.)

+ (AT) Þ(E)R KUEN(E) SINE PRINSINED (B)AD (M)OTO LAN-
ANA KRISTI DONAVISTI GARDIAR IARDIAR
IBODIAR KRISTUS UINKIT KRISTUS REG-
NAT KRISTUS IMPERAT KRISTUS AB OMNI
MALO ME ASAM LIPERET KRUX KRISTI
SIT SUPER ME ASAM HIK ET UBIQUE
+ KHORDA + IN KHORDA + KHORDAE
(I) (M)AGLA + SANGUIS KRISTI SIGNET ME

RUNES, A. D. 1000.*

* This cut is of some of the oldest runes known, giving two lines in Danish and the rest in Latin, as the transliteration shows. It is copied from *The oldest yet found Document in Danish, by Prof. Dr. George Stephens* (Copenhagen, 1888,—from the *Mémoires des Antiquaires du Nord*, 1887). The author says that the leaden tablet on which the runes were cut was found in Odense, Fyn, Denmark, in 1883, and he places the date of it about the year A. D. 1000.

George Stephens's *Handbook of the old Northern Runic Monuments of Scandinavia and England* is a condensation, preserving all the cuts, and making some additions to his larger folio work in 3 vols., *The old-northern Runic monuments of Scandinavia and England, now first collected and deciphered* (London, etc., 1866–68). It does not contain either Icelandic or Green land runes. He says that by the time of the colonization of Iceland "the old northern runes as a system had died out on the Scandinavian main, and were followed by the later runic alphabet. But even this modern Icelandic of the tenth century has not come down to us. If it had, it would be very different from what is now vulgarly so called, which is the greatly altered Icelandic of the thirteenth and fourteenth centuries. . . . The oldest written Icelandic known to us is said to date from about the year 1200. . . . The whole modern doctrine of one uniform Icelandic language all over the immense north in the first one thousand winters after Christ is an impossible absurdity. . . . It is very seldom that any of the Scandinavian runic stones bear a date. . . . No Christian runic gravestone is older than the fourteenth century."

On runes in general, see Mallet, Bohn's ed., pp. 227, 248, following the cut of the Kingektorsoak stone, in Rafn's *Antiq. Americanæ;* Wilson's *Prehist. Man*, ii. 88; Wollheim's *Nat. Lit. der Scandinavier* (Berlin, 1875), vol. i. pp. 2–15; Legis-Glueckselig's *Die Runen und ihre Denkmäler* (Leipzig, 1829); De Costa's *Pre-Columb. Disc.*, pp. xxx; *Revue polit. et lit.*, Jan. 10, 1880.

It is held that runes are an outgrowth of the Latin alphabet. (L. F. A. Wimmer's *Runeskriftens Oprindelse og Udvikling i norden*, Copenhagen, 1874.)

pation on the soil, but nowhere in America, except on an island on the east shore of Baffin's Bay,[1] has any authentic runic inscription been found outside of Greenland. Not a single indisputable grave has been discovered to attest their alleged centuries of fitful occupation. The consistent and natural proof of any occupation of America south of Davis Straits is therefore lacking; and there is not sufficient particularity in the descriptions[2] to remove the suspicion that the story-telling of the fireside has overlaid the reports of the explorer. Our historic sense is accordingly left to consider, as respects the most general interpretation, what weight of confidence should be yielded to the sagas, pre-Columbian as they doubtless are. But beyond this is perhaps, what is after all the most satisfactory way of solving the problem, a dependence on the geographical and ethnical probabilities of the case. The Norsemen have passed into credible history as the most

FROM OLAUS MAGNUS.*

hardy and venturesome of races. That they colonized Iceland and Greenland is indisputable. That their eager and daring nature should have deserted them at this point is hardly conceivable. Skirting the Greenland shores and inuring themselves to the hardships and excitements of northern voyaging, there was not a long stretch of open sea before they could strike the Labrador coast. It was a voyage for which their ships, with courageous crews, were not unfitted. Nothing is more likely than that some ship of theirs may have been blown westerly and unwillingly in the first instance, just as Greenland was in like manner first made known to the Icelanders. The coast once found, to follow it to the south would have been their most consistent action.

We may consider, then, that the weight of probability[3] is in favor of a Northman descent upon the coast of the American mainland at some point,

[1] Dated 1135, and discovered in 1824.

[2] Distinctly shown in the diverse identifications of these landmarks which have been made.

[3] On the probabilities of the Vinland voyages, see Worsaae's *Danes and Norwegians in England*, etc., p. 109.

* Fac-simile of a cut to the chapter "De Alphabeto Gothorum" in the *Historia de Gentibus Septentrionalibus* (Romæ, M.D.LV.).

or at several, somewhere to the south of Greenland; but the evidence is hardly that which attaches to well-established historical records.

The archæological traces, which are lacking farther south, are abundant in Greenland, and confirm in the most positive way the Norse occupation. The ruins of churches and baptisteries give a color of truth to the ecclesiastical annals which have come down to us, and which indicate that after having been for more than a century under the Bishop of Iceland, a succession of bishops of its own was established there early in the twelfth century. The names of seventeen prelates are given by Torfæus, though it is not quite certain that the bishops invariably visited their see. The last known to have filled the office went thither in the early years of the fifteenth century. The last trace of him is in the celebration of a marriage at Gardar in 1409.

The Greenland colonists were equipped with all the necessities of a permanent life. They had horses, sheep, and oxen, and beef is said to have been a regular article of export to Norway. They had buildings of stone, of which the remains still exist. They doubtless brought timber from the south, and we have in runic records evidence of their explorations far to the north. They maintained as late as the thirteenth century a regular commercial intercourse with the mother country,[1] but this trade fell into disuse when a royal mandate constituted such ventures a monopoly of the throne; and probably nothing so much conduced to the decadence and final extinction of the colonies as this usurped and exclusive trade, which cut off all personal or conjoined intercourse.

The direct cause of the final extinction of the Greenland colonies is involved in obscurity, though a variety of causes, easily presumable, would have been sufficient, when we take into consideration the moribund condition into which they naturally fell after commercial restriction had put a stop to free intercourse with the home government.

The Eskimos are said to have appeared in Greenland about the middle of the fourteenth century, and to have manifested hostility to such a degree that about 1342 the imperilled western colony was abandoned. The eastern colony survived perhaps seventy years longer, or possibly to a still later period. We know they had a new bishop in 1387, but before the end of that century the voyages to their relief were conducted only after long intervals.

Before communication was wholly cut off, the attacks of the Skrælings, and possibly famine and the black death, had carried the struggling colonists to the verge of destruction. Bergen, in Norway, upon which they depended for succor, had at one time been almost depopulated by the same virulent disease, and again had been ravaged by a Hanseatic fleet. Thus such intercourse as the royal monopoly permitted had become precarious, and the marauding of freebooters, then prevalent in northern waters, still further served to impede the communications, till at last they wholly ceased, during the early years of the fifteenth century.

[1] *Grönland's Hist. Mindesmaeker*, iii. 9.

It has sometimes been maintained that the closing in of ice-packs was the final stroke which extinguished the last hopes of the expiring colonists.[1] This view, however, meets with little favor among the more enlightened students of climatic changes, like Humboldt.[2]

There has been published what purports to be a bull of Pope Nicholas V,[3] directing the Bishop of Iceland to learn what he could of the condition of the Greenland colonies, and in this document it is stated that part of the colonists had been destroyed by barbarians thirty years before, — the bull bearing date in 1448. There is no record that any expedition followed upon this urging, and there is some question as to the authenticity of the document.[4] In the *Relation* of La Peyrère there is a story of some sailors visiting Greenland so late as 1484; but it is open to question.

Early in the sixteenth century fitful efforts to learn the fate of the colonies began, and these were continued, without result, well into the seventeenth century; but nothing explicable was ascertained till, in 1721, Hans Egede, a Norwegian priest, prevailed upon the Danish government to send him on a mission to the Eskimos. He went, accompanied by wife and children; and the colony of Godthaab, and the later history of the missions, and the revival of trade with Europe, attest the constancy of his purpose and the fruits of his earnestness. In a year he began to report upon certain remains which indicated the former occupation of the country by people who built such buildings as was the habit in Europe. He and his son Paul Egede, and their successors in the missions, gathered for us, first among

[1] The popular confidence in this view is doubtless helped by Montgomery, who has made it a point in his poem on Greenland, canto v. De Courcy (*Hist. of the Church in America*, p. 12) is cited by Howley (*Newfoundland*) as asserting that the eastern colony was destroyed by "a physical cataclysm, which accumulated the ice." On the question of a change of climate in Greenland, see J. D. Whitney's *Climatic Changes* (*Mus. Comp. Zoöl. Mem.*, 1882, vii. 238).

[2] Rink (*Danish Greenland*, 22) is not inclined to believe that there has been any material climatic change in Greenland since the Norse days, and favors the supposition that some portion of the finally remaining Norse became amalgamated with the Eskimo and disappeared. If the reader wants circumstantial details of the misfortunes of their "last man," he can see how they can be made out of what are held to be Eskimo traditions in a chapter of Dr. Hayes's *Land of Desolation*.

Nordenskjöld (*Voyage of the Vega*) holds, such is the rapid assimilation of a foreign stock by a native stock, that it is not unlikely that what descendants may exist of the lost colonists of Greenland may be now indistinguishable from the Eskimo.

Tylor (*Early Hist. Mankind*, p. 208), speaking of the Eskimo, says: "It is indeed very strange that there should be no traces found among them of knowledge of metal-work and of other arts, which one would expect a race so receptive of foreign knowledge would have got from contact with the Northmen."

Prof. Edward S. Morse, in his very curious study of *Ancient and Modern Methods of Arrow Release* (Salem, 1885, — *Bull. Essex Inst.*, xvii.) p. 52, notes that the Eskimo are the only North American tribe practising what he calls the "Mediterranean release," common to all civilized Europe, and he ventures to accept a surmise that it may have been derived from the Scandinavians.

[3] Given by Schlegel, Egede (citing Pontanus), and Rafn; and a French version is in the *Bull. de la Soc. de Géog.*, 2d series, iii. 348. It is said to be preserved in a copy in the Vatican. M. F. Howley, *Ecclesiastical Hist. of Newfoundland* (Boston, 1888), p. 43, however, says: "Abbé Garnier mentions a bull of Pope Nicholas V, of date about 1447, concerning the church of Greenland; but on searching the Bullarium in the Propaganda library, Rome, in 1885, I could not find it."

[4] Laing's *Heimskringla*, i. 146.

modern searchers, the threads of the history of this former people; and, as time went on, the researches of Graah, Nordenskjöld, and other explorers, and the studious habits of Major, Rink, and the rest among the in-

DE I COMMENTARII DEL
Viaggio in Perſia di M. Caterino Zeno il K. & delle guerre fatte nell'Imperio Perſiano, dal tempo di Vſſuncaſſano in quà.
LIBRI DVE.
ET DELLO SCOPRIMENTO dell'Iſole Frislanda, Eslanda, Engrouelanda, Eſtotilanda, & Icaria, fatto ſotto il Polo Artico, da due fratelli zeni, M. Nicolò il K. e M. Antonio.
LIBRO VNO.
CON VN DISEGNO PARTICOLARE DI
tutte le dette parte di tramontana da lor ſcoperte.
CON GRATIA, ET PRIVILEGIO.

IN VENETIA
Per Franceſco Marcolini. M D LVIII.

vestigators, have enabled us to read the old sagas of the colonization of Greenland with renewed interest and with the light of corroborating evidence.[1]

We are told that it was one result of these Northman voyages that the

[1] E. B. Tylor on "Old Scandinavian Civilization among the modern Esquimaux," in the *Journal of the Anthropological Inst.* (1884), xiii. 348, shows that the Greenlanders still preserve some of the Norse customs, arising in part, as he thinks, from some of the lost Scandinavian survivors being merged in the savage tribes. Their recollection of the Northmen seems evident from the traditions collected among them by Dr. Rink in his *Eskimoiske Eventyr og Sagn* (Copenhagen, 1866); and their dress, and some of their utensils and games, as it existed in the days of Egede and Crantz, seem to indicate the survival of customs.

fame of them spread to other countries, and became known among the Welsh, at a time when, upon the death of Owen Gwynedd, who ruled in the northern parts of that country, the people were embroiled in civil strife. That chieftain's son, Prince Madoc, a man bred to the sea, was discontented with the unstable state of society, and resolved to lead a colony to these

DELLO SCOPRIMENTO DEL l'Isole Frislanda, Eslanda, Engroueland Estotilanda, & Icaria, fatto per due fratelli Zeni M. Nicolò il Caualiere, & M. Antonio Libro Vno, col disegno di dette Isole.

E' MILLE, & dugento anni della nostra salute se molto famoso in Venetia M. Marin zeno chiamato per la sua gran uirtù, et destrezza d'ingegno podestà in alcune Republi. d'Italia, ne' gouerni delle quali si portò sempre cosi bene, che era amato, & grandemente riuerito il suo nome da quelli anco, che non l'haueuano mai per presenza conosciuto; e tra l'altre sue belle opere particolarmente si narra,

western lands, where they could live more in peace. Accordingly, in A. D. 1170, going seaward on a preliminary exploration by the south of Ireland, he steered west, and established a pioneer colony in a fertile land. Leaving here 120 persons, he returned to Wales, and fitted out a larger expedition of ten ships, with which he again sailed, and passed out of view forever. The evidence in support of this story is that it is mentioned in early

NOTE. — The cuts above are fac-similes of the title and of the first page of the section on Frisland, etc., from the Harvard College copy. The book is rare. The Beckford copy brought £50; the Hamilton, £38; the Tross catalogue (1882) price one at 150 francs; the Tweitmeyer, Leipzig, 1888, at 250 marks; Quaritch (1885), at £25. Cf. Court Catalogue, no. 378; Leclerc, no. 3002; Dufossé, no. 4965; Carter-Brown, i. 226; Murphy, nos. 2798-99. The map is often in fac-simile, as in the Harvard College copy.

Welsh annals, and that sundry persons have discovered traces of the Welsh tongue among the lighter-colored American Indians, to say nothing of manifold legends among the Indians of an original people, white in color, coming from afar towards the northeast, — proofs not sufficient to attract the confidence of those who look for historical tests, though, as Humboldt contends,[1] there may be no impossibility in the story.

There seems to be a general agreement that a crew of Arabs, somewhere about the eleventh or twelfth century, explored the Atlantic westward, with the adventurous purpose of finding its further limits, and that they reached land, which may have been the Canaries, or possibly the Azores, though the theory that they succeeded in reaching America is not without advocates. The main source of the belief is the historical treatise of the Arab geographer Edrisi, whose work was composed about the middle of the twelfth century.[2]

In the latter part of the fourteenth century,[3] as the story goes, two brothers of Venice, Nicolo and Antonio Zeno, being on a voyage in the North Atlantic were wrecked there, and lived for some years at Frislanda, and visited Engroneland. During this northern sojourn they encountered a sailor, who, after twenty-six years of absence, had returned, and reported that the ship in which he was had been driven west in a gale to an island, where he found civilized people, who possessed books in Latin and could not speak Norse, and whose country was called Estotiland; while a region on the mainland, farther south, to which he had also gone, was called Drogeo, and that here he had encountered cannibals. Still farther south was a great country with towns and temples. This information, picked up by these exiled Zeni, was finally conveyed to another brother in Venice, accompanied by a map of these distant regions. These documents long

1 *Cosmos*, Bohn's ed., ii. 610; *Examen Crit.*, ii. 148.

2 Cf. *Geographie de Edrisi, traduite de l'arabe en français d'après deux manuscrits de la bibliothèque du Roi, et accompagnée de notes, par G. Amédée Jaubert* (Paris, 1836–40), vol. i. 200; ii. 26. Cf. *Recueil des Voyages et Mémoires de la Société de Géographie de Paris*, vols. v., vi. The world-map by Edrisi does not indicate any knowledge of this unknown world. Cf. copies of it in St. Martin's *Atlas*, pl. vi; Lelewel, *Atlas*, pl. x–xii; Peschel's *Gesch. der Erdkunde*, ed. by Ruge, 1877, p. 144; *Amer. Geog. Soc. Journal*, xii. 181; *Allg. Geog. Ephemeriden*, ix. 292; Gerard Stein's *Die Entdeckungsreisen in alter und neuer Zeit* (1883).

Guignes (*Mém. Acad. des Inscriptions*, 1761, xxviii. 524) limits the Arab voyage to the Canaries, and in *Notices et Extraits des MSS. de la bibliothèque du Roi*, ii. 24, he describes a MS. which makes him believe the Arabs reached America; and he is followed by Munoz (*Hist. del Nuevo Mondo*, Madrid, 1793). Hugh Murray (*Discoveries and Travels in No. Amer.*, Lond., 1829, i. p. 11) and W. D. Cooley (*Maritime Discovery*, 1830, i. 172) limit the explorations respectively to the Azores and the Canaries. Humboldt (*Examen Crit.*, 1837, ii. 137) thinks they may possibly have reached the Canaries; but Malte Brun (*Géog. Universelle*, 1841, i. 186) is more positive. Major (*Select Letters of Columbus*, 1847) discredits the American theory, and in his *Prince Henry* agrees with D'Avezac that they reached Madeira. Lelewel (*Géog. du Moyen Age*, ii. 78) seems likewise incredulous. S. F. Haven (*Archæol. U. S.*) gives the theory and enumerates some of its supporters. Peschel (*Geschichte des Zeitalters der Entdeckungen*, 1858) is very sceptical. Gaffarel (*Etudes*, etc., p. 209) fails to find proof of the American theory. Gay (*Pop. History U. S.*, i. 64) limits their voyage to the Azores.

3 Given as A. D. 1380; but Major says, 1390 *Journal Royal Geog. Soc.*, 1873, p. 180.

remained in the family palace in Venice, and were finally neglected and became obscured, until at last a descendant of the family compiled from them, as best he could, a book, which was printed in Venice in 1558 as *Dei Commentarii del Viaggio*, which was accompanied by a map drawn with difficulty from the half obliterated original which had been sent from Frislanda.[1] The original documents were never produced, and the publication took place opportunely to satisfy current curiosity, continually incited

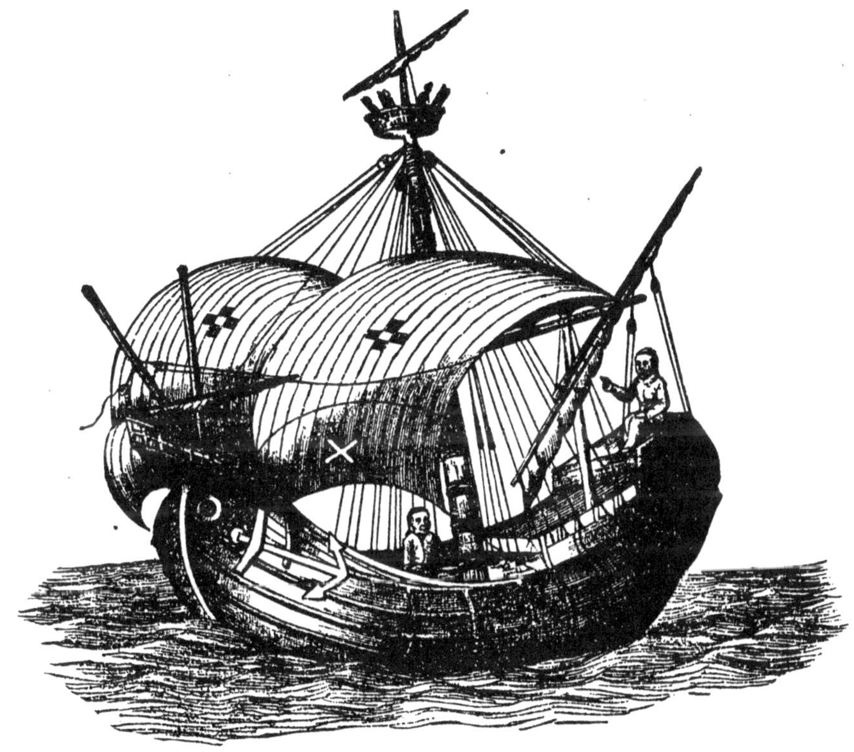

SHIP OF THE FIFTEENTH CENTURY.*

[1] De Costa, *Verrazano the Explorer* (N. Y., 1880), pp. 47, 63, contends that Benedetto Bordone, writing his *Isole del Mondo* in 1521, and printing it in 1528, had access to the Zeno map thirty years and more earlier than its publication. This, he thinks, is evident from the way in which he made and filled in his outline, and from his drawing of "Islanda," even to a like way of engraving the name, which is in a style of letter used by Bordone nowhere else. Humboldt (*Cosmos*, Bohn's ed., ii. 611) has also remarked it as singular that the name Frislanda, which, as he supposed, was not known on the maps before the Zeni publication in 1538, should have been applied by Columbus to an island southerly from Iceland, in his *Tratado de las cinco zonas habitables*. Cf. De Costa's *Columbus and the Geographers of the North* (1872), p. 19. Of course, Columbus might have used the name simply descriptively, — cold land; but it is now known that in a sea chart of perhaps the fifteenth century, preserved in the Ambrosian library at Milan, the name "Fixlanda" is applied to an island in the position of Frislanda in the Zeno chart, while in a Catalan chart of the end of the fifteenth century the same island is apparently called "Frixlanda" (*Studi biog. e bibliog. della soc. geog. ital.*, ii. nos. 400, 404). "Frixanda" is also on a chart, A. D. 1471–83, given in facsimile to accompany Wuttke's "Geschichte der Erdkunde" in the *Jahrbuch des Vereins für Erdkunde* (Dresden, 1870, tab. vi.).

* From the *Isolario* (Venice, 1547).

by the Spanish discoveries. It was also calculated to appeal to the national pride of Italy, which had seen Spain gain the glory of her own sons, Columbus and Vespucius, if it could be established that these distant regions, of which the Zeni brothers so early reported tidings, were really the great new world.[1] The cartography of the sixteenth century shows that the narrative and its accompanying map made an impression on the public mind, but from that day to this it has been apparent that there can be no concurrence of opinion as to what island the Frislanda of the Zeni was, if it existed at all except in some disordered or audacious mind; and, as a matter of course, the distant regions of Estotiland and Drogeo have been equally the subject of belief and derision. No one can be said wholly to have taken the story out of the category of the uncertain.

THE SEA OF DARKNESS.
(From Olaus Magnus.)

The presence of the Basques on the coasts of North America long before the voyage of Columbus is often asserted,[2] and there is no improbability in a daring race of seamen, in search of whales, finding a way to the American waters. There are some indications in the early cartography which can perhaps be easily explained on this hypothesis;[3] there are said to be unusual linguistic correspondences in the American tongues with those of this strange people.[4] There are the reports of the earliest navi-

[1] Irving's *Columbus* takes this view.

[2] J. P. Leslie's *Man's Origin and Destiny*, p. 114, for instance.

[3] Brevoort (*Hist. Mag.*, xiii. 45) thinks that the "Isola Verde" and "Isle de Mai" of the fifteenth-century maps, lying in lat. 46° north, was Newfoundland with its adjacent bank, which he finds in one case represented. Samuel Robertson (*Lit. & Hist. Soc. Quebec*, *Trans.* Jan. 16) goes so far as to say that certain relics found in Canada may be Basque, and that it was a Basque whaler, named Labrador, who gave the name to the coast, which the early Portuguese found attached to it! We find occasional stories indicating knowledge of distant fishing coasts at a very early date, like the following: —

"In the yeere 1153 it is written that there came to Lubec, a citie of Germanie, one canoa with certaine indians, like unto a long barge, which seemed to have come from the coast of Baccalaos, which standeth in the same latitude that Germanie doth" (*Galvano*, Bethune's edition, p. 56).

[4] W. D. Whitney, *Life and Growth of Lan-*

gators, who have left indisputable records that earlier visitors from Europe had been before them, and Cabot may have found some reminders of such;[1] and it is even asserted that it was a Basque mariner, who had been on the Newfoundland banks, and gave to Columbus some premonitions of the New World.[2]

Certain claims of the Dutch have also been advanced;[3] and one for an early discovery of Newfoundland, in 1463–64, by John Vas Costa Cortereal was set forth by Barrow in his *Chronological Hist. of Voyages into the Arctic Regions* (London, 1818); but he stands almost alone in his belief.[4] Biddle in his *Cabot* has shown its great improbability.

In the years while Columbus was nourishing his purpose of a western voyage, there were two adventurous navigators, as alleged, who were breasting the dangers of the Sea of Darkness both to the north and to the south. It

guage, p. 258, says: "No other dialect of the old world so much resembles in structure the American languages." Cf. Farrar's *Families of Speech*, p. 132; Nott and Gliddon's *Indigenous Races*, 48; H. de Charencey's *Des affinités de la langue Basque avec les idiomes du Nouveau Monde* (Paris and Caen, 1867); and Julien Vinson's "La langue basque et les langues Américaines" in the *Compte Rendu, Congrès des Américanistes* (Nancy, 1875), ii. 46. On the other hand, Joly (*Man before Metals*, 316) says: "Whatever may be said to the contrary, Basque offers no analogy with the American dialects."

These linguistic peculiarities enter into all the studies of this remarkable stock. Cf. J. F. Blade's *Etude sur l'origine des Basques* (Paris, 1869); W. B. Dawkins in the *Fortnightly Review*, Sept., 1874, and his *Cave Hunting*, ch. 6, with Brabrook's critique in the *Journal Anthropological Institute*, v. 5; and Julien Vinson on "L'Ethnographie des Basques" in *Mém. de la Soc. d'Ethnographie, Session de 1872*, p. 49, with a map.

[1] But see Vol. III. 45; IV. 3. Forster (*Northern Voyages*, book iii. ch. 3 and 4) contends for these pre-Columbian visits of the European fishermen. Cf. Winsor's *Bibliog. of Ptolemy*, sub anno 1508. The same currents and easterly trade-winds which helped Columbus might easily have carried chance vessels to the American coasts, as we have evidence, apparently, in the stern-post of a European vessel which Columbus saw at Guadaloupe. Haven cites Gumilla (*Hist. Orinoco*, ii. 208) as stating that in 1731 a bateau from Teneriffe was thrown upon the South American coast. Cf. J. P. Casselius, *De Navigationibus fortuitis in Americam, ante Columbum factis* (Magdeburg, 1742); Brasseur's *Popul Vuh*, introd.; Hunt's *Merchants' Mag.* xxv. 275.

[2] Francisque-Michel, *Le Pays Basque*, 189, who says that the Basques were acquainted with the coasts of Newfoundland a century before Columbus (ch. 9).

Humboldt (*Cosmos*, Eng. ed. ii. 142) is not prepared to deny such early visits of the Basques to the northern fishing grounds. Cf. Gaffarel's *Rapport*, p. 212. Harrisse (*Notes on Columbus*, 80) goes back very far: "The Basques and Northmen, we feel confident, visited these shores as early as the seventh century."

There are some recent studies on these early fishing experiences in Ferd. Duro's *Disquisiciones nauticas* (1881), and in E. Gelcich's "Der Fischgang des Gascogner und die Entdeckung von Neufundland," in the *Zeitschrift der Gesellschaft für Erdkunde zu Berlin* (1883), vol. xviii. pp. 249–287.

[3] Cf. M. Hamconius' *Frisia: seu de viris erbusque Frisiæ illustribus* (Franckeræ, 1620), and L. Ph. C. v. d. Bergh's *Nederlands annspraak op de ontdekking van Amerika voor Columbus* (Arnheim, 1850). Cf. Müller's *Catalogue* (1877), nos. 303, 1343.

[4] Watson's bibliog. in Anderson, p. 158.

A Biscayan merchant, a subject of Navarre, is also said to have discovered the western lands in 1444. Cf. André Favyn, *Hist. de Navarre*, p. 564; and G. de Henao's *Averignaciones de las Antigüedades de Cantabria*, p. 25.

Galvano (Hakluyt Soc. ed., p. 72) recounts the story of a Portuguese ship in 1447 being driven westward from the Straits of Gibraltar to an island with seven cities, where they found the people speaking Portuguese; who said they had deserted their country on the death of King Roderigo. "All these reasons seem to agree," adds Galvano, "that this should be that country which is called Nova Spagna."

It was the year (1491) before Columbus' voyage that the English began to send out from Bristol expeditions to discover these islands of the seven cities, and others having the same legendary existence. Cf. Ayala, the Spanish ambassador to England, in *Spanish State Papers*, i. 177. Cf. also Irving's *Columbus*, app. xxiv., and Gaffarel's *Etude sur la rapports*, etc., p. 185.

cannot be said that either the Pole Skolno, in his skirting the Labrador coasts in 1476,[1] or the Norman Cousin, who is thought to have traversed a part of the South American coast in 1488–89,[2] have passed with their exploits into the accepted truths of history; but there was nothing improbable in what was said of them, and they flourish as counter-rumors always survive when attendant upon some great revelation like that of Columbus.

1 See Vol. II. p. 34.

2 See Vol. II. p. 34, where is a list of references, which may be increased as follows: Bachiller y Morales, *Antigüedades Americanas* (Havana, 1845). E. de Freville's *Mémoire sur le Commerce maritime de Rouen* (1857), i. 328, and his *La Cosmographie du moyen age, et les découvertes maritimes des Normands* (Paris, 1860), taken from the *Revue des Sociétés Savantes*. Gabriel Gravier's *Les Normands sur la route des Indes*, (Rouen, 1880). Cf. *Congrès des Américanistes* in *Compte Rendu* (1875), i. 397.

CRITICAL NOTES ON THE SOURCES OF INFORMATION.

A. Early Connection of Asiatic Peoples with the Western Coast of America. — The question of the origin of the Americans, whether an autochthonous one or associated with the continents beyond either ocean, is more properly discussed in another place of the present volume. We can only indicate here in brief such of the phases of the question as suppose an Asiatic connection, and the particular lines of communication.

The ethnic unity of the American races, as urged by Morton and others, hardly meets the requirements of the problem in the opinion of most later students, like Sir Daniel Wilson, for instance; and yet, if A. H. Keane represents, as he claims, the latest ethnological beliefs, the connection with Asia, of the kind that forms ethnic traces, must have been before the history of the present Asiatic races, since the correspondence of customs, etc. is not sufficient for more recent affiliation.[1] It should be remembered also, that if this is true, and if there is the strong physical resemblance between Asiatics and the indigenous tribes of the northwest coast which early travellers and physiologists have dwelt on, we have in such a correspondence strong evidence of the persistency of types.[2]

The Asiatic theory was long a favorite one. So popular a book as Lafitau's *Mœurs des Sauvages* (Paris, 1724) advocated it. J. B. Scherer's *Recherches historiques et géographiques sur le nouveau monde* (Paris, 1777) was on the same side. One of the earliest in this country, Benj. Smith Barton, to give expression to American scholarship in this field held like opinions in his *New Views of the Origin of the Tribes of America* (Philad., 1797).[3] Twenty years later (1816) one of the most active of the American men of letters advocated the same views, — Samuel L. Mitchell in the *Archæologia Americana* (i. 325, 338, 346). The weightiest authority of his time, Alex. von Humboldt, formulated his belief in several of his books: *Vues des Cordillères; Ansichten der Natur; Cosmos.*[4]

1 "Ethnography and Philology of America," in H. W. Bates, *Central America, West Indies, and South America* (Lond., 1882). This was the opinion of Prescott (*Mexico*, Kirk's ed., iii. 398), and he based his judgment on the investigations of Waldeck, *Voyage dans la Yucatan*, and Dupaix, *Antiquités Méxicaines*. Stephens (*Central America*) holds similar views. Cf. Wilson, *Prehistoric Man*, i. 327; ii. 43. Dall (*Third Rep. Bur. Ethnol.*, 146) says: "There can be no doubt that America was populated in some way by people of an extremely low grade of culture at a period even geologically remote. There is no reason for supposing, however, that immigration ceased with these original people."

2 Cf. references in H. H. Bancroft's *Native Races*, v. 39; *Amerika's Nordwest Küste; Neueste Ergebnisse ethnologischer Reisen* (Berlin, 1883), and the English version, *The Northwest Coast of America. Being Results of Recent Ethnological Researches from the collections of the Royal Museums at Berlin. Published by the Directors of the Ethnological Department* (New York, 1883).

3 Cf. his *Observations on some remains of antiquity* (1796).

4 Different shades of belief are abundant: F. Xavier de Orrio's *Solucion del gran problema* (Mexico, 1763); Fischer's *Conjecture sur l'origine des Américaines*; Adair's *Amer. Indians*; G. A. Thompson's *New theory of the two hemispheres* (London, 1815); Adam Hodgson's *Letters from No. Amer.* (Lond., 1824); J. H. McCulloh's *Researches* (Balt., 1829), ch. 10; D. B. Warden's "Recherches sur les Antiquités de

Of the northern routes, that by Behring's Straits is the most apparent, and Lyell says that when half-way over Dover Straits, which have not far from the same dimensions, he saw both the English and French shores at the same time, he was easily convinced that the

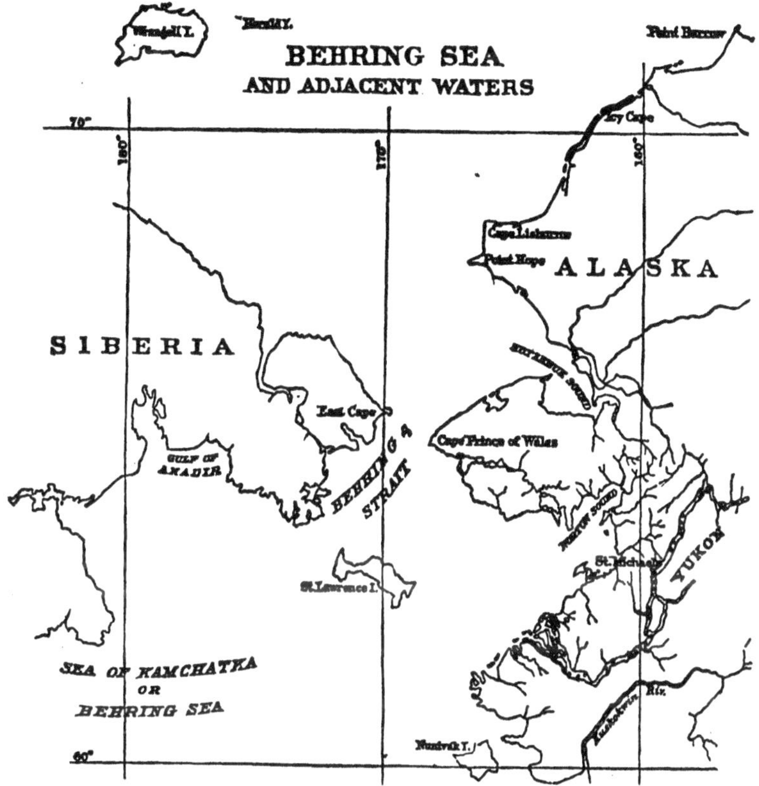

l'Amérique" in the *Antiquités Méxicaines* (Paris, 1834), vol. ii.; E. G. Squier's *Serpent Symbol* (N. Y., 1851); Brasseur de Bourbourg's *Hist. des Nations Civilisées*, i. 7; José Perez in *Revue Orientale et Américaine* (Paris, 1862), vol. viii.; Bancroft's *Native Races*, v. 30, 31, with references; Winchell's *Preadamites*, 397; a paper on Asiatic tribes in North America, in *Canadian Institute Proceedings* (1881), i. 171. Dabry de Thiersant, in his *Origine des Indiens du nouv. monde* (Paris, 1883), reopens the question, and Quatrefages even brings the story of Moncacht-Ape (see *post*, Vol. V. p. 77) to support a theory of frequent Asiatic communication. Tylor (*Early Hist. Mankind*, 209) says that the Asiatics must have taught the Mexicans to make bronze and smelt iron; and (p. 339) he finds additional testimony in the correspondence of myths, but Max Müller (*Chips*, ii. 168) demurs. Nadaillac, in his *L'Amérique préhistorique*, discussed this with the other supposable connections of the American people, and generally disbelieved in them; but Dall, in the English translation, summarily dismisses all consideration of them as unworthy a scientific mind; but points out what the early Indian traditions are (p. 526).

A good deal of stress has been laid at times on certain linguistic affiliations. Barton, in his *New Views*, sought to strengthen the case by various comparative vocabularies. Charles Farcy went over the proofs in his *Antiquités de l'Amérique: Discuter la valeur des documents relatifs à l'histoire de l'Amérique avant la conquête des Européens, et déterminer s'il existe des rapports entre les langues de l'Amérique et celles des tribus de l'Afrique et de l'Asie* (Paris, 1836). H. H. Bancroft (*Native Races*, v. 39) enumerates the sources of the controversy. Roehrig (*Smithsonian Report*, 1872) finds affinities in the languages of the Dakota or Sioux Indians. Pilling (*Bibliog. of Siouan languages*, p. 11) gives John Campbell's contributions to this comparative study. In the *Canadian Institute Proceedings* (1881), vol. i. p. 171, Campbell points out the affinities of the Tinneh with the Tungus, and of the Choctaws and Cherokees with the Ko-

NOTE. — Sketch map from the *U. S. Geodetic Survey*, 1880, App. xvi; also in *Journal Amer. Geog. Soc.*, xv. p. 114. Cf. Bancroft's *Nat. Races*, i. 35.

passage by Behring's Straits solved many of the difficulties of the American problem.[1]

The problem as to the passage by the Aleutian Islands is converted into the question whether primitive people could have successfully crossed an interval from Asia of 130 miles to reach the island Miedna, 126 more to Behring's Island, and then 235 to Attu, the westernmost of the Aleutian Islands, or nearly 500 miles in all, and to have crossed in such numbers as to affect the peopling of the new continent. There are some, like Winchell, who see no difficulty in the case.[2] There are no authenticated relics, it is believed, to prove the Tartar occupancy of the northwest of America.[3] That there have been occasional estrays upon the coasts of British Columbia, Oregon, and California, by the drifting thither of Chinese and Japanese junks, is certainly to be believed; but the argument against their crews peopling the country is usually based upon the probable absence of women in them, — an argument that certainly does not invalidate the belief in an infusion of Asiatic blood in a previous race.[4]

The easterly passage which has elicited most interest is one alleged to have been made by some Buddhist priests to a country called Fusang, and in proof of it there is cited the narrative of one Hœi-Shin, who is reported to have returned to China in A. D. 499. Beside much in the story that is ridiculous and impossible, there are certain features which have led some commentators to believe that the coast of Mexico was intended, and that the Mexican maguey plant was the tree fusang, after which the country is said to have been called. The story was first brought to the attention of Europeans in 1761, when De Guignes published his paper on the subject in the 28th volume (pp. 505–26) of the Academy of Inscriptions.[5] It seems to have attracted little attention till J. H. von Klaproth, in 1831, discredited the American theory in his "Recherches sur le pays de Fousang," published in the *Nouvelles Annales des Voyages* (2d ser., vol. xxi.), accompanied by a chart. In 1834 there appeared at Paris a French translation, *Annales des Empereurs du Japon* (*Nipon o dai itsi rau*), to which (vol. iv.) Klaproth appended an "Aperçu de l'histoire mythologique du Japon," in which he returned to the subject, and convinced Humboldt at least,[6] that the country visited was Japan, and not Mexico, though he could but see striking analogies, as he thought, in the Mexican myths and customs to those of the Chinese.[7]

In 1841, Karl Friedrich Neumann, in the *Zeit-*

riaks. Cf. also *Ibid.*, July, 1884. Dall and Pinart pronounce against any affinity of tongues in the *Contributions to Amer. Ethnology* (Washington), i. 97. Cf. Short, *No. Amer. of Antiq.*, 494; Leland's *Fusang*, ch. 10.

1 Behring's Straits, first opened, as Wallace says, in quaternary times, are 45 miles across, and are often frozen in winter. South of them is an island where a tribe of Eskimos live, and they keep constant communication with the main of Asia, 50 miles distant, and with America, 120 miles away. Robertson solved the difficulty by this route. Cf. *Contributions to Amer. Ethnology* (1877), i. 95–98; Warden's *Recherches;* Maury, in *Revue des deux Mondes*, Ap. 15, 1858; Peschel's *Races of Men*, p. 401; F. von Hellwald in *Smithsonian Report*, 1866; Short, p. 510; Bancroft, *Native Races*, v. 28, 29, 54; and Chavanne's *Lit. of the Polar Regions*, 58, 194 — the last page shows a list of maps. Max Müller (*Chips*, ii. 270) considers this theory a postulate only.

2 *Contrib. to Amer. Ethnology*, i. 96; Lyell's *Principles of Geology*, 8th ed., 368; A. Ragine's *Découverte de l'Amérique du Kamtchatka et des îles Aléoutiennes* (St. Petersburg, 1868, 2d ed.); Pickering's *Races of Men;* Peschel's *Races of Men*, 397; Morgan's *Systems of Consanguinity*. Dall (*Tribes of the Northwest*, in Powell's *Rocky Mountain Region*, 1877, p. 96) does not believe in the Aleutian route.

On the drifting of canoes for long distances see Lyell's *Principles of Geology*, 11th ed., ii. 472; Col. B. Kennon in Leland's *Fousang; Rev. des deux Mondes*, Apr., 1858; Vining, ch. 1. Cf. Alphonse Pinart's "Les Aléoutes et leur origine," in *Mém. de la Soc. d'Ethnographie, session de 1872*, p. 155.

3 Cf. references in H. H. Bancroft's *Nat. Races*, v. 54. We have an uncorroborated story of a Tartar inscription being found. Cf. Kalm's *Reise*, iii. 416; *Archæologia* (London, 1787), viii. 304.

4 Gomara makes record of such floating visitors in the beginning of the sixteenth century. Horace Davis published in the *Amer. Antiq. Soc. Proc.* (Apr., 1872) a record of Japanese vessels driven upon the northwest coast of America and its outlying islands in a paper "On the likelihood of an admixture of Japanese blood on our northwest coast." Cf. A. W. Bradford's *American Antiquities* (N. Y., 1841); Whymper's *Alaska*, 250; Bancroft's *Nat. Races*, v. 52, with references; *Contributions to Amer. Ethnol.*, i. 97, 238; De Roquefeuil's *Journal du Voyage autour du Monde* (1876–79), etc. It is shown that the great Pacific current naturally carries floating objects to the American coast. Davis, in his tract, gives a map of it. Cf. Haven, *Archæol. U. S.*, p. 144; *Bull. Amer. Geog. Soc.* (1883), xv. p. 101, by Thomas Antisell; and *China Review*, Mar., Apr., 1888, by J. Edkins.

5 *Recherches sur les navigations des Chinois du côte de l'Amérique et sur quelques peuples situés à l'extrémité orientale de l'Asie* (Paris, 1761). It is translated in Vining, ch. 1.

6 *Examen Critique*, ii. 65, and *Ansichten der Natur*, or *Views of Nature*, p. 132.

7 Much depends on the distance intended by a Chinese *li*. Klaproth translated the version as given by an

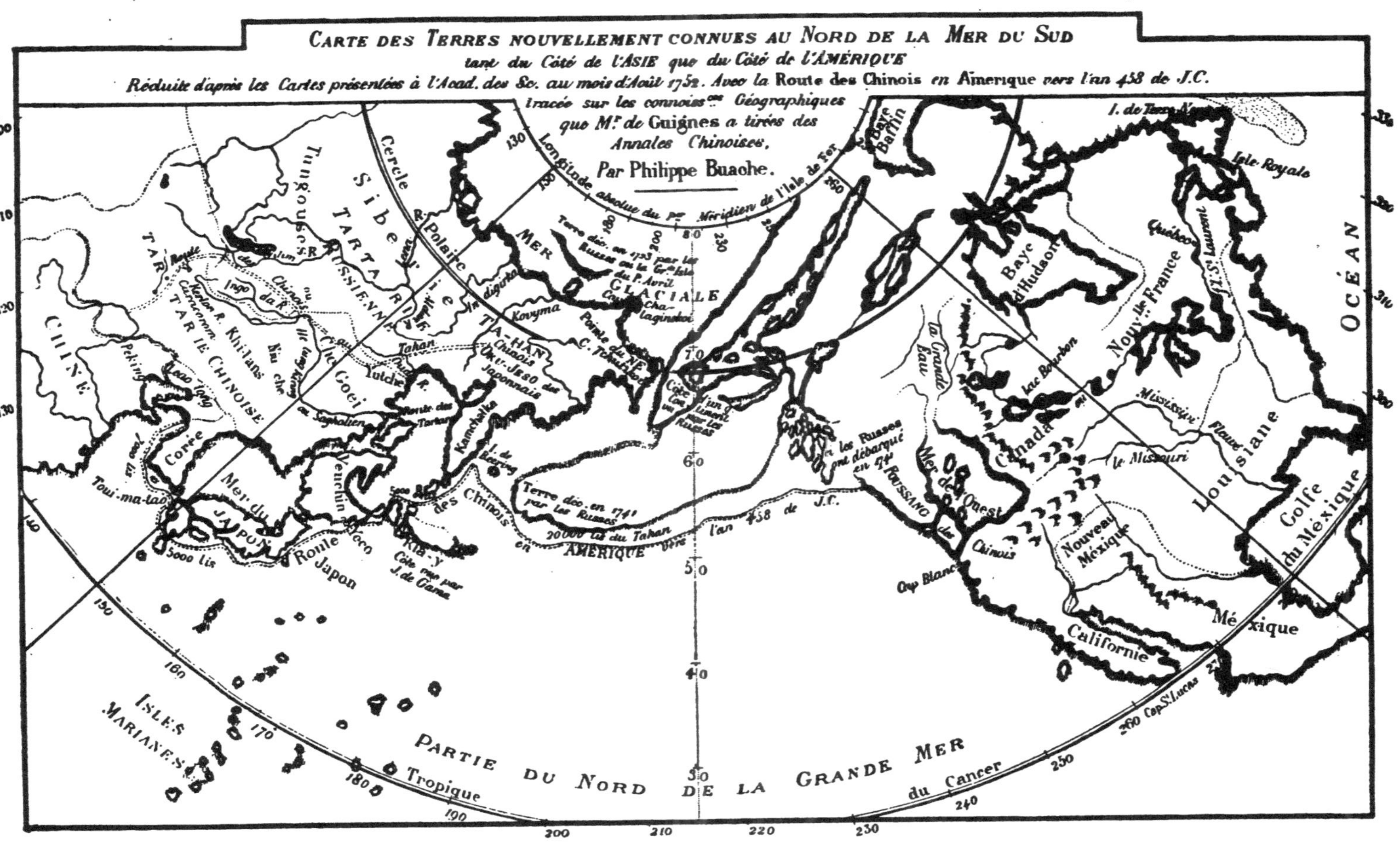

NOTE. — The map of Buache, 1752, showing De Guignes' route of the Chinese emigration to Fusang. Reduced from the copy in the *Congrès internationale des Américanistes, Compte Rendu, Nancy, 1875.*

schrift für allgemeine Erdkunde (new series, vol. xvi.), published a paper on "Ost Asien und West Amerika nach Chinesischen Quellen aus dem fünften, sechsten und siebenten Jahrhundert," in which he gave a version of the Hœi-shin (Hœi-schin, Hui-shĕn) narrative, which Chas. G. Leland, considering it a more perfect form of the original than that given by De Guignes, translated into English in *The Knickerbocker Mag.* (1850), xxxvi. 301, as "California and Mexico in the fifth century."[1]

The next to discuss the question, and in an affirmative spirit, was Charles Hippolyte de Paravey, in the *Annales de Philosophie Chrétienne* (Feb., 1844), whose paper was published separately as *L'Amérique sous le nom de pays de Fou-Sang, est elle citée dès le 5e siècle de notre ère, dans les grandes annales de la Chine*, etc. *Discussion ou dissertation abrégée, où l'affirmative est prouvée* (Paris, 1844); and in 1847 he published *Nouvelles preuves que le pays du Fousang est l'Amérique.*[2]

The controversy as between De Guignes and Klaproth was shared, in 1862, by Gustave d'Eichthal, taking the Frenchman's side, in the *Revue Archéologique* (vol. ii.), and finally in his *Etudes sur les origines Bouddhiques de la civilisation Américaine* (Paris, 1865).[3]

In 1870, E. Bretschneider, in his "Fusang, or who discovered America?" in the *Chinese Recorder and Missionary Journal* (Foochow, Oct., 1870), contended that the whole story was the fabrication of a lying priest.[4]

In 1875 there was new activity in discussing the question. Two French writers of considerable repute in such studies attracted attention: the one, Lucien Adam, in the Congrès des Américanistes at Nancy (*Compte Rendu*, i. 145); and the other, Léon de Rosny, entered the discussions at the same session (*Ibid.* i. p. 131).[5]

The most conspicuous study for the English reader was Charles Godfrey Leland's *Fusang, or The discovery of America by Chinese Buddhist priests in the fifth century* (London, 1875).[6]

The Marquis d'Hervey de Saint Denis published in the *Actes de la Soc. d'Ethnographie* (1869), vol. vi., and later in the *Comptes Rendus* of the French Academy of Inscriptions, a *Mémoire sur le pays connu des anciens Chinois sous le nom de Fou-sang, et sur quelques documents inédits pour servir à l'identifier*, which was afterwards published separately in Paris, 1876, in which he assented to the American theory. The student of the subject need hardly go, however, beyond E. P. Vining's *An inglorious Columbus: or, Evidence that Hwui Shăn and a party of Buddhist monks from Afghanistan discovered America in the fifth century* A. D. (New York, 1885), since the compiler has made it a repository of all the essential contributions to the question from De Guignes down. He gives the geographical reasons for believing Fusang to be Mexico (ch. 20), comparing the original description of Fusang with the early accounts of aboriginal Mexico, and rehearsing the traditions, as is claimed, of the Buddhists still found

early Chinese historian of the seventh century, Li Yan Tcheou, and Klaproth's version is Englished in Bancroft's *Nat. Races*, v. 33–36. Klaproth's memoir is also translated in Vining, ch. 3. Some have more specifically pointed to Saghalien, an island at the north end of the Japan Sea. Brooks says there is a district of Corea called Fusang (*Science*, viii. 402). Brasseur says the great Chinese encyclopædia describes Fusang as lying east of Japan, and he thinks the descriptions correspond to the Cibola of Castañeda.

1 Again with a commentary in *The Continental Mag.* (New York, vol. i.). Subjected to the revision of Neumann, it is reproduced in Leland's *Fusang* (Lond., 1875). Cf. Vining, ch. 6, who gives also (ch. 10) the account in Shan-Hai-king as translated by C. M. Williams in *Mag. Amer. Hist.*, April, 1883.

2 The pamphlets are translated in Vining, ch. 4 and 5. Paravey held to the Mexican theory, and he at least convinced Domenech (*Seven years' residence in the great deserts of No. Amer.*, Lond., 1860). Paravey published several pamphlets on subjects allied to this. His *Mémoire sur l'origine japonaise, arabe et basque de la civilisation des peuples du plateau de Bogota d'après les travaux de Humboldt et Siebold* (Paris, 1835) is a treatise on the origin of the Muyscas or Chibchas. Jomard, in his *Les Antiquités Américaines au point de vue des progrès de la géographie* (Paris, 1817) in the *Bull. de la Soc. Géog.*, had questioned the Asiatic affiliations, and Paravey replied in a *Réfutation de l'opinion émise par Jomard que les peuples de l'Amérique n'ont jamais en aucun rapport avec ceux de l'Asie* (Paris, 1849), originally in the *Annales de philosophie Chrétienne* (May, 1849).

3 Also in the *Rev. Archéologique* (vols. x., xi.), and epitomized in Leland. Cf. also Dr. A. Godron on the Buddhist mission to America in *Annales des Voyages* (Paris, 1864), vol. iv., and an opposing view by Vivien de St. Martin in *L'Année géographique* (1865), iii. p. 253, who was in turn controverted by Brasseur in his *Monuments Anciens du Méxique*.

4 This paper is reprinted in Leland.

5 Cf. also his *Variétés Orientales*, 1872; and his "L'Amérique, etait-elle connue des Chinois à l'époque du déluge?" in the *Archives de la Soc. Amér. de France*, n. s., iii. 191.

6 S. W. Williams, in the *Journal of the American Oriental Soc.* (vol. xi.), in controverting the views of Leland, was inclined to find Fusang in the Loo-choo Islands. This paper was printed separately as *Notices of Fusang and other countries lying east of China in the Pacific ocean* (New Haven, 1881).

by the Spaniards pervading the memories of the natives, and at last (ch. 37) summarizing all the grounds of his belief.[1]

The consideration of the Polynesian route as a possible avenue for peopling America involves the relations of the Malays to the inhabitants of the Oceanic Islands and the capacity of early man to traverse long distances by water.[2]

E. B. Tylor has pointed out the Asiatic relations of the Polynesians in the *Journal of the Anthropological Inst.*, xi. 401. Pickering, in the

[1] A good deal of labor has been bestowed to prove this identity of Fusang with Mexico. It is held to be found in the myths and legends of the two people by Charency in his *Mythe de Votan, étude sur les origines asiatiques de la civilisation américaine* (Alençon, 1871), drawn from the *Actes de la Soc. philologique* (vol. ii.); and he has enforced similar views in the *Revue des questions historiques* (vi. 283), and in his *Djemschid et Quetzalcohuatl. L'histoire légendaire de la Nouvelle-Espagne rapprochée de la source indo-européenne* (Alençon, 1874). Humboldt thought it strange, considering other affinities, — as for instance in the Mexican calendars, — that he could find no Mexican use of phallic symbols; but Bancroft says they exist. Cf. *Native Races*, iii. 501; also see v. 40, 232; Brasseur's *Quatre Lettres*, p. 202; and John Campbell's paper on the traditions of Mexico and Peru as establishing such connections, in the *Compte Rendu, Congrès des Amér.* (Nancy, 1875), i. 348. Dr. Hamy saw in a monument found at Copan an inscription which he thought was the Taë-kai of the Chinese, the symbol of the essence of all things (*Bull. de la Soc. de Géog.*, 1886, and *Journal of the Anthropological Institute*, xvi. 242, with a cut of the stone). Dall controverts this point (*Science*, viii. 402).

Others have dwelt on the linguistic resemblances. B. S. Barton in his *New Views* pressed this side of the question. The presence of a monosyllabic tongue like the Otomi in the midst of the polysyllabic languages of Mexico has been thought strongly to indicate a survival. Cf. Manuel Najera's *Disertacion sobre la lengua Othomi*, Mexico, 1845, and in *Amer. Philos. Soc. Trans.*, n. s., v.; Ampère's *Promenade en Amérique*, ii. 301; Prescott's *Mexico*, iii. 396; Warden's *Recherches* (in Dupaix), p. 125; Latham's *Races of Men*, 408; Bancroft's *Nat. Races*, iii. 737; v. 39, with references. Others find Sanskrit roots in the Mexican. E. B. Tylor has indicated the Asiatic origin of certain Mexican games (*Journal of the Anthropol. Inst.*, xxiv.). Ornaments of jade found in Nicaragua, while the stone is thought to be native only in Asia, is another indication, and they are more distinctively Asiatic than the jade ornaments found in Alaska (*Peabody Mus. Reports*, xviii. 414; xx. 548; *Proc. Mass. Hist. Soc.*, Jan., 1886).

On the general question of the Asiatic origin of the Mexicans see Dupaix's *Antiquités Mexicaines*, with included papers by Lenoir, Warden, and Farcy; the *Report* on a railroad route from the Mississippi, 1853-54 (Washington); Whipple's and other *Reports* on the Indian tribes; John Russell Bartlett's *Personal Narrative* (1854); Brasseur's *Popul Vuh*, p. xxxix; Viollet le Duc's belief in a "yellow race" building the Mexican and Central American monuments, in Charnay's *Ruines Américaines*, and Charnay's traces of the Buddhists in the *Popular Science Monthly*, July, 1879, p. 432; Le Plongeon's belief in the connection of the Maya and Asiatic races in *Amer. Antiq. Soc. Proc.*, Apr. 30, 1879, p. 113; and some papers on the ancient Mexicans and their origin by the Abbé Jolibois, Col. Parmentier, and M. Emile Guimet, which, prepared for the Soc. de Géog. de Lyon, were published separately as *De l'origine des Anciens Peuples du Mexique* (Lyon, 1875).

A few other incidental discussions of the Fusang question are these: R. H. Major in *Select Letters of Columbus* (1847); J. T. Short in *The Galaxy* (1875) and in his *No. Americans of Antiquity*; Nadaillac in his *L'Amérique préhistorique*, 544; Gay's *Pop. Hist. U. S.* calls the story vague and improbable. In periodicals we find: *Gentleman's Mag.*, 1869, p. 333 (reprinted in *Hist. Mag.*, Sept., 1869, xvi. 221), and 1870, reproduced in *Chinese Recorder*, May, 1870; Nathan Brown in *Amer. Philolog. Mag.*, Aug., 1869; Wm. Speer in *Princeton Rev.*, xxv. 83; *Penn Monthly*, vi. 603; *Mag. Amer. Hist.*, Apr., 1883, p. 291; *Notes and Queries*, iii. 58, 78; iv. 19; *Notes and Queries in China and Japan*, Apr., May, 1869; Feb., 1870. Chas. W. Brooks maintained on the other hand (*Proc. California Acad. Sciences*, 1876; cf. Bancroft's *Native Races*, v. 51), that the Chinese were emigrants from America. There is a map of the supposed Chinese route to America in the *Congrès des Américanistes* (Nancy, 1875), vol. i.; and Winchell, *Pre-Adamites*, gives a chart showing different lines of approach from Asia. Stephen Powers (*Overland Monthly*, Apr., 1872, and *California Acad. Sciences*, 1875) treats the California Indians as descendants of the Chinese, — a view he modifies in the *Contrib. to Amer. Ethnology*, vol. iii., on "Tribes of California." It is claimed that Chinese coin of the fifteenth century have been found in mounds on Vancouver's Island. Cf. G. P. Thurston in *Mag. Amer. Hist.*, xiii. p. 457. The principal lists of authorities are those in Vining (app.), and Watson's in Anderson's *America not discovered by Columbus*.

[2] From Easter Island to the Galapagos is 2,000 miles, thence to South America 600 more. On such long migrations by water see Waitz, *Introduction to Anthropology*, Eng. transl., p. 202. On early modes of navigation see Col. A. Lane Fox in the *Journal Anthropological Inst.* (1875), iv. 399. Otto Caspari gives a map of post-tertiary times in his *Urgeschichte der Menschheit* (Leipzig, 1873), vol. i., in which land is made to stretch from the Marquesas Islands nearly to South America; while large patches of land lie between Asia and Mexico, to render migration practicable. Andrew Murray, in his *Geographical Distribution of Mammals*

ethnological chart accompanying the reports of the Wilkes Expedition, makes the original people of Chili and Peru to be Malay, and he connects the Californians with the Polynesians.[1]

The earliest elaboration of this theory was in John Dunmore Lang's *View of the origin and migrations of the Polynesian nations, demonstrating their ancient discovery and progressive settlement of the continent of America* (London, 1834; 2d ed., Sydney, 1877). Francis A. Allen has advanced similar views at the meetings of the Congrès des Américanistes at Luxembourg and at Copenhagen.[2]

The Mongol theory of the occupation of Peru, which John Ranking so enthusiastically pressed in his *Historical researches on the conquest of Peru, Mexico, Bogota, Natchez, and Talomeco, in the thirteenth century, by the Mongols, accompanied with elephants; and the local agreement of history and tradition, with the remains of elephants and mastodontes found in the new world* [etc.] (London, 1827), implies that in the thirteenth century the Mongol emperor Kublai Khan sent a fleet against Japan, which, being scattered in a storm, finally in part reached the coasts of Peru, where the son of Kublai Khan became the first Inca.[3] The book hardly takes rank as a sensible contribution to ethnology, and Prescott says of it that it embodies "many curious details of Oriental history and manners in support of a whimsical theory."[4]

B. IRELAND THE GREAT, OR WHITE MAN'S LAND. — The claims of the Irish to have preceded the Norse in Iceland, and to have discovered America, rest on an Icelandic saga, which represents that in the tenth century Are Marson, driven off his course by a gale, found a land which became known as Huitramannaland, or white man's land, or otherwise as Irland it Mikla.[5] This region was supposed by the colonists of Vinland to lie farther south, which Rafn[6] interprets as being along the Carolina coast,[7] and others have put it elsewhere, as Beauvois in Canada above the Great Lakes; and still others see no more in it than the pressing of some storm-driven vessel to the Azores[8] or some other Atlantic island. The story is also coupled, from another source, with the romance of Bjarni Asbrandson, who sailed away from Iceland and from a woman he loved, because the husband and relatives of the woman made it desirable that

(London, 1866), is almost compelled to admit (p. 25) that as complete a circuit of land formerly crossed the southern temperate regions as now does the northern; and Daniel Wilson, *Prehistoric Man*, holds much the same opinion. The connection of the flora of Polynesia and South America is discussed by J. D. Hooker in the *Botany of the Antarctic Voyage of the Erebus and Terror, 1839–43*, and in his *Flora of Tasmania*. Cf. *Amer. Journal of Science and Arts*, Mar., May, 1854; Jan., May, 1860.

1 *Races of Men*.

2 *Compte Rendu*, 1877, p. 79; 1883, p. 246; the latter being called "Polynesian Antiquities, a link between the ancient civilizations of Asia and America." Further discussions of the Polynesian migrations will be found as follows: A. W. Bradford's *Amer. Antiquities* (N. Y., 1841); Gallatin (*Am. Eth. Soc. Trans.*, i. 176) disputed any common linguistic traces, while Bradford thought he found such; Lesson and Martinet's *Les Polynésiens, leur origine, leurs migrations, leur langage;* Wilson's *Prehistoric Man*, ii. 344; Jules Garnier's "Les migrations polynésiennes" in *Bull. de la Soc. de Géog. de Paris*, Jan., June, 1870; G. d'Eichthal's "Etudes sur l'histoire primitive des races océaniennes et Américaines" in *Mem. de la Soc. Ethnologique* (vol. ii.); Marcoy's *Travels in South America;* C. Staniland Wake's *Chapters on Man*, p. 200; a "Rapport de la Polynésie et l'Amérique" in the *Mémoires de la Soc. Ethnologique*, ii. 223; A. de Quatrefages de Bréau's *Les Polynésiens et leurs migrations* (Paris, 1866), from the *Revue des deux Mondes*, Feb., 1864; O. F. Peschel in *Ausland*, 1864, p. 348; W. H. Dall in *Bureau of Ethnology Rept.*, 1881–82, p. 147. Allen's paper, already referred to, gives references.

3 Bancroft, *Nat. Races*, v. 44, with references, p. 48, epitomizes the story. Cf. Short, 151. There was a tradition of giants landing on the shore (Markham's *Cieza de Leon*, p. 190). Cf. Forster's *Voyages*, 43.

4 A belief in the Asiatic connection has taken some curious forms. Montesinos in his *Memorias Peruanas* held Peru to be the Ophir of Solomon. Cf. Gotfriedus Wegner's *De Navigationis Solomonæis* (Frankfort, 1689). Horn held Hayti to be Ophir, and he indulges in some fantastic evidences to show that the Iroquois, *i. e.* Yrcas, were Turks! Cf. Onffroy de Thoron in *Le Globe*, 1869. C. Wiener in his *L'Empire des Incas* (ch. 2, 4) finds traces of Buddhism, and so does Hyde Clarke in his *Khita-Peruvian Epoch* (1877). Lopez has written on *Les Races Aryennes de Pérou* (1871). Cf. Robert Ellis, *Peruvia Scythica. The Quicha Language of Peru, its derivation from Central Asia with the American languages in general* (London, 1875). Grotius held that the Peruvians were of Chinese stock. Charles Pickering's ethnological map gives a Malay origin to the islands of the Gulf of Mexico and a part of the Pacific coast, the rest being Mongolian.

5 The story is given in English by De Costa (*Pre-Columbian Disc. of America*, p. 85) from the *Landnámabók*, no. 107. Cf. *Saga of Thorfinn Karlsefne*, ch. 13, and that of Erik the Red. Leif is said in the sagas to have met shipwrecked white people on the coasts visited by him (*Hist. Mag.*, xiii. 46).

6 *Antiquitates Americanæ*, 162, 183, 205, 210, 211, 212, 214, 319, 446–51.

7 Brinton in *Hist. Mag.*, ix. 364; Rivero and Tschudi's *Peru*.

8 Schöning's *Heimskringla. Grönlands Historiske Mindesmærker*, i. 150.

he should. Thirty years later, the crew of another ship, wrecked on a distant coast,[1] found that the people who took them prisoners spoke Irish,[2] and that their chieftain was this same renegade, who let them go apparently for the purpose of conveying some token by which he would be remembered to the Thurid of his dreams. Of course all theorists who have to deal with these supposed early discoveries by Europeans connect, each with his own pet scheme, the prevailing legendary belief among the American Indians that white men at an early period made their appearance on the coasts all the way from Central America to Labrador.[3] Whether these strange comers be St. Patrick,[4] St. Brandan even, or some other Hibernian hero, with his followers, is easily to be adduced, if the disposing mind is inclined.

There have been of late years two considerable attempts to establish the historical verity of some of these alleged Irish visits.[5]

C. The Norse in Iceland. — The chief original source for the Norse settlement of Iceland is the famous *Landnamabók*,[6] which is a record by various writers, at different times, of the partitioning and ownership of lands during the earliest years of occupation.[7] This and other contemporary manuscripts, including the *Heimskringla* of Snorre Sturleson and the great body of Icelandic sagas, either at first hand or as filtered through the leading writers on Ice-

1 *Eyrbyggja Saga*, ch. 64, and given in English in De Costa's *Pre-Columbian Discovery*, p. 89. Cf. Sir Walter Scott's version of this saga and the appendix of Mallet's *Northern Antiquities*.

2 Traces of Celtic have been discovered by some of the philologists, when put to the task, in the American languages. Cf. Humboldt, *Relation Historique*, iii. 159. Lord Monboddo held such a theory.

3 Brinton's *Myths of the New World*, 176. One of the earliest accounts which we have of the Cherokees is that by Henry Timberlake (London, 1765), and he remarks on their lighter complexion as indicating a possible descent from these traditionary white men.

4 Richard Broughton's *Monasticon Britannicum* (London, 1655), pp. 131, 187.

5 *A Memoir on the European Colonization of America in ante-historic times* was contributed to the *Proceedings* of the American Ethnological Society in 1851, to which E. G. Squier added some notes, the original paper being by Dr. C. A. A. Zestermann of Leipzig. The aim was to prove, by the similarity of remains, the connection of the peoples who built the mounds of the Ohio Valley with the early peoples of northwestern Europe, a Caucasian race, which he would identify with the settlers of Irland it Mikla, and with the coming of the white-bearded men spoken of in Mexican traditions, who established a civilization which an inundating population from Asia subsequently buried from sight. This European immigration he places at least 1,200 years before Christ. Squier's comments are that the monumental resemblances referred to indicate similar conditions of life rather than ethnic connections.

The other advocate was Eugène Beauvois in a paper published in the *Compte Rendu du Congrès des Américanistes* (Nancy, 1875, p. 4) as *La découverte du nouveau monde par les irlandais et les premières traces du christianisme en Amérique avant l'an 1000*, accompanied by a map, in which he makes Irland it Mikla correspond to the provinces of Ontario and Quebec. Again, in the session at Luxembourg in 1877, he endeavored to connect the Irish colony with the narrative of the seaman in the Zeno accounts, in a paper which he called *Les Colonies Européennes du Markland et de l'Escociland au xiv. Siècle, et les vestiges qui en subsistèrent jusqu'aux xvie et xviie Siècles*, and in which he identifies the Estotiland of the Frislanda mariner. M. Beauvois again, at the Copenhagen meeting of the same body, read a paper on *Les Relations précolumbiennes des Gaels avec le Mexique* (Copenhagen, 1883, p. 74), in which he elicited objections from M. Lucien Adam. Beauvois belongs to that class of enthusiasts somewhat numerous in these studies of pre-Columbian discoveries, who have haunted these Congresses of Americanists, and who see overmuch. Other references to these Irish claims are to be found in Laing's *Heimskringla*, i. 186; Beamish's *Discovery of America* (London, 1841); Gravier's *Découverte de l'Amérique*, p. 123, 137, and his *Les Normands sur la route, etc.*, ch. 1; Gaffarel's *Etudes sur la rapports de l'Amérique*, pp. 201, 214; Brasseur's introd. to his *Popul Vuh;* De Costa's *Pre-Columbian Discovery*, pp. xviii, xlix, lii; Humboldt's *Cosmos* (Bohn), ii. 607; Rask in *Mass. Hist. Soc. Proc.*, xviii. 21; *Journal London Geog. Soc.*, viii. 125; Gay's *Pop. Hist. U. S.*, i. 53; and K. Wilhelmi's *Island, Hvitramannaland, Grönland und Vinland, oder Der Norrmänner Leben auf Island und Grönland und deren Fahrten nach Amerika schon über 500 Jahre vor Columbus* (Heidelberg, 1842).

6 The account in the Landnámabók is briefly rehearsed in ch. 8 of C. W. Paijkull's *Summer in Iceland* (London, 1868).

7 There are various editions, of which the best is called that of Copenhagen, 1843. The *Islendingabók*, a sort of epitome of a lost historical narrative, is considered an introduction to the *Landnámabók*. Much of the early story will be found in Latin in the *Islenzkir Annáler, sive Annales Islandici ab anno Christi 803 ad anno 1430* (Copenhagen, 1847); in the *Scripta historica Islandorum de rebus veterum Borealium*, published by the Royal Soc. of Northern Antiquaries at Copenhagen, 1828–46; and in Jacobus Langebek's *Scriptores Rerum Danicarum medii ævi* (Copenhagen, 1772–1878, — the ninth volume being a recently added index).

landic history, constitute the material out of which is made up the history of Iceland, in the days when it was sending its adventurous spirits to Greenland and probably to the American main.[1]

Respecting the body of the sagas, Laing (*Heimskringla*, i. 23) says: "It does not appear that any saga manuscript now existing has been written before the fourteenth century, however old the saga itself may be. It is known that in the twelfth century, Are Frode, Sæmund and others began to take the sagas out of the traditionary state and fix them in writing; but none of the original skins appear to have come down to our time, but only some of the numerous copies of them." Laing (p. 24) also instances numerous sagas known to have existed, but they are not now recognized;[2] and he gives us (p. 30) the substance of what is known respecting the writers and transcribers of this early saga literature. It is held that by the beginning of the thirteenth century the sagas of the discoveries and settlements had all been put in writing, and thus the history, as it exists, of mediæval Iceland is, as Burton says (*Ultima Thule*, i. 237), more complete than that of any European country.[3]

Among the secondary writers, using either at first or second hand the early MS. sources, the following may be mentioned: —

One of the earliest brought to the attention of the English public was *A Compendious Hist. of the Goths, Swedes and Vandals, and other northern powers* (London, 1650 and 1658), translated in an abridged form from the Latin of Olaus Magnus, which had been for more than a hundred years the leading comprehensive authority on the northern nations. The *Svearikes Historia* (Stockholm, 1746–62) of Olof von Dalin and the similar work of Sven Lagerbring (1769–1788), covering the early history of the north, are of interest for the comparative study of the north, rather than as elucidating the history of Iceland in particular.[4] More direct aid will be got from Mallet's *Northern Antiquities* (London edition, 1847) and from Wheaton's *Northmen.* More special is the *Histoire de l'Island* of Xavier Marmier; and the German historian F. C. Dahlman also touches Iceland with particular attention in his *Geschichte von Dänemark bis zur Reformation, mit Inbegriff von Norwegen und Island* (Hamburg, 1840–43).

A history of more importance than any other yet published, and of the widest scope, was that of Sweden by E. J. Geijer (continued by F. F. Carlson), which for the early period (down to 1654) is accessible in English in a translation by J. H. Turner (London, 1845).[5]

Prominent among the later school of northern historians, all touching the Icelandic annals more or less, have been Peter Andreas Munch in his *Det Norske Folks Historie* (Christiania, 1852–63);[6] N. M. Petersen in his *Danmarks Historie i Hedenold* (Copenhagen, 1854–55); K.

[1] A convenient survey of this early literature is in chapter 1 of the *History of the Literature of the Scandinavian North, from the most ancient times to the present, by Frederick Winkel Horn, revised by the author, and translated by Rasmus B. Anderson* (Chicago, 1884). The text is accompanied by useful bibliographical details. Cf. B. F. De Costa in *Journal Amer. Geog. Soc.* (1880), xii. 159.

[2] Saxo Grammaticus acknowledges his dependence on the Icelandic sagas, and is thought to have used some which had not been yet put into writing.

[3] Baring-Gould in his *Iceland, its Scenes and Sagas* (London, 1863) gives in his App. D a list of thirty-five published sagas, sixty-six local histories, twelve ecclesiastical annals, and sixty-nine Norse annals. Cf. the eclectic list in Laing's *Heimskringla*, i. 17.

Konrad Maurer has given an elaborate essay on this early literature in his *Ueber die Ausdrücke: altnordische, altnorwegische und isländische Sprache* (Munich, 1867), which originally appeared in the *Abhandlungen* of the Bavarian Academy.

G. P. Marsh translated P. E. Müller's "Origin, progress, and decline of Icelandic historical literature" in *The American Eclectic* (N. Y., 1841, — vols. i., ii.). In 1781, Lindblom printed at Paris a French translation of Bishop Troil's *Lettres sur l'Islande*, which contained a catalogue of books on Iceland and an enumeration of the Icelandic sagas. (Cf. Pinkerton's *Voyages*, vol. i.) Chavanne's *Bibliography of the Polar Regions*, p. 95, has a section on Iceland.

Solberg's list of illustrative works, appended to Anderson's version of Horn's *Lit. of the Scandinavian North*, is useful so far as the English language goes. Periodical contributions also appear in *Poole's Index* (p. 622) and *Supplement*, p. 214.

Burton (*Ultima Thule*, i. 239) enumerates the principal writers on Iceland from Arngrimur Jónsson down, including the travellers of this century.

[4] The more general histories of Scandinavia, like Sinding's English narrative, — not a good book, but accessible, — yield the comparisons more readily.

[5] There are also German (Gotha, 1844–75) and French versions (Paris). The best German version, *Geschichte Schwedens* (Hamburg and Gotha, 1832–1887), is in six volumes, a part of the *Geschichte der europäischen Staaten.* Vol. 1–3, by E. G. Geijer, is translated by O. P. Leffler; vol. 4, by F. F. Carlson, is translated by J. G. Petersen; vol. 5, 6, by F. F. Carlson.

[6] Published in German at Lübeck in 1854 as *Das heroische Zeitalter der Nordisch-Germanischen Völker und die Wikinger-Züge.*

Keyser in his *Norges Historie* (Christiania, 1866–67); J. E. Sars in his *Udsigt over den Norske Historie* (Christiania, 1873–77); but all are surpassed by Konrad Maurer's *Island von seiner ersten Entdeckung bis zum Untergange des Freistaates*, — A. D. 800–1262 (Munich, 1874), published as commemorating the thousandth anniversary of the settlement of Iceland, and it has the repute of being the best book on early Icelandic history.[1]

The change from Paganism to Christianity necessarily enters into all the histories covering the tenth and eleventh centuries; but it has special treatment in C. Merivale's *Conversion of the Northern Nations* (Boyle lectures, — London, 1866).[2]

There is a considerable body of the later literature upon Iceland, retrospective in character, and affording the results of study more or less patient as to the life in the early Norse days in Iceland.[3]

G. W. Dasent's introduction to his *Story of Burnt Njal* (Edinburgh, 1861)[4] and his *Norsemen in Iceland* (Oxford Essays, 1858) give what Max Müller (*Chips from a German Workshop*, ii. 191) calls "a vigorous and lively sketch of primitive northern life;" and are well supplemented by Sabine Baring-Gould's *Iceland, its scenes and sagas* (London, 1863 and later), and Richard F. Burton's *Ultima Thule, with an historical introduction* (London, 1875).[5]

D. GREENLAND AND ITS RUINS. — The sagas still serve us for the colonization of Greenland, and of particular use is that of Eric the Red.[6] The earliest to use these sources in the historic spirit was Torfæus in his *Historia Gronlandiæ Antiquæ* (1715).[7] The natural successor of

1 Maurer had long been a student of Icelandic lore, and his *Isländische Volkssagen der Gegenwart gesammelt und verdeutscht* (Leipzig, 1860) is greatly illustrative of the early north. Conybeare (*Place of Iceland in the History of European Institutions*, preface) says: "To any one writing on Iceland the elaborate works of the learned Maurer afford at once a help and difficulty: a help in so far as they shed the fullest light upon the subjects; a difficulty in that their painstaking completeness has brought together well-nigh everything that can be said."

2 What is known as the Kristni Saga gives an account of this change. Cf. Eugène Beauvois, *Origines et fondation du plus ancien évêché du nouveau monde. Le diocèse de Gardhs en Grœnland, 986–1126* (Paris, 1878), an extract from the *Mémoires de la Soc. d'Histoire, etc., de Beaune;* C. A. V. Conybeare's *Place of Iceland in the history of European institutions* (1877); Maurer's *Beiträge zur Rechtsgeschichte des germanischen Nordens;* Wheaton's *Northmen;* Worsaae's *Danes and Norwegians in England*, p. 332; Jacob Rudolph Keyser's *Private Life of the Old Northmen*, as translated by M. R. Barnard (London, 1868), and his *Religion of the Northmen*, as translated by B. Pennock (N. Y., 1854); *Quarterly Review*, January, 1862; and references in McClintock and Strong's *Cyclopædia*, under Iceland.

3 Such are the Swedish work of A. M. Strinhold, known in the German of E. F. Frisch as *Wikingzüge, Staatsverfassung und Sitten der alten Scandinaver* (Hamburg, 1839–41).

A summarized statement of life in Iceland in the early days is held to be well made out in Hans O. H. Hildebrand's *Lifvet på Island under Sagotiden* (Stockholm, 1867), and in A. E. Holmberg's *Nordbon under Hednatiden* (Stockholm). J. A. Worsaae published his *Vorgeschichte des Nordens* at Hamburg in 1878. It was improved in a Danish edition in 1880, and from this H. F. Morland Simpson made the *Prehistory of the North, based on contemporary materials* (London, 1886), with a memoir of Worsaae (d. 1885), the foremost scholar in this northern lore.

4 This book is recognized as one of the best commentaries and most informing books on Icelandic history, and this writer's introduction to Gudbrand Vigfússon's *Icelandic-English Dictionary* (3 vols., Cambridge, Eng., 1869, 1870, 1874) is of scholarly importance.

5 The millennial celebration of the settlement of Iceland in 1874 gave occasion to a variety of books and papers, more or less suggestive of the early days, like Samuel Kneeland's *American in Iceland* (Boston, 1876); but the enumeration of this essentially descriptive literature need not be undertaken here.

6 *Antiquitates Americanæ*, pp. 1–76, with an account of the Greenland MSS. (p. 255). Müller's *Sagenbibliothek.* Arngrimur Jónsson's *Grönlandia* (Iceland, 1688). A fac-simile of the title is in the *Carter-Brown Catalogue*, ii., no. 1356. A translation by Rev. J. Sephton is in the *Proc. Lit. and Philos. Soc. of Liverpool*, vol. xxxiv. 183, and separately, Liverpool, 1880. There is a paper in the *Jahresbericht der geographischen Gesellschaft in München für 1885* (Munich, 1886), p. 71, by Oskar Brenner, on "Grönland im Mittelalter nach einer altnorwegischen Quelle."

Some of the earliest references are: Christopherson Claus' *Den Grölandske Chronica* (Copenhagen, 1608), noticed in the *Carter-Brown Catalogue*, ii., no. 64. Gerald de Veer's *True and perfect description of three voyages* speaks in its title (*Carter-Brown*, ii. 38) of "the countrie lying under 80 degrees, which is thought to be Greenland, where never man had been before." Antoine de la Sale wrote between 1438 and 1447 a curious book, printed in 1527 as *La Salade*, in which he refers to Iceland and Greenland (Gronnellont), where white bears abound (Harrisse, *Bib. Am. Vet.*, no. 140).

7 This book is now rare. Dufossé prices it at 50 francs; F. S. Ellis, London, 1884, at £5.5.0. Before Torfæus, probably the best known book was Isaac de la Peyrère's *Relation du Groenland* (Paris, 1647). It

Torfæus and the book upon which later writers mostly depend is David Crantz's *Historie von Grönland, enthaltend die Beschreibung des Landes und der Einwohner, insbesonders die Geschichten der dortigen Mission. Nebst Fortsetzung* (Barby, 1765–70, 3 vols.). An English translation appeared in London in 1767, and again, though in an abridged form with some changes, in 1820.[1]

Crantz says of his own historic aims, referring to Torfæus and to the accounts given by the Eskimos of the east coast, that he has tried to investigate "where the savage inhabitants came from, and how the ancient Norwegian inhabitants came to be so totally extirpated," while at the same time he looks upon the history of the Moravian missions as his chiefest theme.

The principal source for the identification of the ruins of Greenland is the work compiled by Rafn and Finn Magnusen, *Grönlands Historiske Mindesmærker*,[2] with original texts and Danish versions. Useful summaries and observations will be found in the paper by K. Steenstrup on "Old Scandinavian ruins in South Greenland" in the *Compte Rendu, Congrès des Américanistes* (Copenhagen, 1883, p. 108), and in one on "Les Voyages des Danois au Greenland" in the same (p. 196). Steenstrup's paper is accompanied by photographs and cuts, and a map marking the site of the ruins. The latest account of them is by Lieut. Holm in the *Meddelelser om Grönland* (Copenhagen, 1883), vol. vi. Other views and plans showing the arrangement of their dwellings and the curious circular ruins,[3] which seems to have usually been near their churches, are shown in the Baron Nordenskjöld's *Den andra dicksonska expeditionen till Grönland, dess inre isöken och dess ostkust, utförd år 1883* (Stock-

RUINS OF THE CHURCH AT KATORTOK.*

is one of the earliest books to give an account of the Eskimos. It was again printed in 1674 in *Recueil de Voyages du Nord.* A Dutch edition at Amsterdam in 1678 (*Nauwkenrige Beschrijvingh van Groenland*) was considerably enlarged with other matter, and this edition was the basis of the German version published at Nuremberg, 1679. Peyrère's description will be found in English in a volume published by the Hakluyt Society in 1855, where it is accompanied by two maps of the early part of the seventeenth century. Cf. Carter-Brown, ii., no. 1192, note; Sabin, x. p. 70.

1 Pilling (*Eskimo Bibliog.*, p. 20) gives the most careful account of editions. Cf. Sabin, v. 66. A Dutch translation at Haarlem in 1767 was provided with better and larger maps than the original issue; and this version was again brought out with a changed title in 1786. There was a Swedish ed. at Stockholm in 1769, and a reprint of the original German at Leipzig in 1770, and it is included in the *Bibliothek der neuesten Reisebeschreibungen* (Frankfort, 1779–1797), vol. xx. Cf. Carter-Brown, ii., nos. 1443, 1576, 1577, 1671, 1728.

2 This constitutes in 3 vols. a sort of supplement to the *Antiquitates Americanæ.* Cf. *Dublin Review*, xxvii. 35; *Bulletin de la Soc. de Géog. de Paris*, 3d ser., vol. vi., and a synopsis of the *Mindesmæker* in *The Sacristy*, Feb. 1, 1871 (London).

3 The principal ruin is that of a church, and it will be found represented in the *Antiquitates Americanæ*, and again by Nordenskjöld, Steenstrup, J. T. Smith (*Discovery of America*, etc.), Horsford; and, not to name more, in Hayes's *Land of Desolation* (and in the French version in *Tour du Monde*, xxvi.).

* After a cut in Nordenskjöld's *Den Andra Dicksonska Expeditionen till Grönland*, p. 369, following one in *Efter Meddelelser om Grönland.*

holm, 1885), the result of the ripest study and closest contact.

We need also to scan the narratives of Hans Egede and Graah. Parry found in 1824, on an island on the Baltic coast, a runic stone, commemorating the occupancy of the spot in 1135 (*Antiquitates Americanæ;* Mallet's *Northern Antiquities*, 248); and in 1830 and 1831 other runes were found on old gravestones (Rink's *Danish Greenland*, app. v.; Laing's *Heimskringla*, i. 151). These last are in the Museum at Copenhagen. Most of these imperishable relics have been found in the district of Julianeshaab.[1]

E. The Vinland Voyages. — What Leif and Karlsefne knew they experienced, and what the sagas tell us they underwent, must have just the difference between a crisp narrative of personal adventure and the oft-repeated and embellished story of a fireside narrator, since the traditions of the Norse voyages were not put in the shape of records till about two centuries had elapsed, and we have no earlier manuscript of such a record than one made nearly two hundred years later still. It is indeed claimed that the transmission by tradition in those days was a different matter in respect to constancy and exactness from what it has been known to be in later times; but the assumption lacks proof and militates against well-known and inevitable processes of the human mind.

In regard to the credibility of the sagas, the northern writers recognize the change which came over the oral traditionary chronicles when the romancing spirit was introduced from the more southern countries, at a time while the copies of the sagas which we now have were making, after having been for so long a time orally handed down; but they are not so successful in making plain what influence this imported spirit had on particular sagas, which we

Codex Annal. Regii 2087.

1.

2.

Codex Arna Magn. 420 in 4to Annal. Skalholt. vetustiorum.

3.

1. Bishop Eric's voyage to Vineland in the year 1121.

2. Discovery made by the Iceland clergymen Adalbrand and Thorvald Helgason in the year 1285.

3. A Voyage to Markland (Nova Scotia) in the year 1347.

Chas. C. Rafn.

SAGA MANUSCRIPT.*

[1] Rafn in his *Americas arctiske landes Gamle Geographie efter de Nordiske Oldskrifter* (Copenhagen, 1845) gives the seals of some of the Greenland bishops, various plans of the different ruins, a view of the Katortok church with its surroundings, engraving of the different runic inscriptions, and a map of the Julianehaab district.

* This is a portion of one of the plates in the *Antiquitates Americanæ*, given by Rafn to Charles Sumner, with a key in manuscript by Rafn himself. His signature is from a copy of his *Mémoire* given by him to Edward Everett, and now in Harvard College library.

are asked to receive as historical records. They seem sometimes to forget that it is not necessary to have culture, heroes, and impossible occurrences to constitute a myth. A blending of history and myth prompts Horn to say "that some of the sagas were doubtless originally based on facts, but the telling and re-telling have changed them into pure myths." The unsympathetic stranger sees this in stories that the patriotic Scandinavians are over-anxious to make appear as genuine chronicles.[1] It is certainly unfortunate that the period of recording the older sagas coincides mainly with the age of this southern romancing influence.[2] It is a somewhat anomalous condition when long-transmitted oral stories are assigned to history, and certain other written ones of the age of the recorded sagas are relegated to myth. If we would believe some of the northern writers, what appears to be difference in kind of embellishment was in reality the sign that separated history from fable.[3] Of the interpreters of this olden lore, Torfæus has been long looked upon as a characteristic exemplar, and Horn[4] says of his works that they are "perceptibly lacking in criticism. Torfæus was upon the whole incapable of distinguishing between myth and history."[5]

Erasmus Rask, in writing to Wheaton in

RUIN AT KATORTOK.*

[1] This tendency of the Scandinavian writers is recognized among themselves. Horn (Anderson's translation, 324) ascribes it to "an unbridled fancy and want of critical method rather than to any wilful perversion of historical truth. This tendency owed its origin to an intense patriotism, a leading trait in the Swedish character, which on this very account was well-nigh incorrigible."

[2] Dasent translates from the preface to *Egils Saga* (Reikjavik, 1856): "The sagas show no wilful purpose to tell untruths, but simply are proofs of *the beliefs and turns of thought of men in the age when the sagas were reduced to writing*" (*Burnt Njal*, i. p. xiii).

[3] Rink (*Danish Greenland*, p. 3) says of the sagas that "they exist only in a fragmentary condition, and bear the general character of popular traditions to such a degree that they stand much in need of being corroborated by collateral proofs, if we are wholly to rely upon them in such a question as an ancient colonization of America." So he proceeds to enumerate the kind of evidence, which is sufficient in Greenland, but is wholly wanting in other parts of America, and to point out that the trustworthiness of the sagas of the Vinland voyages exists only in regard to their general scope.

Dasent, in the introduction of Vigfússon's *Icelandic Dictionary*, says of the sagas: "Written at various periods by scribes more or less fitted for the task, they are evidently of very varying authority." The Scandinavian authorities class the sagas as mythical histories, as those relating to Icelandic history (subdivided into general, family, personal, ecclesiastical), and as the lives of rulers.

[4] Anderson's translation, *Lit. of the Scand. North*, p. 81.

[5] Laing (*Heimskringla*, i. 23) says: "Arne Magnussen was the greatest antiquary who never wrote: his judgments and opinions are known from notes, selections, and correspondence, and are of great authority at this day in the saga literature. Torfæus consulted him in his researches."

* After a cut in Nordenskjöld's *Exped. till Grönland*, p. 371, following the *Meddel. om Grönland*, vi. 98.

1831,[1] enumerates eight of the early manuscripts which mention Vinland and the voyages; but Rafn, in 1837, counted eighteen such manuscripts.[2] We know little or nothing about the recorders or date of any of these copies, excepting the *Heimskringla*,[3] nor how long they had existed orally. Some of them were doubtless put into writing soon after the time when such recording was introduced, and this date is sometimes put as early as A. D. 1120, and sometimes as late as the middle or even end of that century. Meanwhile, Adam of Bremen, in the latter part of the eleventh century (A. D. 1073), prepared his *Historia Ecclesiastica*, an account of the spread of Christianity in the north, in which he says he was told by the Danish king that his subjects had found a country to the west, called Winland.[4] A reference is also supposed to be made in the *Historia Ecclesiastica* of Ordericus Vitalis, written about the middle (say A. D. 1140) of the twelfth century. But it was not until somewhere between A. D. 1385 and 1400 that the oldest Icelandic manuscript which exists, touching the voyages, was compiled, — the so-called *Codex Flatoyensis*,[5] though how much earlier copies of it were made is not

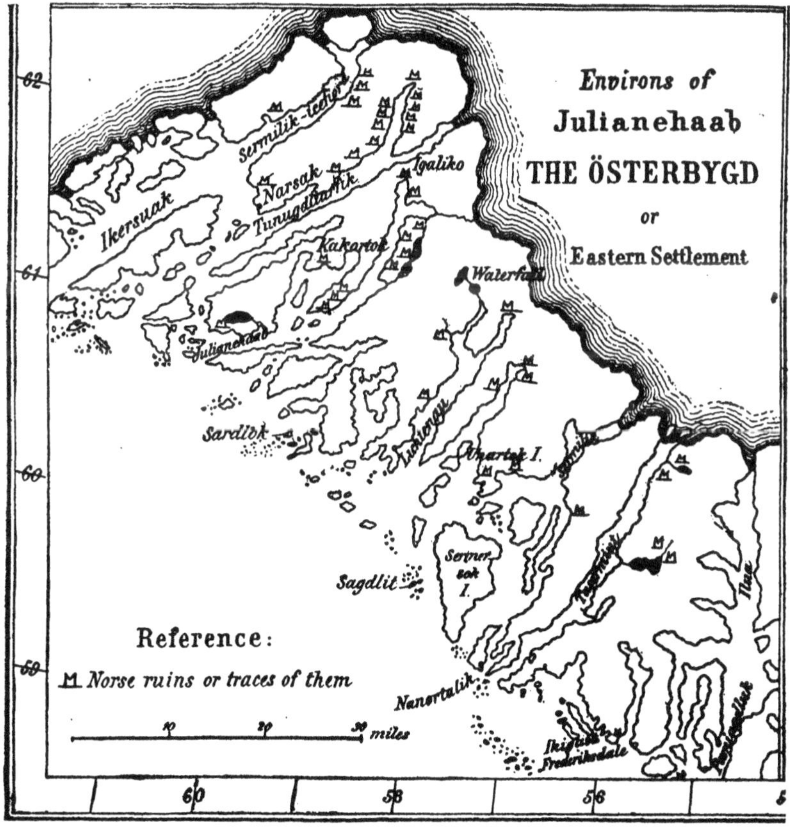

1 *Mass. Hist. Soc. Proc.*, xviii. 20.

2 Oswald Moosmüller's *Europäer in Amerika vor Columbus* (Regensburg, 1879, p. 4) enumerates the manuscripts in the royal library in Copenhagen.

3 A. E. Wollheim's *Die Nat. lit. der Scandinavier* (Berlin, 1875–77), p. 47. Turner's *Anglo Saxons*, book iv. ch. 1. Mallet's *No. Antiq.* (1847), 393.

4 Cf. G. H. Pertz, *Monumenta Germaniæ historica*, 1846, vol. vii. cap. 247. Of the different manuscripts, some call Vinland a "regio" and others an "insula."

5 Discovered in the seventeenth century in a monastery on an island close by the Icelandic coast, and now

NOTE. — The above is a reproduction of a corner map in the map of *Danish Greenland* given in Rink's book of that name. The sea in the southwest corner of the cut is not shaded; but shading is given to the interior ice field on the northern and northeastern part of the map. Rink gives a similar map of the Westerbygd.

known. It is in this manuscript that we find the saga of Olaf Tryggvesson,[1] wherein the voyages of Leif Ericson are described, and it is only by a comparison of circumstances detailed here and in other sagas that the year A. D. 1000 has been approximately determined as the date.[2] In this same codex we find the saga of Eric the Red, one of the chief narratives depended upon by the advocates of the Norse discovery, and in Rask's judgment it "appears to be somewhat fabulous, written long after the event, and taken from tradition." [3]

The other principal saga is that of Thorfinn Karlsefne, which with some differences and with the same lack of authenticity, goes over the ground covered by that of Eric the Red.[4]

RAFN.

in the royal library in Copenhagen. Cf. Laing's introduction to his edition of the *Heimskringla*, vol. i. p. 157. Horn says of this codex: "The book was written towards the end of the fourteenth century by two Icelandic priests, and contains in strange confusion and wholly without criticism a large number of sagas, poems, and stories. No other manuscript confuses things on so vast a scale." Anderson's translation of Horn's *Lit. of the Scandin. North*, p. 60. Cf. *Flateyjarbok. En Samling af Norske Konge-Sagaer med indskudte mindre fortællinger om Begivenheder i og Udenfor Norge samt Annaler* (Christiania, 1860); and Vigfússon's and Unger's edition of 1868, also at Christiania. The best English account of the *Codex Flatoyensis* is by Gudbrand Vigfússon in the preface to his *Icelandic Sagas*, published under direction of the Master of the Rolls, London, 1887, vol. i. p. xxv.

1 For texts, see C. C. Rafn's edition of *Kong Olaf Tryggvesons Saga* (Copenhagen, 1826), and Munch's edition of *Kong Olaf Tryggvesön's Saga* (Christiania, 1853). Cf. also P. A. Munch's *Norges Konge-Sagaer* of Snorri Sturleson, Sturla Thordsson, etc. (Christiania, 1859).

2 The *Codex Flatoyensis* says that it was sixteen winters after the settlement of Greenland before Leif went to Norway, and that in the next year he sailed to Vinland.

3 *Mass. Hist. Soc. Proc.*, xviii. 21.

4 These sagas are given in Icelandic, Danish, and Latin in Rafn's *Antiquitates Americanæ* (Copenhagen,

Of all the early manuscripts, the well-known *Heimskringla* of Snorro Sturleson (b. 1178; d. 1241), purporting to be a history of the Norse kings down to A. D. 1177, is the most entitled to be received as an historical record, and all that it says is in these words: "Leif also found Vinland the Good."[1]

Saxo Grammaticus (d. about 1208) in his *His-*

HISTORIA
VINLANDIÆ ANTIQVÆ,
seu
Partis Americæ Septentrionalis,
ubi
Nominis ratio recensetur,
situs terræ ex dierum brumalium spatio expenditur, soli fertilitas & incolarum barbaries, peregrinorum temporarius incolatus & gesta, vicinarum terrarum nomina & facies
ex
Antiqvitatibus Islandicis in lucem producta exponuntur
per
THORMODUM TORFÆUM
Rerum Norvegicarum Historiographum Regium.

HAVNIÆ,
Ex Typographéo Regiæ Majest. & Universit. 1705.
Impensis Authoris.

1837). Versions or abstracts, more or less full, of all or of some of them are given by Beamish, in his *Discovery of America by the Northmen* (London, 1841), whose text is reprinted by Slafter, in his *Voyages of the Northmen* (Boston, 1877). J. Elliot Cabot, in the *Mass. Quart. Review*, March, 1849, copied in part in Higginson's *Amer. Explorers*. Blackwell, in his supplementary chapters to Mallet's *Northern Antiquities* (London, Bohn's library). B. F. De Costa, in his *Pre-Columbian Discovery of America* (Albany, 1868). Eben Norton Horsford, in his *Discovery of America by Norsemen* (Boston, 1888). Beauvois, in his *Découvertes des Scandinaves en Amérique* (Paris, 1859). P. E. Müller, in his *Sagabibliothek* (Copenhagen' 1816–20), and a German version of part of it by Lachmann, *Sagenbibliothek des Scandinavischen Alterthums in Auszügen* (Berlin, 1816).

1 When, however, Peringskiöld edited the *Heimskringla*, in 1697, he interpolated eight chapters of a more particular account of the Vinland voyages, which drew forth some animadversions from Torfæus in 1705, when he published his *Historia Vinlandiæ*. It was later found that Peringskiöld had drawn these eight chapters

toria Danica begins with myths, and evidently follows the sagas, but does not refer to them except in his preface.[1]

For about five hundred years after this the stories attracted little or no attention.[2] We have seen that Peringskiöld produced these sagas in 1697. Montanus in his *Nieuwe en onbekende Weereld* (Amsterdam, 1671), and Campanius, in 1702, in his *Kort Beskrifning om Provincien Nya Swerige uti America* (Stockholm),[3] gave some details. The account which did most, however, to revive an interest in the subject was that of Torfæus in his *Historia Vinlandiæ Antiquæ* (Copenhagen, 1705), but he was quite content to place the scene of his narrative in America, without attempting to identify localities.[4] The voyages were, a few years later, the subject of a dissertation at the University of Upsala in Sweden.[5] J. P. Cassell, of Bremen, discusses the Adam of Bremen story in another Latin essay, still later.[6]

About 1750, Pieter Kalm, a Swede, brought the matter to the attention of Dr. Franklin, as the latter remembered twenty-five years later, when he wrote to Samuel Mather that "the circumstances gave the account a great appearance of authenticity."[7] In 1755, Paul Henri Mallet (1730–1807), in his *Histoire de Dannemarc*, determines the localities to be Labrador and Newfoundland.[8]

In 1769, Gerhard Schöning, in his *Norges Riges Historie*, established the scene in America. Robertson, in 1777, briefly mentions the voyages in his *Hist. of America* (note xvii.), and, referring to the accounts given by Peringskiöld, calls them rude and confused, and says that it is impossible to identify the landfalls, though he thinks Newfoundland may have been the scene of Vinland. This is also the belief of J. R. Forster in his *Geschichte der Entdeckungen im Norden* (Frankfurt, 1784).[9] M. C. Sprengel, in his *Geschichte der Europäer in Nordamerika* (Leipzig, 1782), thinks they went as far south as Carolina. Pontoppidan's *History of Norway* was mainly followed by Dr. Jeremy Belknap in his *American Biography* (Boston, 1794), who recognizes "circumstances to confirm and none to disprove the relations." In 1793, Muñoz, in his *Historia del Nuevo Mundo*, put Vinland in Greenland. In 1796 there was a brief account

from the *Codex Flatoyensis*, which particular MS. was unknown to Torfæus. When Laing printed his edition of the *Heimskringla*, *The Sea Kings of Norway* (London, 1844), he translated these eight chapters in his appendix (vol. iii. 344). Laing (*Heimskringla*, i. 27) says: "Snorro Sturleson has done for the history of the Northmen what Livy did for the history of the Romans," — a rather questionable tribute to the verity of the saga history, in the light of the most approved comments on Livy. Cf. Horn, in Anderson's translation, *Lit. of the Scandinavian North* (Chicago, 1884), p. 56, with references, p. 59.

1 J. Fulford Vicary's *Saga Time* (Lond., 1887). Some time in the fifteenth century, a monk, Thomas Gheysmer, made an abridgment of Saxo, alleging that he "had said much rather for the sake of adornment than in behalf of truth." The Canon Christiern Pederson printed the first edition of Saxo at Paris in 1514 (Anderson's Horn's *Lit. Scandin. North*, p. 102). This writer adds: "The entire work rests exclusively on oral tradition, which had been gathered by Saxo, and which he repeated precisely as he had heard it, for in the whole chronicle there is no trace of criticism proper. . . . Saxo must also undoubtedly have had Icelandic sagamen as authorities for the legendary part of his work; but there is not the slightest evidence to show that he ever had a written Icelandic saga before him. . . . In this part of the work he betrays no effort to separate fact from fiction, . . . and he has in many instances consciously or unconsciously adorned the original material." Horn adds that the last and best edition is that of P. E. Müller and J. Velchow, *Saxonis Grammatici Historia Danica* (Copenhagen, 1839).

2 Humboldt (*Crit. Exam.*, ii. 120) represented that Ortelius referred to these voyages in 1570; but Palfrey (*Hist. New England*, i. 51) shows that the language cited by Humboldt was not used by Ortelius till in his edition of 1592, and that then he referred to the Zeno narrative.

3 See *post*, Vol. IV. p. 492.

4 His account is followed by Malte Brun in his *Précis de la Géographie* (i. 395). Cf. also *Annales des Voyages* (Paris, 1810), x. 50, and his *Géographie Universelle* (Paris, 1841). Pinkerton, in his *Voyages* (London, 1814), vol. xvii., also followed Torfæus.

5 J. J. Wahlstedt's *Iter in Americam* (Upsala, 1725). Cf. *Brinley Catal.*, i. 59.

6 *Observatio historica ad Frisonum navigatione fortuita in Americam sec. xi. facta* (Magdeburg, 1741).

7 *Franklin's Works*, Philad., 1809, vol. vi.; Sparks's ed., viii. 69.

8 This is the book which furnished the text in an English dress (London, 1770) known as *Northern Antiquities*, and a part of his account is given in the *American Museum* (Philad., 1789). In the Edinburgh edition of 1809 it is called: *Northern antiquities: or a description of the manners, customs, religion and laws, of the ancient Danes, including those of our Saxon ancestors. With a translation of the Edda and other pieces, from the ancient Icelandic tongue. Translated from "L'introduction à l'histoire de Dannemarc, &c.," par. Mons. Mallet. With additional notes by the English translator* [*Bishop Percy*], *and Goranson's Latin version of the Edda.* In 2 vols. The chapters defining the locations are omitted, and others substituted, in the reprint of the *Northern Antiquities* in Bohn's library.

9 There are French and English versions.

in Fritsch's *Disputatio historico-geographica in qua quæritur utrum veteres Americam noverint necne.* H. Stenström published at Lund, in 1801, a short dissertation, *De America Norvegis ante tempora Columbi adita.* Boucher de la Richarderie, in his *Bibliothèque Universelle des Voyages* (Paris, 1808), gives a short account, and cites some of the authorities. Some of the earlier American histories of this century, like Williamson's *North Carolina*, took advantage of the recitals of Torfæus and Mallet. Ebenezer Henderson's *Residence in Iceland* (1814-15)[1] presented the evidence anew. Barrow, in his *Voyages to the Arctic Regions* (London, 1818), places Vinland in Labrador or Newfoundland; but J. W. Moulton, in his *History of the State of New York* (N. Y., 1824), brings that State within the region supposed to have been visited.

A writer more likely to cause a determinate opinion in the public mind came in Washington Irving, who in his *Columbus* (London, 1828) dismissed the accounts as untrustworthy; though later, under the influence of Wheaton and Rafn, he was inclined to consider them of possible importance; and finally in his condensed edition he thinks the facts "established to the conviction of most minds."[2] Hugh Murray, in his *Discoveries and Travels in North America* (London, 1829), regards the sagas as an authority; but he doubts the assigning of Vinland to America. In 1830, W. D. Cooley, in his *History of Maritime and Inland Discovery*,[3] thought it impossible to shake the authenticity of the sagas.

While Henry Wheaton was the minister of the United States at Copenhagen, and having access to the collections of that city, he prepared his *History of the Northmen*, which was published in London and Philadelphia in 1831.[4] The high character of the man gave unusual force to his opinions, and his epitome of the sagas in his second chapter contributed much to increase the interest in the Northmen story. He was the first who much impressed the New England antiquaries with the view that Vinland should be looked for in New England; and a French version by Paul Guillot, issued in Paris in 1844, is stated to have been "revue et augmentée par l'auteur, avec cartes, inscriptions, et alphabet runique."[5] The opinions of Wheaton, however, had no effect upon the leading historian of the United States, nor have any subsequent developments caused any change in the opinion of Bancroft, first advanced in 1834, in the opening volume of his *United States*, where he dismissed the sagas as "mythological in form and obscure in meaning; ancient yet not contemporary." He adds that "the intrepid mariners who colonized Greenland could easily have extended their voyage to Labrador; but no clear historical evidence establishes the natural probability that they accomplished the passage."[6] All this is omitted by Bancroft in his last revised edition; but a paragraph in his original third volume (1840), to the intent that, though "Scandinavians may have reached the shores of Labrador, the soil of the United States has not one vestige of their presence," is allowed to remain,[7] and is true now as when first written.

The chief apostle of the Norseman belief, however, is Carl Christian Rafn, whose work was accomplished under the auspices of the Royal Society of Northern Antiquaries at Copenhagen.[8]

Rafn was born in 1795, and died at Copenhagen in 1864.[9] At the University, as well as later as an officer of its library, he had bent his attention to the early Norse manuscripts and literature,[10] so that in 1825 he was the natural

1 Edinburgh, 1818; Boston, 1831.

2 *Mass. Hist. Soc. Proc.*, 1865, p. 184.

3 *Lardner's Cabinet Cyclopædia.*

4 Allibone, iii. 2667.

5 Irving, in reviewing the book in the *No. Am. Rev.*, Oct., 1832, avoided the question of the Norse discovery. (Cf. his *Spanish Papers*, vol. ii., and Rice's *Essays from the No. Am. Rev.*) C. Robinson, in his *Discoveries in the West* (ch. 1), borrows from Wheaton.

6 Octavo ed., i. pp. 5, 6.

7 Orig. ed., iii. 313; last revision, ii. 132.

8 This society, Kongelige Nordiske Oldskrift-Selskab, since 1825, has been issuing works and periodicals illustrating all departments of Scandinavian archæology (cf. Webb, in *Mass. Hist. Soc. Proc.*, viii. 177), and has gathered cabinets and museums, sections of which are devoted to American subjects. C. C. Rafn's *Cabinet d'antiquités Américaines à Copenhague* (Copenhagen, 1858); *Journal of the Royal Geographical Society*, xiv. 316; Slafter's introd. to his *Voyages of the Northmen.*

9 *Mass. Hist. Soc. Proc.*, viii. 81; *Am. Antiq. Soc. Proc.*, April, 1865; *N. E. Hist. Geneal. Reg.*, 1865, p. 273; *Today*, ii. 176.

10 Professor Willard Fiske has paid particular attention to the early forms of the Danish in the Icelandic literature. In 1885 the British Museum issued a *Catalogue of the books printed in Iceland from A. D. 1578 to 1880 in the library of the British Museum.* In 1886 Mr. Fiske privately printed at Florence *Bibliographical Notices, i.: Books printed in Iceland, 1578-1844, a supplement to the British Museum Catalogue,*

founder of the Royal Society of Northern Antiquaries; and much of the value of its long series of publications is due to his active and unflagging interest.[1] The summit of his American interest, however, was reached in the great folio *Antiquitates Americanæ*,[2] in which he for the first time put the mass of original Norse documents before the student, and with a larger accumulation of proofs than had ever been adduced before, he commented on the narratives and came to conclusions respecting traces of their occupancy to which few will adhere to-day.

The effect of Rafn's volume, however, was marked, and we see it in the numerous presentations of the subject which followed; and every writer since has been greatly indebted to him.

Alexander von Humboldt in his *Examen Critique* (Paris, 1837) gave a synopsis of the sagas, and believed the scene of the discoveries to be between Newfoundland and New York; and in

which enumerates 139 titles with full bibliographical detail and an index. He refers also to the principal bibliographical authorities. Laing's introduction to the *Heimskringla* gives a survey.

1 Cf. list of their several issues in Scudder's *Catal. of Scient. Serials*, nos. 640, 654, and the Rafn bibliography in Sabin, xvi. nos. 67,466–67,486. In addition to its Danish publications, the chief of which interesting to the American archæologist being the *Antiquarisk Tidsskrift* (1845–1864), sometimes known as the *Revue Archéologique et Bulletin*, the society, under its more familiar name of Société Royale des Antiquaires du Nord, has issued its *Mémoires*, the first series running from 1836 to 1860, in 4 vols., and the second beginning in 1866. These contain numerous papers involving the discussion of the Northmen voyages, including a condensed narrative by Rafn, "Mémoire sur la découverte de l'Amérique au 10e siècle," which was enlarged and frequently issued separately in French and other languages (1838–1843), and is sometimes found in English as a *Supplement to the Antiquitates Americanæ*, and was issued in New York (1838) as *America discovered in the tenth century*. In this form (*Mass. Hist. Soc. Proc.*, viii. 187) it was widely used here and in Europe to call attention to Rafn's folio, *Antiquitates Americanæ*.

The *Mémoires* also contained another paper by Rafn, *Aperçu de l'ancienne géographie des régions arctiques de l'Amérique, selon les rapports contenus dans les Sagas du Nord* (Copenhagen, 1847), which also concerns the Vinland voyages, and is repeated in the *Nouvelles Annales des Voyages* (1849), i. 277.

2 *Antiqvitates Americanæ sive scriptores septentrionales rerum ante-Columbianarum in America. Samling af de i nordens oldskrifter indeholdte efterretninger om de gamle nordboers opdagelsesreiser til America fra det 10de til det 14de aarhundrede. Edidit Societas regia antiquariorum Septentrionalium* (Hafniæ, 1837). CONTENTS: Præfatio. — Conspectus codicum membraneorum, in quibus terrarum Americanarum mentio fit. — America discovered by the Scandinavians in the tenth century. (An abstract of the historical evidence contained in this work.) — Pættir af Eireki Rauda ok Grænlendingum. — Saga Þorfinns Karlsefnis ok Snorra Þorbrandssonar. — Breviores relationes: De inhabitatione Islandiæ; De inhabitatione Grœnlandiæ; De Ario Maris filio; De Björne Breidvikensium athleta; De Gudleivo Gudlœgi filio; Excerpta ex annalibus Islandorum; Die mansione Grœnlandorum in locis Borealibus; Excerpta e geographicis scriptis veterum Islandorum; Carmen Færöicum, in quo Vinlandiæ mentio fit; Adami Bremensis Relatio de Vinlandia; Descriptio quorumdam monumentorum Europæorum, quæ in oris Grönlandiæ ocidentalibus reperta et detecta sunt; Descriptio vetusti monumenti in regione Massachusetts reperti; Descriptio vetustorum quorundam monumentorum in Rhode Island. — Annotationes geographicæ; Islandia et Grönlandia; Indagatio Arctoarum Americæ regionum. — Indagatio Orientalium Americæ regionum. — Addenda et emendanda. — Indexes. The larger works are in Icelandic, Danish, and Latin.

Cf. also his *Antiquités Américaines d'après les monuments historiques des Islandais et des anciens Scandinaves* (Copenhagen, 1845). An abstract of the evidence is given in the *Journal of the Royal Geographical Society* (viii. 114), and it is upon this that H. H. Bancroft depends in his *Native Races* (v. 106). Cf. also *Ibid.* v. 115–116; and his *Cent. America*, i. 74. L. Dussieux in his *Les Grands Faits de l'Histoire de la Géographie* (Paris, 1882; vol. i. 147, 165) follows Rafn and Malte-Brun. So does Brasseur de Bourbourg in his *Hist. de Nations Civilisées*, i. 18; and Bachiller y Morales in his *Antigüedades Americanas* (Havana, 1845).

Great efforts were made by Rafn and his friends to get reviews of his folio in American periodicals; and he relied in this matter upon Dr. Webb and others, with whom he had been in correspondence in working up his geographical details (*Mass. Hist. Soc. Proc.*, ii. 97, 107; viii. 189, etc.), and so late as 1852 he drafted in English a new synopsis of the evidence, and sent it over for distribution in the United States (*Ibid.* ii. 500; *New Jersey Hist. Soc. Proc.*, vi.; *N. E. Hist. Geneal. Reg.*, 1853, p. 13). So far as weight of character went, there was a plenty of it in his reviewers: Edward Everett in the *No. Amer. Rev.*, Jan., 1838; Alexander

* Opposite is a section of Rafn's map in the *Antiquitates Americanæ*, giving his identification of the Norse localities. This and the other map by Rafn is reproduced in his *Cabinet d'Antiquités Américaines* (Copenhagen, 1858). The map in the atlas of St. Martin's *Hist. de la Géographie* does not track them below Newfoundland. The map in J. T. Smith's *Northmen in New England* (Boston, 1839) shows eleven voyages to America from Scandinavia, A. D. 861–1285. Cf. map in Wilhelmi's *Island*, etc. (Heidelberg, 1842).

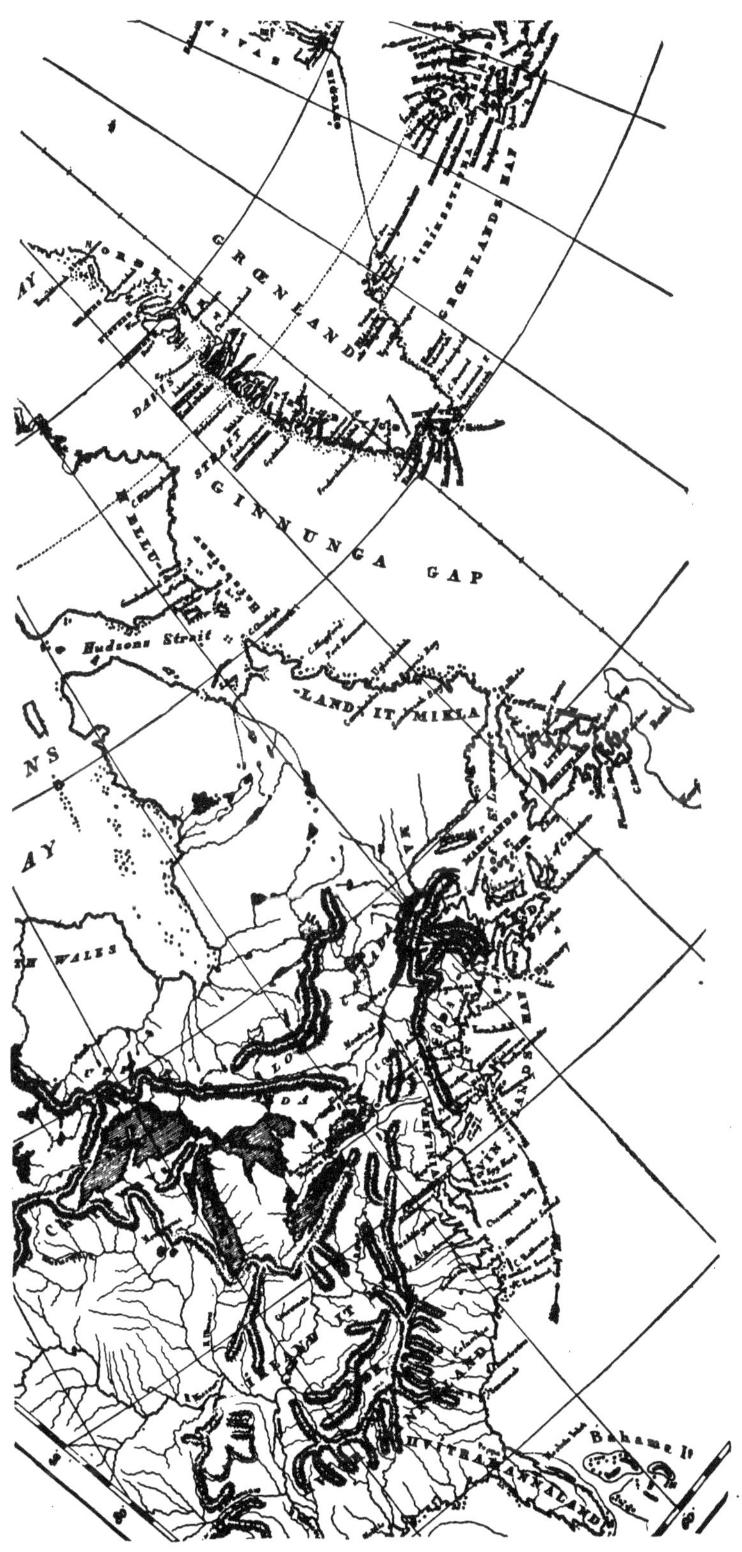

NORSE AMERICA.

his *Cosmos* (1844) he reiterated his views, holding to "the undoubted first discovery by the Northmen as far south as 41° 30′."[1]

Two books which for a while were the popular treatises on the subject were the immediate outcome of Rafn's book. The first of these was *The Northmen in New England*, giving the stories in the form of a dialogue, by Joshua Toulmin Smith (Boston, 1839), which in a second edition (London, 1842) was called *The Discovery of America by the Northmen in the Tenth Century.*

The other book was largely an English version of parts of Rafn's book, translating the chief sagas, and reproducing the maps: Nathaniel Ludlow Beamish's *Discovery of America by the Northmen in the Tenth Century* (London, 1841).[2] Two German books owed almost as much to Rafn, those of K. Wilhelmi[3] and K. H. Hermes.[4] Prescott, at this time publishing the third volume of his *Mexico* (1843), accords to Rafn the credit of taking the matter out of the category of doubt, but he hesitates to accept the Dane's identifications of localities; but R. H. Major, in considering the question in the introduction to his *Select letters of Columbus* (1847), finds little hesitation in accepting the views of Rafn, and thinks "no room is left for disputing the main fact of discovery."

When Hildreth, in 1849, published his *United States*, he ranged himself, with his distrusts, by the side of Bancroft but J. Elliot Cabot, in making a capital summary of the evidence in the *Mass. Quarterly Review* (vol. ii.), accords with the believers, but places the locality visited about Labrador and Newfoundland. Haven in his *Archæology of the United States* (Washington, 1856) regards the discovery as well attested, and that the region was most likely that of Narragansett Bay. C. W. Elliott in his *New England History* (N. Y., 1857) holds the story to be "in some degree mythical." Palfrey in his *Hist. of New England* (Boston, 1858) goes no farther than to consider the Norse voyage as in "nowise unlikely," and Oscar F. Peschel in his *Geschichte des Zeitalters der Entdeckungen* (Stuttgart, 1858) is on the affirmative side. Paul K. Sinding goes over the story with assent in his *History of Scandinavia*, — a book not much changed in his *Scandinavian Races* (N. Y., 1878).[5] Eugène Beauvois did little more than translate from Rafn in his *Découvertes des Scandinaves en*

Everett in the *U. S. Magazine* and *Democratic Review* (1838); George Folsom in the *N. Y. Review* (1838); H. R. Schoolcraft in the *Amer. Biblical Repository* (1839). Cf. *Mass. Hist. Soc. Proc.*, viii. 182–3; *Poole's Index*, 28, 928.

1 Bohn's ed., English transl., ii. 603; Lond. ed., 1849, ii. 233–36. Humboldt expresses the opinion that Columbus, during his visit to Iceland, got no knowledge of the stories, so little an impression had they made on the public mind (*Cosmos*, Bohn, ii. 611), and that the enemies of Columbus in his famous lawsuit, when every effort was made to discredit his enterprise, did not instance his Iceland experience, should be held to indicate that no one in southern Europe believed in any such prompting at that time. Wheaton and Prescott (*Ferdinand and Isabella*, orig. ed., ii. 118, 131) hold similar opinions. (Cf. Vol. II. p. 33.) Dr. Webb says that Irving held back from accepting the stories of the saga, for fear that they could be used to detract from Columbus' fame. Rafn and his immediate sympathizers did not fail to make the most of the supposition that Columbus had in some way profited by his Iceland experience. Laing thinks Columbus *must* have heard of the voyages, and De Costa (*Columbus and the Geographers of the North*) thinks that the bruit of the Northmen voyages extended sufficiently over Europe to render it unlikely that it escaped the ears of Columbus. Cf. further an appendix in Irving's *Columbus*, and Mallet's *Northern Antiquities*, Bohn's ed., 267, in refutation of the conclusions of Finn Magnusen in the *Nordisk Tidsskrift.* It has been left for the unwise and overtopped advocates of a later day, like Goodrich and Marie A. Brown, to go beyond reason in an indiscriminate denunciation of the Genoese. The latter writer, in her *Icelandic Discoverers of America* (Boston, 1888), rambles over the subject in a jejune way, and easily falls into errors, while she pursues her main purpose of exposing what she fancies to be a deep-laid scheme of the Pope and the Catholic Church to conceal the merits of the Northmen and to capture the sympathies of Americans in honoring the memory of Columbus in 1892. It is simply a reactionary craze from the overdone raptures of the school of Roselly de Lorgues and the other advocates of the canonization of Columbus, in Catholic Europe.

2 This book is for the sagas the basis of the most useful book on the subject, Edmund Farwell Slafter's *Voyages of the Northmen to America. Including extracts from Icelandic Sagas relating to Western voyages by Northmen in the 10th and 11th centuries in an English translation by Nathaniel Ludlow Beamish; with a synopsis of the historical evidence and the opinion of professor Rafn as to the places visited by the Scandinavians on the coast of America. With an introduction* (Boston, 1877), published by the Prince Society. Slafter's opinion is that the narratives are "true in their general outlines and important features."

3 *Island, Huitramannaland, Grönland und Vinland* (Heidelberg, 1842).

4 *Die Entdeckung von Amerika durch die Isländer im zehnten und eilften Jahrhundert* (Braunschweig, 1844). Cf. E. G. Squier's *Discovery of America by the Northmen, a critical review of the works of Hermes, Rafn and Beamish* (1849).

5 Cf. his paper in the *Quebec Lit. and Hist. Soc. Trans.*, 1865.

Amérique,—fragments de Sagas Islandaises traduits pour la première fois en français (Paris, 1859)—an extract from the *Revue Orientale et Américaine* (vol. ii.).[1]

Professor Daniel Wilson, of Toronto, has discussed the subject at different times, and with these conclusions: "With all reasonable doubts as to the accuracy of details, there is the strongest probability in favor of the authenticity of the American Vinland. . . . The data are the mere vague allusions of a traveller's tale, and it is indeed the most unsatisfactory feature of the sagas that the later the voyages the more confused and inconsistent their narratives become in every point of detail."[2]

Dr. B. F. De Costa's first book on the subject was his *Pre-Columbian Discovery of America by the Northmen, illustrated by Translations from the Icelandic Sagas, edited with notes and a general introduction* (Albany, 1868). It is a convenient gathering of the essential parts of the sagas; but the introduction rather opposes than disproves some of the "feeble paragraphs, pointed with a sneer," which he charges upon leading opponents of the faith. Professor J. L. Diman, in the *North American Review* (July, 1869), made De Costa's book the occasion of an essay setting forth the grounds of a disbelief in the historical value of the sagas. De Costa replied in *Notes on a Review*, etc. (Charlestown, 1869). In the same year, Dr. Kohl, following the identifications of Rafn, rehearsed the narratives in his *Discovery of Maine* (Portland, 1869), and tracked Karlsefne through the gulf of Maine. De Costa took issue with him on this latter point in his *Northmen in Maine* (Albany, 1870).[3] In the introduction to his *Sailing Directions of Henry Hudson*, De Costa argues that these mariners' guides are the same used by the Northmen, and in his *Columbus and the Geographers of the North* (Hartford, 1872,—cf. *Amer. Church Review*, xxiv. 418) he recapitulates the sagas once more with reference to the knowledge which he supposes Columbus to have had of them. Paul Gaffarel, in his *Etudes sur les rapports de l'Amérique et de l'ancien Continent avant Colomb* (Paris, 1869), entered more particularly into the evidence of the commerce of Vinland and its relations to Europe.

Gabriel Gravier, another French author, was rather too credulous in his *Découverte de l'Amérique par les normands au Xe Siècle* (Paris, 1874), when he assumed with as much confidence as Rafn ever did everything that the most ardent advocate had sought to prove.[4]

There were two American writers soon to follow, hardly less intemperate. These were Aaron Goodrich, in *A History of the Character and Achievements of the so-called Christopher Columbus* (N. Y., 1874), who took the full complement of Rafn's belief with no hesitancy; and Rasmus B. Anderson in his *America not discovered by Columbus* (Chicago, 1874; improved, 1877; again with Watson's bibliography, 1883),[5] in which even the Skeleton in Armor is made to play a part. Excluding such vagaries, the book is not without use as displaying the excessive views entertained in some quarters on the subject. The author is, we believe, a Scandinavian, and shows the tendency of his race to a facility rather than felicity in accepting evidence on this subject.

The narratives were first detailed among our leading general histories when the *Popular History of the United States* of Bryant and Gay appeared in 1876. The claims were presented decidedly, and in the main in the directions indicated by Rafn; but the wildest pretensions of that antiquary were considerately dismissed.

1 Beauvois also made at a later period other contributions to the subject: *Les derniers vestiges du Christianisme prêchés du Xe au XIVe siècles dans le Markland et le Grande-Irlande, les porte-croix de la Gaspésie et de l'Arcadie* (Paris, 1877) which appeared originally in the *Annales de philosophie Chrétiennes*, Apr., 1877; and *Les Colonies européennes du Markland et de l'Escociland au XIVe siècle et les vestiges qui en subsistèrent jusqu'aux XVIe et XVIIe siècle* (Luxembourg, 1878), being taken from the *Compte Rendu* of the Luxembourg meeting of the Congrès des Américanistes.

2 *Prehistoric Man*, 3d ed., ii. 83, 85. Cf. also his *Historic Footprints in America*, extracted from the *Canadian Journal*, Sept., 1864.

3 Joseph Williamson, in the *Hist. Mag.*, Jan., 1869 (x. 30), sought to connect with the Northmen certain ancient remains along the coast of Maine.

4 He was rather caustically taken to account by Henry Cabot Lodge, in the *No. Am. Review*, vol. cxix. Cf. Michel Hardy's *Les Scandinaves dans l'Amérique du Nord* (Dieppe, 1874). An April hoax which appeared in a Washington paper in 1867, about some runes discovered on the Potomac, had been promptly exposed in this country (*Hist. Mag.*, Mar. and Aug., 1869), but it had been accepted as true in the *Annuaire de la Société Américaine* in 1873, and Gaffarel (*Etudes sur les Rapports de l'Amérique avant Columbus*, Paris, 1869, p. 251) and Gravier (p. 139) was drawn into the snare. (Cf. Whittlesey's *Archæol. frauds* in the *Western Reserve Hist. Soc. Tracts*, no. 9, and H. W. Haynes in *Mass. Hist. Soc. Proc.*, Jan., 1888, p. 59.) In a later monograph, *Les Normands sur la route des Indes* (Rouen, 1880), Gravier, while still accepting the old exploded geographical theories, undertook further to prove that the bruits of the Norse discoveries instigated the seamen of Normandy to similar ventures, and that they visited America in ante-Columbian days.

5 There is an authorized German version, *Die erste Entdeckung von Amerika*, by Mathilde Mann (Hamburg, 1888).

During the last score years the subject has been often made prominent by travellers like Kneeland [1] and Hayes,[2] who have recapitulated the evidence; by lecturers like Charles Kingsley;[3] by monographists like Moosmüller;[4] by the minor historians like Higginson,[5] who has none of the fervor of the inspired identifiers of localities, and Weise,[6] who is inclined to believe the sea-rovers did not even pass Davis's Straits; and by contributors to the successive sessions of the Congrès des Américanistes [7] and to other learned societies.[8]

The question was brought to a practical issue in Massachusetts by a proposition raised — at first in Wisconsin — by the well-known musician Ole Bull, to erect in Boston a statue to Leif Ericson.[9] The project, though ultimately carried out, was long delayed, and was discouraged by members of the Massachusetts Historical Society on the ground that no satisfactory evidence existed to show that any spot in New England had been reached by the Northmen.[10] The sense of the society was finally expressed in the report of their committee, Henry W. Haynes and Abner C. Goodell, Jr., in language which seems to be the result of the best historical criticism; for it is not a question of the fact of discovery, but to decide how far we can place reliance on the details of the sagas. There is likely to remain a difference of opinion on this point. The committee say: "There is the same sort of reason for believing in the existence of Leif Ericson that there is for believing in the existence of Agamemnon, — they are both traditions accepted by later writers; but there is no more reason for regarding as true the details related about his discoveries than there is for accepting as historic truth the narratives contained in the Homeric poems. It is antecedently probable that the Northmen discovered America in the early part of the eleventh century; and this discovery is confirmed by the same sort of historical tradition, not strong enough to be called evidence, upon which our belief in many of the accepted facts of history rests." [11]

In running down the history of the literature of the subject, the present aim has been simply to pick out such contributions as have been in some way significant, and reference must be made to the bibliographies for a more perfect record.[12]

Irrespective of the natural probability of the Northmen visits to the American main, other evidence has been often adduced to support the sagas. This proof has been linguistic, ethnological, physical, geographical, and monumental.

Nothing could be slenderer than the alleged correspondences of languages, and we can see in Horsford's *Discovery of America by Northmen* to what a fanciful extent a confident enthusiasm can carry it.[13]

1 *American in Iceland* (Boston, 1876).

2 *Land of Desolation* (New York, 1872). There is a French version in the *Tour du Monde*, xxvi.

3 *Lectures delivered in America* (Philad., 1875), — third lecture.

4 *Europäer in Amerika vor Columbus, nach Quellen bearbeitet von P. Oswald Moosmüller* (Regensburg, 1879).

5 *Larger History of the United States* (N. Y., 1886).

6 *Discoveries of America* (N. Y., 1884).

7 Particularly Beauvois, already mentioned, and Dr. E. Löffler, on the Vinland Excursions of the Ancient Scandinavians, at the Copenhagen meeting, *Compte Rendu* (1883), p. 64. Cf. also Michel Hardy's *Les Scandinaves dans l'Amérique du Nord au Xe Siècle* (Dieppe, 1874).

8 R. G. Haliburton, in *Roy. Geog. Soc. Proc.* (Jan., 1885); Thomas Morgan, in *Roy. Hist. Soc. Trans.* iii. 75.

9 E. N. Horsford's *Discovery of America by the Northmen* (Boston, 1888); Anderson's *America not discovered by Columbus*, 3d ed., p. 30; *N. Y. Nation*, Nov. 17, 1887; *Mag. Amer. Hist.*, Mar., 1888, p. 223.

10 Remarks of Wm. Everett and Chas. Deane in the society's *Proceedings*, May, 1880.

11 *Mass. Hist. Soc. Proc.*, Dec., 1887. The most incautious linguistic inferences and the most uncritical cartological perversions are presented by Eben Norton Horsford in his *Discovery of America by the Northmen — address at the unveiling of the statue of Leif Eriksen, Oct. 29, 1887* (Boston, 1888). Cf. Oscar Brenner in *Beilage zur Allgemeinen Zeitung* (Munich, Dec. 6, 1888). A trustful reliance upon the reputations of those who have in greater or less degree accepted the details of the sagas characterizes a paper by Mrs. Ole Bull in the *Mag. of Amer. Hist.*, Mar., 1888. She is naturally not inclined to make much allowance for the patriotic zeal of the northern writers.

12 The best list is in P. B. Watson's "Bibliog. of Pre-Columbian Discoveries of America," originally in the *Library Journal*, vi. 259, but more complete in Anderson's *America not discovered by Columbus* (3d ed., Chicago, 1883). Cf. also Chavanne's *Literature of the Polar Regions*; Th. Solberg's Bibliog. of Scandinavia, in English, with magazine articles, in F. W. Horn's *Hist. of the lit. of the Scandinavian North* (1884, pp. 413–500). There is a convenient brief list in Slafter's *Voyages of the Northmen* (pp. 127–140), and a not very well selected one in Marie A. Brown's *Icelandic Discoverers*. *Poole's Index* indicates the considerable amount of periodical discussions. The Scandinavian writers are mainly referred to by Miss Brown and Mrs. Bull.

13 Forster finds a corruption of Norvegia (Norway) in Norumbega. Rafn finds the Norse elements in the

The ethnological traces are only less shadowy. Hugo Grotius[1] contended that the people of Central America were of Scandinavian descent. Brasseur found remnants of Norse civilization in the same region.[2] Viollet le Duc[3] discovers great resemblances in the northern religious ceremonials to those described in the *Popul Vuh.* A general resemblance did not escape the notice of Humboldt. Gravier[4] is certain that the Aztec civilization is Norse.[5] Chas. Godfrey Leland claims that the old Norse spirit pervades the myths and legends of the Algonkins, and that it is impossible not to admit that there must have been at one time "extensive intercourse between the Northmen and the Algonkins;" and in proof he points out resemblances between the Eddas and the Algonkin mythology.[6] It is even stated that the Micmacs have a tradition of a people called Chenooks, who in ships visited their coast in the tenth century.

The physical and geographical evidences are held to exist in the correspondences of the coast line to the descriptions of the sagas, including the phenomena of the tides[7] and the length of the summer day.[8] Laing and others, who make no question of the main fact, readily recognize the too great generality and contradictions of the descriptions to be relied upon.[9]

George Bancroft, in showing his distrust, has said that the advocates of identification can no

words Massachusetts, Nauset, and Mount Hope (*Mass. Hist. Soc. Proc.*, viii. 194–198). The word Hole, used as synonymous to harbor in various localities along the Vineyard Sound, has been called a relic of the Icelandic Holl, a hill (*Mag. Amer. Hist.*, June, 1882, p. 431; Jos. S. Fay in *Mass. Hist. Soc. Proc.*, xii. 334; and in Anderson, *America not discovered by Columbus*, 3d ed.).

Brasseur de Bourbourg in his *Nations civilisées du Méxique*, and more emphatically in his *Grammaire Quichée*, had indicated what he thought a northern incursion before Leif, in certain seeming similarities to the northern tongues of those of Guatemala. Cf. also *Nouv. Annales des Voyages*, 6th ser., xvi. 263; *N. Y. Tribune*, Nov. 21, 1855; Bancroft's *Native Races*, iii. 762.

1 *De origine gentium Americanarum* (1642).

2 *Nouv. Ann. des Voyages*, 6th ser., vols. iii. and vi.

3 In Charnay's *Ruines*, etc. (Paris, 1867).

4 *Découverte de l'America par les Normands* (Paris, 1864).

5 H. H. Bancroft, *Nat. Races*, v. 115–16, gives references on the peopling of America from the northwest of Europe.

6 *Trans. Roy. Soc. Lit.*, xiv. 1887; also printed separately as *Mythology, legends and Folk-lore of the Algonquins*. Cf. also his *Algonquin Legends of New England* (1885). Cf. D. G. Brinton in *Amer. Antiquarian*, May, 1885.

7 Mr. Mitchell, of the U. S. Coast Survey, has attended to this part of the subject, and Horsford (p. 28) quotes his MS. He finds on the Massachusetts coast what he thinks a sufficient correspondence to the description of the sagas.

8 So plain a matter as the length of the longest summer day would indubitably point to an absolute parallel of latitude as determining the site of Vinland, if there was no doubt in the language of the saga. Unfortunately there is a wide divergence of opinion in the meaning of the words to be depended upon, even among Icelandic scholars; and the later writers among them assert that Rafn (*Antiq. Amer.* 436) and Magnusen in interpreting the language to confirm their theory of the Rhode Island bays have misconceived. Their argument is summarized in the French version of Wheaton. John M'Caul translated Finn Magnusen's "Ancient Scandinavian divisions of the times of day," in the *Mémoire de la Soc. Roy. des Antiq. du Nord* (1836–37). Rask disputes Rafn's deductions (*Mass. Hist. Soc. Proc.*, xviii. 22). Torfæus, who is our best commentator after all, says it meant Newfoundland. Robertson put it at 58° north. Dahlmann in his *Forschungen* (vol. i.) places it on the coast of Labrador. Horsford (p. 66) at some length admits no question that it must have been between 41° and 43° north. Cf. Laing's *Heimskringla*, i. 173; Palfrey's *New England*, i. 55; De Costa's *Pre-Columbian Disc.*, p. 33; Weise's *Discoveries of America*, 31; and particularly Vigfússon in his *English-Icelandic Dictionary* under "Eykt."

9 "The discovery of America," says Laing (*Heimskringla*, i. 154), "rests entirely upon documentary evidence which cannot, as in the case of Greenland, be substantiated by anything to be discovered in America." Laing and many of the commentators, by some strange process of reasoning, have determined that the proof of these MS. records being written before Columbus' visit to Iceland in 1477 is sufficient to establish the priority of discovery for the Northmen, as if it was nothing in the case that the sagas may or may not be good history; and nothing that it was the opinion entertained in Europe at that time that Greenland and the more distant lands were not a new continent, but a prolongation of Europe by the north. It is curious, too, to observe that, treating of events after 1492, Laing is quite willing to believe in any saga being "filled up and new invented," but is quite unwilling to believe anything of the kind as respects those written anterior to 1492; and yet he goes on to prove conclusively that the *Flatoyensis Codex* is full of fable, as when the saga man makes the eider-duck lay eggs where during the same weeks the grapes ripen and intoxicate when fresh, and the wheat forms in the ear! Laing nevertheless rests his case on the *Flatoyensis Codex* in its most general scope, and calls poets, but not antiquaries, those who attempt to make any additional evidence out of imaginary runes or the identification of places.

farther agree than to place Vinland anywhere from Greenland to Africa.[1]

The earliest to go so far as to establish to a certainty[2] the sites of the sagas was Rafn, who

[1] It must be remembered that this divergence was not so wide to the Northmen as it seems to us. With them the Atlantic was sometimes held to be a great basin that was enclasped from northwestern Europe by a prolongation of Scandinavia into Greenland, Helluland, and Markland, and it was a question if the more distant region of Vinland did not belong rather to the corresponding prolongation of Africa on the south. Cf. De Costa, *Pre-Columbian Disc.*, 108; *Hist. Mag.*, xiii. 46.

[2] He wrote: "Here for the first time will be found indicated the precise spot where the ancient Northmen held their intercourse." The committee of the Mass. Hist. Soc. objected to this extreme confidence. *Proceedings*, ii. 97, 107, 500, 505.

NOTE. — The above map is a fac-simile of one of C. C. Rafn's maps. Cf. the maps in Smith, Beamish Gravier, Slafter, Preble's *Amer. Flag*, etc.

DIGHTON ROCK.*

* Reproduction of part of the plate in the *Antiquitates Americanæ*, after a drawing by J. R. Bartlett. The engravings of the rock are numerous: *Mem. Amer. Acad.*, iii.; the works of Beamish, J. T. Smith, Gravier, Gay, Higginson, etc.; Laing's *Heimskringla;* the French ed. of Wheaton; Hermes' *Entdeckung von Ame-*

placed them on the coast of Massachusetts and Rhode Island, wherein nearly all those have followed him who have thought it worth while to be thus particular as to headland and bay.

In applying the saga names they have, however, by no means agreed, for Krossanes is with some Point Alderton, at the entrance of Boston Harbor, and with others the Gurnet Head; the island where honey dew was found is Nantucket with Rafn, and with De Costa an insular region, Nauset, now under water near the elbow of Cape Cod;[1] the Vinland of Rafn is in Narragansett Bay, that of Dr. A. C. Hamlin is at Merry Meeting Bay on the coast of Maine,[2] and that of Horsford is north of Cape Cod,[3]—not to mention other disagreements of other disputants.

We get something more tangible, if not more decisive, when we come to the monumental evidences. DeWitt Clinton and Samuel L. Mitchell found little difficulty at one time in making many people believe that the earthworks of Onondaga were Scandinavian. A pretended runic inscription on a stone said to have been found in the Grave Creek mound was sedulously ascribed to the Northmen.[4] What some have called a runic inscription exists on a rock near Yarmouth in Nova Scotia, which is interpreted "Hako's son addressed the men," and is supposed to commemorate the expedition of Thorfinn in A. D. 1007.[5] A rock on the little islet of Menana, close to Monhegan, on the coast of Maine, and usually referred to as the Monhegan Rock, bears certain weather marks, and there have been those to call them runes.[6] A similar claim is made for a rock in the Merrimac Valley.[7] Rafn describes such rocks as situated in Tiverton and Portsmouth Grove, R. I., but the markings were Indian, and when Dr. S. A. Green visited the region in 1868 some of them had disappeared.[8]

1 De Costa, *Pre-Col. Disc.*, 29; *N. E. Hist. Geneal. Reg.*, xviii. 37; Gay, *Pop. Hist.*, i. 41; *Mass. Hist. Soc. Coll.*, viii. 72; *Am. Geog. Soc. Journal*, 1870, p. 50; *Amer. Naturalist*, Aug. and Sept., 1879.

2 *Am. Ass. Adv. Science, Proc.* (1856), ii. 214.

3 Cf. paper on the site of Vinland in *Hist. Mag.*, Feb., 1874, p. 94; Alex. Farnum's *Visit of the Northmen to Rhode Island* (*R. I. Hist. Tracts*, no. 2, 1877). The statement of the sagas that there was no frost in Vinland and grass did not wither in winter compels some of the identifiers to resort to the precession of the equinox as accounting for changes of climate (Gay's *Pop. Hist.*, i. 50).

4 E. G. Squier in *Ethnological Journal*, 1848; Wilson's *Prehist. Man*, ii. 98; *Amer. Ethnol. Soc. Trans.*, i. 392; Schoolcraft's *Indian Tribes*, iv. 118; *Mém. de la Soc. royale des Antiq. du Nord*, 1840–44, p. 127.

5 *Amer. Philos. Soc. Proc.*, May 2, 1884 (by Henry Phillips, Jr.); *Numismatic and Antiq. Soc. of Philad., Proc.*, 1884, p. 17; Geo. S. Brown's *Yarmouth* (Boston, 1888).

6 Wilson's *Prehist. Man*, ii. 98; *Amer. Asso. Adv. Science, Proc.*, 1856, p. 214; *Séance annuelle de la Soc. des Antiq. du Nord*, May 14, 1859; H. W. Haynes in *Mass. Hist. Soc. Proc.*, Jan., 1888, p. 56. The Monhegan inscription, as examined by the late C. W. Tuttle and J. Wingate Thornton, was held to be natural markings (*Mag. Amer. Hist.*, ii. 308; *Pulpit of the Revolution*, 410). Charles Rau cites a striking instance of the way in which the lively imagination of Finn Magnusen has misled him in interpreting weather cracks on a rock in Sweden (*Mag. Amer. Hist.*, ii. 83).

7 *N. E. Hist. Geneal. Reg.*, 1854, p. 185.

8 *Antiquitates Americanæ*, 335, 371, 401; *Amer. Antiq. Soc. Proc.*, Oct., 1868, p. 13; W. J. Miller's *Wampanoag Indians.*

rica; Schoolcraft's *Ind. Tribes*, i. 114, iv. 120; Drake's ed., Philad., 1884, i. p. 88; the Copenhagen *Compte Rendu, Congrès des Américanistes*, p. 70, from a photograph. The Hitchcock Museum at Amherst, Mass., had a cast, and one was shown at the Albany meeting (1836) of the Am. Asso. for the Adv. of Science. The rock was conveyed by deed in 1861 to the Roy. Soc. of Northern Antiquaries (*Mass. Hist. Soc. Proc.*, v. 226; vi. 252), but the society subsequently relinquished their title to a Boston committee, who charged itself with the care of the monument; but in doing so the Danish antiquaries disclaimed all belief in its runic character (*Mag. Amer. Hist.*, iii. 236).

NOTE. — The opposite plate is reduced from one in the *Antiq. Americanæ.* They show the difficulty, even before later weathering, of different persons in discerning the same things on the rock, and in discriminating between fissures and incisions. Col. Garrick Mallery (*4th Rept. Bureau of Ethnology*, p. 250) asserts that the inscription has been "so manipulated that it is difficult now to determine the original details." The drawings represented are enumerated in the text. Later ones are numerous. Rafn also gives that of Dr. Baylies and Mr. Gooding in 1790, and that made for the Rhode Island Hist. Society in 1830. The last has perhaps been more commonly copied than the others. Photographs of late years are common; but almost invariably the photographer has chalked what he deems to be the design, — in this they do not agree, of course, — in order to make his picture clearer. I think Schoolcraft in making his daguerreotype was the first to do this. The most careful drawing made of late years is that by Professor Seager of the Naval Academy, under the direction of Commodore Blake; and there is in the Cabinet of the American Antiquarian Society a MS. essay on the rock, written at Blake's request by Chaplain Chas. R. Hale of the U. S. Navy. Haven disputes Blake's statement that a change in the river's bed more nearly submerges the rock at high tide than was formerly the case. Cf. *Am. Antiq. Soc. Proc.*, Oct., 1864, p. 41, where a history of the rock is given; and in Wilson's *Prehistoric Man*, ii. 93.

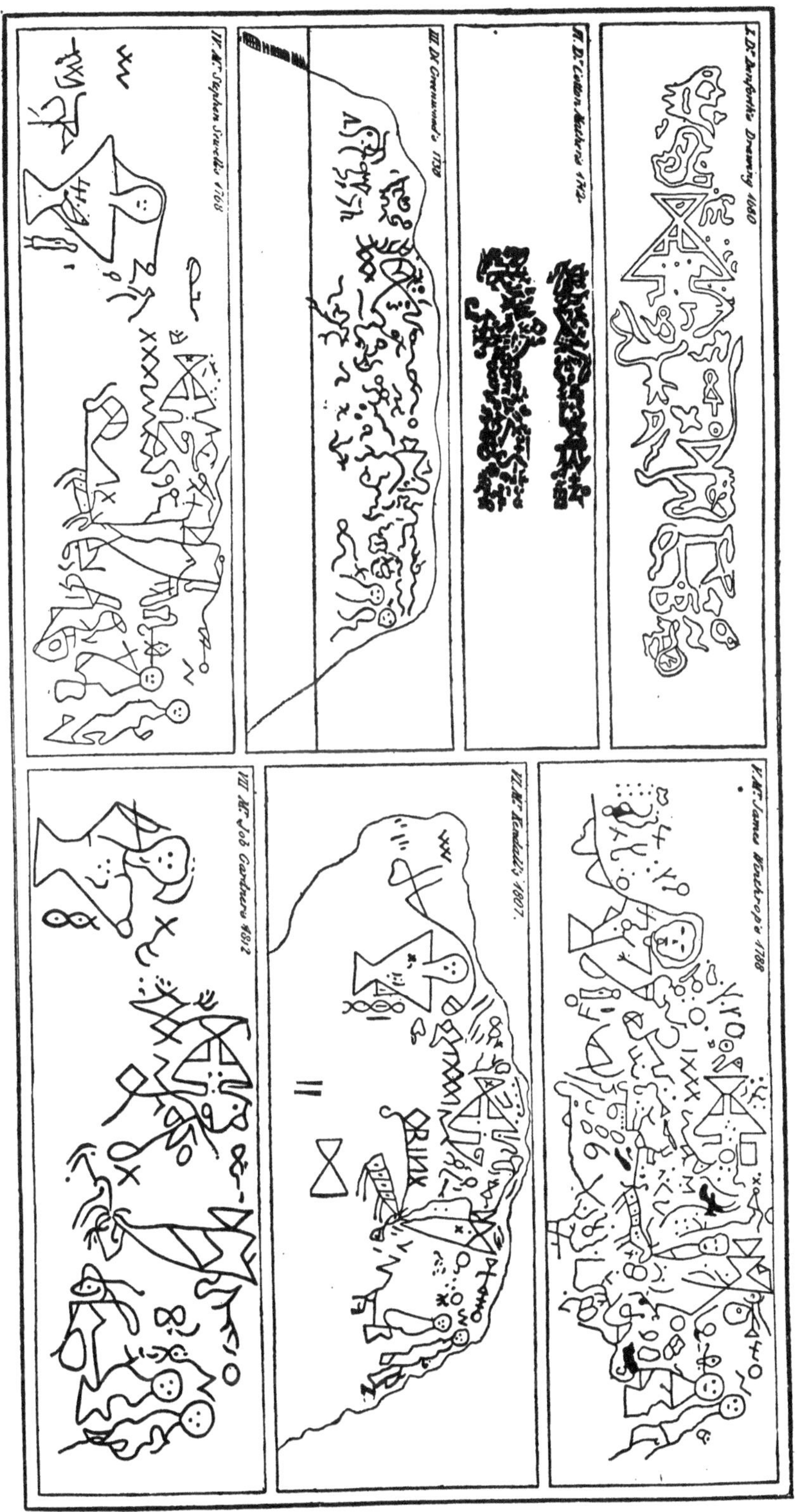

INSCRIPTION ON DIGHTON ROCK. (See p. 102.)

The most famous of all these alleged memorials[1] is the Dighton Rock, lying in the tide on the side of Taunton River, in the town of Berkeley, in Massachusetts.[2] Dr. De Costa thinks it possible that the central portion may be runic. This part is what has been interpreted to mean that Thorfinn with 151 men took possession of the country, and it is said to be this portion of the inscription which modern Indians discard when giving their interpretations.[3] That it is the work of the Indian of historic times seems now to be the opinion common to the best trained archæologists.[4]

Rafn was also the first to proclaim the stone

[1] Cf. list of inscribed rocks in the *Proceedings* (vol. ii.) of the Davenport Acad. of Natural Sciences.

[2] The stone with its inscription early attracted attention, but Danforth's drawing of 1680 is the earliest known. Cotton Mather, in a dedicatory epistle to Sir Henry Ashurst, prefixed to his *Wonderful Works of God commemorated* (Boston, 1690), gave a cut of a part of the inscription; and he communicated an account with a drawing of the inscription to the Royal Society in 1712, which appears in their *Philosophical Transactions.* Dr. Isaac Greenwood sent another draft to the Society of Antiquaries in London in 1730, and their *Transactions* in 1732 has this of Greenwood. In 1768 Professor Stephen Sewall of Cambridge made a copy of the natural size, which was sent in 1774 by Professor James Winthrop to the Royal Society. Dr. Stiles says that Sewall sent it to Gebelin, of the French Academy, whose members judged them to be Punic characters. Stiles himself, in 1783, in an election sermon delivered at Hartford, spoke of "the visit by the Phœnicians, who charged the Dighton Rock and other rocks in Narragansett Bay with Punic inscriptions remaining to this day, which last I myself have repeatedly seen and taken off at large." Cf. Thornton's *Pulpit of the Revolution*, p. 410. The *Archæologia* (London, viii. for 1786) gave various drawings, with a paper by the Rev. Michael Lort and some notes by Charles Vallancey, in which the opinion was expressed that the inscription was the work of a people from Siberia, driven south by hordes of Tartars. Professor Winthrop in 1788 filled the marks, as he understood them, with printer's ink, and in this way took an actual impression of the inscription. His copy was engraved in the *Memoirs of the American Academy of Arts and Sciences* (vol. ii. for 1793). It was this copy by Winthrop which Washington in 1789 saw at Cambridge, when he pronounced the inscription as similar to those made by the Indians, which he had been accustomed to see in the western country during his life as a surveyor. Cf. *Belknap Papers, Mass. Hist. Soc. Coll.*, ii. 76, 77, 81; *Mass. Hist. Soc. Proc.*, x. 114. In 1789 there was also presented to the Academy a copy made by Joseph Gooding under the direction of Francis Baylies (*Belknap Papers*, ii. 160). In the third volume of the Academy's *Memoirs* there are papers on the inscription by John Davis and Edward A. Kendall; Davis (1807) thinking it a representation of an Indian deer hunt, and Kendall later, in his *Travels* (vol. ii. 1809), assigns it to the Indians. This description is copied in Barber's *Historical Collections of Mass.* (p. 117). In 1812 a drawing was made by Job Gardner, and in 1825 there was further discussion in the *Mémoires de la Société de Géographie de Paris*, and in the *Hist. of New York* by Yates and Moulton. In 1831 there was a cut in Ira Hill's *Antiquities of America explained* (Hagerstown, Md.) This was in effect the history of the interest in the rock up to the appearance of Rafn's *Antiquitates Americanæ*, in which for the first time the inscription was represented as being the work of the Northmen. This belief is now shared by few, if any, temperate students. The exuberant Anderson thinks that the rock removes all doubt of the Northmen discovery (*America not discovered by Columbus*, pp. 21, 23, 83). The credulous Gravier has not a doubt. Cf. his *Notice sur le roc de Dighton et le séjour des Scandinaves en Amérique au commencement du XIe siècle* (Nancy, 1875), reprinted from the *Compte Rendu, Congrès des Américanistes*, i. 166, giving Rafn's drawing. The Rev. J. P. Bodfish accepts its evidence in the *Proc. Second Pub. Meeting U. S. Cath. Hist. Soc.* (N. Y., 1886).

[3] *Pre-Columbian Discovery of America*, p. lvii. The *Brinley Catalogue*, iii. 5378, gives Dammartin's *Explification de la pierre de Taunston* (Paris? 1840–50) as finding in the inscription an astronomical theme by some nation foreign to America. Buckingham Smith believed it to be a Roman Catholic invocation, around which the Indians later put their symbols (*Amer. Antiq. Soc. Proc.*, Apr. 29, 1863, p. 32). For discussions more or less extensive see Laing's *Heimskringla*, i. 175; Haven in *Smithsonian Contributions*, 1856, viii. 133, in a paper on the "Archæology of the United States;" Charles Rau in *Mag. Amer. Hist.*, Feb., 1878; Apr., 1879; and in *Amer. Antiquarian*, i. 38; Daniel Wilson's *Prehistoric Man*, ii. 97; J. R. Bartlett in *Rhode Island Hist. Soc. Proc.*, 1872–73, p. 70; Haven and others in *Am. Antiq. Soc. Proc.*, Oct., 1864, and Oct., 1867; H. H. Bancroft's *Native Races*, v. 74; Drake's *N. E. Coast; North American Rev.*, 1874; *Amer. Biblical Repository*, July, 1839; *Historical Mag.*, Dec., 1859, and March, 1869; Lelewel's *Moyen Age*, iii.; H. W. Williams's transl. of Humboldt's *Travels*, i. 157, etc.

[4] Schoolcraft wavered in his opinion. (Cf. Haven, 133.) He showed Gooding's drawing to an Algonkin chief, who found in it a record of a battle of the Indians, except that some figures near the centre did not belong to it, and these Schoolcraft thought might be runic, as De Costa has later suggested; but in 1853 Schoolcraft made no reservation in pronouncing it entirely Indian (*Indian Tribes*, i. 112; iv. 120; pl. 14). Wilson (*Prehist. Man*, ii., ch. 19) is severe on Schoolcraft. On the general character of Indian rock inscriptions, — some of which in the delineations accompanying these accounts closely resemble the Dighton Rock, — see Mallery in the *Bureau of Ethnology, Fourth Report*, p. 19; Lieut. A. M. Wheeler's Report on Indian tribes in *Pacific Rail Road Reports*, ii.; J. G. Bruff on those of Green River in the Sierra Nevada, in

tower now standing at Newport, R. I., as a work of the Northmen; but the recent antiquaries without any exception worth considering, believe that the investigations have shown that it was erected by Governor Arnold of Rhode Island as a windmill, sometime between 1670 and 1680; and Palfrey in his *New England* is thought to have put this view beyond doubt in showing the close correspondence in design of the tower to a mill at Chesterton, in England.[1]

Certain hearthstones which were discovered over twenty-five years ago under a peat bed on Cape Cod were held at the time to be a Norse relic.[2] In 1831 there was exhumed in Fall River, Mass., a skeleton, which had with it what seemed to be an ornamental belt made of metal tubes, formed by rolling fragments of flat brass and an oblong plate of the same metal, — not of bronze, as is usually said,— with some arrow-heads, cut evidently from the same material. The other concomitants of the burial indicated an Indian of the days since the English contact. The skeleton attracted notice in this country by being connected with the Norsemen in Longfellow's ballad, *The Skeleton in Armor*, and Dr. Webb sent such an account of it to the Royal Society of Northern Antiquaries that it was looked upon as another and distinct proof of the identification of Vinland. Later antiquaries have dismissed all beliefs of that nature.[3]

There is not a single item of all the evidence thus advanced from time to time which can be said to connect by archæological traces the presence of the Northmen on the soil of North America south of Davis' Straits. Arguments of this kind have been abandoned except by a few enthusiastic advocates.

That the Northmen voyaging to Vinland encountered natives, and that they were called Skraelings, may be taken as a sufficiently broad statement in the sagas to be classed with those concomitants of the voyages which it is reasonable to accept. Sir William Dawson (*Fossil Men*, 49) finds it easy to believe that these natives were our red Indians; and Gallatin saw no reason to dissociate the Eskimos with other American tribes.[4] That they were Eskimos seems to be the more commonly accepted view.[5]

Smithsonian Rept. (1872); *American Antiquarian*, iv. 259; vi. 119; *Western Reserve Hist. Soc. Tracts*, nos. 42, 44, 52, 53, 56; T. Ewbank's *No. Amer. Rock Writing* (Morrisania, 1866); Brinton's *Myths of the New World*, p. 10; Tylor's *Early Hist. Mankind;* Dr. Richard Andree's *Ethnographische Parallelen und Vergleiche* (Stuttgard, 1878). It is Mallery's opinion that no "considerable information of value in an historical point of view will be obtained directly from the interpretations of the Pictographs in North America."

1 Palfrey, i. p. 57; Higginson's *Larger Hist.*, 44; Gay's *Pop. Hist.*, i. 59, 60; Laing's *Heimskringla*, i. 183; Charles T. Brooks's *Controversy touching the old stone mill in Newport* (Newport, 1851); Peterson's *Rhode Island;* Drake's *New England Coast;* Schoolcraft's *Indian Tribes*, iv. 120; Bishop's *Amer. Manufactures*, i. 118; C. S. Pierce in *Science*, iv. 512, who endeavored by measurement to get at what was the unit of measure used, — an effort not very successful. Cf. references in *Poole's Index*, p. 913.

Gaffarel accepts the Rafn view in his *Etudes sur la rapports*, etc., 282, as does Gravier in his *Normands sur la route*, p. 168; and De Costa (*Pre-Columbian Disc.*, p. lviii) intimates that "all is in a measure doubtful." R. G. Hatfield (*Scribner's Monthly*, Mar., 1879) in an illustrated paper undertook to show by comparison with Scandinavian building that what is now standing is but the central part of a Vinland baptistery, and that the projection which supported the radiating roof timbers is still to be seen. This paper was answered by George C. Mason (*Mag. Amer. Hist.*, iii. 541, Sept., 1879, with other remarks in the *Amer. Architect*, Oct. 4, 1879), who rehearsed the views of the local antiquaries as to its connection with Gov. Arnold. Cf. *Reminiscences of Newport*, by Geo. C. Mason, 1884.

2 *Hist. Mag.*, Apr., 1862, p. 123; *N. E. Hist. Geneal. Reg.*, 1865, p. 372; Abner Morse's *Traces of the Ancient Northmen in America* (Aug., 1861), with a *Supplement* (Boston, 1887).

3 *Mémoires de la Soc. roy. des Antiq. du Nord*, 1843; *New Jersey Hist. Soc. Proc.*, vi.; Stone's *Brant*, ii. 593–94; Schoolcraft's *Ind. Tribes*, i. 127; *Smithsonian Rept.*, 1883, p. 902; Dr. Kneeland in *Peabody Mus. Repts.*, no. 20, p. 543. The skeleton was destroyed by fire about 1843.

4 Dawkins in his *Cave Hunters* accounts them survivors of the cave dwellers of Europe. Cf. Wilson's *Prehistoric Man*. A. R. Grote (*Amer. Naturalist*, Apr., 1877) holds them to be the survivors of the palæolithic man.

5 E. Beauvois' *Les Skroelings, Ancêtres des Esquimaux* (Paris, 1879); B. F. DeCosta in *Pop. Science Monthly*, Nov., 1884; A. S. Packard on their former range southward, in the *American Naturalist*, xix. 471, 553, and his paper on the Eskimos of Labrador, in *Appleton's Journal*, Dec. 9, 1871 (reprinted in Beach's *Indian Miscellany*, Albany, 1877). Humboldt holds them to have been driven across America to Europe (*Views of Nature*, Bohn's ed., 123). Ethnologists are not wholly agreed as to the course of their migrations. The material for the ethnological study of the Eskimos must be looked for in the narratives of the Arctic voyagers, like Scoresby, Parry, Ross, O'Reilly, Kane, C. F. Hall, and the rest; in the accounts by the missionaries like Egede, Crantz, and others; by students of ethnology, like Lubbock (*Prehist. Times*, ch. 14); Prichard (*Researches*, v. 367); Waitz (*Amerikaner*, i. 300); the Abbé Morillot (*Mythologie et légendes des Esquimaux du Groenland* in the *Actes de la Soc. Philologique* (Paris, 1875), vol. iv.); Morgan (*Systems of Consanguinity*,

That the climate of the Atlantic coast of the United States and the British provinces was such as was favorable to the present Arctic dwellers is held to be shown by such evidences as tusks of the walrus found in phosphate beds in South Carolina. Rude implements found in the interglacial Jersey drift have been held by C. C. Abbott to have been associated with a people of the Eskimo stock, and some have noted that palæolithic implements found in Pennsylvania closely resemble the work of the modern Eskimos (*Amer. Antiquarian*, i. 10).[1] Dall remarks upon implements of Innuit origin being found four hundred miles south of the present range of the Eskimos of the northwest coast (*Contributions to Amer. Ethnology*, i. p. 98). Charlevoix says that Eskimos were occasionally seen in Newfoundland in the beginning of the last century; and ethnologists recognize to-day the same stock in the Eskimos of Labrador and Greenland.

The best authority on the Eskimos is generally held to be Hinrich Rink, and he contends that they formerly occupied the interior of the continent, and have been pressed north and across Behring's Straits.[2] W. H. Dall holds similar

HENRIK RINK.*

267), who excludes them from his Ganowanian family; Irving C. Rosse on the northern inhabitants (*Journal Amer. Geog. Soc.*, 1883, p. 163); Ludwig Kumlien in his *Contributions to the natural history of Arctic America*, made in connection with the Howgate polar expedition, 1877–78, in *Bull. of the U. S. Naval Museum* (Washington, 1879), no. 15; and his paper in the *Smithsonian Report* (1878). There are several helpful papers in the *Journal of the Anthropological Institute* (London), vol. i., by Richard King, on their intellectual character; vol. iv. by P. C. Sutherland; vol. vii. by John Rae on their migrations, and W. H. Flower on their skulls; vol. ix. by W. J. Sollars on their bone implements. For other references see Bancroft, *Native Races*, i. 41, 138; *Poole's Index*, p. 424, and *Supplement*, p. 146.

1 This evidence is of course rather indicative of a geological antiquity not to be associated with the age of the Northmen. Cf. Murray's *Distribution of Animals*, 128; Howarth's *Mammoth and Flood*, 285.

2 Rink, born in 1819 in Copenhagen, spent much of the interval from 1853 to 1872 in Greenland. Pilling (*Bibl. Eskimo Language*, p. 80) gives the best account of Rink's publications. His principal book is *Grönland*

* After a likeness given by Nordenskjöld in his *Exped. till Grönland*, p. 121.

views.[1] C. R. Markham, who dates their first appearance in Greenland in 1349, contends, on the other hand, that they came from the west (Siberia) along the polar regions (Wrangell Land), and drove out the Norse settlers in Greenland.[2] The most active of the later students of the Eskimos is Dr. Franz Boas, now of New York, who has discussed their tribal boundaries.[3]

F. The Lost Greenland Colonies. — After intercourse with the colonies in Greenland ceased, and definite tradition in Iceland had died out, and when the question of the re-discovery should arise, it was natural that attention should first be turned to that coast of Greenland which lay opposite Iceland as the likelier sites of the lost colonies, and in this way we find all the settlements placed in the maps of the sixteenth century. The Archbishop Erik Walkendorf, of Lund, in the early part of that century had failed to persuade the Danish government to send an expedition. King Frederick II was induced, however, to send one in 1568; but it accomplished nothing; and again in 1579 he put another in command of an Englishman, Jacob Allday, but the ice prevented his landing. A Danish navigator was more successful in 1581; but the coast opposite Iceland yielded as yet no traces of the Norse settlers. Frobisher's discovery of the west coast seems to have failed of recognition among the Danes; but they with the rest of Europe did not escape noting the importance of the explorations of John Davis in 1585–86, through the straits which bear his name. It now became the belief that the west settlement must be beyond Cape Farewell. In 1605, Christian IV of Denmark sent a new expedition under Godske Lindenow; but there was a Scotchman in command of one of the three ships, and Jacob Hall, who had probably served under Davis, went as the fleet pilot. He guided the vessels through Davis's Straits. But it was rather the purpose of Lindenow to find a northwest passage than to discover a lost colony; and such was mainly the object which impelled him again in 1606, and inspired Karsten Rikardsen in 1607. Now and for some years to come we have the records of voyages made by the whalers to this region, and we read their narratives in Purchas and in such collections of voyages as those of Harris and Churchill.[4] They yield us, however, little or no help in the problem we are discussing. In 1670 and 1671 Christian V sent expeditions with the express purpose of discovering the lost colonies; but Otto Axelsen, who commanded, never returned from his second voyage, and we have no account of his first.

The mission of the priest Hans Egede gave the first real glimmer of light.[5] He was the

geographisch und statistisch beschrieben (Stuttgart, 1860). The English reader has access to his *Tales and Traditions of the Eskimo*, translated by Rink himself, and edited by Dr. Robert Brown (London, 1875); to *Danish Greenland, its people and its products*, ed. by Dr. Brown (London, 1877). Rink says of this work that in its English dress it must be considered a new book. He also published *The Eskimo tribes; their distribution and characteristics, especially in regard to language. With a comparative vocabulary* (Copenhagen, *etc.*, 1887). He also considered their dialects as divulging the relationship of tribes in the *Journal of the Anthropological Institute* (xv. 239); and in the same journal (1872, p. 104) he has written of their descent. Rink also furnished to the *Compte Rendu, Congrès des Américanistes*, a paper on the traditions of Greenland (Nancy, 1875, ii. 181), and (Luxembourg, 1877, ii. 327) another on "L'habitat primitif des Esquimaux."

Dr. Brown has also considered the "Origin of the Eskimo" in the *Archæological Review* (1888), no. 4.

[1] *Alaska and its Resources*, p. 374; and in *Contributions to Amer. Ethnology*, i. 93.

[2] "On the origin and migrations of the Greenland Esquimaux" in the *Journal Royal Geog. Soc.*, 1865; "The Arctic highlanders" in the *Lond. Ethnol. Soc. Trans.* (1866), iv. 125, and in *Arctic Geography and Ethnology* (London, 1875), published by the Royal Geog. Society.

[3] *American Antiquarian*, Jan., 1888. Cf. other papers by him in the *Proc. Roy. Soc. of Canada*, vol. v. "A year among the Eskimos" in the *Journal Amer. Geog. Soc.*, 1887, xix. p. 383; "Reise in Baffinland" in the proceedings of the Berlin Gesellschaft für Erdkunde (1885). Cf. Pilling's *Eskimo Bibliog.*, p. 12; and for linguistic evidences of tribal differences, pp. 69–72, 81–82. Cf. also H. H. Bancroft's *Native Races*, iii. 574, and Lucien Adam's "En quoi la langue Esquimaude, diffère-t-elle grammaticalement des autres langues de l'Amérique du Nord?" in the *Compte Rendu, Congrès des Amér.* (Copenhagen), p. 337.

Anton von Etzel's *Grönland, geographisch und statistisch beschrieben aus Dänischen Quellschriften* (Stuttgart, 1860) goes cursorily over the early history, and describes the Eskimos. Cf. F. Schwatka in *Amer. Magazine*, Aug., 1888.

[4] There is an easy way of tracing these accounts in Joel A. Allen's *List of Works and Papers relating to the mammalian orders of Cete and Sirenia*, extracted from the *Bulletin of Hayden's U. S. Geol. and Geog. Survey* (Washington, 1882). It is necessary to bear in mind that Spitzbergen is often called Greenland in these accounts.

[5] His book, *Det gamle Grönlands nye Perlustration*, etc., was first published at Copenhagen in 1729. Pilling (*Bibliog. of the Eskimo language*, p. 26) was able to find only a single copy of this book, that in the British Museum. Muller (*Books on America*, Amsterdam, 1872, no. 648) describes a copy. This first edition escaped the notice of J. A. Allen, whose list is very carefully prepared (nos. 217, 220, 226, 230, 235). There

earliest to describe the ruins and relics observable on the west coast, but he continued to regard the east settlements as belonging to the east coast, and so placed them on the map. Anderson (Hamburg, 1746) went so far as to place on his map the cathedral of Gardar in a fixed location on the east coast, and his map was variously copied in the following years.

In 1786 an expedition left Copenhagen to explore the east coast for traces of the colonies, but the ice prevented the approach to the coast, and after attempts in that year and in 1787 the effort was abandoned. Heinrich Peter von Eggers, in his *Om Grönlands österbygds sande Beliggenhed* (1792), and *Ueber die wahre Lage des alten Ostgrönlands* (Kiel, 1794), a German translation, first advanced the opinion that the eastern colony as well as the western must have been on the west coast, and his views were generally accepted; but Wormskjöld in the *Skandinavisk Litteraturselskab's Skrifter*, vol. x. (Copenhagen, 1814), still adhered to the earlier

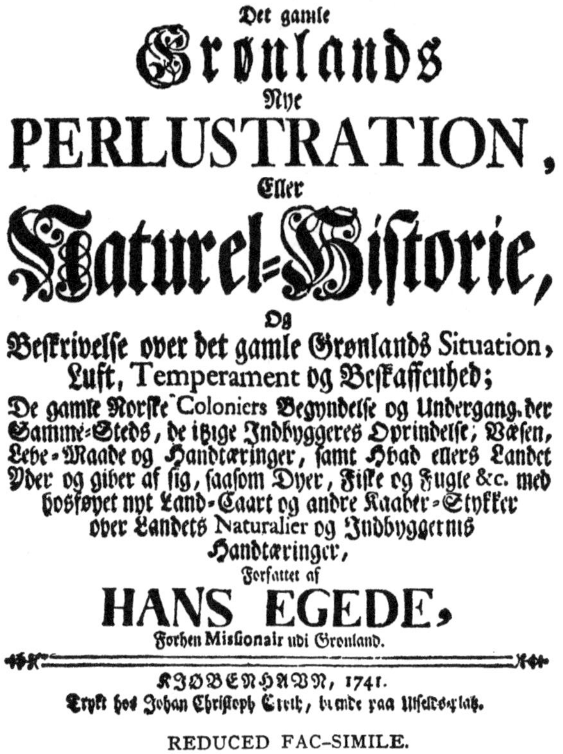

Det gamle
Grønlands
Nye
PERLUSTRATION,
Eller
Naturel-Historie,
Og
Beskrivelse over det gamle Grønlands Situation, Luft, Temperament og Beskaffenhed;
De gamle Norske Coloniers Begyndelse og Undergang der Samme-Steds, de itzige Indbyggeres Oprindelse, Væsen, Leve-Maade og Handteringer, samt Hvad ellers Landet Yder og giver af sig, saasom Dyer, Fiske og Fugle &c. med hosføyet nyt Land-Caart og andre Kaaber-Stykker over Landets Naturalier og Indbyggernis Handteringer,
Forfattet af
HANS EGEDE,
Forhen Missionair udi Grønland.

KIØBENHAVN, 1741.
Trykt hos Johan Christoph Groth, boende paa Ulfelds-Plads.

REDUCED FAC-SIMILE.

[Harvard College Library copy.]

were two German editions of this original form of the book, Frankfort, 1730, and Hamburg, 1740, according to the *Carter-Brown Catalogue* (ii. 448, 647), but Pilling gives only the first. The 1729 edition was enlarged in the Copenhagen edition of 1741, which has a map, "Gronlandia Antiqua," showing the east colony and west colony, respectively, east and west of Cape Farewell. This edition is the basis of the various translations: In German, Copenhagen, 1742, using the plates of the 1741 ed.; Berlin, 1763. In Dutch, Delft, 1746. In French, Copenhagen, 1763. In English, London, 1745; abstracted in the *Philosoph. Transactions Royal Soc.* (1744), xlii. no. 47; and again, London (1818), with an historical introduction based on Torfæus and La Peyrère. Crantz epitomizes Egede's career in Greenland.

The bibliography in Sabin's *Dictionary* (vi. 22,018, etc.) confounds the Greenland journal (1770–78) of Hans Egede's grandson, Hans Egede Saabye (b. 1746; d. 1817), with the work of the grandfather. This journal is of importance as regards the Eskimos and the missions among them. There is an English version: *Greenland: extracts from a journal kept in 1770 to 1778. Prefixed an introduction; illus. by chart of Greenland, by G. Fries. Transl. from the German* [*by H. E. Lloyd*] (London, 1818). The map follows that of the son of Hans, Paul Egede, whose *Nachrichten von Grönland aus einem Tagebuche von Bischof Paul Egede* (Copenhagen, 1790) must also be kept distinct. Pilling's *Bibliog. of the Eskimo language* affords the best guide.

opinions, and Saabye still believed it possible to reach the east coast.

Some years later (1828–31) W. A. Graah made, by order of the king of Denmark, a thorough examination of the east coast, and in his *Undersögelses Reise til Ostkysten af Grönland* (Copenhagen, 1832)[1] he was generally thought to establish the great improbability of any traces of a colony ever existing on that coast. Of late years Graah's conclusions have been questioned, for there have been some sites of buildings discovered on the east side.[2] The Reverend J. Brodbeck, a missionary, described some in *The Moravian Quarterly*, July and Aug., 1882. Nordenskjöld has held that when the east coast is explored from 65° to 69°, there is a chance of discovering the site of an east colony.[3]

R. H. Major, in a paper (*Journal Roy. Geog. Soc.*, 1873, p. 184) on the site of the lost colony, questioned Graah's conclusions, and gave a sketch map, in which he placed its site near Cape Farewell; and he based his geographical data largely upon the chorography of Greenland and the sailing directions of Ivan Bardsen, who was probably an Icelander living in Greenland some time in the fifteenth century.[4]

G. Madoc and the Welsh. — Respecting the legends of Madoc, there are reports, which Humboldt (*Cosmos*, Bohn, ii. 610) failed to verify, of Welsh bards rehearsing the story before 1492,[5] and of statements in the early Welsh annals. The original printed source is in Humfrey Lloyd's *History of Cambria, now called Wales, written in the British language* [by Caradoc] *about 200 years past* (London, 1584).[6] The book contained corrections and additions by David Powell, and it was in these that the passages of importance were found, and the supposition was that the land visited lay near the Gulf of Mexico. Richard Hakluyt, in his *Principall Navigations*, took the story from Powell, and connected the discovery with Mexico in his edition of 1589, and with the West Indies in that of 1600 (iii. p. 1), — and there was not an entire absence of the suspicion that it was worth while to establish some sort of a British claim to antedate the Spanish one established through Columbus.[7]

The linguistic evidences were not brought into prominence till after one Morgan Jones had fallen among the Tuscaroras[8] in 1660, and found, as he asserted, that they could under-

1 An English translation by Macdougall was published in London in 1837 (Pilling, p. 38; Field, no. 619). A French version of Graah's introduction with notes by M. de la Roquette was published in 1835. Cf. *Journal Royal Geog. Soc.*, i. 247. After Graah's publication Rafn placed the Osterbygden on the west coast in his map. Graah's report (1830) is in French in the *Bull. de la Soc. de Géog. de Paris*, 1830.

2 On the present scant, if not absence of, population on the east coast of Greenland, see J. D. Whitney's *Climatic Changes of later geological times* (*Mus. of Comp. Zoöl. Mem.*, vii. p. 303, Cambridge, 1882).

3 The changes in opinion respecting the sites of the colonies and the successive explorations are followed in the *Compte Rendu*, *Congrès des Américanistes* by Steenstrup (p. 114) and by Valdemar-Schmidt, "Sur les Voyages des Danois au Groenland" (195, 205, with references). Cf. on these lost colonies and the search for them *Westminster Review*, xxvii. 139; *Harper's Monthly*, xliv. 65 (by I. I. Hayes); *Lippincott's Mag.*, Aug., 1878; *Amer. Church Rev.*, xxi. 338; and in the general histories, La Peyrère (Dutch transl., Amsterdam, 1678); Crantz (Eng. transl., 1767, p. 272); Egede (Eng. ed., 1818, introd.); and Rink's *Danish Greenland*, ch. 1.

4 The original of Bardsen's account has disappeared, but Rafn puts it in Latin, translating from an early copy found in the Faröe Islands (*Antiquitates Americanæ*, p. 300). Purchas gives it in English, from a copy which had belonged to Hudson, being translated from a Dutch version which Hudson had borrowed, the Dutch being rendered by Barentz from a German version. Major also prints it in *Voyages of the Zeni*. He recognizes in Bardsen's "Gunnbiorn's Skerries" the island which is marked in Ruysch's map (1507) as blown up in 1456 (see Vol. III. p. 9).

5 Hakluyt, however, prints some pertinent verses by Meredith, a Welsh bard, in 1477.

6 *Murphy Catal.*, no. 1489; Sabin, x. p. 322; *Carter-Brown Catal.* for eds. of 1584, 1697, 1702, 1774, 1811, 1832, etc.

7 In the seventeenth century there were a variety of symptoms of the English eagerness to get the claims of Madoc substantiated, as in Sir Richard Hawkins's *Observations* (Hakluyt Soc., 1847), and James Howell's *Familiar Letters* (London, 1645). Belknap (*Amer. Biog.*, 1794, i. p. 58) takes this view of Hakluyt's purpose; but Pinkerton, *Voyages*, 1812, xii. 157, thinks such a charge an aspersion. The subject was mentioned with some particularity or incidentally by Purchas, Abbott (*Brief Description*, London, 1620, 1634, 1677), Smith (*Virginia*), and Fox (*North-West Fox*). Sir Thomas Herbert in his *Relation of some Travaile into Africa and Asia* (London, 1634) tracks Madoc to Newfoundland, and he also found Cymric words in Mexico, which assured him in his search for further proofs (Bohn's *Lowndes*, p. 1049; Carter-Brown, ii. 413, 1166).

The *Nieuwe en onbekende Weereld* of Montanus (Amsterdam, 1671) made the story more familiar. It necessarily entered into the discussions of the learned men who, in the seventeenth century, were busied with the question of the origin of the Americans, as in De Laet's *Notæ ad dissertationem Hugonis Grotii* (Paris, 1643), who is inclined to believe the story, as is Hornius in his *De Originibus Americaniis* (1652).

8 Cf. Catlin's *No. Amer. Indians*, i. 207; ii. 259, 262.

stand his Welsh. He wrote a statement of his experience in 1685–6, which was not printed till 1740.[1]

During the eighteenth century we find Campanius in his *Nye Swerige* (1702) repeating the story; Torfæus (*Hist. Vinlandiæ*, 1705) not rejecting it; Carte (*England*, 1747) thinking it probable; while Campbell (*Admirals*, 1742), Lyttleton (*Henry the Second*, 1767), and Robertson (*America*, 1777) thought there was no ground, at least, for connecting the story with America.

It was reported that in 1764 a man, Griffeth, was taken by the Shawnees to a tribe of Indians who spoke Welsh.[2] In 1768, Charles Beatty published his *Journal of a two months' Tour in America* (London), in which he repeated information of Indians speaking Welsh in Pennsylvania and beyond the Mississippi, and of the finding of a Welsh Bible among them.

In 1772–73, David Jones wandered among the tribes west of the Ohio, and in 1774, at Burlington, published his *Journal of two visits*, in which he enumerates the correspondence of words which he found in their tongues with his native Welsh.[3]

Without noting other casual mentions, some of which will be found in Paul Barron Watson's bibliography (in Anderson's *America not discovered by Columbus*, p. 142), it is enough to say that towards the end of the century the papers of John Williams[4] and George Burder[5] gave more special examination to the subject than had been applied before.

The renewed interest in the matter seems to have prompted Southey to the writing of his

A BRITISH SHIP.*

1 *Gentleman's Magazine.* It is reprinted in H. H. Bancroft's *Native Races*, v. 119, and in Baldwin's *Anc. America*, 286. Cf. John Paul Marana, *Letters writ by a Turkish Spy*, 1691, and later. The story had been told in *The British Sailors' Directory* in 1739 (Carter-Brown, iii. 599).

2 Warden's *Recherches*, p. 157; Amos Stoddard's *Sketches of Louisiana* (Philad., 1812), ch. 17, and *Philad. Med. and Physical Journal*, 1805; with views *pro* and *con* by Harry Toulmin and B. S. Barton.

3 The book was reprinted by Sabin, N. Y., 1865, with an introduction by Horatio Gates Jones.

4 *An inquiry into the truth of the tradition concerning the discovery of America by Prince Madog* (Lond., 1791), and *Further Observations . . . containing the account given by General Bowles, the Creek or Cherokee Indian, lately in London, and by several others, of a Welsh tribe of Indians now living in the western parts of North America* (Lond., 1792, — Field's *Ind. Bibliog.*, nos. 1664–65). Carey's *American Museum* (April, May, 1792), xi. 152, etc., gave extracts from Williams.

5 *The Welsh Indians, or a collection of papers respecting a people whose ancestors emigrated from Wales to America with Prince Madoc, and who are now said to inhabit a beautiful country on the west side of the Mississippi* (London, 1797). He finds these conditions in the Padoucas. Goodson, *Straits of Anian* (Portsmouth, 1793), p. 71, makes Padoucahs out of "Madogwys"!

* After a cut in *The Mirror of Literature*, etc. (London, 1823), vol. i. p. 177, showing a vessel then recently exhumed in Kent, and supposed to be of the time of Edward I, or the thirteenth century. The vessel was sixty-four feet long.

poem *Madoc*, though he refrained from publishing it for some years. If one may judge from his introductory note, Southey held to the historical basis of the narrative. Meanwhile, reports were published of this and the other tribes being found speaking Welsh.[1] In 1816, Henry Kerr printed at Elizabethtown, New Jersey, his *Travels through the Western interior of the United States, 1808–16, with some account of a tribe whose customs are similar to those of the ancient Welsh.* In 1824, Yates and Moulton (*State of New York*) went over the ground rather fully, but without conviction. Hugh Murray (*Travels in North America*, London, 1829) believes the Welsh went to Spain. In 1834, the different sides of the case were discussed by Farcy and Warden in Dupaix's *Antiquités Méxicaines.* Some years later the publication of George Catlin[2] probably gave more conviction than had been before felt,[3] arising from his statements of positive linguistic correspondences in the language of the so-called White[4] Mandans[5] on the Missouri River, the similarity of their boats to the old Welsh coracles, and other parallelisms of custom. He believed that Madoc landed at Florida, or perhaps passed up the Mississippi River. His conclusions were a reinforcement of those reached by Williams.[6] The opinion reached by Major in his edition of *Columbus' Letters* (London, 1847) that the Welsh discovery was quite possible, while it was by no means probable, is with little doubt the view most generally accepted to-day; while the most that can be made out of the claim is presented with the latest survey in B. F. Bowen's *America discovered by the Welsh in 1170 A. D.* (Philad., 1876). He gathers up, as helping his proposition, such widely scattered evidences as the Lake Superior copper mines and the Newport tower, both of which he appropriates; and while following the discoverers from New England south and west, he does not hesitate to point out the resemblance of the Ohio Valley mounds[7] to those depicted in Pennant's *Tour of Wales;* and he even is at no loss for proofs among the relics of the Aztecs.[8]

H. THE ZENI AND THEIR MAP. — Something has been said elsewhere (Vol. III. p. 100) of the influence of the Zeni narrative and its map, in confusing Frobisher in his voyages. The map was reproduced in the Ptolemy of 1561, with an account of the adventures of the brothers, but it was so far altered as to dissever Greenland from Norway, of which the Zeni map had made it but an extension.[9]

The story got further currency in Ramusio (1574, vol. ii.), Ortelius (1575), Hakluyt (1600, vol. iii.), Megiser's *Septentrio Novantiquus* (1613), Purchas (1625), Pontanus' *Rerum Danicarum* (1631), Luke Fox's *North-West Fox* (1633), and in De Laet's *Notæ* (1644), who, as well as Hornius, *De Originibus Americanis* (1644), thinks the story suspicious. It was repeated by Montanus in 1671, and by Capel, *Vorstellungen des Norden*, in 1676. Some of the features of the map had likewise become pretty constant in the attendant cartographical records. But from the close of the seventeenth century for about a hundred years, the story was for the most part ignored, and it was not till 1784 that the interest in it was revived by the publications of Forster[10]

1 *Chambers' Journal*, vi. 411, mentioning the Asguaws.

2 *Letter on the Manners, Customs, and Condition of the No. Amer. Indians* (N. Y., 1842).

3 He convinced, for instance, Fontaine in his *How the World was Peopled*, p. 142.

4 On the variety of complexion among the Indians, see Short's *No. Amer. of Antiq.*, p. 189; McCulloh's *Researches;* Haven, *Archæol. U. S.*, 48; Morton in *Schoolcraft*, ii. 320; *Ethnolog. Journal*, London, July, 1848; App. 1849, commenting on Morton.

5 Pilling, *Bibliog. of Siouan languages* (Washington, 1887, p. 48), enumerates the authorities on the Mandan tongue. The tribe is now extinct. Cf. Morgan's *Systems of Consanguinity*, p. 181.

6 See also *Smithsonian Report*, 1885, Part ii. pp. 80, 271, 349, 449. Ruxton in *Life in the Far West* (N. Y., 1846) found Welsh traces in the speech of the Mowquas, and S. Y. McMaster in *Smithsonian Rept.*, 1865, heard Welsh sounds among the Navajos.

7 Filson in his *Kentucke* has also pointed out this possibility.

8 The bibliography of the subject can be followed in Watson's list, already referred to, and in that in the *Amer. Bibliopolist*, Feb., 1869. A few additional references may help complete these lists: Stephens's *Literature of the Cymry*, ch. 2; the Abbé Domenech's *Seven Years in the Great Desert of America;* Tytler's *Progress of Discovery;* Moosmüller's *Europäer in Amerika vor Columbus* (Regensburg, 1879, ch. 21); Gaffarel's *Rapport* etc., p. 216; *Analytical Mag.*, ii. 409; *Atlantic Monthly*, xxxvii. 305; *No. Am. Rev.* (by E. E. Hale), lxxxv. 305; *Antiquary*, iv. 65; *Southern Presbyterian Rev.*, Jan., April, 1878; *Notes and Queries*, index.

9 This Ptolemy map is reproduced in Gravier's *Les Normands sur la route*, etc., 6th part, ch. 1; and in Nordenskjöld's *Studien und Forschungen* (Leipzig, 1805), p. 25. The Ptolemy of 1562 has the same plate.

10 J. R. Forster's *Discoveries in the Northern Regions.* His confidence was shared by Eggers (1794) in his *True Site of Old East Greenland* (Kiel), who doubts, however, if the descriptions of Estotiland apply to America. It was held to be a confirmation of the chart that both the east and west Greenland colonies were on the side of Davis's Straits.

and Buache,[1] who each expressed their belief in the story.

A more important inquiry in behalf of the narrative took place at Venice in 1808, when Cardinal Zurla republished the map in an essay, and marked out the track of the Zeni on a modern chart.[2]

In 1810, Malte-Brun accorded his belief in the verity of the narrative, and was inclined to believe that the Latin books found in Estotiland were carried there by colonists from Greenland.[3] A reactionary view was taken by Biddle in his *Sebastian Cabot*, in 1831, who believed the publication of 1558 a fraud; but the most effective denial of its authenticity came a few years later in sundry essays by Zahrtmann.[4]

The story got a strong advocate, after nearly forty years of comparative rest, when R. H. Major, of the map department of the British Museum, gave it an English dress and annexed a commentary, all of which was published by the Hakluyt Society in 1873. In this critic's view, the good parts of the map are of the fourteenth century, gathered on the spot, while the

RICHARD H. MAJOR.*

1 Buache reproduced the map, and read in 1784, before the Academy of Inscriptions in Paris, his *Mémoire sur la Frisland*, which was printed by the Academy in 1787, p. 430.

2 *Dissertazione intorno ai viaggi e scoperte settentrionali di Nicolo e Antonio Fratelli Zeni.* This paper was substantially reproduced in the same writer's *Di Marco Polo e degli altri Viaggiatori veneziani più illustri dissertazioni* (Venice, 1818).

3 *Annales des Voyages* (1810), x. 72; *Précis de la Géographie* (1817).

4 *Nordisk Tidsskrift for Oldkyndighed* (Copenhagen, 1834), vol. i. p. 1; *Royal Geog. Soc. Journal* (London, 1835), v. 102; *Annales des Voyages* (1836), xi.

George Folsom, in the *No. Amer. Rev.*, July, 1838, criticised Zahrtmann, and sustained an opposite view. T. H. Bredsdorff discussed the question in the *Grönlands Historiske Mindesmærker* (iii. 529); and La Roquette furnished the article in Michaud's *Biog. Universelle.*

* [After a photograph kindly furnished by himself at the editor's request. — Ed.]

false parts arose from the misapprehensions of the young Zeno, who put together the book of 1558.[1] The method of this later Zeno was in the same year (1873) held by Professor Konrad Maurer to be hardly removed from a fraudulent compilation of other existing material. There has been a marked display of learning, of late years, in some of the discussions. Cornelio Desimoni, the archivist of Genoa, has printed two elaborate papers.[2] The Danish archivist Frederik Krarup published (1878) a sceptical paper in the *Geografisk Tidsskrift* (ii.

BARON NORDENSKJÖLD.*

[1] Major also, in his paper (*Royal Geog. Soc. Journal*, 1873) on "The Site of the Lost Colony of Greenland determined, and the pre-Columbian discoveries of America confirmed, from fourteenth century documents," used the Zeno account and map in connection with Ivan Bardsen's Sailing Directions in placing the missing colony near Cape Farewell. Major epitomized his views on the question in *Mass. Hist. Soc. Proc.*, Oct., 187?. Sir H. C. Rawlinson commented on Major's views in his address before the Royal Geog. Society (*Journal*, 1873, p. clxxxvii).

Stevens (*Bibl. Geographica*, no. 3104) said: "If the map be genuine, the most of its geography is false, while a part of it is remarkably accurate."

[2] *I viaggi e la Carta dei Fratelli Zeno Veneziani* (Florence, 1878), and a *Studio Secondo* (*Estratto dall. Archivio Storico Italiano*) in 1885.

* [From a recent photograph. There is another engraved likeness in the second volume of his *Vega*.]

145).[1] The most exhaustive examination, however, has come from a practical navigator, the Baron A. E. Nordenskjöld, who in working up the results of his own Arctic explorations was easily led into the intricacies of the Zeno controversy. The results which he reaches are that the Zeni narratives are substantially true; that there was no published material in 1558 which could have furnished so nearly an accurate account of the actual condition of those northern waters; that the map which Zahrtmann saw in the University library at Copenhagen, and which he represented to be an original from which the young Zeno of 1558 made his pretended original, was in reality nothing but the Donis map in the Ptolemy of 1482, while the Zeno map is much more like the map of the north made by Claudius Clavis in 1427, which was discovered by Nordenskjöld in a codex of Ptolemy at Nancy.[2]

Since Nordenskjöld advanced his views there have been two other examinations: the one by Professor Japetus Steenstrup of Copenhagen,[3] and the other by the secretary of the Danish Geographical Society, Professor Ed. Erslef, who offered some new illustrations in his *Nye Oplysninger om Broedrene Zenis Rejser* (Copenhagen, 1885).[4]

Among those who accept the narratives there is no general agreement in identifying the principal geographical points of the Zeno map. The main dispute is upon Frislanda, the island where the Zeni were wrecked. That it was Iceland has been maintained by Admiral Irminger,[5] and Steenstrup (who finds, however, the text not to agree with the map), while the map accompanying the *Studi biografici e bibliografici sulla storia della geografia in Italia* (Rome, 1882) traces the route of the Zeni from Iceland to Greenland, under 70° of latitude.

On the other hand, Major has contended for the Faröe islands, arguing that while the engraved Zeno map shows a single large island, it might have been an archipelago in the original, with outlines run together by the obscurities of its dilapidation, and that the Faröes by their preserved names and by their position correspond best with the Frislanda of the Zeni.[6] Major's views have been adopted by most later writers, perhaps, and a similar identification had earlier been made by Lelewel,[7] Kohl,[8] and others.

The identification of Estotiland involves the question if the returned fisherman of the narrative ever reached America. It is not uncommon for even believers in the story to deny that Estotiland and Drogeo were America. That they were parts of the New World was,

1 "Zeniernes Rejse til Norden et Tolkning Forsoeg," with a fac-simile of the Zeni map.

2 Nordenskjöld's *Om bröderna Zenos resor och de äldsta kartor öfner Norden* was published at Stockholm in 1883, as an address on leaving the presidency of the Swedish Academy, April 12, 1882; and in the same year, at the Copenhagen meeting of the Congrès des Américanistes, he presented his *Trois Cartes précolumbiennes, représentant une partie de l'Amérique* (Greenland), which included fac-similes of the Zeno (1558) and Donis (1482) maps with that of Claudius Clavus (1427). This last represents "Islandia" lying midway alone in the sea between "Norwegica Regio" and "Gronlandia provincia." The "Congelatum mare" is made to flow north of Norway, so as almost to meet the northern Baltic, while north of this frozen sea is an Arctic region, of which Greenland is but an extension south and west. The student will find these and other maps making part of the address already referred to, which also makes part in German of his *Studien und Forschungen veranlasst durch meine Reisen im hohen Norden, autorisirte deutsche Ausgabe* (Leipzig, 1885). The maps accompanying it not already referred to are the usual Ptolemy map of the north of Europe, based on a MS. of the fourteenth century; the "Scandinavia" from the *Isolario* of Bordone, 1547; that of the world in the MS. *Insularium illustratum* of Henricus Martellus, of the fifteenth century, in the British Museum, copied from the sketch in José de Lacerda's *Exame dos Viagens do Doutor Livingstone* (Lisbon, 1867); the "Scandinavia" and the "Carta Marina" in the Venetian Ptolemy of 1548; the map of Olaus Magnus in 1567; the chart of Andrea Bianco (1436); the map of the Basle ed. (1532) of Grynæus' *Novis Orbis;* that of Laurentius Frisius (1524). He gives these maps as the material possible to be used in 1558 in compiling a map, and to show the superiority of the Zeno chart. Cf. *Nature*, xxviii. 14; and Major in *Royal Geog. Soc. Proc.*, 1883, p. 473.

3 "Zeni'ernes Reiser i Norden" in the publication of the Royal Society of Northern Antiquaries (Copenhagen, 1883), in which he compares the Zeno Frislanda with the maps of Iceland. He also communicated to the Copenhagen meeting of the Congrès des Américanistes "Les voyages des frères Zeni dans le Nord" (*Compte Rendu*, p. 150).

4 This also appeared in the *Geog. Tidsskrift*, vii. 153, accompanied by fac-similes of the Zeni map, with Ruscelli's alteration of it (1561), and of the maps of Donis (1482), Laurentius Frisius (1525), and of the Ptolemy of 1548.

5 *Roy. Geog. Soc. Journal* (1879), vol. xlix. p. 398, "Zeno's Frisland is Iceland and not the Faröes," — and the same views in "Nautical Remarks about the Zeni Voyages" in *Compte Rendu, Cong. des Amér.* (Copenhagen, 1883), p. 183.

6 "Zeno's Frisland is not Iceland, but the Faröes" in *Roy. Geog. Soc. Journal* (1879), xlix. 412.

7 *Géog. du Moyen Age*, iii. 103.

8 *Discovery of Maine*, 92.

however, the apparent belief of Mercator and of many of the cartographers following the publication of 1558, and of such speculators as Hugo Grotius, but there was little common consent in their exact position.[1]

I. Alleged Jewish Migration. — The identification of the native Americans with the stock of the lost tribes of Israel very soon became a favorite theory with the early Spanish priests settled in America. Las Casas and Duran adopted it, while Torquemada and Acosta rejected it. André Thevet, of mendacious memory, did not help the theory by espousing it. It was approved in J. F. Lumnius's *De extremo Dei Judicio et Indorum vocatione, libri iii.* (Venice and Antwerp, 1569);[2] and a century later the belief attracted new attention in the *Origen de los Americanos de Manasseh Ben Israel*, published at Amsterdam in 1650.[3] It was in the same year (1650) that the question received the first public discussion in English in Thomas Thorowgood's *Jewes in America, or, Probabilities that the Americans are of that Race. With the removall of some contrary reasonings, and earnest desires for effectuall endeavours to make them Christian* (London, 1650).[4] Thorowgood was answered by Sir Hamon L'Estrange in *Americans no Iewes, or Improbabilities that the Americans are of that race* (London, 1652). The views of Thorowgood found sympathy with the Apostle Eliot of Massachusetts; and when Thorowgood replied to L'Estrange he joined with it an essay by Eliot, and the joint work was entitled *Iewes in America, or probabilities that those Indians are Judaical, made more probable by some additionals to the former conjectures: an accurate discourse is premised of Mr. John Eliot (who preached the gospel to the natives in their own language) touching their origination, and his Vindication of the planters* (London, 1660). What seems to have been a sort of supplement, covering, however, in part, the same ground, appeared as *Vindiciæ Judæcorum, or a true account of the Jews, being more accurately illustrated than heretofore*, which includes what is called "The learned conjectures of Rev. Mr. John Eliot" (32 pp.). Some of the leading New England divines, like Mayhew and Mather,[5] espoused the cause with similar faith. Roger Williams also was of the same opinion. William Penn is said to have held like views. The belief may be said to have been general, and had not died out in New England when Samuel Sewall, in 1697, published his *Phænomena quædam Apocalyptica ad aspectum Novi Orbis Configurata*.[6]

[1] Dudley, *Arcano del Mare*, pl. lii, places Estotiland between Davis and Hudson's Straits; but Torfæus doubts if it is Labrador, as is "commonly believed." Lafitau (*Mœurs des Sauvages*) puts it north of Hudson Bay. Forster calls it Newfoundland. Beauvois (*Les colonies Européenes du Markland et de l'Escociland*) makes it include Maine, New Brunswick, and part of Lower Canada. These are the chief varieties of belief. Steenstrup is of those who do not recognize America at all. Hornius, among the older writers, thought that Scotland or Shetland was more likely to have been the fisherman's strange country. Santarem (*Hist. de la Cartographie*, iii. 141) points out an island, "Y Stotlandia," in the Baltic, as shown on the map of Giovanni Leardo (1448) at Venice.

In P. B. Watson's *Bibliog. of Pre-Columbian Discoveries of America* there is the fullest but not a complete list on the subject, and from this and other sources a few further references may be added: Belknap's *Amer. Biography;* Humboldt's *Examen Critique*, ii. 120; Asher's *Henry Hudson*, p. clxiv; Gravier's *Découverte de l'Amérique*, 183; Gaffarel's *Etude sur l'Amérique avant Colomb*, p. 261, and in the *Revue de Géog.*, vii., Oct., Nov., 1880, with the Zeno map as changed by Ortelius; De Costa's *Northmen in Maine;* Weise's *Discoveries of America*, p. 44; Goodrich's *Columbus;* Peschel's *Gesch. des Zeitalters der Entdeckungen* (1858), and Ruge's work of the same title; Guido Cora's *I precursori di Cristoforo Colombo* (Rome, 1886), taken from the *Bollettino della soc. geog. italiana*, Dec., 1885; Gay's *Pop. Hist. U. S.* (i. 76); Foster's *Prehistoric Races; Studi biog. e bibliog. soc. geog. ital.*, 2d ed., 1882, p. 117; P. O. Moosmüller's *Europäer in Amerika vor Columbus*, ch. 24; *Das Ausland*, Oct. 11, Dec. 27, 1886; *Nature*, xxviii. p. 14.

Geo. E. Emery, Lynn, Mass., issued in 1877 a series of maps, making Islandia to be Spitzbergen, with the East Bygd of the Northmen at its southern end; Frisland, Iceland; and Estotiland, Newfoundland.

[2] Sabin, x., no. 42,675.

[3] There are editions with annotations by Robert Ingram, at Colchester, Eng., 1792; and by Santiago Perez Junquera, at Madrid, 1881. Theoph. Spizelius' *Elevatio relationis Montezinianæ de repertis in America tribubus Israeliticis* (Basle, 1661) is a criticism (Leclerc, 547; Field, 1473). One Montesinos had professed to have found a colony of Jews in Peru, and had satisfied Manasseh Ben Israel of his truthfulness.

[4] Cf. collations in Stevens's *Nuggets*, p. 728, and his *Hist. Coll.*, ii. no. 538; Brinley, iii. no. 5463; Field, no. 1551, who cites a new edition in 1652, called *Digitus Dei: new discoveryes, with some arguments to prove that the Jews (a nation) a people . . . inhabit now in America . . . with the history of Ant: Montesinos attested by Mannasseh Ben Israell.* A divine, John Dury, had urged Thorowgood to publish, and had before this, in printing some of the accounts of the work of Eliot and others among the New England Indians, announced his belief in the theory.

[5] Cotton Mather (*Magnalia*, iii. part 2) tells how Eliot traced the resemblances to the Jews in the New England Indians.

[6] 2d ed., 1727. Cf. Sibley's *Harvard Graduates*, ii. p. 361; Carter-Brown, iii. 401.

After the middle of the last century we begin to find new signs of the belief. Charles Beatty, in his *Journal of a two months' tour with a view of promoting religion among the frontier inhabitants of Pennsylvania* (Lond., 1768), finds traces of the lost tribes among the Delawares, and repeats a story of the Indians long ago selling the same sacred book to the whites with which the missionaries in the end aimed to make them acquainted. Gerard de Brahm and Richard Peters, both familiar with the Southern Indians, found grounds for accepting the belief. The most elaborate statement drawn from this region is that of James Adair, who for forty years had been a trader among the Southern Indians.[1] Jonathan Edwards in 1788 pointed out in the Hebrew some analogies to the native speech.[2] Charles Crawford in 1799 undertook the proof.[3] In 1816 Elias Boudinot, a man eminent in his day, contributed further arguments.[4] Ethan Smith based his advocacy largely on the linguistic elements.[5] A few years later an Englishman, Israel Worsley, worked over the material gathered by Boudinot and Smith, and added something.[6] A prominent American Jew, M. M. Noah, published in 1837 an address on the subject which hardly added to the weight of testimony.[7] J. B. Finlay, a mulatto missionary among the Wyandots, was satisfied with the Hebrew traces which he observed in that tribe.[8] Geo. Catlin, working also among the Western Indians, while he could not go to the length of believing in the lost tribes, was struck with the many analogies which he saw.[9] The most elaborate of all expositions of the belief was made by Lord Kingsborough in his *Mexican Antiquities* (1830–48).[10] Since this book there has been no pressing of the question with any claims to consideration.[11]

J. POSSIBLE EARLY AFRICAN MIGRATIONS. — These may have been by adventure or by helpless drifting, with or without the Canaries as a halting-place. The primitive people of the Canaries, the Guanches, are studied in Sabin Berthelot's *Antiquités Canariennes* (Paris, 1879) and A. F. de Fontpertuis' *L'archipel des Canaries, et ses populations primitives*, also in the *Revue de Géographie*, June, 1882, not to mention earlier histories of the Canary Islands (see Vol. II.

1 *The History of the American Indians, particularly those Nations adjoining to the Mississippi, East and West Florida, Georgia, South and North Carolina, and Virginia: Containing an Account of their Origin, Language, Manners, Religious and Civil Customs, Laws, Form of Government, etc., etc., with an Appendix, containing a Description of the Floridas, and the Missisipi Lands, with their productions* (London, 1775). His arguments are given in Kingsborough's *Mex. Antiq.*, viii. Bancroft (*Nat. Races*, v. 91) epitomizes them. Adair's book appeared in a German translation at Breslau (1782).

2 *Observations on the language of the Muhhekaneew Indians, in which . . . some instances of analogy between that and the Hebrew are pointed out* (New Haven, 1788). Cf. on the contrary, Jarvis before the N. Y. Hist. Soc. in 1819.

3 *Essay upon the propagation of the Gospel, in which there are facts to prove that many of the indians in America are descended from the Ten Tribes* (Philad., 1799; 2d ed., 1801).

4 *A Star in the West, or an attempt to discover the long lost Ten Tribes of Israel* (Trenton, N. J., 1816).

5 *View of the Hebrews, or the tribe of Israel in America* (Poultney, Vt., 1825).

6 *A view of the Amer. Indians, shewing them to be the descendants of the Ten Tribes of Israel* (Lond., 1828).

7 *Discourse on the evidences of the Amer. Indians being the descendants of the lost tribes of Israel* (N. Y., 1837). It is reprinted in Maryatt's *Diary in America*, vol. ii.

8 *Hist. of the Wyandotte Mission* (Cincinnati, 1840); Thomson's *Ohio Bibliog.*, 409.

9 *Manners, &c. of the N. Amer. Indians* (Lond., 1841). Cf. *Smithsonian Rept.*, 1885, ii. 532.

10 Mainly in vol. vii.; but see vi. 232, etc. Cf. Short, 143, 460, and Bancroft, *Nat. Races* (v. 26), with an epitome of Kingsborough's arguments (v. 84). Mrs. Barbara Anne Simon in her *Hope of Israel* (Lond., 1829) advocated the theory on biblical grounds; but later she made the most of Kingsborough's amassment of points in her *Ten Tribes of Israel historically identified with the aborigines of the Western Hemisphere* (London, 1836).

11 The recognition of the theory in the Mormon bible is well known. Bancroft (v. 97) epitomizes its recital, following Bertrand's *Mémoires*. There is a repetition of the old arguments in a sermon, *Increase of the Kingdom of Christ* (N. Y., 1831), by the Indian William Apes; and in *An Address* by J. Madison Brown (Jackson, Miss., 1860). Señor Melgar points out resemblances between the Maya and the Hebrew in the *Bol. Soc. Méx. Geog.*, iii. Even the Western mounds have been made to yield Hebrew inscriptions (*Congrès des Amér.*, Nancy, ii. 192).

Many of the general treatises on the origin of the Americans have set forth the opposing arguments. Garcia did it fairly in his *Origen de los Indios* (1607; ed. by Barcia, 1729), and Bancroft (v. 78–84) has condensed his treatment. Brasseur (*Hist. Nat. Civ.*, i. 17) rejects the theory of the ten tribes; but is not inclined to abandon a belief in some scattered traces. Short (pp. 135, 144) epitomizes the claims. Gaffarel covers them in his *Etude sur les rapports de l'Amérique* (p. 87) with references, and these last are enlarged in Bancroft's *Nat. Races*, v. 95–97.

p. 36). Retzius of Stockholm traces resemblances in the skulls of the Guanches and the Caribs (*Smithsonian Rept.*, 1859, p. 266). Le Plongeon finds the sandals of the statue Chacmool, discovered by him in Yucatan, to resemble those of the Guanches (Salisbury's *Le Plongeon in Yucatan*, 57).

The African and even Egyptian origin of the Caribs has had some special advocates.[1] Peter Martyr, and Grotius following him, contended for the people of Yucatan being Ethiopian Christians. Stories of blackamoors being found by the early Spaniards are not without corroboration.[2] The correspondence of the African and South American flora has been brought into requisition as confirmatory.[3]

[1] Varnhagen's *L'origine touranienne des Américains Tupis-Caraïbes et des anciens Egyptiens, indiquée principalement par la philologie comparée: traces d'une ancienne migration en Amérique, invasion du Brésil par les Tupis* (Vienne, 1876). Labat's *Nouveau Voyage aux isles de l'Amérique* (Paris, 1722), vol. ii. ch. 23. Sieur de la Borde's *Relation de l'origine, mœurs, coutumes, etc. des Caraibes* (Paris, 1764). Robertson's *America.* James Kennedy's *Probable origin of the Amer. Indians, with particular reference to that of the Caribs* (Lond., 1854), or *Journal of the Ethnolog. Soc.* (vol. iv.). *London Geog. Journal*, iii. 290.

[2] Cf. Peter Martyr, Torquemada, and later writers, like La Perouse, McCulloh, Haven (p. 48), Gaffarel (*Rapport*, 204), J. Perez in *Rev. Orientale et Amér.*, viii., xii.; Bancroft, *Nat. Races*, iii. 458. Brinton (*Address*, 1887) takes exception to all such views. Cf. Quatrefages' *Human Species* (N. Y., 1879, pp. 200, 202).

[3] Cf. Beccari in *Kosmos*, Apr., 1879; De Candolle in *Géographie botanique* (1855).

THE CARTOGRAPHY OF GREENLAND.

THE oldest map yet discovered to show any part of Greenland, and consequently of America,[1] is one found by Baron Nordenskjöld attached to a Ptolemy Codex in the Stadtbibliothek at Nancy. He presented a colored fac-simile of it in 1883 at the Copenhagen Congrès des Américanistes, in his little brochure *Trois Cartes.* It was also used in illustration of his paper on the Zeni Voyages, published both in Swedish and German. It will be seen by the fac-simile given herewith, and marked with the author's name, Claudius Clavus, that "Gronlandia Provincia" is an extension of a great arctic region, so as to lie over against the Scandinavian peninsula of Europe, with "Islandia," or Iceland, midway between the two lands. Up to the time of this discovery by Nordenskjöld, the map generally recognized as the oldest to show Greenland is a Genovese portolano, preserved in the Pitti Palace at Florence, about which there is some doubt as to its date, which is said to be 1417 by Santarem (*Hist. de la Cartog.*, iii., p. xix), but Lelewel (*Epilogue*, p. 167) is held to be trustier in giving it as 1447.[2] It shows how little influence the Norse stories of their Greenland colonization exerted at this time on the cartography of the north, that few of the map-makers deemed it worth while to break the usual terminal circle of the world by including anything west or beyond Iceland. It was, further, not easy to convince them that Greenland, when they gave it, lay in the direction which the Sagas indicated. The map of Fra Mauro, for instance, in 1459 cuts off a part of Iceland by its incorrigible terminal circle, as will be seen in a bit of it given herewith, the reader remembering as he looks at it that the bottom of the segment is to the north.[3] We again owe to Nordenskjöld the discovery of another map of the north, *Tabula Regionum Septentrionalium*, which he found in a Codex of Ptolemy in Warsaw a few years since, and which he places about 1467. The accompanying partial sketch is reproduced from a fac-simile kindly furnished by the discoverer. The peninsula of "Gronlandia," with its indicated glaciers, is placed with tolerable accuracy as the western extremity of an arctic region, which to the north of Europe is separated from the Scandinavian peninsula by a channel from the "Mare Gotticum" (Baltic Sea), which sweeps above Norway into the "Mare Congelatum." The confused notions arising from an attempt by the compiler of the map to harmonize different drafts is shown by his drawing a second Greenland ("Engronelant") to his "Norbegia," or Norway, and placing just

[1] Santarem, *Hist. de la Cartog.*, iii. 76, refers to maps of the fourteenth century in copies of Ranulphus Hydgen's *Polychronicon*, in the British Museum and in the Advocates' library at Edinburgh, which show a land in the north, called in the one Wureland and in the other Wyhlandia.

[2] *Mag. Am. Hist.*, April, 1883, p. 290. Cf. Vol. II. p. 28. The name used is "Grinlandia."

[3] Mauro's map was called by Ramusio, who saw it, an improved copy of one brought from Cathay by Marco Polo. It is preserved in the Biblioteca Marciana at Venice. It was made by Mauro under the command of Don Alonso V., and Bianco assisted him. The exact date is in dispute; but all agree to place it between 1457 and 1460. A copy was made on vellum in 1804, which is now in the British Museum. Our cut follows one corner of the reproduction in Santarem's *Atlas*. A photographic fac-simile has been issued in Venice by Ongania, and St. Martin (*Atlas*, p. vii) follows this fac-simile. Ruge (*Geschichte des Zeitalters der Entdeckungen*) gives a modernized and more legible reproduction. There are other drawings in Zurla's *Fra Mauro*; Vincent's *Commerce and Navigation of the Ancients* (1797, 1807); Lelewel's *Moyen Age* (pl. xxxiii). Cf. *Studi della Soc. Geografia Italia* (1882), ii. 76, for references.

under it the "Thile"[1] of the ancients, which he makes a different island from "Islandia," placed in proper relations to his larger Greenland.

A few years later, or perhaps about the same time, and before 1471, the earliest engraved map which shows Greenland is that of Nicolas Donis, in the Ulm edition of Ptolemy in 1482. It will be seen from the little sketch which is annexed that the same doubling of Greenland is adhered to.[2] With the usual perversion put

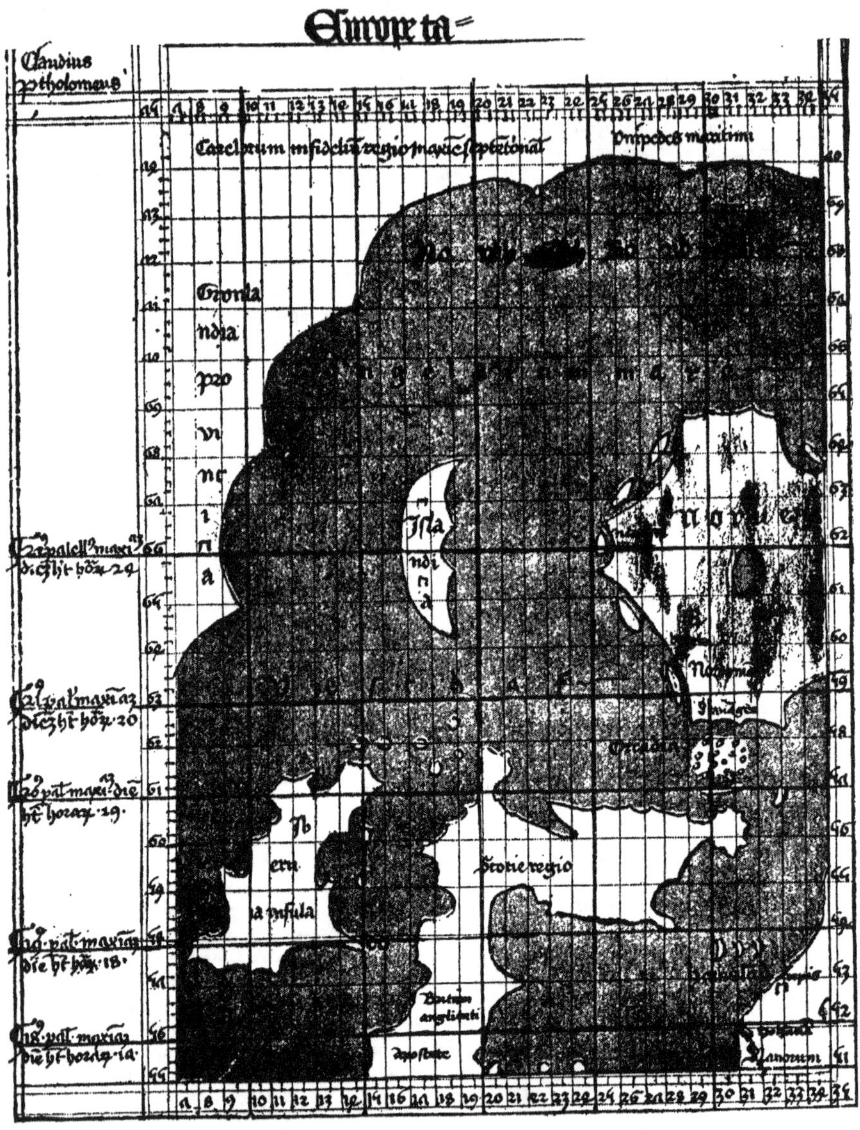

CLAUDIUS CLAVUS, 1427.

[1] Rafn gives a large map of Iceland with the names of A. D. 1000. On the errors of early and late maps of Iceland see Baring-Gould's *Ultima Thule*, i. 253. On the varying application of the name Thule, Thyle, etc., to the northern regions or to particular parts of them, see R. F. Burton's *Ultima Thule, a Summer in Iceland* (London, 1875), ch. 1. Bunbury (*Hist. Anc. Geog.*, ii. 527) holds that the Thule of Marinus of Tyre and of Ptolemy was the Shetlands. Cf. James Wallace's *Description of the Orkney islands* (1693, — new ed., 1887, by John Small) for an essay on "the Thule of the Ancients."

[2] There are other reproductions of the map in full, in Nordenskjöld's *Vega*, i. 51; in his *Broderna Zenos*, and in his *Studien*, p. 31. Cf. also the present *History*, II., p. 28, for other bibliographical detail; Hassler, *Buchdruckergeschichte Ulm's*; D'Avezac's *Waltzemüller*, 23; Wil-

upon the Norse stories, Iceland is made to lie due west of Greenland, though not shown in the present sketch.

At a date not much later, say 1486, it is supposed the Laon globe, dated in 1493, was actually made, or at least it is shown that in some parts the knowledge was rather of the earlier date, and here we have "Grolandia," a small island off the Norway coast.[1]

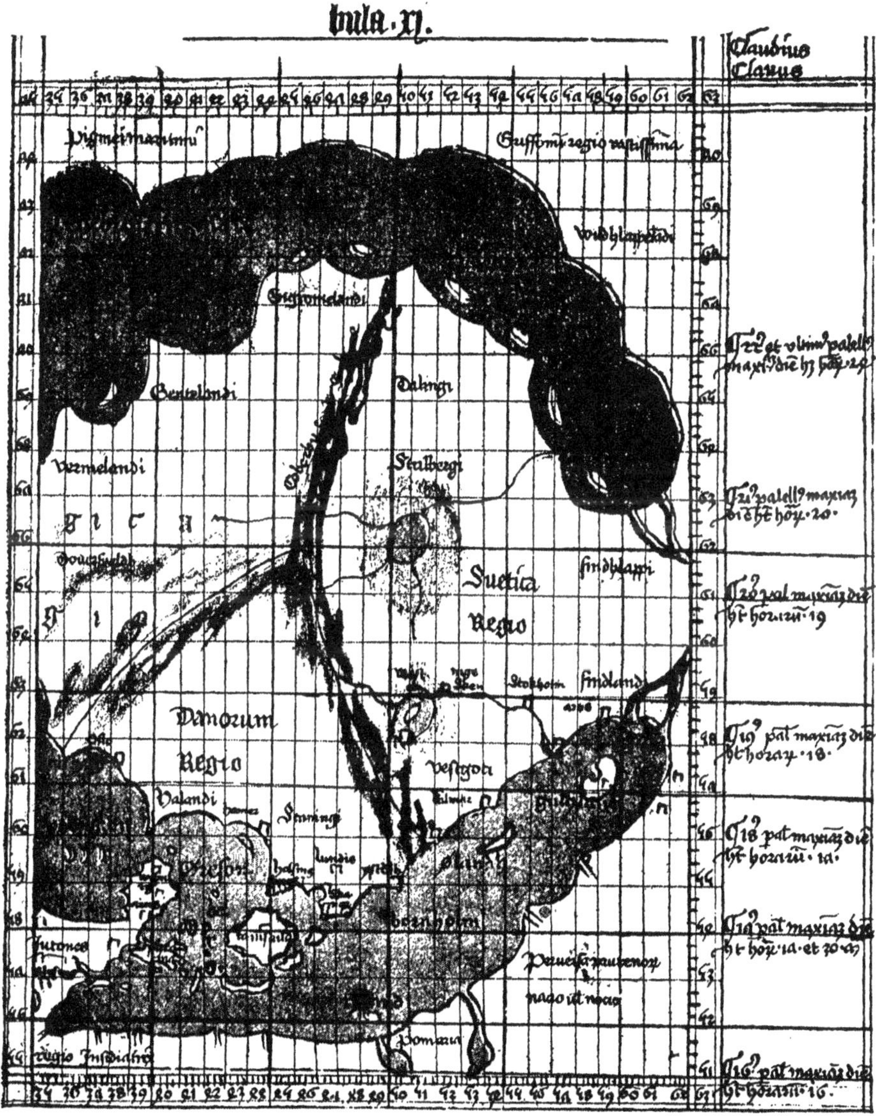

CLAUDIUS CLAVUS, 1427.

We have in 1489–90 a type of configuration, which later became prevalent. It is taken from an *Insularium illustratum Henrici Martelli Germani*, a manuscript preserved in the British Museum, and shows, as seen by the annexed extract, a long narrow peninsula, running southwest from the northern verge of Europe. A sketch of the whole map is given elsewhere.[2]

berforce Eames's *Bibliography of Ptolemy*, separately, and in Sabin's *Dictionary;* and Winsor's *Bibliog. of Ptolemy's Geography*.

[1] Cf. D'Avezac in *Bull. de la Soc. de Géog.*, xx. 417.

[2] See Vol. II. p. 41. There is another sketch in Nordenskjöld's *Studien*, etc., p. 33, which is reduced from a

This seems to have been the prevailing notion of what and where Greenland was at the time of Columbus' voyage, and it could have carried no significance to his mind that the explorations of the Norse had found the Asiatic main, which he started to discover. How far this notion was departed from by Behaim in his globe of 1492 depends upon the interpretation to be given to a group of islands, northwest of Iceland and northeast of Asia, upon the larger of which he writes among its mountains, "Hi man weise Volker."[1]

As this sketch of the cartographical development goes on, it will be seen how slow the map-makers were to perceive the real significance of the Norse discoveries, and how reluctant they were to connect them with the discoveries that followed in the train of Columbus, though occasionally there is one who is possessed with a sort of prevision. The Cantino map of 1502[2] does not settle the question, for a point lying northeast of the Portuguese discoveries in the Newfoundland region only seems to be the southern extremity of Greenland. What was apparently a working Portuguese chart of 1503 grasps pretty clearly the relations of Greenland to Labrador.[3]

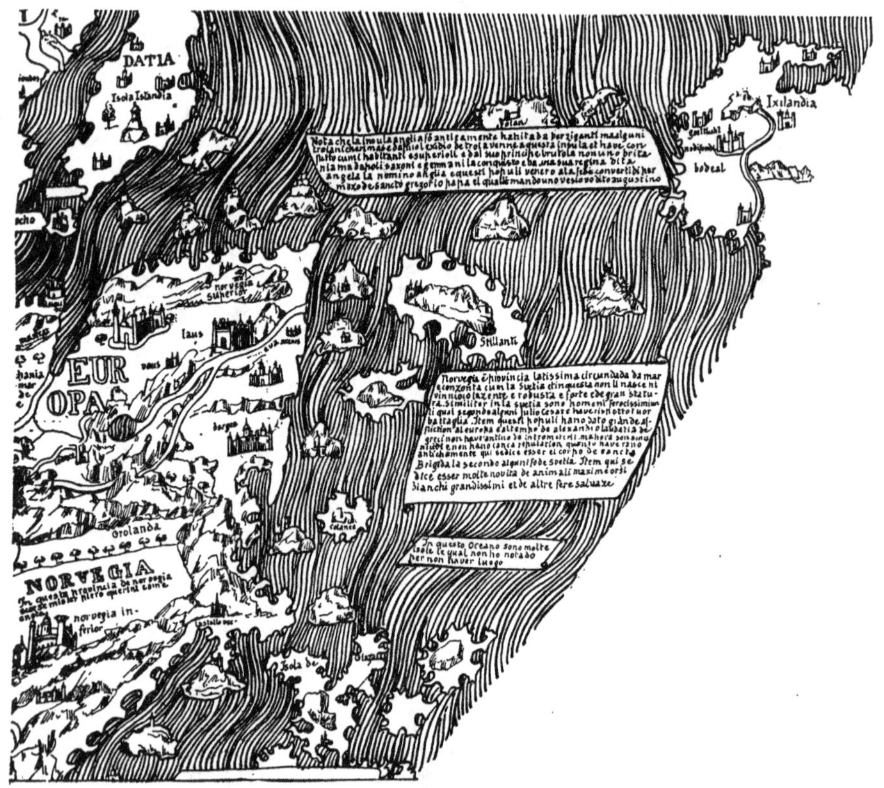

FRA MAURO, 1459.

Lelewel (pl. 43), in a map made to show the Portuguese views at this time,[4] which he represents by combining and reconciling the Ptolemy maps of 1511 and 1513, still places the "Gronland" peninsula in the northwest of Europe, and if his deductions are correct, the Portuguese had as yet reached no clear conception that the Labrador coasts upon which they fished bore any close propinquity to those which the Norse had colonized. Ruysch, in 1508, made a bold stroke by putting "Gruenlant" down as a peninsula of Northeastern Asia, thus trying to reconcile the discoveries of Columbus with the northern sagas.[5] This view was far from acceptable. Sylvanus, in the Ptolemy of 1511, made "Engroneland" a small protuberance on the north shore of Scandinavia, and east of Iceland, evidently choosing between the two theories instead of accepting both, as

fac-simile given in José de Lacerda's *Exame dos Viagens do Doutor Livingstone* (Lissabon, 1867). The present extract is from Santarem, pl. 50. Cf. O. Peschel in *Ausland*, Feb. 13, 1857, and his posthumous *Abhandlungen*, i. 213.

[1] See references in Vol. II. p. 105.

[2] See Vol. II. p. 108.

[3] See *post*, Vol. IV. p. 35; and Kohl's *Discovery of Maine*, p. 174. Cf. Winsor's *Bibliog. of Ptolemy*, sub anno 1511.

[4] He holds that the 1513 Ptolemy map was drawn in 1501–4, and was engraved before Dec. 10, 1508.

[5] See Vol. II. p. 115.

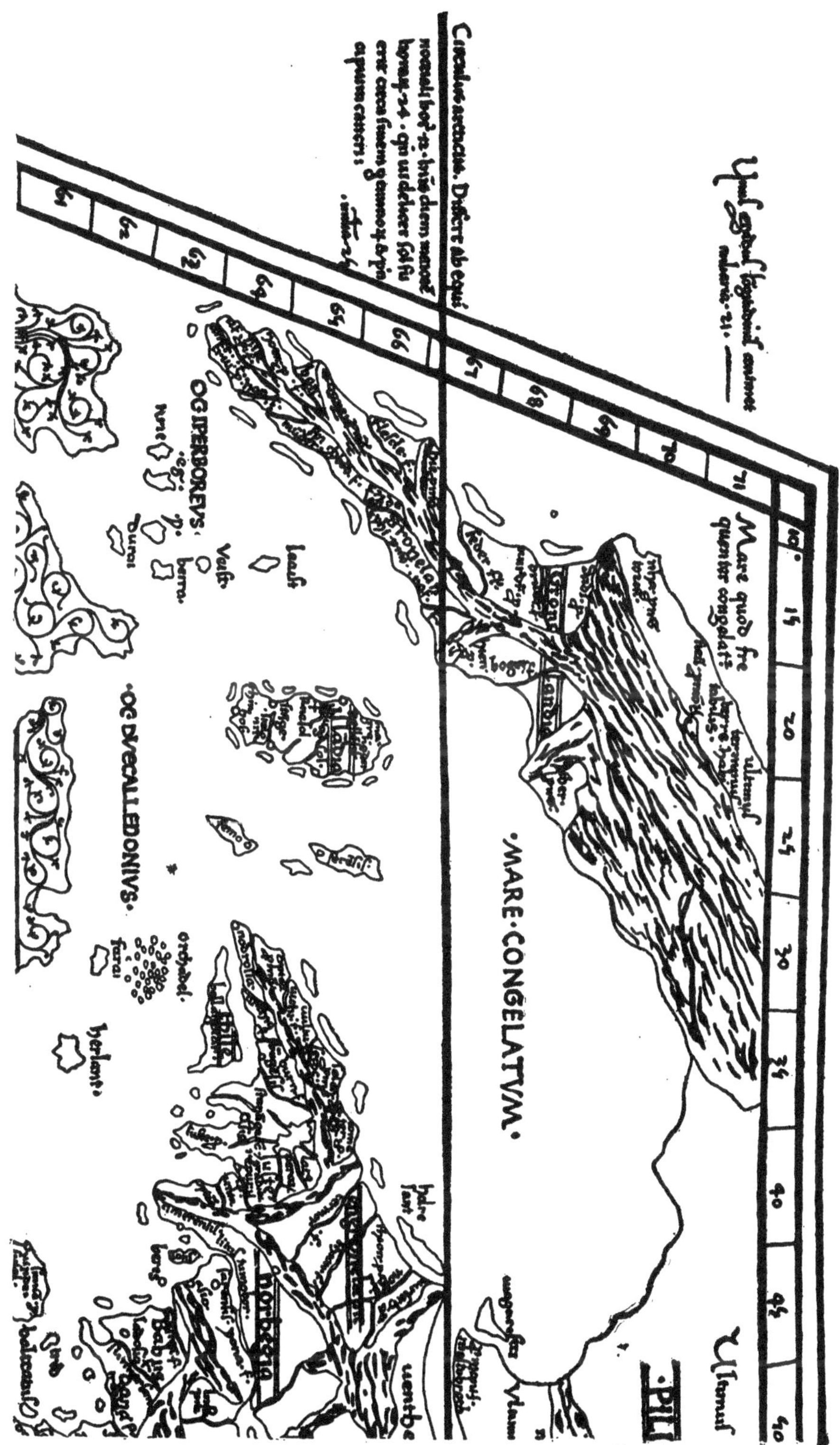

TABULA REGIONUM SEPTENTRIONALIUM, 1467.

was common, in ignorance of their complemental relations.[1] Waldseemüller, in the Ptolemy of 1513, in his "Orbis typus universalis," reverted to and adopted the delineation of Henricus Martellus in 1490.[2]

In 1520, Apian, in the map in Camer's *Solinus*, took the view of Sylvanus, while still another representation was given by Laurentius Frisius in 1522, in an edition of Ptolemy,[3] in which "Gronland" becomes a large

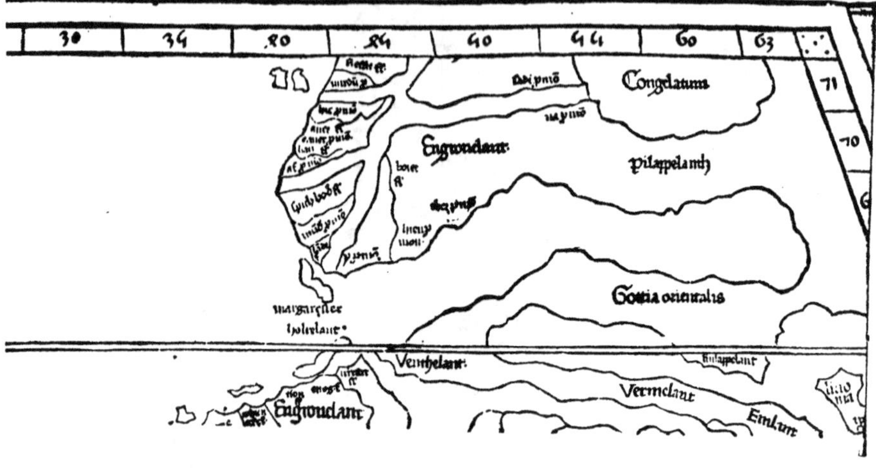

DONIS, 1482.

island on the Norway coast, in one map called "Orbis typus Universalis," while in another map, "Tabula nova Norbegiæ et Gottiæ," the "Engronelant" peninsula is a broad region, stretching from Northwestern Europe.[4] This Ptolemy was again issued in 1525, repeating these two methods of showing Greenland already given, and adding a third,[5] that of the long narrow European peninsula, already familiar in earlier maps — the variety of choice indicating the prevalent cartographical indecision on the point.

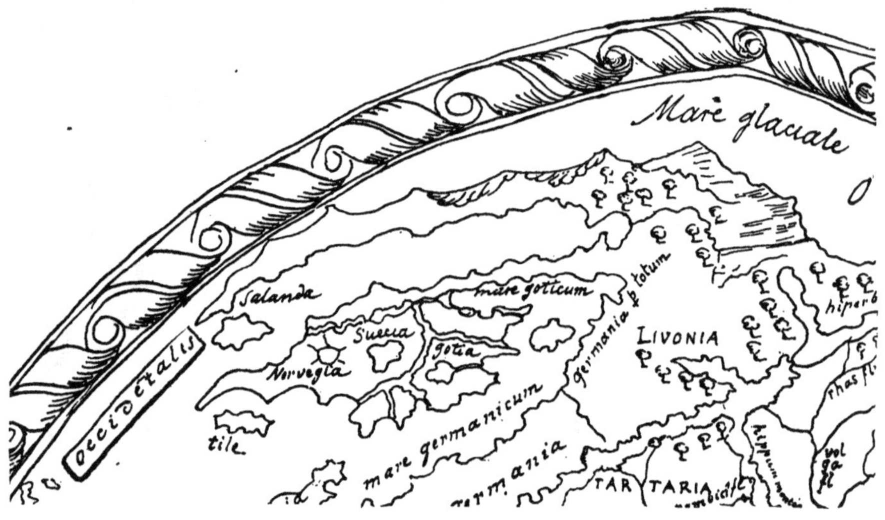

HENRICUS MARTELLUS, 1489–90.

[1] Winsor's *Bibliog. of Ptolemy*, sub anno 1511.

[2] See Vol. II. p. 111. Winsor's *Ptolemy*, sub anno 1513. Reisch, in 1515, seems to have been of the same opinion. Cf. the bibliography of Reisch's *Margarita Philosophia* in Sabin's *Dictionary*, vol. xvi., and separately, prepared by Wilberforce Eames. Reisch's map is given *post*, Vol. II. p. 114. Another sketch of this map, with an examination of the question, where the name "Zoana Mela," applied on it to America, came from, is given by Frank Wieser in the *Zeitschrift für Wissensch. Geographie* (Carlsruhe), vol. v., a sight of which I owe to the author, who believes Waldseemüller made the map.

[3] The map is given, *post*, Vol. II. 175. Cf. also Nordenskjöld, *Studien*, p. 53.

[4] Cf. Winsor's *Bibliog. of Ptolemy*, sub anno 1522.

[5] Winsor's *Bibliog. of Ptolemy*, sub anno 1525. This

Kohl, in his collection of maps,[1] copies from what he calls the Atlas of Frisius, 1525, still another map which apparently shows the southern extremity of Greenland, with "Terra Laboratoris," an island just west

OLAUS MAGNUS, 1539.*

map is no. 49, "Gronlandiæ et Russiæ." Cf. Witsen's *Noord en Oost Tartarye* (1705), vol. ii.

[1] Winsor's *Kohl Collection*, no. 102.

* See Note, p. 125.

OLAUS MAGNUS, 1555.*

* This map, here reproduced on a somewhat smaller scale, is called: *Regnorum Aquilonarum descriptio, hujus Operis subiectum.*

of it, and southwest of that a bit of coast marked "Terra Nova Conterati," which may pass for Newfoundland and the discoveries of Cortereal.

Thorne, the Englishman, in the map which he sent from Seville in 1527,[1] seems to conform to the view which made Greenland a European peninsula, which may also have been the opinion of Orontius Finæus in 1531.[2] A novel feature attaches to an Atlas, of about this date, preserved at Turin, in which an elongated Greenland is made to stretch northerly.[3] In 1532 we have the map in Ziegler's *Schondia*, which more nearly resembles the earliest map of all, that of Claudius Clavus, than any other.[4] The 1538 cordiform map of Mercator makes it a peninsula of an arctic region connected with Scandinavia.[5] This map is known to me only through a fac-simile of the copy given in the *Geografia* of Lafreri, published at Rome about 1560, with which I am favored by Nordenskjöld in advance of its publication in his *Atlas*.

The great *Historia* of Olaus Magnus, as for a long time the leading authority on the northern geography, as well as on the Scandinavian chronicles, gives us some distinct rendering of this northern geographical problem. It was only recently that his earliest map of 1539 has been brought to light, and a section of it is here reproduced from a much reduced fac-simile kindly sent to the editor by Dr. Oscar Brenner of the university at Munich.* Nordenskjöld, in giving a full fac-simile of the Olaus Magnus map of 1567,[6] of which a

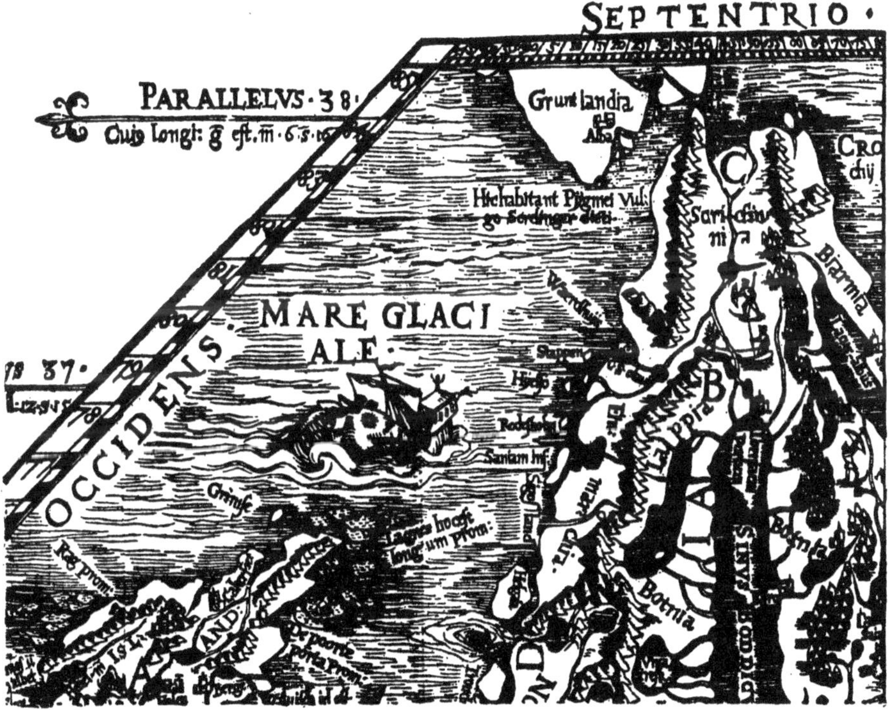

FROM OLAUS MAGNUS' HISTORIA, 1567.

[1] Given *post*, Vol. III. p. 17.

[2] Given *post*, Vol. III. p. 11.

[3] *Jahrb. des Vereins für Erdkunde in Dresden* (1870), tab. vii. A similar feature is in the map described by Peschel in the *Jahresbericht des Vereins für Erdkunde in Leipzig* (1871). It is also to be seen in the Homem map of about 1540 (given in Vol. II. p. 446), and in the map which Major assigns to Baptista Agnese, and which was published in Paris in 1875 as a *Portulan de Charles Quint*. (Cf. Vol. II. p. 445.)

[4] There is a fac-simile of Ziegler's map in Vol. II. 434; also in Goldsmid's ed. of Hakluyt (Edinb., 1885), and in Nordenskjöld's *Vega*, i. 52.

[5] The map (1551) of Gemma Frisius in Apian is much the same.

[6] In the Basle ed. of the *Historia de Gentium*. Cf. Nordenskjöld's *Vega*, vol. i., who says that the map originally appeared in Magnus's *Auslegung und Verklarung der Neuen Mappen von den Alten Goettenreich* (Venice, 1539); and is different from the map which appeared in the intermediate edition of 1555 at Rome, a part of which is also annexed.

NOTE TO MAP ON P. 123.—This fac-simile accompanies a paper appearing in the *Videnskabsselskabs Forhandinger* (1886, no. 15) and separately as *Die ächte karte des Olaus Magnus vom jahre 1539, nach dem exemplar der Münchener Staatsbibliothek* (Christiania, 1886). In this Dr. Brenner traces the history of the great map of Archbishop Olaus Magnus, pointing out how Nordenskjöld is in error in supposing the map of 1567, which that scholar gives, was but a fragment is herewith also given in fac-simile, says that it embodies the views of the northern geographers in separating Greenland from Europe, which was in opposition to those of the geographers of the south of Europe, who united Greenland to Scandinavia. Sebastian Münster in his 1540 edition of Ptolemy introduced a new confusion. He preserved the European elongated peninsula, but called it "Islandia," while to what stands for Iceland is given the old classical name of Thyle.[1] This confusion is repeated in his map of 1545,[2] where he makes the coast of "Islandia" continuous with Baccalaos. This continuity of coast line seemed now to become a common heritage of some of the map-makers,[3] though in the Ulpius globe of 1542 "Groestlandia," so far as it is shown, stands separate from either continent,[4] but is connected with Europe according to the early theory in the *Isolario* of Bordone in 1547.

We have run down the main feature of the northern cartography, up to the time of the publication of the Zeno map in 1558. The chief argument for its authenticity is that there had been nothing drawn and published up to that time which could have conduced, without other aid, to so accurate an outline of Greenland as it gives. In an age when drafts of maps freely circulated over Europe, from cartographer to cartographer, in

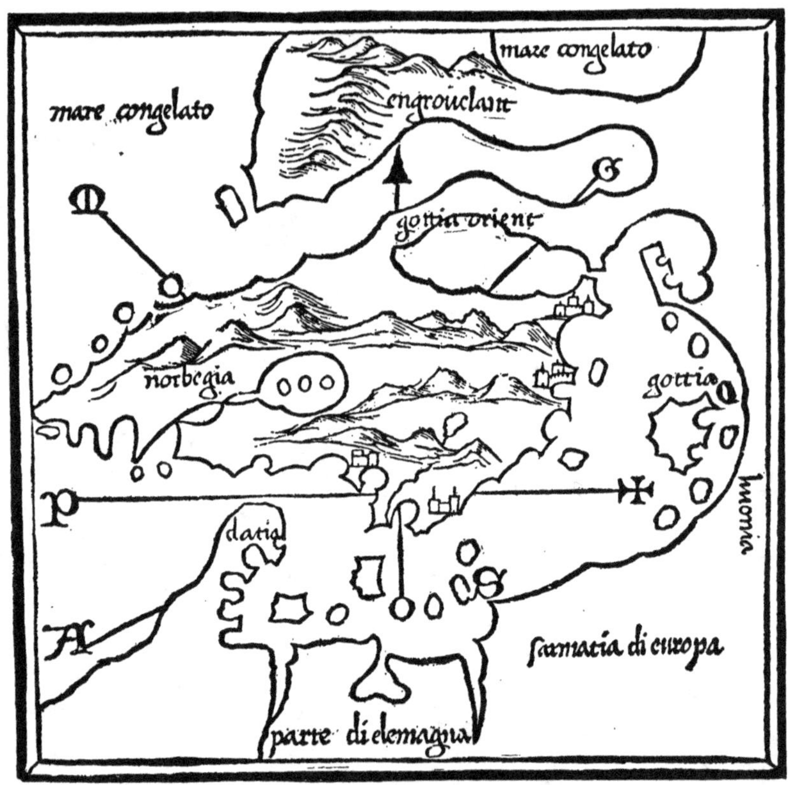

BORDONE'S SCANDINAVIA, 1547.*

[1] The same is done in the Ptolemy of 1548 (Venice). There is a fac-simile in Nordenskjöld's *Studien*, p. 35.

[2] See Vol. IV. p. 84.

[3] We find it in the Nancy globe of about 1540 (see Vol. IV. p. 81); in the Mercator gores of 1541 (Vol. II. p. 177); and in the Ruscelli map of 1544 (Vol. II. p. 432), where Greenland (Grotlandia) is simply a neck connecting Europe with America; and in Gastaldi "Carta Marina," in the Italian Ptolemy of 1548, where it is a protuberance on a similar neck (see Vol. II. 435; IV. 43; and Nordenskjöld's *Studien*, 43). The Rotz map of 1542 seems to be based on the same material used by Mercator in his gores, but he adds a new confusion in calling Greenland the "Cost of Labrador." Cf. Winsor's *Kohl Maps*, no. 104. The "Grutlandia" of the Vopellio map of 1556 is also continuous with Labrador (see Vol. II. 436; IV. 90).

[4] See Vol. IV. pp. 42, 82.

reproduction of the original edition of 1539, which was not known to modern students till Brenner found it in the library at Munich, in March, 1886, and which proves to be twelve times larger than that of 1567. Brenner adds the long Latin address, "Olaus Gothus benigno lectori salutem," with annotations. The map is entitled "Carta Marina et descriptio septentrionalium errarum ac mirabilium rerum in eis contentarum diligentissime elaborata, Anno Dni, 1539." Brenner institutes a close comparison between it and the Zeno chart.

* Reproduced from the fac-simile given in Nordenskjöld's *Studien* (Leipzig, 1885).

manuscript, it does not seem necessary that the search for prototypes or prototypic features should be confined to those which had been engraved. With these allowances the map does not seem to be very exceptional in any feature. It is connected with northwestern Europe in just the manner appertaining to several of the earlier maps. Its shape is no great improvement on the map of 1467, found at Warsaw. There was then

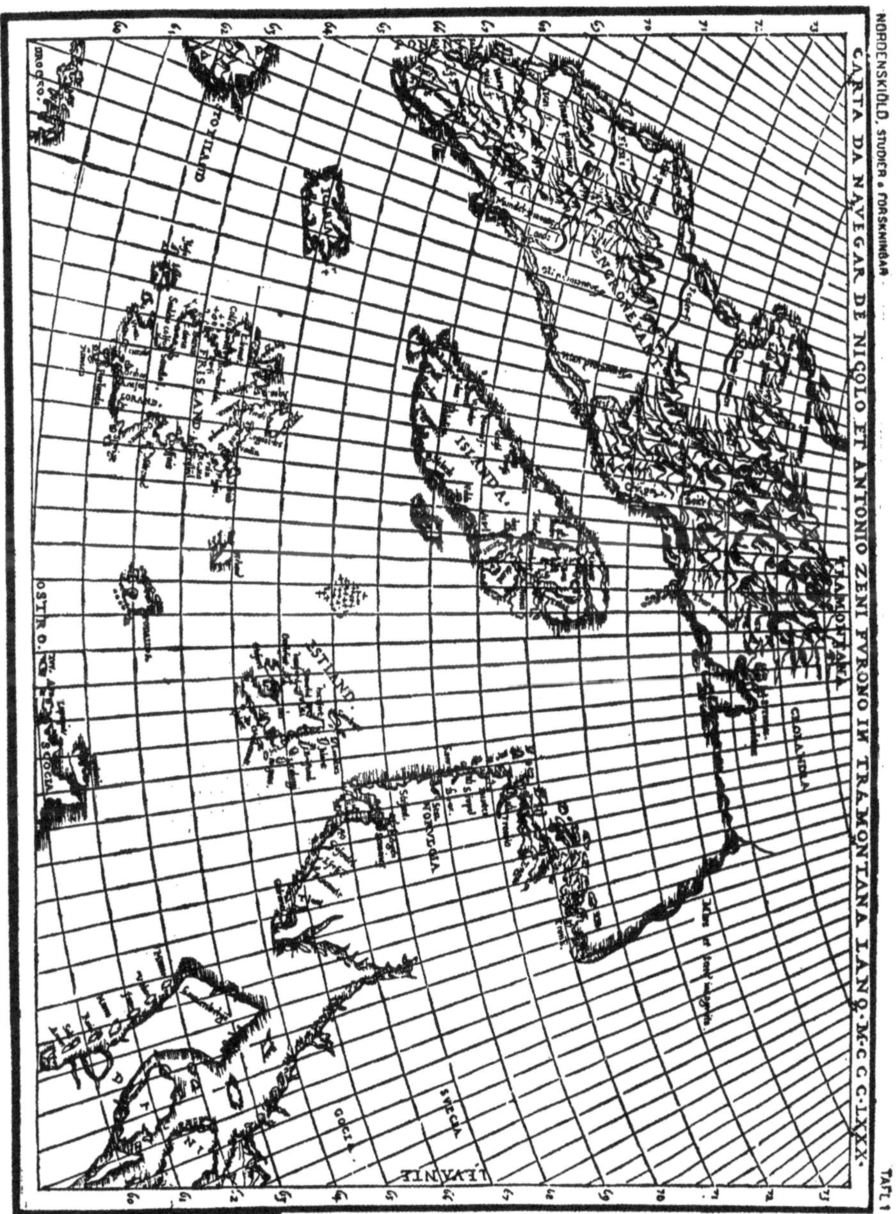

ZENO MAP. (*Reduced.*)*

* The original measures 12×15½ inches. Fac-similes of the original size or reduced, or other reproductions, will be found in Nordenskjöld's *Trois Cartes*, and in his *Studien*; Malte Brun's *Annales des Voyages*; Lelewel's *Moyen Age* (ii. 169); *Carter-Brown Catalogue* (i. 211); Kohl's *Discovery of Maine*, 97; Ruge's *Geschichte des Zeitalters der Entdeckungen*, p. 27; Bancroft's *Central America*, i. 81; Gay's *Pop. Hist. U. S.*, i. 84; Howley's *Ecclesiast. Hist. Newfoundland*, p. 45; Erizzo's *Le Scoperte Artiche* (Venice, 1855), — not to name others.

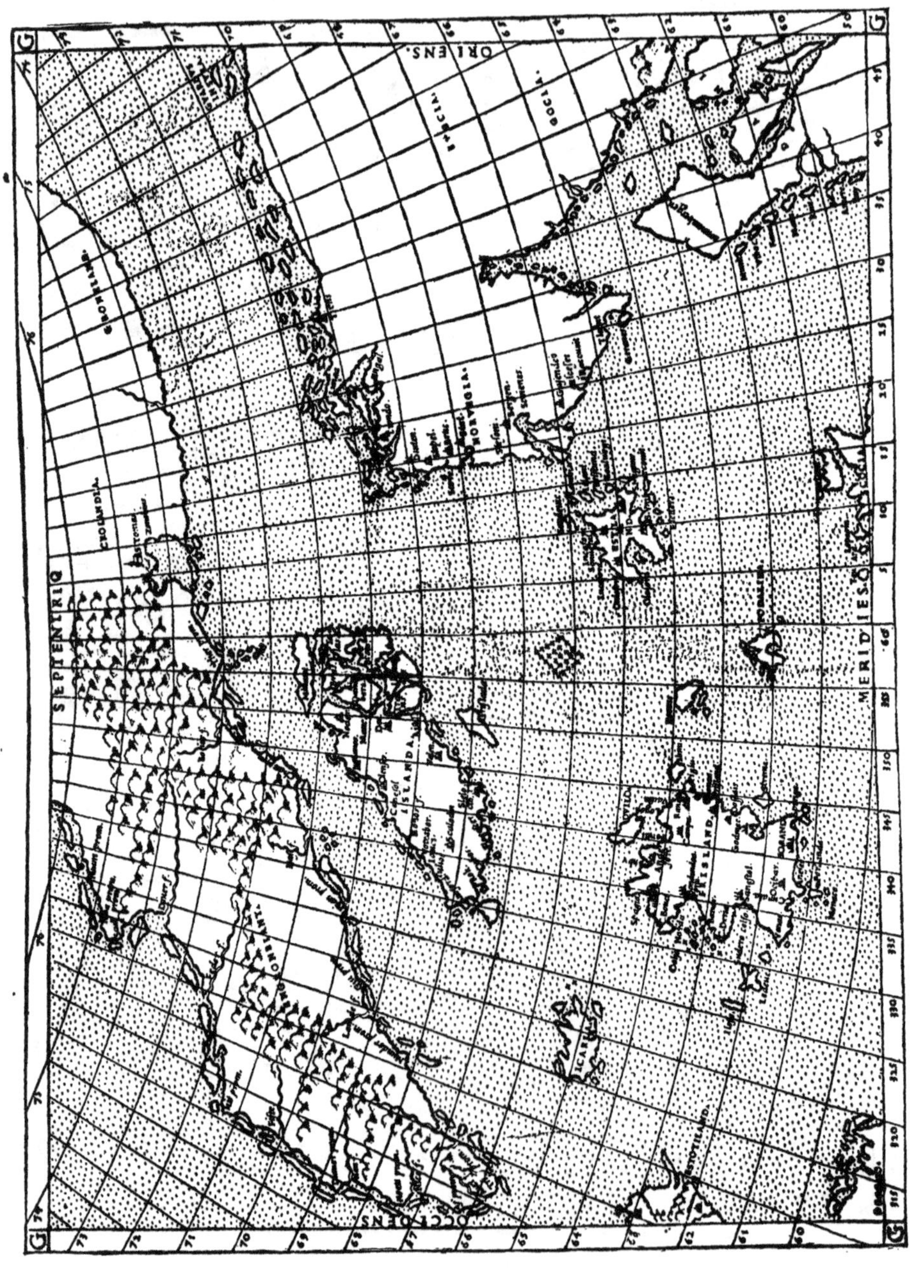

THE PTOLEMY ALTERATION (1561, etc.) OF THE ZENO MAP.

no such constancy in the placing of midsea islands in maps, to interdict the random location of other islands at the cartographer's will, without disturbing what at that day would have been deemed geographical probabilities, and there was all the necessary warranty in existing maps for the most wilfully depicted archipelago. The early Portuguese charts, not to name others, gave sufficient warrant for land where Estotiland and Drogeo appear.

Mention has already been made of the changes in this map, which the editors of the Ptolemy of 1561 made in severing Greenland from Europe, when they reëngraved it.[1] The same edition contained a map of "Schonlandia," in which it seems to be doubtful if the land which stands for Greenland does, or does not, connect with the Scandinavian main.[2] That Greenland was an island seems now to have become the prevalent opinion, and it was enforced by the maps of Mercator (1569 and 1587), Ortelius (1570, 1575), and Gallæus (1585), which placed it lying mainly east and west between the Scandinavian north and the Labrador coast, which it was now the fashion to call Estotiland. In its shape it closely resembled the Zeni outline. Another feature of these maps was the placing of another but smaller island west of "Groenlant," which was called "Grocland," and which seems to be simply a reduplication of the larger island by some geographical confusion,[3] which once started was easily seized upon to help fill out the arctic spaces.[4]

SEPTENTRIONALES REGIONES.*

It was just at this time (1570) that the oldest maps which display the geographical notions of the saga men were drawn, though not brought to light for many years. We note two such of this time, and one of a date near forty years later. One marked "Jonas, Gudmundi filius, delineavit, 1570," is given as are the two others by Torfæus in his *Gronlandia Antiqua*. They all seem to recognize a passage to the Arctic seas between Norway and Greenland, the northern parts of which last are called "Risaland," or "Riseland," and Jonas places "Oster Bygd" and "Wester Bygd" on the opposite sides of a squarish peninsula. Beyond what must be Davis' Straits is "America," and further south "Terra Florida" and "Albania."

If this description is compared with the key of Stephanius' map, next to be mentioned, while we remember

[1] In the edition of 1562, which repeated the map, the cartographer Moletta (Moletius) testified that its geography had been confirmed "by letters and marine charts sent to us from divers parts."

[2] Winsor's *Bibliog. of Ptolemy*, sub anno 1561.

[3] Lok's map of 1582 calls it "Groetland," the landfall of "Jac. Scolvus," the Pole. Cf. Vol. III. 40.

[4] For Mercator's map, see Vol. II. 452; IV. 94, 373. Ortelius' separate map of Scandia is much the same. It is the same with the map of Phillipus Gallæus, dated 1574, but published at Antwerp in 1585 in the *Theatri orbis terrarum Enchiridion*. Gilbert's map in 1576 omits the "Grocland" (Vol. III. 203). Both features, however, are preserved in the Judæis of 1593 (Vol. IV. 97), in the Wytfliet of 1597 (Vol. II. 459), in Wolfe's Linschoten in 1598 (Vol. III. 101), and in Quadus in 1600 (Vol. IV. 101). In the Zaltière map of 1566 (Vol. II. 451; IV. 93), in the Porcacchi map of 1572 (Vol. II. 96, 453; IV. 96), and in that of Johannes Martines of 1578, the features are too indefinite for recognition. Lelewel (i. pl. 7) gives a Spanish mappemonde of 1573.

* From *Theatri orbis Terrarum Enchiridion, per Phillipum Gallæum, et per Hugonem Favolium* (Antwerp, 1585).

that both represent the views prevailing in the north in 1570, it is hard to resist the conclusion that Vinland was north even of Davis' Straits, or at least held to be so at that time.

The second map, that of Stephanius, is reproduced herewith, dating back to the same period (1570); but the third, by Gudbrandus Torlacius, was made in 1606, and is sketched in Kohl's *Discovery of Maine* (p. 109). It gives better shape to "Gronlandia" than in either of the others.

It is not necessary to follow the course of the Greenland cartography farther with any minuteness. As the sixteenth century ended we have leading maps by Hakluyt in 1587 and 1599 (see Vol. III. 42), and De Bry in 1596 (Vol. IV. 99), and Wytfliet in 1597, all of which give Davis's Straits with more or less precision. Barentz's map of 1598 became the exemplar of the circumpolar chart in Pontanus' *Rerum et Urbis Amstelodamensium Historia* of 1611.[1] The chart of Luke Fox, in 1635, marked progress [2] better than that of La Pey-

SIGURD STEPHANIUS, 1570.*

1 In fac-simile in Nordenskjöld's *Vega*, i. 247.

2 Vol. III p. 98.

* Reproduced from the *Saga Time* of J. Fulford Vicary (London, 1887), after the map as given in the publication o the geographical society at Copenhagen, 1885–86, and it is supposed to have been drafted upon the narrative of the sagas. KEY: "*A*. This is where the English have come and has a name for barrenness, either from sun or cold. *B*. This i near where Vineland lies, which from its abundance of useful things, or from the land's fruitfulness, is called Good. Ou countrymen (Icelanders) have thought that to the south it ends with the wild sea and that a sound or fjord separates i from America. *C*. This land is called Rüseland or land of the giants, as they have horns and are called Skrickfinn (Fins that frighten). *D*. This is more to the east, and the people are called Klofinna (Fins with claws) on account o their large nails. *E*. This is Jotunheimer, or the home of the misshapen giants. *F*. Here is thought to be a fjord, o sound, leading to Russia. *G*. A rocky land often referred to in histories. *H*. What island that is I do not know, unles it be the island that a Venetian found, and the Germans call Friesland."

It will be observed under the *B* of the Key, the Norse of 1570 did not identify the Vinland of 1000 with the America c later discoveries.

This map is much the same, but differs somewhat in detail, from the one called of Stephanius, as produced in Kohl' *Discovery of Maine*, p. 107, professedly after a copy given in Torfæus' *Gronlandia Antiqua* (1706). Torfæus quote Theodorus Torlacius, the Icelandic historian, as saying that Stephanius appears to have drawn his map from ancient Icelandic records. The other maps given by Torfæus are: by Bishop Gudbrand Thorlakssen (1606); by Jonas Gudmun (1640); by Theodor Thorlakssen (1666), and by Torfæus himself. Cf. other copies of the map of Stephanius in Malte Brun's *Annales des Voyages*, Weise's *Discoveries of America*, p. 22; *Geog. Tidskrift*, viii. 123, and in Horsford *Disc. of America by Northmen*, p. 37.

rère (1647), though his map was better known.[1] Even as late as 1727, Hermann Moll could not identify his "Greenland" with "Groenland." In 1741, we have the map of Hans Egede in his "Grönland," repeated in

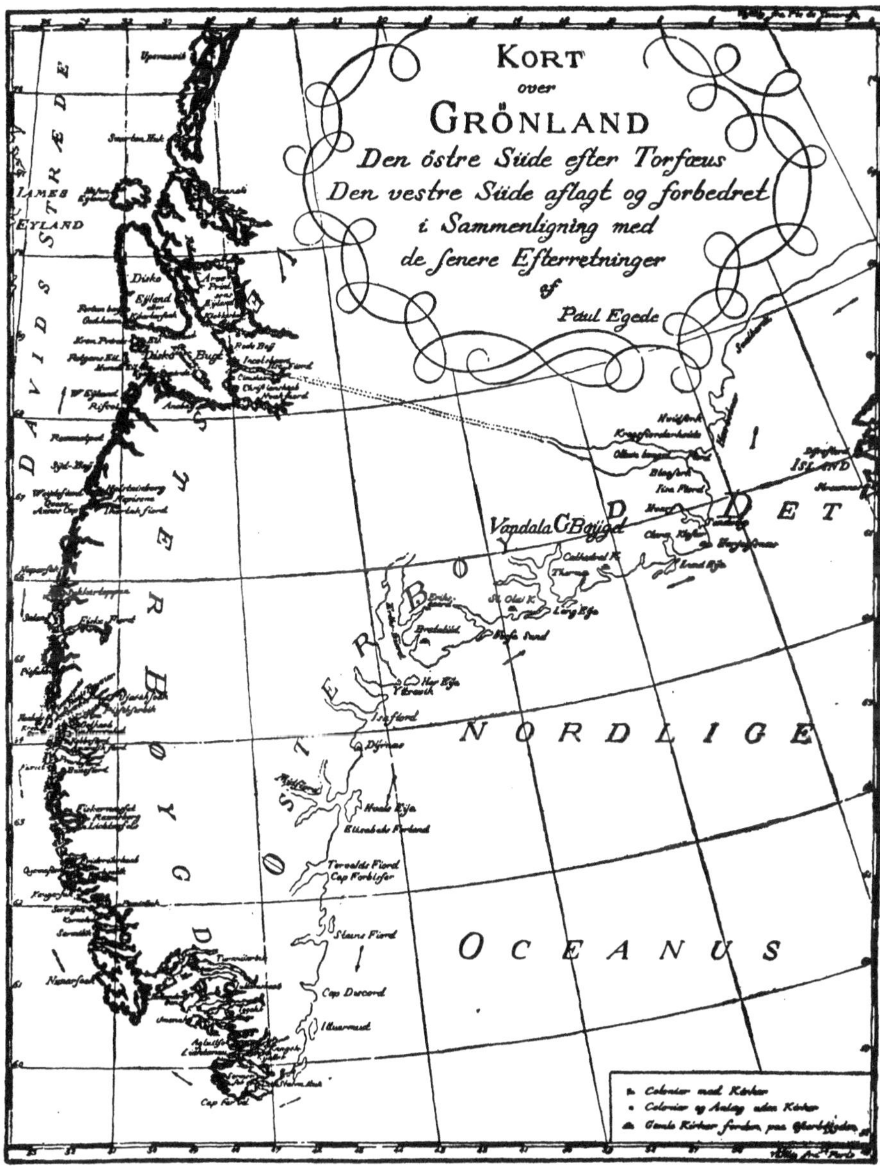

[1] A paper by H. Rink in the *Geografisk Tidskrift* (viii. 139) entitled "Ostgrönländerne i deres Forhold till Vestgrönländerne og de övrige Eskimostammer," is accompanied by drafts of the map of G. Tholacius, 1606, and of Th. Thorlacius, 1668–69, — the latter placing East Bygd on the east coast near the south end. K. J. V. Steenstrup, on Osterbygden in *Geog. Tidskrift*, viii. 123, gives fac-similes of maps of Jovis Carolus in 1634; of Hendrick Doncker in 1669. Sketches of maps by Johannes Meyer in 1652, and by Hendrick Doncker in 1666, are also given in the *Geografisk Tidskrift*, viii. (1885), pl. 5.

NOTE. — The annexed map is a reduced fac-simile of the map in the *Efterretninger om Grönland uddragne af en Journal holden fra 1771 til 1788*, by Paul Egede (Copenhagen, 1789). Paul Egede, son of Hans, was born in 1708, and remained in Greenland till 1740. He was made Bishop of Greenland in 1770, and died in 1789. The above book gives a portrait. There is another fac-simile of the map in Nordenskjöld's *Exped. till Grönland*, p. 234.

late editions, and the old delineation of the east coast after Torfæus was still retained in the 1788 map of Paul Egede.

In the map of 1653, made by De la Martinière, who was of the Danish expedition to the north, Greenland was made to connect with Northern Asia by way of the North pole.[1] Nordenskjöld calls him the Münchhausen of the northeast voyagers; and by his own passage in the "Vega," along the northern verge of Europe, from one ocean to the other, the Swedish navigator has of recent years proved for the first time that Greenland has no such connection. It yet remains to be proved that there is no connection to the north with at least the group of islands that are the arctic outlyers of the American continent.

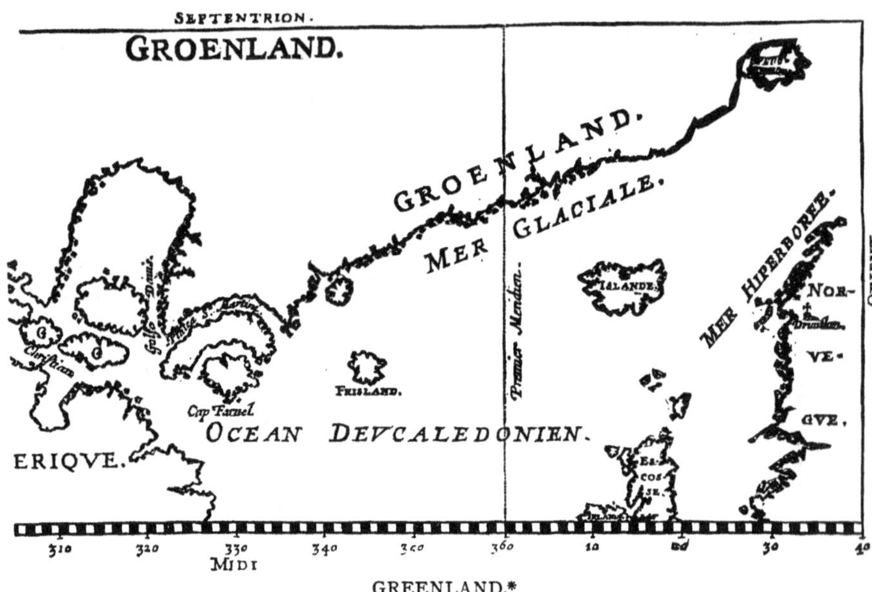

GREENLAND.*

[1] *Voyages des Pais Septentrionaux*, — a very popular book.

* Extracted from the "Carte de Grœnland" in Isaac de la Peyrère's *Relation du Groenland* (Paris, 1647). Cf. Winsor's *Kohl Maps*, no. 122.

CHAPTER III.

MEXICO AND CENTRAL AMERICA.

BY JUSTIN WINSOR.

"THE traditions of the migrations of the Chichimecs, Colhuas, and Nahuas," says Max Müller,[1] "are no better than the Greek traditions about Pelasgians, Æolians, and Ionians, and it would be a mere waste of time to construct out of such elements a systematic history, only to be destroyed again, sooner or later, by some Niebuhr, Grote, or Lewis."

"It is yet too early," says Bandelier,[2] "to establish a definite chronology, running farther back from the Conquest than two centuries,[3] and even within that period but very few dates have been satisfactorily fixed."

Such are the conditions of the story which it is the purpose of this chapter to tell.

We have, to begin with, as in other history, the recognition of a race of giants, convenient to hang legends on, and accounted on all hands to have been occupants of the country in the dimmest past, so that there is nothing back of them. Who they were, whence they came, and what stands for their descendants after we get down to what in this pre-Spanish history we rather presumptuously call historic ground, is far from clear. If we had the easy faith of the native historian Ixtlilxochitl, we should believe that these gigantic Quinames, or Quinametin, were for the most part swallowed up in a great convulsion of nature, and it was those who escaped which the Olmecs and Tlascalans encountered in entering the country.[4] If all this means anything, which may well be doubted, it is as likely as not that these giants were the followers of a demi-god, Votan,[5] who came from over-sea to

[1] *Chips from a German Workshop*, i. 327.

[2] *Archæological Tour*, p. 202.

[3] The earliest fixed date for the founding of Tenochtitlan (Mexico city) is 1325. Brasseur tells us that Carlos de Sigüenza y Gongora made the first chronological table of ancient Mexican dates, which was used by Boturini, and was improved by Leon y Gama, — the same which Bustamante has inserted in his edition of Gomara. Gallatin (*Amer. Ethnol. Soc. Trans.*, i.) gave a composite table of events by dates before the Conquest, which is followed in Brantz Mayer's *Mexico as it was*, i. 97. Ed. Madier de Montjau, in his *Chronologie hiéroglyphico-phonétique des Rois Astéques de 1352 à 1522*, takes issue with Ramirez on some points.

[4] Bancroft (v. 199) gives references to those writers who have discussed this question of giants. Bandelier's references are more in détail (*Arch. Tour*, p. 201). Short (p. 233) borrows largely the list in Bancroft. The enumeration includes nearly all the old writers. Acosta finds confirmation in bones of incredible largeness, often found in his day, and then supposed to be human. Modern zoölogists say they were those of the Mastodon. Howarth, *Mammoth and the Flood*, 297.

[5] See *Native Races*, ii. 117; v. 24, 27.

America,[1] found it peopled, established a government in Xibalba, — if such a place ever existed, — with the germs of Maya if not of other civilizations, whence, by migrations during succeeding times, the Votanites spread north and occupied the Mexican plateau, where they became degenerate, doubtless, if they deserved the extinction which we are told was in store for them. But they had an alleged chronicler for their early days, the writer of the Book of Votan, written either by the hero himself or by one of his descendants, — eight or nine generations in the range of authorship making little difference apparently. That this narrative was known to Francisco Nuñez de la Vega[2] would seem to imply that somebody at that time had turned it into readable script out of the unreadable hieroglyphics, while the disguises of the Spanish tongue, perhaps, as Bancroft[3] suggests, may have saved it from the iconoclastic zeal of the priests. When, later, Ramon de Ordoñez had the document, — perhaps the identical manuscript, — it consisted of a few folios of quarto paper, and was written in Roman script in the Tzendal tongue, and was inspected by Cabrera, who tells us something of its purport in his *Teatro critico Americano*, while Ramon himself was at the same time using it in his *Historia del Cielo y de la Tierra*. It was from a later copy of this last essay, the first copy being unknown, that the Abbé Brasseur de Bourbourg got his knowledge of what Ramon had derived from the Votan narrative, and which Brasseur has given us in several of his books.[4] That there was a primitive empire — Votanic, if you please — seems to some minds confirmed by other evidences than the story of Votan; and out of this empire — to adopt a European nomenclature — have come, as such believers say, after its downfall somewhere near the Christian era, and by divergence, the great stocks of people called Maya, Quiché, and Nahua, inhabiting later, and respectively, Yucatan, Guatemala, and Mexico. This is the view, if we accept the theory which Bancroft has prominently advocated, that the migrations of the Nahuas were from the south northward,[5] and that this was the period of the divergence, eighteen centuries ago or more, of the great civilizing stocks of Mexico and of Central America.[6] We fail to find so early a contact of these two races, if, on the other hand, we accept the old theory that the migrations which established

[1] Sometimes it is said they came from the Antilles, or beyond, easterly, and that an offshoot of the same people appeared to the early French explorers as the Natchez Indians. We have, of course, offered to us a choice of theories in the belief that the Maya civilization came from the westward by the island route from Asia. This misty history is nothing without alternatives, and there are a plenty of writers who dogmatize about them.

[2] *Constituciones diocesanas del obispado de Chiappas* (Rome, 1702).

[3] *Nat. Races*, v. 160.

[4] *Hist. Nations Civilisées*, i. 37, 150, etc. *Popul Vuh*, introd., sec. v. Bancroft relates the Votan myth, with references, in *Nat. Races*, iii. 450. Brasseur identifies the Votanites with the Colhuas, as the builders of Palenqué, the founders of Xibalba, and thinks a branch of them wandered south to Peru. There are some stories of even pre-Votan days, under Igh and Imox. Cf. H. De Charency's "Myth d'Imos," in the *Annales de philosophie Chrétienne*, 1872–73, and references in Bancroft, v. 164, 231.

[5] *Native Races*, ii. 121, etc.

[6] Bancroft (v. 236) points to Bradford, Squier, Tylor, Viollet-le-Duc, Bartlett, and Müller, with Brasseur in a qualified way, as in the main agreeing in this early disjointing of the Nahua stock, by which the Maya was formed through separation from the older race.

the Toltec and Aztec powers were from the north southward,[1] through three several lines, as is sometimes held, one on each side of the Rocky Mountains, with a third following the coast. In this way such advocates trace the course of the Olmecs, who encountered the giants, and later of the Toltecs.

That the Votanic peoples or some other ancient tribes were then a distinct source of civilization, and that Palenqué may even be Xibalba, or the Nachan, which Votan founded, is a belief that some archæologists find the evidence of in certain radical differences in the Maya tongues and in the Maya ruins.[2]

In the Quiché traditions, as preserved in the *Popul Vuh*, and in the *Annals of the Cakchiquels*, we likewise go back into mistiness and into the inevitable myths which give the modern comparative mythologists so much comfort and enlightenment; but Bancroft[3] and the rest get from all this nebulousness, as was gotten from the Maya traditions, that there was a great power at Xibalba,[4] — if in Central America anywhere that place may have been, — which was overcome[5] when from Tulan[6] went out migrating chiefs, who founded the Quiché-Cakchiquel peoples of Guatemala, while others, the Yaqui, — very likely only traders, — went to Mexico, and still others went to Yucatan, thus accounting for the subsequent great centres of aboriginal power — if we accept this view.

As respects the traditions of the more northern races, there is the same choice of belief and alternative demonstration. The Olmecs, the earliest Nahua comers, are sometimes spoken of as sailing from Florida and landing on the coast at what is now Pánuco, whence they travelled to Guatemala,[7] and finally settled in Tamoanchan, and offered their sacrifices farther north at Teotihuacan.[8] This is very likely the Votan legend suited to the more northern region, and if so, it serves to show, unless we discard the whole theory, how the Votanic people had scattered. The other principal source of our suppositions — for we can hardly call it knowledge — of these times is the *Codex Chimalpòpoca*, of which there is elsewhere an account,[9]

[1] Enforced, for instance, by one of the best of the later Mexican writers, Orozco y Berra, in his *Geografía de las lenguas y Carta Ethnografica de México* (Mexico, 1865).

[2] Tylor, *Anahuac*, 189, and his *Early Hist. Mankind*, 184. Orozco y Berra, *Geog.*, 124. Bancroft, v. 169, note. The word Maya was first heard by Columbus in his fourth voyage, 1503–4. We sometimes find it written Mayab. It is usual to class the people of Yucatan, and even the Quiché-Cakchiquels of Guatemala and those of Nicaragua, under the comprehensive term of Maya, as distinct from the Nahua people farther north.

[3] *Nat. Races*, v. 186.

[4] Brinton, with his view of myths, speaks of the attempt of the Abbé Brasseur to make Xibalba an ancient kingdom, with Palenqué as its capital, as utterly unsupported and wildly hypothetical (*Myths*, 251).

[5] Perhaps by Gucumatz (who is identified by some with Quetzalcoatl), leading the Tzequiles, who are said to have appeared from somewhere during one of Votan's absences, and to have grown into power among the Chanes, or Votan's people, till they made Tulan, where they lived, too powerful for the Votanites. Bancroft (v. 187) holds this view against Brasseur.

[6] Perhaps Ococingo, or Copan, as Bancroft conjectures (v. 187).

[7] As Sahagún calls it, meaning, as Bancroft suggests, Tabasco.

[8] Short (p. 248) points out that the linguistic researches of Orozco y Berra (*Geografía de las Lenguas de México*, 1–76) seem to confirm this.

[9] See p. 158.

and from it we can derive much the same impressions, if we are disposed to sustain a preconceived notion.

The periods and succession of the races whose annals make up the history of what we now call Mexico, prior to the coming of the Spaniards, are confused and debatable. Whether under the name of Chichimecs we are to understand a distinct people, or a varied and conglomerate mass of people, which, in a generic way, we might call barbarians, is a question open to discussion.[1] There is no lack of names[2] to be applied to the tribes and bands which, according to all accounts, occupied the Mexican territory previous to the sixth century. Some of them were very likely Nahua forerunners[3] of the subsequent great influx of that race, like the Olmecs and Xicalancas, and may have been the people "from the direction of Florida," of whom mention has been made. Others, as some say, were eddies of those populous waves which, coming by the north from Asia, overflowed the Rocky Mountains, and became the builders of mounds and the later peoples of the Mississippi Valley,[4] passed down the trend of the Rocky Mountains, and built cliff-houses and pueblos, or streamed into the table-land of Mexico. This is all conjecture, perhaps delusion, but may be as good a supposition as any, if we agree to the northern theory, as Nadaillac[5] does, but not so tenable, if, with the contrary Bancroft,[6] we hold rather that they came from the south. We can turn from one to the other of these theorists and agree with both, as they cite their evidences. On the whole, a double compliance is better than dogmatism. It is one thing to lose one's way in this labyrinth of belief, and another to lose one's head.

1 Kirk says (Prescott's *Mexico*): "Confusion arises from the name of Chichimec, originally that of a single tribe, and subsequently of its many offshoots, being also used to designate successive hordes of whatever race." Some have seen in the Waiknas of the Mosquito Coast, and in the Caribs generally, descendants of these Chichimecs who have kept to their old social level. The Caribs, on other authority, came originally from the stock of the Tupis and Guaranis, who occupied the region south of the Amazon, and in Columbus's time they were scattered in Darien and Honduras, along the northern regions of South America, and in some of the Antilles (Von Martius, *Beiträge zur Ethnographie und Sprachenkunde Amerika's zumal Brasiliens*, Leipzig, 1867). Bancroft (ii. 126) gives the etymology of Chichimec and of other tribal designations. Cf. Buschmann's *Ueber die Aztekischen Ortsnamen* (Berlin, 1853). Bandelier (*Archæol. Tour*, 200; *Peabody Mus. Repts.*, ii. 393) says he fails to discover in the word anything more than a general term, signifying a savage, a hunter, or a warrior, Chichimecos, applied to roving tribes. Brasseur says that Mexican tradition applies the term Chichimecs generically to the first occupants of the New World.

2 These names wander and exchange consonants provokingly, and it may be enough to give alphabetically a list comprised of those in Prichard (*Nat. Hist. Man*) and Orozco y Berra (*Geografía*), with some help from Gallatin in the *American Ethno. Soc. Trans.*, i., and other groupers of the ethnological traces: Chinantecs, Chatinos, Cohuixcas, Chontales, Colhuas, Coras, Cuitatecs, Chichimecs, Cuextecas (Guaxtecas, Huastecs), Mazetecs, Mazahuas, Michinacas, Miztecs, Nonohualcas, Olmecs, Otomís, Papabucos, Quinames, Soltecos, Totonacs, Triquis, Tepanecs, Tarascos, Xicalancas, Zapotecs. It is not unlikely the same people may be here mentioned under different names. The diversity of opinions respecting the future of these vapory existences is seen in Bancroft's collation (v. 202). Torquemada tells us about all that we know of the Totonacs, who claim to have been the builders of Teotihuacan. Bancroft gives references (v. 204) for the Totonacs, (p. 206) for the Otomís, (p. 207) for the Mistecs and Zapotecs, and (p. 208) for the Huastecs.

3 Bancroft, ii. 97. Brasseur, *Nat. Civ.*, i. ch. 4, and his *Palenqué*, ch. 3.

4 Called Huehue-Tlapallan, as Brasseur would have it.

5 Following Motolinía and other early writers.

6 *Native Races*, v. 219, 616.

It was the Olmecs who found the Quinames, or giants, near Puebla and Cholula, and in the end overcame them. The Olmecs built, according to one story, the great pyramid of Cholula,[1] and it was they who received the great Quetzalcoatl from across the sea, a white-bearded man, as the legends went, who was benign enough, in the stories told of him, to make the later Spaniards think, when they heard them, that he was no other than the Christian St. Thomas on his missions. When the Spaniards finally induced the inheritors of the Olmecs' power to worship Quetzalcoatl as a beneficent god, his temple soon topped the mound at Cholula.[2] We have seen that the great Nahua occupation of the Mexican plateau, at a period somewhere from the fourth to the seventh century,[3] was preceded by some scattered tribal organizations of the same stock, which had at an early date mingled with the primitive peoples of this region. We have seen that there is a diversity of opinion as to the country from which they came, whether from the north or south. A consideration of this question involves the whole question of the migration of races in these pre-Columbian days, since it is the coming and going of peoples that form the basis of all its history.

In the study of these migrations, we find no more unanimity of interpretation than in other questions of these early times.[4] The Nahua peoples (Toltecs, Aztecs, Mexicans, or what you will), according to the prevalent views of the early Spanish writers, came by successive influxes from the north or northwest, and from a remote place called Tollan, Tula, Tlapallan, Huehue-Tlapallan, as respects the Toltec group,[5] and called Aztlan as

[1] Bandelier, *Archæol. Tour*, 253.

[2] Kingsborough, ix. 206, 460; Veytia, i. 155, 163. Of the Quetzalcoatl myth there are references elsewhere. P. J. J. Valentini has made a study of the early Mexican ethnology and history in his "Olmecas and Tultecas," translated by S. Salisbury, Jr., and printed in the *Amer. Antiq. Soc. Proc.*, Oct. 21, 1882. On Quetzalcoatl in Cholula, see Torquemada, translated in Bancroft, iii. 258.

[3] This wide difference covers intervening centuries, each of which has its advocates. Short carries their coming back to the fourth century (p. 245), but Clavigero's date of A. D. 544 is more commonly followed. Veytia makes it the seventh century. Bancroft (v. 211, 214) notes the diversity of views.

[4] Bancroft (v. 322) in a long note collates the different statements of the routes and sojourns in this migration. Cf. Short, p. 259.

[5] Cf. Kirk in Prescott, i. 10. It must be confessed that it is rather in the domain of myth than of history that we must place all that has been written about the scattering of the Toltec people at Babel (Bancroft, v. 19), and their finally reaching Huehue-Tlapallan, wherever that may have been. The view long prevalent about this American starting-point of the Nahuas, Toltecs, or whatever designation may be given to the beginners of this myth and history, placed it in California, but some later writers think it worth while to give it a geographical existence in the Mississippi Valley, and to associate it in some vague way with the mound-builders and their works (Short, *No. Amer. of Antiq.*, 251, 253). There is some confusion between Huehue-Tlapallan of this story and the Tlapallan noticed in the Spanish conquest time, which was somewhere in the Usumacinta region, and if we accept Tollan, Tullan, or Tula as a form of the name, the confusion is much increased (Short, pp. 217–220). Bancroft (v. 214) says there is no sufficient data to determine the position of Huehue-Tlapallan, but he thinks "the evidence, while not conclusive, favors the south rather than the north" (p. 216). The truth is, about these conflicting views of a northern or southern origin, pretty much as Kirk puts it (Prescott, i. 18): "All that can be said with confidence is, that neither of the opposing theories rests on a secure and sufficient basis." The situation of Huehue-Tlapallan and Aztlan is very likely one and the same question, as looking to what was the starting-point of all the Nahua migrations, extending over a thousand years.

respects the Aztec or Mexican. When, by settlement after settlement, each migratory people pushed farther south, they finally reached Central Mexico This sequence of immigration seems to be agreed upon, but as to where their cradle was and as to what direction their line of progress took, there is a diversity of opinion as widely separated as the north is from the south The northern position and the southern direction is all but universally accepted among the early Spanish writers[1] and their followers,[2] while it is claimed by others that the traditions as preserved point to the south as the starting-point. Cabrera took this view. Brasseur sought to reconcile conflicting tradition and Spanish statement by carrying the line of migration from the south with a northerly sweep, so that in the end Anahuac would be entered from the north, with which theory Bancroft[3] is inclined to agree. Aztlan, as well as Huehue-Tlapallan, by those who support the northern theory, has been placed anywhere from the California peninsula[4] within a radius that sweeps through Wisconsin and strikes the Atlantic at Florida.[5]

[1] Bancroft, v. 217.

[2] Torquemada, Boturini, Humboldt, Brasseur, Charnay, Short, etc.

[3] *Nat. Races* (v. 222).

[4] In support of the California location, Buschmann, in his *Ueber die Spuren der Aztekischen Sprache im nördlichen Mexico und höheren Amerikanischen Norden* (Berlin, 1854), finds traces of the Mexican tongue in those of the recent California Indians. Linguistic resemblances to the Aztec, even so far north as Nootka, have been traced, but later philologists deny the inferences of relationship drawn from such similarity (Bancroft, iii. p. 612). The linguistic confusion in aboriginal California is so great that there is a wide field for tracing likenesses (*Ibid.* iii. 635). In the *California State Mining Bureau, Bulletin no. 1* (Sacramento, 1888), Winslow Anderson gives a description of some desiccated human remains found in a sealed cave, which are supposed to be Aztec. There are slight resemblances to the Aztec in the Shoshone group of languages (Bancroft, iii. 660), and the same author arranges all that has been said to connect the Mexican tongue with those of New Mexico and neighboring regions (iii. 664). Buschmann, who has given particular attention to tracing the Aztec connections at the north, finds nothing to warrant anything more than casual admixtures with other stocks (*Die Lautveränderung Aztekischer Wörter*, Berlin, 1855, and *Die Spuren der Aztekischen Sprachen*, Berlin, 1859). See Short (p. 487) for a summary.

[5] Bancroft (v. 305) cites the diverse views; so does Short to some extent (pp. 246, 258, etc.). Cf. Brinton's *Address* on "Where was Aztlan?" p. 6; Short, 486, 490; Nadaillac, 284; Wilson's *Prehistoric Man*, i. 327.

Brinton (*Myths of the New World*, etc., 89 *Amer. Hero. Myths*, 92) holds that Aztlan is a name wholly of mythical purport, which it would be vain to seek on the terrestrial globe. This cradle region of the Nahuas sometimes appears as the Seven Caves (Chicomoztoc), and Duran places them "in Teoculuacan, otherwise called Aztlan, a country toward the north and connected with Florida." The Seven Caves were explained by Sahagún as a valley, by Clavigero as a city, by Schoolcraft and others as simply seven boats in which the first comers came from Asia; Brasseur makes them and Aztlan the same; others find them to be the seven cities of Cibola, — so enumerates Brinton (*Myths*, 227) who thinks that the seven divisions of the Nahuas sprung from the belief in the Seven Caves and had in reality no existence.

Gallatin has followed out the series of migrations in the *Amer. Ethnol. Soc. Trans.*, i. 162 Dawson, *Fossil Men* (ch. 3), gives his comprehensive views of the main directions of these early migrations. Brasseur follows the Nahua (*Popul Vuh*, introd., sect. ix.). Winchell (*Pre-Adamites*) thinks the general tendency was from north to south. Morgan finds the origin of the Mexican tribes in New Mexico and in the San Juan Valley (*Peabody Mus. Rept.*, xii. 553. Cf. his article in the *North Am. Rev.*, Oct., 1869) Humboldt (*Views of Nature*, 207) touches the Aztec wanderings.

There are two well-known Aztec migration maps, first published in F. G. Carreri's *Giro del Mondo;* in English as "Voyage round the world," in Churchill's *Voyages*, vol. iv., concerning which see Bancroft, ii. 543; iii. 68, 69; Short 262, 431, 433; Prescott, iii. 364, 382. Orozco Berra (*Hist. Antiq. de Mexico*, iii. 61) says tha

The advocates of the southern starting-point of these migrations have been comparatively few and of recent prominence; chief among them are Squier and Bancroft.[1]

With the appearance of a people, which, for want of a better designation, are usually termed Toltecs, on the Mexican table-land in the sixth century or thereabouts,[2] we begin the early history of Mexico, so far as we can make any deductions from the semi-mythical records and traditions which the Spaniards or the later aborigines have preserved for us. This story of the Nahua occupation of Anáhuac is one of strife and shifting vassalage, with rivalries and uprisings of neighboring and kindred tribes, going on for centuries. While the more advanced portion of the Nahuas in Anáhuac were making progress in the arts, that division of the same stock which was living beyond such influence, and without the bounds of Anáhuac, were looked upon rather as barbarians than as brothers, and acquired the name which had become a general one for such rougher natures, Chichimec. It is this Chichimec people under some name or other who are always starting up and overturning something. At one time they unite with the Colhuas and found Colhuacan, and nearly subjugate the lake region. Then the Toltec tarriers at Huehue-Tlapallan come boldly to the neighborhood of the Chichimecs and found Tollan; and thus they turn a wandering community into what, for want of a better name, is called a monarchy. They strengthened its government by an alliance with the Chichimecs,[3] and placed their seat of power at Colhuacan.

these maps follow one another, and are not different records of the same progress. Humboldt (*Vues*, etc., ii. 176) gives an interpretation of them in accordance with Sigüenza's views, which is the one usually followed, and Bancroft (v. 324) epitomizes it. Ramirez says that the copies reproduced in Humboldt, Clavigero, and Kingsborough are not so correct as the engraving given in Garcia y Cubas's *Atlas geográfico, estadistico e histórico de la Republica Mejicana* (April, 1858). Bancroft (ii. 544) gives it as reproduced by Ramirez. It is also in the Mexican edition of Prescott, and in Schoolcraft's *Indian Tribes*. Cf. Delafield's *Inquiry* (N. Y., 1839) and Léon de Rosny's *Les doc. écrits de l'antiq. Amér.* (Paris, 1882). The original is preserved in the Museo Nacional of Mexico. A palm-tree on the map, near Aztlan, has pointed some of the arguments in favor of a southern position for that place, but Ramirez says it is but a part of a hieroglyphic name, and has no reference to the climate of Aztlan (Short, p. 266). F. Von Hellwald printed a paper on "American migrations," with notes by Professor Henry, in the *Smithsonian Report*, 1866, pp. 328–345. Short defines as "altogether the most enlightened treatment of the subject" the paper of John H. Becker, "Migrations des Nahuas," in the *Compte rendu, Congrès des Américanistes* (Luxembourg, 1877), i. 325. This paper finds an identification of the Tulan Zuiva of the Quichés, the Huehue-Tlapallan of the Toltecs, the Amaquemecan of the Chichimecs, and the Oztotlan (Aztlan) of the Aztecs in the valleys of the Rio Grande del Norte and Rio Colorado, as was Morgan's view. Short (p. 249) summarizes his paper. Bancroft (v. 289) shows the diversity of views respecting Amaquemecan.

[1] *Native Races*, v. 167, recapitulates the proofs against the northern theory. J. R. Bartlett, *Personal Narrative*, ii. 283, finds no evidence for it. The successive sites of their sojourns as they passed on their journeys are given as Tlapallan, Tlacutzin, Tlapallanco, Jalisco, Atenco, Iztachnexuca, Tollatzinco, Tollan or Tula, — the last, says Bancroft, apparently in Chiapas. If there was not such confusion respecting the old geography, these names might decide the question.

[2] Writers usually place the beginnings of credible history at about this period. Brasseur and the class of writers who are easily lifted on their imagination talk about traces of a settled government being discernible at periods which they place a thousand years before Christ.

[3] References in Bancroft, v. 247, with Brasseur for the main dependence, in his use of the *Codex Chimalpópoca* and the *Memorial de Colhuacan*.

Then we read of a power springing up at Tezcuco, and of various other events, which happened or did not happen, according as you believe this or the other chronicle. The run of many of the stories of course produces the inevitable and beautiful daughter, and the bold princess, who control many an event. Then there is a league of Colhuacan, Otompan, and Tollan. Suddenly appears the great king Quetzalcoatl, — though it may be we confound him with the divinity of that name; and with him, to perplex matters, comes his sworn enemy Huemac. Quetzalcoatl's devoted labors to make his people give up human sacrifice arrayed the priesthood against him, until at last he fell before the intrigues that made Huemac succeed in Tollan, and that drove his luckless rival to Cholula, where he reigned anew. Huemac followed him and drove him farther; but in doing so he gave his enemies in Tollan a chance to put another on the throne.

Then came a season of peace and development, when Tollan grew splendid. Colhuacan flourished in political power, and Teotihuacan[1] and Cholula were the religious shrines of the people. But at last the end was near.

The closing century of the Toltec power was a frightful one for broil, pestilence, and famine among the people, amours and revenge in the great chieftain's household, revolt among the vassals; with sorcery rampant and the gods angry; with volcanoes belching, summers like a furnace, and winters like the pole; with the dreaded omen of a rabbit, horned like a deer, confronting the ruler, while rebel forces threatened the capital. There was also civil strife within the gates, phallic worship and debauchery, — all preceding an inundation of Chichimecan hordes. Thus the power that had flourished for several hundred years fell, — seemingly in the latter half of the eleventh century.[2] The remnant that was left of the desolated people went hither and thither, till the fragments were absorbed in the conquerors, or migrated to distant regions south.[3]

Whether the term Toltec signified a nation, or only denoted a dynasty, is a question for the archæologists to determine. The general opinion heretofore has been that they were a distinct race, of the Nahua stock, however, and that they came from the north. The story which has been thus far told of their history is the narrative of Ixtlilxochitl, and is repeated by Veytia, Clavigero, Prescott, Brasseur de Bourbourg, Orozco y Berra,

[1] Charnay (Eng. trans., ch. 8 and 9) calls it a rival city of Tula or Tollan, rebuilt by the Chichimecs on the ruins of a Toltec city.

[2] If one wants the details of all this, he can read it in Veytia, Brasseur (*Nat. Civilisées* and *Palenqué*, ch. viii.), and Bancroft, the latter giving references (v. 285).

[3] It is frequently stated that there was a segregated migration to Central America. Bancroft (v. 168, 285), who collates the authorities, finds nothing of the kind implied. He thinks the mass remained in Anáhuac. The old view as expressed by Prescott (i. 14) was that "much the greater number probably spread over the region of Central America and the neighboring isles, and the traveller now speculates on the majestic ruins of Mitla and Palenqué as possibly the work of this extraordinary people." Kirk, as Prescott's editor, refers to the labors of Orozco y Berra (*Geografía de las Lenguas de México*, 122), followed by Tylor, *Anahuac*, 189) as establishing the more recent view that this southern architecture, "though of a far higher grade, was long anterior to the Toltec dominion."

Nadaillac, and the later compilers. Sahagún seems to have been the first to make a distinct use of the name Toltec, and Charency in his paper on *Xibalba* finds evidence that the Toltecs constituted two different migrations, the one of a race that was straight-headed, which came from the northwest, and the other of a flat-headed people, which came from Florida.

Brinton, on the contrary, finds no warrant either for this dual migration, or indeed for considering the Toltecs to be other than a section of the same race, that we know later as Aztecs or Mexicans. This sweeping denial of their ethnical independence had been forestalled by Gallatin;[1] but no one before Brinton had made it a distinct issue, though some writers before and since have verged on his views.[2] Others, like Charnay, have answered Brinton's arguments, and defended the older views.[3] Bandelier's views connect them with the Maya rather than with the Nahua stock,[4] if, as he thinks may be the case, they were the people who landed at Pánuco and settled at Tamoanchan, the Votanites, as they are sometimes called. He traces back to Herrera and Torquemada the identification for the first time of the Toltecs with these people.[5] Bandelier's conclusions, however, are that "all we can gather about them with safety is, that they were a sedentary Indian stock, which at some remote period settled in Central Mexico," and that "nothing certain is known of their language." [6]

[1] *Amer. Ethno. Soc. Trans.*, i.

[2] Bancroft (v. 287) says: "It is probable that the name Toltec, a title of distinction rather than a national name, was never applied at all to the common people."

[3] Brinton's main statement is in his *Were the Toltecs an historic nationality? Read before the American Philosophical Society, Sept. 2, 1887* (Phila., 1887); published also in their *Proceedings*, 1887, p. 229. Cf. also Brinton's *Amer. Hero. Myths* (Phil., 1882), p. 86, where he throws discredit on the existence of the alleged Toltec king Quetzalcoatl (whom Sahagún keeps distinct from the mythical demi-god); and earlier, in his *Myths of the New World* (p. 29), he had suggested that the name Toltec might have "a merely mythical signification." Charnay, who makes the Toltecs a Nahuan tribe, had defended their historical status in a paper on "La Civilisation Tolteque," in the *Revue d'Ethnographie* (iv., 1885); and again, two years later, in the same periodical, he reviewed adversely Brinton's arguments. (Cf. *Saturday Review*, lxiii. 843.) Otto Stoll, in his *Guatemala, Reisen und Schilderungen* (Leipzig, 1886), is another who rejects the old theory.

[4] *Archæol. Tour*, 253.

[5] *Archæol. Tour*, 7. Sahagún identifies the Toltecs with the "giants," and if these were the degraded descendants of the followers of Votan, Sahagún thus earlier established the same identity.

[6] *Archæol. Tour*, 191. The fact that the names which we associate with the Toltecs are Nahua, only means that Nahua writers have transmitted them, as Bandelier thinks. Cf. also Bandelier's citation in the *Peabody Mus. Reports*, vol. ii. 388, where he speaks of our information regarding the Toltecs as "limited and obscure." He thinks it beyond question that they were Nahuas; and the fact that their division of time corresponds with the system found in Yucatan, Guatemala, etc., with other evidences of myths and legends, leads him to believe that the aborigines of more southern regions were, if not descendants, at least of the same stock with the Toltecs, and that we are justified in studying them to learn what the Toltecs were. He finds that Veytia, in his account of the Toltecs, beside depending on Sahagún and Torquemada, finds a chief source in Ixtlilxochitl, and locates Huehue-Tlapallan in the north; and Veytia's statements reappear in Clavigero.

The best narratives of the Toltec history are those in Veytia, *Historia Antigua de Méjico* (Mexico, 1806); Brasseur's *Hist. Nations Civilisées* (vol. i.), and his introduction to his *Popul Vuh;* and Bancroft (v. ch. 3 and 4): but we must look to Ixtlilxochitl, Torquemada, Sahagún, and the others, if we wish to study the sources. In such a study we shall encounter vexatious problems enough. It is practically impossible to arrange chronologically what Ixtlilxochitl says that he got from the picture-writings which he interpreted. Bancroft (v. 209) does the best he can to give it a forced perspicuity. Wilson (*Prehis-*

The desolation of Anáhuac as the Toltecs fell invited a foreign occupation, and a remote people called Chichimecs[1] — not to be confounded with the primitive barbarians which are often so called — poured down upon the country. Just how long after the Toltec downfall this happened, is in dispute;[2] but within a few years evidently, perhaps within not many months, came the rush of millions, if we may believe the big stories of the migration. They surged by the ruined capital of the Toltecs, came to the lake, founded Xoloc and Tenayocan, and encountered, as they spread over the country, what were left of the Toltecs, who secured peace by becoming vassals. Not quite so humble were the Colhuas of Colhuacan, — not to be confounded with the Acolhuas, — who were the most powerful section of the Toltecs yet left, and the Chichimecs set about crushing them, and succeeded in making them also vassals.[3] The Chichimec monarchs, if that term does not misrepresent them, soon formed alliances with the Tepanecs, the Otomis, and the Acolhuas, who had been prominent in the overthrow of the Toltecs, and all the invaders profited by the higher organizations and arts which these tribes had preserved and now imparted. The Chichimecs also sought to increase the stability of their power by marriages with the noble Toltecs still remaining. But all was not peace. There were rebellions from time to time to be put down; and a new people, whose future they did not then apprehend, had come in among them and settled at Chapultepec. These were the Aztecs, or Mexicans, a part of the great Nahua immigration, but as a tribe they had dallied behind the others on the way, but were now come, and the last to come.[4]

Tezcuco soon grew into prominence as a vassal power,[5] and upon the capital city many embellishments were bestowed, so that the great lord of the Chichimecs preferred it to his own Tenayocan, which gave opportunity for rebellious plots to be formed in his proper capital; and here at Tezcuco the next succeeding ruler preferred to reign, and here he became isolated by the uprising of rebellious nobles. The ensuing war was not simply of side against side, but counter-revolutions led to a confusion of tumults, and petty chieftains set themselves up against others here and there. The result was that Quinantzin, who had lost the general headship of the country, recovered it, and finally consolidated his power to a degree surpassing all his predecessors.

toric Man, i. 245) not inaptly says: "The history of the Toltecs and their ruined edifices stands on the border line of romance and fable, like that of the ruined builders of Carnac and Avebury."

[1] Short (page 255) points out that Bancroft unadvisedly looks upon these Chichimecs as of Nahua stock, according to the common belief. Short thinks that Pimentel (*Lenguas indigenas de México*, published in 1862) has conclusively shown that the Chichimecs did not originally speak the Nahua tongue, but subsequently adopted it. Short (page 256) thinks, after collating the evidence, that it is impossible to determine whence or how they came to Anáhuac.

[2] Bancroft, v. 292, gives the different views. Cf. Kirk in Prescott, i. 16.

[3] These events are usually one thing or another, according to the original source which you accept, as Bancroft shows (v. 303). The story of the text is as good as any, and is in the main borne out by the other narratives.

[4] Bancroft, v. 308. Cf., on the arrival of the Mexicans in the valley, Bandelier (*Peabody Mus. Reports*, ii. 398) and his references.

[5] Prescott, i., introduction ch. 6, tells the story of their golden age.

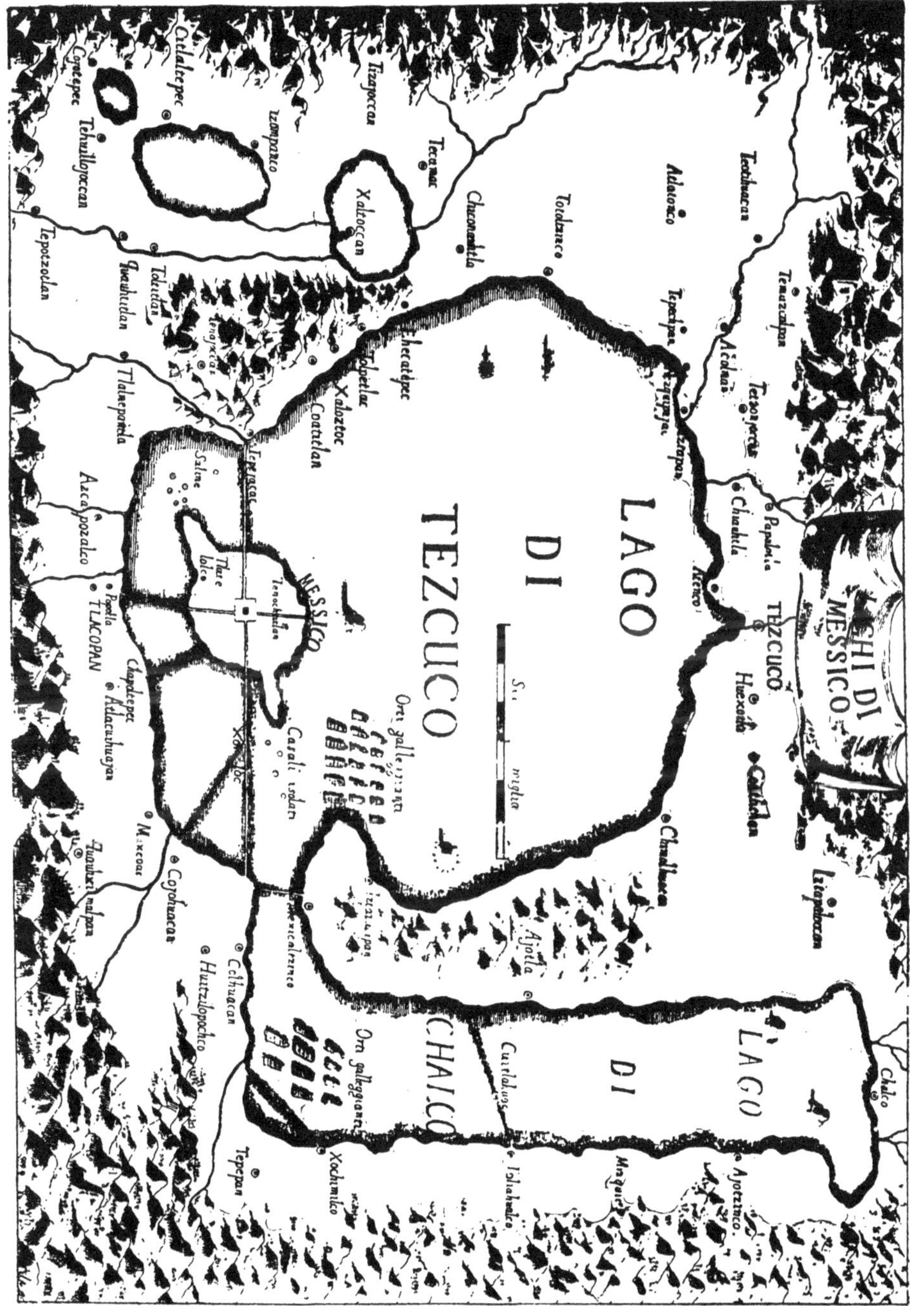

CLAVIGERO'S MEXICO.* (Ed. of 1780, vol. iii.)

* Cf. the map in Lucien Biart's *Les Aztèques* (Paris, 1885). Prescott says the maps in Clavigero, Lopez, and Robertson defy "equally topography and history." Cf. note on plans of the city and valley in Vol. II. pp. 364, 369, 374, to which may be added, as showing diversified views, those in Stevens's *Herrera* (London, 1740), vol. ii.; Bordone's *Libro* (1528); Icazbalceta's *Coll. de docs.*, i. 390; and the Eng. translation of Cortes' despatches, 333.

Meanwhile the Aztecs at Chapultepec, growing arrogant, provoked their neighbors, and were repressed by those who were more powerful. But they abided their time. They were good fighters, and the Colhua ruler courted

CLAVIGERO'S MAP.* (Ed. of 1580, vol. i.)

them to assist him in his maraudings, and thus they were becoming accustomed to warfare and to conquest, and were giving favors to be repaid. This intercourse, whether of association or rivalry, of the Colhuas and Mexicans (Aztecs), was continued through succeeding periods, with a confusion of dates and events which it is hard to make clear. There was mutual distrust and confidence alternately, and it all ended in the Aztecs settling on an island in the lake, where later they founded Tenochtitlan, or Mexico.[1] Here

1 This is placed A. D. 1325. Cf. references in Bancroft (v. 346).

* Clavigero speaks of his map "per servire all storia antica del Messico." A map of the Aztec dominion just before the Conquest is given in Ranking (London, 1827). See note in Vol. II. p. 358.

they developed those bloody rites of sacrifice which had already disgusted their allies and neighbors.

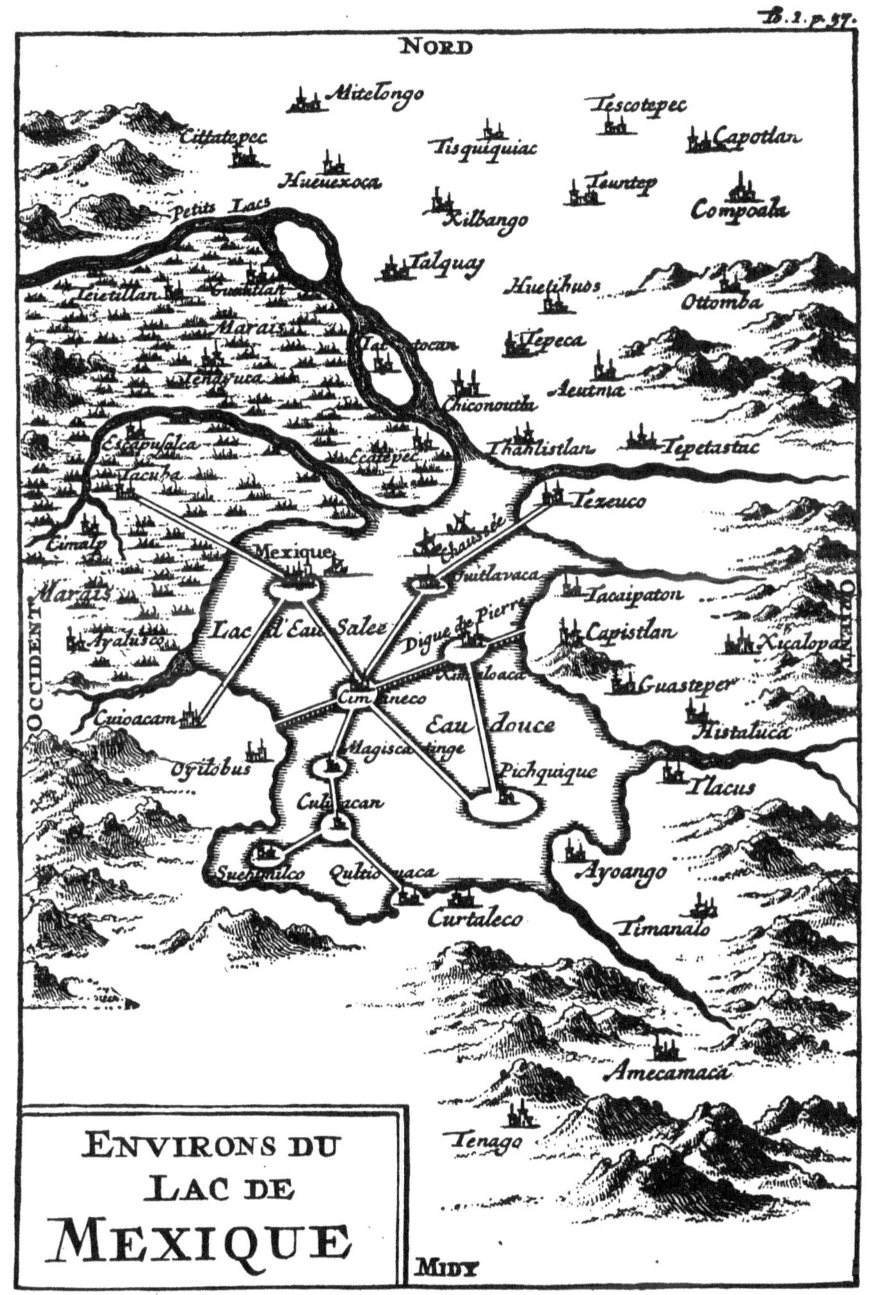

THE LAKE OF MEXICO.*

* A map which did service in different forms in various books about Mexico and its aboriginal localities in the early part of the eighteenth century. It is here taken from the *Voyages de Francois Coreal* (Amsterdam, 1722).

Meanwhile the powers at Colhuacan and Azcapuzalco flourished and repressed uprisings, and out of all the strife Tezozomoc came into prominence with his Tepanecs, and amid it all the Aztecs, siding here and there, gained territory. With all this occurring in different parts of his dominions, the Chichimec potentate grew stronger and stronger, and while by his countenance the old Toltec influences more and more predominated. And so it was a flourishing government, with little to mar its prospects but the ambition of Tezozomoc, the Tepanec chieftain, and the rising power of the Aztecs, who had now become divided into Mexicans and Tlatelulcas. The famous ruler of the Chichimecs, Techotl, died in A. D. 1357, and the young Ixtlilxochitl took his power with all its emblems. The people of Tenochtitlan, or their rulers, were adepts in practising those arts of diplomacy by which an ambitious nation places itself beside its superiors to secure a sort of reflected consequence. Thus they pursued matrimonial alliances and other acts of prudence. Both Tenochtitlan and its neighbor Tlatelulco grew apace, while skilled artisans and commercial industries helped to raise them in importance.

The young Ixtlilxochitl at Tezcuco was not so fortunate, and it soon looked as if the Tepanec prince, Tezozomoc, was only waiting an opportu nity to rebel. It was also pretty clear that he would have the aid of Mexico and Tlatelulco, and that he would succeed in securing the sympathy of many wavering vassals or allies. The plans of the Tepanec chieftain at last ripened, and he invaded the Tezcucan territory in 1415. In the war which followed, Ixtlilxochitl reversed the tide and invaded the Tepanec territory, besieging and capturing its capital, Azcapuzalco.[1] The conqueror lost by his clemency what he had gained by arms, and it was not long before he was in turn shut up in his own capital. He did not succeed in defending it, and was at last killed. So Tezozomoc reached his vantage of ambition, and was now in his old age the lord paramount of the country. He tried to harmonize the varied elements of his people; but the Mexicans had not fared in the general successes as they had hoped for, and were only openly content. The death of Tezozomoc prepared the way for one of his sons, Maxtla, to seize the command, and the vassal lords soon found that the spirit which had murdered a brother had aims that threatened wider desolation. The Mexicans were the particular object of Maxtla's oppressive spirit, and by the choice of Itzcoatl for their ruler, who had been for many years the Mexican war-chief, that people defied the lord of all, and in this they were joined by the Tlatelulcas under Quauhtlatohuatzin, and by lesser allies. Under this combination of his enemies Maxtla's capital fell, the usurper was sacrificed, and the honors of the victory were shared by Itzcoatl, Nezahualcoyotl (the Acolhuan prince whose imperial rights Maxtla had usurped), and Montezuma, the first of the name, — all who had in their several capacities led the army of three or four hundred thousand allies,

[1] On the conquest of the Tecpanecas by the Mexicans, see the references in Bandelier (*Peabody Mus. Reports*, ii. 412).

if we may believe the figures, to their successes, which occurred apparently somewhere between 1425 and 1430. The political result was a tripartite confederacy in Anáhuac, consisting of Acolhua, Mexico, and Tlacopan. In the division of spoils, the latter was to have one fifth, and the others two fifths each, the Acolhuan prince presiding in their councils as senior.[1]

The next hundred years is a record of the increasing power of this confederacy, with a constant tendency to give Mexico a larger influence.[2] The two capitals, Tenochtitlan and Tezcuco, looking at each other across the lake, were uninterruptedly growing in splendor, or in what the historians call by that word,[3] with all the adjuncts of public works, — causeways, canals, aqueducts, temples, palaces and gardens, and other evidences of wealth, which perhaps these modern terms only approximately represent. Tezcuco was taken possession of by Nezahualcoyotl as his ancient inheritance, and his confederate Itzcoatl placed the crown on his head. Together they made war north and south. Xochimilco, on the lake next south of Mexico, yielded; and the people of Chalco, which was on the most southern of the string of lakes, revolted and were suppressed more than once, as opportunities offered. The confederates crossed the ridge that formed the southern bound of the Mexican valley and sacked Quauhnahuac. The Mexican ruler had in all this gained a certain ascendency in the valley coalition, when he died in 1440, and his nephew, Montezuma the soldier, and first of the name,[4] succeeded him. This prince soon had on his hands another war with Chalco, and with the aid of his confederates he finally humbled its presumptuous people. So, with or without pretence, the wars and conquests went on, if for no other reasons, to obtain prisoners for sacrifice.[5] They were diversified at times, particularly in 1449, by contests with the powers of nature, when the rising waters of the lake threatened to drown their cities, and when, one evil being cured, others in the shape of famine and plague succeeded.

[1] For details of the period of the Chichimec ascendency, see Bancroft (v. ch. 5-7), Brasseur (*Nat. Civil.* ii.), and the authorities plentifully cited in Bancroft.

[2] On the nature of the Mexican confederacy see Bandelier (*Peabody Mus. Reports*, ii. 416). He enumerates the authorities upon the point that no one of the allied tribes exercised any powers over the others beyond the exclusive military direction of the Mexicans proper (*Peabody Mus. Reports*, ii. 559). Orozco y Berra (*Geografía*, etc.) claims that there was a tendency to assimilate the conquered people to the Mexican conditions. Bandelier claims that "no attempt, either direct or implied, was made to assimilate or incorporate them." He urges that nowhere on the march to Mexico did Cortés fall in with Mexican rulers of subjected tribes. It does not seem to be clear in all cases whether it was before or after the confederation was formed, or whether it was by the Mexicans or Tezcucans that Tecpaneca, Xochimilca, Cuitlahuac, Chalco, Acolhuacan, and Quauhnahuac, were conquered. Cf. Bandelier in *Peabody Mus. Reports*, ii. 691. As to the tributaries, see *Ibid.* 695.

[3] Cf. Brasseur's *Nations Civ.* ii. 457, on Tezcuco in its palmy days.

[4] Sometimes written Mochtheuzema, Moktezema. The Aztec Montezuma must not, as is contended, be confounded with the hero-god of the New Mexicans. Cf. Bancroft, iii. 77, 171; Brinton's *Myths*, 190; Schoolcraft's *Ind. Tribes*, iv. 73; Tylor's *Prim. Culture*, ii. 384; Short, 333.

[5] This has induced some historians to call these wars "holy wars." Bandelier discredits wholly the common view, that wars were undertaken to secure victims for the sacrificial stone (*Archæol. Tour*, 24). But in another place (*Peabody Mus. Reports*, ii. 128) he says: "War was required for the purpose of obtaining human victims, their religion demanding human sacrifices at least eighteen times every year."

Sometimes in the wars the confederates over-calculated their own prowess, as when Atonaltzin of Tilantongo sent them reeling back, only, however, to make better preparations and to succeed at last. In another war to the southeast they captured, as the accounts say, over six thousand victims for the stone of sacrifice.

The first Montezuma died in 1469, and the choice for succession fell on his grandson, the commander of the Mexican army, Axayacatl, who at once followed the usual custom of raiding the country to the south to get the thousands of prisoners whose sacrifice should grace his coronation. Nezahualcoyotl, the other principal allied chieftain, survived his associate but two years, dying in 1472, leaving among his hundred children but one legitimate son, Nezahualpilli, a minor, who succeeded. This gave the new Mexican ruler the opportunity to increase his power. He made Tlatelulco tributary, and a Mexican governor took the place there of an independent sovereign. He annexed the Matlaltzinca provinces on the west. So Axayacatl, dying in 1481, bequeathed an enlarged kingdom to his brother and successor, Tizoc, who has not left so warlike a record. According to some authorities, however, he is to be credited with the completion of the great Mexican temple of Huitzilopochtli. This did not save him from assassination, and his brother Ahuitzotl in 1486 succeeded, and to him fell the lot of dedicating that great temple. He conducted fresh wars vigorously enough to be able within a year, if we may believe the native records, to secure sixty or seventy thousand captives for the sacrificial stone, so essential a part of all such dedicatory exercises. It would be tedious to enumerate all the succeeding conquests, though varied by some defeats, like that which they experienced in the Tehuantepec region. Some differences grew up, too, between the Mexican chieftain and Nezahualpilli, notwithstanding or because of the virtues of the latter, among which doubtless, according to the prevailing standard, we must count his taking at once three Mexican princesses for wives, and his keeping a harem of over two thousand women, if we may believe his descendant, the historian Ixtlilxochitl. His justice as an arbitrary monarch is mentioned as exemplary, and his putting to death a guilty son is recounted as proof of it.

Ahuitzotl had not as many virtues, or perhaps he had not a descendant to record them so effectively; but when he died in 1503, what there was heroic in his nature was commemorated in his likeness sculptured with others of his line on the cliff of Chapultepec.[1] To him succeeded that Montezuma, son of Axayacatl, with whom later this ancient history vanishes. When he came to power, the Aztec name was never significant of more lordly power, though the confederates had already had some reminders that conquest near home was easier than conquest far away. The policy of the

[1] As to these carvings, which have not yet wholly disappeared, see *Peabody Mus. Reports*, ii. 677, 678. There is a series of alleged portraits of the Mexican kings in Carbajal-Espinosa's *Hist. de Mexico* (Mexico, 1862). See pictures of Montezuma II. in Vol. II. 361, 363, and that in Ranking, p. 313.

last Aztec ruler was far from popular, and while he propitiated the higher ranks, he estranged the people. The hopes of the disaffected within and without Anáhuac were now centred in the Tlascalans, whose territory lay easterly towards the Gulf of Mexico, and who had thus far not felt the burden of Aztec oppression. Notwithstanding that their natural allies, the Cholulans, turned against the Tlascalans, the Aztec armies never succeeded in humbling them, as they did the Mistecs and the occupants of the region towards the Pacific. Eclipses, earthquakes, and famine soon succeeded one another, and the forebodings grew numerous. Hardly anything happened but the omens of disaster[1] were seen in it, and superstition began to do its work of enervation, while a breach between Montezuma and the Tezcucan chief was a bad augury. In this condition of things the Mexican king tried to buoy his hopes by further conquests; but widespread as these invasions were, Michoacan to the west, and Tlascala to the east, always kept their independence. The Zapotecs in Oajaca had at one time succumbed, but this was before the days of the last Montezuma.

His rival across the lake at Tezcuco was more oppressed with the tales of the soothsayers than Montezuma was, and seems to have become inert before what he thought an impending doom some time before he died, or, as his people believed, before he had been translated to the ancient Amaquemecan, the cradle of his race. This was in 1515. His son Cacama was chosen to succeed; but a younger brother, Ixtlilxochitl, believed that the choice was instigated by Montezuma for ulterior gain, and so began a revolt in the outlying provinces, in which he received the aid of Tlascala. The appearance of the Spaniards on the coasts of Yucatan and Tabasco, of which exaggerated reports reached the Mexican capital, paralyzed Montezuma, so that the northern revolt succeeded, and Cacama and Ixtlilxochitl came to an understanding, which left the Mexicans without much exterior support. Montezuma was in this crippled condition when his lookouts on the coast sent him word that the dreaded Spaniards had appeared, and he could recognize their wonderful power in the pictured records which the messenger bore to him.[2] This portent was the visit in 1518 of Juan de Grijalva to the spot where Vera Cruz now stands; and after the Spaniard sailed away, there were months of anxiety before word again reached the capital, in 1519, of another arrival of the white-winged vessels, and this was the coming of Cortés, who was not long in discovering that the path of his conquest was made clear by the current belief that he was the returned Quetzalcoatl,[3] and by

[1] Bancroft (v. 466) enumerates the great variety of such proofs of disaster, and gives references (p. 469). Cf. Prescott, i. p. 309.

[2] Tezozomoc (cap. 106) gives the description of the first bringing of the news to Montezuma of the arrival of the Spaniards on the coast.

[3] Brinton's *Amer. Hero Myths*, 139, etc. See, on the prevalence of the idea of the return at some time of the hero-god, Brinton's *Myths of the New World*, p. 160. "We must remember," he says, "that a fiction built on an idea is infinitely more tenacious of life than a story founded on fact." Brinton (*Myths*, 188) gathers from Gomara, Cogolludo, Villagutierre, and others, instances to show how prevalent in America was the presentiment of the arrival and domination of a white race, — a belief still prevailing among their descendants of the middle regions of America who watch for the coming of Montezuma (*Ibid.* p. 190). Brinton does not seem to recog-

his quick perception of the opportunity which presented itself of combining and leading the enemies of Montezuma.[1]

Among what are usually reckoned the civilized nations of middle America, there are two considerable centres of a dim history that have little relation with the story which has been thus far followed. One of these is that of the people of what we now call Guatemala, and the other that of Yucatan. The political society which existed in Guatemala had nothing of the known duration assigned to the more northern people, at least not in essential data; but we know of it simply as a very meagre and perplexing chronology running for the most part back two or three centuries only. Whether the beginnings of what we suppose we know of these people have anything to do with any Toltec migration southward is what archæologists dispute about, and the philologists seem to have the best of the argument in the proof that the tongue of these southern peoples is more like Maya than Nahua. It is claimed that the architectural remains of Guatemala indicate a departure from the Maya stock and some alliance with a foreign stock; and that this alien influence was Nahuan seems probable enough when we consider certain similarities in myth and tradition of the Nahuas and the Quichés. But we have not much even of tradition and myth of the early days, except what we may read in the *Popul Vuh,* where we may make out of it what we can, or even what we please,[2] with some mysterious connection with Votan and Xibalba. Among the mythical traditions of this mythical period, there are the inevitable migration stories, beginning with the Quichés and ending with the coming of the Cakchiquels, but no one knows to a surety when. The new-comers found Maya-speaking people, and called them mem or memes (stutterers), because they spoke the Maya so differently from themselves.

It was in the twelfth or thirteenth century that we get the first traces of any historical kind of the Quichés and of their rivals the Cakchiquels. Of their early rulers we have the customary diversities and inconsistencies in what purports to be their story, and it is difficult to say whether this or the other or some other tribe revolted, conquered, or were beaten, as we read the annals of this constant warfare. We meet something tangible, however, when we learn that Montezuma sent a messenger, who informed the

nize the view held by many that the Montezuma of the Aztecs was quite a different being from the demigod of the Pueblas of New Mexico.

[1] It is not easy to reconcile the conflicting statements of the native historians respecting the course of events during the Aztec supremacy, such is the mutual jealousy of the Mexican and Tezcucan writers. Brasseur has satisfied himself of the authenticity of a certain sequence and character of events (*Nations Civilisées*), and Bancroft simply follows him (v. 401). Veytia is occupied more with the Tezcucans than with the Aztecs. The condensed sketch here given follows the main lines of the collated records. We find good pictures of the later history of Mexico and Tlascala, before the Spaniards came, in Prescott (i. book 2d, ch. vi., and book 3d, ch. ii.). Bancroft (v. ch. 10) with his narrative and references helps us out with the somewhat monotonous details of all the districts of Mexico which were outside the dominance of the Mexican valley, as of Cholula, Tlascala, Michoacan, and Oajaca, with the Miztecs and Zapotecs, inhabiting this last province.

[2] Bancroft (v. 543-553).

Quichés of the presence of the Spaniards in his capital, which set them astir to be prepared in their turn.

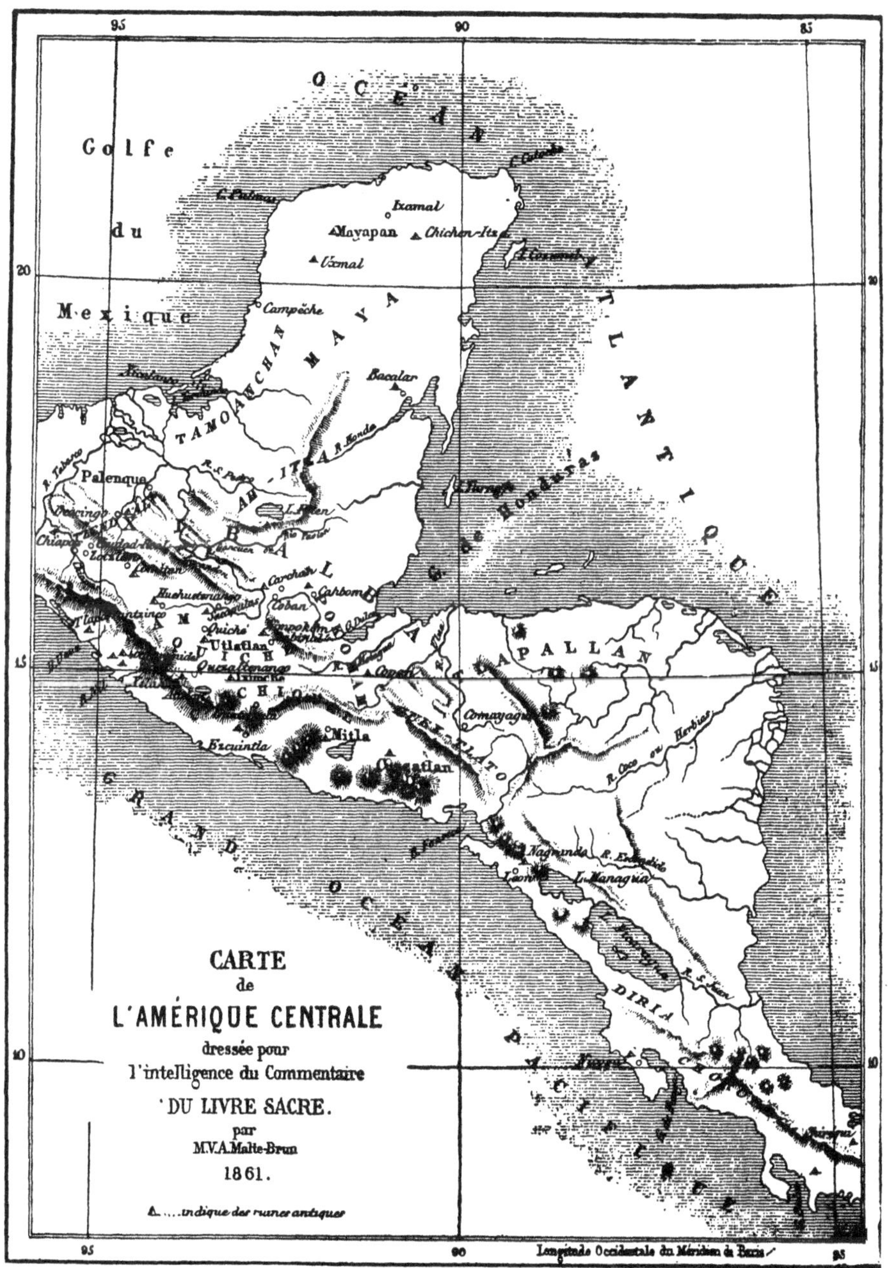

MAP IN BRASSEUR'S POPUL VUH.

It is in the beginning of the sixteenth century that we encounter the rivalries of three prominent peoples in this Guatemala country, and these were the Quichés, the Cakchiquels, and the Zutigils; and of these the Quichés, with their main seat at Utatlan, were the most powerful, though not so much so but the Cakchiquels could get the best of them at times in the wager of war; as they did also finally when the Spaniard Alvarado appeared, with whom the Cakchiquels entered into an alliance that brought the Quichés into sore straits.

A more important nationality attracts us in the Mayas of Yucatan. There can be nothing but vague surmise as to what were the primitive inhabitants of this region; but it seems to be tolerably clear that a certain homogeneousness pervaded the people, speaking one tongue, which the Spaniards found in possession. Whether these had come from the northern regions, and were migrated Toltecs, as some believe, is open to discussion.[1] It has often been contended that they were originally of the Nahua and Toltec blood; but later writers, like Bancroft,[2] have denied it. Brinton discards the Toltec element entirely.

What by a license one may call history begins back with the semi-mythical Zamná, to whom all good things are ascribed — the introduction of the Maya institutions and of the Maya hieroglyphics.[3] Whether Zamná had any connection, shadowy or real, with the great Votanic demigod, and with the establishment of the Xibalban empire, if it may be so called, is a thing to be asserted or denied, as one inclines to separate or unite the traditions of Yucatan with those of the Tzendal, Quiché, and Toltec. Ramon de Ordonez, in a spirit of vagary, tells us that Mayapan, the great city of the early Mayas, was but one of the group of centres, with Palenqué, Tulan, and Copan for the rest, as is believed, which made up the Votanic empire. Perhaps it was. If we accept Brinton's view, it certainly was not. Then Torquemada and Landa tell us that Cukulcan, a great captain and a god, was but another Quetzalcoatl, or Gucumatz. Perhaps he was. Possibly also he was the bringer of Nahua influence to Mayapan, away back in a period corresponding to the early centuries of the Christian era. It is easy to say, in all this confusion, this is proved and that is not. The historian, accustomed to deal with palpable evidence, feels much inclined to leave all views in abeyance.

The Cocomes of Yucatan history were Cukulcan's descendants or followers, and had a prosperous history, as we are told; and there came to live among them the Totul Xius, by some considered a Maya people, who like

[1] It is so held by Stephens, Waldeck, Mayer, Prichard, Ternaux-Compans, not to name others.

[2] Vol. v. 617.

[3] The Maya calendar and astronomical system, as the basis of the Maya chronology, is explained in the version which Perez gave into Spanish of a Maya manuscript (translated into English by Stephens in his *Yucatan*), and which Valentini has used in his "Katunes of Maya History," in the *Amer. Antiq. Soc. Proc.*, Oct. 1879. On the difficulties of the subject see Brasseur's *Nations Civilisées* (ii. ch. 1). Cf. also his *Landa*, section xxxix., and page 366, from the "Cronologia antigua de Yucatan." Cf. further, Cyrus Thomas's *MS. Troano*, ch. 2, and Powell's *Third Report Bur. of Ethn.*, pp. xxx and 3; Ancona's *Yucatan*, ch. xi.; Bancroft's *Nat. Races*, ii. ch. 24, with references; Short, ch. 9; Brinton's *Maya Chronicles*, introduction, p. 50.

the Quichés had been subjected to Nahua influences, and who implanted in the monuments and institutions of Yucatan those traces of Nahua character which the archæologists discover.[1] The Totul Xius are placed in Uxmal in the tenth, eleventh, and twelfth centuries, where they flourished along with the Cocomes, and it is to them that it is claimed many of the ruins which now interest us in Yucatan can be traced, though some of them perhaps go back to Zamná and to the Xibalban period, or at least it would be hard to prove otherwise.

When at last the Cocome chieftains began to oppress their subjects, the Totul Xius gave them shelter, and finally assisted them in a revolt, which succeeded and made Uxmal the supreme city, and Mayapan became a ruin, or at least was much neglected. The dynasty of the Totul Xius then flourished, but was in its turn overthrown, and a period of factions and revolutions followed, during which Mayapan was wholly obliterated, and the Totul Xius settled in Mani, where the Spaniards found them when they invaded Yucatan to make an easy conquest of a divided people.[2]

CRITICAL ESSAY ON THE SOURCES OF INFORMATION.

FROM the conquerors of New Spain we fail to get any systematic portrayal of the character and history of the subjugated people; but nevertheless we are not without some help in such studies from the letters of Cortes,[3] the accounts of the so-called anonymous conqueror,[4] and from what Stephens[5] calls "the hurried and imperfect observations of an unlettered soldier," Bernal Diaz.[6]

We cannot neglect for this ancient period the more general writers on New Spain, some of whom lived near enough to the Conquest to reflect current opinions upon the aboriginal life as it existed in the years next succeeding the fall of Mexico. Such are Peter Martyr, Grynæus, Münster, and Ramusio. More in the nature of chronicles is the *Historia General* of Oviedo (1535, etc.).[7] The *Historia General* of Gomara became generally known soon after the middle of the sixteenth century.[8] The *Rapport*, written about 1560, by Alonzo de Zurita, throws light on the Aztec laws and institutions.[9] Benzoni about this

[1] Bancroft (v. 624) epitomizes the Perez manuscript given by Stephens, the sole source of this Totul Xiu legendary.

[2] Brasseur's *Nations Civilisées* (i., ii.), with the Perez manuscript, and Landa's *Relacion*, are the sufficient source of the Yucatan history. Bancroft's last chapter of his fifth volume summarizes it.

[3] See Vol. II. p. 402.

[4] See Vol. II. p. 397.

[5] *Central America*, ii. 452.

[6] See Vol. II. p. 414.

[7] See Vol. II. p. 343.

[8] See Vol. II. p. 412.

[9] See Vol. II. p. 417. Cf. Prescott's *Mexico*, i. 50; Bancroft (*Nat. Races*, ii. ch. 14) epitomizes the information on the laws and courts of the Nahua; Bandelier (*Peabody Mus. Repts.*, ii. 446), referring to Zurita's Report, which he characterizes as marked for perspicacity, deep knowledge, and honest judgment, speaks of it as embodying the experience of nearly twenty years, — eleven of which were passed in Mexico, — and in which the author gave answers to inquiries put by the king. "If we could obtain," says Bandelier, "all the answers given to these questions from all parts of Spanish America, and all as elaborate and truthful as those of Zurita, Palacio, and Ondegardo, our knowledge of the aboriginal history and ethnology of Spanish America would be much advanced." Zurita's Report in a French translation is in Ternaux-Compans' *Collection;* the original is in Pacheco's *Docs. inéditos*, but in a mutilated text.

time traversed the country, observing the Indian customs.[1] We find other descriptions of the aboriginal customs by the missionary Didacus Valades, in his *Rhetorica Christiana*, of which the fourth part relates to Mexico.[2] Brasseur says that Valades was well

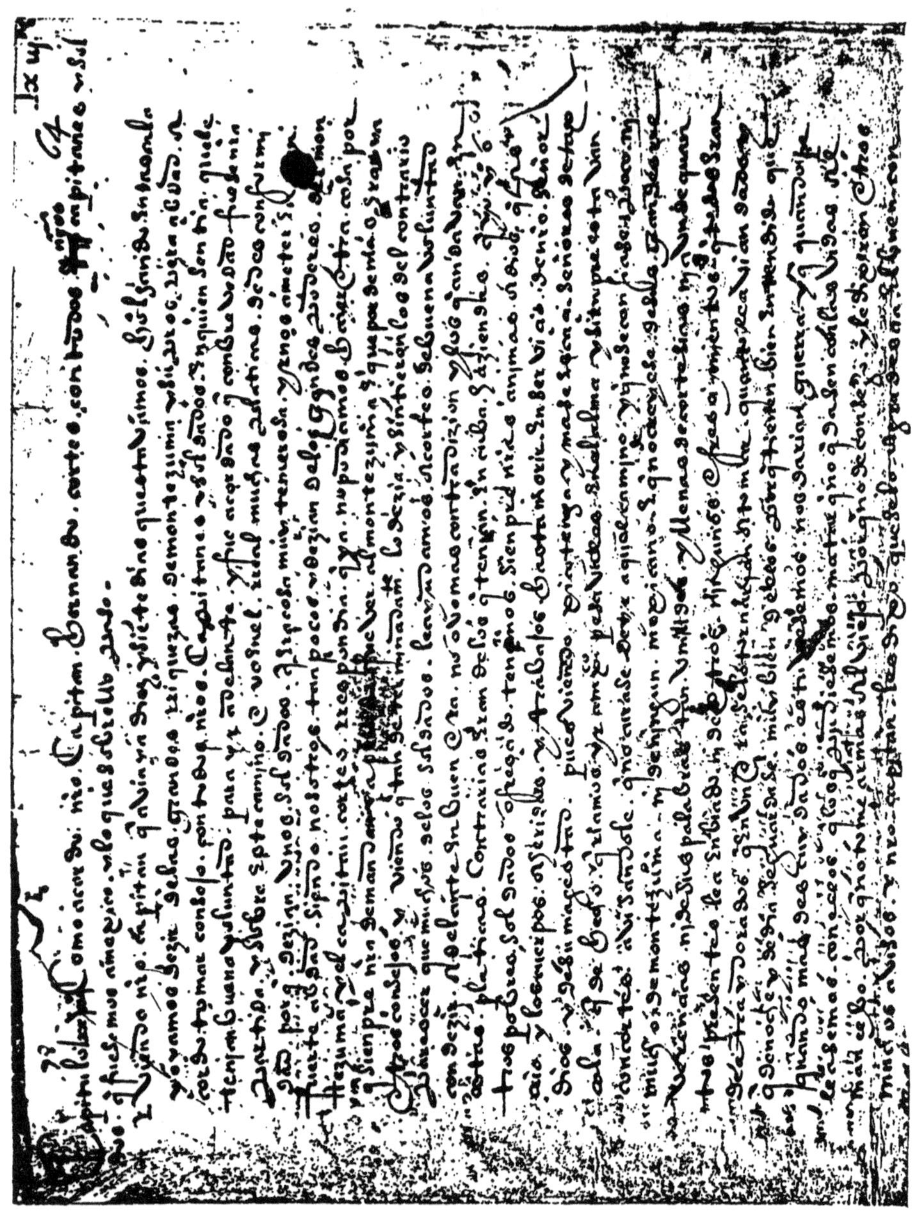

MS. OF BERNAL DIAZ.*

[1] See Vol. II. p. 346.

[2] It is much we owe to the twelve Franciscan friars who on May 13, 1524, landed in Mexico to convert and defend the natives. It is from their

* Fac-simile of the beginning of Capitulo LXXIV. of his *Historia Verdadera*, following a plate in the fourth volume of J. M. de Heredia's French translation (Paris, 1877).

informed and appreciative of the people which he so kindly depicted.[1] By the beginning of the seventeenth century we find in Herrera's *Historia* the most comprehensive of the historical surveys, in which he summarizes the earlier writers, if not always exactly.[2] Bandelier (*Peabody Mus. Repts.*, ii. 387) says of the ancient history of Mexico that "it appears as if the twelfth century was the limit of definite tradition. What lies beyond it is vague and uncertain, remnants of tradition being intermingled with legends and mythological fancies." He cites some of the leading writers as mainly starting in their stories respectively as follows: Brasseur, B. C. 955; Clavigero, A. D. 596; Veytia, A. D. 697; Ixtlilxochitl, A. D. 503. Bandelier views all these dates as too mythical for historical investigations, and finds no earlier fixed date than the founding of Tenochtitlan (Mexico) in A. D. 1325. "What lies beyond the twelfth century can occasionally be rendered of value for ethnological purposes, but it admits of no definite historical use." Bancroft (v. 360) speaks of the sources of disagreement in the final century of the native annals, from the constant tendency of such writers as Ixtlilxochitl, Tezozomoc, Chimalpain, and Camargo, to laud their own people and defame their rivals.

In the latter part of the sixteenth century the viceroy of Mexico, Don Martin Enriquez, set on foot some measures to gather the relics and traditions of the native Mexicans. Under this incentive it fell to Juan de Tobar, a Jesuit, and to Diego Duran, a Dominican, to be early associated with the resuscitation of the ancient history of the country.

To Father Tobar (or Tovar) we owe what is known as the *Codex Ramirez*, which in the edition of the *Crónica Mexicana*[3] by Hernando de Alvarado Tezozomoc, issued in Mexico (1878), with annotations by Orozco y Berra, is called a *Relacion del origen de los Indios que habitan esta nueva España segun sus historias* (José M. Vigil, editor). It is an important source of our knowledge of the ancient history of Mexico, as authoritatively interpreted by the Aztec priests, from their picture-writings, at the bidding of Ramirez de Fuenleal, Bishop of Cuenca. This ecclesiastic carried the document with him to Spain, where in Madrid it is still preserved. It was used by Herrera. Chavero and Brinton recognize its representative value.[4]

To Father Duran we are indebted for an equally ardent advocacy of the rights of the natives in his *Historia de las Indias de Nueva-España y islas de Tierra-Firme* (1579-81), which was edited in part (1867), as stated elsewhere[5] by José F. Ramirez, and after an interval completed (1880) by Prof. Gumesindo Mendoza, of the Museo Nacional, — the perfected work making two volumes of text and an atlas of plates. Both from Tobar and from Duran some of the contemporary writers gathered largely their material.[6]

writings that we must draw a large part of our knowledge respecting the Indian character, condition, and history. These Christian apostles were Martin de Valencia, Francisco de Soto, Martin de Coruña, Juan Xuares, Antonio de Ciudad Rodrigo, Toribio de Benavente, Garcia de Cisneros, Luis de Fuensalida, Juan de Ribas, Francisco Ximenez, Andrés de Cordoba, Juan de Palos.

From the *Historia* of Las Casas, particularly from that part of it called *Apologética historia*, we can also derive some help. (Cf. Vol. II. p. 340.)

[1] Brasseur, *Bib. Mex.-Guat.*, p. 147; Leclerc, p. 168.

[2] Herrera is furthermore the source of much that we read in later works concerning the native religion and habits of life. See Vol. II. p. 67.

[3] Cf. Vol. II. p. 418.

[4] *Anales del Museo Nacional*, iii. 4, 120; Brinton's *Am. Hero Myths*, 78. Bandelier, in *N. Y. Hist. Soc. Proc.*, November, 1879, used a portion of the MS. as printed by Sir Thomas Phillipps (*Amer. Antiq. Soc. Proc.*, i. 115) under the title of *Historia de los Yndios Mexicanos, por Juan de Tovar; Cura et impensis Dni Thomæ Phillipps, Bart.* (privately printed at Middle Hill, 1860. See *Squier Catalogue*, no. 1417). The document is translated by Henry Phillipps, Jr., in the *Proc. Amer. Philosophical Soc.* (Philad.), xxi. 616.

[5] Vol. II. p. 419. Brasseur de Bourbourg's *Bibl. Mex.-Guat.*, p. 59. He used a MS. copy in the Force collection.

[6] This is true of Acosta and Davila Padilla. The bibliography of Acosta has been given elsewhere (Vol. II. p. 420). His books v., vi., and vii. cover the ancient history of the country. He used the MSS. of Duran (Brasseur, *Bibl. Mex.-Guat.*, p. 2), and his correspondence with Tobar, preserved in the Lenox library, has been edited by Icazbalceta in his *Don Fray Zumár-*

We come to a different kind of record when we deal with the Roman script of the early phonetic rendering of the native tongues. It has been pointed out that we have perhaps the earliest of such renderings in a single sentence in a publication made at Antwerp in 1534, where a Franciscan, Pedro de Gante,[1] under date of June 21, 1529, tells the story of his arriving in America in 1523, and his spending the interval in Mexico and Tezcuco, acquiring a knowledge of the natives and enough of their language to close his epistle with a sentence of it as a sample.[2] But no chance effort of this kind was enough. It took systematic endeavors on the part of the priests to settle grammatical principles and determine phonetic values, and the measure of their success was seen in the speedy way in which the interpretation of the old idiograms was forgotten. Mr. Brevoort has pointed out how much the progress of what may be called native literature, which is to-day so helpful to us in filling the picture of their ancient life, is due to the labors in this process of linguistic transfer of Motolinía,[3] Alonzo de Molina,[4] Andrés de Olmos,[5] and, above all, of the ablest student of the ancient tongues in his day, as Mendieta calls Father Sahagún,[6] who, dying in 1590 at ninety, had spent a good part of a long life so that we of this generation might profit by his records.[7]

SAHAGUN.*

raga (Mexico, 1881). Of the *Provincia de Santiago* and the *Varia historia* of Davila Padilla, the bibliography has been told in another place. (Cf. Vol. II. pp. 399–400; Sabin, v. 18780–1; Brasseur de Bourbourg's *Bibl. Mex.-Guat.*, p. 53; *Del Monte Library*, no. 126.) Ternaux was not wrong in ascribing great value to the books.

1 Peter of Ghent. Cf. Vol. II. p. 417.

2 *Chronica Compendiosissima ab exordio mundi per Amandum Zierixcensem, adjectæ sunt epistolæ ex nova maris Oceani Hispania ad nos transmissæ* (Antwerp, 1534). The subjoined letters here mentioned are, beside that referred to, two others written in Mexico (1531), by Martin of Valencia and Bishop Zumárraga (Sabin, i. no. 994; Quaritch, 362, no. 28583, £7 10). Icazbalceta (*Bib. Mex. del Siglo xvi.*, i. p. 33) gives a long account of Gante. There is a French version of the letter in Ternaux's *Collection.*

3 See Vol. II. p. 397. Cf. Prescott, ii. 95. The first part of the *Historia* is on the religious rites of the natives; the second on their conversion to Christianity; the third on their chronology, etc.

4 Cf. Icazbalceta's *Bibl. Mexicana*, p. 220, with references; Pilling's *Proof-sheets*, no. 2600, etc.

5 Pilling, no. 2817, etc.

6 Properly, Bernardino Ribeira; named from his birthplace, Sahagún, in Spain. Chavero's *Sahagún* (Mexico, 1877).

7 A few data can be added to the account of

* After a lithograph in Cumplido's Mexican edition of Prescott's *Mexico.*

Coming later into the field than Duran, Acosta, and Sahagún, and profiting from the labors of his predecessors, we find in the *Monarchia Indiana* of Torquemada[1] the most comprehensive treatment of the ancient history given to us by any of the early Spanish writers. The book, however, is a provoking one, from the want of plan, its chronological confusion, and the general lack of a critical spirit[2] pervading it.

It is usually held that the earliest amassment of native records for historical purposes, after the Conquest, was that made by Ixtlilxochitl of the archives of his Tezcucan line, which he used in his writings in a way that has not satisfied some later investigators. Charnay says that in his own studies he follows Veytia by preference; but Prescott finds beneath the high colors of the pictures of Ixtlilxochitl not a little to be commended. Bandelier,[3] on the other hand, expresses a distrust when he says of Ixtlilxochitl that "he is always a very suspicious authority, not because he is more confused than any other Indian writer, but because he wrote for an interested object, and with a view of sustaining tribal claims in the eyes of the Spanish government."[4]

Among the manuscripts which seem to have belonged to Ixtlilxochitl was the one known in our day under the designation given to it by Brasseur de Bourbourg, *Codex*

Sahagún given in Vol. II. p. 415. J. F. Ramirez completes the bibliography of Sahagún in the *Boletin de la Real Academia de la Historia de Madrid*, vi. 85 (1885). Icazbalceta, having told the story of Sahagún's life in his edition of Mendieta's *Hist. Eclesiastica Indiana* (México, 1870), has given an extended critical and bibliographical account in his *Bibliografia Mexicana* (México, 1886), vol. i. 247–308. Other bibliographical detail can be gleaned from Pilling's *Proof-sheets*, p. 677, etc.; Icazbalceta's *Apuntes*; Beristain's *Biblioteca*; the *Bibliotheca Mexicana* of Ramirez. The list in Adolfo Llanos's *Sahagún y su historia de México* (*Museo Nac. de Méx. Anales*, iii., pt. 3, p. 71) is based chiefly on Alfredo Chavero's *Sahagún* (México, 1877). Brasseur de Bourbourg, in his *Palenqué* (ch. 5), has explained the importance of what Brevoort calls Sahagún's "great encyclopædia of the Mexican Empire." Rosny (*Les documents écrits de l'Antiquité Américaine*, p. 69) speaks of seeing a copy of the *Historia* in Madrid, accompanied by remarkable Aztec pictures. Bancroft, referring to the defective texts of Sahagún in Kingsborough and Bustamante, says: "Fortunately what is missing in one I have always found in the other." He further speaks of the work of Sahagún as "the most complete and comprehensive, so far as aboriginal history is concerned, furnishing an immense mass of material, drawn from native sources, very badly arranged and written." Eleven books of Sahagún are given to the social institutions of the natives, and but one to the conquest. Jourdanet's edition is mentioned elsewhere (Vol. II.).

[1] See Vol. II. p. 421.

[2] Those who used him most, like Clavigero and Brasseur de Bourbourg, complain of this. Torquemada, says Bandelier (*Peabody Mus. Repts.* ii. 119), "notwithstanding his unquestionable credulity, is extremely important on all questions of Mexican antiquities."

[3] *Amer. Antiq. Soc. Proc.*, n. s., i. 105.

[4] Cf. Vol. II. 417; Prescott, i. 13, 163, 193, 196; Bancroft, *Nat. Races*, v. 147; Wilson's *Prehistoric Man*, i. 325. It must be confessed that with no more authority than the old Mexican paintings, interpreted through the understanding of old men and their traditions, Ixtlilxochitl has not the firmest ground to walk on. Aubin thinks that Ixtlilxochitl's confusion and contradictions arise from his want of patience in studying his documents; and some part of it may doubtless have arisen from his habit, as Brasseur says (*Annales de Philosophie Chrétienne*, May, 1855, p. 329), of altering his authorities to magnify the glories of his genealogic line. Max Müller (*Chips from a German Workshop*, i. 322) says of his works: "Though we must not expect to find in them what we are accustomed to call history, they are nevertheless of great historical interest, as supplying the vague outlines of a distant past, filled with migrations, wars, dynasties and revolutions, such as were cherished in the memory of the Greeks in the time of Solon." In addition to his *Historia Chichimeca* and his *Relaciones*, (both of which are given by Kingsborough, while Ternaux has translated portions,) — the MS. of the *Relaciones* being in the Mexican archives, — Ixtlilxochitl left a large mass of his manuscript studies of the antiquities, often repetitionary in substance. Some are found in the compilation made in Mexico by Figueroa in 1792, by order of the Spanish government (Prescott, i. 193). Some were in the Ramirez collection. Quaritch (*MS. Collections*, Jan., 1888, no. 136) held one from that collection, dated about 1680, at £16, called *Sumaria Relacion*, which concerned the ancient Chichimecs. Those which are best known are a *Historia de la Nueva España*, or *Historia del Reyno de Tezcuco*, and a *Historia de Nuestra Señora de Guadalupe*, if this last is by him.

Chimalpopoca,[1] in honor of Faustino Chimalpopoca, a learned professor of Aztec, who assisted Brasseur in translating it. The anonymous author had set to himself the task of converting into the written native tongue a rendering of the ancient hieroglyphics, constituting, as Brasseur says, a complete and regular history of Mexico and Colhuacan. He describes it in his *Lettres à M. le duc de Valmy* (*lettre seconde*) — the first part (in Mexican) being a history of the Chichimecas; the second (in Spanish), by another hand, elucidating the antiquities — as the most rare and most precious of all the manuscripts which escaped destruction, elucidating what was obscure in Gomara and Torquemada.

Brasseur based upon this MS. his account of the Toltec period in his *Nations Civilisées du Mexique* (i. p. lxxviii), treating as an historical document what in later years, amid his vagaries, he assumed to be but the record of geological changes.[2] A similar use was made by him of another MS., sometimes called a Memorial de Colhuacan, and which he named the *Codex Gondra* after the director of the Museo Nacional in Mexico.[3]

Brasseur says, in the *Annales de Philosophie Chrétienne*, that the *Chimalpopoca MS.* is dated in 1558, but in his *Hist. Nat. Civ.*, i. p. lxxix, he says that it was written in 1563 and 1579, by a writer of Quauhtitlan, and not by Ixtlilxochitl, as was thought by Pichardo, who with Gama possessed copies later owned by Aubin. The copy used by Brasseur was, as he says, made from the MS. in the Boturini collection,[4] where it was called *Historia de los Reynos de Colhuacan y México*,[5] and it is supposed to be the original, now preserved in the Museo Nacional de México. It is not all legible, and that institution has published only the better preserved and earlier parts of it, though Aubin's copies are said to contain the full text. This edition, which is called *Anales de Cuauhtitlan*, is accompanied by two Spanish versions, the early one made for Brasseur, and a new one executed by Mendoza and Solis, and it is begun in the *Anales del Museo Nacional* for 1879 (vol. i.).[6]

The next after Ixtlilxochitl to become conspicuous as a collector, was Sigüenza y Gongora (b. 1645), and it was while he was the chief keeper of such records [7] that the Italian traveller Giovanni Francesco Gemelli Carreri examined them, and made some record of them.[8] A more important student inspected the collection, which was later gathered in the College of San Pedro and San Pablo, and this was Clavigero,[9] who manifested a particular interest in the picture-writing of the Mexicans,[10] and has given us a useful account of the antecedent historians.[11]

1 *Annales de Philosophie Chrétienne*, May, 1855, p. 326.

2 In his *Quatre Lettres*, p. 24, he calls it the sacred book of the Toltecs. "C'est le Livre divin lui-même, c'est le Teoamoxtli."

3 Brasseur's *Lettres à M. le duc de Valmy*, *Lettre seconde*.

4 *Catálogo*, pp. 17, 18.

5 Brasseur, *Bibl. Mex. Guat.*, p. 47; *Pinart-Brasseur Catal.*, no. 237.

6 It has been announced that Bandelier is engaged in a new translation of *The Annals of Quauhtitlan* for Brinton's *Aboriginal Literature series*. Cf. Bancroft, iii. 57, 63, and in vol. v., where he endeavors to patch together Brasseur's fragments of it. Short, p. 241.

7 Humboldt says that Sigüenza inherited Ixtlilxochitl's collection; and that it was préserved in the College of San Pedro till 1759.

8 *Giro del mondo*, 1699, vol. vi. Cf. Kingsborough, vol. iv. Robertson attacked Carreri's character for honesty, and claimed it was a received opinion that he had never been out of Italy. Clavigero defended Carreri. Humboldt thinks Carreri's local coloring shows he must have been in Mexico.

9 Cf. the bibliog., in Vol. II., p. 425, of his *Storia Antica del Messico*.

10 We owe to him descriptions at this time of the collections of Mendoza, of that in the Vatican, and of that at Vienna. Robertson made an enumeration of such manuscripts; but his knowledge was defective, and he did not know even of those at Oxford.

11 Robertson was inclined to disparage Clavigero's work, asserting that he could find little in him beyond what he took from Acosta and Herrera "except the improbable narratives and fanciful conjectures of Torquemada and Boturini." Clavigero criticised Robertson, and the English historian in his later editions replied. Prescott points out (i. 70) that Clavigero only knew Sahagún through the medium of Torquemada and later writers. Bancroft (*Nat. Races*, v. 149; *Mexico*, i. 700) thinks that Clavigero "owes his reputation much more to his systematic arrangement and clear narration of traditions that had before been greatly confused, and to the

The best known efforts at collecting material for the ante-Spanish history of Mexico were made by Boturini,[1] who had come over to New Spain in 1736, on some agency for a descendant of Montezuma, the Countess de Santibañez. Here he became interested in the antiquities of the country, and spent eight years roving about the country picking up manuscripts and pictures, and seeking in vain for some one to explain their hieroglyphics. Some action on his part incurring the displeasure of the public authorities, he was arrested, his collection[2] taken from him, and he was sent to Spain. On the voyage an English cruiser captured the vessel in which he was, and he thus lost whatever he chanced to have with him.[3] What he left behind remained in the possession of the government, and became the spoil of damp, revolutionists, and curiosity-seekers. Once again in Spain, Boturini sought redress of the Council of the Indies, and was sustained by it in his petition; but neither he nor his heirs succeeded in recovering his collection. He also prepared a book setting forth how he proposed, by the aid of these old manuscripts and pictures, to resuscitate the forgotten history of the Mexicans. The book[4] is a jumble of notions; but appended to it was what gives it its chief value, a "Catálogo del Museo histórico Indiano," which tells us what the collection was. While it was thus denied to its collector, Mariano Veytia,[5] who had sympathized with Boturini in Madrid, had possession, for a while at least, of a part of it, and made use of it in his *Historia Antigua de Méjico*, but it is denied, as usually stated, that the authorities upon his death (1778) prevented the publication of his book. The student was deprived of Veytia's results till his MS. was ably edited, with notes and an appendix, by C. F. Ortega (Mexico, 1836).[6] Another, who was connected at a later day with the Boturini collection, and who was a more accurate writer than Veytia, was Antonio de Leon y Gama, born in Mexico in 1735. His *Descripcion histórica y Cronológica de las Dos Piedras* (Mexico, 1832)[7] was occasioned by the finding, in 1790, of the great Mexican Calendar Stone and other sculptures in the Square of Mexico. This work brought to bear Gama's great learning to the interpretation of these relics, and to an exposition of the astronomy and mythology of the ancient Mexicans, in a way that secured the commendation of Humboldt.[8]

CLAVIGERO.*

omission of the most perplexing and contradictory points, than to deep research or new discoveries."

[1] See Vol. II. p. 418. Brasseur de Bourbourg's *Hist. des Nations Civilisées*, p. xxxii. Clavigero had described it.

[2] He had collected nearly 500 Mexican paintings in all. Aubin (*Notices*, etc., p. 21) says that Boturini nearly exhausted the field in his searches, and with the collection of Sigüenza he secured all those cited by Ixtlilxochitl and the most of those concealed by the Indians, — of which mention is made by Torquemada, Sahagún, Valadés, Zurita, and others; and that the researches of Bustamante, Cubas, Gondra, and others, up to 1851, had not been able to add much of importance to what Boturini possessed.

[3] This portion of his collection has not been traced. The fact is indeed denied.

[4] *Idea de una nueva historia general de la America septentrional* (Madrid, 1746); Carter-Brown, iii. 817; Brasseur's *Bibl. Mex.-Guat.*, p. 26; Field, *Ind. Bibliog.*, no. 159; Pinart, *Catalogue*, no. 134; Prescott, i. 160.

[5] Brasseur, *Bibl. Mex.-Guat.*, p. 152.

[6] Prescott, i. 24. Harrisse, *Bib. Am. Vet.*, calls Veytia's the best history of the ancient period yet (1866) written.

[7] A second ed. (Mexico, 1832) was augmented with notes and a life of the author, by Carlos Maria de Bustamante; Field, *Ind. Bibliog.*, no. 909; Brasseur's *Bibl. Mex.-Guat.*, p. 68.

[8] Prescott, i. 133. Gama and others collected another class of hieroglyphics, of less importance,

* After a lithograph in Cumplido's Mexican edition of Prescott's *Mexico*, vol. iii.

During these years of uncertainty respecting the Boturini collection, a certain hold upon it seems to have been shared successively by Pichardo and Sanchez, by which in the end some part came to the Museo Nacional, in Mexico.[1] It was also the subject of lawsuits, which finally resulted in the dispersion of what was left by public auction, at a time when Humboldt was passing through Mexico, and some of its treasures were secured by him and placed in the Berlin Museum. Others passed hither and thither (a few to Kingsborough), but not in a way to obscure their paths, so that when, in 1830, Aubin was sent to Mexico by the French government, he was able to secure a considerable portion of them, as the result of searches during the next ten years. It was with the purpose, some

LORENZO BOTURINI.*

but still interesting as illustrating legal and administrative processes used in later times, in the relations of the Spaniards with the natives; and still others embracing Christian prayers, catechisms, etc., employed by the missionaries in the religious instruction (Aubin, *Notice*, etc., 21). Humboldt (vol. xiii., pl. p. 141) gives "a lawsuit in hieroglyphics."

There was published (100 copies) at Madrid, in 1878, *Pintura del Gobernador, Alcaldes y Regidores de México, Codice en geroglíficos Méxicanos y en lengua Castellana y Azteca, Existente en la Biblioteca del Excmo Señor Duque de Osuna*, — a legal record of the later Spanish courts affecting the natives.

[1] Humboldt describes these collections which he knew at the beginning of the century, speaking of José Antonio Pichardo's as the finest.

* After a lithograph in Cumplido's Mexican edition of Prescott's *Mexico*. There is an etched portrait in the *Archives de la Soc. Américaine de France, nouvelle série*, i., which is accompanied by an essay on this "Père de l'Américanisme," and "les sources aux quelles il a puisé son précis d'histoire Américaine," by Léon Cahun.

years later, of assisting in the elucidation and publication of Aubin's collection that the Société Américaine de France was established. The collection of historical records, as

FRONTISPIECE OF BOTURINI'S IDEA.

Aubin held it, was described, in 1881, by himself,[1] when he divided his Mexican picture-writings into two classes, — those which had belonged to Boturini, and those which had not.[2] Aubin at the same time described his collection of the Spanish MSS. of Ixtlilxochitl,[3] while he congratulated himself that he had secured the old picture-writings upon which that native writer depended in the early part of his *Historia Chichimeca.* These Spanish MSS. bear the signature and annotations of Veytia.

We have another description of the Aubin collection by Brasseur de Bourbourg.[4]

[1] *Notice sur une collection d'antiquités Mexicaines,* being an extract from a *Mémoire sur la peinture didactique et l'Écriture figurative des Anciens Mexicains* (Paris, 1851; again, 1859-1861). Cf. papers in *Revue Américaine et Orientale,* 1st ser., iii., iv., and v. Aubin says that Humboldt found that part of the Boturini collection which had been given over to the Mexican archivists diminished by seven eighths. He also shows how Ternaux-Compans (*Crauatés Horribles,* p. 275-289), Rafael Isidro Gondra (in Veytia, *Hist. Ant. de Mex.,* 1836, i. 49), and Bustamante have related the long contentions over the disposition of these relics, and how the Academy of History at Madrid had even secured the suppression of a similar academy among the antiquaries in Mexico, which had been formed to develop the study of their antiquities. It was as a sort of peace-offering that the Spanish king now caused Veytia to be empowered to proceed with the work which Boturini had begun. This allayed the irritation for a while, but on Veytia's death (1769) it broke out again, when Gama was given possession of the collection, which he further increased. It was at Gama's death sold at auction, when Humboldt bought the specimens which are now in Berlin, and Waldeck secured others which he took to Europe. It was from Waldeck that Aubin acquired the Boturini part of his collection. The rest of the collection remained in Mexico, and in the main makes a part at present of the Museo Nacional. But Aubin is a doubtful witness.

Aubin says that he now proposed to refashion the Boturini collection by copies where he could not procure the originals; to add others, embracing whatever he could still find in the hands of the native population, and what had been collected by Veytia, Gama, and Pichardo. In 1851, when he wrote, Aubin had given twenty years to this task, and with what results the list of his MSS., which he appends to the account we have quoted, will show.

These include in the native tongue: —

a. History of Mexico from A. D. 1064 to 1521, in fragments, from Tezozomoc and from Alonso Franco, annotated by Domingo Chimalpain (a copy).

b. Annals of Mexico, written apparently in 1528 by one who had taken part in the defence of Mexico (an original).

c. Several historical narratives on European paper, by Domingo Chimalpain, coming down to A. D. 1591, which have in great part been translated by Aubin, who considers them the most important documents which we possess.

d. A history of Colhuacan and Mexico, lacking the first leaf. This is described as being in the handwriting of Ixtlilxochitl, and Aubin gives the dates of its composition as 1563 and 1570. It is what has later been known as the *Codex Chimalpopoca.*

e. Zapata's history of Tlaxcalla.

f. A copy by Loaysa of an original, from which Torquemada has copied several chapters.

[2] The chief of the Boturini acquisition he enumerates as follows: —

a. Toltec annals on fifty leaves of European paper, cited by Gama in his *Descripcion histórica.* Cf. Brasseur, *Nations Civilisées,* p. lxxvi.

b. Chichimec annals, on Indian paper, six leaves, of which ten pages consist of pictures, the original so-called *Codex Chimalpopoca,* of which Gama made a copy, also in the Aubin collection, as well as Ixtlilxochitl's explanation of it. Aubin says that he has used this account of Ixtlilxochitl to rectify that historian's blunders.

c. Codex on Indian paper, having a picture of the Emperor Xolotl.

d. A painting on prepared skin, giving the genealogy of the Chichimecan chiefs, accompanied by the copies made by Pichardo and Boturini. Cf. *Archives de la Soc. Amér. de France,* 2d ser., i. 283.

e. A synchronical history of Tepechpan and of Mexico, on Indian paper, accompanied by a copy made by Pichardo and an outline sketch of that in the Museo Nacional.

Without specifying others which Aubin enumerates, he gives as other acquisitions the following in particular: —

a. Pichardo's copy of a Codex Mexicanus, giving the history of the Mexicans from their leaving Aztlan to 1590.

b. An original Mexican history from the departure from Aztlan to 1569.

c. Fragments which had belonged to Sigüenza.

[3] *Notice sur une Collection, etc.,* p. 12.

[4] *Hist. des Nations Civilisées* (i. pp. xxxi, lxxvi, etc.; cf. Müller's *Chips,* i. 317, 320, 323). Brasseur in the same place describes his own collection; and it may be further followed in his *Bibl. Mex.-Guat.,* and in the *Pinart Catalogue.* Dr. Brinton says that we owe much for the preservation during late years of Maya MSS. to Don

If we allow the first place among native writers, using the Spanish tongue, to Ixtlilxochitl, we find several others of considerable service: Diego Muñoz Camargo, a Tlaxcallan Mestizo, wrote (1585) a *Historia de Tlaxcallan.*[1] Tezozomoc's *Crónica Mexicana* is probably best known through Ternaux's version,[2] and there is an Italian abridgment in F. C. Marmocchi's *Raccolta di Viaggi* (vol. x.). The catalogue of Boturini discloses a

ICAZBALCETA.*

Juan Pio Perez, and that the best existing collection of them is that of Canon Crescencio Carrillo y Ancona. José F. Ramirez (see Vol. II. p. 398) is another recent Mexican collector, and his MSS. have been in one place and another in the market of late years. Quaritch's recent catalogues reveal a number of them, including his own MS. *Catálogo de Colecciones* (Jan., 1888, no. 171), and some of his unpublished notes on Prescott, not included in those "notas y ecclarecimientos" appended to Navarro's translation of the *Conquest of Mexico* (*Catal.*, 1885, no. 28,502). The several publications of Léon de Rosny point us to scattered specimens. In his *Doc. écrits de l'Antiquité Amér.* he gives the fac-simile of a colored Aztec map. A MS. in the collection of the Corps Legislatif, in Paris, and that of the Codex Indiæ Meridionalis are figured in his *Essai sur le déchiffrement, etc.* (pl. ix, x). In the *Archives de la Soc. Amér. de France, n. s.*, vol. i., etc., we find plates of the Mappe Tlotzin, and a paper of Madier de Montjau, "sur quelques manuscrits figuratifs de l'Ancien Méxique." Cf. also *Anales del Museo*, viii.

Cf. for further mention of collections the *Revue Orientale et Américaine*; Cyrus Thomas in the *Am. Antiquarian*, May, 1884 (vol. vi.); and the more comprehensive enumeration in the introduction to Domenech's *Manuscrit pictographique.* Orozco y Berra, in the introduction to his *Geografía de las Lenguas y Carta Etnográfica* (Mexico, 1864), speaks of the assistance he obtained from the collections of Ramirez and of Icazbalceta.

[1] See Vol. II. p. 418.

[2] See Vol. II. p. 418. Bandelier calls this French version "utterly unreliable."

* [After a photograph kindly furnished by himself at the editor's request. — ED.]

MS. by a Cacique of Quiahuiztlan, Juan Ventura Zapata y Mendoza, which brings the *Crónica de la muy noble y real Ciudad de Tlaxcallan* from the earliest times down to 1689; but it is not now known. Torquemada and others cite two native Tezcucan writers, — Juan Bautista Pomar, whose *Relacion de las Antigüedades de los Indios* [1] treats of the manners of his ancestors, and Antonio Pimentel, whose *Relaciones* are well known. The MS. *Crónica Mexicana* of Anton Muñon Chimalpain (b. 1579), tracing the annals from the eleventh century, is or was among the Aubin MSS.[2] There was collected before 1536, under the orders of Bishop Zumárraga, a number of aboriginal tales and traditions, which under the title of *Historia de los Mexicanos por sus Pinturas* was printed by Icazbalceta, who owns the MS., in the *Anales del Museo Nacional* (ii. no. 2).[3]

As regards Yucatan, Brasseur [4] speaks of the scantiness of the historical material, and Brinton [5] does not know a single case where a Maya author has written in the Spanish tongue, as the Aztecs did, under Spanish influence. We owe more to Dr. Daniel Garrison Brinton than to any one else for the elucidation of the native records, and he had had the advantage of the collection of Yucatan MSS. formed by Dr. C. H. Berendt,[6] which, after that gentleman's death, passed into Brinton's hands.

After the destruction of the ancient records by Landa, considerable efforts were made throughout Yucatan, in a sort of reactionary spirit, to recall the lingering recollections of what these manuscripts contained. The grouping of such recovered material became known as Chilan Balam.[7] It is from local collections of this kind that Brinton selected the narratives which he has published as *The Maya Chronicles*, being the first volume of his *Library of Aboriginal American Literature*. The original texts [8] are accompanied by an English translation. One of the books, the Chilan Balam of Mani, had been earlier printed by Stephens, in his *Yucatan*.[9] The only early Spanish chronicle is Bishop Landa's *Relation des choses de Yucatan*,[10] which follows not an original, but a copy of the bishop's text, written, as Brasseur thinks, thirty years after Landa's death, or about 1610, and which Brasseur first brought to the world's attention when he published his edition, with both Spanish and French texts, at Paris, in 1864. The MS. seems to have been incom-

1 This is Beristain's title. Torquemada, Vetancurt, and Sigüenza cite it as *Memorias histtóricas ;* Brasseur, *Bib. Mexico-Guat.*, p. 122.

2 Cf. "Les Annales Méxicaines," by Rémi Siméon in the *Archives de la Soc. Amér. de France*, n. s., vol. ii.

3 It is cited by Chavero as *Codex Zumárraga.*

4 *Hist. Nat. Civ.*, ii. 577.

5 *Aboriginal Amer. Authors*, p. 29. Cf. Bandelier's *Bibliography of Yucatan* in *Am. Antiq. Soc. Proc.*, n. s., vol. i. p. 82. Cf. the references in Brasseur, *Hist. Nat. Civ.*, and in Bancroft, *Nat. Races*, v.

6 Cf. *Mem. of Berendt*, by Brinton (Worcester, 1884).

7 Cf. Brinton on the MSS. in the languages of Cent. America, in *Amer. Jour. of Science*, xcvii. 222; and his *Books of Chilan Balam, the prophetic and historical records of the Mayas of Yucatan* (Philad., 1882), reprinted from the *Penn Monthly*, March, 1882. Cf. also the *Transactions of the Philad. Numismatic and Antiquarian Soc.*

8 This is in the alphabet adopted by the early missionaries. The volume contains the "Books of Chilan Balam," written "not later than 1595," and also the "Chac Xulub Chen," written by a Maya chief, Nakuk Pech, in 1562, to recount the story of the Spanish conquest of Yucatan.

9 This was in 1843, when Stephens made his English translation from Pio Perez's Spanish version, *Antigua Chronologia Yucateca;* and from Stephens's text, Brasseur gave it a French rendering in his edition of Landa. (Cf. also his *Nat. Civilisées*, ii. p. 2.) Perez, who in Stephens's opinion (*Yucatan*, ii. 117) was the best Maya scholar in that country, made notes, which Valentini published in his "Katunes of Maya History," in the *Pro. of the Amer. Antiq. Soc.*, Oct., 1879 (Worcester, 1880), but they had earlier been printed in Carrillo's *Hist. y Geog. de Yucatan* (Merida, 1881). Bancroft (*Nat. Races*, v. 624) reprints Stephens's text with notes from Brasseur.

The books of Chilan Balam were used both by Cogolludo and Lizana; and Brasseur printed some of them in the *Mission Scientifique au Méxique.* They are described in Carrillo's *Disertacion sobre la historia de lengua Maya ó Yucateca* (Merida, 1870).

10 Brasseur, *Bib. Mex.-Guat.*, p. 30. See Vol. II. p. 429. The Spanish title is *Relacion de las Cosas de Yucatan.*

plete, and was perhaps inaccurately copied at the time. At this date (1864) Brasseur had become an enthusiast for his theory of the personification of the forces of nature in the old recitals, and there was some distrust how far his zeal had affected his text; and moreover he had not published the entire text, but had omitted about one sixth. Brasseur's method of editing became apparent when, in 1884, at Madrid, Juan de Dios de la Rada y Delgado published literally the whole Spanish text, as an appendix to the Spanish translation of Rosny's essay on the hieratic writing. The Spanish editor pointed out some but not all the differences between his text and Brasseur's, — a scrutiny which Brinton has perfected in his *Critical Remarks on the Editions of Landa's Writings* (Philad., 1887).[1]

PROFESSOR DANIEL G. BRINTON.

Landa gives extracts from a work by Bernardo Lizana, relating to Yucatan, of which it is difficult to get other information.[2] The earliest published historical narrative was Cogolludo's *Historia de Yucathan* (Madrid, 1688).[3] Stephens, in his study of the subject,

[1] From the *Proc. of the Amer. Philos. Soc.*, xxiv.

[2] Cf. Bandelier in *Am. Antiq. Soc. Proc.*, n. s., vol. i. p. 88.

[3] The second edition was called *Los tres Siglos de la Dominacion Española en Yucatan* (Campeche and Merida, 2 vols., 1842, 1845). It was edited unsatisfactorily by Justo Sierra. Cf. Vol. II. p. 429; Brasseur, *Bib. Mex.-Guat.*, p. 47.

This, like Juan de Villagutierre Soto-Mayor's *Historia de la Conquista de la Provincia de el Itza, reduccion, y progressos de la de el Lacandon, y otras naciones de Indios Barbaros, de la mediacion de el Reyno de Gautimala, a las Provincias de Yucatan, en la America Septentrional* (Madrid, 1701), (which, says Bandelier, is of importance for that part of Yucatan which has remained unexplored), has mostly to do with the Indians under the Spanish rule, but the books are not devoid of usefulness in the study of the early tribes.

Of the modern comments on the Yucatan ancient history, those of Brasseur in his *Nations Civilisées* are more to be trusted than his introduction to his edition of Landa, which needs to be taken with due recognition of his later

speaks of it as "voluminous, confused, and ill-digested," and says "it might almost be called a history of the Franciscan friars, to which order Cogolludo belonged."[1]

The native sources of the aboriginal history of Guatemala, and of what is sometimes called the Quiché-Cakchiquel Empire, are not abundant,[2] but the most important are the *Popul Vuh*, a traditional book of the Quichés, and the *Memorial de Tecpan-Atitlan*.

The *Popul Vuh* was discovered in the library of the university at Guatemala, probably not far from 1700,[3] by Francisco Ximenez, a missionary in a mountain village of the country. Ximenez did not find the original Quiché book, but a copy of it, made after it was lost, and later than the Conquest, which we may infer was reproduced from memory to replace the lost text, and in this way it may have received some admixture of Christian thought.[4] It was this sort of a text that Ximenez turned into Spanish; and this version, with the copy of the Quiché, which Ximenez also made, is what has come down to us. Karl Scherzer, a German traveller[5] in the country, found Ximenez' work, which had seemingly passed into the university library on the suppression of the monasteries, and which, as he supposes, had not been printed because of some disagreeable things in it about the Spanish treatment of the natives. Scherzer edited the MS., which was published as *Las Historias del Origen de los Indios de Esta Provincia de Guatemala*[6] (Vienna, 1857).

Brasseur, who had seen the Ximenez MSS. in 1855, considered the Spanish version untrustworthy, and so with the aid of some natives he gave it a French rendering, and republished it a few years later as *Popol Vuh. Le Livre sacré et les Mythes de l'antiquité américaine, avec les livres héroïques et historiques des Quichés. Ouvrage original des indigènes de Guatémala, texte Quiché et trad. française en regard, accompagnée de notes philologiques et d'un commentaire sur la mythologie et les migrations des peuples anciens de l'Amérique, etc., composé sur des documents originaux et inédits* (Paris, 1861).

Brasseur's introduction bears the special title: *Dissertation sur les mythes de l'antiquité Américaine sur la probabilité des Communications existant anciennement d'un Continent à l'autre, et sur les migrations des peuples indigènes de l'Amérique,* — in which he took occasion to elucidate his theory of cataclysms and Atlantis. He speaks of his annotations as the results of his observations among the Quichés and of his prolonged studies. He calls the *Popul Vuh* rather a national than a sacred book,[7] and thinks it the original in

vagaries; and Brinton has studied their history at some length in the introduction to his *Maya Chronicles*. The first volume of Eligio Ancona's *Hist. de Yucatan* covers the early period. See Vol. II. p. 429. Brinton calls it "disappointingly superficial." There is much that is popularly retrospective in the various and not always stable contributions of Dr. Le Plongeon and his wife. The last of Mrs. Le Plongeon's papers is one on "The Mayas, their customs, laws, religion," in the *Mag. Amer. Hist.*, Aug., 1887. Bancroft's second volume groups the necessary references to every phase of Maya history. Cf. Charnay, English translation, ch. 15; and Geronimo Castillo's *Diccionario Histórico, biográfico y monumental de Yucatan* (Mérida, 1866). Of Crescencio Carrillo and his *Historia Antigua de Yucatan* (Mérida, 1881), Brinton says: "I know of no other Yucatecan who has equal enthusiasm or so just an estimate of the antiquarian riches of his native land" (*Amer. Hero Myths*, 147). Bastian summarizes the history of Yucatan and Guatemala in the second volume of his *Culturländer des alten Amerika*.

[1] *Yucatan*, ii. 79.

[2] See C. H. Berendt on the hist. docs. of Guatemala in *Smithsonian Report*, 1876. There is a partial bibliography of Guatemala in W. T. Brigham's *Guatemala the land of the Quetzal* (N. Y., 1887), and another by Bandelier in the *Am. Antiq. Soc. Proc.*, n. s., vol. i. p. 101. The references in Brasseur's *Hist. Nations Civilisées*, and in Bancroft's *Native Races*, vol. v., will be a ready means for collating the early sources.

[3] Scherzer and Brasseur are somewhat at variance here.

[4] "There are some coincidences between the Old Testament and the Quiché MS. which are certainly startling." Müller's *Chips*, i. 328.

[5] *Wanderungen durch die mittel-Amerikanischen Freistaaten* (Braunschweig, 1857 — an English translation, London, 1857).

[6] Leclerc, no. 1305.

[7] H. H. Bancroft, *Nat. Races*, ii. 115; iii., ch. 2, and v. 170, 547, gives a convenient condensation of the book, and says that Müller misconceives in some parts of his summary, and that Baldwin in his *Ancient America*, p. 191, follows Müller. Helps, *Spanish Conquest*, iv. App., gives a brief synopsis, — the first one done in English.

some part of the "Livre divin des Toltèques," the Teo-Amoxtli.[1] Brinton avers that neither Ximenez nor Brasseur has adequately translated the Quiché text,[2] and sees no reason to think that the matter has been in any way influenced by the Spanish contact, emanating indeed long before that event; and he has based some studies upon it.[3] In this opinion Bandelier is at variance, at least as regards the first portion, for he believes it to have been *written* after the Conquest and under Christian influences.[4] Brasseur in some of his other writings has further discussed the matter.[5]

The *Memorial of Tecpan-Atitlan*, to use Brasseur's title, is an incomplete MS.,[6] found in 1844 by Juan Gavarrete in rearranging the MSS. of the convent of San Francisco, of Guatemala, and it was by Gavarrete that a Spanish version of Brasseur's rendering was printed in 1873 in the *Boletin de la Sociedad económica de Guatemala* (nos. 29–43). This translation by Brasseur, made in 1856, was never printed by him, but, passing into Pinart's hands with Brasseur's collections,[7] it was entrusted by that collector to Dr. Brinton, who selected the parts of interest (46 out of 96 pp.), and included it as vol. vi. in his *Library of Aboriginal American Literature*, under the title of *The annals of the Cakchiquels. The original text, with a translation, notes, and introduction* (Philadelphia, 1885).

Brinton disagrees with Brasseur in placing the date of its beginning towards the opening of the eleventh century, and puts it rather at about A. D. 1380. Brasseur says he received the original from Gavarrete, and it would seem to have been a copy made between 1620 and 1650, though it bears internal evidence of having been written by one who was of adult age at the time of the Conquest.

Brinton's introduction discusses the ethnological position of the Cakchiquels, who he thinks had been separated from the Mayas for a long period.

The next in importance of the Guatemalan books is the work of Francisco Antonio de Fuentes y Guzman, *Historia de Guatemala, ó Recordación florida escrita el siglo xvii., que publica por primera vez con notas é ilustraciones J. Zaragoza* (Madrid, 1882–83), being vols. 1 and 2 of the *Biblioteca de los americanistas*. The original MS., dated 1690, is in the archives of the city of Guatemala. Owing to a tendency of the author to laud the

[1] Max Müller dissents from this. *Chips*, i. 326. Müller reminds us, if we are suspicious of the disjointed manner of what has come down to us as the *Popul Vuh*, that "consecutive history is altogether a modern idea, of which few only of the ancient nations had any conception. If we had the exact words of the *Popul Vuh*, we should probably find no more history there than we find in the Quiché MS. as it now stands."

[2] Cf. *Aborig. Amer. Authors*, p. 33.

[3] *The names of the gods in the Kiché Myths of Central America* (Philad., 1881), from the *Proc. Amer. Philos. Soc.* He gives his reasons (p. 4) for the spelling *Kiché.*

[4] Cf. *Am. Antiq. Soc. Proc.*, n. s., vol. i. 109; and his paper, "On the Sources of the Aboriginal Hist. of Spanish America," in the *Am. Asso. Adv. Sci. Proc.*, xxvii. 328 (Aug., 1878). In the *Peabody Mus. Eleventh Report*, p. 391, he says of it that "it appears to be for the first chapters an evident fabrication, or at least accommodation of Indian mythology to Christian notions, — a pious fraud; but the bulk is an equally evident collection of original traditions of the Indians of Guatemala, and as such the most valuable work for the aboriginal history and ethnology of Central America."

[5] *Hist. Nat. Civ.*, i. 47. *S'il existe des sources de l'histoire primitive du Méxique dans les monuments égyptiens et de l'histoire primitive de l'ancien monde dans les monuments Américains?* (1864), which is an extract from his *Landa's Relation.* Cf. Bollaert, in the *Royal Soc. of Lit. Trans.*, 1863. Brasseur (*Bib. Mex.-Guat.*, p. 45; Pinart, no. 231) also speaks of another Quiché document, of which his MS. copy is entitled *Titulo de los Señores de Totonicapan, escrito en lengua Quiché, el año de 1554, y traducido al Castellano el año de 1834, por el Padre Dionisio José Chonay, indígena,* which tells the story of the Quiché race somewhat differently from the *Popul Vuh.*

[6] See Vol. II. p. 419.

[7] It stands in Brasseur's *Bib. Mex.-Guat.*, p. 13, as *Memorial de Tecpan-Atitlan (Solola), histoire des deux familles royales du royaume des Cakchiquels d'Iximché ou Guatémala, rédigé en langue Cakchiquèle par le prince Don Francisco Ernantez Arana-Xahila, des rois Ahpozotziles,* where Brasseur speaks of it as analogous to the *Popul Vuh*, but with numerous and remarkable variations. The MS. remained in the keeping of Xahila till 1562, when Francisco Gebuta Queh received it and continued it (*Pinart Catalogue*, no. 35).

natives, modern historians have looked with some suspicion on his authority, and have pointed out inconsistencies and suspected errors.[1] Of a later writer, Ramon de Ordoñez (died about 1840), we have only the rough draught of a *Historia de la creacion del Cielo y de la tierra, conforme al sistema de la gentilidad Americana*, which is of importance for traditions.[2] This manuscript, preserved in the Museo Nacional in Mexico, is all that now exists, representing the perfected work. Brasseur (*Bib. Mex.-Guat.*, 113) had a copy of this draught (made in 1848–49). The original fair copy was sent to Madrid for the press, and it is suspected that the Council for the Indies suppressed it in 1805. Ramon cites a manuscript *Hist. de la Prov. de San Vicente de Chiappas y Goathemala*, which is perhaps the same as the *Crónica de la Prov. de Chiapas y Guatemala*, of which the seventh book is in the Museo Nacional (*Am. Antiq. Soc. Proc.*, n. s., i. 97; Brasseur, *Bib. Mex.-Guat.*, 157).

The work of Antonio de Remesal is sometimes cited as *Historia general de las Indias occidentales, y particular de la gobernacion de Chiapas y Guatemala*, and sometimes as *Historia de la provincia de San Vicente de Chyapa y Guatemala* (Madrid, 1619, 1620).[3]

Bandelier (*Amer. Antiq. Soc. Proc.*, i. 95) has indicated the leading sources of the history of Chiapas, so closely associated with Guatemala. To round the study of the aboriginal period of this Pacific region, we may find something in Alvarado's letters on the Conquest;[4] in Las Casas for the interior parts, and in Alonso de Zurita's *Relacion*, 1560,[5] as respects the Quiché tribes, which is the source of much in Herrera.[6] For Oajaca (Oaxaca, Guaxaca) the special source is Francisco de Burgoa's *Geográfica descripcion de la parte septentrional del Polo Artico de la América*, etc. (México, 1674), in two quarto volumes, — or at least it is generally so regarded. Bandelier, who traces the works on Oajaca (*Amer. Antiq. Soc. Proc.*, n. s., i. 115), says there is a book of a modern writer, Juan B. Carriedo, which follows Burgoa largely. Brasseur (*Bib. Mex.-Guat.*, p. 33) speaks of Burgoa as the only source which remains of the native history of Oajaca. He says it is a very rare book, even in Mexico. He largely depends upon its full details in some parts of his *Nations Civilisées* (iii. livre 9). Alonso de la Rea's *Crónica de Mechoacan* (Mexico, 1648) and Basalenque's *Crónica de San Augustin de Mechoacan* (Mexico, 1673) are books which Brinton complains he could find in no library in the United States.

[1] See Vol. II. 419; Bancroft, *Nat. Races*, v. 564; Bandelier in *Am. Antiq. Soc. Proc.*, i. 105. Bandelier (*Peabody Mus. Repts.*, ii. 391) says that it is now acknowledged that the *Recordacion florida* of Fuentes y Guzman is "full of exaggerations and misstatements." Brasseur (*Bib. Mex.-Guat.*, pp. 65, 87), in speaking of Fuentes' *Noticia histórica de los indios de Guatemala* (of which manuscript he had a copy), says that he had access to a great number of native documents, but profited little by them, either because he could not read them, or his translators deceived him. Brasseur adds that Fuentes' account of the Quiché rulers is "un mauvais roman qui n'a pas le sens commun." This last is a manuscript used by Domingo Juarros in his *Compendio de la historia de la ciudad de Guatemala* (Guatemala, 1808–1818, in two vols. — become rare), but reprinted in the *Museo Guatemalteco*, 1857. The English translation, by John Baily, a merchant living in Guatemala, was published as a *Statistical and Commercial History of Guatemala* (Lond., 1823). Cf. Vol. II. p. 419. Francisco Vazquez depended largely on native writers in his *Crónica de la Provincia de Guatemala* (Guatemala, 1714–16). (See Vol. II. p. 419.)

[2] See note in Bancroft, iii. 451.

[3] Vol. II. 419. Helps (iii. 300), speaking of Remesal, says: "He had access to the archives of Guatemala early in the seventeenth century, and he is one of those excellent writers so dear to the students of history, who is not prone to declamation, or rhetoric, or picturesque writing, but indulges us largely by the introduction everywhere of most important historical documents, copied boldly into the text."

[4] Vol. II. 419.

[5] Vol. II. 417.

[6] E. G. Squier printed in 1860 (see Vol. II. p. vii.) Diego Garcia de Palacio's *Carta dirigida al Rey de España, año 1576*, under the English title of *Description of the ancient Provinces of Guazacupan, Izalco, Cuscatlan, and Chiquimula in Guatemala*, which is also included in Pacheco's *Coleccion*, vol. vi. Bandelier refers to Estevan Aviles' *Historia de Guatemala desde los tiempos de los Indios* (Guatemala, 1663). A good reputation belongs to a modern work, Francisco de Paula Garcia Pelaez's *Memorias para la Historia del antiguo reyno de Guatemala* (Guatemala, 1851–53, in three vols.).

We trace the aboriginal condition of Nicaragua in Peter Martyr, Oviedo, Torquemada, and Ixtlilxochitl.[1]

The earliest general account of all these ancient peoples which we have in English is in the *History of America*, by William Robertson, who describes the condition of Mexico at the time of the Conquest, and epitomizes the early Spanish accounts of the natives. Prescott and Helps followed in his steps, with new facilities. Albert Gallatin brought the powers of a vigorous intellect to bear, though but cursorily, upon the subject, in his "Notes on the semi-civilized nations of Mexico, Yucatan, and Central America," in the *Amer. Ethnological Society's Transactions* (N. Y., 1845, vol. i.), and he was about the first to recognize the dangerous pitfalls of the pseudo-historical narratives of these peoples. The *Native Races*[2] of H. H. Bancroft was the first very general sifting and massing in English of the great confusion of material upon their condition, myths, languages, antiquities, and history.[3] The archæological remains are treated by Stephens for Yucatan and Central America, by Dr. Le Plongeon[4] for Yucatan, by Ephraim G. Squier for Nicaragua and Central America in general,[5] by Adolphe F. A. Bandelier in his communications to the Peabody Museum and to the Archæological Institute of America,[6] and by Professor Daniel G. Brinton in his editing of ancient records[7] and in his mythological and linguistic studies, referred to elsewhere. To these may be added, as completing the English references, various records of personal observations.[8]

1 For details follow the references in Brasseur's *Nat. Civil.*; Bancroft's *Nat. Races*; Stephens's *Nicaragua*, ii. 305, etc. See the introd. of Brinton's *Güegüence* (Philad., 1883), for the Nahuas and Mangues of Nicaragua.

2 Leclerc, no. 1070. Bancroft summarized the history of these ancient peoples in his vol. ii. ch. 2, and goes into detail in his vol. v.

3 He condenses the early Mexican history in his *Mexico*, i. ch. 7. There are recent condensed narratives, in which avail has been had of the latest developments, in Baldwin's *Ancient America*, ch. 4, and Short's *North Americans of Antiquity*.

4 Mrs. Alice D. Le Plongeon has printed various summarized popular papers, like the "Conquest of the Mayas," in the *Mag. Amer. Hist.*, April and June, 1888.

5 A list of Squier's published writings was appended to the *Catalogue of Squier's Library*, prepared by Joseph Sabin (N. Y., 1876), as sold at that time. By this it appears that his earliest study of these subjects was a review of Buxton's *Migrations of the Ancient Mexicans*, read before the London Ethnolog. Soc., and printed in 1848 in the *Edinb. New Philosoph. Mag.*, vol. xlvi. His first considerable contribution was his *Travels in Cent. America, particularly in Nicaragua, with a description of its aboriginal monuments* (London and N. Y., 1852-53). He supplemented this by some popular papers in *Harper's Mag.*, 1854, 1855. (Cf. *Hist. Mag.*, iv. 65; *Putnam's Mag.*, xii. 549.) A year or two later he communicated papers on "Les Indiens Guatusos du Nicaragua," and "Les indiens Xicaques du Honduras," to the *Nouvelles Annales des Voyages* (1856, 1858), and "A Visit to the Guajiquero Indians" to *Harper's Mag.*, 1859. In 1860, Squier projected the publication of a *Collection* of documents, but only a letter (1576) of Palacio was printed (Icazbalceta, *Bibl. Mex.*, i. p. 326). He had intended to make the series more correct and with fewer omissions than Ternaux had allowed himself. His material, then the result of ten years' gathering, had been largely secured through the instrumentality of Buckingham Smith. (See Vol. II. p. vii.)

6 "Art of war and mode of warfare of the Ancient Mexicans" (*Peabody Mus. Rept.*, no. x.).

"Distribution and tenure of lands, and the customs with respect to inheritance among the ancient Mexicans" (*Ibid.* no. xi.).

"Special organizations and mode of government of the ancient Mexicans" (*Ibid.* no. xii.).

These papers reveal much thorough study of the earlier writers on the general condition of the ancient people of Mexico, and the student finds much help in their full references. It was this manifestation of his learning that led to his appointment by the Archæological Institute,—the fruit of his labor in their behalf appearing in his *Report of an Archæological Tour in Mexico, 1881*, which constitutes the second volume (1884) of the *Papers* of that body. In his third section he enlarges upon the condition of Mexico at the time of the Conquest. His explorations covered the region from Tampico to Mexico city.

7 *Library of Aboriginal American Literature*, (Philadelphia.)

8 James H. McCulloh, an officer of the U. S. army, published *Researches on America* (Balt., 1816), expanded later into *Researches, philosophical and antiquarian, concerning the original History of America* (Baltimore, 1829). His fifth and sixth parts concern the "Institutions of the Mex-

During the American Civil War, when there were hopes of some permanence for French influence in Mexico, the French government made some organized efforts to further the study of the antiquities of the country, and the results were published in the *Archives de la Commission Scientifique du Mexique* (Paris, 1864–69, in 3 vols.).[1] The Abbé Brasseur de Bourbourg, who took a conspicuous part in this labor, has probably done more than any other Frenchman to bring into order the studies upon these ancient races, and in some directions he is our ultimate source. Unfortunately his character as an archæological expounder did not improve as he went on, and he grew to be the expositor of some wild notions that have proved acceptable to few. He tells us that he first had his attention turned to American archæology by the report, which had a short run in European circles, of the discovery of a Macedonian helmet and weapons in Brazil in 1832, and by a review of Rio's report on Palenqué, which he read in the *Journal des Savants*. Upon coming to America, fresh from his studies in Rome, he was made professor of history in the seminary at Quebec in 1845–46, writing at that time a *Histoire du Canada*, of little value. Later, in Boston, he perfected his English and read Prescott. Then we find him at Rome poring over the *Codex Vaticanus*, and studying the *Codex Borgianus* in the library of the Propaganda. In 1848 he returned to the United States, and, embarking at New Orleans for Mexico, he found himself on shipboard in the company of the new French minister, whom he accompanied, on landing, to the city of Mexico, being made almoner to the legation. This official station gave him some advantage in beginning his researches, in which Rafael Isidro Gondra, the director of the Museo, with the curators of the viceregal archives, and José Maria Andrade, the librarian of the university, assisted him.

BRASSEUR DE BOURBOURG.*

ican Empire," and "The nations inhabiting Guatemala" (Field, no. 987).

G. F. Lyon's *Journal of a residence and tour in the Republic of Mexico* (Lond., 1826, 1828).

Brantz Mayer's *Mexico as it was and as it is*, and his more comprehensive *Mexico, Aztec, Spanish and Republican* (Hartford, 1853), which includes an essay on the ancient civilization. Mayer had good opportunities while attached to the United States legation in Mexico, but of course he wrote earlier than the later developments (Field, no. 1038).

The distinguished English anthropologist, E. B. Tylor's *Anahuac; or, Mexico and the Mexicans, ancient and modern* (London, 1861), is a readable rendering of the outlines of the ancient history, and he describes such of the archæological remains as fell in his way.

H. C. R. Becher's *Trip to Mexico* (London, 1880) has an appendix on the ancient races.

F. A. Ober's *Travels in Mexico* (1884).

[1] The important papers are:—Tome I. Brasseur de Bourbourg. *Esquisses d'histoire, d'archéologie, d'ethnographie et de linguistique.* Gros. *Renseignements sur les monuments anciens situés dans les environs de Mexico.*—Tome II. Br. de Bourbourg. *Rapport sur les ruines de Mayapan et d'Uxmal au Yucatan.* Hay. *Renseignements sur Texcoco.* Dolfus, Montserrat et Pavie. *Mémoires et notes géologiques.*—Tome III. Doutrelaine. *Rapports sur les ruines de Mitla, sur la pierre de Tlalnepantla, sur un mss. mexicain (avec fac-simile).* Guillemin Tarayre. *Rapport sur l'exploration minéralogique des régions mexicaines.* Siméon. *Note sur la numération des anciens Mexicains.*

* Follows an etching published in the *Annuaire de la Société Américaine de France*, 1875. He died at Nice, Jan. 8, 1874, aged 59 years.

Later he gave himself to the study of the Nahua tongue, under the guidance of Faustino Chimalpopoca Galicia, a descendant of a brother of Montezuma, then a professor in the college of San Gregorio. In 1851 he was ready to print at Mexico, in French and Spanish, his *Lettres pour servir d'introduction à l'histoire primitive des anciennes nations civilisées du Mexique*, addressed (October, 1850) to the Duc de Valmy, in which he sketched the progress of his studies up to that time. He speaks of it as "le premier fruit de mes travaux d'archéologie et d'histoire méxicaines."[1] It was this brochure which introduced him to the attention of Squier and Aubin, and from the latter, during his residence in Paris (1851–54), he received great assistance. Pressed in his circumstances, he was obliged at this time to eke out his living by popular writing, which helped also to enable him to publish his successive works.[2] To complete his Central American studies, he went again to America in 1854, and in Washington he saw for the first time the texts of Las Casas and Duran, in the collection of Peter Force, who had got copies from Madrid. He has given us[3] an account of his successful search for old manuscripts in Central America. Finally, as the result of all these studies, he published his most important work, — *Histoire des nations civilisées du Mexique et de l'Amérique centrale durant les siècles antérieurs à C. Colomb, écrite sur des docs. origin. et entièrement inédits, puisés aux anciennes archives des indigènes* (Paris, 1857–58).[4] This was the first orderly and extensive effort to combine out of all available material, native and Spanish, a divisionary and consecutive history of ante-Columbian times in these regions, to which he added from the native sources a new account of the conquest by the Spaniards. His purpose to separate the historic from the mythical may incite criticism, but his views are the result of more labor and more knowledge than any one before him had brought to the subject.[5] In his later publications there is less reason to be satisfied with his results, and Brinton[6] even thinks that "he had a weakness to throw designedly considerable obscurity about his authorities and the sources of his knowledge." His fellow-students almost invariably yield praise to his successful research and to his great learning, surpassing perhaps that of any of them, but they are one and all chary of adopting his later theories.[7] These were expressed at length in his *Quatre lettres sur le Mexique. Exposition du système hiéroglyphique mexicain. La fin de l'âge de pierre. Époque glaciaire temporaire. Commencement de l'âge de bronze. Origines de la civilisation et des religions de l'antiquité. D'après le Teo-*

[1] He says the work is very rare. A copy given by him is in Harvard College library. *Bib. Mex.-Guat.*, p. 26.

[2] His *Palenqué*, at a later day, was published by the French government (*Quatre Lettres, avant-propos*).

[3] Introduction of his *Hist. Nations Civilisées.*

[4] Tome I. xcii. et 440 pp. *Les temps héroïques et l'histoire de l'empire des Toltèques.* — Tome II. 616 pp. *L'histoire du Yucatan et du Guatémala, avec celle de l'Anahuac durant le moyen âge aztèque, jusqu'à la fondation de la royauté à Mexico.* — Tome III. 692 pp. *L'histoire des Etats du Michoacan et d'Oaxaca et de l'empire de l'Anahuac jusqu'à l'arrivée des Espagnols. Astronomie, religion, sciences et arts des Aztèques, etc.* — Tome IV. vi. et 851 pp. *Conquête du Mexique, du Michoacan et du Guatémala, etc. Etablissement des Espagnols et fondation de l'Eglise catholique. Ruine de l'idolâtrie, déclin et abaissement de la race indigène, jusqu'à la fin du xvie siècle.*

In his introduction (p. lxxiv) Brasseur gives a list of the manuscript and printed books on which he has mainly depended, the chief of which are: Burgoa, Cogolludo, Torquemada, Sahagún, Remesal, Gomara (in Barcia), Lorenzana's *Cortes*, Bernal Diaz, Vetancurt's *Teatro Mexicano* (1698), Valades' *Rhetorica Christiana* (1579), Juarros, Pelaez, Leon y Gama, etc.

[5] Kirk's *Prescott*, i. 10. There are lists of Brasseur's works in his own *Bibliothèque Mex.-Guatémalienne*, p. 25; in the *Pinart Catalogue*, no. 141, etc.; Field, p. 43; Sabin, ii. 7420. Cf. notices of his labors by Haven in *Am. Antiq. Soc. Proc.*, Oct., 1870, p. 47; by Brinton in *Lippincott's Mag.*, i. 79. There is a *Sommaire des voyages scientifiques et des travaux de géographie, d'histoire, d'archéologie et de Philologie américaines, publiés par l'abbé Brasseur de Bourbourg* (St. Cloud, 1862).

[6] *Abor. Amer. Authors*, 57.

[7] Cf. Bandelier, *Am. Antiq. Soc. Proc.*, n. s., i. 93; Field, no. 176; H. H. Bancroft's *Nat. Races*, ii. 116, 780; v. 126, 153, 236, 241, — who says of Brasseur that "he rejects nothing, and transforms everything into historic fact;" but Bancroft looks to Brasseur for the main drift of his chapter on pre-Toltec history. Cf. Brinton's *Myths of the New World*, p. 41.

Amoxtli [etc.] (Paris, 1868), wherein he accounted as mere symbolism what he had earlier elucidated as historical records, and connected the recital of the *Codex Chimalpopoca* with the story of Atlantis, making that lost land the original seat of all old-world and new-world civilization, and finding in that sacred history of Colhuacan and Mexico the secret evidence of a mighty cataclysm that sunk the continent from Honduras (subsequently with Yucatan elevated) to perhaps the Canaries.[1] Two years later, in his elucidation of the *MS. Troano* (1869–70), this same theory governed all his study. Brasseur was quite aware of the loss of estimation which followed upon his erratic change of opinion, as the introduction to his *Bibl. Mex.-Guatémalienne* shows. No other French writer, however, has so associated his name with the history of these early peoples.[2]

In Mexico itself the earliest general narrative was not cast in the usual historical form, but in the guise of a dialogue, held night after night, between a Spaniard and an Indian, the ancient history of the country was recounted. The author, Joseph Joaquin Granados y Galvez, published it in 1778, as *Tardes Américanas: gobierno gentil y católico: breve y particular noticia de toda la historia Indiana: sucesos, casos notables, y cosas ignoradas, desde la entrada de la Gran nacion Tulteca á esta tierra de Anahuac, hasta los presentes tiempos*.[3]

The most comprehensive grouping of historical material is in the *Diccionario Universal de historia y de Geografia* (Mexico, 1853–56),[4] of which Manuel Orozco y Berra was one of the chief collaborators. This last author has in two other works added very much to our knowledge of the racial and ancient history of the indigenous peoples. These are his *Geografia de las lenguas y Carta Etnográfica de México* (Mexico, 1864),[5] and his *Historia antigua y de la Conquista de México* (Mexico, 1880, in four volumes).[6] Perhaps the most important of all the Mexican publications is Manuel Larrainzar's *Estudios sobre la historia de América, sus ruinas y antigüedades, comparadas con lo más notable del otro Continente* (Mexico, 1875-1878, in five volumes).

In German the most important of recent books is Hermann Strebel's *Alt-Mexico* (Hamburg, 1885); but Waitz's *Amerikaner* (1864, vol. ii.) has a section on the Mexicans. Adolph Bastian's "Zur Geschichte des Alten Mexico" is contained in the second volume of his *Culturländer des Alten America* (Berlin, 1878), in which he considers the subject of Quetzalcoatl, the religious ceremonial, administrative and social life, as well as the different stocks of the native tribes.

1 Bancroft, *Nat. Races*, v. 176; Baldwin, *Anc. America*.

2 Reference may be made to H. T. Moke's *Histoire des peuples Américains* (Bruxelles, 1847); Michel Chevalier's "Du Mexique avant et pendant la Conquête," in the *Revue des deux Mondes*, 1845, and his *Le Mèxique ancien et moderne* (Paris, 1863); and some parts of the Marquis de Nadaillac's *L'Amérique préhistorique* (Paris, 1883). A recent popular summary, without references, of the condition and history of ancient Mexico, is Lucien Biart's *Les Aztèques, histoire, mœurs, coutumes* (Paris, 1885), of which there is an English translation, *The Aztecs, their history*, etc., translated by J. L. Garnier (Chicago, 1887).

3 Leclerc, no. 1147; Field, no. 620; Squier, no. 427; Sabin, vii. 28,255; Bandelier in *Am. Antiq. Soc. Proc.*, n. s., i. 116. It has never yet been reprinted. The early date, as well as its rarity, have contributed to give it, perhaps, undue reputation. It is worth from £3 to £4.

4 Leclerc, no. 1119. See Vol. II. p. 415.

5 Leclerc, no. 2079; Brasseur, *Bib. Mex.-Guat.*, p. 113.

6 For the *Historia de Mexico* of Carbajal Espinosa, see Vol. II. p. 428. Cf. Alfred Chavero's *México á través de los Siglos*.

NOTES.

I. The Authorities on the so-called Civilization of Ancient Mexico and Adjacent Lands, and the Interpretation of such Authorities.

The ancient so-called civilization which the Spaniards found in Mexico and Central America is the subject of much controversy: in the first place as regards its origin, whether indigenous, or allied to and derived from the civilizations of the Old World; and in the second place as regards its character, whether it was something more than a kind of grotesque barbarism, or of a nature that makes even the Spanish culture, which supplanted it, inferior in some respects by comparison.[1] The first of these problems, as regards its origin, is considered in another place. As respects the second, or its character, it is proposed here to follow the history of opinions.

In a book published at Seville in 1519, Martin Fernandez d'Enciso's *Suma de geographia que trata de todas las partidas y provincias del mundo: en especial de las Indias*,[2] the European reader is supposed to have received the earliest hints of the degree of civilization — if it be so termed — of which the succeeding Spanish writers made so much. A brief sentence was thus the shadowy beginning of the stories of grandeur and magnificence[3] which we find later in Cortes, Bernal Diaz, Las Casas, Torquemada, Sahagún, Ramusio, Gomara, Oviedo, Zurita, Tezozomoc, and Ixtlilxochitl, and which is repeated often with accumulating effect in Acosta, Herrera, Lorenzana, Solis; Clavigero, and their successors.[4] Bandelier[5] points out how Robertson, in his views of Mexican civilization as in "the infancy of civil life,"[6] really opened the view for the first time of the exaggerated and uncritical estimates of the older writers, which Morgan has carried in our day to the highest pitch, and, as it would seem, without sufficient recognition of some of the contrary evidence.

It has usually been held that the creation among the Mexicans about thirty years after the founding of Mexico of a chief-of-men (Tlacatecuhtli) instituted a feudal monarchy. Bandelier,[7] speaking of the application of feudal terms by the old writers to Mexican institutions, says: "What in their first process of thinking was merely a comparative, became very soon a positive terminology for the purpose of describing institutions to which this foreign terminology never was adapted." He instances that the so-called "king" of these early writers was a translation of the native term, which in fact only meant "one of those who spoke;" that is, a prominent member of the council.[8] Bandelier traces the beginning of the feudal ideas as a graft upon the native systems, in the oldest document issued by Europeans on Mexican soil, when Cortes (May 20, 1519) conferred land on his allies, the chiefs of Axapusco and Tepeyahualco, and for the first time made their offices hereditary. It is Bandelier's opinion that "the grantees had no conception of the true import of what they accepted; neither did Cortes conceive the nature of their ideas." This was followed after the Spanish occupa-

[1] Discrediting Gomara's statement that De Ayllon found tribes near Cape Hatteras who had tame deer and made cheese from their milk, Dr. Brinton says: "Throughout the continent there is not a single authentic instance of a pastoral tribe, not one of an animal raised for its milk, nor for the transportation of persons, and very few for their flesh. It was essentially a hunting race." (*Myths of the New World*, 21.) He adds: "The one mollifying element was agriculture, substituting a sedentary for a wandering life, supplying a fixed dependence for an uncertain contingency."

[2] See Vol. II. p. 98.

[3] It was two years earlier, in 1517, that Hernandez de Cordova had first noticed the ruins of the Yucatan coast, though Columbus, in 1502, near Yucatan had met a Maya vessel, which with its navigators had astonished him.

[4] "No writer," says Bandelier (*Peabody Mus. Repts.* ii. 674), "has been more prolific in pictures of pomp, regal wealth and magnificence, than Bernal Diaz. Most of the later writers have placed undue reliance on his statements, assuming that the truthfulness of his own individual feelings was the result of cool observation. Any one who has read attentively his *Mémoirs* will become convinced that he is in fact one of the most unreliable eye-witnesses, so far as general principles are concerned. . . . Cortes had personal and political motives to magnify and embellish the picture. If his statements fall far below those of his troopers in thrilling and highly-colored details, there is every reason to believe that they are the more trustworthy. . . . In the descriptions by Cortes we find, on the whole, nothing but a barbarous display common to other Indian celebrations of a similar character."

Bandelier's further comment is (*Ibid.* ii. 397): "A feudal empire at Tezcuco was an invention of the chroniclers, who had a direct interest, or thought to have one, in advancing the claims of the Tezcucan tribe to an original supremacy."

Bandelier again (*Ibid.* ii. 385) points out the early statements of the conquerors, and of their annalists, which have prompted the inference of a feudal condition of society; but he refers to Ixtlilxochitl as "the chief originator of the feudal view;" and from him Torquemada draws his inspiration. Wilson (*Prehist. Man*, i. 242) holds much the same views.

[5] *Peabody Mus. Tenth Rept.* vol. ii. 114.

[6] Bandelier ("Art of War, etc.," in *Peabody Mus. Rept.* x. 113) again says of De Pauw's *Recherches philosophiques sur les Américaines*, that it is "a very injudicious book, which by its extravagance and audacity created a great deal of harm. It permitted Clavigero to attack even Robertson, because the latter had also applied sound criticism to the study of American aboriginal history, and by artfully placing both as upon the same platform, to counteract much of the good effects of Robertson's work."

[7] *Peabody Mus. Repts.* ii. 114.

[8] In regard to the nature of the chief-of-men we find, among much else of the first importance in the study of the Mexican government, an exposition in Sahagún (lib. vi. cap. 20), which seems to establish the elective and non-hereditary character of the office. It was "this office and its attributes," says Bandelier (*Peabody Mus. Repts.* ii. 670), "which have been the main stays of the notion that a high degree of civilization prevailed in aboriginal Mexico, in so far as its people were ruled after the manner of eastern despotisms." Bandelier (*Ibid.* ii. 133) says: "It is not impossible that the so-called empire of Mexico may yet prove to have been but a confederacy of the Nahuatlac tribe of the valley, with the Mexicans as military leaders." His argument on the word translated "king" is not convincing.

tion of Mexico by the institution of "repartimientos," through which the natives became serfs of the soil to the conquerors.[1]

The story about this unknown splendor of a strange civilization fascinated the world nearly half a century ago in the kindly recital of Prescott;[2] but it was observed that he quoted too often the somewhat illusory and exaggerated statements of Ixtlilxochitl, and was not a little attracted by the gorgeous pictures of Waldeck and Dupaix. With such a charming depicter, the barbaric gorgeousness of this ancient empire, as it became the fashion to call it, gathered a new interest, which has never waned, and Morgan[3] is probably correct in affirming that it "has called into existence a larger number of works than were ever before written upon any people of the same number and of the same importance."[4] Even those who, like Tylor, had gone to Mexico sceptics, had been forced to the conclusion that Prescott's pictures were substantially correct, and setting aside what he felt to be the monstrous exaggerations of Solis, Gomara, and the rest, he could not find the history much less trustworthy than European history of the same period.[5] It has been told in another place[6] how the derogatory view, as opposed to the views of Prescott, were expressed by R. A. Wilson in his *New Conquest of Mexico*, in assuming that all the conquerors said was baseless fabrication, the European Montezuma becoming a petty Indian chief, and the great city of Mexico a collection of hovels in an everglade, — the ruins of the country being accounted for by supposing them the relics of an ancient Phœnician civilization, which had been stamped out by the inroads of barbarians, whose equally barbarious descendants the Spaniards were in turn to overcome. It cannot be said that such iconoclastic opinions obtained any marked acceptance; but it was apparent that the notion of the exaggeration of the Spanish accounts was becoming sensibly fixed in the world's opinion. We see this reaction in a far less excessive way in Daniel Wilson's *Prehistoric Man* (i. 325, etc.), and he was struck, among other things, with the utter obliteration of the architectural traces of the conquered race in the city of Mexico itself.[7] When, in 1875, Hubert H. Bancroft published the second volume of his *Native Races*, he confessed "that much concerning the Aztec civilization had been greatly exaggerated by the old Spanish writers, and for obvious reasons;" but he contended that the stories of their magnificence must in the main be accepted, because of the unanimity of witnesses, notwithstanding their copying from one another, and because of the evidence of the ruins.[8] He strikes his key-note in his chapter on the "Government of the Nahua Nations," in speaking of it as "monarchical and nearly absolute;"[9] but it was perhaps in his chapter on the "Palaces and Households of the Nahua Kings," where he fortifies his statement by numerous references, that he carried his descriptions to the extent that allied his opinions to those who most unhesitatingly accepted the old stories.[10]

The most serious arraignment of these long-accepted views was by Lewis H. Morgan, who speaks of them as having "caught the imagination and overcome the critical judgment of Prescott, ravaged the sprightly brain of Brasseur de Bourbourg, and carried up in a whirlwind our author at the Golden Gate."[11]

Morgan's studies had been primarily among the Iroquois, and by analogy he had applied his reasoning to the aboriginal conditions of Mexico and Central America, thus degrading their so-called civilization to the level of the Indian tribal organization, as it was understood in the North.[12] Morgan's confidence in its deductions was perfect, and he was not very gracious in alluding to the views of his opponents. He looked upon "the fabric of Aztec romance as the most deadly encumbrance upon American ethnology."[13] The Spanish chroniclers, as he contended, "inaugurated American aboriginal history upon a misconception of Indian life, which has remained

[1] *Peabody Mus. Repts.* ii. 435.

[2] Introd. to *Conquest of Mexico.* See Vol. II. p. 426. In the Appendix to his third volume, Prescott, relying mainly on the works of Dupaix and Waldeck, arrived at conclusions as respects the origin of the Mexican civilization, and its analogies with the Old World, which accord with those of Stephens, whose work had not appeared at the time when Prescott wrote.

[3] *Houses and House Life*, p. 222.

[4] Bancroft (ii. 92) says: "What is known of the Aztecs has furnished material for nine tenths of all that has been written on the American civilized nations in general."

[5] *Anahuac, or Mexico and the Mexicans, Ancient and Modern* (London, 1861). Tylor enlarges upon what he considers the evidences of immense populations; and respecting some of their arts he adds, from inspection of specimens of their handicraft, that "the Spanish conquerors were not romancing in the wonderful stories they told of the skill of the native goldsmiths." On the other hand, Morgan (*Houses and House Life*, 223) thinks the figures of population grossly exaggerated.

[6] Vol. II. p. 427.

[7] When we consider that Rome, Constantinople, and Jerusalem, in spite of rapine, siege and fire, still retain numerous traces of their earliest times, and that not a vestige of the Aztec capital remains to us except its site, we must assume, in Wilson's opinion (*Prehistoric Man*, i. 331), that its edifices and causeways must have been for the most part more slight and fragile than the descriptions of the conquerors implied. Morgan instances as a proof of the flimsy character of their masonry, that Cortes in seventeen days levelled three fourths of the city of Mexico. But, adds Wilson, "so far as an indigenous American civilization is concerned, no doubt can be entertained, and there is little room for questioning, that among races who had carried civilization so far, there existed the capacity for its further development, independently of all borrowed aid" (p. 336). The Baron Nordenskjöld informs me that there is in the library at Upsala a MS. map of Mexico by Santa Cruz (d. 1572) which contains numerous ethnographical details, not to be found in printed maps of that day.

[8] *Native Races*, ii. 159.

[9] *Ibid.* ii. 133.

[10] Bancroft has recently epitomized his views afresh in the *Amer. Antiquarian*, Jan., 1888.

[11] Bancroft wrote in San Francisco, it will be remembered.

[12] It was for Bandelier, in his "Social organization and mode of government of the ancient Mexicans" (*Peabody Mus. Repts.* ii. 557), to demonstrate the proposition that tribal society based, according to Morgan, upon kin, and not political society, which rests upon territory and property, must be looked for among the ancient Mexicans.

[13] Morgan's *Houses*, etc., 225. Bandelier (*Peabody Mus. Rept.*, vol. ii. 114) speaks of the views advanced by Morgan in his "Montezuma's Dinner," as "a bold stroke for the establishment of American ethnology on a new basis." It must be remembered that Bandelier was Morgan's pupil.

substantially unquestioned till recently."[1] He charges upon ignorance of the structure and principles of Indian society, the perversion of all the writers,[2] from Cortes to Bancroft, who, as he says, unable to comprehend its peculiarities, invoked the imagination to supply whatever was necessary to fill out the picture.[3] The actual condition to which the Indians of Spanish America had reached was, according to his schedule, the upper status of barbarism, between which and the beginning of civilization he reckoned an entire ethnical period. "In the art of government they had not been able to rise above gentile institutions and establish political society. This fact," Morgan continues, "demonstrates the impossibility of privileged classes and of potentates, under their institutions, with power to enforce the labor of the people for the erection of palaces for their use, and explains the absence of such structures."[4]

This is the essence of the variance of the two schools of interpretation of the Aztec and Maya life. The reader of Bancroft will find, on the other hand, due recognition of an imperial system, with its monarch and nobles and classes of slaves, and innumerable palaces, of which we see to-day the ruins. The studies of Bandelier are appealed to by Morgan as substantiating his view.[5] Mrs. Zelia Nuttall (*Proc. Am. Assoc. Adv. Sci.*, Aug., 1886) claims to be able to show that the true interpretation of the Borgian and other codices points in part at least to details of a communal life.

The special issues which for a test Morgan takes with Bancroft are in regard to the character of the house in which Montezuma lived, and of the dinner which is represented by Bernal Diaz and the rest as the daily banquet of an imperial potentate. Morgan's criticism is in his *Houses and House Life of the American Aborigines* (Washington, 1881).[6] The basis of this book had been intended for a fifth Part of his *Ancient Society*, but was not used in that publication. He printed the material, however, in papers on "Montezuma's Dinner" (*No. Am. Rev.*, Ap. 1876), "Houses of the Moundbuilders" (*Ibid.*, July, 1876), and "Study of the Houses and House Life of the Indian Tribes" (*Archæol. Inst. of Amer. Publ.*). These papers amalgamated now make the work called *Houses and House Life.*[7]

Morgan argues that a communal mode of living accords with the usages of aboriginal hospitality, as well as with their tenure of lands,[8] and with the large buildings, which others call palaces, and he calls joint tenement houses. He instances, as evidence of the size of such houses, that at Cholula four hundred Spaniards and one thousand allied Indians found lodging in such a house; and he points to Stephens's description of similar communal establishments which he found in our day near Uxmal.[9] He holds that the inference of communal living from such data as these is sufficient to warrant a belief in it, although none of the early Spanish writers mention such communism as existing; while they actually describe a communal feast in what is known as Montezuma's dinner;[10] and while the plans of the large buildings now seen in ruins are exactly in accord with the demands of separate families united in joint occupancy. In such groups, he holds, there is usually one building devoted to the purpose of a Tecpan, or official house of the tribe.[11] Under the pressure to labor, which the

[1] *Ibid.* 222.

[2] Morgan says of his predecessors, "they learned nothing and knew nothing" of Indian society.

[3] *Ibid.* 223.

[4] In this he of course assumes that the ruins in Spanish America are of communal edifices.

[5] Bandelier's papers are in the second volume of the *Reports of the Peabody Museum* at Cambridge. He contends in his "Art of Warfare among the Ancient Mexicans," that he has shown the non-existence of a military despotism, and proved their government to be "a military democracy, originally based upon communism in living." A similar understanding pervades his other essay "On the social organization and mode of government of the ancient Mexicans." Morgan and Bandelier profess great admiration for each other, — Morgan citing his friend as "our most eminent scholar in Spanish American history" (*Houses*, etc., 84), and Bandelier expresses his deep feeling of gratitude, etc. (*Archæolog. Tour*, 32). This affectionate relation has very likely done something in unifying their intellectual sympathies. The *Ancient Society, or researches in the lines of human progress from savagery through barbarism to civilization* (N. Y. 1877), of Morgan is reflected very palpably in these papers of Bandelier. The accounts of the war of the conquest, as detailed in Bancroft's *Mexico* (vol. i.), and the views of their war customs (*Native Races*, ii. ch. 13), contrasted with Bandelier's ideas, — who finds in Parkman's books "the natural parallelism between the forays of the Iroquois and the so-called conquests of the Mexican confederacy" (*Archæol. Tour*, 32), and who reduces the battle of Otumba to an affair like that of Custer and the Sioux (*Art of Warfare*), — give us in the military aspects of the ancient life the opposed views of the two schools of interpreters

[6] Being vol. iv. of the *Contributions to No. Amer. Ethnol.* in Powell's *Survey of the Rocky Mt. Region.* Some of Morgan's cognate studies relating to the aboriginal system of consanguinity and laws of descent are in the *Smithsonian Contributions*, xvii., the *Smithsonian Misc. Coll.* ii., *Amer. Acad. Arts and Sci. Trans.* vii., and *Am. Assoc. Adv. Sci. Proc.*, 1857.

[7] Morgan in this, his last work, condenses in his first chapter those which were numbered 1 to 4 in his *Ancient Society*, and in succeeding sections he discusses the laws of hospitality, communism, usages of land and food, and the houses of the northern tribes, of those of New Mexico, San Juan River, the moundbuilders, the Aztecs, and those in Yucatan and Central America. Among these he finds three distinct ethnical stages, as shown in the northern Indian, higher in the sedentary tribes of New Mexico, and highest among those of Mexico and Central America. S. F. Haven commemorated Morgan's death in the *Am. Antiq. Soc. Proc.*, Apr., 1880.

[8] Cf. Bandelier on "the tenure of lands" in *Peabody Mus. Repts.* (1878), no. xi., and Bancroft in *Nat. Races*, ii. ch. 6, p. 223.

[9] Bandelier (*Peabody Mus. Repts.* ii. 391) points out that when Martin Ursúa captured Tayasál on Lake Petin, the last pueblo inhabited by Maya Indians, he found "all the inhabitants living brutally together, an entire relationship together in one single house," and Bandelier refers further to Morgan's *Ancient Society*, Part 2, p. 181.

[10] Bandelier (*Peabody Mus. Repts.* ii. 673) accepts the views of Morgan, calling it "a rude clannish feast," given by the official household of the tribe as a part of its daily duties and obligations.

[11] On the character of the Tecpan (council house, or official house) of the Mexicans, which the early writers trans-

Spaniards inflicted on their occupants, these communal dwellers were driven, to escape such servitude, into the forest, and thus their houses fell into decay. Morgan's views attracted the adhesion of not a few archæologists, like Bandelier and Dawson; but in Bancroft, as contravening the spirit of his *Native Races*, they begat feelings that substituted disdain for convincing arguments.[1] The less passionate controversialists point out, with more effect, how hazardous it is, in coming to conclusions on the quality of the Nahua, Maya, or Quiché conditions of life, to ignore such evidences as those of the hieroglyphics, the calendars, the architecture and carvings, the literature and the industries, as evincing quite another kind, rather than degree, of progress, from that of the northern Indians.[2]

II. Bibliographical Notes upon the Ruins and Archæological Remains of Mexico and Central America.

Elsewhere in this work some account is given of the comprehensive treatment of American antiquities. It is the purpose of this note to characterize such other descriptions as have been specially confined to the antiquities of Mexico, Central America, and adjacent parts; together with noting occasionally those more comprehensive works which have sections on these regions. The earliest and most distinguished of all such treatises are the writings of Alexander von Humboldt,[3] to whom may be ascribed the paternity of what the French define as the Science of Americanism, which, however, took more definite shape and invited discipleship when the Société Américaine de France was formed, and Aubin in his *Mémoire sur la peinture didactique et l'écriture figurative des Anciens Méxicains* furnished a standard of scholarship. How new this science was may be deduced from the fact that Robertson, the most distinguished authority on early American history, who wrote in English, in the last part of the preceding century, had ventured to say that in all New Spain there was not "a single monument or vestige of any building more ancient than the Conquest." After Humboldt, the most famous of what may be called the pioneers of this art were Kingsborough, Dupaix, and Waldeck, whose publications are sufficiently described elsewhere. The most startling developments came from the expeditions of Stephens and Catherwood, the former mingling both in his *Central America* and *Yucatan* the charms of a personal narrative with his archæological studies, while the draughtsman, beside furnishing the sketches for Stephens's book, embodied his drawings on a larger scale in the publication which passes under his own name.[4] The explorations of Charnay are those which have excited the most interest of late years, though equally significant results have been produced by such special explorers as Squier in Nicaragua, Le Plongeon in Yucatan, and Bandelier in Mexico.

The labors of the French archæologist, which began in 1858, resulted in the work *Cités et ruines Améri-*

late "palace," with its sense of magnificence, see Bandelier (*Peabody Mus. Repts.* ii. 406, 671, etc.), with his references. Morgan holds that Stephens is largely responsible for the prevalence of erroneous notions regarding the Mayas, by reason of using the words "palaces" and "great cities" for defining what were really the pueblos of these southern Indians. Bancroft (ii. 84), referring to the ruins, says: They have "the highest value as confirming the truth of the reports made by Spanish writers, very many, or perhaps most, of whose statements respecting the wonderful phenomena of the New World, without this incontrovertible material proof, would find few believers among the skeptical students of the present day." Bancroft had little prescience respecting what the communal theorists were going to say of these ruins.

[1] Cf. Bancroft's *Cent. America*, i. 317. Sir J. William Dawson, in his *Fossil Men* (p. 83), contends that Morgan has proved his point, and he calls the ruins of Spanish America "communistic barracks" (p. 50). Higginson, in the first chapter of his *Larger History*, which is a very excellent, condensed popular statement of the new views which Morgan inaugurated, says of him very truly, that he lacked moderation, and that there is "something almost exasperating in the positiveness with which he sometimes assumes as proved that which is only probable."

[2] Bancroft in his footnotes (vol. ii.) embodies the best bibliography of this ancient civilization. Cf. Wilson's *Prehistoric Man*, i. ch. 14; C. Hermann Berendt's "Centres of ancient civilization and their geographical distribution," an *Address before the Amer. Geog. Soc.* (N. Y. 1876); Draper's *Intellectual Development of Europe;* Brasseur's *Ms. Troano;* Humboldt's *Cosmos* (English transl. ii. 674); Michel Chevalier in the *Revue de deux Mondes*, Mar.-July, 1845, embraced later in his *Du Méxique avant et pendant la Conquête* (Paris, 1845); Brantz Mayer's *Mexico as it was; The Galaxy*, March, 1876; *Scribner's Mag.* v. 724; *Overland Monthly*, xiv. 468; De Charency's *Hist. du Civilisation du Méxique* (*Revue des Questions historiques*), vi. 283; Dabry de Thiersant's *Origine des indiens du Nouveau Monde* (Paris, 1883); Peschel's *Races of Men*, 441; Nadaillac's *Les premiers hommes et les temps préhistoriques*, ii. ch. 9, etc.

[3] For the bibliography of his works see Brunet, Sabin, Field, etc. The octavo edition of his *Vues* has 19 of the 69 plates which constitute the *Atlas* of the large edition. See the chapter on Peru for further detail.

[4] John Lloyd Stephens, *Incidents of travel in Central America, Chiapas, and Yucatan*, Lond. and N. Y. 1841, — various later eds., that of London, 1854, being "revised from the latest Amer. ed., with additions by Frederick Catherwood." Stephens started on this expedition in 1839, and he was armed with credentials from President Van Buren. He travelled 3000 miles, and visited eight ruined cities, as shown by his route given on the map in vol. i. Cf. references in Allibone, ii. p. 2240; *Poole's Index*, p. 212; his *Incidents of Travel in Yucatan* will be mentioned later.

Frederick Catherwood's *Views of Ancient Monuments in Central America, Chiapas, and Yucatan* (Lond. 1844) has a brief text (pp. 24) and 25 lithographed plates. Some of the original drawings used in making these plates were included in the *Squier Catalogue*, p. 229. (Sabin's *Dict.* iii. no. 11520.) Captain Lindesay Brine, in his paper on the "Ruined Cities of Central America" (*Journal Roy. Geog. Soc.* 1872, p. 354; *Proc.* xvii. 67), testifies to the accuracy of Stephens and Catherwood. These new developments furnished the material for numerous purveyors to the popular mind, some of them of the slightest value, like Asahel Davis, whose *Antiquities of Central America*, with some slight changes of title, and with the parade of new editions, were common enough between 1840 and 1850.

caines: Mitla, Palenqué, Izamal, Chichen-Itza, Uxmal, recueillies et photographiées par Désiré Charnay, avec un Texte par M. Viollet le Duc. (Paris, 1863.) Charnay contributed to this joint publication, beside the photographs, a paper called "Le Méxique, 1858–61, — souvenirs et impressions de Voyage." The Architect Viollet le Duc gives us in the same book an essay by an active, well-equipped, and ingenious mind, but his speculations about the origin of this Southern civilization and its remains are rather curious than convincing.[1]

The public began to learn better what Charnay's full and hearty confidence in his own sweeping assertions was, when he again entered the field in a series of papers on the ruins of Central America which he contributed

THE PYRAMID OF CHOLULA.*

(1879–81) to the *North American Review* (vols. cxxxi.–cxxxiii.), and which for the most part reached the public newly dressed in some of the papers contributed by L. P. Gratacap to the *American Antiquarian*,[2] and in a paper by F. A. Ober on "The Ancient Cities of America," in the *Amer. Geog. Soc. Bulletin*, Mar., 1888. Charnay took moulds of various sculptures found among the ruins, which were placed in the Trocadero Museum in Paris.[3] What Charnay communicated in English to the *No. Amer. Review* appeared in better shape in French in the *Tour du Monde* (1886-87), and in a still riper condition in his latest work, *Les anciens villes du Nouveau Monde: voyages d'explorations au Méxique et dans l'Amérique Centrale. 1857–1882. Ouvrage contenant 214 gravures et 19 cartes ou plans.* (Paris, 1885.)[4]

[1] Viollet le Duc, in his *Histoire de l'habitation humaine depuis les temps préhistoriques* (Paris, 1875), has given a chapter (no. xxii.) to the "Nahuas and Toltecs." Views more or less studied, comprehensive, and restricted are given in R. Cary Long's *Ancient Architecture of America, its historic value and parallelism of development with the architecture of the Old World* (N. Y. 1849), an address from the *N. Y. Hist. Soc. Proc.* 1849, p. 117; R. P. Greg on "the Fret or Key Ornament in Mexico and Peru," in the *Archæologia* (London), vol. xlvii. 157; and a popular summary on "the pyramid in America," by S. D. Peet, in the *American Antiquarian*, July, 1888, comparing the mounds of Cholula, Uxmal, Palenqué, Teotihuacan, Copan, Quemada, Cohokia, St. Louis, etc. John T. Short summarizes the characteristics of the Nahua and Maya styles (*No. Amer. of Antiquity*, 340, 359). There are chapters on their architecture in Bancroft, *Nat. Races*, ii.; but the references in his vol. iv. are most helpful.

[2] Vols. v. vi. vii. on "Ancient Mexican Civilization," "Pyramid of Teotihuacan," "Sacrificial Calendar Stone," "Central America at time of Conquest," "Ruins at Palenque and Copan," "Ruins of Uxmal," etc.

[3] Duplicates were placed in the Nat. Museum at Washington by the liberality of Pierre Lorillard.

[4] The English translation is condensed in parts: *The ancient cities of the New World: being travels and explorations in Mexico and Central America from 1857–1882. Translated from the French by J. Gonino and Helen S. Conant.* (London, 1887.) Some of his notable results were the discovery of stucco ornaments in the province of Iturbide, among ruins which he unfortunately named Lorillard City (Eng. tr. ch. 22). The palace at Tula is also figured in Brocklehurst's *Mexico to-day*, ch. 25. The discovery of what Charnay calls glass and porcelain is looked upon as doubtful by most archæologists, who believe the specimens to be rather traces of Spanish contact.

* After a drawing in Cumplido's Spanish translation of Prescott's *Mexico*, vol. iii. (Mexico, 1846.)

We proceed now to note geographically some of the principal ruins. In the vicinity of Vera Cruz the pyramid of Papantla is the conspicuous monument,[1] but there is little else thereabouts needing particular mention. Among the ruins of the central plateau of Mexico, the famous pyramid of Cholula is best known. The time of its construction is a matter about which archæologists are not agreed, though it is perhaps to be connected with the earliest period of the Nahua power. Duran, on the other hand, has told a story of its erection by the giants, overcome by the Nahuas.[2] Its purpose is equally debatable, whether intended for a memorial, a refuge, a defence, or a spot of worship — very likely the truth may be divided among them all.[3] It is a similar problem for divided opinion whether it was built by a great display of human energy, in accordance with the tradition that the bricks which composed its surface were passed from hand to hand by a line of men, extending to the spot where they were made leagues away, or constructed by a slower process of accretion, spread over successive generations, which might not have required any marvellous array of workmen.[4] The fierce conflict which — as some hold — Cortés had with the natives around the mound and on its slopes settled its fate; and the demolition begun thereupon, and continued by the furious desolaters of the Church, has been aided by the erosions of time and the hand of progress, till the great monument has become a ragged and corroded hill, which might to the casual observer stand for the natural base, given by the Creator, to the modern

GREAT MOUND OF CHOLULA.*

1 Bancroft, iv. 453, and references.

2 Bandelier (p. 235) is confident that it was built by an earlier people than the Nahuas.

3 Cf. Bandelier, p. 247. Short, p. 236.

4 Bancroft (v. 200) gives references on these points, and particular note may be taken of Veytia, i. 18, 155, 199; and Brasseur, *Hist. Nations Civ.* iv. 182. Cf. also Nadaillac, p. 351. Bandelier (*Archæolog. Tour*, 248, 249) favors the gradual growth theory, and collates early sources (p. 250). Bancroft (iv. 474) holds that we may feel very sure its erection dates back of the tenth, and perhaps of the seventh, century.

* After a sketch in Bandelier's *Archæological Tour*, p. 233, who also gives a plan of the mound. The modern Church of Nuestra Señora de los Remedios is on the summit, where there are no traces of aboriginal works. A paved road leads to the top. A suburban road skirts its base, and fields of maguey surround it. The circuit of the base is 3859 feet, and the mound covers nearly twenty acres. Estimates of its height are variously given from 165 to 208 feet, according as one or another base line is chosen. It is built of adobe brick laid in clay, and it has suffered from erosion, slides, and other effects of time. There are some traces of steps up the side. Bandelier (pl. xv.) also gives a fac-simile of an old map of Cholula. The earliest picture which we have of the mound, evidently thought by the first Spaniards to be a natural one, is in the arms of Cholula (1540). There are other modern cuts in Carbajal-Espinosa's *Mexico* (i. 195); *Archæologia Americana* (i. 12); Brocklehurst's *Mexico to-day*, 182. The degree of restoration which draughtsmen allow to themselves, accounts in large measure for the great diversity of appearance which the mound makes in the different drawings of it. There is a professed restoration by Mothes in Armin's *Heutige Mexico*, 63, 68, 72. The engraving in Humboldt is really a restoration (*Vues*, etc., pl. vii., or pl. viii. of the folio ed.). Bandelier gives a slight sketch of a restoration (p 246, pl. viii.).

chapel that now crowns its summit; but if Bandelier's view (p. 249) is correct, that none of the conquerors mention it, then the conflict which is recorded took place, not here, but on the vanished mound of Quetzal-

MEXICAN CALENDAR STONE.*

* After a cut in *Harper's Magazine*. An enlarged engraving of the central head is given on the title-page of the present volume. A photographic reproduction, as the "Stone of the Sun," is given in Bandelier's *Archæological Tour*, p. 54, where he summarizes the history of it, with references, including a paper by Alfredo Chavero, in the *Anales del Museo nacional de México*, and another, with a cut, by P. J. J. Valentini, in *Amer. Antiq. Soc. Proc.*, April, 1878, and in *The Nation*, Aug. 8 and Sept. 19, 1878. Chavero's explanation is translated in Brocklehurst's *Mexico to-day*, p. 186. The stone is dated in a year corresponding to A. D. 1479, and it was early described in Duran's *Historia de las Indias*, and in Tezozomoc's *Crónica mexicana*. Tylor (*Anahuac*, 238) says that of the drawings made before the days of photography, that in Carlos Nebel's *Viaje pintoresco y Arqueológico sobre la República Mejicana*, 1829–1834 (Paris, 1839), is the best, while the engravings given by Humboldt (pl. xxiii.) and others are more or less erroneous. Cf. other cuts in Carbajal's *México*, i. 528; Bustamante's *Mañanas de la Alameda* (Mexico, 1835–36); Short's *No. Amer. of Antiq.*, 408, 451, with references; Bancroft's *Native Races*, ii. 520; iv. 506; Stevens's *Flint Chips*, 309.

Various calendar disks are figured in Clavigero (Casena, 1780); a colored calendar on agave paper is reproduced in the *Archives de la Commission Scientifique du Mexique*, iii. 120. (Quaritch held the original document in Aug., 1888, at £25, which had belonged to M. Boban.)

For elucidations of the Mexican astronomical and calendar system see Acosta, vi. cap. 2; Granados y Galvez's *Tardes Americanas* (1778); Humboldt's essay in connection with pl. xxiii. of his *Atlas;* Prescott's *Mexico*, i. 117; Bollaert in *Memoirs read before the Anthropol. Soc. of London*, i. 210; E. G. Squier's *Some new discoveries respecting the dates on the great calendar stone of the ancient Mexicans, with observations on the Mexican cycle of fifty-two years*, in the *American Journal of Science and Arts*, 2d ser., March, 1849, pp. 153–157; Abbé J. Pipart's *Astronomie, Chronologie et rites des Méxicaines* in the *Archives de la Soc. Amér. de France* (n. ser. i.); Brasseur's *Nat. Civ.*, iii. livre ii.; Bancroft's *Nat. Races*, ii. ch. 16; Short, ch. 9, with ref., p. 445; Cyrus Thomas in Powell's *Rept. Ethn. Bureau*, iii. 7. Cf. Brinton's *Abor. Amer. Authors*, p. 38; Brasseur's "Chronologie historique des Méxicaines" in the *Actes de la Soc. d'Ethnographie* (1872), vol. vi.; Wilson's *Prehistoric Man*, i. 355, for the Toltecs as the source of astronomical ideas, with which compare Bancroft, v. 192; the *Bulletin de la Soc. royale Belge de Géog.*, Sept., Oct., 1886; and Bandelier in the *Peabody Mus. Repts.*, ii. 572, for a comparison of calendars.

Wilson in his *Prehistoric Man* (i. 246) says: "By the unaided results of native science, the dwellers on the Mexican plateau had effected an adjustment of civil to solar time so nearly correct that when the Spaniards landed on their coast, their own reckoning, according to the unreformed Julian calendar, was really eleven days in error, compared with that of the barbarian nation whose civilization they so speedily effaced."

See what Wilson (*Prehistoric Man*, i. 333) says of the native veneration for this calendar stone, when it was exhumed. Mrs. Nuttall (*Proc. Am. Asso. Adv. Sci.*, Aug., 1886) claims to be able to show that this monolith is really a stone which stood in the Mexican market-place, and was used in regulating the stated market-days.

coatl, which in Bandelier's opinion was a different structure from this more famous mound, while other writers pronounce it the shrine itself of Quetzalcoatl.[1]

We have reference to a Cholula mound in some of the earliest writers. Bernal Diaz counted the steps on its side.[2] Motolinía saw it within ten years of the Conquest, when it was overgrown and much ruined. Sahagún says it was built for defensive purposes. Rojas, in his *Relacion de Cholula*, 1581, calls it a fortress, and says the Spaniards levelled its convex top to plant there a cross, where later, in 1594, they built a chapel. Torquemada, following Motolinía and the later Mendieta, says it was never finished, and was decayed in his time, though he traced the different levels. Its interest as a relic thus dates almost from the beginnings of the modern history of the region. Boturini mentions its four terraces. Clavigero, in 1744, rode up its sides on horseback, impelled by curiosity, and found it hard work even then to look upon it as other than a natural hill.[3] The earliest of the critical accounts of it, however, is Humboldt's, made from examinations in 1803, when much more than now of its original construction was observable, and his account is the one from which most travellers have drawn, — the result of close scrutiny in his text and of considerable license in his plate, in which he aimed at something like a restoration.[4] The latest critical examination is in Bandelier's "Studies about Cholula and its vicinity," making part iii. of his *Archæological Tour in Mexico in 1881*.[5]

What are called the finest ruins in Mexico are those of Xochicalco, seventy-five miles southwest of the capital, consisting of a mound of five terraces supported by masonry, with a walled area on the summit. Of late years a cornfield surrounds what is left of the pyramidal structure, which was its crowning edifice, and which up to the middle of the last century had five receding stories, though only one now appears. It owes its destruction to the needs which the proprietors of the neighboring sugar-works have had for its stones. The earliest account of the ruins appeared in the "Descripcion (1791) de los antiqüedades de Xochicalco" of José Antonio Alzate y Ramirez, in the *Gacetas de Literatura* (Mexico, 1790–94, in 3 vols.; reprinted Puebla, 1831, in 4 vols.), accompanied by plates, which were again used in Pietro Marquez's *Due Antichi Monumenti de Architettura Messicana* (Roma, 1804),[6] with an Italian version of Alzate, from which the French translation in

[1] Bandelier's idea (p. 254) is that as the Indians never repair a ruin, they abandoned this remaining mound after its disaster, and transplanted the worship of Quetzalcoatl to the new mound, since destroyed, while the old shrine was in time given to the new cult of the Rain-god.

[2] As Bancroft thinks; but Bandelier says that it was not of this mound, but of the temple which stood where the modern convent stands, that this count was made. *Arch. Tour*, 242.

[3] *Storia Ant. del Messico*, ii. 33.

[4] *Vues*, i. 96; pl. iii., or pl. vii., viii. in folio ed.; *Essai polit.*, 239. The later observers are: Dupaix (*Antiq. Mex.*, and in Kingsborough, v. 218; with iv. pl. viii.). Bancroft remarks on the totally different aspects of Castañeda's two drawings. Nebel, in his *Viaje pintoresco y Arqueolójico sobre la república Mejicana*, 1829–34 (Paris, 1839, folio), gave a description and a large colored drawing. Of the other visitors whose accounts add something to our knowledge, Bancroft (iv. 471) notes the following: J. R. Poinsett, *Notes on Mexico* (London, 1825). W. H. Bullock, *Six Months in Mexico* (Lond., 1825). H. G. Ward, *Mexico in 1827* (Lond., 1828). Mark Beaufoy, *Mex. Illustrations* (Lond., 1828), with cuts. Charles Jos. Latrobe, *Rambles in Mexico* (Lond., 1836). Brantz Mayer, *Mexico as it was* (N. Y., 1854); *Mexico, Aztec, etc.* (Hartford, 1853); and in Schoolcraft, *Ind. Tribes*, vi. 582. Waddy Thompson, *Recoll. of Mexico* (N. Y., 1847). E. B. Tylor, *Anahuac* (Lond., 1861), p. 274. A. S. Evans, *Our Sister Republic* (Hartford, 1870). Summaries later than Bancroft's will be found in Short, p. 369, and Nadaillac, p. 350. Bancroft adds (iv. 471–2) a long list of second-hand describers.

[5] It is illustrated with a map of the district of Cholula (p. 158), a detailed plan of the pyramid or mound (Humboldt is responsible for the former term) as it stands amid roads and fields (p. 230), and a fac-simile of an old map of the pueblo of Cholula (1581).

Bandelier speaks of the conservative tendencies of the native population of this region, giving a report that old native idols are still preserved and worshipped in caves, to which he could not induce the Indians to conduct him (p. 156); and that when he went to see the *Mapa de Cuauhtlantzinco*, or some native pictures of the 16th century, representing the Conquest, and of the highest importance for its history, he was jealously allowed but one glance at them, and could not get another (*Archæol. Tour*, p. 123). He adds: "The difficulty attending the consultation of any documents in the hands of Indians is universal, and results from their superstitious regard for writings on paper. The bulk of the people watch with the utmost jealousy over their old papers . . . They have a fear lest the power vested in an original may be transferred to a copy" (pp. 155–6).

[6] Pinart, no. 590.

NOTE. — The opposite view of the court of the Museum is from Charnay, p. 57. He says: "The Museum cannot be called rich, in so far that there is nothing remarkable in what the visitor is allowed to see." The vases, which had so much deceived Charnay, earlier, as to cause him to make casts of them for the Paris Museum, he at a later day pronounced forgeries; and he says that they, with many others which are seen in public and private museums, were manufactured at Tlatiloco, a Mexican suburb, between 1820 and 1828. See Holmes on the trade in Mexican spurious relics in *Science*, 1886.

The reclining statue in the foreground is balanced by one similar to it at an opposite part of the court-yard. One is the Chac-mool, as Le Plongeon called it, unearthed by him at Chichen-Itza, and appropriated by the Mexican government; the other was discovered at Tlaxcala.

The round stone in the centre is the sacrificial stone dug up in the great square in Mexico, of which an enlarged view is given on another page.

The museum is described in Bancroft, iv. 554; in Mayer's *Mexico as it was*, etc., and his *Mexico, Aztec, etc.*; Fossey's *Mexique*.

On Le Plongeon's discovery of the Chac-mool see *Amer. Antiq. Soc. Proc.*, Apr., 1877; Oct., 1878, and new series, i. 280; Nadaillac, Eng. tr., 346; Short, 400; Le Plongeon's *Sacred Mysteries*, 88, and his paper in the *Amer. Geog. Soc. Journal*, ix. 142 (1877). Hamy calls it the Toltec god Tlaloc, the rain-god; and Charnay agrees with him, giving (pp. 366–7) cuts of his and of the one found at Tlaxcala.

COURT IN THE MEXICO MUSEUM.

Dupaix was made. Alzate furnished the basis of the account in Humboldt's *Vues* (i. 129; pl. ix. of folio ed.) and Waldeck (*Voyage pitt.*, 69) regrets that Humboldt adopted so inexact a description as that of Alzate. From Nebel (*Viage pintoresco*) we get our best graphic representations, for Tylor (*Anahuac*) says that Casteñeda's drawings, accompanying Dupaix, are very incorrect. Bancroft says that one, at least, of these drawings in Kingsborough bears not the slightest resemblance to the one given in Dupaix. In 1835 there were explorations made under orders of the Mexican government, which were published in the *Revista Mexicana* (i. 539, — reprinted in the *Diccionario Universal*, x. 938). Other accounts, more or less helpful, are given by Latrobe, Mayer,[1] and in Isador Löwenstern's *Le Méxique* (Paris, 1843).[2]

The ancient Anahuac corresponds mainly to the valley of Mexico city.[3] Bancroft (iv. 497) shows in a summary way the extent of our knowledge of the scant archæological remains within this central area.[4]

In the city of Mexico not a single relic of the architecture of the earlier peoples remains,[5] though a few movable sculptured objects are preserved.[6]

OLD MEXICAN BRIDGE NEAR TEZCUCO.*

Tezcuco, on the other side of the lake from Mexico, affords some traces of the ante-Conquest architecture, but has revealed no such interesting movable relics as have been found in the capital city.[7] Twenty-five miles north of Mexico are the ruins of Teotihuacan, which have been abundantly described by early writers and modern explorers. Bancroft (iv. 530) makes up his summary mainly from a Mexican official account, Ramon Almaraz's *Memoria de los trabajos ejecutados por la comision cientifica de Pachuca* (Mexico, 1865), adding what was needed to fill out details from Clavigero, Humboldt, and the later writers.[8]

[1] He repeats Alzate's plate of the restoration of the ruins.

[2] Bancroft refers (iv. 483) to various compiled accounts, to which may be added his own and Short's (p. 371). Cf. F. Boncourt in the *Revue d'Ethnographie* (1887).

[3] Prescott, Kirk ed., i. 12. See the map of the plateau of Anahuac in Ruge, *Gesch. des Zeitalters der Entdeck.*, i. 363.

[4] Cf. Gros in the *Archives de la Com. Scient. du Méxique*, vol. i.; H. de Saussure on the *Découverte des ruines d'une ancienne ville Méxicaine située sur le plateau de l'Anahuac* (Paris, 1858, — *Bull. Soc Géog. de Paris*).

[5] The same is true of the earliest Spanish buildings. Icazbalceta (*México en 1554*, p. 74) says that the soil is constantly accumulating, and the whole city gradually sinks.

[6] Bancroft (iv. 505, 516, with references) says that such objects, when brought to light by excavations, have not always been removed from their hiding-places; and he argues that beneath the city there may yet be "thousands of interesting monuments." Cf. B. Mayer's *Mexico as it was*, vol. ii.

Bandelier (*Archæol. Tour*, Part ii. p. 49) gives us valuable "Archæological Notes about the City of Mexico," in which he says that Alfredo Chavero owns a very large oil painting, said to have been executed in 1523, giving a view of the aboriginal city and the principal events of the Conquest. It shows that the ancient city was about one quarter the size of the modern town.

We find descriptions of the city before the conquerors transformed it, in Brasseur's *Hist. Nations Civ.* iii. 187; iv. line 13; and in Bancroft (ii. ch. 18) there is a collation of authorities on Nahua buildings, with specific references on the city of Mexico (ii. p. 567). Bandelier describes with citations its military aspects at the time of the Conquest (*Peabody Mus. Reports*, x. 151).

The movable relics found in Mexico are the following: —

1. The calendar stone. See annexed cut.
2. Teoyamique. See cut in the appendix of this volume.
3. Sacrificial stone. See annexed cut.
4. Indio triste. See annexed cut.
5. Head of a serpent, discovered in 1881. Cf. Bandelier's *Archæol. Tour*, p. 69.
6. Human head. Cf. Bancroft, iv. 518. All of the above, except the calendar stone, are in the Museo Nacional.
7. Gladiatorial stone, discovered in 1792, but left buried. Cf. B. Mayer's *Mexico*, 123; Bancroft, iv. 516; Kingsborough, vii. 94; Sahagún, lib. ii.
8. A few other less important objects. Cf. Bandelier, *Archæol. Tour*, 52.

Antonio de Leon y Gama, who unfortunately had no knowledge of the writings of Sahagún, has discussed most of these relics in his *Descripcion histórico y Cronológico de las dos Piedras &c*. (2d ed. Bustamante, 1832.)

[7] Bancroft, iv. 520, with authorities, p. 523. Cf. *American Antiquarian*, May, 1888.

[8] Bancroft's numerous references make a foot-note (iv. 530). He adds a plan from Almaraz, and says that the description of Linares (*Soc. Mex. Geog. Boletin*, 30, i. 103) is mainly drawn from Almaraz. It is believed, but not absolutely proven, that the mounds were natural ones, artificially shaped (Bandelier, 44). The extent of the ruins is very great, and it is a current belief that the city in its prime must have been very large. The whole region is exceptionally rich in fragmentary and small relics, like pottery, obsidian implements, and terra-cotta heads. Cf. for these last, *Lond. Geog. Soc. Journal*, vii. 10; Thompson's *Mexico*, 140; Nebel, *Viaje*; Mayer's *Mexico as it was*, 227 (as cited in Bancroft, iv. 542); and later publications like T. U. Brocklehurst's *Mexico to-day* (Lond., 1883), and Zelia Nuttall's "Terra Cotta Heads from Teotihuacan," in the *Amer. Journal of Archæology* (June and Sept. 1886), ii. 157, 318.

Bancroft judges that the ruins date back to the sixth century, and says that these mounds served for models of the Aztec teocallis. On the commission already referred to was Antonio García y Cubas, who conducted some personal explorations, and in describing these in a separate publica-

* After a sketch in Tylor's *Anahuac*, who thinks it the original *Puente de las Bergantinas*, where Cortes had his brigantines launched. The span is about 20 feet, and this Tylor thinks "an immense span for such a construction." Cf. H. H. Bancroft, *Native Races*, iv. 479, 528. Bandelier (*Peabody Mus. Reports*, ii. 696) doubts its antiquity.

Bancroft (iv. ch. 10), in describing what is known of the remains in the northern parts of Mexico, gives a summary of what has been written regarding the most famous of these ruins, Quemada in Zacatecas.[1]

THE INDIO TRISTE.*

tion, *Ensayo de un Estudio Comparativo entre las Pirámides Egipcias y Mexicanas* (Mexico, 1871), he points out certain analogies of the American and Egyptian structures, which will be found in epitome in Bancroft (iv. 543). In discussing the monoliths of the ruins, Amos W. Butler (*Amer. Antiquarian*, May, 1885), in a paper on "The Sacrificial Stone of San Juan Teotihuacan," advanced some views that are controverted by W. H. Holmes in the *Amer. Journal of Archæology* (i. 361), from whose footnotes a good bibliography of the subject can be derived. Bandelier (*Archæol. Tour*, 42) thinks that because no specific mention is made of them in Mexican tradition, it is safe to infer that these monuments antedate the Mexicans, and were in ruins at the time of the Conquest.

[1] The early writers make little mention of the place except as one of the halting-places of the Aztec migration. Torquemada has something to say (quoted in *Soc. Mex. Geog. Bol.*, 2°, iii. 278, with the earliest of the modern accounts by Manuel Gutierrez, in 1805). Capt. G. F. Lyon (*Journal of a residence and tour in Mexico*, London, 1828) visited the ruins in 1828. Pedro Rivera in 1830 described them in Márcos de Esparza's *Informe presentado al Gobierno* (Zacatecas, 1830, — also in *Museo Mexicano*, i. 185, 1843). The plan in Nebel's *Viaje* (copied in Bancroft, iv. 582) was made for Governor García, by Berghes, a German engineer, in 1831, who at the time was accompanied by J. Burkart (*Aufenthalt und Reisen in Mexico*, Stuttgart, 1836), who gives a plan of fewer details. Bancroft (iv. 579) thinks Nebel's views of the ruins the only ones ever published, and he enumerates various second-hand writers (iv. 579).

Cf. Fegeux, "Les ruines de la Quemada," in the *Revue d'Ethnologie*, i. 119. The noticeable features of these ruins are their massiveness and height of walls, their absence of decoration and carved idols, and the lack of pottery and the smaller relics. Their history, notwithstanding much search, is a blank.

* After a photograph in Bandelier's *Archæological Tour*, p. 68. He thinks it was intended to be a bearer of a torch, and has no symbolical meaning.

Bancroft (iv. ch. 7) has given a separate chapter to the antiquities of Oajaca (Oaxaca) and Guerrero, as the most southern of what he terms the Nahua people, including and lying westerly of the Isthmus of Tehuantepec, and he speaks of it as a region but little known to travellers, except as they pass through a part of it lying on the commercial route from Acapulco to the capital city of Mexico. Bancroft's summary, with his references, must suffice for the inquirer for all except the principal group of ruins in this region, that of Mitla (or Lyó-Baa), of which a full recapitulation of authorities may be made, most of which are also to be referred to for the lesser ruins, though, as Bancroft points out, the information respecting Monte Alban and Zachila is far from satisfactory. Of Monte Alban, Dupaix and Charnay are the most important witnesses, and the latter says that he considers Monte Alban "one of the most precious remains, and very surely the most ancient of the American civilizations." [1] On Dupaix alone we must depend for what we know of Zachila.

GENERAL PLAN OF MITLA.*

It is, however, of Mitla (sometime Miquitlan, Mictlan) that more considerable mention must be made, and its ruins, about thirty miles southerly from Mexico, have been oftenest visited, as they deserve to be; and we have to regret that Stephens never took them within the range of his observations. Their demolition had begun during a century or two previous to the Spanish Conquest, and was not complete even then. Nature is gloomy, and even repulsive in its desolation about the ruins; [2] but a small village still exists among them. The place is mentioned by Duran [3] as inhabited about 1450; Motolinía describes it as still lived in,[4] and in 1565-74 it had a gobernador of its own. Burgoa speaks of it in 1644.[5]

The earliest of the modern explorers were Luis Martin, a Mexican architect, and Colonel de la Laguna, who examined the ruins in 1802; and it was from Martin and his drawings that Humboldt drew the information with which, in 1810, he first engaged the attention of the general public upon Mitla, in his *Vues des Cordillères*. Dupaix's visit was in 1806. The architect Eduard L. Mühlenpfordt, in his *Versuch einer getreuen Schilderung der Republik Mejico* (Hannover, 1844, in 2 vols.), says that he made plans and drawings in 1830,[6] which, passing into the hands of Juan B. Carriedo, were used by him to illustrate a paper, "Los palacios antiguos de Mitla," in the *Ilustracion Mexicana* (vol. ii.), in which he set forth the condition of the ruins in 1852. Meanwhile, in 1837, some drawings had been made, which were twenty years later reproduced in the ninth volume of the *Smithsonian Contributions to Knowledge*, as Brantz Mayer's *Observations on Mexican history and archæology, with a special notice of Zapotec, remains as delineated in Mr. J. G. Sawkins's drawings of Mitla, etc.* (Washington, 1857). Bancroft points out (iv. 406) that the inaccuracies and impossibilities of Sawkins' drawings are such as to lead to the conclusion that he pretended to explorations which he never made, and probably drafted his views from some indefinite information; and that Mayer was deceived, having no more precise statements than Humboldt's by which to test the drawings. Matthieu Fossey visited the ruins in 1838; but his account in his *Le Mexique* (Paris, 1857) is found by Bancroft to be mainly a borrowed one. G. F. von Tempsky's *Mitla, a narrative of incidents and personal adventure on a journey in Mexico, Guatemala and Salvador, 1853-1855, edited by J. S. Bell* (London, 1858), deceives us by the title into supposing that considerable attention is given in the book to Mitla, but we find him spending but a part of a day there in February, 1854 (p. 250). The book is not prized; Bandelier calls it of small scientific value, and Bancroft says his plates must have been made up from other sources than his own observations.[7] Charnay, here, as well as elsewhere, made for us some important photographs in 1859.[8] This kind of illustration received new accessions of value when Emilio Herbrüger issued a

[1] Cf. Bandelier, p. 320.

[2] Bandelier, p. 276.

[3] Ramirez, ed. 1867.

[4] His brief account is copied by Mendieta and Torquemada, and is cited in Bandelier, p. 324.

[5] *Geog. Descripcion*, ii. cited in Bandelier, 324. Cf. *Soc. Mex. Geog. Boletin*, vii. 170.

[6] Bandelier says (p. 279) that he saw them in the library of the Institute of Oaxaca, and that, though admirable, they have a certain tendency to over-restoration, — the besetting sin of all explorers who make drawings.

[7] Cf. Field, no. 1612.

[8] *Ruines*, etc., 261, and Viollet le Duc, p. 74; *Anciens Villes*, ch. 24.

* After Bandelier's sketch (*Archæological Tour*, p. 276). Key: A, the ruins on the highest ground, with a church and curacy built into the walls. B, C, E, are ruins outside the village. D is within the modern village. F is beyond the river.

series of thirty-four fine plates as *Album de Vistas fotográficas de las Antiguas Ruinas de los palacios de Mitla* (Oaxaca, 1874). In 1864, J. W. von Müller, in his *Reisen in den Vereinigten Staaten, Canada und Mexico* (Leipzig, in 3 vols.), included an account of a visit.[1] The most careful examination made since Bancroft summarized existing knowledge is that of Bandelier in his *Archæological Tour in Mexico in 1881* (Boston, 1885), published as no. ii. of the American series of the *Papers of the Archæological Institute of America*, which is illustrated with heliotypes and sketch plans of the ruins and architectural details in all their geometrical symmetry. Bancroft (iv. 392, etc.) could only give a plan of the ruins based on the sketches of Mühlenpfordt as published by Carriedo, but the student will find a more careful one[2] in Bandelier, who also gives detailed ones of the several buildings (pl. xvii., xviii.)

There is no part of Spanish America richer in architectural remains than the northern section of Yucatan, and Bancroft (iv. ch. 5) has occasion to enumerate and to describe with more or less fullness between fifty and sixty independent groups of ruins.[3] Stephens explored forty-four of these abandoned towns, and such was the native ignorance that of only a few of them could anything be learned in Merida. And yet that this

SACRIFICIAL STONE.*

[1] There is a *Rapport sur les ruines*, by Doutrelaine, in the *Archives de la Commission Scientifique du Mexique* (vol. iii.); Nadaillac (p. 364) and Short (p. 361) have epitomized results, and Louis H. Aymé gives some *Notes on Mitla* in the *Amer. Antiq. Soc. Proc.*, April, 1882, p. 82; Bancroft (iv. 391) enumerates various second-hand descriptions.

[2] I do not understand Bandelier's statement (p. 277) that it is taken from Bancroft's plan, which it only resembles in a general way.

[3] Bancroft classifies their architectural peculiarities (iv. pp. 267-279).

* After a photograph in Bandelier's *Archæological Tour*, p. 67. See on another page, cut of the court-yard of the Museum, where this stone is preserved. Cf. Humboldt, pl. xxi.; Bandelier in *Amer. Antiq.*, 1878; Bancroft, iv. 509; Stevens's *Flint Chips*, 311. There is a discussion of the stone in Orozco y Berra's *El Cuauhxicalli de Tizoc*, in the *Anales del Museo Nacional*, i. no. 1; ii. no. 1. On the sacrificial stone of San Juan Teotihuacan, see paper by Amos W. Butler in the *Amer. Antiq.*, vii. 148. A cut in Clavigero (ii.) shows how the stone was used in sacrifices; the engraving has been often copied. In Mrs. Nuttall's view this stone simply records the periodical tribute days (*Am. Ass. Adv. Sci. Proc.*, Aug. 1886).

country was the land of a peculiar architecture was known to the earliest explorers. Francisco Hernandez de Cordova in 1517, Juan de Grijalva in 1518, Cortés himself in 1519, and Francisco de Montejo in 1527 observed the ruins in Cozumel, an island off the northwest coast of the peninsula, and at other points of the shore.[1] It is only, however, within the present century that we have had any critical notices. Rio heard reports of them merely. Lorenzo de Zavala saw only Uxmal, as his account given in Dupaix shows. The earliest detailed descriptions were those of Waldeck in his *Voyage pittoresque et archéologique dans la province d'Yucatan* (Paris, 1838, folio, with steel plates and lithographs), but he also saw little more than the ruins of Uxmal, in the expedition in which he had received pecuniary support from Lord Kingsborough.[2] It is to John L. Stephens and his accompanying draughtsman, Frederic Catherwood, that we owe by far the most essential part of our knowledge of the Yucatan remains. He had begun a survey of Uxmal in 1840, but had made little progress when the illness of his artist broke up his plans. Accordingly he gave the world but partial results in his *Incidents of Travel in Central America*. Not satisfied with his imperfect examination, he returned to Yucatan in 1841, and in 1843 published at New York the book which has become the main source of information for all compilers ever since, his *Incidents of Travel in Yucatan* (N. Y., 1842; London, 1843; again, N. Y., 1856, 1858). It was in the early days of the Daguerrean process, and Catherwood took with him a camera, from which his excellent drawings derive some of their fidelity. They appeared in his own *Views of Ancient Monuments in Central America* (N. Y., 1844), on a larger scale than in Stephens's smaller pages.

WALDECK.*

Stephens's earlier book had had an almost immediate success. The reviewers were unanimous in commendation, as they might well be.[3] It has been asserted that it was in order to avail of this new interest that a resident of New Orleans, Mr. B. M. Norman, hastened to Yucatan, while Stephens was there a second time, and during the winter of 1841–42 made the trip among the ruins, which is recorded in his *Rambles in Yucatan, or Notes of Travel through the peninsula, including a Visit to the Remarkable Ruins of Chi-chen, Kabah Zayi, and Uxmal* (New York, 1843).[4]

The Daguerrean camera was also used by the Baron von Friederichsthal in his studies at Uxmal and Chichen-Itza, and his exploration seems to have taken place between the two visits of Stephens, as Bancroft determines from a letter (April 21, 1841) written after the baron had started on his return voyage to Europe.[5] In Paris, in October, 1841, under the introduction of Humboldt, Friederichsthal addressed the Academy, and his paper was printed in the *Nouvelles Annales des Voyages* (xcii. 297) as "Les Monuments de l'Yucatan."[6] The camera was not, however, brought to the aid of the student with the most satisfactory results till Charnay, in 1858, visited Izamal, Chichen-Itza, and Uxmal. He gave a foretaste of his results in the *Bulletin de la Soc. de Géog.* (1861, vol. ii. 364), and in 1863 gave not very extended descriptions, relying mostly on his *Atlas* of photographs in his *Cités et Ruines Américaines*, a part of which volume consists of the architectural speculations of Viollet le Duc. Beside the farther studies of Charnay in his *Anciens Villes du Nouveau Monde* (Paris, 1885), there have been recent explorations in Yucatan by Dr. Augustus Le Plongeon and his wife, mainly at Chichen-Itza, in which for a while he had the aid and countenance of Mr. Stephen Salisbury, Jr.,[7] of Worcester, Mass. Le Plongeon's results are decidedly novel and helpful, but they were

[1] See Vol. II. ch. 3. Bancroft (ii. p. 784) collates the early accounts of the habitations of the people, and (iv. 254, 260, 261) the descriptions of the ruins and statelier edifices, as seen by these explorers.

[2] *For. Q. Rev.*, xviii. 251.

[3] Cf. *Poole's Index*, p. 1439.

[4] Bancroft, iv. 145; Field, no. 1138; Leclerc, no. 1217; Pilling, p. 2767; *Dem. Review*, xi. 529. Cf. *Poole's Index*, p. 1439.

[5] *Registro Yucateco*, ii. 437; *Diccionario Universal* (México, 1853), x. 290.

[6] Bandelier, *Am. Antiq. Soc. Proc.*, n. s., i. 92, calls the paper "not very valuable."

[7] This gentleman, since the death of his father, of the same name, succeeded, after an interval, the elder antiquary in the president's chair of the American Antiquarian Society.

* After an etching published in the *Annuaire de la Soc. Amér. de France*. Cf. *Amer. Antiq. Soc. Proc.*, October, 1875.

expressed with more license of explication than satisfied the committee of that society, when his papers were referred to them for publication, and than has proved acceptable to other examiners.[1] Nearly all other descriptions of the Yucatan ruins have been derived substantially from these chief authorities.[2]

DÉSIRÉ CHARNAY.*

[1] Cf. Short, p. 396. Le Plongeon retorts (*Amer. Antiq. Soc. Proc.*, n. s., i. 282) by telling his critic that he had never been in Yucatan. Considering the effect of contact in many of those who have written of the ruins, it may be a question if the implication is valuable as a piece of criticism. Mr. Salisbury and Dr. Le Plongeon reported from time to time in the *Amer. Antiq. Soc. Proc.* the results of the latter's investigations, and the researches to which they gave rise. Those in April, 1876, and April, 1877, of these *Proceedings*, were privately printed by Mr. Salisbury, as *The Mayas*, etc. In April, 1878, Mr. Salisbury reported upon the "Terra-cotta figures from Isla Mujeres." In Oct., 1878, there were communications from Dr. Le Plongeon, and from Alice D. Le Plongeon, his wife. In April, 1879, Dr. Le Plongeon communicated a letter on the affinities of Central America and the East. Since this the Le Plongeons have found other channels of communication. Dr. Le Plongeon expanded his somewhat extravagant notions of Oriental affinities in his *Sacred mysteries among the Mayas and the Quiches, 11,500 years ago; their relation to the sacred mysteries of Egypt, Greece, Chaldea, and India. Freemasonry in times anterior to the temple of Solomon* (New York, 1886).

His preface is largely made up with a rehearsal of his rebuffs and in complaints of the want of public appreciation of his labors. He is, however, as confident as ever, and deciphers the bas-reliefs and mural inscriptions of Chichen-Itza by "the ancient hieratic Maya alphabet" which he claims to have discovered, and shows this alphabet in parallel columns with that of Egypt as displayed by Champollion and Bunsen. Mrs. Le Plongeon published her *Vestiges of the Mayas* in New York, in 1881, and gathered some of her periodical writings in her *Here and There in Yucatan* (N. Y., 1886). Cf. her letter on the ancient records of Yucatan in *The Nation*, xxix. 224.

[2] Baldwin (p. 125), in a condensed way, and likewise Short (ch. 8) and Bancroft (iv. ch. 5), more at length, have mainly depended on Stephens. Cf. references in Bancroft, iv. 147, and Bandelier's list in the *Amer. Antiq. Soc. Proc.*, n. s., i. 82, 95. E. H. Thompson has contributed papers in *Ibid.* Oct., 1886, p. 248, and April, 1887, p. 379, and on the ruins of Kich-Moo and Chun-Kal-Cin in April,

* Reproduced from an engraving in the London edition, 1887, of the English translation of his *Ancient Cities of the New World*.

The principal ruins of Yucatan are those of Uxmal and Chichen-Itza, and references to the literature of each will suffice. Those at Uxmal are in some respects distinct in character from the remains of Honduras and of Chiapas. There are no idols as at Copan. There are no extensive stucco-work and no tablets as at Palenqué. The general type is Cyclopean masonry, faced with dressed stones. The Casa de Monjas, or nunnery (so called), is often considered the most remarkable ruin in Central America; and no architectural

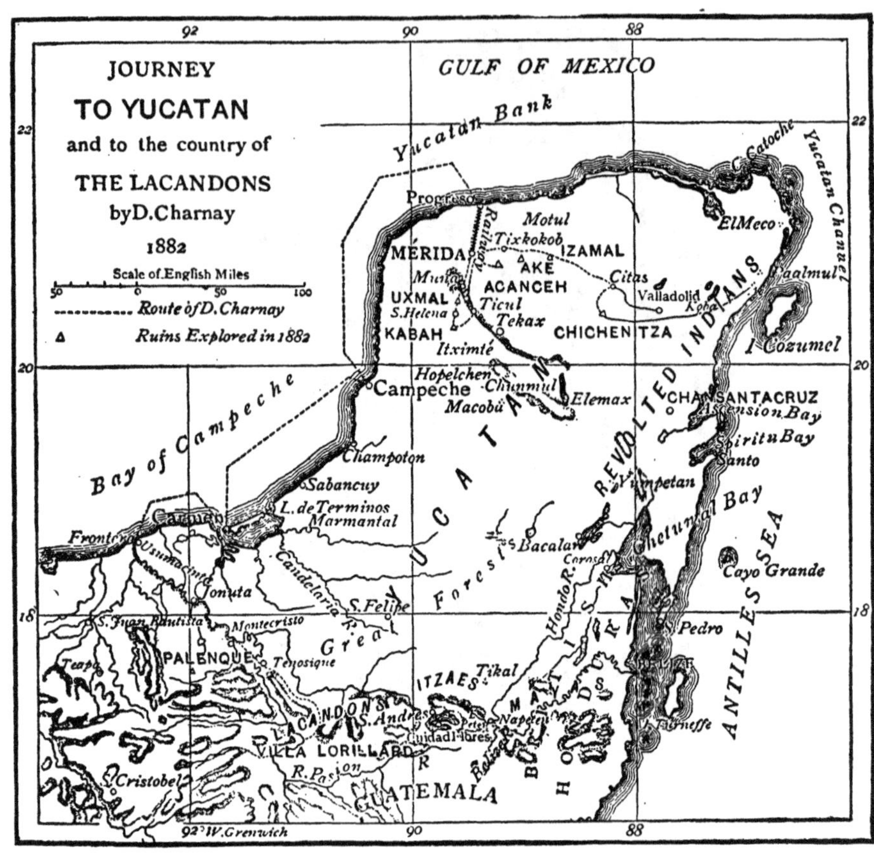

FROM CHARNAY.*

1888, p. 162. Brasseur, beside his *Hist. Nat. Civ.*, ii. 20, has something in his introduction to his *Relation de Landa*.

The description of the ruins at Zayi, which Stephens gives, shows that some of the rooms were filled solid with masonry, and he leaves it as an unaccountable fact; but Morgan (*Houses and House Life*, p. 267) thinks it shows that the builders constructed a core of masonry, over which they reared the walls and ceilings, which last, after hardening, were able to support themselves, when the cores were removed; and that in the ruins at Zayi we see the cores unremoved.

* Also in the *Bull. Soc. de Géog. de Paris*, 1882 (p. 542). The best large (36×28 in.) topographical and historical map of Yucatan, showing the site of ruins, is that of Huebbe and Azuar, 1878. The *Plano de Yucatan*, of Santiago Nigra de San Martin, also showing the ruins, 1848, is reduced in Stephen Salisbury's *Mayas* (Worcester, 1877), or in the *Amer. Antiq. Soc. Proc.*, April, 1876, and April, 1877. V. A. Malte-Brun's map, likewise marking the ruins, is in Brasseur de Bourbourg's *Palenqué* (1866). There are maps in C. G. Fancourt's *Hist. Yucatan* (London, 1854); Dupaix's *Antiquités Mexicaines*; Waldeck's *Voyage dans la Yucatan* (his MS. map was used by Malte-Brun). Cf. the map of Yucatan and Chiapas, in Brasseur and Waldeck's *Monuments Anciens du Mexique* (1866). Perhaps the most convenient map to use in the study of Maya antiquities is that in Bancroft's *Nat. Races*, iv. Cf. Crescentio Carrillo's "Geografía Maya" in the *Anales del Museo nacional de México*, ii. 435.

The map in Stephens's *Yucatan*, vol. i., shows his route among the ruins, but does not pretend to be accurate for regions off his course.

The *Journal of the Royal Geog. Soc.*, vol. xi., has a map showing the ruins in Central America.

The best map to show at a glance the location of the ruins in the larger field of Spanish America is in Bancroft's *Nat. Races*, iv.

feature of any of them has been the subject of more inquiry than the protuberant ornaments in the cornices, which are usually called elephants' trunks.[1] It has been contended that the place was inhabited in the days of Cortes.[2]

The earliest printed account of Uxmal is in Cogolludo's *Yucathan* (Madrid, 1688), pp. 176, 193, 197; but it was well into this century before others were written. Lorenzo de Zavala gave but an outline account in his *Notice*, printed in Dupaix in 1834. Waldeck (*Voyage Pitt.* 67, 93) spent eight days there in May, 1835, and Stephens gives him the credit of being the earliest describer to attract attention. Stephens's first visit in 1840 was hasty (*Cent. Amer.*, ii. 413), but on his second visit (1842) he took with him Waldeck's *Voyage*, and his

RUINED TEMPLE AT UXMAL.*

description and the drawings of Catherwood were made with the advantage of having these earlier drawings to compare. Stephens (*Yucatan*, i. 297) says that their plans and drawings differ materially from Waldeck's; but Bancroft, who compares the two, says that Stephens exaggerated the differences, which are not material, except in a few plates (Stephens's *Yucatan*, i. 163; ii. 264—ch. 24, 25). About the same time Norman and Friederichsthal made their visits. Bancroft (iv. 150) refers to the lesser narratives of Carillo (1845), and another, recorded in the *Registro Yucateco* (i. 273, 361), with Carl Bartholomæus Heller (April, 1847) in his *Reisen in Mexico* (Leipzig, 1853). Charnay's *Ruines* (p. 362), and his *Anciens Villes* (ch. 19, 20), record visits in 1858 and later. Brasseur reported upon Uxmal in 1865 in the *Archives de la Com. Scientifique du Méxique* (ii. 234, 254), and he had already made mention of them in his *Hist. Nations Civ.*, ii. ch. 1.[3]

[1] Cf. the *pros* and *cons* in Waldeck and Charnay. Waldeck first named the ornaments as "Elephants' trunks" (*Voy. Pitt.* p. 74). There are cuts in Stephens, reproduced in Bancroft. There is also a cut in Norman. Cf. E. H. Thompson in *Amer. Antiq. Soc. Proc.*, April, 1887, p. 382.

[2] Stephens, *Yucatan*, ii. 265, gives an ancient Indian map (1557), and extracts from the archives of Mani, which lead him to infer that at that time it was an inhabited Indian town.

[3] Bancroft (iv. 151) gives various references to second-

* After a cut in Ruge's *Gesch. des Zeitalters der Entdeckungen*, p. 357.

The ruins of Chichen-Itza make part of the eastern group of the Yucatan remains. As was not the case with some of the other principal ruins, the city in its prime has a record in Maya tradition; it was known in the days of the Conquest, and has not been lost sight of since,[1] though its ruins were not visited by explorers till well within the present century, the first of whom, according to Stephens, was John Burke, in 1838. Stephens had heard of them and mentioned them to Friederichsthal, who was there in 1840 (*Nouv. Annales des Voyages*, xcii. 300–306). Norman was there in February, 1842 (*Rambles*, 104), and did not seem aware that any one had been there before him; and Stephens himself, during the next month (*Yucatan*, ii. 282), made the best record which we have. Charnay made his observations in 1858 (*Ruines*, 339, — cf. *Anciens Villes*, ch. 18), and gives us nine good photographs. The latest discoverer is Le Plongeon, whose investigations were signalized by the finding (1876) of the statue of Chackmool, and by other notable researches (*Am. Antiq. Soc. Proc.*, April, 1877; October, 1878).[2]

FROM CHICHEN-ITZA.*

FROM CHICHEN-ITZA.†

It seems hardly to admit of doubt that the cities — if that be their proper designation — of Yucatan were the work of the Maya people, whose descendants were found by the Spaniards in possession of the peninsula, and that in some cases, like those of Uxmal and Toloom, their sacred edifices did not cease to be used till some time after the Spaniards had possessed the country. Such were the conclusions of Stephens,[3] the sanest mind that has spent its action upon these remains; and he tells us that a deed of the region where Uxmal is situated, which passed in 1673, mentions the daily religious rites which the natives were then celebrating there, and speaks of the swinging doors and cisterns then in use. The abandonment of one of the buildings, at least, is brought down to within about two centuries, and comparisons of Catherwood's drawings with the descriptions of more recent explorers, by showing a very marked deterioration within a comparatively few years, enable us easily to understand how the piercing roots of a rapidly growing vegetation can make a greater havoc

hand descriptions, noted before 1875, to which may be added those in Short, p. 347; Nadaillac, 334; *Amer. Antiquarian*, vii. 257, and again, July, 1888.

Probably the most accurate of the plans of the ruins is that of Stephens (*Yucatan*, i. 165), which is followed by Bancroft (iv. 153). Brasseur's report has a plan, and others, all differing, are given by Waldeck (pl. viii.), Norman (p. 155), and Charnay (*Ruines*, p. 62). Views and cuts of details are found in Waldeck, Stephens, Charnay, — whence later summarizers like Bancroft, Baldwin, and Short have drawn their copies; while special cuts are copied in Armin (*Das Heutige Mexico*); Larenaudière (*Mexique et Guatemala*, Paris, 1847); Le Plongeon (*Sacred Mysteries*); Ruge (*Zeitalter der Entdeckungen*, p. 357); Morgan (*Houses*, etc., ch. xi.), and in various others. One can best trace the varieties and contrasts of the different accounts of the various edifices in Bancroft's collations of their statements. His constant citation, even to scorn them, of the impertinencies of George Jones's *Hist. of Anc. America* (London, 1842), — the later notorious Count Johannes, — was hardly worth while.

[1] Landa described the ruins. *Relation*, p. 340.

[2] All other accounts are based on these. Bancroft, who gives the best summary (iv. 221), enumerates many of the second-hand writers, to whom Short (p. 396) must be added. Stephens gives a plan (ii. 290) which Bancroft (iv. 222) follows; and it apparently is worthy of reasonable confidence, which cannot be said of Norman's. The ruins present some features not found in others, and the most interesting of such may be considered the wall paintings, one representing a boat with occupants, which Stephens found on the walls of the building called by him the Gymnasium, because of stone rings projecting from the walls (see annexed cut), which were supposed by him to have been used in ball games. Norman calls the same building the Temple; Charnay, the Cirque; but the native designation is Iglesia.

[3] *Yucatan*, i. 94. Cf. Bancroft, *Native Races*, ii. 117; v. 164, 342.

* After a cut in Squier's *Serpent Symbol*. There are two of these rings in the walls of one of the buildings twenty or thirty feet from the ground. They are four feet in diameter. Cf. Stephens's *Yucatan*, ii. 304; Bancroft, iv. 230.

† A bas-relief, one of the best preserved at Chichen-Itza, after a sketch in Charnay and Viollet-le-Duc's *Cités et Ruines Américaines* (Paris, 1863), p. 53, of which Viollet-le-Duc says: "Le profil du guerrier se rapproche sensiblement les types du Nord de l'Europe."

in a century than will occur in temperate climates. The preservation of paint on the walls, and of wooden lintels in some places, also induce a belief that no great time, such as would imply an extinct race of builders, is necessary to account for the present condition of the ruins, and we must always remember how the Spaniards used them as quarries for building their neighboring towns. How long these habitations and shrines stood in their perfection is a question about which archæologists have had many and diverse estimates, ranging from hundreds to thousands of years. There is nothing in the ruins themselves to settle the question, beyond a study of their construction. So far as the traditionary history of the Mayas can determine, some of them may have been built between the third and the tenth century.[1]

We come now to Chiapas. The age of the ruins of Palenqué[2] can only be conjectured, and very indefinitely, though perhaps there is not much risk in saying that they represent some of the oldest architectural structures known in the New World, and were very likely abandoned three or four centuries before the coming of the Spaniards. Still, any confident statement is unwise. Perhaps there may be some fitness in Brasseur's belief that the stucco additions and roofs were the work of a later people than those who laid the foundations.[3] Bancroft (iv. 289) has given the fullest account of the literature describing these ruins. They seem to have been first found in 1750, or a few years before. The report reaching Ramon de Ordoñez, then a boy, was not forgotten by him, and prompted him to send his brother in 1773 to explore them. Among the manuscripts in the Brasseur Collection (*Bib. Mex.-Guat.*, p. 113; Pinart, no. 695) are a *Memoria relativa à las ruinas . . . de Palenqué*, and *Notas de Chiapas y Palenqué*, which are supposed to be the record of this exploration written by Ramon, as copied from the original in the Museo Nacional, and which, in part at least, constituted the report which Ramon made in 1784 to the president of the Audiencia Real. Ramon's view was that he had hit upon the land of Ophir, and the country visited by the Phœnicians. This same president now directed José Antonio Calderon to visit the ruins, and we have his "Informe" translated in Brasseur's *Palenqué* (introd. p. 5). From February to June of 1785, Antonio Benasconi, the royal architect of Guatemala, inspected the ruins under similar orders. His report, as well as the preceding one, with the accompanying drawings, were dispatched to Spain, where J. B. Muñoz made a summary of them for the king. I do not find any of them have been printed. The result of the royal interest in the matter was, that Antonio del Rio was next commissioned to make a more thorough survey, which he accomplished (May–June, 1787) with the aid of a band of natives to fell the trees and fire the rubbish. He broke through the walls in a reckless way, that added greatly to the devastation of years. Rio's report, dated at Palenqué June 24, 1787, was published first in 1855, in the *Diccionario Univ. de Geog.*, viii. 528.[4] Meanwhile, beside the copy of the manuscript sent to Spain, other manuscripts were kept in Guatemala and Mexico; and one of these falling into the hands of a Dr. M'Quy, was taken to England and translated under the title *Description of the Ruins of an Ancient City discovered near Palenque in Guatemala, Spanish America, translated from the Original MS. Report of Capt. Don A. Del Rio; followed by Teatro Critico Americano, or a Critical Investigation and Research into the History of the Americans, by Doctor Felix Cabrera* (London, 1822).[5]

[1] Bancroft collates the views of different writers (iv. 285). He himself holds that these buildings are more ancient than those of Anáhuac; consequently he rejects the arguments of Stephens, that it was by the Toltecs, after they migrated south from Anáhuac, that these constructions were raised (*Native Races*, v. 165, and for references, p. 169). Charnay (*Bull. de la Soc. de Géog.*, Nov., 1881) believes they were erected between the twelfth and fourteenth centuries.

It is well known now that the concentric rings are a useless guide in tropical regions to determine the age of trees, though in the past, the immense size of trees as well as the deposition of soil have been used to determine the supposed ages of ruins. Waldeck counted a ring a year in getting two thousand years for the time since the abandonment of Palenqué; but Charnay (Eng. tr. *Ancient Cities*, p. 260) says that these rings are often formed monthly. Cf. Nadaillac, p. 323.

[2] So called because near a modern village of that name, founded by the Spaniards about 1564. Bancroft (iv. 296) says the ruins are ordinarily called by the natives Casas de Piedra. Ordoñez calls them Nachan, but without giving any authority, and some adopt the Aztec equivalent Culhuacan, city of the serpents. Because Xibalba is held by some to be the name of the great city of this region in the shadowy days of Votan, that name has also been applied to the ruins. Otolum, or the ruined place, is a common designation thereabouts, but Palenqué is the appellation in use by most travellers and writers.

[3] The fact is, that widely distinct estimates have been held, some dating them back into the remotest antiquity, and others making them later than the Conquest. Bancroft (iv. 362) collates these statements. Cf. Dr. Earl Flint in *Amer. Antiquarian*, iv. 289. Morelet identifies them with the Toltec remains, supposing them to be the work of that people after their emigration, and to be of about the same age as Mitla. Charnay (*Anc. Cities of the New World*, p. 260) claims that Cortes knew the place as the religious metropolis of the Acaltecs. On the question of Cortes' knowledge see *Science*, Feb. 27, 1885, p. 171; and *Ibid.* (by Brinton) March 27, 1885, p. 248.

[4] The original is in the Roy. Acad. of Hist. at Madrid (Brasseur, *Bib. Mex.-Guat.*, p. 125), and is called *Descripcion del terreno publacion antigua.*

[5] Field, no. 231; Sabin, xvii. p. 292. The report of Rio was brief, and as we would judge now, superficial. Dupaix treats him disparagingly. The appended essay by Cabrera, an Italian, is said to have been largely filched from Ramon's paper, which had been confidentially placed in his hands (Short, 207). A Spanish text of Cabrera is in the Museo Nacional. Cf. Brasseur (*Bib. Mex.-Guat.*), p. 30; Pinart, no. 186. It is a question if the plates, which constituted the most interesting part of the English book, be Rio's after all; for though they profess to be engraved after his drawings, they are suspiciously like those made by Castañeda, twenty years after Rio's visit (Bancroft, iv. 290). David B. Warden translated Rio's report in the *Recueil de voyages et de Mémoires, par la Soc. de la Géog. de Paris* (vol. ii.), and gave some of the plates. (Cf. Warden's *Recherches sur les antiquités de l'Amérique Septentrionale*, Paris, 1827, in *Mém. de la Soc. de Géog.*) There is a German version, *Beschreibung einer alten Stadt* (Berlin, 1832), by J. H. von Minutoli, which is provided with an introductory essay.

The results of the explorations of Dupaix, made early in the present century by order of Carlos IV. of Spain, long remained unpublished. His report and the drawings of Castañeda lay uncared for in the Mexican archives during the period of the Revolution. Latour Allard, of Paris, obtained copies of some of the drawings, and from these Kingsborough got copies, which he engraved for his *Mexican Antiquities*, in which Dupaix's report was also printed in Spanish and English (vols. iv., v., vi.). It is not quite certain whether the originals or copies were delivered (1828) by the Mexican authorities to Baradère, who a few years later secured their publication with additional matter as *Antiquités méxicaines. Relation des trois expéditions du capitaine*

A RESTORATION BY VIOLLET-LE-DUC.*

Dupaix, ordonnées en 1805, 1806 et 1807, pour la recherche des antiquités du pays, notamment celles de Mitla et de Palenque ; accompagnée des dessins de Castañeda, et d'une carte du pays exploré ; suivie d'un parallèle de ces monuments avec ceux de l'Égypte, de l'Indostan, et du reste de l'ancien monde par Alexandre Lenoir ; d'une dissertation sur l'origine de l'ancienne population des deux Amériques par [*D. B.*] *Warden ; avec un discours préliminaire par M. Charles Farcy, et des notes explicatives, et autres documents par MM. Baradère, de St. Priest* [*etc.*]. (Paris: 1834, texte et atlas.)[1] The plates of this edition

[1] Sabin, x. 209, 213. Cf. *Annales de Philos. Chrétienne*, xi.

* From *Histoire de l'Habitation Humaine, par Viollet-le-Duc* (Paris, 1875). There is a restoration of the Palenqué palace — so called — in Armin's *Das heutige Mexico* (copied in Short, 342, and Bancroft, iv. 323).

are superior to those in Kingsborough and in Rio; and are indeed improved in the engraving over Castañeda's drawings. The book as a whole is one of the most important on Palenqué which we have. The investigations were made on his third expedition (1807–8). A tablet taken from the ruins by him is in the Museo Nacional, and a cast of it is figured in the *Numis. and Antiq. Soc. of Philad. Proc.*, Dec. 4, 1884.

During the twenty-five years next following Dupaix, we find two correspondents of the French and English Geographical Societies supplying their publications with occasional accounts of their observations among the ruins. One of them, Dr. F. Corroy,[1] was then living at Tabasco; the other, Col. Juan Gallindo,[2] was resident in the country as an administrative officer.

SCULPTURES, TEMPLE OF THE CROSS, PALENQUÉ.*

[1] *Bull. de la Soc. de Géog. de Paris*, ix. (1828) 198. Dupaix, i. 2d div. 76.

[2] "Palenque et autres lieux circonvoisins," in Dupaix, i. 2d div. 67 (in English in *Literary Gazette*, London, 1831, no. 769, and in *Lond. Geog. Soc. Journal*, iii. 60). Cf. *Bull. de la Soc. de Géog. de Paris*, 1832. He is over-enthusiastic, as Bandelier thinks (*Amer. Ant. Soc. Proc.*, n. s., i. p. 111).

* These slabs, six feet high, were taken from Palenqué, and when Stephens saw them they were in private hands at San Domingo, near by, but later they were placed in the church front in the same town, and here Charnay took impressions of them, from which they were engraved in *The Ancient Cities*, etc., p. 217, and copied thence in the above cuts. This same type of head is considered by Rosny the Aztec head of Palenqué (*Doc. écrits de la Antiq. Amer.*, 73), and as belonging to the superior classes. In order to secure the convex curve of the nose and forehead an ornament was sometimes added, as shown in a head of the second tablet at Palenqué, and in the photograph of a bas-relief, preserved in the Museo Archeogico at Madrid, given by Rosny (vol. 3), and hypothetically called by him a statue of Cuculkan. This ornament is not infrequently seen in other images of this region.

Bandelier (*Peabody Mus. Repts.*, ii. 126), speaking of the tablet of the Cross of Palenqué, says: "These tablets and figures show in dress such a striking analogy of what we know of the military accoutrements of the Mexicans, that it is a strong approach to identity."

Fréderic de Waldeck, the artist who some years before had familiarized himself with the character of the ruins in the preparation of the engravings for Rio's work, was employed in 1832–34. He was now considerably over sixty years of age, and under the pay of a committee, which had raised a subscription, in which the Mexican government shared. He made the most thorough examination of Palenqué which has yet been made. Waldeck was a skilful artist, and his drawings are exquisite; but he was not free from a tendency to improve or restore, where the conditions gave a hint, and so as we have them in the final publication they have not been accepted as wholly trustworthy. He made more than 200 drawings, and either the originals or copies — Stephens says "copies," the originals being confiscated — were taken to Europe. Waldeck announced his book in Paris, and the public had already had a taste of his not very sober views in some communications which he had sent in Aug. and Nov., 1832, to the Société de Géographie de Paris. Long years of delay followed, and Waldeck had lived to be over ninety, when the French government bought his collection [1] (in 1860), and made preparations for its publication. Out of the 188 drawings thus secured, 56 were selected and were

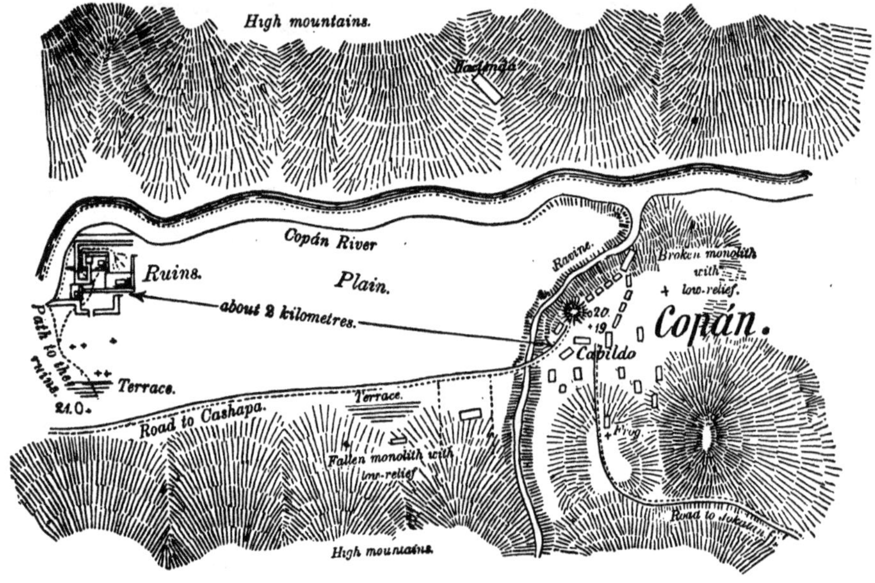

PLAN OF COPAN (RUINS AND VILLAGE).*

admirably engraved, and only that portion of Waldeck's text was preserved which was purely descriptive, and not all of that. Selection was made of Brasseur de Bourbourg, who at that time had never visited the ruins,[2] to furnish some introductory matter. This he prepared in an *Avant-propos*, recapitulating the progress of such studies; and this was followed by an *Introduction aux Ruines de Palenqué*, narrating the course of explorations up to that time; a section also published separately as *Recherches sur les Ruines de Palenqué et sur les origines de la civilisation du Méxique* (Paris, 1886), and finally Waldeck's own *Description des Ruines*, followed by the plates, most of which relate to Palenqué. Thus composed, a large volume was published under the general title of *Monuments anciens du Méxique. Palenqué et autres ruines de l'ancienne civilisation du Méxique. Collection de vues* [*etc.*], *cartes et plans dessinés d'après nature et relevés par M. de Waldeck. Texte rédigé par M. Brasseur de Bou¬bourg*. (Paris, 1864–1866.) [3] While Waldeck's results were still unpublished the ruins of Palenqué were brought most effectively to the attention of the English reader in the *Travels in Central America* (vol. ii. ch. 17) of Stephens, which was illustrated by the drawings of Catherwood,[4] since famous. These better cover the field, and are more exact than those of Dupaix.

Bancroft refers to an anonymous account in the *Registro Yucateco* (i. 318). One of the most intelligent of the later travellers is Arthur Morelet, who privately printed his *Voyage dans l'Amérique Central, Cuba et le Yucatan*, which includes an account of a fortnight's stay at Palenqué. His results would be difficult of access

[1] The report by Angrand, which induced this purchase, is in the work as published.

[2] He had described them in his *Hist. Nat. Civ.*, i. ch. 3.

[3] The book usually sells for about 150 francs.

[4] Given, also enlarged, in the folio known as Catherwood's *Views*.

* From *The Stone Sculptures of Copán and Quiriguá* (N. Y., 1883) of Meye and Schmidt.

except that Mrs. M. F. Squier, with an introduction by E. G. Squier, published a translation of that part of it relating to the main land as *Travels in Central America, including accounts of regions unexplored since the Conquest* (N. Y., 1871).[1]

Désiré Charnay was the first to bring photography to the aid of the student when he visited Palenqué in 1858, and his plates forming the folio atlas accompanying his *Cités et Ruines Américaines* (1863), pp. 72, 411, are, as Bancroft (iv. 293) points out, of interest to enable us to test the drawings of preceding delineators, and to show how time had acted on the ruins since the visit of Stephens. His later results are recorded in his *Les anciennes villes du Nouveau Monde* (Paris, 1885).[2]

YUCATAN TYPES.*

[1] The German version was made from this (Jena, 1872).

[2] Particularly ch. 13, 14. Charnay is the last of the explorers of Palenqué. All the other accounts of the ruins found here and there are based on the descriptions of those who have been named, or at least nothing is added of material value by other actual visitors like Norman (*Rambles in Yucatan*, p. 284). Bancroft (iv. 294) enumerates a number of such second-hand describers. The most important work since Bancroft's summary is Manuel Larrainzar's *Estudios sobre la historia de America, sus ruinas y antigüedades, y sobre el origen de sus habitantes* (Mexico, 1875–78), in five vols., all of whose plates are illustrations from the ruins of Palenqué, which are described and compared with other ancient remains throughout the world. Cf. Brühl, *Culturvölker d. alt. Amerikas.* Plans of the ruins will be found in Waldeck (pl. vii., followed mainly by Bancroft, iv. 298, 307), Stephens (ii. 310), Dupaix (pl. xi.), Kingsborough (iv. pl. 13), and Charnay (ch. 13 and 14). The views of the ruins given by these authorities mainly make up the stock of cuts in all the popular narratives.

The most interesting of the carvings is what is known as the Tablet of the Cross, which was taken from one of the minor buildings, and is now in the National Museum at Washington. It has often been engraved, but such representations never satisfied the student till they could be tested by the best of Charnay's photographs. (Engravings in Brasseur and Waldeck, pl. 21, 22; Rosny's *Essai sur le déchiffrement*, etc.; Minutoli's *Beschreibung einer alten Stadt in Guatimala* (Berlin, 1832); Stephens's *Cent. Amer.*, ii.; Bancroft, *Nat. Races*, iv. 333; Charnay, *Les anciens Villes*, and Eng. transl. p. 255; Nadaillac, 325; *Powell's Rept.*, i. 221; cf. p. 234; *Amer. Antiquarian*, vii. 200.) The most important discussion of the tablet is Charles Rau's *Palenqué Tablet in the U. S. National Museum* (Washington, 1879), being the *Smithsonian Contri. to Knowledge*, no. 331, or vol. xxii. It contains an account of the explorations that have been made at Palenqué, and a chapter on the "Aboriginal writing in Mexico, Central America, and Yucatan, with some account of the attempted translations of Maya hieroglyphics." Rau's conclusion is that it is a Phallic symbol. Cf. a summary in *Amer. Antiquarian*, vi., Jan., 1884, and in *Amer. Art Review*, 1880, p. 217. Rau's paper was translated into Spanish and French: *Tablero del Palenque en el Museo nacional de los Estados-Unidos* [traducido por Joaquin Davis y Miguel Perez], in the *Anales del Museo nacional.* Tomo 2, pp. 131–203. (México, 1880.) *La Stèle de Palenqué du Musée national des Etats-Unis, à Washington. Traduit de l'Anglais avec autorisation de l'auteur.* In the *Annales du Musée Guimet*, vol. x. (Paris, 1887.) Rau's views were criticised by Morgan.

There are papers by Charency on the interpretation of the hieroglyphs in *Le Muséon* (Paris, 1882, 1883).

The significance of the cross among the Nahuas and Mayas has been the subject of much controversy, some connecting it with a possible early association with Christians in ante-Columbian days (Bancroft, iii. 468). On this later point see Bamps, *Les traditions relatives à l'homme blanc et au signe de la cruz en Amérique à l'Epoque précolumbienne*, in the *Compte rendu, Congrès des Américanistes* (Copenhagen, 1883), p. 125; and "Supposed vestiges of early Christian teaching in America," in the *Catholic Historical Researches* (vol. i., Oct., 1885). The symbolism is variously conceived. Bandelier (*Archæol. Jour.*) holds it to be the emblem of fire, indeed an ornamented fire-drill, which later got mixed up with the Spanish crucifix. Brinton (*Myths of the New World*, 95) sees in it the four cardinal points, the rain-bringers, the symbol of life and health, and cites (p. 96) various of the early writers in proof. Brinton (*Am. Hero Myths*, 155) claims to have been the first to connect the Palenqué cross with the four cardinal points.

* Given by Rosny, *Doc. Écrits de la Antiq. Amér.*, p. 73, as types of the short-headed race which preceded the Aztec occupation. They are from sculptures at Copan. Cf. Stephens's *Cent. America*, i. 139; Bancroft, iv. 101.

There have been only two statues found at Palenqué, in connection with the Temple of the Cross,[1] but the considerable number of carved figures discovered at Copan,[2] as well as the general impression that these latter ruins are the oldest on the American continent,[3] have made in some respects these most celebrated of the Honduras remains more interesting than those of Chiapas. It is now generally agreed that the ruins of Copan[4] do not represent the town called Copan, assaulted and captured by Hernando de Choves in 1530, though the identity of names has induced some writers to claim that these ruins were inhabited when the Spaniards came.[5] The earliest account of them which we have is that in Palacio's letter to Felipe II., written (1576) hardly more than a generation after the Conquest, and showing that the ruins then were much in the same condition as later described.[6] The next account is that of Fuentes y Guzman's *Historia de Guatemala* (1689), now accessible in the Madrid edition of 1882; but for a long time only known in the citation in Juarros' *Guatemala* (p. 56), and through those who had copied from Juarros.[7] His account is brief, speaks of Castilian costumes, and is otherwise so enigmatical that Brasseur calls it mendacious. Colonel Galindo, in visiting the ruins in 1836, confounded them with the Copan of the Conquest.[8] The ruins also came under the scrutiny of Stephens in 1839, and they were described by him, and drawn by Catherwood, for the first time with any fullness and care, in their respective works.[9]

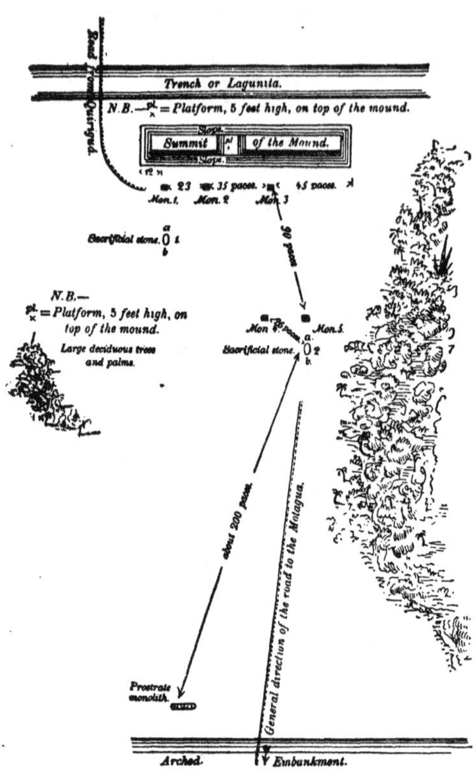

PLAN OF THE RUINS OF QUIRIGUA.*

Always associated with Copan, and perhaps even older, if the lower relief of the carvings can bear that interpretation, are the ruins near the village of Quiriguá, in Guatemala, and

The bird and serpent — the last shown better in Charnay's photograph than in Stephens's cut — is (*Myths*, 119) simply a rebus of the air-god, the ruler of the winds. Brinton says that Waldeck, in a paper on the tablet in the *Revue Américaine* (ii. 69), came to a similar conclusion. Squier (*Nicaragua*, ii. 337) speaks of the common error of mistaking the tree of life of the Mexicans for the Christian symbol. Cf. Powell's *Second Rept., Bur. of Ethnol.*, p. 208; the *Fourth Rept.*, p. 252, where discredit is thrown upon Gabriel de Mortillet's *Le Signe de la cross avant le Christianisme* (Paris, 1866); Joly's *Man before Metals*, 339; and Charnay's *Les Anciens Villes* (or Eng. transl. p. 85). Cf. for various applications the references in Bancroft's index (v. p. 671).

1 Both were alike, and one was broken in two. There are engravings in Waldeck, pl. 25; Stephens, ii. 344, 349; Squier's *Nicaragua*, 1856, ii. 337; Bancroft, iv. 337.

2 These have been the subject of an elaborate folio, thought, however, to be of questionable value, *Die Steinbildwerke von Copán und Quiriguá, aufgenommen von Heinrich Meye; historisch erläutert und beschrieben von Dr. Julius Schmidt* (Berlin, 1883), of which there is an English translation, *The stone sculptures of Copán and Quiriguá;* translated from the German by A. D. Savage (New York, 1883). It gives twenty plates, Catherwood's plates, and the cuts in Stephens, with reproductions in accessible books (Bancroft, iv. ch. 3; Powell's *First Rept. Bur. Ethn.* 224; Ruge's *Gesch. des Zeitalters; Amer. Antiquarian*, viii. 204-6), will serve, however, all purposes.

3 Squier says: "There are various reasons for believing that both Copan and Quirigua antedate Olosingo and Palenqué, precisely as the latter antedate the ruins of Quiché, Chichen-Itza, and Uxmal, and that all of them were the work of the same people, or of nations of the same race, dating from a high antiquity, and in blood and language precisely the same that was found in occupation of the country by the Spaniards."

4 Named apparently from a neighboring village.

5 Ref. in Bancroft, iv. 79.

6 This account can be found in Pacheco's *Col. Doc. inéd.* vi. 37, in Spanish; in Ternaux's *Coll.* (1840), imperfect, and in the *Nouv. Annales des Voyages*, 1843, v. xcvii. p. 18, in French; in Squier's *Cent. America*, 242, and in his ed. of Palacio (N. Y. 1860), in English; and in Alexander von Frantzius's *San Salvador und Honduras im Jahre* 1576, with notes by the translator and by C. H. Berendt.

7 Stephens, *Cent. Am.*, i. 131, 144; Warden, 71; *Nouvelles Annales des Voyages*, xxxv. 329; Bancroft, iv. 82; *Bull. de la Soc. de Géog. de Paris*, 1836, v. 267; Short, 56, 82, — not to name others.

8 His account is in the *Amer. Antiq. Soc. Trans.*, ii.; *Bull. Soc. de Géog.* 1835; Dupaix, a summary, i. div. 2, p. 73; Bradford's *Amer. Antiq.*, in part. Galindo's drawings are unknown. Stephens calls his account "unsatisfactory and imperfect."

9 *Central America*, i. ch. 5-7; *Views of Anc. Mts.* It is Stephens's account which has furnished the basis of those given by Bancroft (iv. ch. 3); Baldwin, p. 111; Short, 356;

* From Meye and Schmidt's *Stone Sculptures of Copán and Quiriguá* (N. Y., 1883).

known by that name. Catherwood first brought them into notice;[1] but the visit of Karl Scherzer in 1854 produced the most extensive account of them which we have, in his *Ein Besuch bei den Ruinen von Quiriguá* (Wien, 1855).[2]

The principal explorers of Nicaragua have been Ephraim George Squier, in his *Nicaragua*,[3] and Frederick Boyle, in his *Ride across a Continent* (Lond. 1868),[4] and their results, as well as the scattered data of others,[5] are best epitomized in Bancroft (iv. ch. 2), who gives other references to second-hand descriptions (p. 29). Since Bancroft's survey there have been a few important contributions.[6]

III. Bibliographical Notes on the Picture-Writing of the Nahuas and Mayas.

In considering the methods of record and communication used by these peoples, we must keep in mind the two distinct systems of the Aztecs and the Mayas;[7] and further, particularly as regards the former, we must not forget that some of these writings were made after the Conquest, and were influenced in some degree by Spanish associations. Of this last class were land titles and catechisms, for the native system obtained for some time as a useful method with the conquerors for recording the transmission of lands and helping the instruction by the priests.[8]

It is usual in tracing the development of a hieroglyphic system to advance from a purely figurative one — in which pictures of objects are used — through a symbolic phase; in which such pictures are interpreted conventionally instead of realistically. It was to this last stage that the Aztecs had advanced; but they mingled the two methods, and apparently varied in the order of reading, whether by lines or columns, forwards, upwards, or backwards. The difficulty of understanding them is further increased by the same object holding different meanings in different connections, and still more by the personal element, or writer's style, as we should call it, which was impressed on his choice of objects and emblems.[9] This rendered interpretation by no means easy to the aborigines themselves, and we have statements that when native documents were referred

Nadaillac, 328, and all others. Bancroft in his bibliog. note (iv. pp. 79–81), which has been collated with my own notes, mentions others of less importance, particularly the report of Center and Hardcastle to the Amer. Ethnol. Soc. in 1860 and 1862, and the photographs made by Ellerley, which Brasseur (*Hist. Nat. Civ.* i. 96; ii. 493; *Palenqué*, 8, 17) found to confirm the drawings and descriptions of Catherwood and Stephens.

Stephens (*Cent. Am.*, i. 133) made a plan of the ruins reproduced in *Annales des Voyages* (1841, p. 57), which is the basis of that given by Bancroft (iv. 85). Dr. Julius Schmidt, who was a member of the Squier expedition in 1852–53, furnished the historical and descriptive text to a work which in the English translation by A. D. Savage is known as *Stone Sculptures of Copán and Quiriguá, drawn by Heinrich Meye* (N. Y., 1883). What Stephens calls the Copan idols and altars are considered by Morgan (*Houses and House Life*, 257), following the analogy of the customs of the northern Indians, to be the grave-posts and graves of Copan chiefs. Bancroft (iv. ch. 3) covers the other ruins of Honduras and San Salvador; and Squier has a paper on those of Tenampua in the *N. Y. Hist. Soc. Proc.*, 1853.

[1] Stephens's *Central America*, ii. ch. 7; and *Nouvelles Annales des Voyages*, vol. lxxxviii. 376, derived from Catherwood.

[2] Other travellers who have visited them are John Baily, *Central America* (Lond. 1850); A. P. Maudsley, *Explorations in Guatemala* (Lond. 1883), with map and plans of ruins, in the *Proc. Roy. Geog. Soc.* p. 185; W. T. Brigham's *Guatemala* (N. Y., 1886). Bancroft (iv. 109) epitomizes the existing knowledge; but the remains seem to be less known than any other of the considerable ruins. There are a few later papers: G. Williams on the Antiquities of Guatemala, in the *Smithsonian Report*, 1876; Simeon Habel's "Sculptures of Santa Lucia Cosumalhuapa in Guatemala" in the *Smithson. Contrib.* xxii. (Washington, 1878), or "Sculptures de Santa (Lucia) Cosumalwhuapa dans le Guatémala, avec une rélation de voyages dans l'Amérique Centrale et sur les côtes occidentales de l'Amérique du Sud, par S. Habel. Traduit de l'anglais, par J. Pointet," with eight plates, in the *Annales du Musée Guimet*, vol. x. pp. 119–259 (Paris, 1887); Philipp Wilhelm Adolf Bastian's "Stein Sculpturen aus Guatemala," in the *Jahrbuch der k. Museen zu Berlin*, 1882, or "Notice sur les pierres sculptées du Guatémala récemment acquises par le Musée royal d'ethnographie de Berlin. Traduit avec autorisation de l'auteur par J. Pointet," in the *Annales du Musée Guimet*, vol. x. pp. 261–305 (Paris, 1887); and C. E. Vreeland and J. F. Bransford, on the *Antiquities at Pantaleon, Guatemala* (Washington, 1885), from the *Smithsonian Report* for 1884.

[3] *Nicaragua; its people, scenery, monuments, and the proposed interoceanic canal* (N. Y., 1856; revised 1860), a portion (pp. 303–362) referring to the modern Indian occupants. Squier was helped by his official station as U. S. chargé d'affaires; and the archæological objects brought away by him are now in the National Museum at Washington. He published separate papers in the *Amer. Ethnol. Soc. Trans.* ii.; *Smithsonian Ann. Rept.* v. (1850); *Harper's Monthly*, x. and xi. Cf. list in Pilling, nos. 3717, etc.

[4] His explorations were in 1865–66. He carried off what he could to the British Museum.

[5] Like Bedford Pim and Berthold Seemann's *Dottings on the Roadside in Panama, Nicaragua, and Mosquito* (Lond., 1869).

[6] J. F. Bransford's "Archæological Researches in Nicaragua," in the *Smithsonian Contrib.* (Washington, 1881). Karl Bovallius's *Nicaraguan Antiquities*, with plates (Stockholm, 1886), published by the Swedish Society of Anthropology and Geography, figures various statues and other relics found by the author in Nicaragua, and he says that his drawings are in some instances more exact than those given by Squier before the days of photography. In his introduction he describes the different Indian stocks of Nicaragua, and disagrees with Squier. He gives a useful map of Nicaragua and Costa Rica.

[7] It is only of late years that they have been kept apart, for the elder writers like Kingsborough, Stephens, and Brantz Mayer, confounded them.

[8] The Father Alonzo Ponce, who travelled through Yucatan in 1586, is the only writer, according to Brinton (*Books of Chilan Balam*, p. 5), who tells us distinctly that the early missionaries made use of aboriginal characters in giving religious instruction to the natives (*Relacion Breve y Verdadera*).

[9] Leon y Gama tells us that color as well as form seems to have been representative.

to them it required sometimes long consultations to reach a common understanding.[1] The additional step by which objects stand for sounds, the Aztecs seem not to have taken, except in the names of persons and places, in which they understood the modern child's art of the rebus, where such symbol more or less clearly stands for a syllable, and the representation was usually of conventionalized forms, somewhat like the art of the European herald. Thus the Aztec system was what Daniel Wilson[2] calls "the pictorial suggestion of associated ideas."[3] The phonetic scale, if not comprehended in the Aztec system, made an essential part of

de las partes otro, y assi viene a hazer in infinitum como
se podra ver en el siguiente exemplo. Le, quiere dezir laço
y caçar con el, para escrivirle con sus caratares aviendo
les nosotros hecho entender que son dos letras lo escrivian
ellos con tres poniendo a la aspiracion de la l, la vocal e,
que antes de si trae, y en esto no hierran aunque usen de e si
quisieren ellos de su curiosidad. Exemplo.
despues al cabo le pegan la parte junta. Ha que quiere dezir
agua porque la hache tiene a. h. ante de si lo ponen ellos al
principio con a. y al cabo desta manera. También
lo escriven a partes de la una y otra manera yo
no pusiera aqui ni tratara dello sino por dar cuenta entera
de las cosas desta gente. Ma in kati quiere dezir no quiero, ellos
lo escriven a partes desta manera.
Siguese su a, b, c.
De las letras que aqui faltan carece esta lengua
y tiene otras añadidas de la nuestra para otras
cosas que las ha menester, y ya no usan para nada destos
sus carateres especialmente la gente moça que an aprendido
los nuestros

FAC-SIMILE OF A PART OF LANDA'S MS.*

[1] See references on the accepted difficulties in *Native Races*, ii. 551. Mrs. Nuttall claims to have observed certain complemental signs in the Mexican graphic system, "which renders a misinterpretation of the Nahuatl picture-writings impossible" (*Am. Asso. Adv. Science, Proc.*, xxxv. (Aug., 1886); *Peabody Mus. Papers*, i. App.

[2] *Prehist. Man*, ii. 57, 64, for his views.

[3] Bancroft, *Native Races*, ii. ch. 17 (pp. 542, 552) gives a good description of the Aztec system, with numerous references; but on this system, and on the hieroglyphic element in general, see Gomara; Bernal Diaz; Motolinía in Icazbalceta's *Collection*, i. 186, 209; Ternaux's *Collection*, x. 250; Kingsborough, vi. 87; viii. 190; ix. 201, 235, 287, 325; Acosta, lib. vi. cap. 7; Sahagún, i. p. iv.; Torquemada, i. 29, 30, 36, 149, 253; ii. 263, 544; Las Casas's *Hist. Apologética;* Purchas's *Pilgrimes*, iii. 1069; iv. 1135; Clavigero, ii. 187; Robertson's *America;* Boturini's *Idea*, pp. 5, 77, 87, 96, 112, 116; Humboldt's *Vues*, i. 177, 192; Veytia, i. 6, 250; Gallatin in *Am. Ethn. Soc. Trans.* i. 126, 165; Prescott's *Mexico*, i. ch. 4; Brasseur's *Nat. Civ.*, i. pp. xv, xvii; Domenech's *Manuscrit pictographique*, introd.; Mendoza, in the *Boletin Soc. Mex.*

* After a fac-simile in the *Archives de la Soc. Amér. de France, nouv. ser.*, ii. 34. (Cf. pl. xix. of Rosny's *Essai sur le déchiffrement*, etc.) It is a copy, not the original, of Landa's text, but a nearly contemporary one (made thirty years after Landa's death), and the only known.

NOTE TO OPPOSITE CUT. — This representation of Yucatan hieroglyphics is a reduction of pl. i. in Léon de Rosny's *Essai sur le déchiffrement de l'écriture hiératique de l'Amérique Centrale*, Paris, 1876. Cf. Bancroft, iv. 92; Short, 403.

the Maya hieroglyphics, and this was the great distinctive feature of the latter, as we learn from the early descriptions,[1] and from the alphabet which Landa has preserved for us. It is not only in the codices or books of the Mayas that their writing is preserved to us, but in the inscriptions of their carved architectural remains.[2]

When the Abbé Brasseur de Bourbourg found, in 1863, in the library of the Royal Academy of History at Madrid, the MS. of Landa's *Relacion*, and discovered in it what purported to be a key to the Maya alphabet, there were hopes that the interpretation of the Maya books and inscriptions was not far off. Twenty-five years, however, has not seen the progress that was wished for; and if we may believe Valentini, the alphabet of Landa is a pure fabrication of the bishop himself;[3] and even some of those who account it genuine, like Le Plongeon, hold that it is inadequate in dealing with the older Maya inscriptions.[4] Cyrus Thomas speaks of this alphabet as simply an attempt of the bishop to pick out of compound characters their simple elements on the supposition that something like phonetic representations would be the result.[5] Landa's own description[6] of the alphabet accompanying his graphic key[7] is very unsatisfactory, not to say incomprehensible. Brasseur has tried to render it in French, and Bancroft in English; but it remains a difficult problem to interpret it intelligibly.

Brasseur very soon set himself the task of interpreting the Troano manuscript by the aid of this key, and he soon had the opportunity of giving his interpretation to the public when the Emperor Napoleon III. ordered that codex to be printed in the sumptuous manner of the imperial press.[8] The efforts of Brasseur met

Geog., 2de ed. i. 896; Madier de Montjau's *Chronologie hiéroglyphico-phonetic des rois Aztèques, de 1322 à 1522*, with an introduction "sur l'Ecriture Méxicaine;" Lubbock's *Prehistoric Times*, 279, and his *Origin of Civilization*, ch. 2; E. B. Tylor's *Researches into the Early Hist. of Mankind*, 89; Short's *No. Amer. of Antiq.*, ch. 8; Müller's *Chips*, i. 317; The Abbé Jules Pipart in *Compte-rendu, Congrès des Amér.* 1877, ii. 346; Isaac Taylor's *Alphabets*; Foster's *Prehistoric Races*, 322; Nadaillac, 376, not to cite others. Bandelier has discussed the Mexican paintings in his paper "On the sources for aboriginal history of Spanish America" in *Am. Asso. Adv. Science, Proc.*, xxvii. (1878). See also *Peabody Mus. Reports*, ii. 631; and Orozco y Berra's "Códice Mendozino" in the *Anales del Museo Nacional*, vol. i. Mrs. Nuttall's views are in the *Peabody Mus., Twentieth Report*, p. 567. Quaritch (*Catal.* 1885, nos. 29040, etc.) advertised some original Mexican pictures; a native MS. pictorial record of a part of the Tezcuco domain (supposed A. D. 1530), and perhaps one of the "pinturas" mentioned by Ixtlilxochitl; a colored Mexican calendar on a single leaf of the same supposed date and origin; with other MSS. of the fifteenth and sixteenth centuries. (Cf. also his *Catal.*, Jan., Feb., 1888.)

The most important studies upon the Aztec system have been those of Aubin. Cf. his *Mémoire sur la peinture didactique et l'écriture figurative des Anciens Méxicains*, in the *Archives de la Soc. Amér. de France*, iii. 225 (*Revue Orient. et Amér.*), in which he contended for the rebus-like character of the writings. He made further contributions to vols. iv. and v. (1859-1861). Cf. his "Examen des anciennes peintures figuratives de l'ancien Méxique," in the new series of *Archives*, etc., vol. i.; and the introd. to Brasseur's *Nations Civilisées*, p. xliv.

[1] Bancroft (*Nat. Races*, ii. ch. 24) translates these from Landa, Peter Martyr, Cogulludo, Villagutierre, Mendieta, Acosta, Benzoni, and Herrera, and thinks all the modern writers (whom he names, p. 770) have drawn from these earlier ones, except, perhaps, Medel in *Nouv. Annales des Voyages*, xcvii. 49. Cf. Wilson, *Prehistoric Man*, ii. 61. It will be seen later that Holden discredits the belief in any phonetic value of the Maya system. But compare on the phonetic value of the Mexican and Maya systems, Brinton in *Amer. Antiquarian* (Nov. 1886); Lazarus Geiger's *Contrib. to the Hist. of the Development of the Human Race* (Eng. tr. by David Asher). London, 1880, p. 75; and Zelia Nuttall in *Am. Ass. Adv. Sci. Proc.*, Aug. 1886.

[2] Dr. Bernoulli, who died at San Francisco, in California, in 1878, and whose labors are commemorated in a notice in the *Verhandlungen der Naturforschenden Gesellschaft* (vi. 710) at Basle, found at Tikal, in Guatemala, some fragments of sculptured panels of wood, bearing hieroglyphics as well as designs, which he succeeded in purchasing, and they were finally deposited in 1879 in the Ethnological Museum in Basle, where Rosny saw them, and describes them, with excellent photographic representations, in his *Doc. Ecrits de l'Antiq. Amér.* (p. 97). These tablets are the latest additions to be made to the store already possessed from Palenqué, as given by Stephens in his *Central America, Chiapas, and Yucatan*; those of the Temple of the Cross at Palenqué, after Waldeck's drawings in the *Archives de la Soc. Amér. de France* (ii., 1864); that from Kabah in Yucatan, given by Rosny in his *Archives Paléographiques* (i. p. 178; Atlas, pl. xx.), and one from Chichen-Itza, figured by Le Plongeon in *L'Illustration*, Feb. 10, 1882; not to name other engravings. Rosny holds that Rau's *Palenqué Tablet* (Washington, 1879) gives the first really serviceably accurate reproduction of that inscription. Cf. on Maya inscriptions, Bancroft, ii. 775; iv. 91, 97, 234; Morelet's *Travels*; and Le Plongeon in *Am. Antiq. Soc. Proc.*, n. s., i. 246. This last writer has been thought to let his enthusiasm — not to say dogmatism — turn his head, under which imputation he is not content, naturally (*Ibid.* p. 282).

[3] "Landa's alphabet a Spanish fabrication," appeared in the *Amer. Antiq. Soc. Proc.*, April, 1880. In this, Philipp J. J. Valentini interprets all that the old writers say of the ancient writings to mean that they were pictorial and not phonetic; and that Landa's purpose was to devise a vehicle which seemed familiar to the natives, through which he could communicate religious instruction. His views have been controverted by Léon de Rosny (*Doc. Ecrits de la Antiq. Amér.* p. 91); and Brinton (*Maya Chronicles*, 61), calls them an entire misconception of Landa's purpose.

[4] *Am. Antiq. Soc. Proc.*, n. s., i. 251.

[5] *Troano MS.*, p. viii

[6] *Relation*, Brasseur's ed., section xli.

[7] This is given in the *Archives de la Soc. Amér. de France*, ii. pl. iv.; in Brasseur's ed. of Landa; in Bancroft's *Nat. Races*, ii. 779; in Short, 425; Rosny (*Essai sur le déchiff.* etc., pl. xiii.) gives a "Tableau des caractères phonétique Mayas d'après Diégo de Landa et Brasseur de Bourbourg."

[8] *Manuscrit Troano Etudes sur le système graphique et la langue des Mayas* (Paris, 1869-70) — the first volume containing a fac-simile of the Codex in seventy plates, with Brasseur's explications and partial interpretation. In the second volume there is a translation of Gabriel de Saint Bonaventure's *Grammaire Maya*, a "Chrestomathie" of Maya extracts, and a Maya lexicon of more than 10,000 words. Brasseur published at the same time (1869) in the *Mémoires de la Soc. d'Ethnographie* a *Lettre à M. Léon de Rosny sur la découverte de documents relatifs à la haute antiquité américaine, et sur le déchiffrement et l'interprétation de l'écriture phonétique et figurative de la langue Maya* (Paris, 1869). He explained his application of Landa's alphabet in the introduction to the *MS. Troano*,

with hardly a sign of approval. Léon de Rosny criticised him,[1] and Dr. Brinton found in his results nothing to commend.[2]

No one has approached the question of interpreting these Maya writings with more careful scrutiny than Léon de Rosny, who first attracted attention with his comparative study, *Les écritures figuratives et hiéroglyphiques des différens peuples anciens et moderns* (Paris, 1860; again, 1870, augmentée). From 1869 to 1871 he published at Paris four parts of *Archives paléographiques de l'Orient et de l'Amérique, publiées avec des notices historiques et philologiques*, in which he included several studies of the native writings, and gave a bibliography (pp. 101–115) of American paleography up to that time. His *L'interprétation des anciens textes Mayas* made part of the first volume of the *Archives de la Soc. Américaine de France* (new series). His chief work, making the second volume of the same, is his *Essai sur le déchiffrement de l'écriture hiératique de l'Amérique Central* (Paris, 1876), and it is the most thorough examination of the problem yet made.[3] The last part (4th) was published in 1878, and a Spanish translation appeared in 1881.

PALENQUÉ HIEROGLYPHICS.*

Wm. Bollaert, who had paid some attention to the paleography of America,[4] was one of the earliest in England to examine Brasseur's work on Landa, which he did in a memoir read before the Anthropological Society,[5] and later in an "Examination of the Central American hieroglyphs by the recently discovered Maya alphabet."[6] Brinton[7] calls his conclusions fanciful, and Le Plongeon claims that the inscription in Stephens, which Bollaert worked upon, is inaccurately given, and that Bollaert's results were nonsense.[8] Hyacinthe de Charency's efforts have hardly been more successful, though he attempted the use of Landa's alphabet with something like scientific care. He examined a small part of the inscription of the Palenqué tablet of the Cross in his *Essai de déchiffrement d'un fragment d'inscription palenquéene*.[9]

Dr. Brinton translated Charency's results, and, adding Landa's alphabet, published his *Ancient phonetic alphabet of Yucatan* (N. Y., 1870), a small tract.[10] His continued studies were manifest in the introduction on "The graphic system and the ancient records of the Mayas" to Cyrus Thomas's *Manuscript Troano*.[11] In this paper Dr. Brinton traces the history of the attempts which have thus far been made in solving this perplexing problem.[12] The latest application of the scientific spirit is that of the astronomer E. S. Holden,

i. p. 36. Brasseur later confessed he had begun at the wrong end of the MS. (*Bib. Mex.-Guat.*, introd.). The pebble-shape form of the characters induced Brasseur to call them *calculiform*; and Julien Duchateau adopted the term in his paper "Sur l'écriture calculiforme des Mayas" in the *Annuaire de la Soc. Amér.* (Paris, 1874), iii. p. 31.

[1] *L'écriture hiératique*, and *Archives de la Soc. Am. de France*, n. s., ii. 35.

[2] *Ancient Phonetic Alphabets of Yucatan* (N. Y., 1870), p. 7.

[3] It is the development of a paper given at the Nancy session of the Congrès des Américanistes (1875). Landa's alphabet with the variations make 262 of the 700 signs which Rosny catalogues. He printed his "Nouvelles Recherches pour l'interpretation des caractères de l'Amérique Centrale" in the *Archives*, etc., iii. 118. There is a paper on Rosny's studies by De la Rada in the Compte-rendu of the Copenhagen session (p. 355) of the Congrès des Américanistes. Rosny's *Documents écrits de l'antiquité Américaine* (Paris, 1882), from the *Mémoires de la Société d'Ethnographie* (1881), covers his researches in Spain and Portugal for material illustrative of the pre-Columbian history of America. Cf. also his "Les sources de l'histoire anté columbienne du nouveau monde," in the *Mémoires de la Soc. d'Ethnographie* (1877). For the titles in full of Rosny's linguistic studies, see Pilling's *Proof-sheets*, p. 663.

[4] *Anthropol. Review*, May, 1864; *Memoirs of the Anthropol. Soc.*, i.

[5] *Memoirs*, etc., ii. 298.

[6] *Memoirs*, etc., 1870, iii. 288; *Trans. Anthrop. Inst. Gt. Britain.*

[7] Introd. to Cyrus Thomas's *MS. Troano.*

[8] *Am. Antiq. Soc. Proc.*, *n. s.*, i. 250.

[9] *Actes de la Soc. philologique*, March, 1870. Cf. *Revue de Philologie*, i. 380; *Recherches sur le Codex Troano* (Paris, 1876); *Actes*, etc., March, 1878; Baldwin's *Anc. America*, App.

[10] Cf. *Sabin's Amer. Bibliopolist*, ii. 143.

[11] *Contributions to N. A. Ethnology*, *Powell's Survey*, vol. v. Cf. also his *Phonetic elements in the graphic system of the Mayas and Mexicans* in the *Amer. Antiquarian* (Nov., 1886), and separately (Chicago, 1886), and his *Ikonomic method of phonetic writing* (Phila., 1886). Thomas in *The Amer. Antiquarian* (March, 1886) points out the course of his own studies in this direction.

[12] Cf. Short, p. 425. Dr. Harrison Allen in 1875, in the

* After a cut in Wilson's *Prehistoric Man*, ii. p. 63. It is also given in Bancroft (iv. 355), and others. It is from the Tablet of the Cross.

who sought to eliminate the probabilities of recurrent signs by the usual mathematical methods of resolving systems of modern cipher.[1]

There are few examples of the aboriginal ideographic writings left to us. Their fewness is usually charged to the destruction which was publicly made of them under the domination of the Church in the years following

LÉON DE ROSNY.*

Amer. Philosophical Society's Transactions, made an analysis of Landa's alphabet and the published codices. Rau, in his *Palenqué Tablet of the U. S. Nat. Museum* (ch. 5), examines what had been done up to 1879. In the same year Dr. Carl Schultz-Sellack wrote on "Die Amerikanischen Götter der vier Weltgegenden und ihre Tempel in Palenqué," touching also the question of interpretation (*Zeitschrift für Ethnologie*, vol. xi.); and in 1880 Dr. Förstemann examined the matter in his introduction to his reproduction of the Dresden Codex.

[1] *Studies in Central American picture-writing* (Washington, 1881), extracted from the *First Report of the Bureau of Ethnology*. His method is epitomized in *The Century*, Dec., 1881. He finds Stephens's drawings the most trustworthy of all, Waldeck's being beautiful, but they embody "singular liberties." His examination was confined to the 1500 separate hieroglyphs in Stephens's *Central America*. Some of Holden's conclusions are worth noting: "The Maya manuscripts do not possess to me the same interest as the stones, and I think it may be certainly said that all of them are younger than the Palenqué tablets, and far younger than the inscriptions at Copan." "I distrust the methods of Brasseur and others who start from the misleading and unlucky alphabet handed down by Landa," by forming variants, which are made "to satisfy the necessities of the interpreter in carrying out some preconceived idea." He finds a rigid adherence to the standard form of a character prevailing throughout the same inscription. At Palenqué the inscriptions read as an English inscription would read, beginning at the left and proceeding line by line downward. "The system employed at Palenqué and Copan was the same in its general character, and almost identical even in details." He deciphers three proper names: "all of them have been pure picture-writing, except in so far as their rebus character may make them in a sense phonetic." Referring to Valentini's *Landa Alphabet a Spanish Fabrication*, he agrees in that critic's conclusions. "While my own," he adds, "were reached by a study of the stones and in the course of a general examination, Dr. Valentini has addressed himself successfully to the solution of a special problem." Holden thinks his own solution of the three proper names points of departure for subsequent decipherers. The Maya method was "pure picture-writing. At Copan this is found in

* After a photogravure in *Les Documents écrits de l'antiquité Américaine* (Paris, 1882). Cf. cut in *Mém. de la Soc. d'Ethnographie* (1887), xiii. p. 71.

the Conquest.[1] The alleged agents in this demolition were Bishop Landa, in 1562, at Mani, in Yucatan,[2] and Bishop Zumárraga at Tlatelalco, or, as some say, at Tezcuco, in Mexico.[3] Peter Martyr[4] has told us something of the records as he saw them, and we know also from him, and from their subsequent discovery in European collections, that some examples of them were early taken to the Old World. We have further knowledge of them from Las Casas and from Landa himself.[5] There have been efforts made of late years by Icazbalceta and Canon Carrillo to mitigate the severity of judgment, particularly as respects Zumárraga.[6] The first, and indeed the only attempt that has been made to bring together for mutual illustration all that was known of these manuscripts which escaped the fire,[7] was in the great work of the Viscount Kingsborough (b. 1795, d. 1837). It was while, as Edward King, he was a student at Oxford that this nobleman's passion for Mexican antiquities was first roused by seeing an original Aztec pictograph, described by Purchas (*Pilgrimes*, vol. iii.), and preserved in the Bodleian. In the studies to which this led he was assisted by some special scholars, including Obadiah Rich, who searched for him in Spain in 1830 and 1832, and who after Kingsborough's death obtained a large part of the manuscript collections which that nobleman had amassed (*Catalogue of the Sale*, Dublin, 1842). Many of the Kingsborough manuscripts passed into the collection of Sir Thomas Phillipps (*Catalogue*, no. 404), but the correspondence pertaining to Kingsborough's life-work seems to have disappeared. Phillipps had been one of the main encouragers of Kingsborough in his undertaking.[8] Kingsborough, who had spent £30,000 on his undertaking, had a business dispute with the merchants who furnished the printing-paper, and he was by them thrown into jail as a debtor, and died in confinement.[9]

Kingsborough's great work, the most sumptuous yet bestowed upon Mexican archæology, was published between 1830 and 1848, there being an interval of seventeen years between the seventh and eighth volumes. The original intention seems to have embraced ten volumes, for the final section of the ninth volume is signatured as for a tenth.[10] The work is called: *Antiquities of Mexico; comprising facsimiles of Ancient Mexican Paintings and Hieroglyphics, preserved in the Royal Libraries of Paris, Berlin, and Dresden; in the Imperial Library of Vienna; in the Vatican Library; in the Borgian Museum at Rome; in the Library of the Institute of Bologna; and in the Bodleian Library at Oxford; together with the Monuments of New Spain, by M. Dupaix; illustrated by many valuable inedited MSS.* With the theory maintained by Kingsborough throughout the work, that the Jews were the first colonizers of the country, we have nothing to do here; but as the earliest and as yet the largest repository of hieroglyphic material, the book needs to be examined. The compiler states where he found his MSS., but he gives nothing of their history, though something more is now known of their descent. Peter Martyr speaks of the number of Mexican MSS. which had in his day been taken to Spain, and Prescott remarks it as strange that not a single one given by Kingsborough was found in that country. There are, however, some to be seen there now.[11] Comparisons which have been made of Kingsborough's plates show that they are not inexact; but they almost necessarily lack the validity that the modern photographic processes give to fac-similes.

Kingsborough's first volume opens with a fac-simile of what is usually called the *Codex Mendoza*, preserved in the Bodleian. It is, however, a contemporary copy on European paper of an original now lost, which was sent by the Viceroy Mendoza to Charles V. Another copy made part of the Boturini collection, and from this Lorenzana[12] engraved that portion of it which consists of tribute-rolls. The story told of the fate of the orig-

its earliest state; at Palenqué it was already highly conventionalized."

[1] See references in Bancroft's *Nat. Races*, ii. 576.

[2] Cogulludo's *Hist. de Yucatan*, 3d ed., i. 604.

[3] Prescott, i. 104, and references.

[4] Dec. iv., lib. 8.

[5] Brasseur de Bourbourg's *Troano MS.*, i. 9. Cf. on the Aztec books Kirk's Prescott, i. 103; Brinton's *Myths*, 10; his *Aborig. Amer. Authors*, 17; and on the Mexican paper, Valentini in *Amer. Antiq. Soc. Proc.*, 2d s., i. 58.

[6] Cf. Icazbalceta's *Don Fray Juan de Zumárraga, primer Obispo y Arzobispo de México (1529-48). Estudio biográfico y bibligráfico. Con un apéndice de documentos inéditos ó raros* (Mexico, 1881). A part of this work was also printed separately (fifty copies) under the title of *De la destruccion de antigüedades mexicanas atribuida á los misioneros en general, y particularmente al Illmo. Sr. D. Fr. Juan de Zumárraga, primer Obispo y Arzobispo de México* (Mexico, 1881). In this he exhausts pretty much all that has been said on the subject by the bishop himself, by Pedro de Gante, Motolinía, Sahagún, Duran, Acosta, Davila Padilla, Herrera, Torquemada, Ixtlilxochitl, Robertson, Clavigero, Humboldt, Bustamante, Ternaux, Prescott, Alaman, etc. Brasseur (*Nat. Civil.*, ii. 4) says of Landa that we must not forget that he was oftener the agent of the council for the Indies than of the Church. Helps (iii. 374) is inclined to be charitable towards a man in a skeptical age, so intensely believing as Zumárraga was. Sahagún relates that earlier than Zumárraga, the fourth ruler of his race, Itzcohuatl, had caused a large destruction of native writings, in order to remove souvenirs of the national humiliation.

[7] Humboldt was one of the earliest to describe some of these manuscripts in connection with his *Atlas*, pl. xiii.

[8] Cf. *Catal. of the Phillipps Coll.*, no. 404. An original colored copy of the *Antiquities of Mexico*, given by Kingsborough to Phillipps, was offered of late years by Quaritch at £70–£100; it was published at £175. The usual colored copies sell now for about £40–£60; the uncolored for about £30–£35. It is usually stated that two copies were printed on vellum (British Museum, Bodleian), and ten on large paper, which were given to crowned heads, except one, which was given to Obadiah Rich. Squier, in the *London Athenæum*, Dec. 13, 1856 (Allibone, p. 1033), drew attention to the omission of the last signature of the *Hist. Chichimeca* in vol. ix.

[9] Rich, *Bibl. Amer. Nova*, ii. 233; *Gentleman's Mag.*, May, 1837, which varies in some particulars. Cf. for other details Sabin's *Dictionary*, ix. 485; De Rosny in the *Rev. Orient et Amér.*, xii. 387. R. A. Wilson (*New Conquest of Mexico*, p. 68) gives the violent skeptical view of the material.

[10] Sabin, ix., no. 37,800.

[11] Léon de Rosny (*Doc. écrits de l'Antiq. Amér.*, p. 71) speaks of those in the Museo Archæológico at Madrid.

[12] *Hist. Nueva España.*

inal is, that on its passage to Europe it was captured by a French cruiser and taken to Paris, where it was bought by the chaplain of the English embassy, the antiquary Purchas, who has engraved it.[1] It was then lost

FAC-SIMILE OF PLATE XXV OF THE DRESDEN CODEX.*

[1] *Pilgrimes*, vol. iii. (1625). It is also included in Thevenot's *Coll. de Voyages* (1696), vol. ii., in a translation. Clavigero (i. 23) calls this copy faulty. See also Kircher's *Œdipus Ægypticus;* Humboldt's plates, xiii., lviii., lix. with his text, in which he quotes Du Palin's *Study of Hieroglyphics*, vol. i. See the account in Bancroft, ii. 241.

* From Cyrus Thomas's *Manuscript Troano.*

sight of, and if Prescott's inference is correct it was not the original, but the Bodleian copy, which came into Purchas' hands.[1]

Beside the tribute-rolls,[2] which make one part of it, the MS. covers the civil history of the Mexicans, with a third part on the discipline and economy of the people, which renders it of so much importance in an archæological sense.[3] The second reproduction in Kingsborough's first volume is what he calls the *Codex Telleriano-Remensis*, preserved in the Bibliothèque Nationale at Paris, and formerly owned by M. Le Tellier.[4] The rest of this initial volume is made up of fac-similes of Mexican hieroglyphics and paintings, from the Boturini and Selden collections, which last is in the Bodleian.

The second Kingsborough volume opens with a reproduction of the *Codex Vaticanus* (the explanation[5] is in volume vi.), which is in the library of the Vatican, and it is known to have been copied in Mexico by Pedro de los Rios in 1566. It is partly historical and partly mythological.[6] The rest of this volume is made up of fac-similes of other manuscripts, — one given to the Bodleian by Archbishop Laud, others at Bologna,[7] Vienna,[8] and Berlin.

The third volume reproduces one belonging to the Borgian Museum at Rome, written on skin, and thought to be a ritual and astrological almanac. This is accompanied by a commentary by Frabega.[9] Kingsborough gives but a single Maya MS., and this is in his third volume, and stands with him as an Aztec production. This is the *Dresden Codex*, not very exactly rendered, which is preserved in the royal library in that city, for which it was bought by Götz,[10] at Vienna, in 1739. Prescott (i. 107) seemed to recognize its difference from the Aztec MSS., without knowing precisely how to class it.[11] Brasseur de Bourbourg calls it a religious and astrological ritual. It is in two sections, and it is not certain that they belong together. In 1880 it was reproduced at Dresden by polychromatic photography (Chromo-Lichtdruck), as the process is called, under the editing of Dr. E. Förstemann, who in an introduction describes it as composed of thirty-nine oblong sheets folded together like a fan. They are made of the bark of a tree, and covered with varnish. Thirty-five have drawings and hieroglyphics on both sides; the other four on one side only. It is now preserved between glass to prevent handling, and both sides can be examined. Some progress has been made, it is professed, in deciphering its meaning, and it is supposed to contain "records of a mythic, historic, and ritualistic character."[12]

Another script in Kingsborough, perhaps a Tezcucan MS., though having some Maya affinities, is the *Fejérvary Codex*, then preserved in Hungary, and lately owned by Mayer, of Liverpool.[13]

Three other Maya manuscripts have been brought to light since Kingsborough's day, to say nothing of three others said to be in private hands, and not described.[14] Of these, the *Codex Troano* has been the subject of much study. It is the property of a Madrid gentleman, Don Juan Tro y Ortolano, and the title given to the manuscript has been somewhat fantastically formed from his name by the Abbé Etienne Charles Brasseur

1 Prescott, i. 106. He thinks that a copy mentioned in Spineto's *Lectures on the Elements of Hieroglyphics*, and then in the Escurial, may perhaps be the original. Humboldt calls it a copy.

2 Humboldt placed some tribute-rolls in the Berlin library, and gave an account of them. See his pl. xxxvi.

3 Cf. references in Bancroft's *Native Races*, ii. 529. The "Explicacion" of the MS. is given in Kingsborough's volume v., and an "interpretation" in vol. vi.

4 Kingsborough's "explicacion" and "explanation" are given in his vols. v. and vi. Rosny has given an "explication avec notes par Brasseur de Bourbourg" in his *Archives paléographiques* (Paris, 1870–71), p. 190, with an atlas of plates. Cf. references in Bancroft, ii. 530; and in another place (iii. 191) this same writer cautions the reader against the translation in Kingsborough, and says that it has every error that can vitiate a translation. Humboldt thinks his own plates, lv. and lvi., of the codex carefully made.

5 Prescott says (i. 108) of this that it bears evident marks of recent origin, when "the hieroglyphics were read with the eye of faith rather than of reason." Cf. Bancroft, *Nat. Races*, ii. 527.

6 Portions of it are also reproduced in the *Archives de la Soc. Amér. de France*; in Rosny's *Essai sur le déchiffrement de l'Ecriture Hiératique*; and in Powell's *Third Rept. Bur. of Ethnology*, p. 56. Cf. also Humboldt's *Atlas*, pl. xiii.; and H. M. Williams's translation of his *Vues*, i. 145.

7 It is known to have been given in 1665 by the Marquis de Caspi by Count Valerio Zani. There is a copy in the museum of Cardinal Borgia at Veletri.

8 Known to have been given in 1677 by the Duke of Saxe-Eisenach to the Emperor Leopold. Some parts are reproduced in Robertson's *America*, Lond., 1777, ii. 482.

9 Humboldt, *Vues des Cordillères*, p. 89; pl. 15, 27, 37; Prescott, i. 106. There is a single leaf of it reproduced in Powell's *Third Rept. Bur. of Eth.*, p. 33.

10 Cf. his *Denkwürdigkeiten der Dresdener Bibliothek* (1744), p. 4.

11 Stephens (*Central America*, ii. 342, 453; *Yucatan*, ii. 292, 453) was in the same way at a loss respecting the conditions of the knowledge of such things in his time. Cf. also Orozco y Berra, *Geografia de las Lenguas de México*, p. 101.

12 *Die Mayahandschrift der königlichen öffentlichen Bibliothek zu Dresden; herausgegeben von E. Förstemann* (Leipzig, 1880). Only thirty copies were offered for sale at two hundred marks. There is a copy in Harvard College library. Parts of the manuscript are found figured in different publications: Humboldt's *Vues des Cordillères*, ii. 268, and pl. 16 and 45; Wuttke's *Gesch. der Schrift. Atlas*, pl. 22, 23 (Leipzig, 1872); *Archives de la Soc. Amér. de France*, n. s., vol. i. and ii.; Silvestre's *Paléographie Universelle*; Rosny's *Les Ecritures figuratives et hiéroglyphiques des peuples anciens et modernes* (Paris, 1860, pl. v.), and in his *Essai sur le déchiffrement*, etc.; Ruge, *Zeitalter der Entdeckungen*, p. 559. Cf. also Le Noir in *Antiquités Méxicaines*, ii. introd.; Förstemann's separate monographs, *Der Maya apparat in Dresden* (*Centralblatt für Bibliothekswesen*, 1885, p. 182), and *Erläuterungen zur Mayahandschrift der königlichen öffentlichen Bibliothek zu Dresden* (Dresden, 1886); Schellhas' *Die Maya-Handschrift zu Dresden* (Berlin, 1886); C. Thomas on the numerical signs in *Arch. de la Soc. Am. de France*, n. s., iii. 207.

13 Cf. Powell's *Third Rept. Eth. Bureau*, p. 32.

14 Brinton's *Maya Chronicles*, 66; Brasseur de Bourbourg's *Troano* (1868).

CODEX CORTESIANUS.*

* From a fac-simile in the *Archives de la Société Américaine de France, nouv. ser.*, ii. 30.

de Bourbourg, who was instrumental in its recognition about 1865 or 1866, and who edited a sumptuous two-volume folio edition with chromo-lithographic plates.[1]

While Léon de Rosny was preparing his *Essai sur le déchiffrement de l'Ecriture hiératique* (1876), a Maya manuscript was offered to the Bibliothèque Impériale in Paris and declined, because the price demanded was too high. Photographic copies of two of its leaves had been submitted, and one of these is given by Rosny in the *Essai* (pl. xi.). The Spanish government finally bought the MS., which, because it was supposed to have once belonged to Cortes, is now known as the *Codex Cortesianus.* Rosny afterwards saw it and studied it in the Museo Archeológico at Madrid, as he makes known in his *Doc. Ecrits de la Antiq. Amér.*, p. 79, where he points out the complementary character of one of its leaves with another of the MS. Troano, showing them to belong together, and gives photographs of the two (pl. v. vi.), as well as of other leaves (pl. 8 and 9). The part of this codex of a calendar character (Tableau des Bacab) is reproduced from Rosny's plate by Cyrus Thomas [2] in an essay in the *Third Report of the Bureau of Ethnology*, together with an attempted restoration of the plate, which is obscure in parts. Finally a small edition (85 copies) of the entire MS. was published at Paris in 1883.[3]

CODEX PEREZIANUS.*

The last of the Maya MSS. recently brought to light is sometimes cited as the *Codex Perezianus*, because the paper in which it was wrapped, when recognized in 1859 by Rosny,[4] bore the name "Perez"; and sometimes designated as Codex Mexicanus, or Manuscrit Yucatèque No. 2, of the National Library at Paris. It was a few years later published as *Manuscrit dit Méxicain No. 2 de la Bibliothèque Impériale, photographié par ordre de S. E. M. Duruy, ministre de l'instruction publique* (Paris, 1864, in folio, 50 copies). The original is a fragment of eleven leaves, and Brasseur [5] speaks of it as the most beautiful of all the MSS. in execution, but the one which has suffered the most from time and usage.[6]

[1] It constitutes vol. ii. and iii. of the series.

Mission scientifique au Mèxique et dans l'Amèrique Centrale. Ouvrages publiés par ordre de l'Empereur et par les soins du Ministre de l'Instruction publique (Paris, 1868–70), under the distinctive title: *Linguistique, Manuscrit Troano. Etudes sur le système graphique et la langue des Mayas, par Brasseur de Bourbourg* (1869–70).

Rosny, who compared Brasseur's edition with the original, was satisfied with its exactness, except in the numbering of the leaves; and Brasseur (*Bibl. Mex.-Guat.*, 1871) confessed that in his interpretation he had read the MS. backwards. The work was reissued in Paris in 1872, without the plates, under the following title: *Dictionnaire, Grammaire et Chrestomathie de la langue maya, précédés d'une étude sur les système graphique des indigènes du Yucatan (Mèxique)* (Paris, 1872).

Brasseur's *Rapport, addressé à son Excellence M. Duruy*, included in the work, gives briefly the abbé's exposition of the MS. Professor Cyrus Thomas and Dr. D. G. Brinton, having printed some expositions in the *American Naturalist* (vol. xv.) united in an essay making vol. v. of the *Contributions to North American Ethnology* (Powell's survey) under the title: *A Study of the Manuscript Troano by Cyrus Thomas, with an introduction by D G. Brinton* (Washington, 1882), which gives fac-similes of some of the plates. Thomas calls it a kind of religious calendar, giving dates of religious festivals through a long period, intermixed with illustrations of the habits and employments of the people, their houses, dress, utensils. He calls the characters in a measure phonetic, and not syllabic. Cf. Rosny in the *Archives de la Soc. Am. de France*, n. s., ii. 28; his *Essai sur le déchiffrement*, etc. (1876); Powell's *Third Rept. Bur. of Eth.*, xvi.; Bancroft's *Nat. Races*, ii. 774; and Brinton's *Notes on the Codex Troano and Maya Chronology* (Salem, 1881).

[2] Cf. *Science*, iii. 458.

[3] *Codex Cortesianus. Manuscrit hiératique des anciens Indiens de l'Amèrique centrale conservé au Musée archéologique de Madrid. Photographié et publié pour la première fois, avec une introduction, et un vocabulaire de l'écriture hiératique yucatèque par Léon de Rosny* (Paris, 1883). At the end is a list of works by De Rosny on American archæology and paleography.

[4] *Archives de la Soc. Am. de France*, n. s., ii. 25.

[5] *Bib. Mex.-Guat.*, p. 95.

[6] Cf. Rosny in *Archives paléographiques* (Paris, 1869–71), pl. 117, etc.; and his *Essai sur le déchiffrement*, etc., pl. viii., xvi.

* One of the leaves of a MS. No. 2, in the Bibliothèque Nationale, Paris, following the fac-simile (pl. 124) in Léon de Rosny's *Archives paléographiques* (Paris, 1869).

NOTE. — This Yucatan bas-relief follows a photograph by Rosny (1880), reproduced in the *Mém. de la Soc. d'Ethnographie*, no. 3 (Paris, 1882).

www.ingramcontent.com/pod-product-compliance
Lightning Source LLC
LaVergne TN
LVHW011201110826
845150LV00006B/1287

* 9 7 8 1 4 2 5 5 7 2 5 6 3 *